Handbook of
Multicultural Assessment

Lisa A. Suzuki, Paul J. Meller,
Joseph G. Ponterotto, Editors

Handbook of Multicultural Assessment

. . . .

Clinical, Psychological, and Educational Applications

Jossey-Bass Publishers
San Francisco

Substantial discounts on bulk quantities of Jossey-Bass books are available to corporations, professional associations, and other organizations. For details and discount information, contact the special sales department at Jossey-Bass Inc., Publishers (415) 433–1740; Fax (800) 605–2665.

For sales outside the United States, please contact your local Simon & Schuster International Office.

 Manufactured in the United States of America on Lyons Falls Pathfinder Tradebook. This paper is acid-free and 100 percent totally chlorine-free.

Chapter 6: Excerpt from Thorndike, R. L., Hagen, E. P., & Sattler, J. M. *The Stanford-Binet Intelligence Scale,* Fourth Edition: Technical Manual, copyright © 1986. Reproduced with permission of the Riverside Publishing Company, Chicago, IL.

Chapter 12: Excerpt from "Speech and Language of the Limited English Proficient Child" reprinted with permission from *Seminars in Speech and Language,* vol. 9, number 4, 1988, Thieme Medical Publishers, Inc.

Chapter 12: Excerpt from BEST PRACTICES IN SCHOOL SPEECH-LANGUAGE PATHOLOGY: 2nd Edition. Copyright © 1992 by The Psychological Corporation. Reproduced by permission. All rights reserved.

Library of Congress Cataloging-in-Publication Data

Handbook of multicultural assessment : clinical, psychological, and
   educational applications / Lisa A. Suzuki, Paul J. Meller, Joseph G.
   Ponterotto.
        p. cm. — (Jossey-Bass social and behavioral science series)
     Includes bibliographical references and index.
     ISBN 0-7879-0191-1
     1. Psychological tests—Social aspects. 2. Psychometrics—Social
   aspects. 3. Educational tests and measurements—Social aspects.
   4. Multiculturalism. I. Suzuki, Lisa A., 1961–   . II. Meller,
   Paul J. III. Ponterotto, Joseph G. IV. Series.
   BF176.H36 1996
   153.9'3'08'693—dc20   95–23643
                                                                            CIP

FIRST EDITION
HB Printing   10 9 8 7 6 5 4 3 2 1

Contents

Foreword

The *Handbook of Multicultural Assessment* is an ambitious undertaking. It encompasses assessment in the conventional culture of the United States, plus assessment in the variety of new cultures introduced by the large numbers of new immigrants. It permits focusing on the number of prejudices already existing about what assessment is and how it should be undertaken as well as raising issues that will add to such questions.

There has been severe criticism of the use of personality and cognitive measures with diverse ethnic populations. Even the most widely used measures of achievement have been attacked because of claimed cultural and ethnic bias, while measures of aptitude have fared even worse. While much research has addressed these issues conducted by individuals and by publishing companies to refute the claims of bias in their publications, the information remains unintegrated, and much is scattered across various disciplines, especially in the fields of education and psychology.

The *Handbook of Multicultural Assessment* brings together contributions by scholars in the areas of psychometrics, assessment, and evaluation who have expertise in the application of testing and assessment in multicultural environments. Considering the changing demographics of the country and the need for valid and reliable measurement of psychological constructs, the *Handbook of Multicultural Assessment* fills an important need. It not only provides a comprehensive view of various cultural issues but offers updated information pertaining to the usage of major psychological instruments. Special stress is placed on the fact that, in addition to the cultural differences incorporated in the construction of the items themselves, the normative data are primarily based on samples of U.S. participants rather than on those of the specific subculture to which the individual to be assessed belongs.

The tendency to ignore the variability existing among subcultures within a commonly accepted subculture is explored, and many illustrations such as the differences in Spanish vocabulary between Mexican and Puerto Rican children are given. For the relatively few U.S. tests for which a translation into a single language exists, warnings as to errors in interpretation by clinicians are prevalent.

The topics covered are extensive and range from a review and integration of the most current literature on multicultural assessment issues to information about the usage cross-culturally of the most popular psychological measures. For example, there are such interesting chapters as "Multicultural Usage of the MMPI-2" and "Language Assessment: Multicultural Considerations."

Every educational or social program is initiated, continues, or is discarded because of some form of evaluation that is buttressed by various types of assessment. One's major concerns should be to ascertain that the assessments are systematic and that the value implications are explicit. The authors of the *Handbook of Multicultural Assessment* have this objective in mind. The various topical chapters provide important information to assessment educators and students as well as to practitioners in the field. In view of its competitive focus, the book will have utility for most mental health professionals.

Syracuse University   Eric F. Gardner
November 1995

Preface

· ·

The use of personality and cognitive assessment instruments and methods with diverse racial and ethnic populations has been a source of controversy. Clinicians and educators have questioned the usage of personality and intellectual measures with diverse populations. Questions have been raised regarding whether these instruments discriminate against members of minority communities, for example, by underestimating their potential or overpathologizing their symptoms.

While much research has addressed issues of cultural bias and racial or ethnic differences on various measures, the information remains unintegrated and scattered across various disciplines in psychology and education. This text brings together writings by experts of national stature in the areas of psychometrics, assessment, and evaluation. The chapter authors are scholars with expertise in the application of testing constructs to multicultural assessment. The authors' contributions, prepared for this book by invitation, do not represent a consensus. Instead, a diversity of multicultural perspectives is presented.

Numerous articles and only a few books have been written addressing the general topic of multicultural assessment or usage of particular psychological measures with diverse populations. However, an integrative text does not currently exist. Given the changing demographics of this country and the need for accurate and sensitive measurement of psychological constructs, this text fulfills a great need in the field for a comprehensive review of various multicultural issues and updated information pertaining to usage of major psychological instruments.

This book is based in part on "Multicultural Assessment for Clinicians and Educators," an institute held in 1993 at Fordham University, Lincoln Center. Many of the chapter authors presented at this institute, which was attended by clinicians in the field (psychologists, social workers, counselors), as well as by educators and administrators. The institute enabled authors to meet with practitioners, students, and academicians regarding multiculturalism and assessment. Many of the participants asked that a text be developed based on the topics presented, given the importance of the information to clinical practice and training. This book represents an answer to this call.

The chapters represent reviews of the most current literature on multicultural assessment issues and usage of the most popular psychological measures cross-culturally. The text provides important information to educators, students, and practitioners. This book is appropriate for graduate courses in multicultural counseling and therapy and in assessment (both personality and cognitive). Given the comprehensive focus, it has utility for all mental health professionals.

It is beyond the scope of any text to cover all of the tests currently used in educational and clinical settings. The editors and authors have attempted to cover as many areas as possible. For example, the achievement chapter focuses primarily on the usage of group achievement tests, while the cognitive chapter highlights usage of popular, individually administered intelligence tests. In each case, it is hoped that the reader will obtain information that will be helpful in the selection of other instruments, and background information on general multicultural considerations regarding test use and interpretation.

Important key issues are discussed throughout the text. For example, acculturation and language issues are mentioned in numerous chapters.

The topics are arranged into four sections, each addressing a particular area of measurement and preceded by short introductory comments by the editors. Part I consists of two introductory chapters that provide foundational information regarding cross-cultural sensitivity and ethics. Part II encompasses social and emotional assessment issues including reviews of the major instruments and procedures used in this area. Part III targets cognition and educational assessment. Part IV focuses on emerging issues in assessment. It encompasses a range of contemporary topics relevant to multicultural assessment, and concludes with summary information and conclusions about present trends and future directions in multicultural assessment by the editorial team.

It is our hope that this book will stimulate interest and further debate regarding appropriate multicultural assessment practices. The complexities of the process make this a challenging area for research and open discussion regarding appropriate clinical practice.

Lisa A. Suzuki
Paul J. Meller
Joseph G. Ponterotto

Acknowledgments

We would like to sincerely thank the following students for their assistance in reviewing and editing the various chapters of this book: Shari Baum (Hofstra University), Glenn Matchett (University of Oregon), and Anne Robertson (University of Oregon). Without their assistance and constructive feedback, the publication of this text would have been much more difficult. We wish them continued success in their academic programs and professional growth.

Anthony A. Cancelli, former associate dean, Graduate School of Education, Fordham University, was instrumental in facilitating the Multicultural Assessment Institute from which the ideas for this book were created. His encouragement, patience, and understanding were greatly appreciated.

We would like to acknowledge the support and assistance of Rebecca McGovern, senior editor of the Jossey-Bass Social and Behavioral Science/Health Series, and Katie Levine, our editorial assistant. We are thankful for their patience with respect to various time delays.

Completion of this book was an extremely time-consuming task. The support of our families and significant others was critical. For their continuing love, understanding, and tolerance we will always be grateful.

The Editors

. . . .

Lisa A. Suzuki is assistant professor of counseling psychology at New York University. She joined this faculty in the fall of 1995. Most of the work on this text was completed while Suzuki was on an academic appointment at the University of Oregon (1993–1995). Her first academic appointment was in the counseling psychology program at Fordham University.

Suzuki received her B.A. degree (1983) in psychology from Whitman College, her M.Ed. degree (1985) in counselor education from the University of Hawaii, Manoa, and her Ph.D. degree (1992) in counseling psychology from the University of Nebraska, Lincoln.

Suzuki's main research interests have been in the areas of multicultural assessment and training. She is coeditor of the *Handbook of Multicultural Counseling* and coauthor of numerous chapters and encyclopedia entries focusing on multicultural assessment and intelligence testing.

Paul J. Meller is assistant professor in the combined clinical and school psychology program at Hofstra University. He received his B.A. degree (1982) in psychology from the State University of New York, Stony Brook, his M.A. degree (1984) in developmental psychology from Teachers College, Columbia University, and his Ph.D. degree (1988) in school psychology from Syracuse University. He has worked as a school psychologist or consulting psychologist in numerous school districts, head-start programs, and community mental health centers.

Meller's principal research activities have involved the prevention of school adjustment difficulties and the promotion of social competence in young children who are at high risk. He has authored numerous papers in the area of prevention and social competence, as well as on authentic assessment, social validity of interventions, and cross-cultural consultation.

Meller has been active in numerous professional organizations, including the New York Association of School Psychologists, the National Association of School Psychologists, and the Division of School Psychology of the American Psychological Association.

Joseph G. Ponterotto is a professor in the counseling psychology program at Fordham University, Lincoln Center, New York City. He received his B.A. degree (1980) in psychology from Iona College in New Rochelle, New York, and his M.A. degree (1981) in counseling and his Ph.D. degree (1985) in counseling psychology from the University of California, Santa Barbara. His first academic appointment was in the counseling psychology program at the University of Nebraska, Lincoln. He moved to Fordham University in 1987.

Ponterotto's professional focus is in the area of multicultural counseling, multicultural education, and diversity training. He is an active consultant on multicultural issues to school districts, universities, and a variety of organizations. His recent coauthored and coedited books include the *Handbook of Multicultural Counseling; Preventing Prejudice: A Guide for Counselors and Educators;* the *Handbook of Racial/Ethnic Minority Counseling Research;* and *Affirmative Action on Campus.*

The Contributors

Warren Stanley Adamson is a School based Prevention of Abuse through Rehabilitation and Knowledge (SPARK) counselor at Automotive High School in New York City. There he counsels adolescents and facilitates cognitive-behavioral training focusing on substance abuse, HIV, and violence prevention. He is pursuing an M.S. Ed. degree in guidance and counseling at Hunter College, City University of New York. Adamson has conducted anger control training at Hunter College. He is working on an anger control training experimental study, his thesis project.

Charlene M. Alexander received her B.A. degree (1983) in psychology and her M.S. degree (1985) in counseling from Creighton University. She received her Ph.D. degree (1992) in counseling psychology from the University of Nebraska, Lincoln. Alexander is coeditor of the *Handbook of Multicultural Counseling* and coauthor of a chapter entitled "Creative Approaches to Multicultural Counseling." Her work focuses on utilizing creative aspects of various cultures in the counseling process, including games, dance, music, and food.

Sabrina Teresa Arena is a doctoral student in Fordham University's urban school psychology program, where she is also a graduate assistant. She received her B.S. degree (1992) in psychology from St. John's University and her M.S. degree (1995) in bilingual psychology from Fordham University while acting as head research assistant for an infant cognitive development project.

Scott K. Baker is a research associate in the Division of Learning and Instructional Leadership at the University of Oregon. He received his B.S. degree (1981) in psychology from Longbeach State University, his M.S. degree (1984) in psychology from Western Washington University, and his Ph.D. degree (1993) in school psychology from the University of Oregon. His research interests include alternative assessment strategies with diverse learners, including those students for whom English is not their native language, and the development of early literacy skills for students at risk for academic failure.

Lorrie E. Bryant is a doctoral candidate in school psychology in the educational psychology department at the University of Nebraska, Lincoln. She received her B.A. degree (1977) in psychology from Hastings College and her M.A. degree (1979) in developmental psychology from the University of Nebraska, Omaha. She has extensive practical experience in schools and private and public agencies providing assessment and direct service to children and adults with special needs and their families. She also provides consultation and training to staff regarding effective educational and management strategies.

Anthony A. Cancelli is professor of school psychology at Fordham University, where he has been an educator in the school psychology program since 1981. He also coordinates the school psychology program and has served as associate dean and director of graduate studies in Fordham's Graduate School of Education. He received his B.S. degree (1970) from St. Joseph's University, his M.Ed. degree (1973) from West Chester State College, and his Ed.D. degree (1976) from Oklahoma State University.

Robert J. Clayton is a neuropsychology examiner with Neurobehavioral Assessments. He received his B.S. degree (1978) in psychology from Georgetown University. He pursued graduate study in psychology at the State University of New York, Stony Brook. He is senior author on presentations at the American Psychological Association, the International Neuropsychology Society, and the New York Neuropsychology Group, in association with the New York Academy of Science. His presentations have focused on neuropsychological function and brain electromagnetic topography.

Jane Close Conoley is professor of educational psychology at the University of Nebraska, Lincoln (UNL). She is also associate dean of research for UNL's Teachers College. She received her B.A. degree (1969) from the College of New Rochelle and her Ph.D. degree (1976) in school psychology, with a secondary area of systems theory and analysis, from the University of Texas, Austin. Her areas of primary interest are interventions with handicapped and seriously emotionally disturbed and aggressive children and youths, and family interventions. She is also well known for her work in measurement and serves as an editor of the *Mental Measurement Yearbook* series, published by the Buros Institute of Mental Measurements.

Carol A. Friedman is coordinator of the head trauma program at the Institute for Child Development at Hackensack Medical Center, and clinical assistant professor of pediatrics at the University of Medicine and Dentistry of New Jersey. She received her B.A. degree (1978) in psychology and her B.S. degree in elementary education from the University of Pennsylvania and her M.A. (1983) and Ph.D. (1986) degrees from the State University of New York, Stony Brook.

Eric F. Gardner is Margaret O. Slocum Professor emeritus of psychology and education at Syracuse University. He was chairman of the psychology department and director of the Psychological Services and Research Center at Syracuse University and was the senior author of the Stanford Achievement Test and other widely used tests. He is currently working on a revision of *ABLE (Adult Basic Learning Examination)* and on the *Syracuse Scales of Infant and Toddler Development*. He received his B.A. degree (1935) in mathematics from Harvard College, his M.A. degree (1936) from the University of Massachusetts, Boston, and his Ed.D. degree (1947) in measurement and statistics from Harvard University.

Leo Goldman is adjunct professor at Hunter College and project associate at the Center for Advanced Study in Education at the Graduate School; both are units of the City University of New York. He is retired from the City University of New York (1982) and Fordham University (1991). He is author of *Using Tests in Counseling* and editor of *Research Methods for Counselors*. He was editor of the *Personnel & Guidance Journal* (now the *Journal of Counseling and Development*). He is a diplomate in counseling psychology.

Roger L. Greene is professor of clinical training at Pacific Graduate School of Psychology. He received his B.A. degree (1966) in psychology from the University of Colorado, his M.S. degree (1967) in psychology from New Mexico Highlands University, and his Ph.D. degree (1974) in clinical psychology from Washington State University. He teaches, writes, and conducts research in the area of objective personality assessments.

Irma Guadarrama is associate professor in the School of Education at the University of Houston, where she teaches and conducts research in the Bilingual Education and ESL teacher training program. She received her B.S. degree (1971) in elementary education from Texas Christian University, her M.A. degree (1975) from the University of Texas, San Antonio, and her Ph.D. degree (1982) in curriculum and instruction from the University of Texas, Austin.

Abigail M. Harris is associate professor of school psychology at Fordham University. She works internationally in the area of testing and validity of assessment practices. She received her B.A. degree in sociology from University of Delaware, her M.A. degree (1973) from Michigan State University in educational psychology: learning and cognition, and her Ph.D. degree (1987) in school psychology from the University of California, Berkeley.

Kenneth W. Howell is professor of special education in the Woodring College of Education at Western Washington University. Howell has published extensively in the areas of assessment and evaluation. He received his B.A. degree (1971) in education and his M.A. degree (1972) in special education from Arizona State University, and his Ph.D. degree (1978) in special education with a concentration in school psychology from the University of Oregon. Howell also works nationally developing and monitoring special education programs for incarcerated children and youth.

Merle A. Keitel is associate professor of counseling and counseling psychology in the Graduate School of Education at Fordham University, where she is also director of training. Her research interests are in the areas of health psychology, stress and coping, and women's health issues. She received her B.A. degree (1980) in psychology from the State University of New York, Binghamton, and her Ph.D. degree (1987) in counseling psychology from the State University of New York, Buffalo.

Henry M. Koegel is a Ph.D. candidate in counseling psychology in the Division of Psychological and Educational Services at Fordham University, Lincoln Center. His area of specialization is multicultural counseling. He received his B.A. degree (1976) in psychology from Hofstra University and his M.A. degree (1989) in college counseling and student development from Hunter College of the City University of New York.

Eric L. Kohatsu is assistant professor of psychology at California State University, Los Angeles. He received his B.A. (1982) and M.A. (1985) degrees in religion from the University of Hawaii, Manoa, his Ed.M. degree (1987) in counseling psychology from Rutgers University, and his Ph.D. degree (1992) in counseling psychology from the University of Maryland, College Park. His research interests are in racial identity theory and its applications, Asian American mental health, cross-cultural counseling, racism and prejudice, research methodology, and religious/spiritual issues.

Mary Kopala is assistant professor in the Division of Educational Foundations and Counseling at Hunter College, City University of New York, and is a licensed psychologist. She received her B.S. degree (1971) in education, her M.Ed. degree (1980) in counseling, and her Ph.D. degree (1987) in counseling psychology, all from Pennsylvania State University. Her professional interests focus on qualitative methods and their application to diverse populations, for example, the experiences of immigrant children, including post-traumatic stress disorder. Additional areas include multicultural aspects of ethics, supervision, and health counseling.

John F. Kugler is a school psychologist for the New York City Board of Education. He is also an adjunct professor at Fordham University and former director of the School Consultation Center at Fordham. He received his B.A. degree (1982) in psychology from Brooklyn College, and his M.S. degree (1985) in educational psychology and his Ph.D. degree (1993) in urban school psychology from Fordham University.

S. Alvin Leung is associate professor of counseling psychology in the Department of Educational Psychology at the University of Houston. He received his B.S. degree (1980) in psychology, and his M.S. degree (1982) and Ph.D. degree (1988) in counseling psychology from the University of Illinois, Urbana-Champaign. His major research areas include career behavior of ethnic minorities, career assessment, and cross-cultural counseling and training.

Antonio Medina is graduate adviser of EOP/retention services at Chico State University, where he is also career adviser in career services. He received his B.A. degree (1993) in psychology from Sonoma State University and his M.Ed. degree (1994) in counseling from the University of San Diego. Antonio is currently transferring Ph.D. programs from the University of Texas, Austin, to the University of Nevada, Reno, where he will continue his doctoral studies in counselor education with an emphasis in student services.

Norweeta G. Milburn is assistant professor of psychology in the Department of Psychology at Hofstra University. She received her B.A. degree (1976) in psychology at Wesleyan University, and her M.A. degree (1978) in community/organizational psychology and her Ph.D. degree (1982) in community psychology at the University of Michigan, Ann Arbor.

Kevin L. Moreland is associate professor of psychology at Fordham University, where he is also assistant chair for graduate studies. He is also adjunct associate professor of psychology in psychiatry at Cornell University Medical College, and is on the editorial boards of four journals dedicated to psychological assessment. He received his B.A. degree (1976) in psychology from Florida State University and his Ph.D. degree (1981) in clinical psychology from the University of North Carolina, Chapel Hill.

Phyllis S. Ohr is assistant professor in the psychology department at Hofstra University. She received her B.A. degree (1976) in psychology from the State University of New York, Buffalo, and her P.D. degree (1983) in school psychology and her Ph.D. degree (1990) in clinical child psychology from St. John's University. Her expertise is in early childhood development, and she has served as consultant for early intervention programs and child care centers.

Amado M. Padilla is professor of education and chairman of the graduate program in language, literacy, and culture in the School of Education at Stanford University. He is the founding editor of the *Hispanic Journal of Behavioral Sciences* and author of 150 articles and chapters on numerous topics. He received his B.A. degree (1964) in psychology from New Mexico Highlands University, his M.S. degree (1966) in experimental psychology from Oklahoma State University, and his Ph.D. degree (1969) in experimental psychology from the University of New Mexico. He is active in numerous professional and community organizations and was elected to the Palo Alto Unified School District Board of Education.

Richard J. Rankin is professor emeritus of educational psychology at the University of Oregon. He obtained his B.A. degree (1953) in psychology, his M.A. degree (1954) in educational psychology, and his Ph.D. degree (1957) in individual differences and research design from the University of California. His academic appointments include the psychology departments at Chico State College (1958–1960) and Oklahoma State University (1960–1967), and the educational psychology department at the University of Oregon (1967–1995). His interests include the study of individual differences, multivariate research, fishing, and woodworking.

Marilyn A. Reynolds is a bilingual school psychologist and a student in the Fordham University school psychology doctoral program. She received her B.A. degree (1972) in romance languages from Queens College, her M.S. degree (1979) in elementary education from Long Island University, C. W. Post campus, and a professional diploma (1992) in school psychology from Fordham University. She has been a bilingual general and special education teacher as well as coordinator for bilingual special education for several districts in New York City.

Tina Q. Richardson is assistant professor in the Department of Counseling Psychology, School Psychology, and Special Education at Lehigh University. She is a graduate of the counseling psychology program at the University of Maryland. She received her B.A. degree (1985) in psychology, her M.A. degree (1987), and her Ph.D. degree (1991) in counseling psychology from the University of Maryland. Her research interests include multicultural issues in psychology, racial identity development, gender identity development, and counseling women.

Barry A. Ritzler is professor of psychology at Long Island University, in addition to his private practice and his consultation at Yeshiva University, City College of New York, and a New Jersey state prison. He is president of the Society for Personality Assessment, and also is a member of the faculty of Rorschach Workshops, Inc. He has been director of clinical training at the University of Southern Mississippi and Fairleigh Dickinson University. He received his B.A. degree (1964) from Manchester College and his Ph.D. degree (1969) from Wayne State University.

Robert Rueda is professor and chairperson of the Division of Educational Psychology in the School of Education at the University of Southern California, where he also teaches in the language, literacy, and learning program. He received his B.A. degree (1972) in psychology from the University of California, Los Angeles, his M.S.W. degree (1974) in clinical social work from the University of Southern California, and his Ph.D. degree (1979) in educational psychology and special education from the University of California, Los Angeles.

Mitchell L. Schare is associate professor of psychology at Hofstra University, where he is assistant director for clinical psychology in the doctoral program in clinical/school psychology. He received his B.A. degree (1978) in psychology from the State University of New York, Stony Brook. He received his M.A. (1982) and Ph.D.

(1985) degrees in clinical psychology from the State University of New York, Binghamton, following an internship at Brown University Medical School Consortium.

Mark R. Shinn is associate professor and director of the University of Oregon school psychology program. He received his B.A. degree (1974) in psychology from Gustavus Adolphus College and his Ph.D. degree (1981) in school psychology from the University of Minnesota. For two years, he was a full-time school psychologist with St. Paul Public Schools' Limited English Proficiency (LEP) team. He has published over sixty articles and book chapters, and he also edited *Curriculum-Based Measurement: Assessing Special Children*, the best-selling book in the Guilford School Practitioner series.

Ellen L. Shulman is a bilingual speech-language pathologist in the City School District in Rochester, New York. She received her B.A. (1979) and M.A. (1980) degrees in communication disorders from the State University of New York, Buffalo. She also received her Certificate of Advanced Studies in educational administration (1987) from the State University of New York, Brockport. She has published journal articles and instructional materials, and presented many workshops on multicultural topics.

Richard R. Valencia is associate professor of educational psychology in the College of Education at the University of Texas, Austin. He has published extensively in the areas of ethnic minority assessment issues and the psychological and social foundations of Mexican American education. He received his B.A. degree (1970) in psychology, his M.A. degree (1972) in educational psychology, and his Ph.D. degree (1977) in early childhood education, all from the University of California, Santa Barbara.

Damian A. Vraniak is an American Indian psychologist (Ojibwe-Sioux) who has worked with American Indian children and families for twenty years. He helped develop the Northwind Warriors, a gifted program for Indian children, and started the Minneapolis Indian Health Board mental health unit. In addition, he created the graduate-level national training program for Indian psychologists at Utah State University, and developed a new integrated family-centered service delivery form that is being implemented in three reservation and two urban Indian communities in Wisconsin and Minnesota. He obtained his B.S. degree (1973) in psychology from Mankato State University, his M.A. degree (1976) in psychology from George Peabody College, and his Ph.D. degree (1980) in clinical counseling and school psychology from Vanderbilt University.

Edward A. Yansen is director of pupil personnel services in the Rochester City School District in Rochester, New York, and is a practicing school psychologist. He has been an assistant elementary school principal, coauthored articles on multicultural assessment, and conducted seminars and workshops on this topic at the state and national levels. He received his B.S. (1974) and M.S. (1977) degrees in psychology from Pace University. He is completing his doctoral studies in educational administration at the University of Rochester.

Christine Zalewski is associate professor of psychology at Pacific Graduate School of Psychology, where she currently coordinates the psychological assessment sequence. She received her B.A. degree (1983) in psychology from the University of Rochester and her M.A. (1986) and Ph.D. (1989) degrees in clinical psychology from the University of Virginia. She both teaches and conducts research in the areas of psychopathology and psychological assessment.

Handbook of
Multicultural Assessment

Part I

· ·

General Issues in Multicultural Assessment

P art I of the *Handbook of Multicultural Assessment* focuses on general issues related to the process of assessment. The chapters included in this section focus on thematic issues that will impact usage of tests and testing procedures throughout the various areas covered in the text.

In Chapter One, Amado Padilla and Antonio Medina highlight major issues, considerations, and recommendations in using tests "sensitively" with diverse populations. Important considerations regarding societal issues, demographic features of the individuals tested, appropriate standardization procedures, language issues, high-stakes versus low-stakes assessment, and factors influencing testing procedures are highlighted. In addition, the authors identify the assumptions that often underlie the inappropriate usage of tests with linguistic and cultural minority groups. Recommendations in terms of test selection, behavioral observation, and usage of translated measures are presented.

In Chapter Two, Merle Keitel, Mary Kopala, and Warren Adamson critically examine the ethical issues and potential dilemmas that may arise in multicultural assessment. The authors specifically address areas of ethical concern in servicing minority communities and the importance of culturally congruent interventions. Keitel, Kopala, and Adamson cite specific studies in the literature to illustrate potential areas of bias present in the assessment procedure, diagnosis of mental illness in minority groups, and strategies for assuring ethical practice in multicultural settings. A case is provided to illustrate various ethical concerns in the assessment process.

· ·

Cross-Cultural Sensitivity in Assessment
Using Tests in Culturally Appropriate Ways

Amado M. Padilla and Antonio Medina

There is a long-standing debate regarding appropriate testing and assessment strategies for use with minority populations including women, ethnic minorities, limited standard-English speakers, and the physically challenged. According to Gregory and Lee (1986), psychoeducational assessment is an area of professional practice that has been particularly subject to complaints about the differential treatment of racial and ethnic minorities. Korchin (1980) and Olmedo (1981) have noted that it is possible for standardized testing to contribute to the perpetuation of social, economic, and political barriers confronting racial and ethnic minorities. Gregory and Lee note that standardized tests are used primarily for selecting and screening; consequently, if tests or their users are discriminatory toward particular groups, such groups may be unfairly denied access to educational and career opportunities.

Researchers, educators, and scholars familiar with minority communities argue that instruments normed on majority group populations or developed on Eurocentric approaches cannot be blindly applied to people of color. Anyone intent on using tests with ethnic minorities needs to understand and appreciate the heterogeneity within the specific ethnic group. The reason is simply this: The validity and reliability of a test used with individuals of different cultural or linguistic groups who were not included in the standardization group are questionable. Thus it is important to recognize that diversity may exist between test examiners and examinees even when the differences may not be easily apparent. An example would be the case of a Latino adolescent who appears acculturated to the test examiner, but who nonetheless is more adept in Spanish than English (Padilla, 1992) or who is not adept in the deeper cultural nuances of living in the United States. Also, the experiential background of ethnic minorities differs significantly from that of the mainstream on whom the tests were standardized, and this difference leads to questions about the validity of the test instrument.

In this chapter, we will discuss the challenges of using tests in culturally appropriate ways. This topic is not easily confined to a few pages, but we will summarize the major issues and offer recommendations for using assessment instruments and procedures in ways that are culturally sensitive.

What Is Culturally Sensitive Assessment?

We believe that assessment is made culturally sensitive through a continuing and open-ended series of substantive and methodological insertions and adaptations designed to mesh the process of assessment and evaluation with the cultural characteristics of the group being studied. The insertions and adaptations span the entire assessment and evaluation process, from the development or adaptation of instruments, including translation, to the administration of the measure and to the analysis, scoring, and interpretation of the scores. Assessment is also made culturally sensitive through an incessant, basic, and active preoccupation with the culture of the group or individual being assessed.

Cultural sensitivity in assessment becomes more complex when test users become conscious of culturally specific behaviors or areas of development such as ethnic identity or acculturation, which have not been viewed as significant concerns for most White, middle-class individuals. The important consideration regarding acculturation, for example, is that the relationship between change in cultural orientation, psychological adjustment, and educational attainment is in need of more attention. Issues of residence (rural, urban, suburban), English language proficiency, generation in the United States, and level of acculturation are particularly important for Latinos and Asian Americans.

There are three major ways in which tests may be biased: the very content or construction of test items may be biased; incidental features such as formatting, mode of test administration, or even examiner personality factors may be biased; and bias may be found in inappropriate use of a test, such as to select applicants deemed qualified for a desired position. In the case of the first type of bias, the content of a test can be easily manipulated to favor one cultural or social group over another. In the second type of bias, speed tests are a good example of an administrative procedure that can serve to penalize test takers who are not proficient in English. And finally, tests have sometimes been used to select individuals for a particular job when the test really had little bearing on the tasks to be carried out in the performance of the job.

The search for culturally fair strategies or selection rules is hampered by the lack of consensus on what constitutes "cultural fairness" (Williams, 1983). This is an important problem because it demonstrates some of the relevant activities of the measurement community in attempting to find solutions to bias selection (Williams, 1983). Bias in the selection process may result in unfair treatment and unequal opportunity or access for some groups. Williams (1983) also notes that consideration of selection rules is important because such rules are tools for determining potentially successful or unsuccessful applicants for purposes of admission or employment.

Bracken and Barona (1991) note that practitioners' need for appropriate instrumentation to use in the assessment of children from different cultural and linguistic backgrounds has long been a pervasive problem in education and psychology. This situation has become a major concern in education today because approximately

10 percent of all school-age children nationally come from non-English-language homes (Waggoner, 1988). This problem is even more critical in certain states. For example, in California about one-fourth of all students in kindergarten through twelfth grade enter school as limited English proficient (LEP) (California State Department of Education, 1994). A similar situation occurs in other states with large immigrant, school-age populations such as New York, Texas, Arizona, New Mexico, Illinois, Florida, and Massachusetts.

Research results have shown that, because of varying cultural backgrounds, approximately 5 million students are inappropriately tested each year by standardized assessment instruments—including standardized achievement tests (Torres, 1991). The issue of inappropriate assessment is of major concern in California because in the academic year of 1994–95 there were 1.2 million out of 4.5 million students in kindergarten through twelfth grade who were identified as limited English proficient (LEP). Furthermore, demographic information indicates that one out of every five people in California was born outside of the United States. Lastly, as a result of mandated testing, it has been estimated that, on the average, each student in the U.S. public school system takes three district- or state-mandated standardized tests each year (Coffman, 1985).

There is also the debate on whether psychometricians and other consumers of tests should use a test that would be considered biased or culturally bound in some way with someone who is not middle class. Tests may be considered biased if they project only predominant values and attitudes and do not reflect the linguistic and cultural experiences of minority groups. Such testing procedures definitely affect the assessment, interpretation, or placement outcomes of lower socioeconomic status individuals. The implication here is that test performance of an individual who comes from a different cultural background or is lower in social class may be affected in ways not intended by the test maker. Thus, while normative test information is very helpful and important in some regards, we need to know what the test or measure assesses when it is used with social groups for which it was not standardized (Sommers, 1989).

Johnson, Vickers, and Williams (1987) note that PL 94–142 (1975), the Education for All Handicapped Children Act, in part, provided impetus for the use of techniques for nonbiased assessment: "Among other guidelines for evaluation, it requires the establishment of procedures for the selection and use of a variety of tests that are not racially or culturally discriminatory" (p. 334). While there are arguments to be made for a purely technical definition of bias and validity, there are strong arguments to be made for the inclusion of politics, values, and culture in considering the full context of test interpretation and test use in which issues of test bias arise (Messick, 1989).

Low-Stakes Versus High-Stakes Testing

The major concern that arises when culturally sensitive testing procedures are not followed has to do with how the test outcomes are used. In today's test-conscious environment, where tests have acquired such prominence for diagnosis, selection, certification, and accountability, it is vitally important to contextualize this discussion in the language of "low-stakes" and "high-stakes" decision making. An example of low-stakes testing would be the use of assessment instruments to determine what the student knows or does not know and then to use such information to aid in instruction. Low-stakes testing is most commonplace in kindergarten to twelfth grade. One of the difficulties of such testing is that it may result in classifications and labels between students, which may not be followed by effective educational support for students identified as at risk, in need of remedial help, or not ready for promotion (McCarty and Cardenas, 1986).

On the other hand, high-stakes testing results in decision making that has an important and long-term effect regarding academic placement, scholarship awards, graduation, or professional and graduate school entry. Once test scores become numbers in a file, they provide the basis for high-stakes decisions concerning certification, selection, placement, and promotion that are made without consideration of inequities imposed by the original testing situation (Lam, 1993). Examples of high-stakes testing would be the use of a test score to determine eligibility for promotion to a supervisory position in an organization or a minimal score on the Graduate Record Examination (GRE) for admission to an elite graduate department or institution of higher education. A much more extended discussion of the impact of high-stakes testing on minority students can be found in Chapter Eighteen.

It is well known that important decisions are made in education, employment, and mental health services based on information provided by test results. Latinos and Asian Americans are becoming more prominent in the workforce because of their increasing numbers and youth relative to White Americans, who are more heavily distributed among the aging sector of the population (Hayes-Bautista, Schink, and Chapa, 1988). Padilla (1992) believes that these facts attest to the need to consider seriously the problem inherent in the psychological testing of Latinos and Asian Americans in order to ensure their educational and occupational opportunity and success. In so doing, the social well-being of all Americans is fostered. Furthermore, because so many crucial life decisions are in one way or another based on high-stakes testing, it is important to recognize the heterogeneity within the U.S. population and the difficulties that this poses for test developers and consumers alike.

In spite of the fact that standardized achievement tests have long been criticized for their potential bias against minority students (Lam, 1993) and the fact that educators, evaluators, and administrators have been reprimanded for inappropriate use of test scores, it is still a common practice in education to use assessment procedures to track students into vocationally or academically oriented classes. Educators driven by the need to be accountable to school boards and state-level educational agencies feel that they are assisting the students in selection and academic placement according to their intellectual capacity, personal skills, and interests. Many educators argue that assessment instruments are necessary for determining which students have the relevant knowledge and to what degree, and who are thus adequately prepared to complete college-oriented, high-track classes.

The challenges of culturally appropriate testing become even more interesting in the use of SAT and GRE scores. While college admission officers insist on applying the traditional test-score criteria and seek to recruit the cream of the crop of minority students, some officers of higher education argue that spoon-feeding the minority student and programming instruction to make up for past educational and cultural deprivation are not the proper roles of the university. Tests, they claim, are not unfair, they merely demonstrate the unfairness of the educational system. Next there are those extremists who insist on interpreting the relatively lower average scores of minorities as indicative of the inherent incapacity of some ethnic groups to undertake serious academic pursuits, and therefore condemn attempts to compensate for underachieving students. The latest version of this argument is presented by Herrnstein and Murray (1994) in their book *The Bell Curve*. In spite of the countless arguments leveled against these interpretations of racial differences in IQ, there is an audience for books such as *The Bell Curve*.

Psychometricians also claim that tests have been misused and misinterpreted by counselors, teachers, admission officers, and administrators. They argue that those who use tests should be aware of the meaning of the results and should not interpret the scores on IQ tests as implying permanent, innate, or irremediable deficiency (Samuda, 1975). Test results for some merely indicate the degree of the individual's atypical level of function. Tests may highlight the unfairness of life—not the unfairness of the test. According to Samuda, it is the job of our educational system to gear instruction to the special needs of the student and to bring him or her up to par.

Although tests are not perfect and infallible instruments, it is important to point out that tests have allowed merit to shine through and have opened doors to a more equitable distribution of opportunities (Samuda, 1975). Actually, this was one of the original intents of tests, and the goal is still an important one when using cognitive-based tests. However, the measurement of achievement and aptitude is so confounded by social class, quality of schooling, and cultural differences that the ideal for which tests were intended is often hopelessly entangled with the human drama of equality of opportunity for minority individuals and the politics of science and human well-being.

Questions about the validity of aptitude and achievement tests were discussed by a Latino psychologist more than sixty years ago (Sanchez, 1932a, 1932b), but little attention was given to Sanchez's critique at that time despite his intimate knowledge of Latino culture and the fact that he published his critiques in reputable journals of the day. We might ask, if questions were raised about the validity of tests by Sanchez and others beginning sixty years ago, and such concerns have continued to the present, why has so little attention been given to these problems? The answer to this rhetorical question probably is that people of color have not had the political clout, either in society generally or in the field of psychological assessment specifically, to insist that their concerns be taken seriously (Padilla, 1992).

Sanchez's work deserves further comment. First of all, Sanchez was Mexican American and familiar with all the nuances of his own culture—language, family dynamics, and socioeconomic conditions, and was trained with certain skills in the administration and interpretation of psychological data bearing on achievement and education (Padilla, 1988). This gave him the qualifications to assess and interpret with significant insight research findings about Mexican Americans. Padilla noted that although Sanchez identified problems with psychological tests and suggested resolutions more than sixty years ago, Latino and other ethnic minority individuals are nevertheless still confronted today by many of the same dilemmas in testing.

Over the years, numerous other investigators have criticized the administration of tests in English to linguistic minority children. The argument has long been that such testing is not valid and numerous recommendations to assist in appropriate assessment of limited English speakers or otherwise unacculturated individuals have been offered. For example, nearly sixty years ago, Mitchell (1937) suggested that a corrective factor be added to the mental test score of a Spanish language dominant child if tested in English, a correction that would more accurately reflect the child's level of intellectual functioning. Mitchell arrived at this recommendation after noting that children perform better in Spanish than in English on the Otis Group Intelligence Scale. This innovative idea was not implemented at the time since it was considered too radical, but is reminiscent of a procedure developed four decades later by Mercer (1979), who offered a System of Multicultural Pluralistic Assessment (SOMPA) that includes four sociocultural scales (urban acculturation, SES, family structure, and family size) combined with the WISC-R to determine an IQ score for children from minority backgrounds.

Although Mitchell's early recommendation for a corrective scoring procedure did eventually become a reality with Mercer's SOMPA procedure, we continue to be a long way from any type of implementation of an unbiased assessment system when it comes to certain categories of individuals such as limited English proficient speakers or less than fully acculturated ethnic minority people. At the least, we need more research on how nondominant proficiency in English interacts with other variables to predict performance on tests where speed is important (Llabre, 1991).

According to Pennock-Roman (1992), many of the same factors shown here to be associated with test scores for Latino students—quality of educational background, parental socioeconomic status, familiarity with tests, experience with time limits, and test-taking strategies—are also related to the test performance of other ethnic groups. In addition, she adds that for Latino students and linguistic minorities, language background is an important influence

on scores. Hence, she concludes that most, and perhaps all, aptitude tests cannot be considered "pure" measures of cognitive abilities for any student.

Readers might raise the question: If assessment instruments are
considered biased toward certain groups, then why are they still
being used? One apparent answer is that psychological assessment
is big business in the United States. It is estimated that approximately $900 million alone is spent on the assessment of students
in kindergarten through twelfth grade. This dollar amount does not
include total revenues from all facets of the testing industry, which
is closer to $5 billion a year. As a society, we are very test conscious
and use assessments for multiple purposes ranging from selection
of individuals for employment and promotion to objective methods of demonstrating program effectiveness. To gauge the multiple
uses of tests, all the reader has to do is examine the table of contents of this volume.

Concerns in Culturally Sensitive Testing

Bracken and Barona (1991) note that there is evidence to suggest
that children from different cultural backgrounds interpret test
items differently, bring to the test situation a different set of expectations and knowledge, and generally do not score as high as members of the mainstream culture on standardized tests. While
adequately translated tests can greatly enhance the accuracy of test
results, Bracken and Barona point out that examiners should not
ignore the important influence of the examinee's cultural experience and history on the assessment process. "The specific individual experience of non-majority culture individuals will greatly
influence their educational, emotional and language development"
(p. 129). Thus it is important to consider the test taker's cultural
and individual differences, in addition to language, in the assessment process. Also, when trying to fully understand minority test
takers, it is important to consider information related to their immi-

gration and educational status (Bracken and Barona, 1991). Furthermore, the implementation of culturally sensitive psychological and educational practice would be an added feature of culturally sensitive assessment practice.

Gregory and Lee (1986) note that the consumers of the results of psychoeducational assessments include not only parents but also helping professionals including therapists, teachers, and social workers. These professionals need to include the synthesizing of complex information to judge the validity of the test data. Decisions about the validity of test results can be particularly complex when test data are used to make high-stakes decisions for certain groups or ethnic populations.

It should be added here that the "Ethical Principles of Psychologists and Code of Conduct" (American Psychological Association [APA], 1992) direct professionals to provide thorough discussion of the limitations of their data, especially where their work touches on social policy or might be construed to the detriment of persons in specific age, sex, ethnic, or socioeconomic groups. Gregory and Lee (1986) add that the "Standards for Educational and Psychological Testing" (APA, 1985) suggest that it is essential that test users avoid bias in test selection, administration, and interpretation; they should avoid even the appearance of discriminatory practice. It is the appearance of discriminatory practice, however, that has led to the familiar controversy over the issue of test bias.

According to Lam (1993), five assumptions about a test taker's characteristics are usually made by developers of standardized achievement tests. These assumptions are especially pertinent to the testing of language minority students, because they are the students who are most frequently improperly assessed (Lam, 1993). The following five assumptions are interrelated.

1. *Developers assume that test takers have no linguistic barriers that inhibit their performance on the test.* It would be an ideal world if this were true, but the fact of the matter is that there are many

individuals who are not proficient in English and whose score may not reflect their true ability level, which would be obtained only if assessed in their dominant language. Valdés and Figueroa (1994) put this problem into perspective when they state: "When a bilingual individual confronts a monolingual test, developed by monolingual individuals, and standardized and normed on a monolingual population, both the test taker and the test are asked to do something that they cannot. The bilingual test taker cannot perform like a monolingual. The monolingual test can't 'measure' in the other language." (p. 172) Obviously, there are few easy routes around this complex problem, and all one can do is keep in mind the limitations of tests.

2. *The content of the test at any particular level is suitable and of nearly equal difficulty for test takers at a particular age or educational level.* There are today (because of immigration) many individuals who were raised and educated in other countries, for whom the cultural content of a test is problematic. In addition, there are numerous minority children whose education in inner-city schools has ill-prepared them for the educational content inherent in many tests.

3. *Test takers are familiar with or have the test sophistication for taking standardized tests.* It is quite probable that minority students are less familiar with standardized achievement testing and thus less testwise than majority students, most of whom have been exposed to standardized testing over an extended time. Another consideration is that more educated parents who are more testwise themselves engage in more coaching with their children to instruct them on strategies known to be useful on multiple-choice tests and in the importance of balancing speed and accuracy in objective type tests. This type of coaching and practice is generally not found in the homes of lower socioeconomic status children because their parents may not be knowledgeable themselves of good test-taking practices.

4. *Test takers are properly motivated to do well on the test.* In other words, there is an absence of motivational test bias that prevents test takers from performing to their full ability. However, for many

students the consequences of testing have not been favorable, and thus they may not be as motivated to perform on a test to their full ability, especially if they have the belief that tests are socially or culturally biased in the first place.

5.   *Test takers do not have strong negative psychological reactions to testing.* Developers of tests may not fully understand the adverse psychological impact experienced by an individual who is not confident in taking a test for linguistic, cultural, or social reasons. Prior experience with tests may have shown an individual that the speed requirements of tests create special difficulties when trying to access information in a second language or that certain content—especially in the areas of history, literature, and acceptable standards of behavior in the United States—may be difficult because of different educational, cultural, or life experiences. Thus, the absence of confidence on a test may create undue stress and anxiety for the test taker, depressing performance below what it might be under more optimal and relaxed conditions.

Aside from postulating a normal distribution of the population, standardization procedures have also been based on the assumption that the Euro-White, middle-class standards, values, attitudes, beliefs, experience, and knowledge are the only correct ones, thereby denying minority groups and poor Whites the recognition of their cultural distinctiveness (Samuda, 1975). In other words, minority individuals have been forced to compete on unequal terms with Euro-White, middle-class persons, giving the latter a marked advantage. It is not surprising, then, that scores on tests of all types are consistently lower for individuals who differ from the normative population. In short, when a test designed for one cultural group is administered to a different cultural group, the test automatically favors the first group and gives lower outcomes for the other group. Williams (1983) also notes that the match or mismatch between a student's cultural experiences and those of the school environment calls into question the validity of both predictor and criterion variables.

Standardized achievement testing procedures that are insensitive to linguistic and cultural needs of minority students can deflate students' test performances, and the resulting scores in turn result in inappropriate academic labeling and placement, such as retention in grade or low-expectation education tracks. These erroneous educational decisions reduce self-esteem and academic interest and can directly or indirectly lead students to leave school prematurely or achieve at lower levels than they might have were it not for inappropriate testing practices and policies. A more thorough discussion can be found in Chapter Nine, which specifically examines issues of achievement testing with diverse students.

According to Sommers (1989), the pragmatic element of language militates against both measures of reliability and validity, since an individual's language has been shown to be influenced by factors outside of those found in the formal testing atmosphere of normative studies. Sommers also notes that since individual children are more or less influenced by these pragmatic factors, standardized samples fail to reflect the diversity of their language understanding and use, and standardization language measures may consequently lack validity. It also has been suggested that age equivalent scores should be considered less reliable than other scores, such as standard scores or percentile ranks.

Sommers (1989) further mentions that a related problem is the use of norm-referenced language tests with children from minority populations. Efforts to modify norm-referenced tests to make them fairer and more accurate representations of some aspects of children's linguistic abilities by changing their content and form of administration are rarely completed, particularly prior to the publication of the test.

Sommers (1989) lastly mentions that based upon the effectiveness of the criterion measure as an overall indicator of the comprehensive use of language by kindergarten children, each of the screening tests lacked effectiveness in the accurate identification of children at risk for language disorders. From a theoretical standpoint, the model used to assess language performance and competence is based on a monocultural and monolingual view of language acquisition and functioning. Its underlying assumption is that individuals must attain and demonstrate certain competencies in English deemed essential for effective functioning as members of society. However, as was noted earlier, there is a large population of children for whom English is not the first and only language they must learn. In fact, bilingualism is the norm around the world rather than monolingualism, which is the prevailing view from an assessment perspective. Thus, another part of culturally appropriate assessment must incorporate features that credit individuals for bilingual skills and bicultural knowledge.

Similarly, Bernal (1990) states that there is something about the test(s) or testing situations that affects how minority subjects perform and suggests that English-language proficiency, socioeconomic status, testwiseness, motivation, and degree of acculturation all have an impact on an examinee's performance. As Marin (1992), Olmedo (1981) and Padilla (1980) point out, acculturative, linguistic, psychological, and sociocultural factors must all be considered in order to understand how a person fits within his or her own culture as well as within the dominant culture. An understanding of each individual's acculturation level and biculturalism should help to explain how culture differentially influences academic and test-taking performance (Barona and Pfeiffer, 1992).

In many instances, behaviors that may characterize individuals who are in the process of learning English or becoming acculturated into U.S. society may be interpreted as indicators of learning disabilities. When such tests are used with individuals coming from cultural or language backgrounds different from that of the normative population, the opportunities for inaccurate interpretation of test results increase (Santos de Barona and Barona, 1991). Thus, such scales may lack usefulness for the interpretation of the performance of individuals from diverse backgrounds. Such an assessment will require a skilled individual who is fluent in the examinee's language and who can separate problems "related to issues of language competence and those that are associated with deficits in learning" (Barona and Santos de Barona, 1987, p. 192).

The latter is important in that individuals who speak the same language but originate from different geographic regions may use different expressions to describe the same object, situation, or phenomenon (Santos de Barona and Barona, 1991). Psychologists who are bilingual have noted that failure to account for such differences can inappropriately penalize individuals for using those terms which are acceptable within their particular cultural framework. The issues surrounding the assessment of language are many. The challenges are compounded when trying to assess linguistic proficiency in English in native speakers of other languages. The challenges and many helpful suggestions to language assessment are discussed in Chapter Twelve.

In sum, children or adolescents with limited or no English language skills must be assessed carefully within the context of their cultural environment if appropriate educational or psychological services are to be provided. Such modifications, however, should not merely be static adjustments but should instead consider the unique circumstances of each child on an individual basis. It is well known that lower socioeconomic class and minority ethnic membership are associated with lower levels of performance on assessment measures of all types. With the demographic shifts taking place in our society today and projected to continue on into the future, it is time to acknowledge that assessment measures and practices need to reflect the richer cultural fabric that now constitutes the U.S. population.

Outcomes of Poor Testing Practices

In essence, identical treatment, the definition most consonant with accurate prediction, presupposes access to the same experiences: this is especially true of cognitive type testing. According to Williams

(1983), this supposition is not met in our educational system because of bias in placement—a substantial amount of research documents that minority and White children are indeed exposed to different curricula through the practice of ability tracking. The poor learning environment must lead to poor performance on the achievement tests, and thus it accounts for the accurate predictive validity cited by researchers.

Gregory and Lee (1986) note that standardized tests are used to select and screen. They further add that if these tests or their users discriminate negatively toward particular groups, such groups are unfairly denied access to educational and career opportunities. According to Padilla (1988), the result of inappropriate assessment procedures has long been the overrepresentation of Mexican American children in special education classes. Padilla further explains that more recent studies have shown that this practice continues, but in modified form. For example, a study of special education referral practices in large urban school settings found that over 60 percent of the Mexican American students referred were diagnosed as learning disabled or as language impaired, categories that were almost nonexistent a decade earlier.

The overrepresentation of Mexican Americans in special education classes has resulted in at least one court suit. In *Diana v. California State Board of Education* (1970), the suit questioned the practice of testing children in English when this was not their dominant language. Padilla (1988) notes that although this case was settled out of court and in favor of *Diana*, it has had little impact on professional practice and the overrepresentation of students in special classes.

Most culturally diverse children of preschool age have not interacted extensively in structured group situations. It has been estimated that fewer than one out of four minority children aged four years or younger have attended preschool programs (Fradd, 1987). For these children, most learning has occurred through the family, which itself may be isolated experientially from the mainstream culture (Santos de Barona and Barona, 1991).

Extrapolating to success in higher education, Samuda notes that scores on a test of scholastic aptitude or developed ability to reason with words and numbers posing college-level problems, inform the user about how much trouble a student may expect to have in moving immediately into college work. They say nothing about the odds against which the student has had to struggle in developing those particular abilities or about the energy and determination the individual will put into college work (Samuda, 1975). A student's ability to solve problems posed in a different language or cultural context may or may not be reflected in the scores, depending on how widely divergent the two cultures at issue may be.

For a student whose schooling has been poor or whose home and perhaps predominant community language is other than English, a moderate score may represent a triumph of ability, devotion to study, and resilience in the face of educational adversity. The test scores by themselves are not designed to reflect these characteristics, not because the qualities themselves are unimportant but because testing has not yet produced ways to measure them. In educational assessment and selection practices, the student's biographical record, demonstrated interest, and long-term perseverance as reflected in school grades, especially as further illuminated by the comments of those who know his or her history, are the indispensable bases for understanding the meaning of the scores resulting from the test.

Bracken and Barona (1991) mention that the practice of translating tests from a source language into a second target language has not generally provided an acceptable solution to the pervasive problem of inappropriate assessment for many reasons, among which are the following:

1. Test directions are frequently too psychotechnical, difficult, stilted, or "foreign" to allow for easy translation.

2. Practitioner-produced translations are rarely back-and-forth translated (Brislin, 1980) to provide equivalent meanings across languages.

3. The underlying psychological constructs assessed by translated tests are sometimes not universal across cultures (Van de Vijver and Poortinga, 1982).

4. Content assessed on achievement tests can differ in importance across cultures or languages (Fouad and Bracken, 1986).

5. Examinee test-taking behaviors and orientations toward test directions and procedures can vary from one culture to another (Butcher and Pancheri, 1976).

6. There has been a general failure to develop workable translation procedures or standards against which to systematically judge the equivalence of translations and constructs across languages or cultures (Brislin, 1970).

Each of these potential threats to translation validity highlights the need for special care and attention to be paid to the procedures used in producing translations of tests for multicultural and multilingual assessment (Bracken and Barona, 1991).

Werner and Campbell (1970) offer five basic recommendations to facilitate the production of quality test translation. They point out that test items should consist of simple sentences, pronouns should be avoided in test directions and items and nouns should be repeated instead, test items should not contain metaphors or colloquialisms, the passive voice in test directions and items should be avoided, and hypothetical phrasing and subjunctive mood in test directions and items should be avoided.

Because the translation of any test is difficult, time consuming, and inherently error prone, it is important that an instrument selected for translation be psychometrically sound and of potential use in a translated form. Obviously, it would not be sensible to translate an instrument of marginal quality (Padilla, 1992).

A comprehensive, multistep translation and validation process is essential for the successful translation of tests from their source language to one or more target languages (Bracken and Barona, 1991). Test translators should not strive to make the test "as easy as possible" or "more easily understood" than the source-language version; they should strive to render a translation that is as nearly identical in structure and format to the source-language version as possible, without compromising the cultural uniqueness of the target population for whom the translation is intended (p. 123).

Bracken and Barona (1991) lastly note that the back-translation should be contrasted with the original version of the test to compare grammatical structure, comparability of concepts, level of word complexity and overall similarity in meaning, wording, and format. "As with the original translator, the back-translator should be well educated, fully bilingual and familiar with the psychotechnical concepts and language employed in the source tests materials" (p. 123).

As previously mentioned, testing procedures and outcomes can be placed within a framework of low-stakes and high-stakes testing. Low-stakes testing is used for such things as implementation of curriculum to increase children's knowledge or to diagnose deficiencies and determine what children need to know. On the other hand, high-stakes testing results in decision making that has an important and long-term effect ranging from placement in special education classes to high-ability classes, scholarships, professional and graduate school admission, and job promotion. Clearly, the concern for appropriate assessment is critical because students who do poorly on a low-stakes test will not be prepared to do well in a high-stakes test, the result of which may be vocational tracking or gatekeeping from higher education. The concern for such consequences is even more important with the increased discussion of national testing standards and educational accountability. As this move takes hold, the need for fair and authentic assessment measures and practices is more critical. A more detailed discussion of the challenges inherent in alternative assessment procedures can be found in Chapter Seven.

Recommendations for Nonbiased Assessment Practices

Duffey, Salvia, Tucker, and Ysseldyke (1981) described biased assessment as constant error in decisions, predictions, and inferences about members of particular groups. Historically, strategies employed to eliminate these discriminatory aspects included attempts to minimize the cultural and verbal components of testing or so-called fair testing (Cattell, 1950). One of the most publicized approaches to nonbiased assessment has been the use of pluralistic norms, such as the System of Multicultural Pluralistic Assessment (SOMPA; Mercer, 1979). Johnson, Vickers, and Williams (1987) note that while these techniques are available, the extent that they are being used has not been determined. Some researchers, in fact, have suggested that few school psychologists are trained in the area of nonbiased assessment, and therefore know little about these procedures for evaluating children from minority group backgrounds. The finding is generally supported by critics who have suggested that frequently psychologists neglect to use techniques that can reduce bias during assessment of students from minority groups. Complex judgments concerning appropriate and equitable use can best be made by test administrators such as school psychologists and teachers familiar with the students and the environment in which the test is administered (Lam, 1993, p. 180).

Eurocentric approaches to the study of ethnic minority populations in education is based on the fact that these approaches have frequently resulted in misguided interpretations because of specific biases inherent in the paradigms themselves. Research emphasis is also usually placed on a comparative approach that uses similar measures to compare groups of people who differ across culture, ethnic origins, or languages. We must keep in mind the importance of understanding how the cultural background that the ethnic respondent brings to the task of completing interviews, surveys, and multiple-choice tests determines the response patterns that emerge. A more appropriate or bias-free sample may be a more likely outcome when the ethnic community is involved in the psychological assessment enterprise. All consumers of assessment measures need to address the relevance of mainstream paradigms that test developers use to define their approach.

As the authors in this book indicate, users of tests, regardless of the context, must question the absence of critical information when it comes to assessing culturally diverse populations. Further, the competence necessary for becoming culturally sensitive in assessment procedures is not an easy task. Psychologists who employ tests as part of their professional responsibility may be unaware of how their linguistic, social class, and cultural experiences influence their construction of knowledge, selection of particular tests, and interpretations they derive from psychological assessment procedures. Standard norms in assessment usually reflect the values of the dominant social group and any deviations from this are interpreted as deficits or differences that possibly require intervention.

A paradigm shift is required wherein the study of a specific ethnic group is valued for its own sake and need not be compared to another group, especially if the comparison is likely to be biased. Instruments that are biased and that favor a particular group should not be used to evaluate differences between culturally distinct groups of people. Psychological research should not examine individuals from the perspective of their failures, but rather should concentrate on success experiences for the purpose of building on these to achieve even greater success. Further, instruments must also be appropriate for properly assessing changes in learning or behavior due to instruction or some other intervention program. However, if assessment devices are inappropriate in a pretest context, they will also be poor measures of postintervention learning or behavior changes.

Test makers and users need to be aware of how test performance is influenced by social class, inequality in educational opportunity, parent's educational attainment, cultural orientation of the home, language background of examinees, proficiency in English, prior socialization experiences, family structure and dynamics, and level of motivation to do well. When sufficient information is obtained beforehand about possible confounding variables in deciding to test a particular individual or group, a more informed decision can be made about the suitability of the assessment instruments to be used.

In order to increase the cross-cultural assessment competency of test examiners, such individuals must be knowledgeable and comfortable with the traditional customs and communicative styles of many individuals who do not represent the prototypical middle-class person on whom most assessment instruments are based. We recommend that test users find ways to involve the minority community members in the selection of instruments to be used in schools, places of employment, placement centers, and so forth. This practice will increase the trust and rapport that the minority community will have in testing practices and will result in more appropriate assessment measures, practices, and decision making.

In conclusion, it continues to be important to expose and sensitize professionals to possible discriminatory assessment practices while continuing to broaden our options in multicultural assessment methods. In advocating for an approach to multicultural assessment that is culturally sensitive, it is also evident that as professionals we must redouble our efforts to increase the pool of qualified minority psychologists who are trained in psychometric theory and test construction. Further, we need to train individuals who can become experts in psychological assessment of all types, who will assume leadership positions in their respective fields. To date, there are too few psychologists with the expertise necessary to advance our challenge for a culturally sensitive approach to assessment beyond that which has prevailed for the past twenty-five years. As we near the twenty-first century, we look forward to assessment practices that better reflect the multicultural face of our country.

References

American Psychological Association (1992). *Ethical principles of psychologists and code of conduct.* Washington, DC: Author.

American Psychological Association (1985). *Standards for educational and psychological testing.* Washington, DC: Author.

Barona, A., & Pfeiffer, S. I. (1992). Effects of test administration procedures and acculturation level on achievement scores. *Journal of Psychoeducational Assessment, 10,* 124–132.

Barona, A., & Santos de Barona, M. (1987). A model for the assessment of limited English proficient students referred for special education services. In S. H. Fradd & W. J. Tikunoff (Eds.), *Bilingual education and bilingual special education: A guide for administrators* (pp. 183–210). Boston: College Hill Press.

Bernal, M. E. (1990). Increasing the interpretative validity and diagnostic utility of Hispanic children's scores on tests of achievement and intelligence. In F. C. Serafica, A. I. Schwebel, R. K. Russell, P. D. Isaac, & L. B. Myers (Eds.), *Mental health of ethnic minorities* (pp. 108–138). New York: Praeger.

Bracken, B. A., & Barona, A. (1991). State of the art procedures for translating, validating and using psychoeducational tests in cross-cultural assessment. *School Psychology International, 12,* 119–132.

Brislin, R. W. (1970). Back translation for cross-cultural research. *Journal of Cross-Cultural Psychology, 1,* 185–216.

Brislin, R. W. (1980). Translation and content analysis of oral and written material. In H. C. Triandis & J. W. Berry (Eds.), *Handbook of cross-cultural psychology: Vol. 2: Methodology.* Needham Heights, MA: Allyn & Bacon.

Butcher, J. N., & Pancheri, P. (1976). *A handbook of cross-national MMPI research.* Minneapolis: University of Minnesota Press.

California State Department of Education. (1994). *Fall language survey results for school year 1993–1994.* Sacramento: Office of Bilingual Education.

Cattell, R. (1950). *Culture-free intelligence test.* Champaign, IL: Institute for Personality and Ability Testing.

Coffman, W. E. (1985). *Testing in the schools: A historical perspective.* Los Angeles: University of California, Center for the Study of Evaluation.

Diana v. California State Board of Education (1970), Civ. No. C-70–37 RFP (N.D. Cal., 1970).

Duffey, J., Salvia, J., Tucker, J., & Ysseldyke, J. (1981). Nonbiased assessment: A need for operationalism. *Exceptional Children, 47,* 427–433.

Fouad, N., & Bracken, B. (1986). Cross-cultural translation and validation of two U.S. psychoeducational assessment instruments. *School Psychology International, 7,* 167–172.

Fradd, H. S. (1987). *Bilingual education and bilingual special education: A guide for administrators.* Boston: Little, Brown.

Gregory, S., & Lee, S. (1986). Psychoeducational assessment of racial and ethnic minority groups: Professional implications. *Journal of Counseling Psychology and Development, 14,* 635–637.

Hayes-Bautista, D. E., Schink, W. O., & Chapa, J. (1988). *The burden of support: Young Latinos in an aging society.* Stanford, CA: Stanford University Press.

Herrnstein, R. J., & Murray, C. (1994). *The bell curve: Intelligence and class structure in American life*. New York: Free Press.

Johnson, B. A., Vickers, L., & Williams, C. (1987). School psychologists' use of techniques for nonbiased assessment. *College Student Journal, 21,* 334–339.

Korchin, S. J. (1980). Clinical psychology and minority problems. *American Psychologist, 35,* 262–269.

Lam, T.C.M. (1993). Testability: A critical issue in testing language minority students with standardized achievement tests. *Measurement and Evaluation in Counseling and Development, 26,* 179–191.

Llabre, M. M. (1991). Time as a factor in the cognitive test performance of Latino college students. In J. Deneen, G. Keller, & R. Magallan (Eds.), *Assessment and access: Hispanics and higher education* (pp. 95–104). New York: SUNY Press.

Marin, G. (1992). Issues in the measurement of acculturation among Hispanics. In K. F. Geisinger (Ed.), *Psychological testing of Hispanics* (pp. 235–252). Washington, DC: American Psychological Association.

McCarty, J., & Cardenas, J. (1986). A minority view on testing. *Educational Measurement, 5,* 6–11.

Mercer, J. R. (1979). *Technical Manual: System of Multicultural Pluralistic Assessment (SOMPA)*. New York: Psychological Corporation.

Messick, S. (1989). Validity. In R. L. Linn (Ed.), *Educational measurement* (3rd ed.). New York: Macmillan.

Mitchell, A. J. (1937). The effect of bilingualism in the measurement of intelligence. *Elementary School Journal, 38,* 29–37.

Olmedo, E. L. (1981). Testing linguistic minorities. *American Psychologist, 36*(10), 1078–1085.

Padilla, A. M. (1980). The role of cultural awareness and ethnic loyalty in acculturation. In A. M. Padilla, (Ed.), *Acculturation: Theory, models and some new findings* (pp. 47–84). Boulder, CO: Westview Press.

Padilla, A. M. (1988). Early psychological assessment of Mexican-American children. *Journal of the History of the Behavioral Sciences, 24,* 113–115.

Padilla, A. M. (1992). Reflections on testing: Emerging trends and new possibilities. In K. F. Geisinger (Ed.), *Psychological testing of Hispanics* (pp. 271–284). Washington, DC: American Psychological Association.

Pennock-Roman, M. (1992). Interpreting test performance in selective admissions for Hispanic students. In K. F. Geisinger (Ed.), *Psychological testing of Hispanics* (pp. 99–136). Washington, DC: American Psychological Association.

Public Law 94–142. (1975). *Education for All Handicapped Children Act of 1975*, 20 U.S. § 1401.

Samuda, R. J. (Ed.). (1975). *Psychological testing of American minorities: Issues and consequences. Alternatives to traditional standardized tests*. New York: HarperCollins.

Sanchez, G. I. (1932a). Group differences in Spanish-speaking children: A critical review. *Journal of Applied Psychology, 40,* 223–231.

Sanchez, G. I. (1932b). Scores of Spanish-speaking children on repeated tests. *Journal of Genetic Psychology, 40,* 223–231.

Santos de Barona, S. M., & Barona, A. (1991). The assessment of culturally and linguistically different preschoolers. *Early Childhood Research Quarterly, 6,* 363–376.

Sommers, R. K. (1989). Language assessment: Issues in the use and interpretation of tests and measures. *School Psychology Review, 18,* 452–462.

Torres, J. (1991). Equity in education and the language minority student. *Forum, 14*(4), 1–3.

Valdés, G., & Figueroa, R. A. (1994). *Bilingualism and testing: A special case of bias*. Norwood, NJ: Ablex.

Van de Vijver, F.J.R., & Poortinga, Y. H. (1982). Cross-cultural generalization and universality. *Journal of Cross-Cultural Psychology, 13,* 387–408.

Waggoner, D. (1988). Foreign born children in the United States in the eighties. *NABE: Journal of the National Association for Bilingual Education, 12,* 23–49.

Werner, O., & Campbell, D. (1970). Translating, working through interpreters, and the problem of decentering. In R. Naroll & R. Cohen (Eds.), *A handbook of method in cultural anthropology* (pp. 398–420.) New York: Natural History Press.

Williams, T. S. (1983). Some issues in the standardized testing of minority students. *Journal of Education, 165,* 192–208.

Ethical Issues in
Multicultural Assessment

Merle A. Keitel, Mary Kopala, and
Warren Stanley Adamson

Counselors, social workers, and psychologists are responsible for promoting the well-being of their clients (for example, American Association for Counseling and Development [AACD], 1988; American Psychological Association [APA], 1992). Ethical dilemmas arise when mental health professionals encounter situations in which it is necessary to consider more than one competing ethical principle. For example, a psychologist may assess his or her client as not having the psychological or intellectual resources to adequately care for a child. The professional may consider taking a paternalistic action and removing the child from the home in spite of the risk that this may do psychological harm to the client. While ethical guidelines and standards of practice provide some structure, they cannot respond to every potential situation and are meant to be used primarily as an heuristic for practice. Consequently, ethical decision making is frequently anxiety provoking for mental health professionals (Sileo and Kopala, 1993).

Ethical questions in assessment become even more complex when multicultural issues are involved. Mental health professionals who understand individuals within their cultural context improve the accuracy and usefulness of psychological assessment results (Pope and Vasquez, 1991). While culture, ethnicity, and race are identified as important variables to be considered while engaged in the assessment process, how to incorporate these variables when conducting assessments is seldom discussed in the literature. This chapter will identify cultural factors related to ethical assessment procedures, present guidelines for the assessment of minority group members, and describe a case for the purposes of illustrating the many variables that counselors need to consider when completing an assessment of a minority group member.

Ethical Multicultural Practice

Ethical practice in general requires that mental health professionals be sensitive to and aware of the special needs of minorities. It has been recommended that mental health professionals advocate against agency policies that may impose obstacles for some groups of individuals and not others (such as hours of operation, forms to be completed, or wheel chair access), and develop strategies that enhance the quality of life for ethnic minorities who are living in poverty and are subject to poor living quarters and violence. In addition, mental health professionals need to understand and be alert to possible biases when interpreting research findings, be aware that many assessment instruments did not include minority members in their normative samples (or are culturally loaded to reflect the psychological constructs relevant to U.S. culture), avoid discriminating against individuals based on their ethnic-racial status or gender (this discrimination may be subtle and unintentional), and understand the context in which clients live in order to understand the distress they feel (Pope and Vasquez, 1991).

In addition, clients must be helped to understand, maintain, and resolve their sociocultural identity (see *Guidelines for Providers of Services to Ethnically and Culturally Diverse Populations*, APA, 1990). Potential risks and benefits must be clearly explained. When working with a client from a different cultural background, the mental health professional must consider the client's level of acculturation. A client may be highly acculturated to the dominant culture, and the counselor, therefore, should not mistakenly assume that the client's world view is compatible with his or her culture of origin (Ibrahim and Arredondo, 1986).

Limitations of Using Tests with Minorities

Knowing the limitations of various tests with people of color is imperative. The tests themselves may not be biased if they are used in the ways in which they were intended. Other chapters in this book describe these limitations in detail.

Potential Bias in Test Administration

Bias may be introduced during the administration of tests because of the examiner's feelings, beliefs, and attitudes toward the client on the basis of his or her racial-ethnic membership, gender, sexual orientation, or other characteristics. When the test taker's primary language is different from that of the examiner, miscommunication is likely. Word, Zanna, and Cooper (1974) note differences between how White interviewers behaved with White versus Black interviewees; that is, more physical distance, more speech errors, and less eye contact with Black versus White interviewees. White interviewers were trained to use both styles with all White interviewees. White interviewees who were interviewed in the manner in which Blacks were typically interviewed performed less well on a series of objective measures used during the assessment interview. Although this study is twenty years old and should be replicated, it still alerts individual professionals to be aware of how their attitudes can influence the outcome of assessments.

Potential Bias in Ratings

Sackett and DuBois (1991) compared data from three sources: their own large-scale civilian study; a large-scale military study (Pulakos, White, Oppler, and Borman, 1989); and a meta-analytic study (Kraiger and Ford, 1985) that examined performance ratings of peers and supervisors. In the civilian and military studies, Whites received higher ratings than did Blacks from both Black and White raters. In contrast, the results of the Kraiger and Ford meta-analytic study indicate that Blacks rated Blacks higher and Whites rated Whites higher. This was not supported in Sackett and DuBois' reanalysis of the data from Kraiger and Ford's study for several reasons: mostly peer ratings were included in the meta-analysis; studies were not sorted according to type prior to computing effect sizes; and only fourteen samples of the seventy-four studies reviewed in the meta-analysis had Black raters. In the reanalysis, Sackett and DuBois separated the fourteen samples into laboratory studies, peer rating studies, and supervisor rating studies. The effect sizes were computed and data again analyzed. They concluded that Black supervisors do not rate Black supervisees higher than they rate Whites.

Differences were found when peers rated each other versus when supervisors rated their supervisees. Blacks tended to rate their Black peers higher than their White peers, while both Black and White supervisors tended to rate Whites higher than Blacks, and there was essentially no difference in the ratings received by White supervisees. Black supervisors tended to rate the Black supervisees higher than did White supervisors.

Potential Bias in Interpretation of Test Results

Psychological assessment instruments and techniques may not be biased, but bias may be introduced when the results are interpreted. For example, Pope and Vasquez (1991) cite Bache's (1894) early studies of reaction time that reported that men had faster reaction times than women. Bache interpreted this as evidence of men's superior intellect. In later comparisons between Whites and Blacks, he wrote, "That the Negro is, in the truest sense, a race inferior to that of the whites, can be proven by many facts, and among these, the quickness of his automatic movements as compared with those of the white" (cited in Pope and Vasquez, 1991, p. 134). In other words, when men were found to have faster reaction times than women, reaction time was interpreted as being an index of intelligence. However, when Blacks were found to have faster reaction times than Whites, reaction time was interpreted as having an inverse relationship with intelligence. Bache reasoned that Whites had slower reflexes to compensate for the advancement of their intellect.

Obvious differences in language might alert the examiner to be cautious when interpreting test results. However, when one's client appears to be fluent or has great facility in the dominant language, the examiner may draw erroneous conclusions about the client's abilities. It is possible that the client may be constructing the second language according to the rules of the primary language. This could lead the tester to question the logic of the responses. (See Chapter Twelve for further discussion of language issues in assessment.)

If the professional could understand or identify the patterns of construction, entirely different conclusions could be reached. For example, a Chinese woman responding to open-ended questions on a personality measure may be misperceived by the examiner as being disorganized because of the sequencing of words.

The content of the message itself can be misconstrued, as illustrated by the following scenario. An Iranian man wrote to his American female pen pal: "Please write anything you want to me until I send for you." The receiver of the letter was so fearful that she never wrote back. We can assume that the letter's author was expressing that he was waiting for further correspondence rather than planning a trip to kidnap the young woman. Such misinterpretations during an assessment could lead to serious consequences such as hospitalization, dismissal from a job, placement in the wrong educational setting, loss of freedom, refusal to continue one's education, among others. We refer readers to *Standards for Educational and Psychological Testing* (APA, 1985) for a specific discussion of testing linguistic minorities.

Diagnosis of Mental Illness in Minorities

Minority people have been diagnosed with mental illness more often than members of the dominant culture. For example, a recent study indicates that Blacks and Hispanics in state and county mental hospitals were more apt to be diagnosed as schizophrenic at the time of admission (56.3 percent and 43.9 percent, respectively) as compared to Whites (31.5 percent). Similarly, those admitted to psychiatric units of nonfederal general hospitals exhibited differential percentages of schizophrenia diagnoses, that is, Blacks 38.0 percent, Hispanics 36.7 percent, and Whites 22.7 percent. A similar pattern is evident in private psychiatric hospital admissions for schizophrenia (Blacks 35.7 percent, Hispanics 27.2 percent, and Whites 19.2 percent) (Snowden and Cheung, 1990).

Involuntary psychiatric hospitalization also occurs at different rates for members of minority groups. Involuntary psychiatric criminal commitment occurs 3.5 times more often for other racial groups than it does for Whites, and involuntary noncriminal commitment occurs 2.4 times as often (Rosenstein, Milazzo-Sayre, MacAskill, and Manderscheid, 1987). Bias in evaluation may account for the differential rates of diagnosis and involuntary hospitalization across cultural groups rather than actual differences in rates of occurrence of specific mental disorders (Snowden and Cheung, 1990).

Mental health professionals must be aware of environmental stressors that may influence how people behave. Those who are not subject to discrimination on a regular basis may pathologize minority persons as hostile or paranoid when in fact their behavior may be viewed as ways to cope with the poverty or prejudice they are experiencing. Many minority group members report being followed or ignored by sales personnel when they are in retail shops. Such reports should not necessarily be construed by professionals as paranoid ideation. There is a good possibility that this has, in fact, occurred.

Another explanation for why minority group members tend to have higher rates of mental illness is that disproportionate numbers of minority populations tend to fall in the lower socioeconomic status (SES) categories. SES and race are highly correlated in the United States with some ethnic minority groups having lower SES. Income is also the variable most consistently correlated with well-being. Therefore, distress experienced by low-income individuals may be due to economic circumstances rather than race. Further, SES is also highly related to measures of intelligence, as those from higher SES background appear to score higher on these measures.

In response to authors' criticisms of the DSM-III and DSM-III-R when diagnosing minority group members, (Velasquez, Johnson, and Brown-Cheatham, 1993) the DSM-IV (American Psychiatric Association, 1994) has incorporated some information about cultural factors. It alerts clinicians who do not share the same cultural background as their clients that errors could occur in making assessments. Unless the clinician is familiar with the nuances of the culture, misinterpretation is quite possible since some behaviors that are considered normal in one culture may be considered abnormal in another. Cultures vary in their communication styles, ways of coping, and so forth, and therefore applying personality disorder criteria across cultures is not appropriate.

The DSM-IV has improved on the DSM-III-R by including an appendix that gives general instructions on how to understand the impact of culture on the presenting symptoms and descriptions of culture-bound syndromes, including symptom patterns and idioms for describing distress. It also explains how disorders may be influenced by culture in that, for example, in some cultures depression appears primarily as somatic symptoms rather than sadness. The references to culture are minimal, but more emphasis is given to environmental stressors in formulating a diagnosis. Previously, Axis 4 asked the practitioner to rate the severity of psychosocial stressors as experienced by most individuals. Now, Axis 4 requires the practitioner to list specific current environmental stressors that may impact the mental well-being of the client. Experiences of discrimination or recent migration to the United States are examples of stressors that might be specified on Axis 4. Further, the authors of DSM-IV urge practitioners to use all Axes when diagnosing a client rather than depending on Axes 1 and 2 only.

The DSM-IV acknowledges the importance of cultural variables and provides a schema for incorporating their importance when working with a client from a different cultural background. This is an important first step. Now the ethical practitioner must utilize the system as it was intended to be used. Further, the cultural information incorporated in the DSM-IV is limited for some disorders and, consequently, it is critical that practitioners not rely solely on the DSM-IV for information regarding the influence of cultural factors in mental functioning. Finally, in creating the DSM-IV, a panel of international experts contributed information about the impact of culture and a new V code, acculturative stress, has been included.

Strategies for Assuring Ethical Multicultural Assessments

Mental health professionals should be familiar with the following publications: *Ethical Standards* (AACD, 1988) with particular attention to Section C, Measurement and Evaluation; *Ethical Principles of Psychologists* (APA, 1992) with attention to Principle 8, Assessment Techniques; *Guidelines for Computer-Based Tests and Interpretation* (APA, 1986); *Casebook on Ethical Principles of Psychologists* (APA, 1987); *Guidelines for Providers of Services to Ethnically and Culturally Diverse Populations* (APA, 1990); and *Standards for Educational and Psychological Testing* (APA, 1985).

Psychologists must be trained in the administration and interpretation of specific tests. Further, they must be competent in the application of particular tests to clients of specific cultural backgrounds, for example, Puerto Rican Americans, Mexican Americans, African Americans, Caribbean Americans, and other identifiable origins. Psychologists must also be cognizant of differences among individuals within these groups.

Both graduate and postgraduate training in multicultural assessment and ethical decision making is valuable. Classes and workshops with a multicultural focus sponsored by professional associations and cultural groups can help sensitize the professional to these issues. Specifically, training in hands-on clinical assessment with multicultural populations is helpful. Cultural education can also help the professional to understand the world in which a client lives.

Clinical supervision of multicultural assessment may be necessary. This can be achieved via observation, case conferences, review of audio- or videotaped assessments, and peer supervision groups. Specific feedback on the professional's performance during multicultural assessments is essential for skills improvement (see Chapter Twenty for further discussion).

Guidelines for Conducting Ethical Multicultural Assessments

In assessing minority group members, acculturation level must be determined, appropriate tests must be selected, the client must be informed about the testing process and how the results will be used, the tests must be administered in an unbiased manner, and the results must be interpreted to the client in ways that ensure a clear understanding.

Assessing Acculturation Level

Level of acculturation is an important variable when evaluating an individual. Cultures clearly differ according to their nonverbal behaviors, lifestyle patterns, expressions and uses of language. For example, lack of eye contact is considered to be a sign of anxiety or inter- and intrapersonal problems in Western culture. In other cultures, such as some Asian cultures, it is viewed as a sign of respect for elders or authority figures. Likewise, a lack of assertive behavior may signify deference rather than disinterest or pathology. A mental health professional who is not aware of this potential difference may misinterpret an Asian client's lack of eye contact as a sign of pathology.

A strong correlation exists between generational status and acculturation. Acculturation levels of extended family members, significant others, friends, and peers may influence the behavior of the client. The psychologist must consider this factor during the assessment and interpretation process.

On the other hand, misinterpretation is equally likely if the mental health professional assumes that because the client is from a particular culture, he or she will manifest the behavior patterns of that culture. In other words, it is more appropriate to assess an individual who is highly acculturated in a way similar to a member of the dominant culture. For example, a highly acculturated Asian client who does not maintain eye contact may not be accurately assessed by a mental health professional who has assumed that eye contact is not a relevant variable simply because the client is Asian.

Selecting Appropriate Tests

When selecting a test, it is important to consider several issues related to the construction and validation of the tests. It is critical to explore the nature of the group on which the test was normed. If the manual has dated information, then it is suggested that the test authors be contacted for the most recent norms to determine if they include racial and ethnic minorities, men, and women.

The language of the test is another important consideration. Frequently, tests are written in English but then are translated for use with individuals whose language is not English. It is important for the test user to examine the manual to ensure that the specific guidelines for translations have been followed so that the constructs are equivalent across cultures (Dana, 1993).

The items of the measures must be examined for invasiveness.

In some cultures, personal information is not readily shared with individuals outside the family system, therefore, tests that require the client to reveal personal information may be regarded as invasive or even offensive.

Cross-cultural validation is critical if tests are to be applied to individuals who are newly arrived in the United States. One must determine if the construct exists in the language or culture of the individual, and if it does exist, whether it is similar to the way the authors of the instrument defined it (Dana, 1993). Practitioners may decide not to use a test that seems to be biased against a particular group. However, in actuality these tests may not be biased if they reflect actual differences between groups on the construct being measured. As long as the test score is highly correlated with the criterion measure, then the test is valid even though certain groups are not performing as well as others.

Ensuring Informed Consent

Mental health professionals are ethically required to inform clients about the purposes for the testing, the way the information will be used, and types of methods used. Prior to the testing, clients must voluntarily agree to participate and understand the right to refuse. Simultaneously, they also must be aware that refusal to participate may result in consequences, for example, refusal to sit for the Graduate Record Examination (GRE) may result in one's not being accepted to graduate school. Once the testing has been completed, the results must be interpreted fully to the client and must be relevant to the concerns expressed by the client.

Administering and Interpreting the Test

Nonverbal behavior must be assessed. Because of the differences in nonverbal behavior across cultures, there is the potential for inaccurate interpretation. For example, Blacks may project a facial expression called "the cool pose" (Majors and Billson, 1992), which may be interpreted as detachment or flat affect. This could lead to an inappropriate diagnosis of schizophrenia (Jewell, 1989). Mental health professionals must carefully avoid giving nonverbal cues, for example, increased physical distance and diminished eye contact, that may decrease test performance by minority clients.

Another example of a subtle cue is the tester's attitude toward the test taker's abilities. High expectations on the part of the administrator will more often result in useable results, while low expectations will likely prompt substandard test performance. Here the social orientation of the test taker is of prime importance. A test taker from a culture with a personal orientation such as the Puerto Rican culture will respond to good rapport with the tester. Lack of a therapeutic rapport with the tester and a perfunctory attitude on the part of the administrator may result in marginally useful data from the testee.

Experiences of racial discrimination may lead to distrust and defensive behaviors on the part of the client. Consequently, he or she may have serious difficulty with self-disclosure that can hamper the assessment process. Verbal behavior is also a key component during the assessment process. The client ideally should be tested in his or her language of choice. Particular attention must be paid to the client's understanding of test content. Although the client may prefer to be tested in English, he or she may not fully understand the language used, which would produce faulty data for assessment. Language switching by the client during assessment may signal the elicitation of especially important and emotional material. The professional must guard against mistaking this documented phenomenon for evidence of pathology.

Client motivation should also be assessed. The professional must, in addition to informed consent, carefully assess the client's motivation to participate in the assessment. If the client does not feel the assessment process is valuable, this attitude will also produce substandard data. During an initial discussion of the assessment process, the professional should help the client understand that information from an assessment may be utilized to make decisions of personal and social importance to the client, for example, for a judge to determine child custody in a client's case.

The professional must consider cultural variations in disorders when making a diagnosis. For instance, individuals in certain cultural groups might exhibit depressive symptoms via somatization without diminished affect or defective cognitive functioning. Furthermore, diagnoses should not be based solely on test data without examining alternative nonpathological explanations for behaviors, cognitions, and beliefs. For example, believers in Santeria "may report hearing voices, communicating with the dead, altered states of consciousness, or dissociative states that are often perceived as schizophrenic symptoms" (Jewell, 1989, p. 304). Similarly, Nigerians may be misdiagnosed for paranoid schizophrenia because of their strong belief in the practice of hexing (Jewell, 1989). Lack of sensitivity to such culturally sanctioned behavior may partially contribute to a clinician's mistakenly making a diagnosis of schizophrenia.

Case Example

Though some commentators may critique the following case as stereotypical, it was created as a composite of several actual cases. In particular, the responses to the WAIS-R test provide an illustration of how data may be misinterpreted if the client's cultural context is not considered. This individual's (mal)adaptive responses must be interpreted in the context of living in a hostile environment fraught with racism and discrimination. Furthermore, this case is not a flat representation, which is the main characteristic of a stereotypical picture, but rather a multifaceted, realistic one. The discussion evolves not from one symptom to a single interpretation but instead from multiple symptoms to a variety of possible assessments.

Background

P. is a thirty-year-old Puerto Rican male who came to the United States five years ago. He voluntarily presented for a psychological assessment at the urging of his priest. He currently resides with his wife and his parents in their home in a drug-infested, low-income neighborhood inhabited primarily by African Americans and other Hispanics. Presenting symptoms include irritability, fitful sleep, and violent behaviors.

P. has recently been throwing and breaking objects and hitting the walls. He has made his family members targets of his angry outbursts, and they have sought the help of their parish priest, who has referred P. for psychological assessment.

P. admits past use of alcohol and other substances but denies any substance use or abuse at this time. He boasts about owning a number of weapons, including assault weapons and ammunition. P. has a history of violence and admits to abusing his wife, who is a polysubstance abuser. He sees her failure to help his mother with the housekeeping and her use of drugs as signs of disrespect. In an attempt to "straighten her out," he has frequently hit her. He has also forced her to have sex with him against her will. He sees this behavior "as his right." In order to protect her, he has made threats against various drug dealers.

Partial Test Data

The WAIS-R and Rorschach are administered as part of the standard procedure in the hospital where P. was assessed. On the WAIS-R, the client defined "winter" as a "cold season when things die, sometimes the cold kills people." When P. was asked why a free press was important in a democracy, he responded, "Free press, ha! Goddamned reporters are fucking liars! I don't believe anything they say." He defined commence as "Ready, Aim, Fire!" while "terminate" was defined as "to murder." In response to various Rorschach cards, P. saw dead, bloody animals and mutilated insects.

Discussion of the Case

Since P. was referred by his parish priest, the psychologist must clearly explain the assessment process and respective roles to P. prior to assessment. In particular, he must include a detailed explanation of confidentiality and reporting requirements for violent behavior. This explanation is particularly important here, because psychological services are often unavailable and underutilized by the Puerto Rican population (Rogler, Malgady, Constantino, and Blumenthal, 1987).

An assessment of acculturation of this subject may yield useful information. The assessment would include a personal history of the subject, including his experiences since his immigration to the United States five years ago and an assessment of his family's level of acculturation. The clinician must also assess subject motivation to participate in this assessment. Although this referral was deemed voluntary, it is possible the subject is participating merely out of respect for his family and priest, and may be ambivalent or even uncooperative in his motivation and behavior during this assessment. Also, the subject—due to minority membership, minimal acculturation, and possible drug involvement—may be distrustful of the clinician and the assessment process.

The subject's fluency in English may be a factor in this assessment. If the subject is not fluent in English, then the assessment should be conducted in Spanish. If a bilingual clinician is not available, an interpreter may be used, although this is not ideal. Assessment instruments written in Spanish should be used where possible.

The subject's plans, if any, to commit violent acts must be assessed. His boasting about ownership of assault weapons and his disclosures of striking his wife require immediate evaluation of imminent danger to others. This is made problematic by the subject's history of substance abuse, which calls into question the accuracy of any self-report. The evaluation may be accomplished by interviewing the subject and, for a possibly more objective viewpoint, his wife and family. The wife, due to Puerto Rican tradition, may out of respect for the client (as well as fear of retribution) not disclose information to the clinician. Information from friends and peers may be helpful, although obtaining such additional information would require the client's written consent.

Puerto Rican culture promotes the theme of *machismo*. Expectations are that men will be strong and protect women and the family. This client may have perversely interpreted this notion as physical dominance or abuse of his wife. Abuse is a clear contradiction of protection. If he does not believe he is in control of "his woman," he may feel humiliated because his manhood may be threatened, and he may lose face among his peers.

His self-reported threats directed at drug dealers may be the client's attempt to "impress" the psychologist. These threats may be construed as "macho" posturing, but the psychologist should be wary. These threats may in fact be real, in which case they must be interpreted as severely maladaptive and self-destructive, since drug dealers routinely commit murder. Threatening drug dealers could result in his death. In addition, the client's logic is faulty, since threatening drug dealers does not protect his wife from her substance abuse.

The ethical dilemma in this case can be framed in terms of balancing confidentiality and autonomy for the client with beneficence for the wife, family, and possibly society. Informed consent, including a detailed discussion of confidentiality and professional reporting requirements with the client, is indicated in this, as in all cases.

If the professional is unfamiliar with typical normal and pathological responses of Puerto Rican males on the WAIS-R, he or she should consult with a culturally knowledgeable supervisor or clinician on this case as well as review the clinical literature. The professional must consider a variety of possible explanations for the subject's WAIS-R and interview responses. For instance, the subject's aggressive associations might reflect, among other possibilities, imminent aggressive responses or, conversely, depressive coping responses of a relatively powerless and ineffectual individual. In other words, the boasting might be a warning of dangerous action or a purely personal stress response. Nonpsychological explanations also must be considered. WAIS-R responses may stem from the realities of living in an impoverished urban environment where drug activity and violence permeate the neighborhood. After having experienced discrimination due to his ethnicity, he may have a reality-based "paranoia" about the "White establishment" and the press. If these same WAIS-R responses were given by a White Anglo-Saxon Protestant living in an affluent community in Middle America, different interpretations could be made.

Psychologists must remain alert to possible countertransference. In this case, the practitioner may experience a strong dislike for the client or feel frightened by the client's potential for violence. These countertransferential feelings may affect the assessment in several ways. Bias may be introduced in the administration of tests in that the conscious or unconscious feelings of the tester may affect his or her behavior. If experiencing fear, the administrator could become arrogant, intimidating, or condescending as a way to defend against these feelings. Fear may also manifest itself as physical or psychological distance, or reduced eye contact and withdrawal. In either case, the client's test performance may be impaired.

Repulsion or alienation from the client may result in punitive action on the part of the psychologist. He or she may overestimate the client's potential for violence and be more inclined to recommend hospitalization than he or she would with a White, middle-class client.

Summary and Conclusions

Mental health professionals who conduct evaluations or psychological assessments of minority group members need specific skills and knowledge. To ensure competent and ethical practice, we recommend that students and practitioners learn about different cultures and their attitudes toward people who may differ from themselves. Practitioners must be educated as to how their biases can affect assessment outcomes, even when objective tests are being administered.

Of course, the fact that within-group differences are greater than between-group differences must be emphasized. Just because an individual is Korean, it does not mean that he or she will behave in ways that are promoted in the Korean culture. He or she may be highly acculturated and more similar to an "American" than to a newly arrived immigrant from Korea. Assessing level of acculturation and understanding clients within their cultural contexts allows more meaningful interpretation of test responses to be made.

To be ethical in their practice, psychologists should carefully choose tests that are not culturally loaded to reflect Western culture and that include members of the client's specific ethnic group in the normative sample. When language barriers threaten an accurate assessment, referral to a bilingual psychologist should be made. If none are available, the practitioner should consider the assistance of an interpreter.

The DSM-IV represents a good beginning in the effort to incorporate cultural factors, but more research and clearer guidelines for assessment are needed. There is an obvious need for more bilingual psychologists, and training programs should make every effort to recruit bilingual students. Training programs must also infuse discussion of cultural issues into all coursework rather than having one isolated course in multicultural issues. More specifically, cultural issues must be incorporated into classes on ethics and psychological assessment.

References

American Association for Counseling and Development. (1988). *Ethical standards* (Rev. ed.). Alexandria, VA: Author.

American Psychiatric Association. (1994) *Diagnostic and statistical manual of mental disorders: DSM-IV* (4th ed.). Washington, DC: Author.

American Psychological Association. (1985). *Standards for educational and psychological testing.* Washington, DC: Author.

American Psychological Association. (1986). *Guidelines for computer-based tests and interpretations.* Washington, DC: Author.

American Psychological Association. (1987). *Casebook on ethical principles of psychologists.* Washington, DC: Author.

American Psychological Association. (1990). *Guidelines for providers of services to ethnically and culturally diverse populations.* Washington, DC: Author.

American Psychological Association. (1992). Ethical principles of psychologists and code of conduct. *American Psychologist, 47,* 1597–1611.

Bache, R. M. (1894). Reaction time with reference to race. *Psychological Review, 1,* 475–486.

Dana, R. H. (1993). *Multicultural assessment perspectives for professional psychology.* Needham Heights, MA: Allyn & Bacon.

Ibrahim, F. A., & Arredondo, P. M. (1986). Ethical standards for cross-cultural counseling, counselor preparation, practice, assessment, and research. *Journal of Counseling and Development, 60,* 349–352.

Jewell, D. A. (1989). Cultural and ethnic issues. In S. Wetzler & M. M. Katz (Eds.), *Contemporary approaches to psychological assessment* (pp. 299–309). New York: Brunner/Mazel.

Kraiger, K., & Ford, J. K. (1985). A meta-analysis of ratee race effects in performance rating. *Journal of Applied Psychology, 70,* 56–65.

Majors, R., & Billson, J. M. (1992). *Cool pose: The dilemmas of black manhood.* Lexington, MA: Lexington Books.

Pope, K. S., & Vasquez, M.J.T. (1991). *Ethics in psychotherapy and counseling: A practical guide for psychologists.* San Francisco: Jossey-Bass.

Pulakos, E. D., White, L. A., Oppler, S. H., & Borman, W. C. (1989). Examination of race and sex effects on performance ratings. *Journal of Applied Psychology, 74,* 770–780.

Rogler, L. H., Malgady, R. G., Constantino, G., & Blumenthal, R. (1987). What do culturally sensitive mental health services mean? *American Psychologist, 42,* 565–570.

Rosenstein, M. J., Milazzo-Sayre, L. J., MacAskill, R. L., & Manderscheid, R. W. (1987). Use of inpatient services by special populations. In R. W. Manderscheid & S. A. Barrett (Eds.), *Mental health, United States, 1987* (DHHS Publication No. ADM 87–1518). Washington, DC: U.S. Government Printing Office. 59–74.

Sackett, P. R., & DuBois, C.L.Z. (1991). Rater-ratee race effects on performance evaluation: Challenging meta-analytic conclusions. *Journal of Applied Psychology, 76*, 873–877.

Sileo, F. J., & Kopala, M. (1993). An A-B-C-D-E worksheet for promoting beneficence when considering ethical issues. *Counseling and Values, 37*, 89–95.

Snowden, L. R., & Cheung, F. K. (1990). Use of inpatient mental health services by members of ethnic minority groups. *American Psychologist, 45*, 347–355.

Velasquez, R. J., Johnson, R., & Brown-Cheatham, M. (1993). Teaching counselors to use the DSM-III-R with ethnic minority: A paradigm. *Counselor Education and Supervision, 32*, 323–331.

Word, C., Zanna, M. P., & Cooper, J. (1974). The nonverbal mediation of self-fulfilling prophecies in interracial interaction. *Journal of Experimental Social Psychology, 10*, 109–120.

Part II

• •

Social and Emotional Assessment

Part II of the *Handbook of Multicultural Assessment* focuses on the usage of major tests and procedures in assessing social and emotional functioning. Clinicians have often raised questions as to whether testing procedures can be used cross-culturally. Specifically, some have asked whether personality measures "overpathologize" and discriminate against members of minority groups. It is imperative that clinicians and educators be aware of the literature pertaining to appropriate multicultural practice.

Chapter Three, by Kevin Moreland, examines issues pertaining to social and emotional assessment. He identifies sources of controversy in the assessment of personality indicators cross-culturally, psychometric issues to be considered in test use, sources of bias in the assessment procedure, and recommendations for appropriate usage of these measures.

In Chapter Four, Christine Zalewski and Roger Greene examine one of the most well-researched and utilized personality measures—the Minnesota Multiphasic Personality Inventory (MMPI). The authors review current literature with respect to the MMPI and MMPI-2. Important factors in understanding cross-cultural differences on this measure are addressed. These include methodological concerns in research studies, validity, acculturation issues, and moderator variables (such as education, socioeconomic status, and intelligence). Summaries are provided with respect to Black-White,

Hispanic-White, Native American-White, and Asian-White comparisons. Guidelines for appropriate multicultural administration and interpretation of the MMPI-2 are highlighted. The chapter concludes with a case example demonstrating the integration of multicultural issues into MMPI usage.

Chapter Five, by Barry Ritzler, examines multicultural issues in the usage of projective methods. The Rorschach, TEMAS and Early Memories Procedures are highlighted in this section. Studies regarding the validity and reliability of these methods are summarized. Risk factors that should be considered in the usage of these measures are elaborated. Ritzler provides information regarding an appropriate assessment procedure and issues related to referral questions and dissemination of results. This chapter also provides a case example to illustrate the appropriate usage of projective methods.

Persistent Issues in Multicultural Assessment of Social and Emotional Functioning

Kevin L. Moreland

Before the turn of the century, there was much commentary on questions that are now the subject matter of social science, but empirical research, as we now know it, did not exist. Thus, for example, thinkers have long commented on supposed "national personalities"—while rigorous investigations can probably only be dated from Wundt's (1900–1909) *Volkerpsychologie*. Shortly after Wundt's massive publication, anthropologists and psychologists began the seminal investigations of the social and emotional characteristics— that is, the *personality*—of cultural and ethnic minority populations in the United States (Kluckhohn and Murray, 1954).

For many years, the controversies generated by multicultural investigations of personality were entirely academic. Even those controversies were not about the applicability of personality assessment devices in different cultures (Lonner, 1975). It was assumed that responses to instruments like the Rorschach had the same meaning irrespective of the respondent's ethnic or cultural background. The early, unsophisticated research undoubtedly ill-served

Note: I would like to thank Nancy A. Busch, Lee Anna Clark, Kurt F. Geisinger, Diana Knauf, and Sarah I. Pratt for their extensive help in the preparation of this chapter. None will be completely happy with what I have done—so, naturally, I am solely responsible for any errors or omissions in this chapter.

the interests of the groups that were studied. However, that research was probably not harmful to individual participants.

By 1960, several psychologists had expressed concern that personality assessment devices developed in Euro-American culture might not perform well with members of minority groups. Specifically, evidence began to accumulate suggesting that the MMPI did not function the same way for African Americans and Euro-Americans (Ball, 1960; Caldwell, 1954; Hokanson and Calden, 1960; Panton, 1959). This research generated a lasting interest in this problem for two reasons. It coincided with the rise of our current insistence that all persons be treated fairly without regard for factors such as ethnic and cultural background. Moreover, the MMPI and similar instruments are used routinely to help make important decisions about individuals, such as whether they should be hired for a job. Thus, to paraphrase Gynther (1972), the application to minorities of personality instruments developed in Euro-American culture may be a prescription for discrimination.

The remainder of this chapter will focus on what we know about detection and eradication of such discrimination from personality assessment. Before embarking on that task, it is important to say that I believe this area is pervaded by more opinion and fewer good data than most. This is due in part to the fact that this has been a sorely neglected area of investigation. It is also due to the inherent difficulty of doing research in an area where one cannot even try to maintain the pretense of engaging in value-free science. I now turn to some of those sources of difficulty.

Sources of Confusion and Controversy

Dana (1993) and S. Sue (1991) have identified several unspoken sources of confusion in professional practice with ethnic and cultural minorities. These sources of practical confusion have also been sources of scholarly controversy. These issues must always be recognized and explored because they can affect the usefulness of multicultural assessment research and the acceptability of assessment services to minority clients. (For the sake of simplicity, the term *client* will be used to refer both to recipients of professional services and to research subjects.)

Euro-American Model of Science

Koch (1981) points out that American psychologists—I would say social scientists—are trained in a scientific attitude that Kimble (1984) has characterized as emphasizing objectivity, data, elementism, concrete mechanisms, nomothesis, determinism, and scientific values. Dana (1993) holds that multicultural research and practice should emanate from a human science perspective characterized by the opposite of the foregoing terms: intuition, theory, holism, abstract concepts, idiography, indeterminism, and humanistic values. I believe this is an artificial dichotomy. A balance of these two perspectives is required for effective assessment regardless of the assessee's ethnic or cultural background. However, since the human science perspective has been neglected, I will emphasize its importance for personality assessment.

Dana's (1993) view has several implications for all research and practice in personality assessment. Person-environment fit should be emphasized to a greater extent than has heretofore been the case. Traditional in-office assessment via client interviews and tests needs to be supplemented with increased reliance on informants and *in vivo* behavioral observations. Traditional personality assessment has also focused on the individual client. A systems view involving consideration of influences ranging from genes to societal institutions will produce a more complete picture of an individual's personality functioning (Taplin, 1980). Family, community, and society, in particular, have greater salience for members of some American minorities than for Euro-Americans (Sampson, 1988). Lastly, the traditional barrier between the assessor and the client needs to be razed. The assessor and the client should collaborate to elucidate the multiple causal influences impinging on the client (Finn and

Tonsager, in press; Fischer, 1993). This is especially important for the multicultural client whose cultural experience and world view may differ from the assessor's.

Universal or Culture-Sensitive?

Psychologists have traditionally preferred a perspective that emphasizes presumed universals among human beings. They frequently assume that measures are universal when, in the absence of evidence to the contrary, it is safest to assume that the measures reflect the dominant culture in which they were developed. Less often, psychologists assume a culture-sensitive perspective, examining behavior using criteria from within a culture.

Most popular personality assessment techniques impose a middle-class, Euro-American perspective (Dana, 1993) as if it were universal. The items for the tests discussed in the next two chapters, the scoring procedures for them (that is, scales), and their norms, were developed by middle-class Euro-Americans or their Western European ancestors working with subject samples that were also overwhelmingly Euro-American or European and predominantly middle class. The usefulness of such measures in multicultural assessment rests on two considerations. First, do the data produced by such measures have the same meaning for minority clients and Euro-American clients? The jury is still out on this question. Few studies have addressed this question for most instruments (see, for example, Velasquez and Callahan, 1992). Even when many data have accumulated, their interpretation remains controversial. Almost four decades of research involving thousands of subjects has convinced Gynther that MMPI scores do not have the same meaning for African Americans and Euro-Americans; however, as he noted in his 1989 "review of reviews," other experts have examined the same data and reached the opposite conclusion.

If none of the available instruments is truly universal, you can reject such assessment entirely or collaborate with minority clients to decide whether it is fairer to impose a dominant-culture perspective on them. This frequently is not an easy decision. In American society, many clients remain rooted in their original culture while simultaneously enmeshed in the social and economic realities of the middle-class, predominantly Euro-American culture. On one hand, rejection of a Euro-American perspective may force reliance on techniques of unknown or dubious validity. On the other hand, assessment from a Euro-American perspective may be equally invalid with such clients.

Fortunately, well-developed, culture-sensitive instruments are becoming increasingly common. For example, one group of Hispanic researchers developed a culturally relevant measure of stress (Cervantes, Padilla, and de Snyder, 1990, 1991), while another developed a picture-story technique for Hispanic children (Costantino, Malgady, and Rogler, 1988). When such instruments are not available, clients may decide that it is best, under the circumstances, to impose a dominant-culture perspective on themselves. Given the state of personality assessment technology, it is not at all unrealistic for an ethnic minority client to be faced with choices among techniques of known validity for Euro-Americans and techniques of unknown validity designed to be appropriate for their culture. I believe clients should be informed of the pros and cons of all approaches and should work with you to decide how to proceed. (Since I will offer several similar opinions in this chapter, the reader should know that I am a middle-class, Euro-American male.) A minority client trying to decide whether he or she has the personality characteristics of a successful accountant should be allowed to decide how much to trust the dominant-culture perspective afforded by the 16PF and the culturally sensitive, interview-based subjective judgment of a vocational counselor.

Assimilation or Pluralism?

Is it desirable for multicultural people to assimilate into mainstream society, or should they endeavor to maintain essential ingredients of their unique and historic identities while still trying to participate fully as citizens? My feeling is that, when it comes to assessment, you should take the clients where you find them. If you feel that a client has not carefully considered the potential consequences of the desire to assimilate fully or never to venture outside their subcultural enclave, a referral for counseling may be appropriate. A client who states a firm, well-considered rejection of middle-class, Euro-American standards should be assessed using methods that reflect the standards of the preferred culture. Likewise, an individual desiring to assimilate fully may wish to be assessed according to the standards of the dominant society. That wish should be honored.

Many multicultural clients will be neither fully identified with their culture of origin nor fully assimilated into mainstream society. In such cases, measures of acculturation can be used to assess degree of assimilation (such as Dana, 1993, pp. 111–139; Olmedo, 1979). The process of acculturation is itself a significant psychosocial stressor (Berry and Kim, 1988). This stress, like any other, will color many other manifestations of personality (for example, Whatley and Dana, 1989, cited in Dana, 1993). In the context of counseling and mental health care, Gaw (1982) suggests that acculturation levels may affect the nature of symptoms, presenting problems, and clients' beliefs about the origins of symptoms. Other experts believe that acculturation level is related to the likely success of different treatment approaches (for example, D. W. Sue, 1981; S. Sue and Morishima, 1982). Although the research evidence remains sparse, it appears that acculturation may be a useful interpretive moderator when the personality of multicultural persons is assessed with instruments developed for Euro-Americans (for example, Dana, 1988).

Culture or Socioeconomic Status?

In the United States, race and ethnicity are highly correlated with socioeconomic status (Laosa, 1978). When this confound is controlled, apparent personality differences among cultural groups often disappear (R. L. Greene, 1987). An additional layer of complexity is added by the fact that social class structure itself differs among at least some multicultural groups (Bass, 1982). Researchers need to be careful to control for socioeconomic status, while practitioners need to be skeptical of the many published studies in which the implications of socioeconomic status have not been examined.

Group Personality or Individual Differences?

Group personality research includes studies of the average or modal personality pattern of citizens of entire nations (for example, Inkeles and Levinson, 1969), and ethnic and cultural groups (for example, Kaplan, 1961). It is critical that we do not reify such data, allowing them to become stereotyped images of culturally different persons that may introduce bias into subsequent test interpretations (Dana, 1993). It is important to remember that variation *within* such encompassing groups is likely to be at least as large as differences *between* groups (Argyle, 1969). Assuming within-group homogeneity causes measurement error and subject variability to be confused, a problem for both research and practical application.

Racism

Racism continues to be a problem in American society, even though it is no longer officially tolerated (Jaynes and Williams, 1989). Unintentional racism may still hamper the efforts of even the most well-intentioned social scientists. Concerned that minorities were unfairly portrayed as genetically deficient (for example, Shuey, 1966), well-meaning scholars expended a great deal of effort attempting to understand and remediate the cultural deprivation (that is, differences from middle-class Euro-American culture) that "really" caused minorities' problems (Moynihan, 1965). I do not believe the contention of some that we are all racists; however, I do believe that most educators and health care professionals know little about multicultural issues. Most doctoral programs in clinical psychology, for example, do not mandate training in multicultural issues (Bernal and Castro, 1994). It is incumbent on those working with multicultural persons to recognize the pernicious, if subtle, effects of such igno-rance and to take remedial steps (Myers, Wohlford, Guzman, and Echemendia, 1991, Appendix D).

Psychometric Issues

The development of culture-sensitive assessment tools is no dif-ferent from the development of their dominant-culture counter-parts. However, most multicultural assessment is carried out using instruments developed in the dominant culture, such as the CPI, MMPI, Rorschach, and 16PF. Sometimes the dominant-culture instruments are adapted to the needs of multicultural groups, the most frequent adaptation being translation into another language. Performing such adaptations and evaluating their adequacy in-volves consideration of psychometric concepts specific to the adap-tation process as well as psychometric concepts universally important in the test development.

Equivalence

Lonner (1979) identified four kinds of equivalence that need to be considered when deciding whether an assessment procedure devel-oped in one culture can legitimately be used with persons from another culture.

The term *functional equivalence* comes from anthropology and refers to the functions of rituals, institutions, and customs in differ-ent cultures. In some cultures, a belch is a compliment while in oth-ers it is an insult (Lonner, 1979). Functional equivalence can be assessed using the variety of expert-judgment-based procedures developed to investigate content-related validity (Messick, 1989). In this case, the experts need to understand the functions embod-ied in the test items under consideration in both the culture in which they originated and the culture to which they are to be gen-eralized. It may also be possible to make changes in test items that render them functionally equivalent across cultures. Translated literally, the MMPI item referring to *Alice in Wonderland* is meaningless to most Asians, but it is possible to develop equivalents for those cultures by construing the function of *Alice* as "a story most children know and like" (Cheung, 1985; Clark, 1985).

Conceptual equivalence refers to equivalence of meanings individuals give to concepts; these concepts might be specific stimuli, procedures, or constructs used in multicultural work. "Depression" provides an extreme example of this issue. Marsella (1980) noted that some Asian languages do not include a word that translates as "depression," apparently because those speaking the language conceive of no such malady. Like functional equivalence, it may be possible to establish conceptual equivalence via expert judgment. Since construct-related validity presupposes conceptual equivalence, errors by the judges will be revealed by the less subjective procedures used to establish construct-related validity. If, for example, the construct "depression" does not exist in a culture, then factor analysis should not reveal a depression factor in that culture (Ben-Porath, 1990; Butcher and Han, in press).

Linguistic equivalence refers to the problem of translation. This may be translation of written matter or translation that takes place during an interview. The former area has received a good deal of attention, with Brislin and his colleagues (see Brislin, 1986; Brislin, Lonner, and Thorndike, 1973) recommending *back-translation* as a method of ensuring linguistic equivalence. In a nutshell, back-translation involves translation from the original language to the target language and translation, by a second translator, back into the original language. Ideally, this process should be repeated with different translators until the concepts rather than the language are central to the translated version.

When you are dealing with language barriers in an interview, the issue is more complex and no less important (Vasquez-Nuttal and Ivey, 1986). Marcos, Alpert, Urcuyo, and Kesselman (1973) found that bilingual Hispanic patients received higher psychopathology ratings when interviewed in English than when interviewed in Spanish. I believe the best solution to this problem is the development of more semistructured interviews for multicultural use. The causes of differences among interviews conducted in different languages remain unclear and are, no doubt, complex. They certainly deserve much further study. The greater the structure of interviews, the easier it will be to identify and eliminate unwanted sources of variance.

Metric equivalence refers to the meanings of score differences. Poortinga (1975) asserts that in order for a measure to be comparable across cultures it must relate to other measures in the same way and it must measure the same construct at the same level in different societies. In my view, this carries things too far. Measures held to this standard will be unable to detect genuine differences across cultures (Sharma, 1977).

Some metric differences are spurious, and it is important to eliminate those. For example, test formats sometimes yield spurious differences among groups. Individuals unfamiliar with computers perform less well on computer versions of tests than those who have used computers (Johnson and White, 1980). Nobody should be penalized for lack of familiarity with computers unless computer skills are being assessed. Current interest in replacing multiple-choice academic achievement tests with "authentic assessment" methods such as portfolios of classroom work compiled by students has been fueled, in part, by the belief that the former unfairly penalize multicultural groups (Lidz, 1987).

I do not believe that metric equivalence should be mandatory when norms alone yield differences across cultures. Lonner (1981) points out that, in personality measurement, the more one set of norms departs from another culture's set, the more questionable is the multicultural interpretation of the measure. For example, if different raw scores on the CPI yield the same T scores in different cultures, then different sets of endorsed items are yielding the same T scores. Do these "equivalent" T scores have the same meaning? Perhaps, but it seems more likely that equivalent raw scores will have the same meaning for individuals while differences in the corresponding T scores will tell us something meaningful about cultural differences. Clark (1987) notes that metric equivalence does not require equal means as long as the relations within and among variables remain constant.

Ironically, when I worked for a test publisher I learned that most customers believed that group-specific norms (and, if necessary, translation) were *the* solution to the problem of multicultural application of dominant-culture instruments. That is, their question was always "Does that test have separate norms for African Americans (Asian Americans, Hispanics . . .)?" Nobody ever asked about functional or conceptual equivalence or the traditional forms of reliability and validity.

Reliability

Reliability is less influenced by cultural differences than are other psychometric properties (Sundberg and Gonzales, 1981). Nevertheless, it is wise to ascertain test stability, internal consistency and, if multiple forms are available, equivalence of those forms in all populations in which a measure is to be used rather than relying on values obtained for the development population.

Validity

The following brief discussion will focus on the validation of dominant-culture measures for multicultural use. It goes without saying that the validity of culture-sensitive measures needs to be investigated in much the same way.

Concerns about content-related validity involve the multicultural comparability of item sampling in the relevant domain of interest. As noted above, functional equivalence is established using methods developed to establish content-related validity. If functional equivalence is established, you can be sure that all the items in the measure are *relevant* for multicultural use. You cannot, however, be sure of the measure's content *representativeness*. That is, it may be necessary to add items to the measure in order to make sure it samples all areas relevant to the construct in the new culture.

Most research on the applicability of tests like the MMPI and Rorschach to multicultural populations has relied, implicitly or explicitly, on criterion-related validation. Implicit reliance on criterion-related validation characterized virtually all of the MMPI studies reviewed by R. L. Greene (1987). Those studies involved comparisons of test profiles of Euro-Americans and members of multicultural groups drawn from the *same* broad population (for example, psychiatric patients, or pregnant women). Mean differences in such studies are taken as evidence that multicultural interpretation of the score is not warranted (see Pritchard and Rosenblatt, 1980). In my view, this is a classic example of confusing measurement error and subject variability owing to an unwarranted assumption of within group homogeneity (see "Group Personality Versus Individual Differences," earlier in this chapter). Lachar, Dahlstrom, and Moreland (1986) report several more traditional analyses of the criterion-related validity of the MMPI for members of racial and ethnic minorities. They found that equations developed to predict staff symptom ratings from the MMPI scores of Euro-American psychiatric inpatients cross-validated as well with African Americans as with Euro-Americans. This is an excellent means of demonstrating the multicultural applicability of dominant-culture instruments, provided the criterion measures are accurate measures for both the majority and minority groups (Irvine and Carroll, 1980).

Even if the conceptual equivalence of a measure has been established by expert judgment, it should be verified by gathering evidence of construct-related validity. Factor analysis is commonly used to verify that the internal structure of a measure is stable across populations, while evidence of convergent and discriminant validity is obtained via techniques like the multitrait-multimethod matrix (Campbell and Fiske, 1959). Irvine and Carroll (1980) made the sensible but seldom-followed suggestion that convergent and discriminant validity be evaluated using both culture-sensitive and purportedly universal measures. Determining whether a measure is free from bias is one form of discriminant validation (Geisinger, 1992).

Psychometric Bias

Failure to establish any of the forms of equivalence, reliability, or validity described above may lead to psychometric bias. That is, the measure may give rise to inferences about members of one multicultural group that are less accurate than those about members of another (Cole and Moss, 1989). At this point, it is important to note that, as will be detailed below, a lack of psychometric bias *does not* guarantee accurate assessment.

Administration

In a paper that deserves to be better known, Fink and Butcher (1972) demonstrate that a lack of rapport between assessor and client frequently compromises the usefulness of the results of even an "objective" personality measure like the MMPI. Assessors need to be conscious of the additional fact that efforts to establish rapport will go awry if they are not sensitive to their multicultural clients' expectations and beliefs about the nature of the assessment process. A couple of examples should suffice to vivify this point.

Euro-American professional ethics emphasizes maintenance of a professional distance from clients, including a lack of contact outside the service delivery context and a focus on professional service during contacts. If you adopt this stance with Native American clients, you probably will not obtain much useful information. Many Native Americans are reluctant to trust an assessor they have never met outside the assessor's office (LaFromboise, Dauphinais, and Rowe, 1980). Once in the office, Plains Indians are not going to be comfortable diving immediately into a discussion of their personality. Such clients will expect you to begin the meeting with informal small talk about matters of mutual interest and understanding (Hornby, 1985, cited in Dana, 1993). Continuation of the in-office relationship may be conditioned on increased involvement outside the service delivery context.

Efforts to establish rapport commonly have nonverbal components that may not have the desired effect with a multicultural client. For example, a traditional Asian American woman may be embarrassed by your efforts to make eye contact (D. W. Sue and Sue, 1977). Leaning forward in your seat, commonly interpreted by Euro-Americans as a desirable expression of the assessor's interest, may be viewed by the Asian American client as an unseemly invasion of her personal space. In both instances, her reticence is likely to increase.

Responses to projective techniques are known to be especially sensitive to situational factors even in Euro-American culture (Klopfer and Taulbee, 1976). Therefore, assessors using projective techniques with multicultural populations need to be especially cognizant of the potential influence of the foregoing factors (Abel, 1973).

Interpretation

Assessors working with multicultural clients need to be aware that bias may occur even if the equivalence, reliability, and validity of dominant culture measures for multicultural use have been thoroughly documented. Indeed, it may occur even if culture-sensitive measures are employed. Assessors also need to be aware of tools they can employ at the interpretation phase to overcome bias, even psychometric bias.

Assessor Bias

Dana (1993) warned against the harmful effects of assessor bias. Even if you use psychometrically sound measures, you may bias interpretations because of unquestioned and unacknowledged, but inappropriate, beliefs in assimilation (B. A. Greene, 1985), the use of theory that is bound to the wrong culture (Mays, 1985), or stereotyped expectations about members of another cultural group (Wyatt, Powell, and Bass, 1982).

Obviously, assessor bias is most effectively reduced by increasing cultural sensitivity; a number of training programs are available for that purpose (Pedersen, 1988). Increasing cultural sensitivity is a multistep process that involves consciousness raising, cognitive and experiential understanding, and skills training. Needless to say, while increased cultural sensitivity may be most important to the proper interpretation of assessment data, it will positively influence all steps in the assessment process, from selecting the proper measurement tools to providing feedback to assessees.

Personality theories commonly embraced by American psychologists have been criticized as providing an inadequate basis for counseling racial and ethnic minority clients (for example, Ponterotto and Casas, 1991, pp. 49–66). There is no reason to believe that those theories are any more useful when it comes to assessment. Cross-culturally robust theories, like the five-factor model of personality, which is now coming into clinical use, should help ameliorate this problem (see Costa and Widiger, 1994). Ultimately, culture-sensitive personality theories, which are only just now being developed, will also reduce chances of biased assessment (Dana, 1990, pp. 11–14).

Moderator Variables

Competent assessment of the personality of multicultural persons can be accomplished only by clearly delineating the contribution of culture. This is especially true when it comes to "abnormal" personality—that is, psychopathology (Rogler, 1993). Interpretation of personality data can be moderated (that is, modified) by information about the impact of culture. Many potential moderators have been proposed (Dana, 1993, pp. 111–139; Ponterotto and Casas, 1991, pp. 101–117), several of which will be discussed below.

Acculturation

Acculturation entails changes in an individual's psychological patterns owing to continuous contact with a culture different from the original one (Berry, 1980). It is usually thought of as consisting of at least three components: birth and generational history; culture-specific behaviors such as language use; and culture-specific attitudes including, for example, adherence to a culture's values (Smith, 1980). Outcomes of acculturation range from assimilation into the dominant culture to retention of the original culture and separation from the dominant culture. Obviously, well-conceived measures of acculturation provide a rather direct assessment of the impact of culture on an individual.

There are two broad types of acculturation instruments. Monolevel instruments assess the degree to which an individual retains his or her original culture, while bilevel instruments additionally measure the individual's identification with the dominant culture (Olmedo, 1979). The latter are preferable to the former because they permit detection of the bicultural person who has integrated aspects of both cultures and, in some cases, the marginal person who is not strongly identified with either culture. (Note that the marginal person who is not strongly identified with any culture is probably the hardest to accurately assess.)

In general, the weaker a client's identification with the dominant culture, the more circumspect you need to be in the interpretation of dominant-culture measures. Unfortunately, little is known about the specific parameters of exercising such care. It may be wisest in such cases to ignore the results of dominant-culture measures, but no precise acculturation "cutting score" is available to inform that decision. On the other hand, you should not automatically reject the results of dominant-culture measures just because they have been shown to be related to acculturation. Whatley and Dana (1989, cited in Dana, 1993) found that several MMPI scales were correlated with several stages of acculturation among African American college students. These correlations are not surprising given the fact that the stages of acculturation are described using terms like alienation, anxiety, confusion, guilt, rage, pain, and psychological disturbance (Cross, 1978).

Value Orientations

Kluckhohn (1951) developed a set of five value dimensions based on his belief that there are a limited number of problems for which all humans must find solutions. He believed we must all develop beliefs about human nature and about our relationship to mother nature. Humans also, he believed, develop a characteristic temporal focus and conception of what activity ought to occupy their time. People also decide how best to define their relationships with others. Szapocznik, Scopetta, Aranalde, and Kurtines (1978) and Ibrahim and Kahn (1987) have developed instruments for measuring these value orientations for several American cultural groups.

Kluckhohn's (1951) value orientations have a great deal of intuitive appeal irrespective of a person's racial or ethnic group. If a client sees individual as opposed to group goals as paramount, intrapsychic theories may be most helpful in understanding his or her personality (McAdams, 1994). Feedback based on humanistic explanations of personality may make the most sense to persons who believe humans are innately good. The special usefulness of these value orientations with multicultural clients stems from the fact that racial and ethnic groups differ systematically along Kluckhohn's dimensions (Dana, 1993, p. 12).

The topic of this section is often called *world view* (as in Ibrahim and Kahn, 1987). However, world view is also frequently used to denote a concept that is more inclusive than the "value orientations" discussed here (for example, Katz, 1985). I therefore suggest that Kluckhohn's (1951) terminology be retained when the discussion is limited to his concepts.

Other Influences

Despite sincere efforts to establish rapport, multicultural clients may not feel comfortable providing the depth and breadth of information commonly provided by Euro-American clients (for example, see Franco, Malloy, and Gonzalez, 1984). It does not seem possible to use self-disclosure as a true moderator in the assessment of individuals; after all, you cannot know what you have not been told! However, data from an instrument like the Self-Disclosure Situations Survey (see Chelune, 1978) will increase your sensitivity to the possibility that you not have all the pieces of the puzzle so that you can be cautious in your conclusions. In particular, care should be taken not to label culturally mediated reticence as defensiveness.

Response styles that plague the interpretation of self-reports by Euro-Americans may be especially problematic with some multicultural groups. For example, acquiescence may be a problem with clients of Asian origin, for whom affirmative responses may be a form of politeness (Chun, Campbell, and Yoo, 1974). Similarly, Hispanics' expectations of high frequencies of positive social behaviors and low frequencies of negative social behaviors (Triandis, Marin, Lisansky, and Betancourt, 1984) may cause social desirability to be a problem when working with that population (Ross and Mirowsky, 1984). Like self-disclosure, it does not seem possible to employ response styles as true moderators in individual cases (for example, see Jackson and Paunonen, 1980). A number of response style measures are available, several of which are embedded in the MMPI-2, to help you decide when you need to make your interpretations more tentative than they otherwise would be (Paulhus, 1991).

Recommendations for Practice

Traditionally, personality assessment has not been a collaborative enterprise (Dana, 1985). The client provided the raw data and may have been informed of the assessor's conclusions, but he or she was not asked to help formulate the questions to be answered, nor to help make sense of the data. This is a mistake in the assessment of Euro-Americans (Finn and Tonsager, in press; Fischer, 1993) and it can be an even bigger mistake in the assessment of ethnic and racial minority persons (Dana, 1993). Unless the assessor is thoroughly familiar with the client's culture, there is a serious risk of posing irrelevant questions for the assessment and coming up with wrong answers to them besides.

Dana (1993, pp. 217–219) proposes a model for the assessment of multicultural clients that I cannot improve. He suggests that the establishment of a collaborative relationship be followed by an

assessment of the client's level of acculturation. Level of acculturation would guide the choice of assessment techniques. Clients who
are identified with Euro-American culture can safely be assessed
with the techniques ordinarily used with Euro-Americans. Clients
who remain strongly identified with their original culture will probably be most accurately assessed via a set of culture-sensitive techniques. This may include instruments originally developed in the
dominant culture that meet the requirements for multicultural use
described in the bulk of this chapter, along with culture-sensitive
methods. This mix of techniques may also prove most useful with
the individual who is not strongly identified with either the original culture or the dominant culture. Finally, bicultural persons
should be provided information that will allow them to choose the
combination of techniques they would feel most comfortable with.

Assessment results should be explored with the client and, in
many cases, others important in the multicultural person's extended
sense of his or her "self" (see Sampson, 1988). This maximizes the
chances that the import of the results will be accepted and, hence,
that recommendations for action will be acceptable. Finally, in
keeping with the collaborative approach, the assessor should seek
feedback about the client's satisfaction with the assessment process
(for example, see Attkisson and Greenfield, 1994).

References

Abel, T. M. (1973). *Psychological testing in cultural contexts*. New Haven, CT:
    College and University Press.

Argyle, M. (1969). *Social interaction*. New York: Atherton.

Attkisson, C. C., & Greenfield, T. K. (1994). Client Satisfaction Questionnaire-
    8 and Service Satisfaction Scale-30. In M. E. Maruish (Ed.), *The use of
    psychological testing for treatment planning and outcome assessment* (pp.
    402–422). Hillsdale, NJ: Erlbaum.

Ball, J. C. (1960). Comparison of MMPI profile differences among Negro-White
    adolescents. *Journal of Clinical Psychology, 16*, 304–307.

Bass, B. A. (1982). The validity of socioeconomic factors in the assessment and
    treatment of Afro-Americans. In B. A. Bass, G. E. Wyatt, & G. J. Powell

(Eds.), *The Afro-American family: Assessment, treatment, and research issues* (pp. 69–83). Philadelphia: Grune & Stratton.

Ben-Porath, Y. S. (1990). Cross-cultural assessment of personality: The case for replicatory factor analysis. In J. N. Butcher & C. D. Spielberger (Eds.), *Advances in personality assessment* (Vol. 8, pp. 27–48). Hillsdale, NJ: Erlbaum.

Bernal, M. E., & Castro, F. G. (1994). Are clinical psychologists prepared for service and research with ethnic minorities? Report of a decade of progress. *American Psychologist, 49,* 797–805.

Berry, J. W. (1980). Acculturation as varieties of adaptation. In A. M. Padilla (Ed.), *Acculturation: Theory, models and some new findings* (pp. 9–25). Boulder, CO: Westview Press.

Berry, J. W., & Kim, U. (1988). Acculturation and mental health. In P. R. Dasen, J. W. Berry, & N. Sartorious (Eds.), *Health and cross-cultural psychology: Toward applications* (pp. 207–236). Newbury Park, CA: Sage.

Brislin, R. W. (1986). The wording and translation of research instruments. In W. J. Lonner & J. W. Berry (Eds.), *Field methods in cross-cultural research* (pp. 137–164). Newbury Park, CA: Sage.

Brislin, R. W., Lonner, W. J., & Thorndike, R. M. (1973). *Cross-cultural research methods.* New York: Wiley.

Butcher, J. N., & Han, K. (in press). Methods of establishing cross-cultural equivalence. In J. N. Butcher (Ed.), *International adaptation of the MMPI-2: A handbook of research and clinical applications.* Minneapolis: University of Minnesota Press.

Caldwell, M. G. (1954). Case analysis method for the personality study of offenders. *Journal of Criminal Law, Criminology and Police Science, 45,* 291–298.

Campbell, D. T., & Fiske, D. W. (1959). Convergent and discriminant validation by the multitrait-multimethod matrix. *Psychological Bulletin, 56,* 81–105.

Cervantes, R. C., Padilla, A. M., & de Snyder, N. S. (1990). Reliability and validity of the Hispanic Stress Inventory. *Hispanic Journal of Behavioral Sciences, 12,* 76–82.

Cervantes, R. C., Padilla, A. M., & de Snyder, N. S. (1991). The Hispanic Stress Inventory: A culturally relevant approach to psychosocial assessment. *Psychological Assessment, 3,* 438–447.

Chelune, G. J. (1978). Nature and assessment of self-disclosing behavior. In P. McReynolds (Ed.), *Advances in psychological assessment* (Vol. 4, pp. 278–320). San Francisco: Jossey-Bass.

Cheung, F. M. (1985). Cross-cultural considerations for the translation and adaptation of the Chinese MMPI in Hong Kong. In J. N. Butcher & C. D. Spielberger (Eds.), *Advances in personality assessment* (Vol. 4, pp. 131–158). Hillsdale, NJ: Erlbaum.

Chun, K., Campbell, J., & Yoo, J. (1974). Extreme response style in cross-cultural research: A reminder. *Journal of Cross-Cultural Psychology, 5,* 465–480.

Clark, L. A. (1985). A consolidated version of the MMPI in Japan. In J. N. Butcher & C. D. Spielberger (Eds.), *Advances in personality assessment* (Vol. 4, pp. 95–130). Hillsdale, NJ: Erlbaum.

Clark, L. A. (1987). Mutual relevance of mainstream and cross-cultural psychology. *Journal of Consulting and Clinical Psychology, 55,* 461–470.

Cole, N. S., & Moss, P. A. (1989). Bias in test use. In R. L. Linn (Ed.), *Educational measurement* (3rd ed., pp. 201–219). New York: Macmillan.

Costa, P. T., Jr., & Widiger, T. A. (Eds.). (1994). *Personality disorders and the five-factor model of personality.* Washington, DC: American Psychological Association.

Costantino, G., Malgady, R. G., & Rogler, L. H. (1988). *TEMAS (Tell-Me-A-Story) manual.* Los Angeles: Western Psychological Services.

Cross, W. E., Jr. (1978). The Thomas and Cross models of psychological nigrescence: A literature review. *Journal of Black Psychology, 5,* 13–31.

Dana, R. H. (1985). A service delivery paradigm for personality assessment. *Journal of Personality Assessment, 49,* 598–604.

Dana, R. H. (1988). Culturally diverse groups and MMPI interpretation. *Professional Psychology: Research and Practice, 19,* 490–495.

Dana, R. H. (1990). Cross-cultural and multi-ethnic assessment. In J. N. Butcher & C. D. Spielberger (Eds.), *Advances in personality assessment* (Vol. 8, pp. 1–26). Hillsdale, NJ: Erlbaum.

Dana, R. H. (1993). *Multicultural assessment perspectives for professional psychology.* Needham Heights, MA: Allyn & Bacon.

Fink, A., & Butcher, J. N. (1972). Reducing objections to personality inventories with special instructions. *Educational and Psychological Measurement, 32,* 631–639.

Finn, S. E., & Tonsager, M. (in press). *Therapeutic assessment: Using psychological testing to help clients change.* Washington, DC: American Psychological Association.

Fischer, C. T. (1993). *Individualizing psychological assessment* (2nd ed.). Hillsdale, NJ: Erlbaum.

Franco, J. N., Malloy, T., & Gonzalez, R. (1984). Ethnic and acculturation differences in self-disclosure. *Journal of Social Psychology, 122,* 21–32.

Gaw, A. (1982). *Cross-cultural psychiatry.* Littleton, MA: Wright.

Geisinger, K. F. (1992). Fairness and selected psychometric issues in the psychological testing of hispanics. In K. F. Geisinger (Ed.), *Psychological testing of Hispanics* (pp. 17–42). Washington, DC: American Psychological Association.

Greene, B. A. (1985). Considerations in the treatment of Black patients by White therapists. *Psychotherapy, 22,* 389–393.

Greene, R. L. (1987). Ethnicity and MMPI performance: A review. *Journal of Consulting and Clinical Psychology, 55,* 497–512.

Gynther, M. D. (1972). White norms and Black MMPIs: A prescription for discrimination? *Psychological Bulletin, 78,* 386–402.

Gynther, M. D. (1989). MMPI comparisons of Blacks and Whites: A review and commentary. *Journal of Clinical Psychology, 45,* 878–883.

Hokanson, J. E., & Calden, G. (1960). Negro-White differences on the MMPI. *Journal of Clinical Psychology, 16,* 32–33.

Hornby, R. (1985, May). Mental health services delivery to the Rosebud Sioux. In R. Dana (Chair), *Cross-cultural services for native Americans.* Symposium conducted at the meeting of the Southern Anthropological Society, Fayetteville, AR.

Ibrahim, F. A., & Kahn, H. (1987). Assessment of world views. *Psychological Reports, 60,* 163–176.

Inkeles, A., & Levinson, D. J. (1969). National character: The study of modal personality and sociocultural systems. In G. Lindzey & E. Aronson (Eds.), *The handbook of social psychology* (Vol. 4, 2nd ed., pp. 418–506). Reading, MA: Addison-Wesley.

Irvine, S. H., & Carroll, W. K. (1980). Testing and assessment across different cultures: Issues in methodology and theory. In H. C. Triandis & J. W. Berry (Eds.), *Handbook of cross-cultural psychology, Vol. 2: Methodology* (pp. 181–243). Needham Heights, MA: Allyn & Bacon.

Jackson, D. N., & Paunonen, S. V. (1980). Personality structure and assessment. *Annual Review of Psychology, 31,* 503–551.

Jaynes, G. D., & Williams, R. M., Jr. (Eds.). (1989). *A common destiny: Blacks and American society.* New York: National Research Council.

Johnson, D. F., & White, C. B. (1980). Effects of training on computerized test performance in the elderly. *Journal of Applied Psychology, 65,* 357–358.

Kaplan, B. (1961). Cross-cultural use of projective techniques. In F.L.K. Hsu (Ed.), *Psychological anthropology* (pp. 235–254). Homewood, IL: Dorsey.

Katz, J. H. (1985). The sociopolitical nature of counseling. *The Counseling Psychologist, 13*, 615–624.

Kimble, G. A. (1984). Psychology's two cultures. *American Psychologist, 39*, 833–839.

Klopfer, W. G., & Taulbee, E. S. (1976). Projective tests. *Annual Review of Psychology, 27*, 543–568.

Kluckhohn, C. (1951). Values and value orientations in the theory of action. In T. Parsons & E. A. Shields (Eds.), *Toward a general theory of action* (pp. 388–433). Cambridge, MA: Harvard University Press.

Kluckhohn, C., & Murray, H. A. (Eds.). (1954). *Personality in nature, society, and culture*. New York: Knopf.

Koch, S. (1981). The nature and limits of psychological knowledge. *American Psychologist, 36*, 257–269.

Lachar, D., Dahlstrom, W. G., & Moreland, K. L. (1986). Relationship of ethnic background and other demographic characteristics to MMPI patterns in psychiatric samples. In W. G. Dahlstrom, D. Lachar, & L. E. Dahlstrom (Eds.), *MMPI patterns of American minorities* (pp. 139–178). Minneapolis: University of Minnesota Press.

LaFromboise, T. D., Dauphinais, P., & Rowe, W. (1980). Indian students' perception of positive helper attitudes. *Journal of American Indian Education, 111*, 11–15.

Laosa, L. M. (1978). Maternal teaching strategies in Chicano families of varied educational and socioeconomic levels. *Child Development, 49*, 1129–1135.

Lidz, C. (Ed.) (1987). *Dynamic assessment*. New York: Guilford.

Lonner, W. J. (1975). An analysis of the pre-publication evaluation of cross-cultural manuscripts: Implications for future research. In R. W. Brislin, S. Bochner, & W. J. Lonner (Eds.), *Cross-cultural perspectives in learning* (pp. 305–320). New York: Halstead Press.

Lonner, W. J. (1979). Issues in cross-cultural psychology. In A. J. Marsella, R. Tharp, & T. Ciborowski (Eds.), *Perspectives on cross-cultural psychology* (pp. 17–45). New York: Academic Press.

Lonner, W. J. (1981). Psychological tests and intercultural counseling. In P. B. Pedersen, J. G. Draguns, W. J. Lonner, & J. E. Trimble (Eds.), *Counseling across cultures* (2nd ed., pp. 275–303). Honolulu: University of Hawaii Press.

Marcos, L. R., Alpert, M., Urcuyo, L., & Kesselman, M. (1973). The effect of interview language on the evaluation of psychopathology in Spanish-American schizophrenic patients. *American Journal of Psychiatry, 130*, 549–553.

Marsella, A. J. (1980). Depressive experience and disorder across cultures. In H. C. Triandis & J. G. Draguns (Eds.), *Handbook of cross-cultural psychology, Vol. 6: Psychopathology* (pp. 237–289). Needham Heights, MA: Allyn & Bacon.

Mays, V. M. (1985). The Black American and psychotherapy: The dilemma. *Psychotherapy, 22,* 379–387.

McAdams, D. P. (1994). *The person: An introduction to personality psychology* (2nd ed.). Orlando, FL: Harcourt Brace Jovanovich.

Messick, S. (1989). Validity. In R. L. Linn (Ed.), *Educational measurement* (3rd ed., pp. 13–103). New York: Macmillan.

Moynihan, D. P. (1965). Employment, income and the ordeal of the negro family. *Daedalus, 4,* 745–770.

Myers, H. F., Wohlford, P., Guzman, L. P., & Echemendia, R. J. (Eds.) (1991). *Ethnic minority perspectives on clinical training and services in psychology.* Washington, DC: American Psychological Association.

Olmedo, E. L. (1979). Acculturation: A psychometric perspective. *American Psychologist, 34,* 1061–1070.

Panton, J. H. (1959). Inmate personality differences related to recidivism, age and race as measured by the MMPI. *Journal of Correctional Psychology, 4,* 28–35.

Paulhus, D. L. (1991). Measurement and control of response bias. In J. P. Robinson, P. R. Shaver, & L. S. Wrightsman (Eds.), *Measures of Personality and Social Psychological Attitudes* (Vol. 1, pp. 17–60). San Diego: Academic Press.

Pedersen, P. (1988). *A handbook for developing multicultural awareness.* Alexandria, VA: American Counseling Association.

Ponterotto, J. G., & Casas, J. M. (1991). *Handbook of racial/ethnic minority counseling research.* Springfield, IL: Thomas.

Poortinga, Y. H. (1975). Some implications of three different approaches to intercultural comparison. In J. W. Berry & W. J. Lonner (Eds.), *Applied cross-cultural psychology* (pp. 327–332). Lisse, The Netherlands: Swets & Zeitlinger.

Pritchard, D. A., & Rosenblatt, A. (1980). Racial bias in the MMPI: A methodological review. *Journal of Consulting and Clinical Psychology, 48,* 263–267.

Rogler, L. H. (1993). Culturally sensitizing psychiatric diagnosis. *Journal of Nervous and Mental Disease, 181,* 401–408.

Ross, C. E., & Mirowsky, J. (1984). Socially-desirable response and acquiescence in a cross-cultural survey of mental health. *Journal of Health and Social Behavior, 25,* 189–197.

Sampson, E. E. (1988). The debate on individualism: Indigenous psychologies of the individual and their role in personal and societal functioning. *American Psychologist, 43*, 15–22.

Sharma, S. (1977). Cross-cultural comparisons of anxiety: Methodological problems. *Topics in Culture Learning, 5*, 166–173.

Shuey, A. (1966). *The testing of Negro intelligence*. New York: Social Science Press.

Smith, T. W. (1980). Ethnic measurement and identification. *Ethnicity, 7*, 78–95.

Sue, D. W. (1981). *Counseling the culturally different: Theory and practice*. New York: Wiley.

Sue, D. W., & Sue, D. (1977). Barriers to effective cross-cultural counseling. *Journal of Counseling Psychology, 24*, 420–429.

Sue, S. (1991). Ethnicity and culture in psychological research and practice. In J. D. Goodchilds (Ed.), *Psychological perspectives on human diversity in America* (pp. 51–85). Washington, DC: American Psychological Association.

Sue, S., & Morishima, J. K. (1982). *The mental health of Asian Americans: Contemporary issues in identifying and treating mental problems*. San Francisco: Jossey-Bass.

Sundberg, N. D., & Gonzales, L. R. (1981). Cross-cultural and cross-ethnic assessment: Overview and issues. In P. McReynolds (Ed.), *Advances in psychological assessment*. (Vol. 5, pp. 460–541). San Francisco: Jossey-Bass.

Szapocznik, J., Scopetta, M. A., Aranalde, M., & Kurtines, W. (1978). Cuban value structures: Treatment implications. *Journal of Consulting and Clinical Psychology, 46*, 961–970.

Taplin, J. R. (1980). Implication of general systems theory for assessment and intervention. *Professional Psychology, 11*, 722–727.

Triandis, H. C., Marin, G., Lisansky, J., & Betancourt, H. (1984). *Simpatia* as a cultural script of Hispanics. *Journal of Personality and Social Psychology, 47*, 1363–1375.

Vasquez-Nuttal, E., & Ivey, A. E. (1986). The diagnostic interview process. In H. M. Knoff (Ed.), *Child and adolescent personality* (pp. 111–113). New York: Guilford.

Velasquez, R. J., & Callahan, W. J. (1992). Psychological testing of Hispanic Americans in clinical settings: Overview and issues. In K. F. Geisinger (Ed.), *Psychological testing of Hispanics* (pp. 253–265). Washington, DC: American Psychological Association.

Whatley, P. R., & Dana, R. H. (1989). *Racial identity and MMPI group differences*.

Unpublished paper, Department of Psychology, University of Arkansas, Fayetteville.

Wundt, W. (1900–1909). *Volkerpsychologie* (10 vols.). Leipzig: Englemann.

Wyatt, G. E., Powell, G. J., & Bass, B. A. (1982). The survey of Afro-American behavior: Its development and use in research. In B. A. Bass, G. E. Wyatt, & G. J. Powell (Eds.), *The Afro-American family: Assessment, treatment, and research issues* (pp. 13–33). Philadelphia: Grune & Stratton.

. . . .

4

Multicultural Usage of the MMPI-2

Christine Zalewski and Roger L. Greene

The Minnesota Multiphasic Personality Inventory (MMPI; Hathaway and McKinley, 1967) is the most widely researched and clinically employed objective personality inventory (for example, see Dahlstrom, Welsh, and Dahlstrom, 1975; Lubin, Larsen, Matarazzo, and Seever, 1985). Multicultural assessment with the MMPI is extensive (for example, Dana, 1993) although the implications for the cross-cultural use of the instrument are not yet fully understood. There have been numerous empirical studies published in this area as well as several reviews of the literature. Dahlstrom, Lachar, and Dahlstrom (1986) have provided a thorough, in-depth analysis of the influence of ethnic group membership on MMPI performance, and Dana (1993) has provided a general overview of multiethnic assessment with the MMPI. Also, there have been a number of other reviews of the research in this area that should be consulted for a variety of perspectives on this topic (Costello, Tiffany, and Gier, 1972; Dana and Whatley, 1991; Greene, 1987; Gynther, 1972, 1979, 1989; Velasquez, 1992). However, the interplay between the complicated nature of the issues involved and the methodologic variation in the literature precludes definitive resolution to most culturally related concerns. In fact, reviewers of the same literature have reached remarkably different conclusions (see Gynther and Green, 1980; Pritchard and Rosenblatt, 1980a, 1980b).

Note: Portions of this chapter have been adapted from _Specific Groups: Adolescents, the Aged, Blacks, and Other Ethnic Groups,_ in Greene, 1991.

The MMPI also has been translated into a number of different languages for use around the world, which allows for the investigation of the effects of cultural factors on MMPI performance from an international perspective. Given the space limitations in this chapter, however, neither international studies or those related to the validity of foreign language versions of the MMPI-2 are systematically reviewed. The reader interested in this perspective should consult Butcher (1985), Butcher and Clark (1979), Butcher and Pancheri (1976), and Dana (1993) for additional information.

This chapter provides an overview of the issues involved in using the MMPI-2 in cross-cultural applications. The chapter begins with a brief overview of the MMPI and changes from the MMPI to the MMPI-2. Next, the literature related to cross-cultural research is summarized, by reviewing methodological issues and then general findings related to specific cultural groups. Within each section, results related to the basic clinical and validity scales are presented first, followed by results related to validation research, the supplementary scales, and item analysis, respectively. Additionally, guidelines for multicultural administration and interpretation of the MMPI-2 are offered, as is a case example.

For those unfamiliar with derivation of the MMPI, a brief review will be helpful before discussing its use cross-culturally. The MMPI is a 566-item, true-false, self-report inventory containing thirteen standard validity and clinical scales (listed in Table 4.1). Additional published subscales, supplementary scales, content scales, and special scales number in the hundreds (Dahlstrom, Welsh, and Dahlstrom, 1975). Standard texts recommend a sixth-grade reading level for standard administration (Dahlstrom, Welsh, and Dahlstrom, 1972; Friedman, Webb, and Lewak, 1989; Graham, 1987; Greene, 1980).

The clinical scales of the MMPI were created using the method of empirical keying. Specifically, item responses of individuals within specific criterion groups (for example, uncomplicated hypochondriasis) were compared to normal controls. Those items

Table 4.1. MMPI-2 Validity and Clinical Scales.

Scale Name	Abbreviation	Number
Lie	L	
F	F	
K	K	
Hypochondriasis	Hs	1
Depression	D	2
Hysteria	Hy	3
Psychopathic Deviate	Pd	4
Masculinity–Femininity	Mf	5
Paranoia	Pa	6
Psychasthenia	Pt	7
Schizophrenia	Sc	8
Hypomania	Ma	9
Social Introversion	Si	0

on which the two groups differed significantly were included in the final scales, weighted in the "deviant" direction. Thus, elevations on the clinical scales correspond to increasing response-pattern similarity to the criterion psychiatric groups.

The primary normative group for the MMPI consisted of 724 White men and women who brought friends or relatives to the University Hospitals in Minneapolis in the late 1930s. The individuals in the group ranged in age from sixteen to fifty-five, and were similar to the Minnesota population regarding demographic variables such as gender and marital status. This normative group still serves as the reference for determining the standard MMPI profile.

Because the original normative group differs so greatly from many individuals currently assessed with the MMPI, the validity of the instrument in cross-cultural settings has been questioned. In fact, the nonrepresentative nature of the original normative sample was one of the primary concerns resulting in the MMPI-2, the current revision of the MMPI (Butcher, Dahlstrom, Graham, Tellegen, and Kaemmer, 1989). However, the introduction of the MMPI-2, while addressing several cross-cultural limitations, also has increased the complexity of the conclusions that can be drawn from the empirical literature.

Changes from the MMPI to the MMPI-2

Restandardization of the MMPI was undertaken to provide current norms for the inventory, develop a nationally representative and larger normative sample, provide appropriate representation of minority groups, and update item content where necessary (see Butcher and others, 1989). New criterion groups and item derivation procedures were *not* used on the standard validity and clinical scales to maximize continuity between the two instruments. One hundred and six items on the original MMPI were eliminated from the MMPI-2, including the 16 repeated items and 13 items from the standard validity and clinical scales. Seven of the latter 13 items were religious in content and three were related to bowel and bladder functioning. An additional 68 items were reworded and 107 items were added, although the new items are not included in the standard validity and clinical scales.

The MMPI-2 was standardized on a sample of 2,600 subjects from seven states (California, Minnesota, North Carolina, Ohio, Pennsylvania, Virginia, and Washington). Efforts were made to reflect the national census regarding demographic variables such as age, marital status, ethnicity, education, and so forth. The normative sample for the MMPI-2 differed significantly from that of the original MMPI in years of education, occupational status, and representation of Black, Hispanic, Native American, and Asian American individuals. Although the MMPI-2 normative sample more accurately reflects the current United States population than does the original normative sample, it still varies from census parameters for education level and occupational status. Specifically, 70.4 percent of the normative sample had completed at least some college compared to 33.1 percent in the census. Similarly, 40.8 percent of the MMPI-2 normative sample held professional jobs compared to 15.6 percent of the census (see Butcher and others, 1989). However, the actual impact of the relatively high education and occupational level of the MMPI-2 normative group on the standard validity and clinical scales and codetype interpretation remains to be determined empirically. This is especially true as it relates to cross-cultural usage, particularly regarding interaction effects of SES and cultural group membership.

Other changes from the MMPI to the MMPI-2 include the adoption of *uniform* T scores in the place of *linear* T scores, the introduction of fifteen new content scales, the restriction to individuals over the age of eighteen, and an increase in reading level from sixth to eighth grade.

Considerable controversy has arisen regarding whether the correlates of the individual scales and the codetypes that were derived on the MMPI can be applied to the MMPI-2 (for example, see Adler, 1990; Caldwell, 1990; Nichols, 1991). This issue is of particular relevance to the cross-cultural MMPI research given that the nonrepresentative nature of the all-White Minnesota sample was one of the primary reasons for the development of the MMPI-2. Additionally, other changes from the MMPI may differentially affect individuals from varying cultures, such as the omission of seven religious items, the higher educational and occupational level of the normative sample, the increase in reading level, and so on.

Several important issues are relevant to understanding the cross-cultural implications of MMPI-2 usage. The first is whether cultural group membership is related to differences in MMPI-2 scores after controlling for potentially confounding factors such as socioeconomic status and educational level. If minority group status does affect MMPI-2 scale scores when these factors are controlled, the critical issue becomes whether MMPI-2 interpretations based on census-representative or specific cultural group norms are more valid. Finally, since the vast majority of the cross-cultural research was conducted with the MMPI, the extent to which these results are applicable to the MMPI-2 has yet to be determined empirically. Thus, caution should be exercised when generalizing cross-cultural MMPI results to practice with the MMPI-2.

Cross-Cultural Research with the MMPI and MMPI-2

A great variety of terms are used in the literature to denote specific cultural groups, and many are used interchangeably. For instance, the term *Asian* may be used to describe Asian Americans, foreign Asian college students studying in the United States, or Japanese, Chinese, or Vietnamese citizens living in their own countries. Because the specific groups falling under the general rubric of "Asian," "Hispanic," or "Black" may differ from one another as much as the general groups differ from the original White Minnesota sample, specificity in reporting the results of prior research is imperative. Thus, for the purposes of this chapter, the general headings of "Black," "Asian," "Hispanic," and "Native American" will be used for general groupings: However, the specific terms employed in original articles will be used when summarizing previous research.

Methodologic Issues

Historically, the prototypic investigation of the effect of cultural group membership on MMPI performance consisted of plotting the mean MMPI profile of a particular cultural sample against the original normative group or another specific cultural group. If differences occurred between the two groups on any scale, the typical conclusion was that the MMPI as a whole, or some subset of scales, was affected by membership in that cultural group. This often led researchers to recommend specific norms for particular cultural groups, procedures for adjusting scores for use with individuals within specific groups, or prohibition of using the MMPI with various groups (for example, Gynther, Lachar, and Dahlstrom, 1978).

However, a number of points must be considered before the conclusion is justified that observed group mean differences reflect cultural group membership. Greene (1987) has summarized several methodologic issues present in cross-cultural MMPI studies that can potentially affect the interpretation of any cultural group differences that are found. These included determination of ethnic group membership, profile validity, role of moderator variables, use of appropriate statistical analyses, adequate sample size, and effect size.

Most studies summarized by Greene (1987) provided information regarding demographic characteristics of the samples, the role of moderator variables such as education, socioeconomic status, and intelligence, and basic MMPI information such as types of scores analyzed and criteria used for determining profile validity. However, because any of these parameters can profoundly influence the results of a study, complete information related to each of them should be included in any published report.

Researchers were casual in reporting the criteria used to specify membership within the target cultural groups under examination. Most often, the persons were described as Black, Hispanic, Asian American, and so on, with little consideration of whether they actually identified with their respective cultural groups. Sometimes Hispanic subjects, and less frequently, Asian American subjects, were classified on the basis of their surname, which at least strongly suggests that, at some point in their family heritage, there was either membership in the ethnic group or marriage to a member. However, a surname does not determine whether persons actually are members of the ethnic group, or more important, whether they have any identification with that group.

Recently, some researchers have used measures of acculturation or cultural group identification such as the Acculturation scale for Mexican Americans (Cuellar, Harris, and Jasso, 1980) as moderator variables in examining MMPI performance in individuals within specific cultural groups (for example, see Montgomery and Orozco, 1985). Although numerous measures of acculturation and cultural group identification have been published in recent years, such as the Suinn-Lew Asian Self-Identity Acculturation scale (Suinn, Rickard-Figueroa, Lew, and Vigil, 1987), the usage of such instruments in cross-cultural MMPI studies is still more the exception than the rule.

Finally, and most importantly, in order to determine that the MMPI-2, or any other instrument, is affected by cultural group membership and in need of pluralistic norms, differences in criterion-related validity must be demonstrated. Group mean differences, regardless of their resiliency to methodologic control, are insufficient to warrant changes in interpretive procedures. Unfortunately, the cross-cultural literature on the MMPI/MMPI-2 continues to be profoundly lacking in criterion-related empirical research.

Thus, although the cross-cultural MMPI literature will be summarized below, the reader is encouraged to seek original sources and apply these methodologic criteria to best understand the extent to which the results can be generalized to clinical practice or various research paradigms.

General Findings

The literature will be divided primarily according to Black, Hispanic, Native American, and Asian American comparisons to White samples. Although a number of recent researchers have made comparisons across non-White groups (such as Barefoot and others, 1991; Bernstein, Teng, Grannemann, and Garbin, 1987; Cannon, Bell, Fowler, Penk, and Finkelstein, 1990; Knatz, Inwald, Brockwell, and Tran, 1992; Penk and others, 1989), the stated subdivision of this literature will be retained for several reasons. First, most of the research has been conducted with the MMPI, which was normed on an all-White sample. Second, the normative sample for the MMPI-2, which was more culturally representative, still was composed primarily of White subjects (81.4 percent). Thus, if specific groups, such as Hispanics or Asian Americans, do reliably differ on their MMPI-2 scores, their modest representation (2.8 percent and .7 percent, respectively) in the normative sample is unlikely to have a meaningful effect on the normative mean scores. Finally, limited space precludes examination of the multitude of cross-cultural comparisons that can be made. Thus, the interested reader is encouraged to seek original sources for multigroup comparisons across cultures.

Black-White Comparisons

Greene (1991) summarized fifty-four studies, including eighty-one comparisons of various groups of Blacks and Whites on the MMPI standard validity and clinical scales. Since MMPI performance varies as a function of the setting in which the test is administered, Greene subdivided the studies by their use of normal, prison, substance abuse, medical-welfare, or psychiatric samples. Because there was no consistent pattern of group-related score differences found across the studies, no global statement regarding Black-White differences was supported. Even within specific populations, there were few generalizations that could be made in a reliable manner.

For example, in normal populations it is routinely assumed that Blacks frequently score higher on Scales *F*, 8, and 9 than do Whites. However, a majority of the twenty-five comparisons within normal samples found no reliable differences on these three scales, although when differences did occur, Blacks did score higher than Whites. In fact, there was no scale on which a majority of the comparisons were consistently higher either in Blacks or Whites in any setting. Consequently, it appears inappropriate to conclude that Blacks routinely score higher than Whites on any of the standard MMPI validity or clinical scales in any setting thus far examined.

Findings from more recent studies examining Black-White differences on the basic validity and clinical scales have continued to be difficult to summarize concisely. For instance, Robyak and Byers (1990) examined the effects of race and severity of alcoholism on Black and White male hospitalized alcoholics matched for age and education. They found significant effects for race and severity, but no interaction. Blacks scored significantly higher than Whites on Scales *F*, *1*, and *9*, one or more of which had been previously reported as higher in Whites (see Penk, Woodward, Robinowitz, and Hess, 1978; Sutker, Archer, and Allain, 1978, 1980), although only on Scales *1* and *9* were these differences five *T* score points or more.

Penk and others (1989) compared MMPI validity and clinical scale scores of Black, Hispanic, and White male Vietnam veterans who were seeking treatment for addiction disorders. The groups were similar regarding age, education, and SES, and were subdivided into three combat exposure levels. The main effect for ethnicity was significant for Scales 2, 4, 5, 6, 9, and 0. Scale scores were relatively similar among the three ethnic groups under the No and Light combat exposure conditions. However, differences occurred within the Heavy combat exposure condition, with Blacks scoring higher than both Hispanics and Whites on those subscales found to differ among the groups.

Cannon and others (1990) examined the effect of age and race on MMPI scores of alcohol-, drug-, and mixed-substance abusers who were inpatients at a Veterans Administration medical center. For purposes of analysis, the patients were dichotomized on the basis of non-Hispanic Whites versus all others, who were primarily Black and Hispanic. White patients had significantly higher means on Scales 1, 5, and 0, and significantly lower means on Scale 9. Although no group mean differences were reported, the correlations between the significant MMPI scales and dichotomously dummy coded racial group membership were .19 or lower, suggesting minimal differences that would be unlikely to have clinical meaning. In addition, because the Black and Hispanic subjects were grouped together, the pattern of differences attributable to each ethnicity remains unknown.

Finally, the normative sample for the MMPI-2 provides some information regarding Black-White differences, especially as a function of gender and educational level. Although the subjects in the normative sample were subdivided into Asian, Black, Hispanic,

Native American, and White groups, only the Black and White groups contained sufficient numbers to support such comparisons. Examination of these differences within the MMPI-2 normative sample is particularly important given the relatively high level of education evident therein, including the Black subsample. Specifically, 58.7 percent of Black males and 61.7 percent of Black females completed at least some college education or more (Butcher and others, 1989).

When the Black women, White women, Black men, and White men are compared across five educational levels, including part high school, high school, part college, college, and post college, mean score scale differences vary considerably in magnitude. For instance, Scale 2 differs by two T points or less among the educational groups for White men, whereas the mean score for Scale 8 is thirteen T points higher for Black women with part high school education ($T = 60$) than for Black women with post college education ($T = 47$) (Butcher and others, 1989). Space limitations in this chapter preclude detailed presentation of these comparisons and discussion related to the possible reasons for the differences. However, the implications are sufficient to warrant cross-validation of the findings, especially given the variability in size among the ethnicity by gender groupings (ranging from $n = 9$ to $n = 343$) in the Black and White samples.

In summary, the findings across research examining group mean differences for Blacks and Whites have been inconsistent, with some significant differences reported in opposite directions in separate studies. However, as Gynther and Green (1980) point out, box scores for differences and tabular summaries of findings, although tempting, may be overly simplistic and obscure important differences. For instance, it is possible that the Black samples in various studies may have differed in SES, concomitant pathology, or their identification with a Black culture, which may have obscured real differences or, alternatively, implied differences where none truly exist.

The specific population that is being examined also appears to be an important influence on the nature of Black-White differences. For instance, in substance abuse samples, Whites rather frequently score higher than, or similar to, Blacks on certain scales, whereas in psychiatric samples the differences often are found in opposite directions.

One final comment about Black-White differences on the standard validity and clinical scales seems warranted. The more rigorously that moderator variables and profile validity issues are controlled by an investigator, the less likely it becomes that Black-White differences will be found. For example, Costello and others (1972) reported that no Black-White differences were found if invalid profiles were excluded. Similarly, Penk and his colleagues (Penk, Roberts, Robinowitz, Dolan, Atkins, and Woodward, 1982; Penk, Robinowitz, Roberts, Dolan, and Atkins, 1981) have found no Black-White differences in substance abuse patients when age, education, socioeconomic status, and intelligence were controlled statistically.

Thus, it appears that moderator variables, such as SES, education, and intelligence, as well as profile validity issues, are important factors to be controlled in any MMPI-2 research, and particularly when the potential effect of ethnic status is being examined. Rather than discussing the fact that normals from an ethnic minority tend to have more elevated scores on the standard validity and clinical scales than White normals, it seems much more important to consider the role of the moderator variables listed above.

The paucity of studies that have examined the relative validity of the MMPI across cultural groups is in direct contrast to the numerous studies examining simple Black-White differences. Greene (1987, 1991) summarized this literature and found that while some researchers found different correlates for Blacks and Whites on the MMPI (such as Gynther, Altman, and Warbin, 1973), others did not (such as Elion and Megargee, 1975; Genthner and Graham, 1976).

Only a few studies have investigated whether there are differences in the discriminability of Blacks and Whites within and between diagnostic groups using the MMPI. Both Cowan, Watkins, and Davis (1975) and Davis (1975) examined Black-White differences in matched groups of schizophrenics and nonschizophrenics and found no significant differences for ethnicity. Cowan and others did find that Blacks with less than twelve years of education were more likely to be misclassified than either Blacks with twelve years or more of education or Whites. Their results appear to be compatible with Rosenblatt and Pritchard (1978), who found race differences only in patients with IQs below 94.

Strauss, Gynther, and Wallhermfechtel (1974) examined Black-White differences between groups of patients with diagnoses of either behavior disorder or functional psychosis. The authors reported substantially higher rates of misdiagnosis among Blacks than Whites. However, Shore (1976) indicated that these results were subject to computational errors, and concluded that Black-White differences were not clearly supported by the data presented.

More recently, Knatz and others (1992) evaluated 3,391 Black, 3,349 White, and 1,547 Hispanic male correction officers on their job status and histories of absence, lateness, and disciplinary interviews. Discriminant function analyses revealed no significant bias in prediction accuracy of any counterproductive job behavior measure.

Johnson and Brems (1990) compared MMPI profiles of twenty-two Black and twenty-two White clients carefully matched regarding age, gender, and Axis I and Axis II diagnoses. They found no significant differences on either the validity scales or ten clinical scales between the two races. The authors suggest that the need for separate Black and White MMPI norms may be overstated, and in inpatient psychiatric settings, previously reported MMPI differences may be due more to moderator variables than race.

Because of the limited amount of research and the dated nature of many of the existing studies, it is difficult to conclude whether there are Black-White differences between various diagnostic groups as assessed by the MMPI. The interested reader should consult Pritchard and Rosenblatt (1980a, 1980b) for a critical view of this research before assuming the reliability of any previously reported correlational differences. There does appear to be, however, a tendency for persons with limited education and below-average IQs to score differently than the normative group on the MMPI, and the clinician should consider this when interpreting such a client's MMPI. Clearly, additional research is needed to investigate the clinical correlates of Black-White differences in MMPI performance when the potential influence of moderator variables have been controlled adequately.

There has been very little research on Black-White differences for the numerous MMPI supplementary scales. Greene (1987, 1991) summarized the limited research in this area, which demonstrated few reliable Black-White differences despite the failure of most studies to control for moderator variables. One interesting finding was that Black and White substance abusers scored similarly on the MacAndrew Alcoholism scale (MacAndrew, 1965) (for example, see McCreary and Padilla, 1977; Snyder, Kline, and Podany, 1985; Walters, Greene, Jeffrey, Kruzich, and Haskin, 1983), yet normal Blacks score higher than Whites (Walters and others, 1983). In the MMPI-2 normative sample, MacAndrew Alcoholism Scale-Revised scores differed as a function of education within each of the gender by ethnicity groupings, ranging from 5 (White women) to 13 (Black men) T points in difference from part high school to post college. Since the MacAndrew Alcoholism scale is used so widely in spite of criticism of its validity (see Gottesman and Prescott, 1989), considerably more research on this topic is necessary.

Two additional studies have been published since Greene's more recent (1991) review. The first examined the effects of race and the validity of Megargee, Cook, and Mendelsohn's Overcontrolled-Hostility (O-H) scales using 412 male forensic psychiatric inpatients (Hutton, Miner, Blades, and Langfeldt, 1992). A stepwise multiple regression on O-H scores was performed using instant offense, psychiatric diagnosis, education, employment history, incidents of hospital physical assault, and race as predictor variables. The only significant predictor of O-H score was race, with Black patients scoring approximately 6 T score points higher than White patients, and obtaining a relatively high proportion of O-H scores greater than 69 (43 percent).

The second study, Barefoot and others (1991), found that the Cook-Medley Hostility scale (Ho) scores were correlated with race (White and non-White), years of education, occupation, and income in a national survey sample of 2,536 adults. Higher Ho scores were found in non-Whites, with the greatest Ho score differences occurring among those with the lowest incomes. Within the category of non-Whites, there were no significant differences on Ho between Black Americans (n = 302), and Asian, Hispanic, and Native Americans (n = 168).

A number of investigators have reported Black-White differences at the item level on the MMPI (Costello, 1973, 1977; Gynther and Witt, 1976; Harrison and Kass, 1967, 1968; Jones, 1978; Miller, Knapp, and Daniels, 1968; Witt and Gynther, 1975). Although from 58 to 213 items have been found to differentiate Blacks from Whites in a given study, there has been limited overlap among these items across the various investigations.

Additionally, many of the studies examining Black-White item responses are dated, and their generalizability is limited due to the general trend for response-pattern change over time (for example, see Colligan, Osborne, Swenson, and Offord, 1983; Dahlstrom, Lachar, and Dahlstrom, 1986). Consequently, there does not appear to be any real conclusion that can be drawn from these findings other than that item-level endorsement frequencies may vary in different samples with a small number of items consistently differentiating Blacks and Whites.

Bernstein and others (1987) compared the principal component structure of the MMPI's validity and clinical scales (excluding Scale 5) in a sample of over 13,000 Hispanic, White, Black, and Native

American subjects. They found the factor structure to be invariant across the groups, which is a necessary, but not sufficient, condition for the MMPI to be viewed as unbiased. The authors particularly noted the fact that the pattern and structure loadings of Scales F and 8, which are most frequently cited as biased, were at least as high for Blacks as for the other groups. This finding challenges the notion that these scales relate less well to general maladjustment in Blacks, although they cannot address the possibility of intercept bias, or the equivalence of scale elevations across groups.

In contrast, Beck and others (1989) found some differences in the factor structure between Black (n = 2,712) and White (n = 18,148) psychiatric inpatients and outpatients. The items that make up the traditional validity and clinical scales were factored by the principal components method, followed by Varimax rotations of six through twenty-five factors. The results suggest that there was reasonable correspondence between Blacks and Whites for some factors, such as Neurotic Symptoms, but that many others replicated poorly. In addition, the authors noted that inspection and interpretation of the factor loadings sometimes revealed that factors with the same labels were characterized by low coefficients of congruence.

Hispanic-White Comparisons

Greene (1987, 1991) summarized the literature examining Hispanic-White differences on the standard validity and clinical scales of the MMPI. The results from the thirteen studies making up the literature did not suggest any clear pattern to the comparisons, and there were few data to support the contention that Hispanics frequently score higher on the L scale and lower on Scale 5 (see Greene, 1980), although when differences were found they tended to be in that direction. There did appear to be, however, a tendency for fewer Hispanic-White differences to be found than when Black-White comparisons were made.

Velasquez and his colleagues (Velasquez, 1984; Velasquez and

Callahan, 1990a, 1990b; Velasquez, Callahan, and Carrillo, 1989; Velasquez, Callahan, and Carrillo, 1991; Velasquez, Callahan, and Young, 1993; Velasquez and Gimenez, 1987) have provided the most systematic research on the use of the MMPI with Hispanics.

Velasquez and Gimenez (1987) found few MMPI differences among three diagnostic groups (schizophrenia, antisocial personality disorder, and affective disorder with unipolar depression) of Mexican American psychiatric inpatients. However, this failure to find a strong pattern of association between the MMPI and specific diagnostic categories has been reported frequently in samples other than Mexican American inpatients (see Greene, 1988).

Velasquez and Callahan (1990a) found that Hispanic American alcoholics had lower scores on Scales 4, 5, and 0 than White alcoholics, similar to the relationship found in Black-White comparisons among alcoholics. This latter finding that Hispanic alcoholics, like Black alcoholics, have lower scores on the MMPI when differences are found, requires that any study of ethnic differences on the MMPI include the setting as a potential confounding factor.

Velasquez and others (1993) found that Hispanic-White MMPI differences were not eliminated when both groups were matched on three key moderator variables—age, education, and psychiatric diagnosis (Schizophrenia, Depression, Antisocial). Differences in MMPI response pattern between Hispanics and Whites were more likely to occur in schizophrenic and depressed patients, rather than their antisocial counterparts. Discriminant function analysis indicated that Scales L, 9, 5, 8, and 6 were the most useful in discriminating between ethnic groups and examination of the group mean differences revealed T score differences of five or more points for each of these scales.

Velasquez and others (1991) examined the effect of gender differences on the MMPI among sixty Mexican American psychiatric inpatients, who are described as sharing "similar" DSM-III diagnoses, although little diagnostic information was given beyond the modal admission diagnosis, which was atypical depression. Mexican

American males obtained significantly higher scores than their female counterparts on Scales F, 5, and 6. They concluded that researchers should account for gender when conducting cross-ethnic MMPI comparisons, and that the practice of grouping Mexican American men and women together for MMPI comparisons with other ethnic groups should be discontinued in favor of comparisons that consider the effects of both gender and ethnicity. However, the lack of diagnostic information available for the groups, combined with known gender-related differences in diagnostic base rates, undermines the foundation for their conclusions.

Other recent studies of Hispanic-White differences on the MMPI have explored an assortment of topics with varying degrees of methodologic control. Weisman, Anglin, and Fisher (1989) examined the differences in MMPI profiles between Chicano and Anglo narcotics addicts who had histories of incarceration that began either before or after narcotics use. The ethnicity effect was significant for Scale F and all clinical Scales except 2 and 0. Where scale differences were significant, Anglo addicts consistently had higher mean scale scores than Chicanos. Chicano addicts' MMPI profiles, unlike the profiles of Anglos, did not differ as a result of whether incarceration took place before or after narcotics use.

Whitworth (1988) compared Anglo college students (n = 150) to Mexican American college students who completed the MMPI in Spanish (n = 150) and English (n = 150), all of whom were matched for gender and age. He found significant language and ethnicity differences among the three groups on ten of the thirteen MMPI scales, including L, F, 1, 2, 4, 5, 6, 7, 8, and 0. The Mexican Americans who took the test in Spanish scored higher than both Anglos and Mexican Americans tested in English on all the previously significant MMPI scales, with the exception of Scale 7, on which Mexican Americans tested in Spanish scored significantly higher than Anglos, but not Mexican Americans tested in English. Mexican Americans tested in English scored significantly higher than Anglos on only Scale L, which is consistent with the previous findings of Lawson, Kahn, and Heiman (1982).

Venn (1988) compared sixteen Native American and sixteen Mexican American inpatient alcoholic men who were matched with White American men on the basis of age and marital status. The Mexican American men scored significantly higher than Whites on Scale *L*, which was the only statistically significant difference between the groups. The small sample sizes, however, preclude determination that there actually are few differences between these two groups.

One recent study, Whitworth and McBlaine (1993), examined the MMPI-2 in Hispanic students. One hundred and ten Anglo and 173 Hispanic American college students completed a combined version of the MMPI and MMPI-2, from which K-corrected *T* scores for each instrument were computed. The Hispanic students obtained higher scores on Scale *L*, and the Anglo students obtained higher scores on Scales *K*, *3*, and *4*. However, none of these statistically significant results reflected group mean differences of five *T* score points or more. The authors concluded that the pattern of results was consistent with previous research on the MMPI, and suggested that any differences on the MMPI between these two groups of Anglos and Hispanics will be essentially the same on the MMPI-2.

Three studies mentioned earlier, Penk and others (1989), Knatz and others (1992), and Bernstein and others (1987), reported no differences between Hispanics and Whites on the standard MMPI scales, the prediction accuracy of the MMPI, or the principal component structure of the instrument, respectively.

Two additional studies (Anderson, Thompson, and Boeringa, 1993; Clark, Velasquez, and Callahan, 1992), reported frequently occurring codetypes among various diagnostic groups. Anderson and others examined the profiles of nineteen outpatient Mexican American Vietnam veterans diagnosed with PTSD, and Clark and others examined two-point codetypes among diagnostic groups of Hispanic adults who completed a Spanish version of the MMPI. However, neither of these studies employed control groups, limiting the generalizability of their findings.

DuAlba and Scott (1993) examined the differences between

male Hispanic (n = 60) and White (n = 60) workers' compensation applicants on somatization and malingering as assessed by the MMPI. Somatization was assessed as present when Scales 1, 2, and 3 were greater than or equal to a T score of 70. Malingering was assessed by the MMPI dissimulation index of $F - K > + 9$. Most (93 percent) of the Hispanic applicants were classified as somatizers, whereas only 55 percent of the Whites were so classified. There were no differences for malingering between the races.

Few studies have examined Hispanic-White differences on the MMPI supplementary scales. McCreary and Padilla (1977) found no differences between Mexican American and White male offenders, and Page and Bozlee (1982) found no differences between Hispanic American and White male alcoholics on the MacAndrew Alcoholism scale (MacAndrew, 1965). McCreary and Padilla reported that Hispanics scored higher on the Overcontrolled-Hostility scale (Megargee, Cook, and Mendelsohn, 1967), and Dolan, Roberts, Penk, Robinowitz, and Atkins (1983) found no differences larger than five T points on any of the Wiggins (1966) Content scales.

In contrast, Montgomery, Arnold, and Orozco (1990) reported differences between Mexican American and Anglo-American college students on the Wiggins Content scales, as well as the Harris-Lingoes subscales and the Serkownek subscales. Mexican American students scored higher on eight of the thirteen Wiggins Content scales, including Depression, Poor Moral, Authority Conflict, Psychoticism, Organic Symptoms, Manifest Hostility, Phobias, and Poor Health. However, when acculturation and age were covaried, no significant group differences remained. The authors determined that acculturation and age are important moderator variables because most of the statistically significant differences between Mexican Americans' and Anglos' performance on the MMPI supplemental scales could be suppressed by statistically controlling them. The interested reader is referred to the original article for a more detailed description of the analyses, as well as the results from the many other scales examined.

In summary, the MMPI literature regarding Hispanic-White comparisons is varied, both in terms of the specific scales examined and methodologic control. Although there was no scale found to differ between Hispanics and Whites in every study, higher Scale *L* scores in Hispanic groups as compared to White groups has been the most consistent finding.

One final note worth mentioning is that recent MMPI studies have tended to better inform the reader about the criteria used for determining Hispanic group membership (for example, see Clark and others, 1992; Velasquez and others, 1991). This is a substantial improvement given the importance of this issue and the relative lack of attention it received in the earlier literature.

Native American-White Comparisons

Greene (1987, 1991) summarized the literature that examined Native American-White differences on the standard validity and clinical scales of the MMPI. For the first time, there appeared to be a clear pattern for normal Native Americans to score higher on the clinical scales than their White counterparts, although they did not obtain higher scores on Scale *F*. However, only two studies were conducted in this area, the most recent of which was published in 1966. In addition, there were no similar trends evident in the remaining five studies examining psychiatric and substance abuse samples.

One study not included in Greene's reviews compared sixteen Native American inpatient alcoholic males to a White American sample matched for age and marital status, and found no significant differences on any validity or clinical scales (Venn, 1988). However, as mentioned earlier, the power in this study was quite low due to the small sample size, and may account for the lack of significant differences. In contrast, Bernstein and others (1987) employed a sample of over 13,000 subjects and found the principal component structure of the validity and clinical scales to remain invariant across several racial groups, including Native Americans.

Only two studies have investigated the performance of Native American samples on any of the MMPI supplementary scales. Uecker, Boutilier, and Richardson (1980) found no differences between Indian and White substance abusers on the MacAndrew Alcoholism scale (MacAndrew, 1965). The authors did not report data from a non-substance-abuse–Native American sample, so it is not known whether they also would elevate the MacAndrew Alcoholism scale as previously described in normal Blacks.

Barefoot and others (1991) found that the Cook-Medley Hostility scale (Ho) scores were higher among non-Whites, a group that included Native Americans, and that the greatest Ho score differences between the races occurred among those with the lowest incomes. However, the authors did not report the number of Native Americans contained in the non-White group, and the extent to which they influenced the results remains unknown.

Clearly, empirical studies related to the validity of the MMPI for use with Native American populations are sadly lacking. In addition, the dated nature of those few studies that have been published warrants extreme caution in the generalization of their results to current usage.

Asian American-White Comparisons

Despite Greene's (1987) conclusion that more research is necessary to understand potential differences between Asian Americans and Whites on MMPI performance, few empirical findings have been published in the ensuing years. Most of the literature has examined group mean differences on the standard MMPI validity and clinical scales, or characteristics related to differences in the expression of distress, such as somatization, or to a lesser extent, hostility. A large proportion of this literature has been conducted with college students, perhaps reflective of the recent rise in enrollment of Asian Americans in institutions of higher education (National Center for Education Statistics, 1991).

Marsella, Sanborn, Kameoka, Shizuru, and Brennan (1975) found that nonclinical samples of Chinese American and Japanese

American college students scored higher than White Americans on Scale 2, the only MMPI scale examined in their study. Sue and Sue (1974) also found differences between Asian American and "non-Asian" students from a university psychiatric clinic on several MMPI scales. Asian American males scored higher on Scales L, F, 1, 2 4, 6, 7, 8, and 0 whereas Asian American females scored higher on Scales L, F, 6, 7, 8, and 0 than their White counterparts. In addition, the authors reported that Asian Americans scored higher than Whites on a set of ten items reflecting somatic complaints and on a set of six items reflecting family problems.

Cogburn, Zalewski, Farrell, and Mendoza (1993) found that Asian American college students scored higher on Scales L, F, 1, 2, 4, 6, 7, 8, and 0, and scored lower on Scale K, than did their White counterparts. They found an ethnicity-gender interaction for Scales 5 and 0, with Asian American females scoring highest and White males scoring lowest on Scale 0, and similarly, Asian American females scored highest whereas Asian American males scored lowest on Scale 5. Asian Americans also scored higher than Whites on the Social Discomfort and Health Concerns content scales, on a set of critical items related to somatic symptoms, and on the ten somatic items previously examined by Sue and Sue (1974). All of the standard validity and clinical scales except L and 1 differed by five T score points or more. However, because no diagnostic measures were collected, it remains unknown whether these differences in scores reflect actual differences in pathology or differences in reporting style.

Stevens, Kwan, and Graybill (1993) found differences between foreign Chinese (n = 25) and White American students (n = 22). Chinese males, relative to White males, scored higher on Scale 0. Chinese females obtained higher scores on Scales L, K, 2, 3, and lower scores on Scale 5, than White females. However, because of the vastly different experiences of foreign and U.S. Asian groups, caution must be exercised in generalizing findings from foreign Asian samples to Asian American samples.

In contrast to these studies, Tsushima and Onorato (1982)

found, after controlling for type of pathology, Japanese American and White neurological and medical patients responded similarly on the clinical and validity scales. The one exception to this was Scale 5, which demonstrated a Gender by Race interaction. In this study, White males obtained the highest scores on Scale 5, conflicting with the findings of Cogburn and others (1993).

Little research has examined Asian American performance on any supplementary scales. In a study of Type A behavior and hostility, Fukunishi, Nakagawa, Nakamura, Ogawa, and Nakagawa (1993) compared the MMPI Cook-Medley Hostility scale (Ho) scores of 228 Japanese and 121 American college students. The Ho scores were significantly higher in the American than the Japanese group. Conversely, Barefoot and others (1991) found that Ho scores were lower for Whites than non-Whites, a group that contained an unspecified number of Asian Americans. Because these authors did not compare the Asians to other cultural groups within the non-White sample, their impact on the Ho scores remains unknown.

In summary, while considerable literature suggests that Asian Americans score higher on items reflecting somatic concerns relative to other psychological symptoms, other findings are inconsistent, and suggest that elevations may occur on scales reflecting a wide range of psychological distress. Given the relative shortage of empirical studies in this area and the inconclusive nature of existing findings, further research is necessary to clearly delineate any differential response patterns associated with Asian American group membership.

Guidelines for Multicultural Usage of the MMPI-2

The first consideration in multicultural administration and interpretation of the MMPI-2 relates to the complexity of the literature. The conclusions that can be drawn from the empirical studies are *not* conducive to simplified rules of thumb—or even standard practices for interpretation.

Second, the role of moderator variables is essential for understanding the profile of any individual, regardless of cultural identification. Education, income level, occupation, and other measures of socioeconomic status play an important role in the observation of differences across cultural groups. Stated briefly, the more closely groups are matched for these variables, the fewer differences are found, and the magnitude of the differences that remain tends to be greatly decreased.

Third, the frequent failure in the literature to assess in any manner persons' identification with their ethnic group is quite notable. It seems very questionable to discuss the effects of ethnic status on MMPI-2 performance without some means of ensuring that the persons actually identify with and belong to the ethnic group. Thus, investigations of the effect of ethnic status on MMPI-2 performance need to refrain from assuming that identity with the minority culture is defined by the person's race or surname. Practitioners relying on empirical research in making clinical decisions should be aware of the ethnic group membership criteria employed in the studies they consider. This is especially true, given that level of acculturation and cultural group identification appear to be important factors in the determination of any changes to standard interpretive procedures.

Fourth, the effect sizes reported within specific areas should be incorporated into decisions for clinical practice. Group mean differences under five T points, regardless of statistical significance, are unlikely to have clinical meaning in any setting. Also, when differences are found, it is important to determine whether or not there are associated clinical correlates.

The fact that fewer than ten studies actually have examined the empirical correlates of ethnic status and MMPI performance should indicate the direction for future MMPI-2 research. A related topic concerns the nature of those group differences that are reported in the literature. It is almost always unknown whether group mean differences reflect a trend for most of the persons in one group to differ slightly, or for a very small subsample to differ greatly. In addition, few researchers report information regarding the percentage of clin-ically elevated profiles across various cultural groups, or other infor-mation that might be more helpful to the practitioner than simple group mean differences.

Fifth, there is a profound lack of studies on the multitude of MMPI-2 supplementary scales in any cultural group. Since a num-ber of these supplementary scales are scored routinely, research is needed to examine the effect of ethnic status on performance on these scales. Until further empirical study is completed, clinicians should be cautious in their cross-cultural use of the supplementary scales.

Sixth, few researchers have addressed within-cultural-group dif-ferences on the MMPI/MMPI-2. Subgroups of many cultures can differ in religion, beliefs, values, and behaviors as much as the over-arching cultures can differ from one another. Thus, studies using broadly based cultural samples may miss true and important differ-ences, or alternatively, imply differences where none exist. Practi-tioners using the MMPI-2 in multicultural settings should be aware of these important differences and avoid generalizing results from studies of broadly based cultural differences to more narrowly defined subcultures.

Seventh, the advances of the MMPI-2 toward employing a more nationally representative normative sample should not be construed as evidence of the instrument's cultural fairness. Although current and representative normative samples are desirable, they are not sufficient to ensure that the instrument is unbiased. If no cultural group differences truly exist, the inclusion of specific cultural groups in the normative sample is irrelevant. If they do exist, then their inclusion in small numbers will in no way aid the clinician in inter-preting profiles across cultures.

Finally, and perhaps most importantly, it is imperative that clin-icians apply common sense when using the MMPI-2 cross-culturally. For instance, reading level, if in question, always should be assessed prior to standard administration. Similarly, the risk-benefit ratio asso-ciated with specific instances of cross-cultural use of the MMPI-2 should be examined carefully, given the inconclusive nature of much of the empirical literature. The adage "first do no harm" should be paramount in the minds of any practitioners interested in employing the MMPI-2 cross-culturally. In this "soft" science, clinicians routinely contend with the use of imperfect instruments. The MMPI-2 is no different in this respect, and should be treated accordingly.

Case Example

The subject of this case example, Gary Blake, was referred for psychological testing after voluntary admission to a locked psychiatric unit in Northern California. Identifying information and a number of facts regarding this individual have been altered to protect his anonymity. Interested readers are referred to standard interpretive manuals (such as Friedman, Webb, and Lewak, 1989; Graham, 1990; Greene, 1991) for references to research supporting the clinical interpretations.

Mr. Blake, a twenty-nine-year-old Black man, drove himself to the emergency room at a local teaching hospital, where he complained of "feeling down" and fleeting thoughts of suicide. When Mr. Blake stated that he could not be sure that he would refrain from harming himself in the foreseeable future, he was offered voluntary admission to an inpatient unit, which he readily accepted. Mr. Blake had a history of polysubstance abuse, which included cocaine, alcohol, marijuana, and various prescription medications, and to a lesser extent, heroin. He had participated in several substance-related rehabilitation programs, which he believed "helped for a while." The emergency room staff did not believe Mr. Blake to be under the influence of any substance at the time of the initial contact. Psychological evaluation was conducted in order to aid in diagnosis and dispositional planning. At the time of testing, approximately twenty-four hours after admission, Mr. Blake was friendly and socially engaging. He was casually but neatly dressed, and fully cooperative in completing the MMPI-2.

Mr. Blake's scores on Scales *L, F,* and *K* meet the criteria for one of the four commonly encountered validity scale configurations (see Figure 4.1). Specifically, Scales *L* and *K* are elevated above *T* scores of at least 60, and *F* is near to, or below, a *T* score of 50.

The authors have heard many novice clinicians discount the elevations on Scale *L* in Black clients because "Blacks tend to produce higher scores on Scale *L* than Whites." However, many studies demonstrating these differences were conducted using "normal" samples. In studies examining subjects with substance abuse (a primary diagnosis for this individual) or those in psychiatric settings (as in this case), Black-White differences on Scale *L* have been strikingly absent. In addition, given the known impact of SES on Scale *L,* consideration of the client's educational and family background is imperative. In this instance, the client completed four years of college in a prestigious university, and both of his parents were prominent professionals.

Thus, standard interpretation of his validity scales suggest that he was attempting to avoid or deny unacceptable impulses, difficulties,

Figure 4.1. MMPI-2 Profile for Mr. Blake.

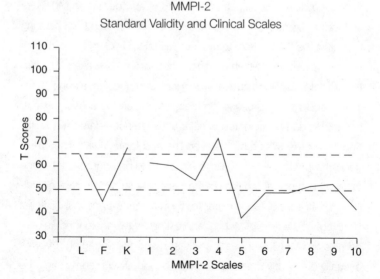

MMPI-2
Standard Validity and Clinical Scales

and feelings, and present himself as well as possible. Deliberate defensiveness and denial of psychopathology often is seen in individuals obtaining this type of configuration. Although the F-K Index score is not the optimal measure for examining the underreporting of psychopathology, Mr. Blake's score of −21 is noteworthy.

In spite of the defensiveness evident from the validity scales, Mr. Blake obtained a Spike 4 clinical codetype. All of Mr. Blake's supplementary scale scores were subclinical in elevation, as were all of his MMPI-2 Content scale scores. Only one of the Harris-Lingoes subscales for Scale 4 reached a clinical elevation (Family Discord, T = 65). However, the small number of items contained on these subscales decreases their reliability, and thus they should be interpreted with caution. The largest subsets of critical items endorsed by Mr. Blake were substance-related in content or suggestive of behavioral problems. Mr. Blake did not endorse any of the suicide-related items that were introduced in the MMPI-2.

As with elevations on Scale L, the literature does not support the supposition that Blacks obtain higher scores than Whites on Scale 4 in substance abuse or psychiatric settings. Standard codetype interpretation for this profile suggests a high probability of impulsive behavior, low frustration tolerance, lack of insight, rebelliousness, and problems with substance abuse, the latter of which clearly was correct in Mr. Blake's case. Individuals with this codetype often form superficial relationships rather quickly, but have difficulty in initiating or maintaining closer interpersonal ties. Interestingly, Mr. Blake, through his socially engaging nature, had become friendly with a number of other patients as well as several staff members, but requested that no members of his family be contacted regarding his hospitalization.

Typically, individuals with Spike 4 codetypes have little insight into their life problems, often externalizing blame and failing to take responsibility for their own actions. Behavior change through treatment is improbable, especially in instances of subclinical Scale 2 elevations, as is seen in Mr. Blake's profile.

What was unusual in Mr. Blake's case is that both his validity scale configuration and his Spike 4 codetype are associated with the tendency to avoid treatment. Typically, clients who obtain Spike 4 profiles are poor candidates for psychotherapy. When they are seen in clinical settings, often resulting from mandatory referral by social agencies, they are likely to discontinue therapy when it is no longer required. However, Mr. Blake was self-referred, appeared comfortable seeking help, and was amenable to admission on an inpatient unit. This apparent contradiction was explained two days after testing, when Mr. Blake requested discharge from the unit. He told his therapist that for the past several months he had collected car payments from three friends with whom he had jointly purchased a fairly expensive recreational vehicle. Instead of paying his monthly bill, Mr. Blake used the money to buy cocaine, a plan that worked until the vehicle was repossessed. Mr. Blake stated that his friends were "out of control" and threatening him with bodily harm, at which point he determined it would be best to "lay low" for a while. After driving around town for several hours, he decided to attempt admission into a hospital, where during previous stays for rehabilitation, he said he felt safe and secure. Mr. Blake said that he phoned an uncle who was sending him the money to reimburse his friends, who were apparently appeased by this news.

In this case, the patient's MMPI-2 profile was consistent with his psychiatric history, current symptomatology, and, unfortunately, therapeutic outcome. Had standard interpretive procedures been abandoned or discounted due to his racial or cultural group status, it is unlikely the testing would have been efficacious. Clearly, important moderator variables, such as educational level, intelligence, and family background were essential to the decision-making process in this instance.

. . . .

Summary

After reviewing the research regarding the MMPI/MMPI-2 performance of various ethnic groups, a number of comments seem warranted. First, the failure to find any consistent pattern of scale differences between Whites and any other ethnic, cultural, or racial groups in any setting would suggest that the endorsement of pluralistic norms is premature. It appears that moderator variables, such as SES, education, and intelligence, as well as profile validity, are more important determinants of MMPI performance than cultural group status. Definitely, further research is needed to examine the role of identified cultural factors on MMPI performance when appropriate controls are instituted for the multitude of factors that can affect the results.

As more attention is directed toward the multicultural use of the MMPI-2, sustained efforts should be made toward integrating empirical study with clinical practice. Demonstration of group mean differences, however interesting, is of limited value in comparison to the determination of differential validity. Should future research demonstrate reliable differences in the validity of the MMPI-2 across cultural groups, then the same methods used to examine those differences must be incorporated into clinical practice. For instance, if Black-White differences are found as a function of cultural group identification, then an identification measure must be administered clinically to interpret MMPI-2 profiles accurately. In the absence of this clinical practice, the product of decades of research would be irrelevant to the actual cross-cultural usage of the instrument.

References

Adler, T. (1990, April). Does the 'new' MMPI beat the 'classic'? *APA Monitor*, 18–19.

Anderson, T. R., Thompson, J. P., & Boeringa, J. A. (1993). *MMPI-2 and Mississippi scale profiles of Hispanic veterans with post-traumatic stress disorder.* Paper presented at the annual meeting of the American Psychological Association, Toronto.

Barefoot, J. C., Peterson, B. L., Dahlstrom, W. G., Siegler, I. C., Anderson, N. B., & Williams, R. B., Jr. (1991). Hostility patterns and health implications: Correlates of Cook-Medley Hostility Scales Scores in a national survey. *Health Psychology, 10*, 18–24.

Beck, N. C., McRae, C., Hendrichs, T. F., Sneider, L., Horowitz, B., Rennier, G., Thomas, S., & Hedlund, J. (1989). Replicated item level factor structure of the MMPI: Racial and sexual differences. *Journal of Clinical Psychology, 45*, 553–560.

Bernstein, I. H., Teng, G., Grannemann, B. D., and Garbin, C. P. (1987). Invariance in the MMPI's component structure. *Journal of Personality Assessment, 51*, 522–531.

Butcher, J. N. (1985). Current developments in MMPI use: An international perspective. In C. D. Spielberger & J. N. Butcher (Eds.), *Advances in personality assessment* (Vol. 4, pp. 83–94). Hillsdale, NJ: Erlbaum.

Butcher, J. N., & Clark, L. A. (1979). Recent trends in cross-cultural MMPI research and application. In J. N. Butcher (Ed.), *New developments in the use of the MMPI* (pp. 69–111). Minneapolis: University of Minnesota Press.

Butcher, J. N., Dahlstrom, W. G., Graham, J. R., Tellegen, A. M., & Kaemmer, B. (1989). *Minnesota Multiphasic Personality Inventory-2 (MMPI-2): Manual for administration and scoring.* Minneapolis: University of Minnesota Press.

Butcher, J. N., & Pancheri, P. (1976). *A handbook of cross-national MMPI research.* Minneapolis: University of Minnesota Press.

Caldwell, A. B. (1990, August). *MMPI, MMPI-2, and the measurement of the human condition.* Paper presented at the annual meeting of the American Psychological Association, Boston.

Cannon, D. S., Bell, W. E., Fowler, D. R., Penk, W. E., & Finkelstein, A. S. (1990). MMPI differences between alcoholics and drug abusers: Effect of age and race. *Psychological Assessment: A Journal of Consulting and Clinical Psychology, 2*, 51–55.

Clark, S. A., Velasquez, R. J., & Callahan, W. J. (1992). MMPI–ER two point codes of industrially injured Hispanic workers by DSM-III-R diagnosis. *Psychological Reports, 71*, 107–112.

Cogburn, M., Zalewski, C., Farrell, S., & Mendoza, M. (1993, April). *Comparison of Asian American and White college students on the MMPI-2.* Paper presented at the annual convention of the Western Psychological Association, Phoenix.

Colligan, R. C., Osborne, D., Swenson, W. M., & Offord, K. P. (1983). *The MMPI: A contemporary normative study.* New York: Praeger.

Costello, R. M. (1973). Item level racial differences on the MMPI. *Journal of Social Psychology, 91*, 161–162.

Costello, R. M. (1977). Construction and cross-validation of an MMPI Black-White scale. *Journal of Personality Assessment, 41*, 514–519.

Costello, R. M., Tiffany, D. W., & Gier, R. H. (1972). Methodological issues and racial (Black-White) comparisons on the MMPI. *Journal of Consulting and Clinical Psychology, 38*, 161–168.

Cowan, M. A., Watkins, B. A., & Davis, W. E. (1975). Level of education, diagnosis and race-related differences in MMPI performance. *Journal of Clinical Psychology, 31*, 442–444.

Cuellar, I., Harris, L. C., & Jasso, R. (1980). An acculturation scale for Mexican-American normal and clinical populations. *Hispanic Journal of Behavioral Science, 2*, 199–217.

Dahlstrom, W. G., Lachar, D., & Dahlstrom, L. E. (1986). *MMPI patterns of American minorities*. Minneapolis: University of Minnesota Press.

Dahlstrom, W. G., Welsh, G. S., & Dahlstrom, L. E. (1972). *An MMPI handbook: Vol. I. Clinical interpretation* (Rev. ed.). Minneapolis: University of Minnesota Press.

Dahlstrom, W. G., Welsh, G. S., & Dahlstrom, L. E. (1975). *An MMPI handbook: Vol. II. Research applications* (Rev. ed.). Minneapolis: University of Minnesota Press.

Dana, R. H. (1993). *Multicultural assessment perspectives for professional psychology*. Needham Heights, MA: Allyn & Bacon.

Dana, R. H., & Whatley, P. R. (1991). When does a difference make a difference? MMPI scores and African-Americans. *Journal of Clinical Psychology, 47*, 400–406.

Davis, W. E. (1975). Race and the differential "power" of the MMPI. *Journal of Personality Assessment, 39*, 138–140.

Dolan, M. P., Roberts, W. R., Penk, W. E., Robinowitz, R., & Atkins, H. G. (1983). Personality differences among Black, White, and Hispanic-American male heroin addicts on MMPI content scales. *Journal of Clinical Psychology, 39*, 807–813.

DuAlba, L., & Scott, R. L. (1993). Somatization and malingering for workers' compensation applicants: A cross-cultural MMPI study. *Journal of Clinical Psychology, 49*, 913–917.

Elion, V. H., & Megargee, E. I. (1975). Validity of the MMPI Pd scale among Black males. *Journal of Consulting and Clinical Psychology, 43*, 166–172.

Friedman, A. F., Webb, J. T., & Lewak, R. (1989). *Psychological assessment with the MMPI*. Hillsdale, NJ: Erlbaum.

Fukunishi, I., Nakagawa, T., Nakamura, H., Ogawa, J., & Nakagawa, T. (1993). A comparison of Type A behavior pattern, hostility, and typus melancholicus in Japanese and American students: Effects of defensiveness. *International Journal of Social Psychiatry, 39*, 58–63.

Genthner, R. W., & Graham, J. R. (1976). Effects of short-term public psychiatric hospitalization for both Black and White patients. *Journal of Consulting and Clinical Psychology, 44,* 118–124.

Gottesman, I. I., & Prescott, C. (1989). Abuses of the MacAndrew MMPI alcoholism scale: A critical review. *Clinical Psychology Review, 9,* 223–242.

Graham, J. R. (1987). *The MMPI: A practical guide* (2nd ed.). New York: Oxford.

Graham, J. R. (1990). *MMPI-2: Assessing personality and psychopathology.* New York: Oxford.

Greene, R. L. (1980). *The MMPI: An interpretive manual.* Philadelphia: Grune & Stratton.

Greene, R. L. (1987). Ethnicity and MMPI performance: A review. *Journal of Consulting and Clinical Psychology, 55,* 497–512.

Greene, R. L. (1988). *The MMPI: Use with specific populations.* Philadelphia: Grune & Stratton.

Greene, R. L. (1991). *The MMPI-2/MMPI: An interpretive manual.* Needham Heights, MA: Allyn & Bacon.

Gynther, M. D. (1972). White norms and Black MMPIs: A prescription for discrimination? *Psychological Bulletin, 78*(5), 386–402.

Gynther, M. D. (1979). Ethnicity and personality: An update. In J. N. Butcher (Ed.), *New developments in the use of the MMPI* (pp. 113–140). Minneapolis: University of Minnesota Press.

Gynther, M. D. (1989). MMPI comparisons of Blacks and Whites: A review and commentary. *Journal of Clinical Psychology, 45,* 878–883.

Gynther, M. D., Altman, H., & Warbin, R. (1973). Interpretation of uninterpretable MMPI profiles. *Journal of Consulting and Clinical Psychology, 40,* 78–83.

Gynther, M. D., & Green, S. B. (1980). Accuracy may make a difference, but does a difference make for accuracy?: A response to Pritchard and Rosenblatt. *Journal of Consulting and Clinical Psychology, 48,* 268–272.

Gynther, M. D., Lachar, D., & Dahlstrom, W. G. (1978). Are special norms for minorities needed? Development of an MMPI F scale for Blacks. *Journal of Consulting and Clinical Psychology, 46,* 1403–1408.

Gynther, M. D., & Witt, P. H. (1976). Windstorms and important persons: Personality characteristics of Black educators. *Journal of Clinical Psychology, 32,* 613–616.

Harrison, R. H., & Kass, E. H. (1967). Differences between Negro and White pregnant women on the MMPI. *Journal of Consulting Psychology, 31,* 454–463.

Harrison, R. H., & Kass, E. H. (1968). MMPI correlates of Negro acculturation in a northern city. *Journal of Personality and Social Psychology, 10,* 262–270.

Hathaway, S. R., & McKinley, J. C. (1967). *MMPI manual* (Rev. ed.). New York: Psychological Corporation.

Hutton, H. E., Miner, M. H., Blades, J. R., & Langfeldt, V. C. (1992). Ethnic differences on the MMPI Overcontrolled-Hostility scale. *Journal of Personality Assessment, 58,* 260–268.

Johnson, M. E., & Brems, C. (1990). Psychiatric inpatient MMPI profiles: An exploration for potential racial bias. *Journal of Counseling Psychology, 37,* 213–215.

Jones, E. E. (1978). Black-White personality differences: Another look. *Journal of Personality Assessment, 42,* 244–252.

Knatz, H. F., Inwald, R. E., Brockwell, A. L., & Tran, L. N. (1992). IPI and MMPI predictions of counterproductive job behaviors by racial group. *Journal of Business and Psychology, 7,* 189–201.

Lawson, H. H., Kahn, M. W., & Heiman, E. M. (1982). Psychopathology, treatment outcome, and attitude toward mental illness in Mexican-American and European patients. *International Journal of Social Psychology, 28,* 20–26.

Lubin, B., Larsen, R. M., Matarazzo, J. D., & Seever, M. (1985). Psychological test usage patterns in five professional settings. *American Psychologist, 40,* 857–861.

MacAndrew, C. (1965). The differentiation of male alcoholic outpatients from nonalcoholic psychiatric outpatients by means of the MMPI. *Quarterly Journal of Studies on Alcohol, 26,* 238–246.

McCreary, C., & Padilla, E. (1977). MMPI differences among Black, Mexican-American, and White male offenders. *Journal of Clinical Psychology, 33,* 171–177.

Marsella, A. J., Sanborn, K. O., Kameoka, V., Shizuru, L., & Brennan, J. (1975). Cross-validation of self-report measures of depression among normal populations of Japanese, Chinese, and White ancestry. *Journal of Clinical Psychology, 31,* 281–287.

Megargee, E. I., Cook, P. E., & Mendelsohn, G. A. (1967). Development and validation of an MMPI scale of assaultiveness in overcontrolled individuals. *Journal of Abnormal Psychology, 72,* 519–528.

Miller, C., Knapp, S. C., & Daniels, C. W. (1968). MMPI study of Negro mental hygiene clinic patients. *Journal of Abnormal Psychology, 73,* 168–173.

Montgomery, G. T., Arnold, B., & Orozco, S. (1990). MMPI supplemental scale performance of Mexican Americans and level of acculturation. *Journal of Personality Assessment, 54,* 328–342.

Montgomery, G. T., & Orozco, S. (1985). Mexican Americans' performance on the MMPI as a function of level of acculturation. *Journal of Clinical Psychology, 41,* 203–212.

National Center for Education Statistics. (1991). *Digest of Education Statistics, 1991*. Washington, DC: U.S. Government Printing Office.

Nichols, D. (1991, March). Wish list for an early course correction. In D. S. Nichols (Chair), *The Minnesota earthquake: Looking forward from the MMPI-2 temblor*. Plenary Session presented at the Midwinter Meeting of the Society For Personality Assessment, New Orleans.

Page, R. D., & Bozlee, S. (1982). A cross-cultural MMPI comparison of alcoholics. *Psychological Reports, 50*, 639–646.

Penk, W. E., Roberts, W. R., Robinowitz, R., Dolan, M. P., Atkins, H. G., & Woodward, W. A. (1982). MMPI differences of Black and White polydrug abusers seeking treatment. *Journal of Consulting and Clinical Psychology, 50*, 463–465.

Penk, W. E., Robinowitz, R., Black, J., Dolan, M., Bell, W., Dorsett, D., Ames, M., & Noriega, L. (1989). Ethnicity: Post-traumatic stress disorder (PTSD) differences among Black, White, and Hispanic veterans who differ in degrees of exposure to combat in Vietnam. *Journal of Clinical Psychology, 45*, 729–735.

Penk, W. E., Robinowitz, R., Roberts, W. R., Dolan, M. P., & Atkins, H. G. (1981). MMPI differences of male Hispanic-American, Black, and White heroin addicts. *Journal of Consulting and Clinical Psychology, 49*, 488–490.

Penk, W. E., Woodward, W. A., Robinowitz, R., & Hess, J. L. (1978). Differences in MMPI scores of Black and White compulsive heroin users. *Journal of Abnormal Psychology, 87*, 505–513.

Pritchard, D. A., & Rosenblatt, A. (1980a). Racial bias in the MMPI: A methodological review. *Journal of Consulting and Clinical Psychology, 48*, 263–267.

Pritchard, D. A., & Rosenblatt, A. (1980b). Reply to Gynther and Green. *Journal of Consulting and Clinical Psychology, 48*, 273–274.

Robyak, J. E., & Byers, P. H. (1990). Effects of race and severity of alcoholism on MMPI's of male alcoholics. *Journal of Social Behavior and Personality, 5*, 409–416.

Rosenblatt, A. I., & Pritchard, D. A. (1978). Moderators of racial differences on the MMPI. *Journal of Consulting and Clinical Psychology, 46*, 1572–1573.

Shore, R. E. (1976). A statistical note on "Differential misdiagnosis of Blacks and Whites by the MMPI." *Journal of Personality Assessment, 40*, 21–23.

Snyder, D. K., Kline, R. B., & Podany, E. C. (1985). Comparison of external correlates of MMPI substance abuse scales across sex and race. *Journal of Consulting and Clinical Psychology, 53*, 520–525.

Stevens, M. J., Kwan, K., & Graybill, D. (1993). Comparison of MMPI-2 scores of foreign Chinese and Caucasian-American students. *Journal of Clinical Psychology, 49,* 23–27.

Strauss, M. E., Gynther, M. D., & Wallhermfechtel, J. (1974). Differential misdiagnosis of Blacks and Whites by the MMPI. *Journal of Personality Assessment, 38,* 55–60.

Sue, S., & Sue, D. W. (1974). MMPI comparisons between Asian-American and non-Asian students utilizing a student health psychiatric clinic. *Journal of Counseling Psychology, 21,* 423–427.

Suinn, R. M., Rickard-Figueroa, K., Lew, S., & Vigil, P. (1987). The Suinn-Lew Asian self-identity acculturation scale: An initial report. *Educational and Psychological Measurement, 47,* 401–407.

Sutker, P. B., Archer, R. P., & Allain, A. N. (1978). Drug abuse patterns, personality characteristics, and relationships with sex, race, and sensation seeking. *Journal of Consulting and Clinical Psychology, 46,* 1374–1378.

Sutker, P. B., Archer, R. P., & Allain, A. N. (1980). Psychopathology of drug abusers: Sex and ethnic considerations. *The International Journal of the Addictions, 15,* 605–613.

Tsushima, W. T., & Onorato, V. A. (1982). Comparison of MMPI scores of White and Japanese-American medical patients. *Journal of Consulting and Clinical Psychology, 50,* 150–151.

Uecker, A. E., Boutilier, L. R., & Richardson, E. H. (1980). "Indianism" and MMPI scores of men alcoholics. *Journal of Studies on Alcohol, 41,* 357–362.

Velasquez, R. J. (1984). *An atlas of MMPI group profiles on Mexican-Americans.* Los Angeles: Spanish Speaking Mental Health Research Center.

Velasquez, R. J. (1992). Hispanic-American MMPI research (1949–1992): A comprehensive bibliography. *Psychological Reports, 70,* 743–754.

Velasquez, R. J., & Callahan, W. J. (1990a). MMPI comparisons of Hispanic- and White-American veterans seeking treatment for alcoholism. *Psychological Reports, 67,* 95–98.

Velasquez, R. J., & Callahan, W. J. (1990b). MMPIs of Hispanic, Black, and White DSM-III schizophrenics. *Psychological Reports, 66,* 819–822.

Velasquez, R. J., Callahan, W. J., & Carrillo, R. (1989). MMPI profiles of Hispanic-American inpatient and outpatient sex offenders. *Psychological Reports, 65,* 1055–1058.

Velasquez, R. J., Callahan, W. J., & Carrillo, R. (1991). MMPI differences among Mexican-American male and female psychiatric inpatients. *Psychological Reports, 68,* 123–127.

Velasquez, R. J., Callahan, W. J., & Young, R. (1993). Hispanic-White MMPI comparisons: Does psychiatric diagnosis make a difference? *Journal of Clinical Psychology, 49,* 528–534.

Velasquez, R. J., & Gimenez, L. (1987). MMPI differences among three diagnostic groups of Mexican-American state hospital patients. *Psychological Reports, 60,* 1071–1074.

Venn, J. (1988). MMPI profiles of Native-, Mexican-, and Caucasian-American male alcoholics. *Psychological Reports, 62,* 427–432.

Walters, G. D., Greene, R. L., Jeffrey, T. B., Kruzich, D. J., & Haskin, J. J. (1983). Racial variations on the MacAndrew Alcoholism scale of the MMPI. *Journal of Consulting and Clinical Psychology, 51,* 947–948.

Weisman, C. P., Anglin, M. D., & Fisher, D. G. (1989). The MMPI profiles of narcotics addicts. II. Ethnic and criminal history effects. *The International Journal of the Addictions, 24,* 881–896.

Whitworth, R. H. (1988). Anglo- and Mexican-American performance on the MMPI administered in Spanish or English. *Journal of Clinical Psychology, 44,* 891–897.

Whitworth, R. H., & McBlaine, D. D. (1993). Comparison of the MMPI and MMPI–2 administered to Anglo- and Hispanic-American university students. *Journal of Personality Assessment, 61,* 19–27.

Wiggins, J. S. (1966). Substantive dimensions of self-report in the MMPI item pool. *Psychological Monographs, 80* (22, Whole No. 630).

Witt, P. H., & Gynther, M. D. (1975). Another explanation for Black-White MMPI differences. *Journal of Clinical Psychology, 31,* 69–70.

5

Projective Methods for Multicultural Personality Assessment

Rorschach, TEMAS, and the Early Memories Procedure

Barry A. Ritzler

Multicultural circumstances create problems for psychological assessment, particularly when the focus is on personality assessment. Interpretation of personality style and behavior patterns may lose their validity when the following conditions exist:

1. The subject of the assessment is not acculturated to the culture of the psychologist administering the test or the psychologist interpreting the results.

2. The assessment methods are administered in a language other than the native language of the subject.

3. The assessment methods are not sensitive to the cultural background of the unacculturated subject.

4. The psychologist interpreting the assessment results does not understand the cultural background of the subject.

5. The referral question is not appropriate for the native culture of the unacculturated subject.

6. In reporting results, the psychologist does not explain the cultural effects in a way that can be understood by referring

professionals with cultural backgrounds different from that of the subject.

The projective methods evaluated in this chapter have been selected because they are particularly well suited for addressing the problems of multicultural assessment. First, in the case of the Rorschach (Exner, 1993), the test stimuli (inkblots) are sufficiently ambiguous to eliminate cultural bias. It may be that members of some cultures have more familiarity with the concept of using inkblots for personality assessment, but it is unlikely that any culture provides more than occasional experience with actual Rorschach Method. Taking a Rorschach is a novel experience for nearly everyone, regardless of culture.

Second, an apperception method such as the TEMAS (Costantino, Malgady, and Rogler, 1988) provides direct control for cultural factors by presenting picture stimuli that are culturally relevant.

Finally, the Early Memories Procedure (Bruhn, 1989) uses material that is available to individuals in all cultures and does not rely on test stimuli that might have cultural bias.

Before the projective methods are evaluated for the adequacy with which they address the multicultural assessment problems outlined above, a brief description will be given of each method followed by a more elaborate consideration of the various threats to test validity.

Methods

The three projective assessment methods chosen for this chapter have been selected because they are the only projective methods that have established reliability and validity for multicultural assessment.

The question of when reliability and validity are adequately established is a debatable issue. Indeed, the debates regarding reliability and validity of projective techniques have been going on for decades and often become quite heated and political (Mischel, 1976; Weiner, 1989, 1991). Consequently, the choice of assessment methods for this discussion, though based on considerable research evidence of reliability and validity, is somewhat arbitrary because all projective methods are less than perfectly reliable and incontestably valid. Nevertheless, the three methods discussed here emerge as having defensible reliability and validity. Conspicuous by their absence are the various types of figure drawing methods (such as Hammer, 1958) and the Bender Gestalt Test (Bender, 1938)— methods used by far too many psychologists considering their lack of reliability and validity as methods of personality assessment (Motta, Little, and Tobin, 1993; Margolis, Williger, Greenlief, Dunn, and Gfeller, 1989).

Of the methods considered acceptable for this discussion, the Rorschach has had fairly extensive cross-cultural and multicultural application with at least some recent research relevant to multicultural reliability and validity (Meernhout and Mukendi, 1980; Krall, 1983; Takeuchi and Scott, 1986; DeVos and Boyer, 1989; Hernandez-Guzman, Rey-Clericus, San Martin-Petersen, and Vinet-Reichhardt, 1989; Howes and DeBlassie, 1989; Spigelman, Spigelman, and Englesson, 1991). The thematic apperception methods only recently have had promising multicultural application with the development of the TEMAS method for multicultural assessment of children from urban ethnic groups, specifically Hispanic and African American (Costantino and Malgady, 1983). The Early Memories Procedure is a relatively unknown method with, nevertheless, promising reliability and validity credentials (Bruhn, 1985; Bruhn and Bellow, 1984, 1987; Bruhn and Schiffman, 1982; Tobey and Bruhn, 1992); the procedure, however, has had little multicultural application.

Rorschach

The Rorschach Method presents ten standard inkblots to the subject with the simple instruction, What might this be? (This describes the standard administration procedure of the Comprehensive System; see Exner, 1993.) After responses to the ten blots have been obtained and transcribed verbatim, the examiner takes the subject through the ten blots again in order to conduct a non-leading inquiry to obtain adequate information to code each response according to an elaborate scoring system. Several standard scoring systems have existed for fifty years or more, most notably Rorschach's original system (1921) and comparable systems by Klopfer (Klopfer and Kelley, 1942), Beck (1944), Rapaport (Rapaport, Gill, and Schafer, 1946), Piotrowski (1957), and Hertz (1970). In the early 1970s, a scoring system was developed by Exner (1974), who systematically surveyed the previously mentioned systems and selected scoring variables that passed stringent requirements for reliability and validity. The result was the Comprehensive System, which has become the most frequently used scoring method for the Rorschach. The Beck and Klopfer systems continue to be used by substantial minorities of psychologists, with the Rapaport system having a smaller but loyal following. The Piotrowski and Hertz systems are rarely, if ever, used. Many of the variables from the original Rorschach system were incorporated in the Comprehensive System.

Proper application of the Rorschach Method requires a standard administration followed by a complete scoring of all responses and subsequent interpretation based on the established validity of the variables in the scoring system. Direct content analysis is an important part of the interpretation technique but is not acceptably valid without integration with interpretations derived from the summary scores. Substantial norms exist to delineate the range of scores typical of individuals without serious psychological problems. Using these norms, certain psychological problems and deficiencies can be detected, but the primary use of the Rorschach Method is to describe the unique personality style of the subject. This is accomplished by describing how the subject's performance differs from the normative pattern of scores. The many variables in the scoring systems (approximately 170 in the Comprehensive System) enable the psychologist to obtain information about many components of personality functioning such as cognition, emotional expression, behavior control, self-image, and the perception of interpersonal relations. Content analysis combined with interpretation of scores also enables the psychologist to describe significant psychodynamic issues.

TEMAS

Thematic apperception methods typically present the subject with a picture (usually a photograph or a drawing) depicting scenes in which people appear to be involved in some kind of psychological experience. The subject is instructed to tell a story that includes what is happening in the picture, what led up to the scene, what the people are thinking and feeling, and how the story ends. The oldest and most frequently used apperception method is the Thematic Apperception Test (Murray, 1943), which has no inquiry period and no commonly used scoring system. The TEMAS (Costantino, Malgady, and Rogler, 1988; an acronym for *Tell Me A Story* but also the Spanish word for "theme"), however, includes a highly structured inquiry period and an elaborate scoring system that takes into account the thematic "pull" of each stimulus picture. The resulting scoring system enables the psychologist to interpret such personality components as cognition, interpersonal relations, achievement motivation, delay of gratification, self-concept, sexual identity, moral judgment, reality testing, and affect. The pictures, in contrast to the TAT pictures, are brightly colored, often involving a greater number of people, and covering a more dramatic range of personal experience and fantasy themes. The TEMAS method is normed for children and adolescents only and uses alternate forms for White and minority (Hispanic and African American) children (Costantino, Malgady, Rogler, Casullo, and Castillo, 1988).

Early Memories Procedure

The Early Memories Procedure (EMP) (Bruhn, 1989) asks the subject for fifteen to twenty early memories starting with the five earliest and continuing until memories have been reconstructed involving critical topics such as relationships with parents and siblings, school, embarrassment, and other important personal issues. Subjects are asked to rate their memories for clarity and positive versus negative impact.

Interpretation of the EMP usually involves a joint consideration of the memories by the psychologist and the subject. The psychologist presents a generalized psychological precis of the memory in the form of implications for current functioning, and the subject is asked to appraise the validity of these low-inference interpretations. The EMP allows for interpretation of general world view, attitudes toward relationships, sense of self, emotional expressivity, coping strategies, insight, and cognitive complexity.

Elaboration of Risk Factors

The following sections will elaborate on several risk factors for multicultural projective assessment. Discussion will include specific ways in which these risks interfere with the validity of personality assessment and some suggestions for reducing or eliminating these effects.

Acculturation

Individuals who move across cultures show different levels of adaptation. Some accommodate completely to the new culture. Their behavior style and even their attitudes become those of the new culture, and the ways and sensibilities of the old culture are left behind. Such wholesale acculturation is rare, however. Many individuals continue to show some personality characteristics more consistent with the old than the new culture, even though considerable acculturation is apparent. Others adapt with a blend of the old and new so that the result is a nearly equal representation of both cultures. Still others keep the ways and attitudes of the old culture while accommodating to the new culture just enough to avoid major conflicts and misunderstandings. Finally, it is not rare to find individuals who resist, avoid, or fail to form even the most surface of accommodations and continue to be identified as true adherents to the old ways (Cross, 1991).

Because acculturation covers such a wide spectrum, a psychologist must be able to determine the extent of acculturation in the individual client. Several reasonably adequate methods for assessing acculturation exist depending on the subject's culture of origin (such as Cuellar, Harris, and Jasso, 1980; Franco, 1983; Marin, Sabogal, VanOss-Marin, Otero-Sabogal, and Perez-Sable, 1987; Mendoza, 1989; Olmedo, Martinez, and Martinez, 1978; Suinn, Rickard-Figueroa, Lew, and Vigil, 1987). By using such methods, the psychologist can arrive at a useful estimate of the extent to which the client is culturally different. When acculturation is minimal, much caution must be exercised in projective personality assessment or the psychologist must take the low degree of acculturation into account when administering the assessment methods and interpreting their results. Unfortunately, methods for assessing acculturation do not exist for many of the major cultures of origin of individuals who immigrate to the United States.

Language Differences

Although knowing the client's level of acculturation is essential, it usually is not enough to assure valid assessment. It is apparent that even the most acculturated clients will respond to projective methods differently in their native language than in English (Dana, 1993). Even when English is the native language, differences in dialect can result in different test performances if the dialect is different from the dialect used in the test administration. And when acculturation is minimal, the language factor looms larger even when the client speaks fluent English (Hoffman, Dana, and Bolton,

1985; Malgady, Rogler, and Costantino, 1987). The example cases presented at the end of this chapter will illustrate this point.

Because of the frequently significant language factor in multicultural projective assessment, it usually is advisable to administer the methods in the client's native language. This tactic is less important (and may lead to invalid results) when the client is highly acculturated.

Cross-Cultural Sensitivity

Knowing the level of acculturation and administering the methods in the native language will not suffice if the assessment methods are not sensitive to personality characteristics indigenous to the client's culture. Personality characteristics that develop from cultural experiences may be misidentified or missed altogether by assessment methods that have emerged from cultures much different from that of the client (Low, 1985). For instance, the normal social reticence of the Finnish culture may appear as pathological isolation on the TEMAS (an assessment method developed out of the socially intense culture of minority neighborhoods of large American urban centers) or may escape the notice of a psychologist using the EMP because the instructions usually call for socially involved memories.

A corollary to this problem arises when there are no norms for the projective method for the culture of the client being assessed. Empirically-based projective methods such as the Rorschach Comprehensive System and the TEMAS require adequate norms for effective use. Few such norms currently exist for the most promising methods of projective assessment. This lack will be further discussed in the section evaluating the three projective methods covered in this chapter.

Multicultural Awareness

Knowledge of the client's level of acculturation, choice of the correct language for administration, and appropriately sensitive assess-

ment methods will not be sufficient if the psychologist is not adequately attuned to the cultural factors in the client's test performance (a problem discussed in detail in Chapter Twenty). This risk
factor often is the most crucial in invalidating multicultural projective assessment because its remedy requires that the psychologist
be a native of the client's culture or be adequately informed about
and experienced with that culture (Ramirez, 1984). The example
of the Hispanic culture in an area such as New York City illustrates
the difficulty of finding the appropriate match. The psychologist
may be Hispanic and may speak Spanish fluently but may still come
from a culture dramatically different from that of the Hispanic
client. Such combinations as Cuban and Haitian or Mexican and
South American may result in cultural gaps that can not be com-
pensated for by proper management of the other multicultural projective assessment risk factors. Even if the psychologist comes from
the same country as the client, the cultural gap may be too great.
Take, for example, the differences between an African American
client from New York City and an African American psychologist
born and raised in rural Alabama. A psychologist can bridge such a
gap by diligently learning about the client's culture, but sufficient
knowledge probably requires rather lengthy first-hand experience—
an opportunity not easily available to most professionals (Sue and
Zane, 1987).

Inappropriate Referral Questions

A factor seldom considered in multicultural personality assessment
is whether the question asked in the referral is relevant to the culture of the client. For instance, a referral asking for the evaluation of
an American Indian's suitability for psychoanalysis would fail to
take into account the fact that the Native American culture typically does not dispose individuals to find the psychoanalytic experience meaningful (Gibbs, 1980). Consequently, an American
Indian client may show all of the Rorschach signs that suggest a
likelihood of success in psychoanalysis, but cultural incompatibility

with the therapy approach would make the recommendation of psychoanalysis a poor choice. An appropriately selected, administered, and interpreted projective method cannot address culturally inappropriate referral questions.

Culturally Inappropriate Dissemination of Results

Projective methods do not lend themselves well to computerized reporting of results. Typically, interpretive hypotheses are formed, modified, and integrated into a rather complex—but hopefully comprehensive and understandable—report. The task is difficult enough without the further complication of multicultural factors. Consequently, the assessment task can still fail when the correct methods have been chosen, the proper administrative techniques used, and the psychologist is adequately trained and sensitive in regard to multicultural issues. The failure can come at the last stage of reporting the results. Usually, the psychologist is reporting to professionals who lack sufficient understanding of the client's cultural issues. For the report to have a meaningful and useful effect, the psychologist must apprise the reader or listener of the cultural implications and how they alter the interpretations and comprehensive integration necessary to understand personality (Dana, 1994). This task of making the culturally different client understandable is formidable, but vitally essential. Fortunately, projective methods such as those covered in this chapter can facilitate effective assessment dissemination.

Evaluation of Multicultural Projective Methods

In this section, each of the three projective methods proposed as acceptable for multicultural assessment will be evaluated for their current and potential effectiveness. As this section unfolds, it will become apparent that there is a wide discrepancy between the confidence that currently is warranted in these methods as multicultural techniques and the potential they hold for doing the job much better after they have been further developed as multicultural instruments. Although some multicultural norms exist for the Rorschach

(Meernhout and Mukendi, 1980; Mattlar, 1986; Spigelman and others, 1991; Rausch-deTraubenberg, Block-Laine, Duplant, and Martin, 1993) and the TEMAS (Costantino, Malgady, and Rogler, 1986) and some validation has been done with the TEMAS as a multicultural method (Costantino and Malgady, 1983; Costantino, Malgady, and Rogler, 1986, 1988; Costantino, Malgady, Rogler, Casullo, and others, 1988; Costantino, Malgady, Rogler, and Tsui, 1988; Costantino, Malgady, and Vazquez, 1981), research in this area is in its infancy. Nevertheless, these three methods are, in the author's opinion, by far the best available.

In spite of the lack of sufficient research validation, projective methods are prime candidates for multicultural assessment because an argument can be made that the stimulus material reduces cultural biases more than any other class of assessment methods. It is well known that most extensively validated, widely used intelligence tests are hopelessly biased (Cattell, 1962). Even those designated as "culture-free" do not eliminate the effects of previous cultural experiences, both of impoverishment and enrichment. Language factors greatly affect performance, and some of the tasks used to measure intelligence have little or no relevance for cultures very different from the Anglo-European.

Paper-and-pencil inventories such as the MMPI and other interview-related self-report assessment methods also are closely tied with cultural bias (Charles, 1988; Hoffman, Dana, and Bolton, 1985; Keefe, Sue, Enomoto, Durvasula, and Chao, 1994). The language problems are inherent, and the cultural specificity of the item wording is nearly inescapable. Also, unacculturated individuals from a culture different from that of the psychologist may be highly reluctant to give an open, nondefensive self-report. Low acculturation is closely associated with guarded self-presentation and suspicion regarding the intention of those culturally different others (such as psychologists) who are trying to gain information by asking directly (Helms, 1990).

Projective methods, on the other hand, keep language factors to a minimum by using very simple instructions and further minimize cultural bias by keeping these questions and instructions purposely ambiguous: What might this be? Tell me a story, and What do you remember about . . . ? are easily understood without losing their ambiguity. Cultural bias has much less of a chance of influencing performance when the specific nature of the required performance is unclear to the client.

Rorschach

The Rorschach has the most sets of multicultural norms: French (Rausch-deTraubenberg and others, 1993), Swedish (Spigelman and others, 1991), Finnish (Mattlar, 1986), and Zairian (Meernhout and Mukendi, 1980), to name a few. Comparison of these norms indicates that performance of nonpatient adults does not vary widely between countries. When educational sophistication is controlled, even the general content of responses varies little across cultures. For the Rorschach, there is much more difference between depressed and nondepressed samples than there is between samples of nonpatients from countries that have very different cultures (Exner, 1993). Unfortunately, very little research has been done on the Rorschach to test its validity as a method sensitive to multicultural issues. The examples in the last section of this chapter illustrate the preliminary findings of an ongoing study of the multicultural sensitivity of the Rorschach Comprehensive System. Much more needs to be done, however, before the Rorschach can claim indisputable validity for multicultural assessment. Its standardized administration methods, its empirically based quantification, and its sensitivity to subtle personality processes make it a prime candidate as a detector of cultural influence on personality functioning.

TEMAS

The TEMAS (Costantino, Malgady, and Rogler, 1988) is the purest multicultural method of the three covered in this chapter. With matching sets of minority and Caucasian cards, it provides a direct assessment of cultural influence on test performance. Furthermore, even though its specific pictures make it the least ambiguous of the three, the large number of pictures and the scoring system, which takes into account the stimulus "pull" of the drawings, allows the psychologist to directly assess cultural issues and to separate them from personality issues that are not based on cultural influence.

Only three current problems limit the use of the TEMAS as a multicultural assessment method. The first is that the norms have been established and the picture scenes are based on minority group experience in large urban centers (specifically, New York City). The assessment of multicultural influences is likely to be much less valid for African American and Hispanic groups in small cities and rural areas. This problem could be simply remedied by establishing norms for these areas and by modifying the pictures to appear less urban-ized. (Some of the pictures do, indeed, show country scenes, but a large majority are clearly depicting life in a big city.)

A second problem for the TEMAS is that its validation has not had time to reach the proportions of the Rorschach empirical base. Judging from the industry of the original developers and the popu-larity already gained by the method, this problem of limited vali-dation should continue to fade. Also, the TEMAS success is encouraging to psychologists who work with cultural groups other than African Americans and Hispanics. There is good reason to believe that the construction of stimulus pictures appropriate for any culture of interest could result in clinical validity by adapting the TEMAS scoring and interpretation system.

The final current problem with the TEMAS is that it has only been used with children and adolescents. Again, however, adapta-tion for use with adults is a very feasible possibility and would appear only to require a concentrated research and development effort.

Early Memories Procedure

The Early Memories Procedure (Bruhn, 1989), an elaborate adap-tation of an assessment method with a long history (for example, see Charry, 1959; Eisenstein and Ryerson, 1951; Friedman, 1952; Mosak, 1958), has no quantified norms of any sort and has not been used as a multicultural instrument. Nevertheless, the universal nature of early memories and the simple, low-inference interpretation method makes it a promising candidate for multicultural assessment. About as much validation exists as there is for the TEMAS, but none of it has a multicultural emphasis. Because it uses no stimulus material, it may have the greatest potential as a culture-free method. It seems reasonable to assume that nearly every human culture has particular interest in memories. Having a memory is such an essentially human process that it is difficult to imagine that a culture exists in which the members are not intimately familiar with memories. Furthermore, the interpretation of memories—or at least using them to influence behavior—is a procedure inherent in human personality functioning.

Effects of Acculturation on Language Risk Factor

Acculturation, or the development of competence in a new culture, is an important moderating variable in multicultural assessment. It is reasonable to assume that the greater the acculturation, the less the effect of the risk factors outlined in this chapter. In other words, if an individual has become very well integrated into a new culture, testing may not have to be administered in the native language, and the interpreting psychologist may not need to be sensitive to cultural issues.

As a test of this assumption, a study is being conducted at Long Island University to compare the Rorschachs of highly acculturated individuals and minimally acculturated individuals (Rosenberg and Ritzler, in preparation). The Rorschach is administered to each subject in English and in the native language. The general hypothesis is that nonacculturated individuals will show a greater discrepancy between the English and native language Rorschachs and that the native language Rorschach will show a higher level of adjustment.

It also is anticipated that highly acculturated individuals will show better adjustment in their English Rorschachs.

The examples in this chapter are taken from this study, which continues in progress. The first subject is a forty-eight-year-old housewife from an affluent metropolitan suburb. She was born in Israel and lived there until she was fourteen years old, when she came with her family to the United States. Her native language is Hebrew, which she continues to speak fluently. Although she is ethnically Jewish in much of her social activities and observance of holidays, she is not particularly religious. Her hobby is Israeli dancing, which she practices three or four nights a week.

The second subject is a thirty-two-year-old psychiatric resident at a metropolitan medical center. He lives in an apartment in the city. Although he speaks English fluently, he has lived in Spain all his life. He has been in the United States for only ten months. He attended medical school in Spain, and his native language is Spanish.

Neither subject has a history of psychiatric symptoms or treatment. At the time of testing, the first subject's husband was embroiled in legal proceedings that threatened his self-owned business. Shortly after the testing, the court case was decided in his favor. No other situational stresses were apparent for either subject.

The Rorschach was administered twice to each subject. The first time it was administered in English and the second time in the subject's native language. Both administrations were conducted by a psychologist who spoke the native language and was from a cultural background similar to that of the subject. The responses for each administration were scored according to the Rorschach Comprehensive System, and standard scores were calculated. Table 5.1 contains a summary of the significant findings.

Inspection of Table 5.1 reveals contrasting findings for the two subjects. The acculturated Israeli woman clearly shows a better adjustment on her English Rorschach. Her English Rorschach shows more personality resources available, less stress, less emotional

Table 5.1. Summary of Significant Rorschach Differences in Acculturated and Nonacculturated Example.

Variable	Definition	Acculturated S		Nonacculturated S	
		Eng.	Nat. Lang.	Eng.	Nat. Lang.
EA	Available resources	6.5	6.0	5.0	7.5
EA – es	Stress tolerance	2.5	0.0	.5	1.0
FC	Emotional constraint	1	2	4	1
X+ percent	Reality testing	74	67	60	76
DQ+	Cognitive maturity	7	5	3	6
3r+(2)/R	Self-esteem	.47	.33	.21	.47

constraint, better reality testing, greater cognitive maturity, and higher self-esteem. In contrast, the Spanish subject's native language Rorschach shows the better adjustment with essentially the same pattern as the Israeli woman's English Rorschach. Consequently, the findings are consistent with the notion that projective methods can track the effects of acculturation (cultural competence). Indeed, the Israeli woman's cultural competence has increased so far in her adopted culture as to seemingly outdistance her native cultural competence.

Conclusions

Projective methods hold significant potential for multicultural assessment. Full realization of this potential, however, will require considerably more investigation and development of these methods as multicultural techniques. Although it may be premature to limit the multicultural use of projective methods to the three covered in this chapter, there do not appear to be any challengers on the horizon. Surely, the Rorschach, TEMAS, and EMP give psychologists much opportunity to explore projective multicultural assessment.

The enumerated risk factors must receive major consideration whenever multicultural psychological assessment is attempted. Projective methods offer possible means for circumventing, or at least reducing, some of the hinderance caused by the existence of risk factors. Also, projective methods will enable psychologists to better determine when such risk factors are likely to have significant impact. These methods may enable psychologists to identify the "culture-free" personality in individuals whose cultural differences interfere with the accuracy of nonprojective assessment methods.

References

Beck, S. (1944). *Rorschach's test I: Basic processes.* Philadelphia: Grune & Stratton.

Bender, L. (1938). *A visual motor gestalt test and its clinical use.* New York: American Orthopsychiatric Association.

Bruhn, A. (1985). Using early memories as a projective technique: The Cognitive-Perceptual method. *Journal of Personality Assessment, 49,* 587–597.

Bruhn, A. (1989). *The early memories procedure.* (Available from Arnold R. Bruhn, 4704 Hunt Avenue, Chevy Chase, MD 20815).

Bruhn, A., & Bellow, S. (1984). Warrior, general, and president: Dwight David Eisenhower and his earliest memories. *Journal of Personality Assessment, 48,* 371–377.

Bruhn, A., & Bellow, S. (1987). The cognitive-perceptual approach to the interpretation of early memories: The earliest memories of Golda Meir. In C. D. Spielberger & J. N. Butcher (Eds.), *Advances in personality assessment* (Vol. 6, pp. 69–87). Hillsdale, NJ: Erlbaum.

Bruhn, A., & Schiffman, H. (1982). Prediction of locus of control stance from the earliest childhood memory. *Journal of Personality Assessment, 46,* 380–390.

Cattell, R. (1962). *Handbook for Culture Fair Intelligence Test: Scale I.* Champaign, IL: Institute for Personality and Ability Testing.

Charles, K. (1988). *Culture-specific MMPI norms for a sample of northern Ontario Indians.* Unpublished master's thesis, Lakehead University, Thunder Bay, Ontario, Canada.

Charry, J. (1959). Childhood and teen-age memories in mentally ill and normal groups. *Dissertation Abstracts International, 20,* 1073.

Costantino, G., & Malgady, R. (1983). Verbal fluency of Hispanic, Black, and White children on TAT and TEMAS. *Hispanic Journal of Behavioral Sciences, 5,* 199–206.

Costantino, G., Malgady, R., & Rogler, L. (1986). *Standardization and validation of TEMAS, a pluralistic thematic apperception test.* New York: Fordham University, Hispanic Research Center.

Costantino, G., Malgady, R. G., & Rogler, L. (1988). *TEMAS (Tell-Me-A-Story) manual.* Los Angeles: Western Psychological Services.

Costantino, G., Malgady, R., Rogler, L., Casullo, M., & Castillo, A. (1988). *Cross-cultural validation of TEMAS (Minority and Nonminority Versions).* Paper presented at the 96th Annual Convention of the American Psychological Association, Atlanta.

Costantino, G., Malgady, R., Rogler, L., & Tsui, E. (1988). Discriminant analysis of clinical outpatients and public school children by TEMAS: A thematic apperception test for Hispanic and Black children. *Journal of Personality Assessment, 52,* 670–678.

Costantino, G., Malgady, R., & Vazquez, C. (1981). A comparison of the Murray-TAT and a new thematic apperception test for urban Hispanic children. *Hispanic Journal of Behavioral Sciences, 3,* 291–300.

Cross, W. E., Jr. (1991). *Shades of Black: Diversity in African-American identity.* Philadelphia: Temple University Press.

Cuellar, I., Harris, L. C., & Jasso, R. (1980). An acculturation scale for Mexican-American normal and clinical populations. *Hispanic Journal of Behavioral Science, 2,* 199–217.

Dana, R. H. (1993). *Multicultural assessment perspectives for professional psychology.* Needham Heights, MA: Allyn & Bacon.

Dana, R. H. (1994). Workshop on multicultural personality assessment. Presented at the Midwinter Meeting of the Society for Personality Assessment, Chicago.

DeVos, G., & Boyer, B. (1989). *Symbolic analysis crossculturally.* Berkeley: University of California Press.

Eisenstein, V., & Ryerson, R. (1951). Psychodynamic significance of the first conscious memory. *Bulletin of the Menninger Clinic, 15,* 213–220.

Exner, J. (1974). *The Rorschach: A comprehensive system* (Vol. 1). New York: Wiley.

Exner, J. (1993). *The Rorschach: A comprehensive system* (Vol. 1, 3rd ed.) New York: Wiley.

Franco, J. (1983). An acculturation scale for Mexican-American children. *Journal of General Psychology*, *108*, 175–181.

Friedman, A. (1952). Early childhood memories of mental patients. *Journal of Child Psychiatry*, *2*, 266–269.

Gibbs, J. (1980). The interpersonal orientation in mental health consultation: Toward a model of ethnic variations in counseling. *Journal of Community Psychology*, *8*, 195–207.

Hammer, E. (1958). *The clinical application of projective drawings*. Springfield, IL: Thomas.

Helms, J. E. (Ed.) (1990). *Black and White racial identity: Theory, research, and practice*. New York: Greenwood Press.

Hernandez-Guzman, P., Rey-Clericus, R., San Martin-Petersen, C., & Vinet-Reichhardt, E. (1989). Differences between Anglo-American and Latin-American cultures in responses given to the Rorschach Psychodiagnostic Test (translation). *Terapia Psicologica*, *8*, 62–66.

Hertz, M. (1970). *Frequency tables for scoring Rorschach responses*. Cleveland, OH: Case Western Reserve University Press.

Hoffman, T., Dana, R., & Bolton, B. (1985). Measured acculturation and MMPI-168 performance of Native American adults. *Journal of Cross-Cultural Psychology*, *16*, 243–256.

Howes, R., & DeBlassie, R. (1989). Model errors in the cross cultural use of the Rorschach. *Journal of Multicultural Counseling and Development*, *17*, 79–84.

Keefe, K., Sue, S., Enomoto, K., Durvasula, R., & Chao, R. (1994). Asian American and White college students' performance on the MMPI-2. In J. Butcher (Ed.), *Handbook of international MMPI-2 research*, pp. 204–235. New York: Oxford University Press.

Klopfer, B., & Kelley, D. (1942). *The Rorschach technique*. Yonkers-on-Hudson, NY: World Book.

Krall, V. (1983). Rorschach norms for inner city children. *Journal of Personality Assessment*, *47*, 155–157.

Low, S. (1985). Culturally interpreted symptoms or culture-bound syndromes: A cross-cultural review of nerves. *Social Science and Medicine*, *21*, 187–196.

Malgady, R., Rogler, L., & Costantino, G. (1987). Ethnocultural and linguistic bias in mental health evaluation of Hispanics. *American Psychologist*, *42*, 228–234.

Margolis, R., Williger, N., Greenlief, C., Dunn, E., & Gfeller, P. (1989). The sensitivity of the Bender Gestalt Test as a screening instrument for neuropsychological impairment in older adults. *Journal of Psychology*, *123*, 670–678.

Marin, G., Sabogal, F., VanOss-Marin, B., Otero-Sabogal, R., & Perez-Sable, E. (1987). Development of a short acculturation scale for Hispanics. *Hispanic Journal of Behavioral Sciences, 9,* 183–205.

Mattlar, C. (1986). Finnish Rorschach responses in cross-cultural context: A normative study. *Psychology and Social Research, 58,* 166–200.

Meernhout, M., & Mukendi, N. (1980). Rorschach responses from another culture: A sample of rural Zairians (translation). *Bulletin de Psychologie Scolaire et d'Orientation, 29,* 61–70.

Mendoza, R. (1989). An empirical scale to measure type and degree of acculturation in Mexican-American adolescents and adults. *Journal of Cross-Cultural Psychology, 20,* 372–385.

Mischel, W. (1976). *Introduction to personality* (2nd ed.). Troy, MO: Holt, Rinehart, & Winston.

Mosak, H. (1958). Early recollections as a projective technique. *Journal of Projective Techniques, 22,* 302–311.

Motta, R., Little, S., & Tobin, M. (1993). The use and abuse of human figure drawings. *School Psychology Quarterly, 8,* 162–169.

Murray, H. (1943). *Thematic Apperception Test manual.* Cambridge, MA: Harvard University Press.

Olmedo, E., Martinez, J., & Martinez, S. (1978). Measure of acculturation for Chicano adolescents. *Psychological Reports, 42,* 159–170.

Piotrowski, Z. (1957). *Perceptanalysis.* New York: Macmillan.

Ramirez, M. (1984). Assessing and understanding biculturalism-multiculturalism in Mexican-American adults. In J. Martinez & R. Martinez (Eds.), *Chicano psychology* (pp. 77–94). Orlando, FL: Academic Press.

Rapaport, D., Gill, M., & Schafer, R. (1946). *Diagnostic Psychological Testing* (Vols. 1 & 2). Chicago: Yearbook Publishers.

Rausch-deTraubenberg, N., Block-Laine, F., Duplant, N., & Martin, M. (1993). The Rorschach in adolescence: Psychic functioning in a normal population (translation). *Bulletin de la Societe du Rorschach et des Methodes Projectives de Langue Française, 37,* 7–39.

Rorschach, H. (1921). *Psychodiagnostik.* Bern, Switzerland: Bircher. (Transl. Hans Huber Verlag, 1942).

Rosenberg, D., & Ritzler, B. (in preparation). Acculturation as a factor in the validity of cross-cultural Rorschach assessment.

Spigelman, A., Spigelman, G., & Englesson, I. (1991). Cross cultural differences between American and Swedish children regarding their Egocentricity Index. *Tidsskrift for Norsk Psykologforening, 28,* 316–319.

Sue, S., & Zane, N. (1987). The role of culture and cultural techniques in psychotherapy: A critique and reformulation. *American Psychologist, 42,* 37–45.

Suinn, R. M., Rickard-Figueroa, K., Lew, S., & Vigil, P. (1987). The Suinn-Lew Asian Self-Identity Acculturation Scale: An initial report. *Educational and Psychological Measurement, 47,* 401–407.

Takeuchi, M., & Scott, R. (1986). Educational productivity and Rorschach location responses of preschool Japanese and American children. *Psychology in the Schools, 23,* 368–373.

Tobey, L., & Bruhn, A. (1992). Early memories and the criminally dangerous. *Journal of Personality Assessment, 59,* 137–152.

Weiner, I. (1989). On competence and ethicality in psychodiagnostic assessment. *Journal of Personality Assessment, 53,* 827–831.

Weiner, I. (1991). Developments in research in personality assessment. *Journal of Personality Assessment, 56,* 370–372.

Part III

. . . .

Cognition and Educational Assessment

Part III of the *Handbook of Multicultural Assessment* includes chapters focusing on cognitive and educational testing with racial or ethnic minority groups. Many controversies have evolved in this area due to concerns regarding score discrepancies between groups. Moratoriums on ability testing in particular states and numerous court cases focusing on test usage are evidence of these concerns.

The section begins with a brief invited commentary by Richard Rankin. He was asked to share his perspective, given his knowledge of historical and contemporary issues in cognitive and educational testing. This information provides a good framework to examine and integrate information from the substantive chapters in this section.

Chapter Six focuses on issues pertaining to cognitive assessment across cultures. Lisa Suzuki, Damian Vraniak, and John Kugler focus primarily on the usage of individual intelligence measures—WISC-III, WAIS-R, and the Stanford-Binet (4th Edition). Brief highlights from the literature in this area are presented. Specific factors influencing test selection and appropriate usage of intelligence tests are covered. The chapter concludes with a case example to illustrate the various multicultural issues involved in the assessment process.

In Chapter Seven, Mark Shinn and Scott Baker examine the use of curriculum-based measurement (CBM) with diverse learners. The authors begin by providing information regarding the CBM procedure and how it differs from traditional assessment practices.

Examples of how CBM can address issues of illiteracy and special education decision making are specifically addressed, as is usage of CBM as a problem-solving model. Actual cases are used to illustrate the application of CBM procedures with minority children.

In Chapter Eight, Abigail Harris, Marilyn Reynolds, and Henry Koegel explore the usage of nonverbal assessment practices. Distinctions are made between nonreading, nonlanguage, and performance tests. Issues affecting the interpretation of nonverbal assessment data are identified. The authors also critically examine the most popular nonverbal assessment instruments.

Kenneth Howell and Robert Rueda provide information regarding achievement testing with culturally and linguistically diverse students in Chapter Nine. Specific characteristics of standardized or criterion-referenced achievement tests are identified. Factors impacting the usage of these measures with minority students are discussed. Criteria for determining test quality in the achievement area are also noted. Alternatives to traditional achievement testing are also presented.

Chapter Ten, by Carol Friedman and Robert Clayton, presents multicultural considerations in neuropsychological assessment. Risk factors are identified with respect to diverse populations and moderator variables such as socioeconomic status and educational attainment. Sources of bias during the neuropsychological procedures are identified. Finally, case studies are presented to illustrate the multicultural issues highlighted in the chapter.

Performance-based assessment is the focus of Chapter Eleven by Anthony Cancelli and Sabrina Arena. The authors discuss this procedure as an alternative to standardized multiple-choice tests. Issues of validity and reliability are specifically addressed. Multicultural issues are integrated throughout the identified process of performance-based assessment.

Invited Commentary
A Historical Perspective of Cognitive and Educational Assessment

Richard J. Rankin

Humans have a compulsion to study performance differences among their kind. This is nothing new, nor is it limited to academic areas. The cultural myths include speculation that Italians can sing, women cannot hit a curve ball, and White men cannot jump. That there are measurable differences in performances including achievement and intelligence is not in much doubt, and why these differences occur is of great dispute and may be even more resistant to scientific answers than the great religious debates. In an early work, Anastasi and Foley (1949) make three major points: racial typing is hard to do, as within-group differences are greater than between-group differences in relation to many psychological constructs; the proposed criteria of racial performance differences have been proven inadequate because of the specificity of what each culture calls higher mental processes, that is, what is considered intellect is itself culturally conditioned; different races live under varied cultural conditions, therefore, it is difficult to compare them directly and impossible to determine the relative contribution of heredity and environment.

The intervening forty-five years have not changed the landscape of research in racial and cultural differences very much. There have been heated discussions and quite a bit of name calling. Jensen (1980) wrote a compelling text titled *Bias in Mental Testing*, in which he points out that lower scores for some groups and higher scores for other groups are obvious, but differences in mean scores do not prove bias. Racial and cultural differences have been used to justify programs for the disadvantaged, while similar data can be used to justify the uselessness of the same programs. *The Bell Curve* (Herrnstein and Murray, 1994) asserts that intelligence levels differ among ethnic groups. Neither I nor anyone else in the field is of the opinion that there are no differences in measured intelligence across groups. The real issue is the misuse of these findings when they are used to make performance predictions for individuals and to close off educational and employment opportunities for groups.

It is impossible to make valid statements that genetic intelligence levels differ among ethnic groups. This point has been documented from the beginning of the testing movement and has had advocates from the beginning of testing, notably Binet himself. Further statements such as "Based on national norms, high percentages of minority children remain in the bottom decile of IQ after the mother's IQ has been controlled" (Herrnstein and Murray, 1994) prove nothing. Without a randomized experimental design, terms like "controlling for" do not make sense, and so far, we have not discovered a way to randomly assign people to racial and intellectual groups.

References

Anastasi, A. & Foley, J. P. (1949). *Differential psychology: Individual and group differences in behavior*. New York: Macmillan.

Herrnstein, R. J., & Murray, C. (1994). *The bell curve: Intelligence and class structure in American life*. New York: Free Press.

Jensen, A. R. (1980). *Bias in mental testing*. New York: Free Press.

6

Intellectual Assessment Across Cultures

Lisa A. Suzuki, Damian A. Vraniak, and John F. Kugler

For centuries, different cultural groups have developed ways to quantify abilities and distinguish people performing at different levels through various forms of measurement (Azar, 1995; Vane and Motta, 1990). The cultural component was and is an important variable in the measurement of what we now term "intelligence." Recent works in this area—books such as *The Bell Curve* (Herrnstein and Murray, 1994), publications in major psychological journals (for example, Jensen, 1995; Yee, Fairchild, Weizmann, and Wyatt, 1993), and articles in the popular press ("Mainstream Science on Intelligence," 1994)—attest to the continued importance and controversy of this area.

The purpose of this chapter is to highlight important considerations in the usage of intelligence measures with racial or ethnic minority groups. Certainly, these issues could be comprehensively examined as the topic of an entire book. However, it is our intent to provide information regarding problems surrounding the theoretical construct of intelligence, the deficit-discrepancy hypothesis, mainstream science on intelligence, racial-ethnic ability profiles, and frequently cited variables to be considered in intelligence testing. In addition, this chapter will provide brief summaries with regard to the most commonly used intelligence tests (such as the Wechsler Intelligence Scale for Children-III (Wechsler, 1991), the Wechsler Adult Intelligence Scale-Revised (Wechsler, 1981), and the Stanford-Binet (4th Edition) (Thorndike, Hagen, and Sattler, 1986). Finally, specific assumptions for appropriate assessment practice will be provided along with a case example illustrating the issues presented. This chapter focuses primarily on the usage of individual intelligence measures and only a brief discussion of group intelligence tests is provided.

Although much of the research cited in this chapter focuses on group differences, it is imperative that professionals remember that racial or ethnic group differences do not necessarily apply to individuals being tested. Within-group differences clearly exceed between-group differences (Kaufman, 1990). Herrnstein and Murray (1994) note: "The first thing to remember is that the differences among individuals are far greater than the differences between groups. If all the ethnic differences in intelligence evaporated overnight, most of the intellectual variation in America would endure" (p. 271). It is equally important to remember that knowledge and sensitivity to group differences in formulating hypotheses and interpreting test scores with respect to individuals from diverse backgrounds is imperative in the assessment process.

Multiple Definitions and Theories of Intelligence

As one becomes familiar with the area of intelligence assessment, it becomes clear that there exist numerous definitions and theories regarding this construct. Intelligence has been defined by some researchers as the ability to reason abstractly, to give correct answers, to adapt to novel situations, and so on. Theorists have defined intelligence in very different ways—consider Spearman (1927), Thurstone (1941), Cattell (1963), Guilford (1988), Sternberg (1988), and Gardner (1987). Spearman indicated that intelligence was made up of a general ("g") factor and numerous subabilities. Thurstone, on the other hand, identified seven primary abilities that constituted intelligence. These included: verbal comprehension, word fluency, number facility, spatial visualization, reasoning (inductive and deductive), perceptual speed, and memory.

Cattell (1963) suggested that intelligence could be divided into two forms: crystallized and fluid abilities. Crystallized abilities were those based upon cultural assimilation (Sattler, 1992). Development of these abilities was influenced by formal and informal educational factors throughout life, and they included both acquired skills and knowledge. Fluid abilities were viewed as more nonverbal and "culture free." As Sattler (1992) noted, these abilities involved adaptive learning capabilities. "It is through the exercise of fluid abilities that crystallized intelligence develops" (p. 48).

Guilford (1988) believed that these theories were not exhaustive with respect to the entire domain of human abilities; they did not encompass all of the possible tasks involved in assessing intelligence. Thus, he devised a schematic model of human abilities that took the form of a three-dimensional cube addressing psychological operations (for example, cognition and memory), material or content (for example, figural, symbolic, or behavioral), and the form of the information as a product (for example, units, classes, and systems).

Sternberg (1988) wrote about a componential and triarchic theory that recognized some aspects of intelligence as universal, while others differed between cultures. Sternberg noted that "if one considers intelligence as a whole, both its nature and the ways in which it is appropriately measured do differ, at least potentially, from one culture to another" (p. 68). He defined intelligence as "the mental activity underlying purposive adaptation to, shaping of, and selection of real-world environments relevant to one's life" (p. 69).

Gardner (1987) argued for the concept of "multiple intelligences," challenging the notion of a singular "g" factor. These multiple intelligences include: intrapersonal, interpersonal, linguistic, logical-mathematical, bodily-kinesthetic, musical, and spatial. Gardner defined intelligence as the "ability to solve a problem or to fashion a product which is valued in one or more cultural settings" (p. 25). He indicated that intelligence is a culturally relative construct.

In practice, each measure of intelligence is based upon a slightly varied definition of this construct. It is imperative that one understand the definition upon which a test is based. The lack of an agreed-upon definition of intelligence and theoretical context have stimulated a great deal of controversy, which has impacted the field of intelligence testing. Some have stated that intelligence may simply be what intelligence tests measure (Boring, 1923).

Problems in definition have also contributed to the controversies surrounding the usage of intelligence tests with minority populations. If researchers cannot agree upon what intelligence is and how it should be measured, then the field is open to debate and disagreement.

Measured Intelligence and the Deficit-Discrepancy Hypothesis

The focus of much of the research has been based upon a deficit-discrepancy hypothesis. According to this hypothesis, differences in intelligence between racial or ethnic groups are a result of deficits within the individual members of various ethnic groups, which result in the lower scores on intelligence measures. A major assumption of this hypothesis is the following: "A community under conditions of poverty (for it is the poor who are the focus of attention, and disproportionate numbers of the poor are members of minority ethnic groups) is a disorganized community, and this disorganization expresses itself in various forms of deficit(s)" (Cole and Bruner, 1971, p. 867). Fallows (1980) reports that the first crude IQ tests were used for racial and ethnic exclusion. He notes that in 1912, Henry Goddard "scientifically proved that 83 percent of Jews were 'feebleminded,' along with 90 percent of Hungarians, 79 percent of Italians, and 87 percent of Russians" (cited in Fallows, 1980, p. 39).

Currently, the hardest hit by this deficit focus have been racial or ethnic minority children in the schools, specifically Black, Hispanic, and American Indian children (Dana, 1993; McShane, 1989; McShane and Plas, 1984a, 1984b). Academic environments are often the places in which intellectual measures are used to classify and determine eligibility for services. In the 1960s and 1970s, disproportionate numbers of Black and Spanish-surnamed youth were identified as mentally retarded based upon standardized IQ measures (President's Committee on Mental Retardation, 1969). The phrase the "six hour retardate" was coined as they were functionally retarded only while they were in school, not while they were at home or in their communities. The students appeared "retarded" in terms of academic skills in the school environment but demonstrated much higher potential in terms of survival and adaptability skills in their respective communities. Court cases challenging the usage of intelligence tests and Black psychologists calling for a moratorium on the usage of standardized intelligence tests with Black children (Jackson, 1975) are just a few of the issues that have arisen as test data have been misused and misinterpreted to the detriment of particular racial or ethnic groups. For a review of representative court cases regarding assessment and placement of racial or ethnic minority children in the educational system, the reader is referred to Sattler (1992).

Mainstream Science with Respect to Intelligence

In 1994, the *Wall Street Journal* published a statement titled "Mainstream Science on Intelligence," highlighting conclusions in mainstream science with respect to intelligence. The statement was signed by fifty-two professors identified as experts in intelligence and allied fields. The statement was issued by this group of professors to promote a more "reasoned discussion" of this controversial area with respect to empirical research findings. Issues pertaining to the meaning and measurement of intelligence were addressed. In the article, intelligence was defined as: "A very general mental capability that, among other things, involves the ability to reason, plan, solve problems, think abstractly, comprehend complex ideas, learn quickly and learn from experience" (p. A18). Based on this definition, the statement indicates that intelligence can be measured and "intelligence tests measure it well" (p. A18). According to this article, intelligence tests are "not culturally biased against American

Blacks or other native-born, English-speaking peoples in the U.S. Rather, IQ scores predict equally accurately for all such Americans, regardless of race or social class" (p. A18). Suggestions are made for those who do not speak English to be given a nonverbal test or a measure in their own language.

The article states that there is no "persuasive evidence that the IQ bell curves for different racial-ethnic groups are converging" (p. A18). The authors go on to state that the reasons for these differences include both environment and heredity.

While not the focus of this chapter, no discussion regarding IQ differences between racial or ethnic groups can escape the heredity versus environment debate. Based upon an extensive review of the literature, Kaufman (1990) reports that general intelligence has "an estimated broad heritability index of 52 percent, indicating that about half of the variability in IQ scores is due to genetic factors" (p. 33). Environmental influences in IQ are extremely complex, as no one factor (for example, socioeconomic status, schooling, or region) has been identified as accounting for a significant proportion of the variance in IQ with different ethnic groups (Vernon, 1979). Kaufman (1990) notes that environmental factors vary between racial or ethnic groups and may differ significantly within cultures, therefore, due to insufficient data, differences in IQ between groups cannot be attributed to genetic factors.

What are the differences in IQ among different racial-ethnic groups? Common findings of racial-ethnic group differences in overall IQ scores are reported as: Whites 100, Blacks 85, Hispanics midway between Blacks and Whites, and Asians and Jews somewhere above 100 ("Mainstream Science," 1994).

The controversy of the bell curve differences between racial or ethnic groups on intelligence continues. The need for accurate and appropriate assessment procedures is imperative, as challenges continue to be raised regarding the usage of standardized intelligence tests with racial or ethnic minority children. Examination of general findings as presented in the "Mainstream Science on Intelligence" article (1994) does not represent the complexity of issues that impact usage of IQ tests with racial or ethnic minority group members. Issues pertaining to the bell curve controversy will be addressed in this chapter.

Racial or Ethnic Profiles of Abilities

Examination of overall IQ scores (Full Scale IQ; FSIQ) does not represent the complete picture with respect to the intelligence of racial or ethnic groups, as differences are noted in ability profiles. In a study by Suzuki and Gutkin (1993) incorporating a total of 6,869 children from various racial or ethnic groups, Whites scored at a mean of 10 (average) across visual-reasoning and verbal-reasoning subtests. The American Indian and Hispanic groups demonstrated relative strengths in visual-reasoning in comparison to verbal-reasoning abilities. The sample of Blacks obtained a relatively flat profile with scores consistently below the White average. The Japanese international sample obtained the most distinct profile, with overall strengths noted in visual- and numerical-reasoning abilities. Suzuki and Gutkin (1993) indicate that these results should be interpreted with caution, as within-group differences were found among Native American tribal groups and possibly between Hispanic subgroups. Regional differences were also evident among samples of Black children.

Other studies have reported similar findings regarding relative strengths of particular racial or ethnic groups. Researchers have repeatedly noted higher visual-reasoning abilities relative to verbal-reasoning abilities for American Indians (Browne, 1984; McShane, 1980; McShane and Plas, 1984a; Sattler, 1992; Wilgosh, Mulcahy, and Watters, 1986), and Mexican Americans and Hispanics (Laosa, 1984; McShane and Cook, 1985; Taylor and Richards, 1991; Whitworth and Gibbons, 1986). Asian profiles have also indicated nonverbal-reasoning strengths along with high mathematical abilities (Lynn, 1977; Lynn and Hampson, 1985–86). While numerous studies have been conducted to examine Black profiles on various IQ measure, the results have been unclear and somewhat inconsistent (Reynolds, Willson, and Hickman, 1988). Some studies have indicated relative strengths in verbal reasoning (Taylor and Richards, 1991; Vance, Hankins, and McGee, 1979; Vance, Huelsman, and Wherry, 1976) and short-term memory (Jensen and Reynolds, 1982; Reynolds and others, 1988). However, the exact nature of the profile of abilities for Blacks remains elusive.

Variables Considered in the Assessment Process

The process of multicultural intelligence assessment is complex. Researchers have examined the role of significant variables that should be considered in this process. These include socioeconomic status, educational level, health issues, residential and regional differences, language, and acculturation factors.

Socioeconomic Status

One variable often included in discussions regarding racial or ethnic group differences in IQ is socioeconomic status (SES). An early study by Lesser, Fifer, and Clark (1965) indicates that differences in social class (for example, poor, middle-income, high-income) were associated with significant differences in measured levels of mental ability in a comparison of four ethnic groups—Chinese, Jewish, Black, and Puerto Rican. This study indicated that increases in socioeconomic status were correlated with increases in overall IQ. It is believed that social and economic deprivation will influence measured intelligence, especially in the area of verbal comprehension (Vance and Hankins, 1978). However, SES does not account for all of the variance in IQ. "Mainstream Science" (1994) indicates that when SES is equated, differences in IQ become smaller but remain substantial for individuals from the same socioeconomic background. "Black students from prosperous families tend to score higher in IQ than blacks from poor families, but they score no higher, on average, than whites from poor families" (p. A18). Therefore, SES is not the only variable accounting for the variance in racial or ethnic group intelligence.

Educational Attainment

Years of education have a significant impact on intelligence test performance. However, as Kaufman (1990) reports, it is unclear whether people score higher on IQ tests because of their educational attainment, or whether people stay in school longer because they are brighter (higher IQ). On the WAIS-R, differences due to educational attainment were significant: college graduates obtained overall IQs 32½ points higher than those with seven years or less schooling. This variable is important given that particular racial or ethnic groups tend to have disproportionately higher drop-out rates from the educational system.

Health Factors

Performance on IQ measures can also be influenced by health factors. Kaufman (1994) notes that children with undetected visual or hearing problems may score poorly on IQ tests based upon sensory losses. For example, McShane (1989) notes that hearing loss due to high rates of otitis media among American Indian children will impact the assessment process. McShane and Berry (1988) cite research linking otitis media and resulting hearing loss to decreases in language ability, lower academic achievement in reading, and mathematics.

Another health issue that has been linked to low IQ is blood lead level. Even low levels of lead absorption have been found to be significantly related to children's IQ (Hawk and others, 1986; McShane and Plas, 1984a). Findings were especially of concern with low-SES populations; particularly with Blacks and American Indians who have been identified as being at risk for higher blood lead levels (McShane and Plas). Other health factors to be considered in the assessment process include malnutrition during critical periods of development, drugs, fetal alcohol syndrome, and so forth.

Residential and Regional Issues

Early studies indicated the existence of regional differences in IQ. For example, Black children living in the South were found to have lower IQs than Black children living in other regions of the country (Sowell, 1978). Sowell attributed this to environmental variables such as poorer schooling and social constraints placed upon Blacks in the South.

Current studies have indicated that regional differences in IQ have diminished over time despite earlier reports. Regional differences are considered by some to be trivial and nonsignificant (Kaufman, 1990).

Studies have also indicated urban versus rural differences on IQ tests. Early findings indicated that children living in rural areas scored lower than those in urban areas (Vernon, 1979). More recent studies have obtained differences that are small and clinically nonsignificant. Kaufman (1990) attributes decreases in residential differences to the availability of mass media, increased communication, and improved educational services. These factors have ended the isolation of rural areas, "making the kinds of facts and problems assessed by intelligence tests readily accessible to almost everyone" (p. 166).

This variable regarding rural or urban residence, however, should continue to be examined in those communities that may still be relatively isolated with respect to the media. For example, some American Indian reservations do not have ready access to the media—that is, they have few television sets and newspapers (Tanner-Halverson, Burden, and Sabers, 1993). McShane and Cook (1985) also report urban and rural residence as significantly impacting IQ scores in their review of studies focusing on Hispanic abilities.

Language

Assessment becomes a greater challenge when English is not the examinee's primary language. There exists a need for bilingual professionals who can obtain information from individuals in their primary language (Dana, 1993). Recommendations have been made indicating that bilingual individuals be tested in both languages as appropriate assessment practice (Rogers, 1993). Examiners must also attend to dialectal differences.

Problems often arise in using translated measures. Although high-quality translation procedures may have been used in the development process, direct translations of tests are often not possible as psychological constructs may have relevance in one culture but not another. Usage of translators and interpreters also poses concerns. Just because the content of the items is preserved does not automatically ensure that the item taps the same ability or that it has the same meaning within the cultural context of the individual being tested. Dana (1993) notes that translations of standardized instruments "have not resolved the problems due to archaisms, contaminations, Anglicisms, and alterations of word meanings" (p. 187).

In reference to language issues, it is also important for examiners to recognize that some racial or ethnic cultures are less verbally oriented. For example, the American Indian and Asian cultures place an emphasis on nonverbal communication (McShane and Plas, 1984a). This may play a role in the development of relative strengths in visual-reasoning abilities in comparison to verbal reasoning.

Acculturation

Understanding the acculturation issues of the individual is important as culture impacts problem solving strategies and familiarity with test formats. The process of testing a person who has recently arrived in the United States will be contextually different than testing a third- or fourth-generation individual. Indeed, professionals may opt to postpone the administration of a standardized IQ test until such time as the individual has become accustomed to the dominant culture of the United States—that is, its educational system, language, community norms. Descriptive indicators (for example, behavioral observations), curriculum-based measures, and past records from the individual's homeland may be much more useful in capturing the potential intelligence and skills of the individual being tested than a standardized IQ test. For more information regarding acculturation variables as they impact specific racial or ethnic groups, the reader is referred to Dana (1993).

Individual Intelligence Tests

The Wechsler scales and the Stanford-Binet (4th Edition) (SB-IV) are representative of the premiere tests in the area of individually administered intelligence scales. The Wechsler scales consist of the Wechsler Preschool and Primary Scale of Intelligence-Revised (WPPSI-R; Wechsler, 1989), which is designed for young children ages three years to seven years, three months; the Wechsler Intelligence Scale for Children-Third Edition (WISC-III; Wechsler, 1991) for ages six years to sixteen years, eleven months; and the Wechsler Adult Intelligence Scale-Revised (WAIS-R; Wechsler, 1981) for ages sixteen to seventy-four. The WPPSI-R will not be covered in this chapter; see Chapter Seventeen for information regarding this test and discussions of other intelligence measures including the K-ABC and the McCarthy scales.

The WISC-III, WAIS-R, and SB-IV have a long history of development, revision, and restandardization based upon data from the U.S. Census. The following discussion does not focus on the numerous reliability and validity data available on these measures. The Wechsler scales and the SB-IV have withstood criticisms regarding their usage with racial or ethnic minority children, adolescents, and adults. In general, studies have indicated that the scales are reliable and valid with respect to racial or ethnic minority group members. Instead, the development of the scales is emphasized along with scoring differences between various racial or ethnic groups.

Wechsler Intelligence Scale for Children-Third Edition

David Wechsler identified intelligence as a unitary construct that could be reflected in an individual's ability to adapt to novel situations. Therefore, he believed that tests must present to the individual a variety of tasks to tap into the multidimensional facets of intelligence. He also saw it as a clinical tool and only one aspect of personality. The Wechsler Intelligence Scale for Children-Third Edition (WISC-III) (Wechsler, 1991) is the most recently updated

Wechsler scale. It has been described as the model for redevelopment of intellectual measures (Helms, 1992). The WISC-III yields three composite scores: Verbal, Performance, and Full Scale IQs. The subtests of the WISC-III are designed to assess multiple facets of a child's intellectual abilities. Wechsler writes: "all of these abilities are valued to varying degrees by our culture, and all relate to behavior that is generally accepted as intelligent behavior in one way or another" (p. 1).

Four factor-based index scores can be computed based upon the subtest scores. These include: Verbal Comprehension (Information, Similarities, Vocabulary, Comprehension), Perceptual Organization (Picture Completion, Picture Arrangement, Block Design, Object Assembly), Freedom from Distractibility (Arithmetic, Digit Span), and Processing Speed (Coding, Symbol Search). Little (1992) notes weaknesses in this factor structure and recommends caution in interpreting the Freedom from Distractibility factor.

The goals of the restandardization for the WISC-III were to improve subtest content, administration, and scoring rules, update the norms, and enhance the factor structure, while maintaining the basic structure and overall content of the WISC-R. A primary focus of the subtest revisions was to minimize bias in content. In general, research on the WISC-R had indicated minimal evidence of ethnic bias. Despite these findings, several methods were used to examine possible bias in items (for example, item statistics were examined to test for ethnic, gender, and regional bias). The few items that were identified in this process were those in the Information, Vocabulary, and Comprehension subtests. These were replaced in the final item pool. Item-bias analyses were conducted on the WISC-III tryout data. As an "oversample," approximately four hundred minority children were tested and their scores analyzed for bias (Wechsler, 1991, p. 12).

An item-review panel composed of psychologists familiar with the racial or ethnic bias studies on the WISC-R was also given the revised items and evaluations of the former WISC-R items to review. The test developers also examined the artwork presented in the Performance subtests. Care was taken to ensure that a balanced number of males and females were represented and that a "wide variety of ethnically identifiable persons, names, and topics" were included in the items (Wechsler, 1991, p. 13).

The standardization of the WISC-III was based on the 1988 U.S. Census and stratified with respect to age, gender, race-ethnicity, geographic region, and parent-guardian education. A total of 2,200 children participated in the standardization process—200 children in each of eleven age groups. Equal numbers of males and females were included. Children were categorized into racial or ethnic group classifications: White, Black, Native American, Eskimo, Aleut, Asian, Pacific Islander, or other. The parents were asked to indicate whether their child was of Hispanic origin. The Native American, Eskimo, Aleut, Asian, and Pacific Islander groups were collapsed and combined to form the "other" category. Racial or ethnic proportions were maintained within each age group, gender, geographic region, and parent education level. Based on the percentages provided in the manual, the total numbers representing each racial or ethnic group are as follows: Hispanic (n = 242), Black (n = 339), Other (n = 77), and White (n = 1542). Information was not available with respect to IQ scores for each racial or ethnic group in the standardization sample.

Given its relatively short history, few research studies have been conducted looking at various racial or ethnic groups and how they score on the WISC-III. One study by Weiss, Prifitera, and Roid (1993) examined fairness in predicting achievement across racial or ethnic and gender groups on the WISC-III. Achievement was assessed using school grades and nationally standardized achievement test scores for reading, writing, and math. Results indicate that in general the WISC-III predicts academic achievement fairly across ethnic and gender groups.

Tanner-Halverson and others (1993) examined usage of the WISC-III with Tohono O'odham Native American children. The average Tohono O'odham student's Verbal and Full Scale IQs (VIQ 84.5, FSIQ 86.8) are approximately one standard deviation below the national average of 100. The group's PIQ was in the average range at 91.9. Based upon their findings these researchers stress the need for developing local norms on the WISC-III for particular samples like the Tohono O'odham.

The authors also report that despite improvements in the WISC-III, items still appear irrelevant or biased against these Native American children. In particular, items that picture an umbrella or a supermarket will be unfamiliar to these children, who live in a desert community and do not have access to grocery stores. References to pianos (Similarities subtest) and newspapers (Comprehension subtest) are also unfamiliar to these children, given their current environment. The authors also note that many homes on the reservation do not have television or electricity. "A practical way to reduce the impact of such cultural and linguistic content is to derive norms from the examinee's cultural group" (Tanner-Halverson and others 1993, p. 127).

Wechsler Adult Intelligence Scale-Revised

The Wechsler Adult Intelligence Scale-Revised (WAIS-R) shares much in common with the WISC-III (Wechsler, 1981). The WAIS-R factor structure is similar to the WISC-III and many of the subtests parallel each other. The WAIS-R has been identified as "by far the most popular intelligence test for adults" (Harrison, Kaufman, Hickman, and Kaufman, 1988, p. 197). Kaufman (1990) refers to the WAIS-R as "king among assessment tools used to assess adult functioning in numerous domains and has no peer in the intelligence domain" (p. 18). The WAIS-R was designed to assess the intellectual abilities of individuals aged sixteen to seventy-four years.

The purposes of the revisions to the WAIS were to update content, provide new normative data, and eliminate or reduce gender and racial bias. The standardization sample consisted of 1,880 individuals stratified according to the 1970 U.S. Census. Stratification variables included gender, race, geographic region, residence, education, and occupation. The reported IQs of different racial or ethnic groups in the standardization sample were as follows: White (n = 1,664), VIQ 101.2, PIQ 101.3, FSIQ 101.4; Black (n = 192), VIQ 87.9, PIQ 87.3, FSIQ 86.9; Others including Asians and American Indians (n = 24) VIQ 94.2, PIQ 96.5, FSIQ 94.0 (Reynolds, Chastain, Kaufman, and McLean, 1987).

A study by Whitworth and Gibbons (1986) of Black, White, and Mexican American male college students yielded the following WAIS-R scores: White (VIQ 109.2, PIQ 112.5, and FSIQ 111.9); Mexican American (VIQ 97.7, PIQ 106.7, and FSIQ 101.4); and Black (VIQ 96.3, PIQ 99.9, and FSIQ 97.4).

Numerous studies have been conducted with respect to the validity, reliability, and psychometric qualities of the WAIS-R. Overall, results indicate that this measure is valid and reliable with respect to different racial or ethnic minority groups when used appropriately (Kaufman, McLean, and Reynolds, 1991; Sattler, 1992). Dana (1993) notes, however, that the factor structure of the Wechsler scales (that is, WAIS-R, WISC-R) may vary across different racial or ethnic minority groups. For example, McShane and Plas (1984a) indicate that the Freedom from Distractibility factor for members of the American Indian population is "misleading." They also note significant intertribal variations. Kaufman's review of the literature on Black-White differences also notes that loadings on "g" (general intelligence) are different for Blacks in comparison to Whites on the WAIS-R subtests (Kaufman, 1990).

Kaufman (1990) reports that some clinicians use abbreviated forms of the WAIS-R, relying upon the Vocabulary-Block Design subtests for clinical screening. These two subtests will "consistently underestimate" the intelligence of Blacks "because it emphasizes their areas of greatest weakness" (p. 163). Thus, he does not recommend usage of abbreviated versions of the WAIS-R with particular minority groups.

Stanford-Binet (4th Edition)

The Stanford-Binet (4th Edition) (SB-IV; Thorndike and others, 1986) was designed to assess the cognitive abilities of individuals age two years to adulthood. This test has a long history with predecessors like the Stanford-Binet Form L-M. The discussion that follows focuses only on the SB-IV.

The SB-IV is based on a theoretical model of "g" or general intelligence. The test authors state that "It is our strong belief that the best measure of g—and consequently broadly effective prediction—will stem from a diverse set of cognitive tasks that call for relational thinking in a diversity of contexts" (p. 6). The theoretical model consists of a three-level hierarchy with "g" at the top; "g" is divided into crystallized abilities, fluid-analytic abilities, and short-term memory. Crystallized abilities are divided into verbal reasoning and quantitative reasoning. The fluid-analytic abilities consist of abstract and visual reasoning.

The SB-IV utilizes an adaptive testing format, as no examinee is administered all of the items. Instead, each is tested on a variety of tasks closest to their ability level.

The test authors report that the test was designed to provide the professional with opportunities to obtain qualitative information as the examinee is exposed to a variety of tasks. Thus, the examiner can observe the examinee's flexibility and reaction to frustration, success, and failure.

Criteria for item inclusion were as follows (Thorndike and others, 1986, p. 10):

1. They have been shown to be acceptable measures of verbal reasoning, quantitative reasoning, abstract-visual reasoning, or short term memory.
2. They could be scored reliably.
3. They were generally recognized as being relatively free of ethnic and gender bias.

4. They functioned adequately over a wide range of age groups.

Items that had been criticized in the past for ethnic bias were eliminated by item-fairness review teams made up of people selected to represent various minority groups. Independent experts were also selected to review items to examine ethnic balance and representativeness of geographic regions. A total of eleven Black, five Hispanic, four American Indian, and four Asian professionals participated in the item review process. Minority students were oversampled to conduct reliable item-bias analyses. Following preliminary tryouts, field trials, and revisions, the final form of the SB-IV had fifteen tests. Six were new item types not in previous editions. The SB-IV yields Standard Age Scores (SAS) in four areas (Verbal Reasoning, Abstract-Visual Reasoning, Quantitative Reasoning, and Short-Term Memory) and a Composite SAS score.

The standardization process involved 500 examiners testing more than 5,000 subjects across forty-seven states and the District of Columbia (Thorndike and others, 1986). The standardization sample was designed to reflect the 1980 U.S. Census, incorporating seven primary variables: geographic region, community size, ethnic group, parental education, occupation, age, and gender. Four ethnic groups were proportionally represented in the standardization sample: White, Black, Hispanic, and Asian-Pacific Islander. The manual notes that American Indians were also included. The standardization sample included: Hispanic ($n = 313$), Asian ($n = 107$), Black ($n = 711$), American Indian ($n = 82$), Other ($n = 109$), and White ($n = 3,691$). The average for the Weighted standardization sample Composite Score across the age range was 99.7 with a standard deviation of 16.1. Scoring differences between the racial or ethnic groups are reported in the manual in three age groupings. Sattler (1992) computed the median scores of the three age groups and reported mean racial or ethnic group scores as: Asian 99.9, Black 91.0, Hispanic 94.9, American Indian 94.7, and White 103.5.

Thorndike, Hagen, and Sattler (1986) note that with respect to racial or ethnic groups:

> Three ethnic groups—Hispanics, Asians, and Blacks—
> had distinctive patterns of mean scores that were consis-
> tent across age groups. Hispanics had higher mean scores
> in Abstract/Visual Reasoning, Quantitative Reasoning,
> and Short-Term Memory than in Verbal Reasoning. His-
> panic examinees, at all ages, had their highest mean score
> in Abstract/Visual Reasoning. Asian examinees, at all
> ages, had higher mean scores in Abstract/Visual Reason-
> ing and Quantitative Reasoning than in Verbal Reason-
> ing. In two of the three age groups, Asian examinees also
> had higher mean scores in Abstract/Visual Reasoning
> and Quantitative Reasoning than in Short-Term Mem-
> ory. The Black examinees had their highest scores in
> Short-Term Memory [p. 37].

No summary statements were made with regard to the Native American sample cited in the technical manual.

Concerns in Group Intelligence Testing

Usage of group intelligence tests has been criticized for the same reasons as the individualized measures. In a review of group intelligence tests, Vane and Motta (1990) note that attacks have focused on the way in which the tests are used, conclusions drawn based upon obtained IQ scores, theories underlying the tests, and the tests themselves. Group intelligence tests have been identified as discriminating against particular minority groups. Results of the tests have at times been misused to indicate the inferiority of particular minority groups.

The controversial book, *The Bell Curve: Intelligence and Class Structure in American Life* (Herrnstein and Murray, 1994), is based in part upon cognitive test scores on the Armed Forces Qualification

Test (AFQT). The authors state that this instrument is "highly g-loaded," which translates into "it is a good measure of cognitive ability" (p. 120). Herrnstein and Murray (1994) use IQ statistics (these statistics are also suspect) to make statements regarding the relationship of IQ and race to social policy, education, and so on. Implied within their discussion is the notion of the inferiority of some racial or ethnic minority groups. Since the publication of *The Bell Curve*, books have been written to dispute the interpretations and conclusions made in the Herrnstein and Murray book. Two such edited texts are: *The Bell Curve Wars: Race, Intelligence and the Future of America* (Fraser, 1995), and *The Bell Curve Debate* (Jacoby and Glauberman, 1995).

Group intelligence tests have been criticized for the following: "that they do not predict adequately what they are designed to predict, that they tend to favor groups who are sophisticated test takers, that the test scores are subject to improvement with coaching or repetition, that they emphasize unimportant aspects at the expense of aspects crucial for success in school or employment, and that they have not been standardized adequately on certain populations" (Vane and Motta, 1990, p. 105).

Group intelligence tests correlate highly with one another. Vane and Motta (1990) note that some of the group tests we are familiar with have quite different titles: Scholastic Aptitude Test, the Medical College Admission Test, The Law School Aptitude Test, and the Graduate Record Examination. These tests have been identified as the "gatekeepers" to higher education. Reschly (1990) notes that these general aptitude tests "are not different in any significant respect from traditional general intelligence tests" (p. 151).

To their credit, developers of these major instruments have become sensitized to the multicultural issues that can impact performance on these measures. For example, one of the "gatekeeper" instruments to graduate schools in the United States is the Graduate Record Examination (GRE) published by the Educational Testing Service (ETS). Materials describing the GRE clearly state: "It should be remembered that the GRE tests provide measures of certain types of developed abilities and achievement, reflecting educational and cultural experience over a long period. Special care is required in interpreting the GRE scores of students who may have had an educational and cultural experience somewhat different from that of the traditional majority" (ETS, 1994, p. 14).

ETS also provides GRE information as part of Project 1000—an initiative to recruit and retain minority students in graduate level programs. Given scoring differences between racial or ethnic groups, ETS now sends a breakdown of GRE scores by ethnic group with the minority Project 1000 applicant's test scores. In addition, a statement that the scores should be interpreted with caution accompanies this information (ETS, 1988).

Assumptions for Appropriate Use of Intelligence Measures

The accuracy and appropriateness of the intellectual assessment process is based upon a number of assumptions. A listing of the assumptions as identified by Kaufman (1990,* 1994) is presented in this section, with each assumption followed by brief discussion designed to highlight multicultural issues as they impact the assessment process.

1. *"The focus of any assessment is the person being assessed, not the test"* (Kaufman, 1990, p. 24).

Professionals often become preoccupied with IQ scores to the detriment of the individual being assessed. An individual is not best represented by a sum of subtest scores. Kaufman (1990, 1994) reminds professionals that IQ tests are first and foremost "clinical instruments," designed to provide information regarding multiple facets of an individual's functioning. In addition to the abilities tapped by traditional IQ measures, professionals can gain valuable information regarding frustration tolerance, problem-solving

*From Kaufman, A. S. *Assessing adolescent and adult intelligence.* Copyright 1990 by Allyn and Bacon. Adapted by permission.

strategies, response styles, and so forth by observing the individual during the assessment process. These behavioral observations should be interpreted with respect to racial or ethnic differences in terms of approaches to the task, familiarity with the examination format, test taking strategies, and so on.

Kaufman (1994) reports the importance of individualizing the WISC-III interpretation based upon language and dialect, subculture and home life, educational, racial, and gender-based factors. For example, differences in dialect should be considered "different" but not "deficient."

2.   *"The goal of any examiner is to be better than the tests he or she uses"* (Kaufman, 1990, p. 25).

While any person who reads and memorizes a test manual can administer the IQ test in a standardized manner, it requires skill, knowledge, and experience to complete a comprehensive intelligence assessment. Knowledge of theory and research should be integrated into the assessment process. This knowledge should include familiarity with how different groups score on particular measures. Sensitivity to multicultural issues and information obtained from clinical interviews, observations, and supplementary tests should be incorporated into the interpretation of the assessment results.

It is important for professionals to be trained adequately in the process of assessment so that they can demonstrate the skills necessary to do the job noted above. As one colleague stated, "we have become proficient at training testers . . . we need to focus on making them good clinical assessors." Therefore, training in intelligence testing must focus not only on the theory, research, and standardized administration of particular IQ tests, but include specific instruction regarding the multicultural issues that can impact the assessment process. Students should have knowledge regarding how different groups score on particular tests. They need to recognize cultural variables within case examples that may influence interpretation of test results. Students will benefit from training experience testing children, adolescents, and adults from different cultural backgrounds.

Armour-Thomas (1992) presents recommendations for training and practice in IQ testing, including a concentration in the following areas: intelligence theory and cross-cultural issues, qualitative assessment (for example, clinical interviewing, behavioral observation), inclusion of culturally relevant data in reporting of test results, and consultative services to teachers and other professionals regarding interpretation of intelligence profiles of racial or ethnic minority group members.

3.   *"Intelligence tests measure what the individual has learned"* (Kaufman, 1990, p. 25).

Kaufman notes that the "content of all tasks, whether verbal or nonverbal, is learned within a culture" (p. 25). Learning takes place in a variety of settings including school, home, and community. This assumption brings to the forefront the point that all tests are "culturally loaded." Cultural loading refers to the degree of cultural specificity present in a particular test. All tests are tied in some way to the unique aspects of the culture in which they were developed (Reynolds, 1982). With respect to intelligence, tests must be relevant to the definition of "smart" behavior within a particular culture. "As a measure of past learning, the IQ test is best thought of as a kind of achievement test, not as a simple measure of aptitude" (Kaufman, 1990, p. 25).

As noted earlier, the Tanner-Halverson and others (1993) study of the Tohono O'odham Indians demonstrates the importance of attending to the cultural loading of particular items and subtests of the IQ measures being selected. Modifications can be made in interpretation based upon sound clinical judgment. For example, the examiner can report that "The Verbal and/or Full Scale IQ is not considered to be an accurate reflection of the child's intellectual ability because of his/her bilingual, culturally different background" (p. 126).

4.   *"The tasks composing intelligence tests are illustrative samples of behavior and are not meant to be exhaustive"* (Kaufman, 1990, p. 26).

The various IQ tests discussed in this chapter consist of subtests designed to obtain behavioral samples of an individual from a variety of perspectives. The tasks are not exhaustive and therefore there are inherent limitations. Kaufman (1990) suggests that IQ tests be supplemented with other informal and formal measures of functioning to obtain a broader indication of an individual's abilities.

Collateral information in multicultural assessment is important. The cultural and experiential background of individual test takers will influence their understanding of the tasks presented during the administration of a standardized IQ test. In addition, this cultural information is vitally important in providing a context for interpretation of the results obtained.

5. *"Intelligence tests assess mental functioning under fixed experimental conditions"* (Kaufman, 1990, p. 26).

The assessment process is influenced by a number of factors — rapport between examiner and examinee, environmental conditions (noise, lighting, temperature), examiner skill in administration (accurate and efficient presentation of the test materials), examiner skill in observing behavior, and so on.

It is the role of the clinician to establish rapport and facilitate the individuals being tested in doing their best. This will help provide the most accurate picture of their strengths and needs. Sensitivity to cultural norms is beneficial in this process.

Armour-Thomas (1992) indicates the need to understand sociolinguistic variables—"courtesies and conventions of discourse that govern interpersonal interactions" (p. 556). Sociolinguistic variables impact the student's motivation depending upon the compatibility, understanding, and sensitivity demonstrated by the examiner in the assessment process.

For example, McShane (1989) suggests that sociolinguistic adaptations be made in testing American Indian children. These include the following considerations:

- Examiners should allow more time during untimed tests.

- Examiners should not look directly at children during tests like the Digit Span subtest, given the meaning of eye contact in this culture.

- Touching behavior should not be used during the assessment process.

- Examiners must be sensitive to speech tone differences and adjust to American Indian children's generally lower levels of speech and accommodate rather than ask the child to speak louder since louder speech could be interpreted as indicating anger.

- Examiners should be aware that the response style of Indian children may be short, quick responses. Awareness of this style will enable the examiner to "catch responses" without asking children to repeat their answers.

- Examiners should be aware that the child may use variations on nonverbal cues. For example, when asked to "point," they may use a facial grimace or other gesture to indicate their response.

- Examiners who are familiar with the language of the child should still attend to possible dialectal differences.

- Examiners should be aware of cultural interactions. For example, McShane (1989) suggests that examiners sit across and to the side of the child being tested. The examiner can observe the child without having to stare directly at the child. Also, if the child shifts position, this could indicate discomfort in the testing situation.

By being sensitive to culturally appropriate behavior during the assessment process, the skilled clinician can establish rapport more easily and likely obtain the most accurate indication of the child's intellectual potential as measured by the IQ test.

In addition to the sociolinguistic variable, Williams (1987) notes the importance of incorporating culturally appropriate reinforcers in the assessment process. Similar considerations should be made for all racial or ethnic groups.

6.   *IQ tests must be interpreted on an individual basis by a "shrewd and flexible detective"* (Kaufman, 1990, p. 27).

Often the assessment process may yield what appears to be discrepant information. Teachers' reports may differ from information provided by family members or the individual being tested. The examiner must investigate in order to provide a comprehensive picture of the individual in his or her own cultural context based upon appropriate assessment practices. Knowing the community and culture in which the individual resides can provide vital information to supplement the IQ tests. Examiners familiar with a particular community can obtain cultural informants and consultants who create bridges into the culture and can be invaluable during the assessment process.

Testing the limits is also recommended to obtain valuable information regarding the individual's thought processes (Kaufman, 1994). The chapter authors often will go back over item responses and ask individuals to elaborate on their answers. For example, on a Picture Arrangement item, an examinee may be asked "tell me about your story." Questions can be raised as to whether the individual conceptualizes the story in an organized fashion. Kaufman (1994) notes that items may be failed based on the child's "cultural and subcultural background, which may teach different interpretations of situations that depict social interactions" (p. 88).

7.   *"Intelligence tests are best used to generate hypotheses of potential help to the person; they are misused when the results lead to harmful outcome"* (Kaufman, 1990, p. 27).

In the past, data obtained on standardized IQ tests have been used to indicate the inferiority of particular racial or ethnic groups. Numerous court cases have arisen when psychologists have failed to use tests appropriately (Sattler, 1992). Earlier, we wrote of the "six hour retardate" as an example of how tests have been used to the detriment of particular racial or ethnic groups. Unfortunately, there are many other examples that could be cited. It is important for the examiner to remember that hypotheses should be generated based upon multiple sources, including information from the clinical interview, behavioral observations, past records, collateral reports (for example, from teachers), supplementary tests, and others familiar with the culture to provide context, (Kaufman, 1994).

Case Example

Born to Ojibwa (American Indian) parents in 1960, Sue was referred for a diagnostic evaluation at the age of eight due to "uncontrolled" behavior. For the next thirteen years, her abilities and needs were assessed by a variety of well-known professionals from various disciplines. The following are brief excerpts from the various reports obtained from several agencies during this time period. Four major areas of diagnoses are represented: mental capacity, perceptual abilities, speech and language, and behavior.

Mental capacity. Evaluations noted signs of organic brain damage, citing problems in visual-motor functioning and slow speech. Results of an encephalogram indicated a large lesion in the right hemisphere of the brain and later reports suggested the possibility of a severe seizure disorder of major motor type.

Physicians and psychologists indicated that Sue scored within the mildly mentally retarded range with an overall Stanford-Binet IQ estimate of 60 on one testing and 75 on the next. Reports also revealed that Sue scored within the educable retarded range on verbal abilities, but performance abilities were higher. Entries in professional records stated the following: "I think Sue is disabled for any sort of economic independence, even with supervision in the future, and because of retardation and convulsive disorders she is totally and permanently incapacitated at this time." "Reports indicate both physical and mental impairment, Sue is certainly disabled for any sort of economic independence . . ." "Sue has severely reduced visual and auditory memory that precludes acquisition of even functional skills in reading, spelling or math."

There were, however, indicators of higher functioning that were not weighted as highly. A first-year intern who worked daily with Sue reported that he did not feel that she was retarded. Other physicians noted that Sue was capable of attending to her own personal needs. Despite these indicators, professionals continued to attribute Sue's low academic achievement to severely reduced mental ability.

Based on these test results, Sue was moved to a special rehabilitation school for the mentally retarded where she remained for approximately twelve years.

Perceptual abilities. Reports pertaining to Sue's perceptual-motor abilities indicated higher intellectual potential. Professionals at the rehabilitation school noted that Sue had adequate perceptual skills to learn to read; her perception of spatial relationships was especially well developed, her visual-motor coordination was good, she possessed excellent eye-hand coordination skills, artistic talent, good athletic ability, and good finger dexterity.

A rehabilitation school art teacher commented that Sue possessed unique art skills and produced precise beadwork. At a downtown arts center, another art teacher observed that Sue did a lot of beadwork, was a very capable designer, copied drawings from old masters, and drew from her imagination. Sue was able to sell some of her crafts for money.

Speech and language abilities. Over the years, physicians found that Sue had many attacks of acute otitis media, she had speech and hearing defects, and her eardrums showed scarring typical of chronic otitis media. Another physician charted thirty- to forty-decibel hearing loss in the left ear on a pure tone audiometer.

A consulting professional found that Sue knew letters but could not pronounce any words. Her "slow speech" was attributed to her "obvious" intellectual retardation. A speech pathologist remarked that Sue failed to grasp concepts requiring a higher level of conceptualization and mispronounced some words, had severely reduced auditory sequencing, poor sound blending and closure. However, he found her speech intelligible.

Sue's maternal grandparents (her caregivers from age four to six) spoke only Chippewa. It was noted that Sue's speech in English was broken and poorly enunciated. Teachers suggested that Sue had limited knowledge of many middle-class institutions and concepts, and poor speech and grammar—which, instead of indicating mental deficiency, may have been due to a lack of early childhood opportunity to learn proper speech. When pushed to work on a task that proved difficult for her, Sue was observed to "regress." During a "regression," her speech would take on a sing-song, teasing tone and become unintelligible.

Behavior. Records indicate that Sue had a history of uncontrolled aggression and disruptive classroom behavior. She was expelled from school because she was considered a menace to the class. Records indicated that Sue could be moderately cooperative although somewhat detached, and at times she appeared dazed. Sue was also observed to ramble incoherently.

Sue spent a great deal of time at home after being expelled from both kindergarten and first grade. According to social histories, Sue appeared to prefer to be alone, always liked to be busy, insisted on doing housework, and was not a discipline problem at home. She also had poor impulse control, and ventilated anger at others. However, her behavior showed improvement when she was placed in the new school. Her teachers described her as friendly, bright-eyed, alert, liking school, being no discipline problem at the new school, able and willing to follow directions, and having a good attention span when she wished. She did, however, display low tolerance for frustration, resulting in oppositional behavior characterized by regression to babyish type behavior. Sue displayed a definite talent for role playing and was described as a "very imaginative" young girl who "often acts out something she wants to explain."

Sue's teachers noted excellent progress in academic areas: "artistic skills and perseverance are major strengths," "model student with her personal qualities and her classroom behaviors," "shown more initiative and assertiveness this year, top salesperson."

What happened? Sue was considered mentally retarded because she was deficient in speech and language skills, obtained low scores on two IQ tests, and did poorly in school. The official diagnosis of retardation was based also on an accumulation of records and the clinical impressions of various observers. In fact, however, Sue's speech and language difficulties can be better explained as an accumulation of physiological, psychosocial, and cultural problems than by a basic lack of mental ability.

Sue was given the Stanford-Binet (note, older version) test of intelligence, an instrument that has been found to be inappropriate for use with American Indian subjects since it consistently underestimates their abilities (for example, see Guilliams, 1975; Rowe, 1914). She was also given one of the Wechsler Intelligence scales. Her scores followed the usual pattern for Indian subjects: a wide discrepancy between Verbal IQ (VIQ) and Performance IQ (PIQ), with the former serving to reduce her Full Scale IQ (McShane, 1980; McShane and Plas, 1984a). This profile, which often suggests the need for further evaluation when seen in White populations, is frequently observed in Indians. For the Indian population, a discrepancy between VIQ and PIQ may be viewed as normative. Sue's PIQ, the best estimate of overall cognitive ability for American Indians, fell in the low average range; in no way should it have been stretched to suggest retardation. In terms of educational achievement, although teachers remarked that Sue made progress at times, she was so often absent from school she had little opportunity to learn. In fact, she did not attend school consistently until about age eight or nine, at which point she entered a special school.

In addition to misinterpreting data and information, miscommunication of diagnostic inferences occurred between professionals. Although a school psychologist, a neurologist, and a physician suggested brain damage (specifically a right hemisphere lesion), a later computerized tomography (CT) scan displayed no cerebral abnormalities. Professionals' perceptions of Sue's mental abilities became more negative over the years: "mild mental deficiency," "educable range of mentally defective," "obviously intellectually retarded," progressed to "severely reduced mental ability," "disabled for any sort of economic independence (even with supervision), because of retardation" and finally to "totally and permanently incapacitated." This increasingly pessimistic forecast continued despite evidence to the contrary, such as an increase in IQ from one testing session to the next, demonstrated economic success (making and selling quality beadwork), and good academic progress during periods of consistent school attendance.

There were diametrically opposed views of Sue's perceptual abilities. At least two physicians stated that, as a result of severe perceptual problems, Sue would never be able to read, do math, and so on. However, her PIQ scores, her beautiful beadwork and drawing, good athletic ability, and several comments by individual professionals, clearly demonstrated that the young Indian girl possessed at least average (and in some specific areas, exceptional) visual-spatial abilities and visual-motor skills.

Sue was perceived to have "slow speech" and specific problems in certain areas. Evidence in the records stated that she suffered repeated bouts of tonsillitis and middle ear infection before the age of five. As already noted, her eardrums showed scarring typical of chronic otitis media and by age eight she had a thirty- to forty-decibel loss in at least one ear. A speech and language assessment showed severely reduced ability in auditory sequencing, closure, and producing multisyllable words, deficits often associated with the type of conductive hearing loss Sue suffered. Unremediated, such hearing loss has been found not only to cause verbal impairment and language delay, but also reduced verbal IQ, lowered educational achievement, and emotional difficulties (McShane, 1980). Although she was expelled from both kindergarten and first grade, no one ever addressed her hearing problem.

In addition to her physiological problems, there were two psychosocial influences on her language development to be considered. From age four to six, Sue was cared for by her paternal grandparents, who spoke only Chippewa. It is likely that a two-year experience with another language at this critical age period would affect her acquisition of English.

Finally, Sue was taking at least three drugs for seizure control. These drugs have specific behavioral effects, such as slow or slurred speech, lethargy, and confusion, all of which might create the impression of speech problems and limited ability. Given the high doses in which she was taking these drugs, it is perhaps surprising that Sue could communicate as well as she did. In summary, the speech and language problems Sue exhibited could be related to hearing loss, to lack of educational experience, to psychocultural influences, and to possible drug side effects.

Sue was frequently absent from school. On more than one psychological assessment, Sue displayed a preoccupation with threatening, destructive topics, often with sexual overtones, as well as "babyish" regressive behavior. Bizarre ideation as well as aggressive and withdrawn behaviors in school eventually resulted in her being expelled. However, none of her many examiners explored the possibility that, because of negative life events, Sue might have severe psychological and psychosocial problems that might necessitate in-depth psychotherapy and psychosocial intervention. In fact, it was discovered only late in her history that Sue had suffered from the drinking and sexual acting-out of her stepfather and that this had begun when she was very young. Ironically, before this was revealed, Sue had been placed in the custody of her stepfather and mother, who used her "disability" checks for purposes other than to secure proper clothing and food for her. Although Sue had made attempts to communicate her extreme situation, little seriousness was attached to these unreliable "incoherencies" concerning sexual abuse.

This case highlights the importance of integrating test scores with information obtained from multiple sources and contextualizing the assessment process. The serious consequences that can occur as a result of the inappropriate use of test scores are evidenced in this case. Specific multicultural issues are indicated as well as more general concerns regarding appropriate psychological assessment practices.

Summary and Conclusions

In this chapter, we have attempted to provide the reader with information regarding the assessment process and usage of intelligence measures with diverse populations. While we have not covered all of the intelligence instruments currently available, nor provided an exhaustive review of the literature pertaining to the tests highlighted, we hope that readers have gained an understanding of the importance of following an assessment guide in gathering vital information in intelligence assessment. This process involves observing the individual in different settings, selecting appropriate test instruments, and integrating the information into a comprehensive interpretation of the individual at a particular point in time. Bias in assessment can be significantly reduced or prevented through appropriate test selection and sensitive administration and interpretation of scores within a cultural and environmental context.

References

Armour-Thomas, E. (1992). Intellectual assessment of children from culturally diverse backgrounds. *School Psychology Review, 21*(4), 552–565.

Azar, B. (1995, January). Search for intelligence beyond 'g'. *The APA Monitor, 26*(1), 1.

Boring, E. G. (1923, June). Intelligence as the tests test it. *New Republic,* 35–37.

Browne, D. B. (1984). WISC-R scoring pattern among Native Americans of the northern plains. *White Cloud Journal, 3*(2), 3–16.

Cattell, R. B. (1963). Theory of fluid and crystallized intelligence: A critical experiment. *Journal of Educational Psychology, 54*(1), 1–22.

Cole, M., & Bruner, J. S. (1971). Culture difference and inferences about psychological processes. *American Psychologist, 26,* 867–876.

Dana, R. H. (1993). *Multicultural assessment perspectives for professional psychology*. Needham Heights, MA: Allyn & Bacon.

Educational Testing Service. (1988). A summary of data collected from Graduate Student Record Examinations test takers during 1986–87, *Data Summary Report #12*. Princeton, NJ: Author.

Educational Testing Service. (1994). *GRE: 1994–1995 guide to the use of the Graduate Record Examinations program*. Princeton, NJ: Author.

Fallows, J. (1980). The tests and the "brightest." How fair are the college boards? *The Atlantic, 245*(2), 37–48.

Fraser, S. (Ed.). (1995). *The bell curve wars: Race, intelligence, and the future of America*. New York: HarperCollins.

Gardner, H. (1987). The theory of multiple intelligences. *Annals of Dyslexia, 37*, 19–35.

Guilford, J. P. (1988). Some changes in the structure-of-intellect model. *Educational and Psychological Measurement, 48*(1), 1–4.

Guilliams, C. (1975). *Item analysis of American and Chicano responses of the vocabulary scales of the Stanford-Binet LM and Wechsler batteries*. (ERIC Document Reproduction Service No. ED 346 082).

Harrison, P. L., Kaufman, A. S., Hickman, J. A., & Kaufman, N. L. (1988). A survey of tests used for adult assessment. *Journal of Psychoeducational Assessment, 6*, 188–198.

Hawk, B. A., Schroeder, S. R., Robinson, G., Otto, D., Mushak, P., Kleinbaum, D., & Dawson, G. (1986). Relation of lead and social factors to IQ of low-SES children: A partial replication. *American Journal of Mental Deficiency, 91*(2), 178–183.

Helms, J. E. (1992). Why is there no study of cultural equivalence in standardized cognitive ability testing? *American Psychologist, 47*(9), 1083–1101.

Herrnstein, R. J., & Murray, C. (1994). *The bell curve: Intelligence and class structure in American life*. New York: Free Press.

Jackson, G. D. (1975). Another psychology view from the Association of Black Psychologists. *American Psychology, 30*, 88–93.

Jacoby, R., & Glauberman, N. (Eds.). (1995). *The bell curve debates*. New York: Random House.

Jensen, A. R. (1995). Psychological research on race differences. *American Psychologist, 50*(1), 41–42.

Jensen, A. R., & Reynolds, C. R. (1982). Race, social class, and ability patterns on the WISC-R. *Personality and Individual Differences, 3*(4), 423–438.

Kaufman, A. S. (1990). *Assessing adolescent and adult intelligence*. Needham Heights, MA: Allyn & Bacon.

Kaufman, A. S. (1994). *Intelligent testing with the WISC-III*. New York: Wiley.

Kaufman, A. S., McLean, J. E., & Reynolds, C. R. (1991). Analysis of WAIS-R factor patterns by sex and race. *Journal of Clinical Psychology, 47*(4), 548–557.

Laosa, L. M. (1984). Ethnic, socioeconomic, and home language influences upon early performance on measures of ability. *Journal of Educational Psychology, 76*(6), 1178–1198.

Lesser, G. S., Fifer, G., & Clark, D. H. (1965). Mental abilities of children from different social-class and cultural groups. *Monographs of the Society for Research in Child Development, 30*(4, Whole No. 102).

Little, S. G. (1992). The WISC-III: Everything old is new again. *School Psychology Quarterly, 7*(2), 136–142.

Lynn, R. (1977). The intelligence of the Japanese. *Bulletin of the British Psychological Society, 30*, 69–72.

Lynn, R., & Hampson, S. (1985–86). The structure of Japanese abilities: An analysis in terms of the hierarchical model of intelligence. *Current Psychological Research and Reviews, 4*(4), 309–322.

Mainstream science on intelligence. (1994, December 13). *The Wall Street Journal*, p. A18.

McShane, D. (1980). A review of scores of American Indian children on the Wechsler intelligence scale. *White Cloud Journal, 1*(4), 3–10.

McShane, D. (1989, April). *Testing and American Indians, Alaska Natives*. Sponsored by the National Commission on Testing and Public Policy. Symposium concerning the effects of testing on American Indian and Alaska Natives, Albuquerque, NM.

McShane, D., & Berry, J. W. (1988). Native North Americans: Indian and Inuit abilities. In S. H. Irvine & J. W. Berry (Eds.), *Human abilities in a cultural context* (pp. 385–426). New York: Cambridge University Press.

McShane, D. A., & Cook, V. J. (1985). Transcultural intellectual assessment: Performance by Hispanics on the Wechsler scales (pp. 737–785). In B. B. Wolman (Ed.), *Handbook of intelligence: Theories, measurement, and applications*, New York: Wiley.

McShane, D. A., & Plas, J. M. (1984a). The cognitive functioning of American Indian children: Moving from the WISC to the WISC-R. *School Psychology Review, 13*(1), 61–73.

McShane, D. A., & Plas, J. M. (1984b). Response to a critique of the McShane and Plas review of American Indian performance on the Wechsler Intelligence Scales. *School Psychology Review, 13*(1), 83–88.

President's Committee on Mental Retardation. (1969). *The six-hour retarded child: A report on a conference on problems of education of children in the inner city* (pp. 1–26). Washington, DC: U.S. Government Printing Office.

Reschly, D. J. (1990). Aptitude tests in educational classification and placement. In G. Goldstein & M. Hersen (Eds.), *Handbook of psychological assessment* (2nd ed., pp. 148–172). New York: Pergamon Press.

Reynolds, C. R. (1982). The problem of bias in psychological assessment. In C. R. Reynolds & T. B. Gutkin (Eds.), *The handbook of school psychology* (pp. 178–208). New York: Wiley.

Reynolds, C. R., Chastain, R. L., Kaufman, A. S., & McLean, J. E. (1987). Demographic characteristics and IQ among adults: Analysis of the WAIS-R standardization sample as a function of the stratification variables. *Journal of School Psychology, 25*, 323–342.

Reynolds, C. R., Willson, V. L., & Hickman, J. A. (1988). Black-White differences in American children's patterns of information processing independent of overall ability differences. In D. H. Saklofske & S.B.G. Eysenck (Eds.), *Individual differences in children and adolescents* (pp. 303–312). Sevenoaks, Kent, Great Britain: Hodder & Stoughton.

Rogers, M. R. (1993). Psychoeducational assessment of racial/ethnic minority children and youth. In H. B. Vance (Ed.), *Best practices in assessment for school and clinical settings* (pp. 399–440). Brandon, VT: Clinical Psychology Publishing Company.

Rowe, E. C. (1914). Five hundred forty-seven White and two hundred sixty-eight Indian children tested by the Binet-Simon tests. *Pedagogical Seminary, 21*, 454–468.

Sattler, J. M. (1992). *Assessment of children* (Revised and updated 3rd ed.). San Diego: Author.

Sowell, T. (1978). Race and IQ reconsidered. In T. Sowell (Ed.), *Essays and data on American ethnic groups* (pp. 203–229). New York: Urban Institute.

Spearman, C. (1927). *The abilities of man.* New York: Macmillan.

Sternberg, R. J. (1988). A triarchic view of intelligence in cross-cultural perspective. In S. H. Irvine & J. W. Berry (Eds.), *Human abilities in cultural context* (pp. 60–85). New York: Cambridge University Press.

Suzuki, L. A., & Gutkin, T. B. (1993, August). *Racial/ethnic ability patterns on the WISC-R and theories of intelligence.* Paper presented at the 101st annual convention, American Psychological Association, Toronto, Canada.

Tanner-Halverson, P., Burden, T., & Sabers, D. (1993). WISC-III normative data for Tohono O'odham Native-American children. *Journal of Psychoeducational Assessment: WISC-III Monograph*, 125–133.

Taylor, R. L, & Richards, S. B. (1991). Patterns of intellectual differences of Black, Hispanic and White children. *Psychology in the Schools, 28*, 5–8.

Thorndike, R. L., Hagen, E. P., & Sattler, J. M. (1986). *Technical manual for the Stanford-Binet Intelligence Scale* (4th ed.). Chicago: Riverside.

Thurstone, L. L. (1941). *Factorial studies of intelligence.* Chicago: University of Chicago Press.

Vance, H. B., & Hankins, N. (1978). Analysis of cognitive ability for rural White culturally different children. *The Journal of Psychology, 98*, 15–21.

Vance, H. B., Hankins, N., & McGee, H. (1979). A preliminary study of Black and White differences on the revised Wechsler Intelligence Scale for Children. *Journal of Clinical Psychology, 35*(4), 815–819.

Vance, H. B., Huelsman, C. B., & Wherry, R. J. (1976). The hierarchical factor structure of the Wechsler Intelligence Scale for Children as it relates to disadvantaged White and Black children. *The Journal of Genetic Psychology, 95*, 287–293.

Vane, J. R., & Motta, R. W. (1990). Group intelligence tests. In G. Goldstein & M. Hersen (Eds.), *Handbook of psychological assessment* (2nd ed., pp. 102–122). New York: Pergamon Press.

Vernon, P. E. (1979). *Intelligence: Heredity and environment.* San Francisco: Freeman.

Wechsler, D. (1981). *Manual for the Wechsler Adult Intelligence Scale-Revised.* San Antonio, TX: The Psychological Corporation.

Wechsler, D. (1991). *Manual for the Wechsler Intelligence Scale for Children-Third Edition.* San Antonio, TX: Psychological Corporation.

Wechsler, D. (1989). *Manual for the Wechsler Preschool and Primary Scale of Intelligence-Revised.* San Antonio, TX: Psychological Corporation.

Weiss, L. G., Prifitera, A., & Roid, G. (1993). The WISC-III and the fairness of predicting achievement across ethnic and gender groups. *Journal of Psychoeducational Assessment: WISC-III Monograph*, 35–42.

Whitworth, R. H., & Gibbons, R. T. (1986). Cross-racial comparison of the WAIS and WAIS-R. *Educational and Psychological Measurement, 46*, 1041–1049.

Wilgosh, L., Mulcahy, R., & Watters, B. (1986). Identifying gifted Canadian Inuit children using conventional IQ measures and nonverbal (performance) indicators. *Canadian Journal of Special Education, 2*(1), 67–74.

Williams, C. L. (1987). Issues surrounding psychological testing of minority patients. *Hospital and Community Psychiatry, 38*(2), 184–189.

Yee, A. H., Fairchild, H. H., Weizmann, F., & Wyatt, G. E. (1993). Addressing psychology's problems with race. *American Psychologist, 48*, 1132–1140.

7

The Use of Curriculum-Based Measurement with Diverse Learners

Mark R. Shinn and Scott K. Baker

To many readers of this chapter, its contents likely will appear to be quite different from the other chapters in this book. In fact, a significant number of readers will be very unfamiliar with the content. The topic is Curriculum-Based Measurement (CBM), the use of standardized, short-duration fluency measures of basic literacy and math skills (that is, reading, spelling, written expression, and mathematics computation) to make decisions about instructional effectiveness (Deno, 1989; Fuchs, 1993; Shinn, 1989a). Our use of CBM is likely to be more familiar to readers of the special education or school psychology literature than to other psychologists or mental health professionals.

Familiarity issues aside, this chapter is likely to be perceived as noticeably different from the others in the beliefs and premises that underlie the use of CBM with students from diverse backgrounds. First, this chapter is predicated on a belief that what should be assessed is not the uniqueness of coming from a minority or

Note: The development of this chapter was supported, in part, by Grant No. H023C10151 from the U.S. Department of Education, Office of Special Education Research, to conduct research in using Curriculum-Based Measurement to facilitate reintegration of students with mild disabilities into general education classrooms. The views expressed within this paper are not necessarily those of the U.S. Department of Education. Portions of the case studies were presented in Shinn (1995) and Shinn, Collins, and Gallagher (in press).

linguistically different background; *uniqueness should not be the predominant focus of assessment*. Other chapters will identify various special ways of collecting or interpreting data (for example, intelligence or personality testing) that are specific to members of a particular group (such as language minority or African American students). We are not proposing that what should be assessed is always the same in every instance or that cultural difference is unimportant to human behavior and should be ignored. Instead, we argue that what should be assessed to the greatest degree possible are the *commonalities* of all children's needs as they relate to becoming successful members of society. We propose that one of the fundamental commonalities is the development of literacy skills.

Second, we believe that this chapter differs from others in the focus of assessment, or of the *why* and *how* we assess. Instead of focusing our efforts primarily at assessing individual differences at the learning characteristic levels (such as intellectual ability or learning or processing abilities) for purposes of diagnosis, we propose assessing individual differences in regard to the students' responsiveness to instruction. We propose shifting the purpose of assessment from diagnosis of (dis)abilities to examining the effectiveness of our interventions to enhance student achievement of important educational outcomes. Our assessment focus should be to find instructional practices that work to meet the academic needs of children from diverse backgrounds (Shinn and Good, 1993). The most important technical feature of our assessment activities therefore should be treatment validity (Hayes, Nelson, and Jarrett, 1987); assessment should lead to development of interventions that result in significantly improved student outcomes. This assessment approach requires us to shift how we assess from a summative evaluation approach (that is, determining what a student has learned) to a formative evaluation approach (that is, determining what a student is learning). Formative evaluation requires us to collect data on an ongoing basis because currently we do not have the technical expertise to know in advance how well an instructional program will work for any individual student (Deno, 1986). For more information on this approach, see Deno (1991).

Finally, this chapter is likely different from the others in our selection of who we assess; the target population with whom CBM is best used is general education students in Grades 1 to 3 or 4 who are in the process of acquiring and mastering basic literacy skills. Many of these students have been referred for, or receive, remedial services such as Chapter I or bilingual education, or special education services under the mild disabilities categories of learning disabilities, educational mental retardation, or behavior disorder. We believe that a great deal of educational attention should be focused on students at these ages to prevent the development of severe learning problems and that early intervention maximizes the likelihood that all children will experience successful educational outcomes.

Problems of Illiteracy

It is well established that significant numbers of Americans are functionally illiterate. Estimates of current adult illiteracy are between 21 percent and 23 percent (Office of Educational Research and Improvement [OERI], 1992). The problem of illiteracy in America is actually worsening. Literacy scores of young adults are 11 to 14 points lower today than they were in 1985. The problem of illiteracy is more severe for persons from diverse backgrounds. For example, Adams (1990) reports that illiteracy rates among minority youth are approximately 40 percent. According to *The Condition of Education Report* (National Center for Education Statistics [NCES], 1992) at ages nine, thirteen, and seventeen, Black and Hispanic students score 1⅓ SD (20 points) below Whites on reading and math achievement tests. According to the *Trends in Academic Progress Report* (National Assessment of Educational Progress, 1991) this gap has not narrowed since 1982. For example, Hispanic nine- and thirteen-year-olds are reading at the same level in 1990 as 1975.

The consequences of illiteracy are well established. For example, illiteracy is strongly associated with high rates of school drop out (Ysseldyke, Algozzine, and Thurlow, 1992), which are estimated to be around 30 percent nationally for high school students (Center for the Study of Social Policy, 1991) Drop-out rates are even higher rates for students from diverse cultural backgrounds. Hispanic students, for example, are almost two-and-a-half times more likely to drop out than White students (33 percent versus 12.4 percent). Some school districts where Hispanic students constitute the majority report drop-out rates as high as 50 percent (OERI, 1991). In major urban settings, this figure can approach 70 percent (Arias, 1986). Among the most serious consequences for school dropouts is limited career earning power. Students without a high school education have twice the unemployment rate and a standard of living that is more than 40 percent lower than twenty years ago in constant dollars (Carnegie Council on Adolescent Development, 1989). Illiteracy also is strongly associated with unemployment and crime. Of the chronically unemployed, approximately 85 percent are functionally illiterate (Adams, 1990). Of the prison population, illiterate adults make up 60 percent.

In sum, the illiteracy problem is severe, especially among diverse learners. The consequences of the problem are known, and the situation is not improving. We remain optimistic that with the right focus, including assessment, the problem of illiteracy can be addressed effectively. Of the social ills that trouble America, illiteracy is among the most solvable. In addition, solving the literacy problem will undoubtedly have a positive affect on other social problems including crime, unemployment, drug abuse, and teenage pregnancy. As stated by McGill-Franzen and Allington (1991), "It is a question of will. We know how to accelerate the literacy development of low achieving schools . . . we can organize our schools so that all children are entitled to literacy. . . . We have evidence that better programs can be implemented and for long-term costs not substantially different than what we now spend" (pp. 28–29).

One of the most powerful effects educators can have to ensure full literacy development as well as to facilitate school success is to have all students attain adequate levels of reading by the time they move into content-area subjects, usually around the fourth grade (Adams, 1990). Stanovich (1986) has outlined some of the long-term negative consequences of not acquiring adequate reading skills during the first years of schooling. Juel's longitudinal study (1988) has demonstrated how unlikely it is that students will catch up with their average-achieving peers if they do not get off to a good start in reading acquisition.

Current Testing Practices

Most current assessment efforts are designed to search for within-the-child explanations for why children are failing to acquire the necessary academic skills to become literate. Assessors test students to find their processing problems, memory problems, attention problems, psychological problems, plus a number of other deficiencies. With respect to reading problems, reading experts generally agree that this type of testing approach is not correct. For example, McGill-Franzen and Allington (1991) state that despite our good intentions, poor general education reading programs and separate specialized programs for students with reading problems are to blame for the bulk of reading problems observed in school today. Bardon (1988) also argues that a search for within-student pathology is misplaced and that more emphasis needs to be devoted to what students must learn to be successful.

Problems with Current Approaches

Garcia and Pearson (1994) indicate that two reasons for the current educational assessment reform movement are that reliance on traditional published tests with their multiple-choice format was responsible for many of the current problems in public education, and that data from published tests has a "pernicious influence on the lives and well-being of students, particularly low-income students" (p. 338). Discussions of assessment strategies with students from diverse backgrounds invariably emphasize the latter, including a section on the harmful effects published tests have had on the welfare of students. The tests themselves are blamed, as this quote from Garcia and Pearson (1994) indicates: "The political logic of those who rely on assessment as an instrument of reform seems, ironically, to stem from a deep-seated belief that assessment has been responsible for many of our current educational woes: Since curriculum-narrowing, standardized, multiple-choice tests created the problems from which schools, teachers, and students now suffer, the key to a liberating curriculum must be an assessment system in which broader, more challenging, and more authentic educational values are operationalized and promoted" (p. 337). Garcia and Pearson's summation of published tests can be discussed most usefully in the context of test validity. We argue that validity is not a thing or a number that tests have or do not have but rather a process that individuals use to make decisions that affect people. For example, in the criminal justice system, a valid decision-making process can be thought of in the jury's attempt to weigh evidence from multiple sources to arrive at a verdict that accurately reflects the quality and quantity of the evidence before them.

Messick's conceptualization of test validity (1989) echoes components of the criminal judgment system: "Validity is an *integrated evaluative judgment* of the degree to which empirical evidence and theoretical rationales support the adequacy and appropriateness of inferences and actions based on test scores or other modes of assessment" (p. 13, emphasis added). If validity is an integrated evaluative judgment, then the burden of proof for documenting the validity of using any test score to make a decision about a student does not depend on the absolute "reliability and validity" of the test but on educators who make decisions based on test scores and other data. Clearly, the strongest evidence of test validity is derived from documentation that the inferences and actions educators make on the basis of test scores lead to positive outcomes for students.

Many different assessment solutions have been offered to address the needs of students from diverse backgrounds. Most of these have threatened to merely reconfirm the usual approach of utilizing published tests in decision making. The tendency has been to search for the right test or procedure and to think only cursorily about the purposes behind data collection. For example, Mercer (1979) proposed the System of Multicultural Pluralistic Assessment (SOMPA) to assess in a culturally fair way the performance of low-income students. The SOMPA modifies students' WISC-R scores on the basis of age and sociocultural background to predict student potential. In general, the modified WISC-R scores predict achievement less well than traditional WISC-R scores (Figueroa and Sassenrath, 1989), and critics also have argued that separate norms are too costly to develop, do not provide for important comparisons with the general population, and do not in truth take into account the complexity of cultural identity despite giving the appearance of doing so (Mercer, 1989; Samuda, 1975).

With students from non-English-dominant backgrounds, a popular practice has been to translate English tests such as the WISC-R into languages such as Spanish and then test students in their native language (Caterino, 1990; Figueroa, 1990). Many educators have pointed out the numerous problems associated with this practice. For example, Figueroa (1990) concludes that a "translated test is a mystery test whose scores defy interpretation" (p. 98). Olmedo (1981) points out that "translated items may exhibit psychometric properties substantially different from those of the original English items" (p. 1083). Finally, the *Standards for Educational and Psychological Testing* (American Educational Research Association, American Psychological Association, and National Council on Measurement in Education, 1985) stated that "When a test is translated from one language or dialect to another, its reliability and validity for the uses intended in the linguistic groups to be tested should be established" (p. 75). Establishing the reliability and validity of translated tests is done rarely, if ever (Figueroa, 1990).

Changing the Focus

We concur that published tests have played too large a role in educational and psychological decision making, not just with students from diverse backgrounds. As stated by Deno, "it is not that we lack data, but that we collect the wrong data" (1986, p. 358). We do not believe the data are "wrong" because they are obtained from tests that are "standardized." In fact, we argue that standardized tests (that is, tests that are created, administered, and interpreted in a consistent manner) are necessary to make between-person comparisons and within-person comparisons over time. What we consider to be the "wrong data" is information that does not lead to solutions that address the needs of students from diverse backgrounds; in other words, data that do not lead to better instructional decisions.

A general consensus is beginning to build among educators that assessment and instruction should be integrally related. That is, assessment data should reflect instruction and the results of assessment data should be used to drive further instruction. Garcia and Pearson (1994) propose two solutions to link assessment to intervention more effectively. Both solutions fall under that category of alternative assessment strategies. The first is *authentic assessment,* which is defined as "how students are approaching, processing and completing 'real-life' tasks in a particular domain" (p. 357). Clearly, reading would fall under the category of a real-life task, and its authenticity in most primary classrooms in the country is without question. The second is *performance assessment* that represents or closely simulates performance in real-world settings, is inherently entangled with instruction, is grounded in the essence of the discipline being assessed, and includes in its scoring procedures something about the "reasonableness" of the procedures used to carry out the task or solve the problem.

The strength of these alternative assessment strategies is that they attempt to assess tasks that are part of important classroom instruction, assess performance on things that are important long-term skills and knowledge, and require that students actually engage in meaningful response formats during assessment. The disadvantages are also important. First, as with most recently developed educational concepts, various terms mean different things to different people. In other words, the distinctions between authentic, performance-based, and portfolio assessment are not yet clear. Second, the psychometric standards for decision making, which have provided a valuable anchor for traditional assessment practices, have not have not been well established with alternative assessment strategies. In fact, there is debate about whether traditional standards of psychometric evidence should apply to new forms of assessment (Moss, 1994). Third, a clear delineation of how alternative assessment strategies will be used in educational decision making has not been established. For example, distinctions between using data to determine student eligibility for special programs, monitoring student progress toward long-term goals, planning instructional programs, and evaluating the effectiveness of interventions either require that different data be collected or that extant data be examined differently.

What Is Curriculum-Based Measurement?

Curriculum-Based Measurement (CBM) is a specific type of a newer approach to assessing students' academic skills called Curriculum-Based Assessment (CBA). In brief, CBA approaches can be defined as any testing strategy that uses students' curriculum as the basis for decision making (Deno, 1986). Although the use of curriculum as testing materials is common to all types of CBA, they range from generally widespread approaches such as informal reading inventories (IRIs) to more specific testing and decision-making practices such as Curriculum-Based Assessment for Instructional Design (C-BAID; Gickling and Thompson, 1985). For more detail on a comparison of CBA approaches, see Shinn, Rosenfield, and Knutson (1989), Marston (1989), or Tindal (1993).

CBM differs from other CBA strategies on a number of dimensions.

Testing is accomplished using a limited number of standardized and validated measures of student performance in the basic skill areas of reading, spelling, mathematics computation, and written expression:

1. *In reading, students read aloud from basal readers for one minute.* The number of words read correctly per minute (that is, oral reading fluency) is the score of interest, with errors and accuracy scores as additional interpretive aids. Maze, a multiple-choice close reading technique, also has been validated as a CBM testing strategy (Fuchs and Fuchs, 1992). The number of correct word choices per five minutes is the primary metric.

2. *In spelling, students write words that are dictated at specified intervals (either five, seven, or ten seconds) for two minutes.* The number of correct letter sequences and words spelled correctly are counted.

3. *In written expression, students write a story for three minutes after being given a story starter* (for example, "Pretend you are playing on the playground and a spaceship lands. A little green person comes out and calls your name and . . . "). The number of words written, spelled correctly, or correct word sequences are counted.

4. *In mathematics, students write answers to computational problems via two-minute probes.* The number of correctly written digits is counted.

These simple measures were designed to be Dynamic Indicators of Basic Skills (DIBS), measuring "vital signs" or serving as "academic thermometers" of student achievement. See Deno (1992) for more background on the history of CBM. The measures are curriculum-based in that they are derived from the general education curriculum all students are expected to learn. Unlike commercially available achievement tests that are broad band (that is, they sample across numerous years of achievement with few items at a particular grade level), CBM employs a more narrow-band strategy and numerous test items. All test items on a particular CBM measure come from a student's annual curriculum. However, the tests also are not so narrow (that is, sampled only from a specific lesson) that they measure only recent and highly specific learning. For more detail on this topic see Fuchs (1993) and Fuchs and Deno (1991).

When this sampling procedure is combined with the use of a fluency metric, the result is an instrument that is Dynamic (D): that is, it is sensitive to between- and within-person change in a given area. This sensitivity allows for more precision in differentiating academic skills among students at one point in time (for example, identifying poor readers in a class) and evaluating an individual's progress over time (for example, identifying better reading now than two weeks earlier).

Furthermore, by relying on short-duration tests (that is, one to three minutes), these measures can be administered frequently, allowing change to be assessed on a routine, ongoing basis. Therefore, the short-term effects (over, say, four to six weeks) of instructional interventions can be measured. Effective instructional interventions can be maintained and ineffective interventions modified to improve student learning.

In addition to being dynamic, CBM scores are Indicators (I) of Basic Skills (BS) or literacy. They were validated to be correlates of key academic behaviors in reading, spelling and written expression, and mathematics computation. CBM measures were not designed to measure *all* behaviors in an academic domain. In reading, for example, oral reading is an excellent index of general reading proficiency including comprehension, but it does not provide information about such things as whether a student can separate fact from fiction or identify the compellingness of an author's argument. It is important to note that the use of CBM does not preclude using other specific skill measures of interest.

When used as DIBS, Curriculum-Based Measures work like an

educational thermometer. A thermometer does four things especially well. It can:

- Tell whether there is a health problem that warrants further investigation (for example, a temperature of 104.5 degrees F).

- Help understand the severity of the problem (a temperature of 104 is more severe than a temperature of 101).

- Inform a treatment provider whether a given intervention is effective (the temperature is reduced to 100.3 after aspirin).

- Tell when there is no longer a problem (the temperature is reduced to 98.6 degrees).

It is important to note that indicators such as thermometers typically do not tell you specifically what is wrong. For example, a thermometer would not inform a physician whether the cause of a high fever was a bacterial or viral infection or an attack of appendicitis.

Since 1978, an extensive program of research has validated the use of CBM tests in educational decision making. See Marston (1989) for an extensive summary of these validation studies. Most of the validation research has been conducted on CBM reading measures. Results suggest strongly that oral reading works well as an indicator of general reading proficiency, including comprehension, for most students. Efforts have supported the validity for students from diverse or minority backgrounds (Baker and Good, in press). Evidence has demonstrated construct validity (Shinn, Good, Knutson, Tilly, and Collins, 1992) as well as traditional conceptions of criterion-related validity, including correlations with accepted published measures of reading proficiency (for example, Deno, Mirkin, and Chiang, 1982; Fuchs, Fuchs, and Maxwell, 1988) and teacher ratings of reading achievement (Fuchs, Fuchs, and Deno, 1982).

Most importantly, across the domains of reading, spelling, and mathematics computation, CBM has been shown to have treatment validity. The use of CBM to evaluate the effects of instructional interventions and adjust them when necessary has resulted in significantly improved student achievement outcomes (Fuchs, Deno, and Mirkin, 1984; Fuchs and Fuchs, 1986; Fuchs, Fuchs, and Hamlett, 1989; Fuchs, Fuchs, Hamlett, and Allinder, 1991; Fuchs, Fuchs, Hamlett, and Stecker, 1991).

Reducing Illiteracy

We conceptualize three times when we can intervene to ensure that students develop basic literacy skills: before the skill or competency is actually needed (that is, a *preventative* approach); at the time the skill or competency is actually needed (that is, an *instructional* approach); and after the skill or competency is actually needed (that is, a *remedial* approach). The validity of the assessment procedures is tied directly to the effectiveness of our interventions. It is our perspective that increased attention to effective instructional approaches in general education classrooms should occur at the time a skill is needed (that is, during instruction) rather than later; this approach may reduce the need for later remediation.

Peer-Referenced Comparisons

CBM reading measures in the early grades can be used evaluate important skills at the time they are needed by documenting the distribution of reading skills for students from different backgrounds and by monitoring directly and frequently individual student reading progress over time. Illustrating the distribution of reading skills for students from diverse backgrounds, Figure 7.1 represents CBM reading performance data for all first- and second-grade students in a rural school district with a Hispanic population of over 60 percent. The per capita income in the community is the third lowest in the state, and 29.1 percent of the residents live below the official poverty line. Clearly, educators in this district have a legitimate reason to be

Figure 7.1 Distribution of CBM Reading Scores by Group by Grade.

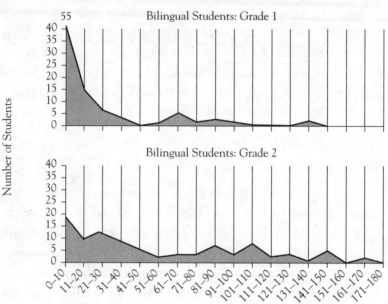

Words Read Correctly in English

concerned about student literacy because of the strong relation between poverty and literacy (Stanovich, 1986) and because of the connection between language minority status and the attainment of English literacy (NCES, 1992).

In Figure 7.1, the performance of all the students in Grades 1 and 2 in the district who were either monolingual English speakers or bilingual speakers with skills in Spanish and English is presented. A high percentage of the bilingual students received some form of bilingual education service or had otherwise been referred for remedial services because of low academic achievement. These data were collected in the winter, so not surprisingly in Grade 1 a very high percentage of the English-speaking students (34 percent) and the bilingual students (61 percent) were reading between 0 and 10 words correctly when administered a CBM reading probe from first-

Figure 7.1 Distribution of CBM Reading Scores by Group by Grade, Cont'd.

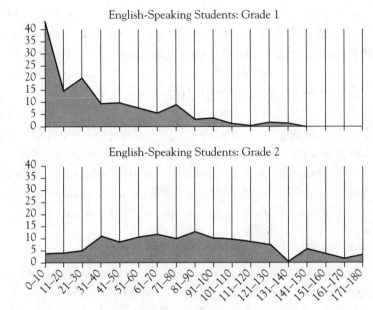

Words Read Correctly in English

grade reading material. By Grade 2, however, the percentage of English-speaking students reading between 0 and 10 words correctly per minute in second-grade material dropped to 3 percent, indicating that reading instruction from first to second grade was resulting in strong reading improvement for the vast majority of students. A similar pattern, although less dramatic, occurred with the bilingual students. By Grade 2, the percentage of bilingual students who were essentially nonreaders dropped from 61 percent to 18 percent. The higher percentage of bilingual students in the nonreading category may have been influenced by many variables, including differential instructional emphasis on English reading acquisition between groups of students and higher numbers of bilingual students with only rudimentary English skills.

The evidence does not suggest, however, that the CBM normative data are any less valid for the bilingual students than they are for the English-speaking students. In this same district, a sample of English-speaking second-grade students (n = 25) and second-grade bilingual students (n = 21) were administered the Reading Comprehension Subtest of the Stanford Diagnostic Reading Test (SDRT; Karlsen and Gardner, 1985). Not only was the magnitude of the correlation between the CBM reading fluency measure and the SDRT Reading Comprehension Subtest higher for the bilingual students compared to the English-speaking students (.73 versus .56), but the magnitude of the correlation is within the range of correlations typically reported between CBM reading measures and published measures of reading comprehension (Marston, 1989).

Individually Referenced Comparisons

Another way to consider these normative first- and second-grade CBM reading data is to consider what the educational implications might be for individual students. For example, in Figure 7.2 the progress monitoring data of two second-grade bilingual students who were administered CBM reading probes two times per week for ten weeks are presented. Their initial data point in the ten-week data collection period was their winter normative score, so it is possible to compare these two students to other Spanish- and English-speaking students in the district. In addition, a within-student comparison can be made over time. That is, Carmen and Miguel's reading performance can be compared over time to their previous performance. One of the significant advantages of CBM is that as short duration fluency measures, data can be collected frequently to make formative evaluations of student progress over time.

When the CBM norming data were collected, the average reading fluency score of bilingual students (n = 108) was fifty-three words read correctly. The average score for the English-speaking students (n = 127) was seventy-eight words read correctly. Both Carmen (score = 34) and Miguel (score = 42) scored below these means at the time of the winter norming. In terms of the individ-

Figure 7.2. Rates of Reading Progress for Carmen and Miguel.

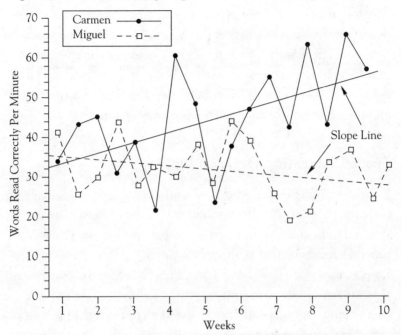

ual progress each student made over time, however, very different conclusions would be made about Carmen and Miguel. Carmen obviously is making much better progress than Miguel, and to the extent these different rates of progress represent important indicators of essential literacy skills, the value of a CBM progress monitoring system can be clearly seen. This value is enhanced when the reliability of these one-minute measures of reading are considered. For example, with the bilingual students in this study, a one-minute measure of reading was estimated to be .92. The reliability of the aggregate of five to ten one-minute measures was .99.

Some of the interesting considerations about the reading progress data of Carmen and Miguel are that not only did both students begin in the winter at about the same level of reading performance, but they also were in the same school, attended the same general education classroom, had the same reading teacher, and received essentially the same type of reading instruction. Different conclusions about the effectiveness of reading instruction might be drawn on the basis of whether one was talking about the progress of Carmen or Miguel. The point about evaluating the effectiveness of reading instruction may be extremely important as educators look for valid ways to assess how effective and sensitive instructional approaches are to the individual differences of students.

Special Education Decision Making

Even the most effective general education programs are unlikely to meet the needs of all students. Some students may need more intensive and individualized instructional programs than are provided in general education (that is, special education). As the preceding section detailed, CBM can be used in general education classrooms in the primary grades to identify systemic instructional deficiencies that require wide-scale intervention efforts to track the progress of individual students as they acquire literacy skills. This allows for instructional program deficiencies to be rectified for individual students in general education classrooms. To date, however, the primary use of CBM has been in special education decision-making practices.

In special education decision making, CBM is used in a Problem-Solving Model. This model is made up of five related but different steps: Problem Identification, Problem Certification, Exploring Solutions, Evaluating Solutions, and Problem Solution. Data collected during one step of the model may be used to facilitate decision making at subsequent steps. Descriptions of the Problem-Solving Model decisions and corresponding CBM procedures are presented in Table 7.1.

The need for additional assessment information is determined on a sequential basis. Sometimes, assessment activities stop after the first decision (Problem Identification) if a problem is not validated. Other times, assessment and decision making occur on a repeated basis throughout a student's educational career.

Table 7.1. CBM Problem-Solving Model Decisions, Measurement Activities, and Evaluation Activities.

Problem-Solving Decision	Measurement Activities	Evaluation Activities	Specific Tasks
Problem Identification	Observe and record student differences, if any, between actual and expected performance	Decide that a performance discrepancy exists	Peer-Referenced Assessment
Problem Certification	Describe the magnitude of differences between actual and expected performance in the context of likelihood of general education alone solving the problem	Decide if discrepancies are important enough that special services may be required for problem resolution	Survey-Level Assessment and identification of alternative intervention options
Exploring Solutions	Determine options for annual goals	Decide on annual goal(s) and actual content of intervention to be implemented	Write annual goal based on Survey-Level Assessment; Identify specific skill or strategy deficits
Evaluating Solutions	Monitor intervention implementation and changes in student performance	Determine if intervention is effective or should be modified	Collect progress monitoring data and compare with aimline
Problem Solution	Observe and record student differences, if any, between actual and expected performance	Decide if current discrepancies, if any, are not enough and special services may be reduced or eliminated	Repeat Peer-Referenced Assessment and Survey-Level Assessment

As described by Deno (1989), the Problem-Solving Model is predicated on a number of important assumptions. Among its most important tenets is that a problem is defined situationally, that is, as a discrepancy between what is expected and what occurs. Academic problems exist when a specific student does not perform the academic behavior(s) expected in a particular curriculum in a particular school or community. In other words, "Maurice is not learning to read the Scribner reading curriculum like the other students in third grade in Longfellow School." It is important to note that the corollary to this tenet is that a problem in one situation may not be a problem in another. In a different community with different expectations (that is, where typical students perform differently from typical Longfellow third graders), Maurice may *not* be considered to have a problem learning to read. Decisions about the need for additional resources are based on the severity of student academic need in the general education curriculum relative to local achievement expectations (Deno, 1986, 1989; Deno, Marston, and Tindal, 1985).

A second important assumption of the Problem-Solving Model is that educators must "generate many possible plans of action prior to attempting problem solution," (Deno, 1989, p. 11) and must evaluate the effects of the program actually implemented. Presently, we lack the assessment technology to say with certainty what instructional program will work with any student. We cannot say that Maurice will benefit from special education (or peer tutoring or Chapter I) in School A before we try it out. Therefore, we need to treat all of our interventions as testable hypotheses that must be evaluated formatively for each individual student. Interventions that show strong positive effects when they are evaluated are maintained; ineffective interventions are discarded or modified (Stoner and Green, 1992).

Using CBM in a Problem-Solving Model

Selected case studies will be used to illustrate how CBM is used within a Problem-Solving Model in special education decision making. For more detail about the specifics of using CBM in a Problem-Solving Model, the reader is encouraged to read Shinn (1989a).

Problem Identification

When a problem is suspected, it is important that time-efficient data are collected to help determine its relative importance. Problem Identification decisions involve collecting data to determine whether a problem warranting further investigation exists. As stated earlier, a problem is defined as a discrepancy between expected and actual student performance in the area of concern. When CBM is used within a Problem-Solving Model, *expected performance* represents the academic skill level that typical general education students display in typical general education curricula at the time a specific student is referred for a potential problem. This expected skill level is estimated by deriving same-grade "local norms" that represent students with similar acculturation or learning opportunities. *Actual performance* represents the academic skill level of the referred student in the same material used to generate the local norms. A potential problem is validated when a student's score is significantly below the typical performance of same-grade peers. If a referred student's performance is *not* significantly different from typical peers, it would be difficult to consider it a problem of sufficient magnitude to warrant assessment for special education eligibility, especially in light of the principle of the Least Restrictive Environment (LRE). For more information on this topic, see Shinn (1989b) or Shinn and Hubbard (1992). Two case studies—Anthony (a fifth-grade Hispanic student) and Dewanna (a fifth-grade African American student)—provide illustrations of the Problem Identification procedures.

Anthony

Anthony's mother requested that he be tested for special education eligibility because of her perceptions of his low math and reading skills. An important question is whether Anthony's mother's perceptions (or any other person's) are sufficiently accurate to warrant a time-consuming and expensive comprehensive assessment process. To attempt to validate a problem, Anthony was tested using samples of his fifth-grade math and reading curriculum materials with CBM procedures. His scores then were compared to the performances of fifth-grade peers who had been sampled randomly across Anthony's school district at around the same time of the school year. This norming process took place during the fall, winter, and spring of the school year. Alternatively, for Problem Identification decisions, his scores could have been compared to fifth graders from his own classroom or from his own school. For more information on developing CBM local norms see Habedank (1995) or Shinn (1989a).

Anthony was tested in math and reading for three to five days using repeated samples to obtain a broad sample of his skills. Shorter, yet repeated, samples can provide information on performance variability and reduce effects of "bad" days and examiner familiarity. In math, Anthony completed three randomly selected math probes, one each day, from the computational objectives of the district's general education fifth-grade math curriculum. The median number of digits Anthony completed correctly on the math probes (32 CD) was determined and compared to fifth-grade math norms (26 CD). In reading, Anthony read three different randomly selected passages each day from Level 5 of *Houghton Mifflin,* the district's general education reading series. The median number of words read correctly (WRC) and errors were determined. The overall reading median of 79 WRC then was compared to fifth-grade reading norm of 115 WRC.

The results of Anthony's Problem Identification testing compared to the school district's fifth-grade normative sample are presented in Table 7.2. These data are displayed graphically in Figure 7.3 to facilitate understanding by administrators, teachers, and parents. Three types of information are included on the graph:

- Anthony's daily math scores and median reading scores represented by the black dots.

Table 7.2. Results of CBM Problem Identification Testing for
Anthony, a Fifth Grader.

Academic Area Tested	Day 1	Day 2	Day 3	Overall Median	Peer Median
Math Grade 5 Probes					
CD	32	30	35	32 CD	26 CD
Reading Grade 5 Passages					
WRC Passage 1	77	89	68		
WRC Passage 2	80	85	70		
WRC Passage 3	79	78	75		
WRC Daily Median	79	85	70	79 WRC	115 WRC

Note: WRC = words read correctly; CD = correct digits.

- The median performance of his fifth-grade peers is represented by the heavy dark lines.

- The *cutting score* that Anthony's skills consistently had to fall below to be considered significantly discrepant from his peers is represented by the double lines.

In this example, the cutting scores were based on the sixteenth percentile and were the raw score that corresponded to that percentile rank. For more information on determining cutting scores for use in the Problem-Solving Model, see Shinn (1989b).

Decisions are made by comparing Anthony's scores to the cutting score and by examining any obvious explanations for any performance discrepancies. If his scores are *above* the cutting score, an important discrepancy warranting special education assessment may not exist. If Anthony's score is *below* the cutting score, a problem exists that may need to be assessed in further detail, *if* alternative explanations such as hearing, vision, health, school attendance, and behavior problems do not account for the problem.

Anthony's daily math scores consistently were above the math cutting score. Thus, no significant math problem was identified, and a more extensive mathematics skills assessment was not warranted.

Figure 7.3. Results of Anthony's Problem Identification Testing in Grade 5 Reading and Math Probes—Compared to Same-Grade Peers.

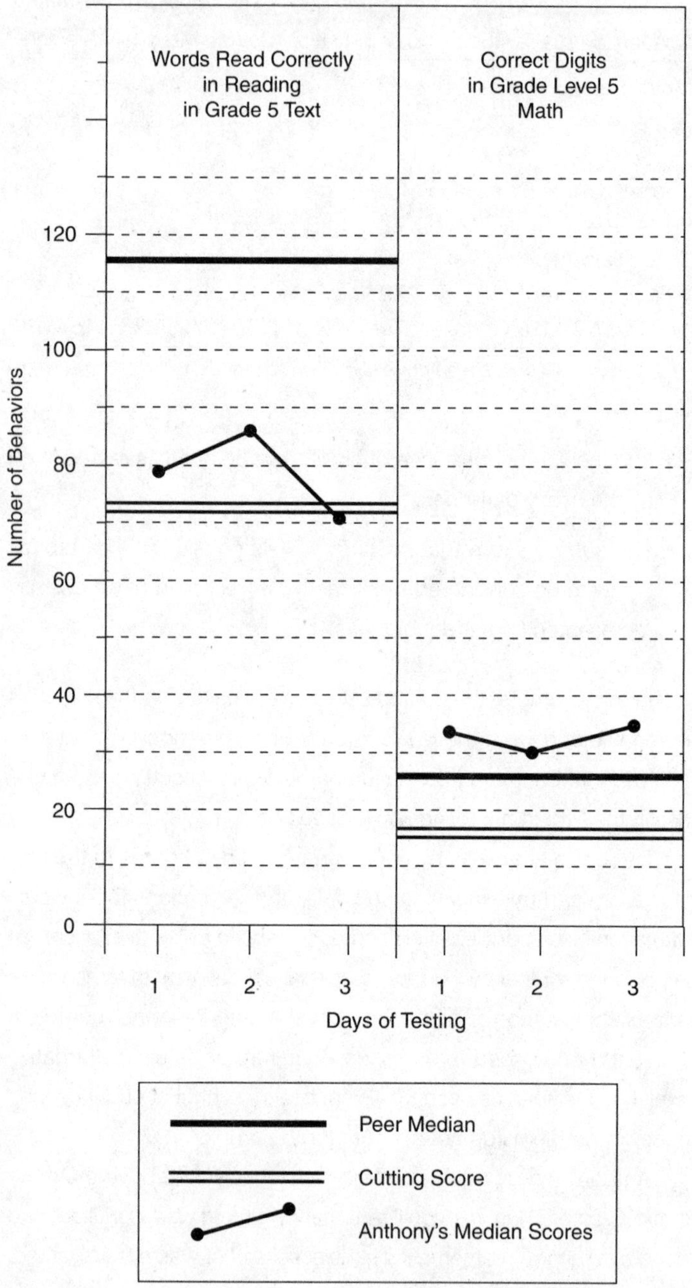

A similar conclusion was reached in reading. The data were helpful in assisting Anthony's teacher to develop a better general education reading program because qualitative information on his reading skills are embedded in the CBM reading measures. Skill strengths and deficiencies and strategies that may be contributing to his reading difficulties were identified, including: reading accuracy, type of reading errors, self-correction of reading errors, and speed of word recognition. Anthony read with a high degree of accuracy (96 percent) and his few reading errors seldom changed or interfered with the original meaning of the passages. Most of his errors involved omission of word endings ("ing" and "s") or articles ("a" and "the"). Anthony also frequently self-corrected his reading errors, a behavior that suggests he was reading for meaning. Most obviously, Anthony read slowly, which was potentially problematic because slowness often interferes with reading comprehension (Laberge and Samuels, 1974) and prevents students from completing schoolwork in a timely manner. To improve Anthony's reading rate, it was suggested that he engage in "repeated-reading" activities to supplement his classroom reading instruction.

Dewanna

Dewanna was referred for special education by her general education teacher because of potentially significant difficulties in math and reading. The testing procedures used to assess Dewanna's math and reading skills were identical to those described for Anthony. Dewanna's math and reading skills were assessed using typical fifth-grade math and reading material, and the results were compared to the math and reading scores of fifth-grade peers comprising the school district's norming sample. Dewanna's Problem Identification scores are presented in Table 7.3 and Figure 7.4. Because Dewanna was tested during the winter quarter, the cutting scores were based on winter norms from fifth graders sampled randomly from her school district.

Table 7.3. Results of CBM Problem Identification Testing for Dewanna, a Fifth Grader.

Academic Area Tested	Day 1	Day 2	Day 3	Overall Median	Peer Median
Math Grade 5 Probes					
CD	26	22	19	22 CD	41 CD
Reading Grade 5 Passages					
WRC Passage 1	52	43	50		
WRC Passage 2	46	45	49		
WRC Passage 3	43	41	42		
WRC Daily Median	46	43	49	46 WRC	128 WRC

Note: WRC = words read correctly; CD = correct digits.

Dewanna's reading and math scores fell at or below the cutting scores in math and reading. These data indicate that significant problems were identified and that additional testing might be necessary to resolve the problem. Because no obvious alternative explanations for these skill discrepancies were found (for example, chronic school attendance problems), it was decided that additional academic testing was necessary to determine the extent of Dewanna's educational needs and to provide resources for resolving her math and reading difficulties.

Problem Certification

The next decision of the Problem-Solving Model requires data to determine the severity of the problem. If a problem is of sufficient magnitude, additional resources (for example, special education) may be necessary. A problem is considered serious when a significant discrepancy between what is expected and what occurs is observed at grade level and lower levels of the general education curriculum. To measure this discrepancy and determine problem magnitude, a Survey-Level Assessment (SLA) using CBM is conducted in each academic area in which a problem has been identified. SLA involves testing the student in successive levels of the general education curriculum until a level is found at which the student performs success-

Figure 7.4. Results of Dewanna's Problem Identification Testing in Grade 5 Reading and Math Probes—Compared to Same-Grade Peers.

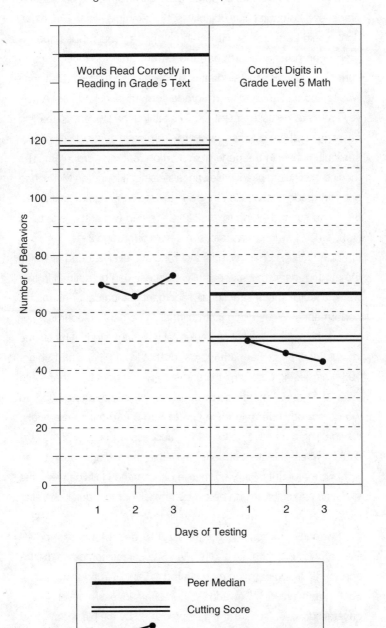

fully. A survey-level *math* assessment involves testing the student on math probes with items selected randomly from each successive grade-level computational objectives. For example, a fifth-grade student would be tested on fifth-grade computational probes, fourth-grade computational probes, and so on, until the level of math curriculum in which the student is successful is identified. Dewanna was tested on fifth- and fourth-grade computational probes. A survey-level *reading* assessment requires testing the student on reading passages that are selected randomly from each successive book or curriculum level in the general education reading curriculum. The reading curriculum used in Dewanna's district (Houghton Mifflin) had one fifth-grade text, one fourth-grade text, two third-grade texts (3–2, 3–1), two second-grade texts (2–2, 2–1), and two first-grade texts (1–2, 1–1). Dewanna was tested in Levels 5 through 2–1.

SLA testing continues until a curriculum level is found at which the student performs successfully. Success can be defined in two ways, according to instructional placement standards, or normative performance. When using instructional placement standards, success is the highest level of curriculum at which the student meets the instructional placement standards for that level (Fuchs and Shinn, 1989) or reading between forty and sixty words correctly per minute in Grade 1 and 2 materials, or between seventy and one hundred words correctly per minute in Grade 3 to 6 curriculum materials. When using normative performance, success is the level of the curriculum where the student performs within the average range of the local norm. Most typically normative performance falls between the sixteenth and eighty-fourth percentile ranks. For more detail on defining successful performance, see Shinn (1989b, 1995).

Normative performance was used to define success in Dewanna's district. Her math and reading SLA scores compared to fifth- and fourth-grade norms are presented in Table 7.4 and Figure 7.5. Each graph includes Dewanna's scores in successive levels of the general education curriculum, as represented by the black dots, and successive grade-level norms, as represented by the boxes.

Table 7.4. Results of CBM Problem Certification Testing Using
Survey-Level Assessment for Dewanna.

Academic Area	Curriculum Level	Dewanna's Median Performance	Grade-Level Peer Performance	Dewanna's Percentile Rank
Math	5	22	41	10th
	4	37	26	75th
Reading	5	46	128	2nd
	4	46	108	4th
	3–2	38	*	*
	3–1	37	90	7th
	2–2	59	*	*
	2–1	79	79	50th

Note: * = Local norms were developed only from one level of curriculum per grade. Therefore, no norms are available for these curriculum levels.

In math, according to the normative performance definition, Dewanna performed successfully in the computational curriculum for Grade 4. Her performance of thirty-seven correct digits fell within the average range of the Grade 4 math norm (seventy-fifth percentile). In reading, Dewanna performed most successfully in Level 2–1 of Houghton Mifflin. Her performance of seventy-nine words read correctly on Level 2–1 passages fell within the average range of the Grade 2 reading norm (fiftieth percentile).

Problem Certification decisions are based on student eligibility and need. In Dewanna's district, she could be determined eligible for special education services if her performance in problem areas fell below the sixteenth percentile in material one grade level below her current grade placement. Dewanna's scores were *above* the eligibility cutting score in math; she would not be considered eligible for special education because of mathematics needs. Observations of her math skills on the CBM tasks showed that although she completed many of the problems, a significant number were solved inaccurately. She frequently miscounted by one on addition problems and

Figure 7.5. Results of Dewanna's Survey-Level Assessment in Math, Comparing Her Performance to Same- and Other-Grade General Education Students.

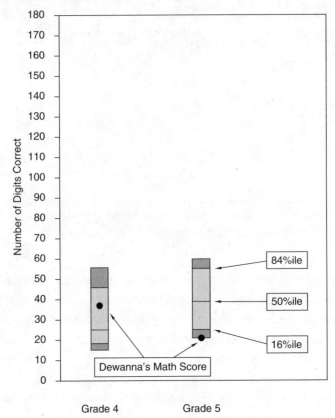

Curriculum Levels and Grade-Level Normative Ranges

added when she was supposed to subtract and multiply. However, she accurately solved addition, subtraction, and single-digit multiplication problems in isolation. This outcome indicates Dewanna did not attend to the math operation and worked carelessly. To address Dewanna's difficulties with multiple-digit multiplication problems, it was suggested that she be taught and given adequate opportunity to practice systematic strategies for solving multiple-digit multiplication problems and for self-monitoring the accuracy of her work.

In contrast, Dewanna's median reading score on the fourth-grade reading passages fell below the eligibility cutting score, meaning she could be found eligible for special education if it were determined that general education resources only were insufficient to resolve the reading problem. After considering the magnitude of Dewanna's reading problem and the resources necessary for implementing the recommendations, it was decided that Dewanna's reading problem likely would not be resolved using general education resources only, and thus she was found eligible for special education with an IEP objective required in reading.

Exploring Solutions

Thus far, this chapter has described the use of the Problem-Solving Model to provide a needs-based alternative assessment approach that arguably works as well or better than conventional eligibility determination activities (Shinn, 1989a). Unfortunately, psychologists and educators are less practiced and proficient in assessing students for the purposes of intervention planning and evaluation. Using CBM within the Problem-Solving Model can remedy this situation when students have academic problems. The Problem-Solving Model makes explicit the importance of assessment for intervention planning during the Exploring Solutions decision, in which a direct linkage between assessment for eligibility purposes and intervention planning occurs.

The purpose of Exploring Solutions is threefold: to specify the data-based goals of the intervention; the *content* of the intervention, or "what to teach"; and the *way* to deliver the intervention, or "how to teach." CBM is most useful for the goal-setting component of Exploring Solutions. The data collected during Problem Identification and Problem Certification are used for this purpose (Fuchs and Shinn, 1989). The mechanism for goal setting is the annual goal of a student's Individualized Education Plan (IEP). The basic idea is simple and works much like conventional practice; annual goals are based on identifying "where the student is now" and where the IEP team would like the student to perform in one year, if the intervention is successful. This process is illustrated using the following case study.

Sara

Sara, a third-grade African American student, was found eligible for special education in reading in the fall after Problem Identification and Certification decisions were made. As shown in Table 7.5, her SLA data showed her as "successful" in the Grade 1, Level 3 general education reading book. In one year, according to the publisher's scope-and-sequence, typical students would be *expected* to perform proficiently in Level 2 of the Grade 2 basal. If the IEP team wanted to write a goal that facilitated Sara's "catching up" with her peers (that is, reducing the discrepancy), they may want her to perform proficiently in a third-grade or even fourth-grade level of the basal series in one year. In Sara's case, the IEP team decided that they would consider the special education program to be successful if she performed proficiently in the Level 3–2 general education basal reader in one year.

CBM IEP goals use a long-term approach to goal setting. In this approach, measurement of progress toward the goal is designed to answer the question, Is the student becoming more proficient in reading, math, writing, or spelling in the general education curriculum? The advantages of using CBM and a long-term goal approach are discussed in more detail in Fuchs (1993) and Fuchs and Deno (1991).

The goal-setting process begins with identifying the academic area in which the goal is to be written so that the dynamic indicator for that content becomes the behavior to measure. Because Sara requires an annual goal in reading, the behavior component of the goal is oral reading. The second step is establishing the goal's *conditions*. The *time frame* is the time at which the goal is expected to be accomplished. In Sara's school system, all IEP goals expired on

Table 7.5. Reading Survey-Level Assessment for Sara, with Curriculum Level and Performance Relative to Local Norms.

Level of Ginn Curriculum	Sara's Median Performance	Grade-Level Peer Performance	Sara's Percentile Rank
3–2	27	100	2nd
3–1	27	NA	NA
2–2	32	NA	NA
2–1	37		15
1–3	49	NA	NA
1–2	55	**	**

Note: * = Local norms were developed only from one level of curriculum per grade level. Therefore, no norms are available for these curriculum levels. ** = No first-grade students were tested in the fall because most students entered with limited reading skills.

their anniversary date, one year from the time of writing. Therefore, Sara's annual goal would begin "In thirty-six weeks (one academic year), . . ." The next task is *specification of the level of curriculum* the student will be expected to perform proficiently in one year. This task requires knowledge of the general education curriculum scope-and-sequence, a judgment of how much is expected to be accomplished and the ramifications of how the problem is defined. See Fuchs and Shinn (1989) for more detail on this topic. Because Sara's IEP team specified Level 3–2 as the annual goal material, when combined with the time frame and the behavior, her goal so far would read as follows: "In 36 weeks, when given a randomly selected passage from Level 3–2 of the ABC Curriculum, Sara will read aloud . . ."

The final task in setting annual goals requires specification of a *criterion for performance.* The question for Sara is, How well do we want her to read the Level 3–2 basal, if her intervention program is to be considered successful? Two broad approaches can be used to identify a criterion for success, with or without local norms. In Sara's case, a local norm was used to set the criterion for success; the goal was written so that Sara would be expected to read as well as the typical third-grader in the fall, or one hundred words read correctly. In the absence of local norms, other strategies may be used to identify a criterion for success on the annual goal, including expert judgment or instructional placement standards.

The actual IEP annual goal written by Sara's IEP team was as follows: "In 36 weeks, when given a randomly selected passage from Level 3–2 of the ABC Curriculum, Sara will read aloud one hundred words correctly per minute." The team also added an accuracy criterion that she would read a randomly selected passage with five or fewer errors (approximately 95 percent accuracy). This goal was based on a rationale that a successful program would have Sara reading proficiently in an end-of-third-grade reader by the time she was in fourth grade.

Evaluating Solutions

The use of CBM Survey-Level Assessment data to write annual IEP goals links assessment for eligibility decision making to intervention planning. The use of CBM IEP goals links intervention planning to intervention evaluation by providing a standard for determining intervention effectiveness. The purpose of Evaluating Solutions is to monitor student progress toward IEP goals and in this way determine an intervention's effectiveness.

As with other decisions in the Problem-Solving Model detailed earlier, the annual goal can be represented graphically as shown in Figure 7.6 to clarify communication of expectations. In the figure, the expected rate of progress is translated into an aimline showing number of words to be read correctly in each week of the academic year. Her initial Survey-Level data in Level 3–2, the annual goal material, represents her current performance. The intersection of the criterion for success (100 words read correctly) and the goal date (36 weeks) forms her *aim*. The line drawn from her current performance to her aim forms her aimline or *expected rate of progress.*

Sara's actual rate of progress, or trendline, is traced in Figure 7.7. By comparing her *trendline,* determined by collecting samples of her reading from Level 3–1 over time, with her expected rate of progress,

Figure 7.6. Graphic Display of Sara's IEP Goal Translated into Expected Rate of Student Progress.

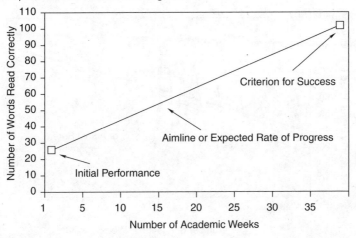

a decision can be made about treatment effectiveness and the need for program modification. When the actual rate of progress exceeds the expected rate of progress, the student's goal is raised. When the actual rate of progress is below the expected rate of progress, the student's intervention program is changed.

Progress monitoring data usually are collected once or twice per week by a special education teacher delivering the intervention or via a microcomputer (Fuchs, 1988; Fuchs, Hamlett, and Fuchs, 1990). In reading, students read one probe each testing occasion. Testing items are selected from a pool that represents the domain of *all* the items from the goal level of the curriculum. With Sara, this would represent a sample from all passages in the Level 3–2 basal reader. Probes are created by randomly selecting subsets of items from this large pool and student progress is measured repeatedly on these probes.

The results of testing Sara one to two times per week using randomly selected reading probes from Level 3–2 are shown in Figure 7.7. The data are plotted soon after testing on an equal interval graph. A minimum of ten data points are suggested before a reliable

Figure 7.7 Graphic Display of Sara's Rate of Progress Relative to Her IEP Goal.

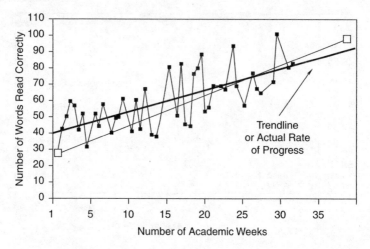

decision can be made about the effectiveness of an intervention program (Good and Shinn, 1990). On Sara's graph, after the first ten data points, it is clear that she is meeting or exceeding her expected rate of progress; nine of the ten data points are above the aimline. This is a good indication that the instructional intervention is effective and should be maintained. As the school year continued, Sara's teacher continued to evaluate her progress routinely, and by the end of the academic year, she had been tested forty-seven times during the thirty-week period. Her overall rate of progress, the trendline, is represented by the heavy black line that is calculated by drawing an ordinary least squares regression line through all the data points. The trendline corresponds closely to the slope of the aimline, indicating an intervention program that is effective.

As mentioned earlier in the chapter, when the effects of instructional interventions are examined systematically and continuously, educators can make data-based decisions about whether to maintain or change interventions. Students need not receive instructional programs for long periods of time that do not meet their needs. Unsuccessful interventions can be changed and successful interventions can be maintained. The net result of this type of approach is that student achievement outcomes are improved significantly (Fuchs and others, 1984; Fuchs and Fuchs, 1986).

Problem Solution

It can be argued persuasively that the kinds of testing activities that characterize long-term decisions about students' educational needs (for example, annual reviews or special education exit reviews) are little more than psychometric superstitious behavior. Annual reviews rely heavily on published achievement tests that are not designed to evaluate the progress of individual students (Carver, 1974; Marston, 1989).

A Problem-Solving Model resolves some problems in determining students' long-term needs and the appropriateness of continued special education services. Problem Solution decisions are tied conceptually to the assessment activities that defined the problem in the first place: Is there *still* a discrepancy between what is expected for the student and how the student performs? Procedurally, the discrepancy is measured again and is augmented by study of the special education student's rate of progress toward the IEP annual goal.

The logical time to make Problem Solution decisions is during the periodic and annual reviews that are required by law for students in special education (Rothstein, 1990). Periodic reviews are conducted with two pieces of CBM assessment data, the student progress graph and new Problem Identification testing (that is, peer-referenced testing) results. These data are used to answer the questions: Is the student making progress? and if so, is the progress "important?" The first question is answered by examining the student's graph showing the rate of progress toward the IEP annual goal. As in making Evaluating Solutions decisions, intervention effectiveness is determined by comparing the student's trendline to the aimline.

The second question, about the "importance" of student progress, helps separate issues of intervention effectiveness and goal appropriateness. Student change is defined as "important" if it results in *reduced discrepancies.* Data to make this decision are collected by testing the special education student in a peer-referenced manner as was done in Problem Identification. Random samples of the curriculum from the student's expected grade placement are used for testing. However, unlike Problem Identification, this testing takes place in one sitting rather than by collecting repeated samples over time. The student's scores are compared to same-grade peers, using the type of summary metric that was employed in Problem Identification. Reduced discrepancies indicate that the special education student has made meaningful, important growth.

In Sara's case, a periodic review was conducted the first trimester after her special education certification (winter), approximately ten weeks after her special education placement. Her IEP progress graph at Week 10 showed her consistently scoring at or above her aimline (see Figure 7.7). Sara also was tested using three randomly selected passages from the same level of the reading series as her initial Problem Identification testing. This process took less than ten minutes. Her scores, summarized in percentile ranks, are shown in Table 7.6. The number of words she read correctly increased to fifty-two and the magnitude of the discrepancy decreased from performance at the second percentile compared to same-grade peers to the fourth percentile. Both pieces of data indicate that the progress she is making toward her IEP goal is educationally meaningful. She is reducing her reading skill discrepancy compared to her peers, and her later reading scores show a consistent increase above her early reading scores.

The annual review process is simply a more in-depth assessment of a student's skill level and rates of progress. Again, progress toward the IEP annual goal is investigated by comparing actual versus expected student progress on the student performance graph. As can be seen in Sara's graph, at Week 30 when the annual review was conducted her actual rate of progress paralleled her expected rate. Thus, the special education intervention could be considered effective. Information on the current severity of the problem is obtained

Table 7.6. Periodic and Annual Review Reading Assessment as
Part of Problem Solution Decisions for Sara.

Level of Curriculum	*Sara's Fall Median WRC	*Sara's Fall Percentile	**Sara's Winter Median WRC	Sara's Winter Percentile	*Sara's Spring Median WRC	*Sara's Spring Percentile
3–2	27	2nd	53	4th	69	6th
3–1	27	NA			66	NA
2–2	32	NA			81	NA
2–1	37	15			80	26th
1–3	49	NA			106	NA
1–2	55	NA			123	89th

Notes: * = Based on Survey-Level Assessment; ** = Peer-Referenced Testing compared to same-grade students only.

with a new Survey-Level Assessment. The obtained information is used to determine problem severity and to write the annual goal for the next year. The results of Sara's annual review Survey-Level Assessment are also presented in Table 7.6. Sara's number of words read correctly improved again in third-grade material and the discrepancy from peers was reduced as she improved from the 4th to the 6th percentile. Her reading skills also improved significantly from fall in all levels of the general education reading series.

Summary

Significant numbers of students are failing to acquire the basic academic skills necessary for success in school and life. On the whole, efforts to resolve this problem have not succeeded. Assessment practices that place sole emphasis on identification of potential disabilities within the student have contributed to the problem because they are linked to dangerous assumptions about the nature of student learning difficulties and do not increase the likelihood that students will be placed and maintained in effective programs.

Curriculum-Based Measurement (CBM), when used within the Problem-Solving Model, is an alternative approach to assessment and decision making that is not tied to dangerous assumptions about the nature of student learning. The use of this model also increases the likelihood that children will be placed in effective programs. CBM is a consistent and continuous measurement system that was designed to function as Dynamic Indicators of Basic Skills (DIBS). These DIBS are to be used as educational thermometers, that is, tools to identify an academic problem and decide whether the intervention for that problem is effective. CBM is inextricably tied to the Problem-Solving Model, in which data are used to guide decision making. Decisions are tied to general education curricula and often to how typical students perform in each curriculum. The critical feature that defines CBM is the collection of data on repeated standard tasks for *individual* students. When used to evaluate and modify instructional intervention programs for individual students, research findings consistently have found significantly improved outcomes.

References

Adams, M. J. (1990). *Beginning to read: Thinking and learning about print*. Cambridge, MA: MIT Press.

American Educational Research Association, American Psychological Association, & National Council on Measurement in Education (1985). *Standards for educational and psychological testing*. Washington, DC: Authors.

Arias, M. B. (November, 1986). The context of education for Hispanic students: An overview. *American Journal of Education*, 26–57.

Baker, S. K., & Good, R. (in press). The appropriateness of a curriculum-based reading measure with bilingual students. *School Psychology Review*.

Bardon, J. I. (1988). Alternative educational delivery approaches: Implications for school psychology. In J. L. Graden, J. E. Zins, & M. C. Curtis (Eds.), *Alternative educational delivery systems: Enhancing instructional options for all students* (pp. 563–571). Washington, DC: National Association of School Psychologists.

Carnegie Council on Adolescent Development. (1989). *Turning points: Preparing American youth for the 21st century*. No. Carnegie Corporation of New York.

Carver, R. P. (1974). Two dimensions of tests: Psychometric and edumetric. *American Psychologist, 29*, 512–518.

Caterino, L. C. (1990). Step-by-step procedure for the assessment of language-minority children. In A. Barona & E. E. Garcia (Eds.), *Children at risk: Poverty, minority status, and other issues of educational equality* (pp. 269–282). Washington, DC: National Association of School Psychologists.

Center for the Study of Social Policy. (1991). *Kids count data book*. Washington, DC: Author.

Deno, S. L. (1986). Formative evaluation of individual student programs: A new role for school psychologists. *School Psychology Review, 15*, 358–374.

Deno, S. L. (1989). Curriculum-based measurement and alternative special education services: A fundamental and direct relationship. In M. R. Shinn (Ed.), *Curriculum-Based Measurement: Assessing special children* (pp. 1–17). NY: Guilford.

Deno, S. L. (1991). Individual differences and individual difference: The essential difference of special education. *The Journal of Special Education, 24*(2), 160–173.

Deno, S. L. (1992). The nature and development of curriculum-based measurement. *Preventing School Failure, 36*(2), 5–10.

Deno, S. L., Marston, D., & Tindal, G. (1985). Direct and frequent curriculum-based measurement: An alternative for educational decision making. *Special Services in the Schools, 2*, 5–28.

Deno, S. L., Mirkin, P., & Chiang, B. (1982). Identifying valid measures of reading. *Exceptional Children, 49*(1), 36–45.

Figueroa, R. A. (1990). Best practices in the assessment of bilingual children. In A. T. Thomas & J. Grimes, (Eds.), *Best practices in school psychology-II* (pp. 93–106). Washington, DC: National Association of School Psychologists.

Figueroa, R. A., & Sassenrath, J. M. (1989). A longitudinal study of the predictive validity of the System of Multicultural Pluralistic Assessment (SOMPA). *Psychology in the Schools, 26*, 5–19.

Fuchs, L. S. (1988). Effects of computer-managed instruction on teachers' implementation of systematic monitoring programs and student achievement. *Journal of Educational Research, 81*, 294–304.

Fuchs, L. S. (1993). Enhancing instructional programming and student achievement with curriculum-based measurement. In J. Kramer (Ed.), *Curriculum-based measurement* (pp. 65–104). Lincoln, NE: Buros Institute of Mental Measurements.

Fuchs, L. S., & Deno, S. L. (1991). Paradigmatic distinctions between instructionally relevant measurement models. *Exceptional Children, 57*(6), 488–500.

Fuchs, L. S., Deno, S. L., & Mirkin, P. (1984). The effects of frequent curriculum-based measurement and evaluation on pedagogy, student achievement and student awareness of learning. *American Educational Research Journal, 21*, 449–460.

Fuchs, L. S., & Fuchs, D. (1986). Effects of systematic formative evaluation on student achievement: A meta-analysis. *Exceptional Children, 53*, 199–208.

Fuchs, L. S., & Fuchs, D. (1992). Identifying a measure for monitoring student reading progress. *School Psychology Review, 21*(1), 45–58.

Fuchs, L. S., Fuchs, D., & Deno, S. L. (1982). Reliability and validity of curriculum-based informal reading inventories. *Reading Research Quarterly, 18*, 6–26.

Fuchs, L. S., Fuchs, D., & Hamlett, C. L. (1989). Effects of instrumental use of curriculum-based measurement to enhance instructional programs. *Remedial and Special Education, 10*(2), 43–52.

Fuchs, L. S., Fuchs, D., Hamlett, C. L., & Allinder, R. M. (1991). The contribution of skills analysis to Curriculum-Based Measurement in spelling. *Exceptional Children, 57*(5), 443–452.

Fuchs, L. S., Fuchs, D., Hamlett, C. L., & Stecker, P. M. (1991). Effects of curriculum-based measurement and consultation on teaching planning and student achievement in mathematics operations. *American Educational Research Journal, 28*, 617–641.

Fuchs, L. S., Fuchs, D., & Maxwell, L. (1988). The validity of informal reading comprehension measures. *Remedial and Special Education, 9*, 20–28.

Fuchs, L. S., Hamlett, C. L., & Fuchs, D. (1990). Monitoring basic skills progress. Austin, TX: Pro-Ed.

Fuchs, L. S., & Shinn, M. R. (1989). Writing CBM IEP Objectives. In M. R. Shinn (Ed.), *Curriculum-based measurement: Assessing special children* (pp. 132–154). NY: Guilford.

Garcia, G. E., & Pearson, P. D. (1994). Assessment and diversity. In L. Darling-Hammond (Ed.), *Review of research in education* (20th ed., pp. 337–391). Washington, DC: American Educational Research Association.

Gickling, E., & Thompson, V. (1985). A personal view of curriculum-based assessment. *Exceptional Children, 52*, 153–165.

Good, R. H., & Shinn, M. R. (1990). Forecasting accuracy of slope estimates for reading curriculum-based measurement: Empirical evidence. *Behavioral Assessment, 12*, 179–193.

Habedank, L. K. (1995). The effects of reintegrating students with mild disabilities in reading. In A. Thomas & J. Grimes (Eds.), *Best practices in school psychology*. Silver Spring, MD: National Association of School Psychologists.

Hayes, S. C., Nelson, R. O., & Jarrett, R. B. (1987). The treatment utility of assessment: A functional approach to evaluating assessment quality. *American Psychologist, 42*(11), 963–974.

Juel, C. (1988). Learning to read and write: A longitudinal study of 54 children from first through fourth grades. *Journal of Educational Psychology, 80,* 837–847.

Karlsen, B., & Gardner, E. (1985). *Stanford Diagnostic Reading Test (3rd Ed.).* San Antonio, TX: Psychological Corporation.

Laberge, D., & Samuels, S. J. (1974). Toward a theory of automatic information processing in reading. *Cognitive Psychology, 6,* 293–323.

Marston, D. (1989). Curriculum-based measurement: What is it and why do it? In M. R. Shinn (Ed.), *Curriculum-based measurement: Assessing special children* (pp. 18–78). NY: Guilford.

McGill-Franzen, A., & Allington, R. L. (1991). The gridlock of low reading achievement: Perspectives on practice and policy. *Remedial and Special Education, 12*(3), 20–30.

Mercer, J. R. (1979). *Technical Manual: System of Multicultural Pluralistic Assessment (SOMPA).* New York: Psychological Corporation.

Mercer, J. (1989). Alternative paradigms for assessment in a pluralistic society. In J. A. Banks & C.A.M. Banks (Eds.), *Multicultural education: Issues and perspectives* (pp. 289–304). Needham Heights, MA: Allyn & Bacon.

Messick, S. (1989). Validity. In R. L. Linn (Ed.), *Educational measurement* (3rd ed., pp. 13–103) New York: Macmillan.

Moss, P. A. (1994). Can there be validity without reliability? *Educational Researcher, 23*(2), 5–12.

National Assessment of Educational Progress. (1991). *Trends in academic progress: Achievement of American students in science, 1969–70 to 1990, mathematics, 1973–1990, reading, 1971 to 1990, writing, 1984 to 1990.* Washington, DC: Author.

National Center for Education Statistics. (1992). *The condition of education report.* Washington, DC: Author.

Office of Educational Research and Improvement of the U.S. Department of Education. (1992). *Meeting goal 3: How well are we doing?* (OR 92–3071). Washington, DC: U.S. Government Printing Office.

Olmedo, E. L. (1981). Testing linguistic minorities. *American Psychologist, 36*(10), 1078–1085.

Rothstein, L. F. (1990). *Special education law.* New York: Longman.

Samuda, R. J. (Ed.). (1975). *Psychological testing of American minorities: Issues and consequences. Alternatives to traditional standardized tests.* New York: HarperCollins.

Shinn, M. R. (Ed.). (1989a). *Curriculum-based measurement: Assessing special children*. New York: Guilford.

Shinn, M. R. (1989b). Identifying and defining academic problems: CBM screening and eligibility procedures. In M. R. Shinn (Ed.), *Curriculum-based measurement: Assessing special children* (pp. 90–129). New York: Guilford.

Shinn, M. R. (1995). Curriculum-based measurement and its use in a problem-solving model. In A. Thomas & J. Grimes (Eds.), *Best practices in school psychology*. Silver Spring, MD: National Association of School Psychologists.

Shinn, M. R., Collins, V. L., & Gallagher, S. (in press). Assessing students from minority backgrounds: Contemporary solutions to old problems. In L. Meyer & C. A. Utley (Eds.), *The school reform movement: Implementing effective schooling practices and intervention strategies for multicultural students with mild disabilities*. New York: Brookes.

Shinn, M. R., & Good, R. H. (1993). CBA: An assessment of its current status and a prognosis for its future. In J. Kramer (Ed.), *Curriculum-based measurement*. Lincoln, NE: Buros Institute of Mental Measurements.

Shinn, M. R., Good, R. H., Knutson, N., Tilly, W. D., & Collins, V. (1992). Curriculum-based reading fluency: A confirmatory analysis of its relation to reading. *School Psychology Review, 21*(3), 458–478.

Shinn, M. R., & Hubbard, D. D. (1992). Curriculum-based measurement and problem-solving assessment: Basic procedures and outcomes. *Focus on Exceptional Children, 24*(5), 1–20.

Shinn, M. R., Rosenfield, S., & Knutson, N. (1989). Curriculum-based assessment: A comparison and integration of models. *School Psychology Review, 18*, 299–316.

Stanovich, K. E. (1986). Matthew effects in reading: Some consequences of individual differences in the acquisition of literacy. *Reading Research Quarterly, 21*, 360–406.

Stoner, G., & Green, S. K. (1992). Reconsidering the scientist-practitioner model for school psychology practice. *School Psychology Review, 21*, 155–166.

Tindal, G. (1993). A review of curriculum-based procedures on nine assessment components. In J. Kramer (Ed.), *Curriculum-based measurement* (pp. 25–64). Lincoln, NE: Buros Institute of Mental Measurements.

Ysseldyke, J. E., Algozzine, B. J., & Thurlow, M. L. (Eds.). (1992). *Critical issues in special education*. Boston: Houghton Mifflin.

8

Nonverbal Assessment
Multicultural Perspectives

Abigail M. Harris, Marilyn A. Reynolds,
and Henry M. Koegel

In the wake of concerns about bias in traditional ability tests and with growing numbers of limited standard-English speakers in the United States, there is increased interest in nonverbal assessment. Educators and psychologists hope that by reducing the emphasis on verbal skills or removing language altogether from the testing process, they can minimize the impact of culturally based linguistic differences on assessment results and outcomes.

This chapter discusses current issues surrounding the use of nonverbal ability measures with multicultural populations, particularly children. In the first section, definitions of the major types of nonverbal ability measures are provided. The second section highlights some of the relevant issues and the implications for best practice. The third section reviews commonly used nonverbal assessment instruments. A final section summarizes some of the issues in light of recent discussions of intelligence testing in decision-making.

Definitions

Typically, when nonverbal is used to describe an ability measure, it refers to the conditions required for administering the test, what the test purports to measure (for example, nonverbal reasoning), or both. In its most inclusive definition, nonverbal has been used to describe any test that does not require the examinee to be literate (Anastasi, 1988). By this definition, orally administered tests of vocabulary and comprehension (typically considered to be measures of verbal ability) would be considered nonverbal. A more restrictive definition, and one that is generally more accepted, is that nonverbal refers to those ability measures that use a "nonverbal medium" to assess intellectual functioning (Naglieri and Prewett, 1990) and do not require written or spoken language from the examinee (Sattler, 1988). In either case, inclusive or more restricted, these descriptions focus on how the assessment is conducted and emphasize the conditions required for test administration.

In addition to emphasizing the medium of test administration, Naglieri and Prewett (1990) extend the definition to include a consideration of what is being measured. They propose that "'Nonverbal intelligence tests' are those that are designed to measure a theoretical construct called 'nonverbal intelligence' . . . no reading or other language variable should influence the individual's score" (pp. 348–349). This further restriction on what constitutes a nonverbal ability measure is useful in that it acknowledges that nonverbal measures may assess a unique construct within a larger framework of intellectual functioning. However, from a practical standpoint, this aspect of the definition is difficult to operationalize. As will be discussed later, the specific aptitudes examinees draw upon when responding to a task are very difficult to ascertain, and response styles may vary from one examinee to another. Thus, in this chapter, we will focus on tests that use a nonverbal medium for administration, and we will consider what each test purports to measure.

There is no one accepted framework for classifying nonverbal assessment tests. We have chosen to adapt a taxonomy proposed by Anastasi (1988). She distinguishes between nonreading (which she labels nonverbal), nonlanguage, and performance tests. While the boundaries of these categories overlap, this organization illustrates the broad range of tasks that have come under the nonverbal assessment rubric. It also highlights a core difference between these instruments and the corresponding implications for practice.

Nonreading tests require no reading or writing by the examinee, although they tend to make use of oral instructions and communication on the part of the examiner. Examples include tasks that use simple vocabulary to convey a social, logical, or mathematical reasoning problem. While some writers also include tasks that actually measure verbal comprehension (for example, Anastasi, 1988), others limit this category to those tasks that may use oral language in the directions but are not intended to measure language or vocabulary (Jensen, 1980; Naglieri and Prewett, 1990).

Nonlanguage tests typically require no language on the part of either examiner or examinee. The instructions can be demonstrated, gestured, or pantomimed, with little or no use of oral or written language. Typically, the cognitive demand of the task does not involve words, either written or spoken, and the task does not require the examinee to respond using oral or written language. Often, these tests begin with sample items that are so simple that most examinees can understand the requirements of the task without verbal directions. Examples include mazes, copying of geometric designs, drawing human figures, and identifying missing pieces or rotated shapes.

Nonverbal performance tests are nonlanguage tests that require the examinee to perform some action or manipulation of concrete objects, although the intent of the performance is not to measure manipulative skill or manual dexterity per se. Examples are paper folding, form boards, jigsaw puzzles, and block designs. As with nonlanguage paper and pencil tests, typically the directions can be demonstrated, and there are sample questions or tasks before the testing begins to ensure that the examinee understands what is expected.

As is evident from these definitions, nonverbal tests are distributed across a range from tasks that rely on language and actually measure some facility with language, to tasks that attempt to eliminate language altogether from the assessment process. In between are tasks that involve varying degrees of language in the administration process or in the task demand. Awareness of these gradations is useful in making decisions about which tests to administer and how to interpret the generalizability of the results.

Issues and Implications for Best Practice

Central to this section is the belief that the challenge of all assessment, including multicultural assessment, is to capture within the assessment process the full range of the examinee's potential. The danger to be avoided is underestimating an examinee's potential by using assessment practices that limit or fail to provide sufficient and diverse opportunities for the examinee to demonstrate aptitude. From a best practice standpoint, this means that psychologists and educators engaged in multicultural assessment must be alert for any indication or clue that some aspect of the examinee's capabilities is being missed, underestimated, or misrepresented. Instead of following a prescribed assessment plan, the assessor should be sensitive to such clues and adapt the assessment process to follow up on these leads as they emerge during the assessment process. In keeping with the belief stated above, interpretations resulting from multicultural assessment should be presented accurately and without overstating the meaningfulness of findings that are not supported by valid and reliable data. These and several other issues affecting the interpretation of nonverbal assessment data are discussed below.

Nonverbal assessment limits the range of abilities that can be sampled. Assessment represents a sampling of behavior. Typically, we rely on standardized measures that are either norm or criterion referenced to allow us to sample specific behaviors and locate the examinee's performance within a meaningful context. When verbal and nonverbal measures can be used, the opportunities for sampling from a broad spectrum of domains are only limited by the time and energy of those involved.

When the use of verbally based instruments is either not possible or not advisable, the options remaining for sampling behavior using standardized or norm-referenced procedures are drastically reduced. Therefore, assessment plans that must rely heavily or exclusively on nonverbal measures should be designed to sample from as many domains as possible. When it is possible to use non-reading measures, results from some of these instruments may provide the only available window into the examinee's verbal reasoning in his or her native language. While using the norms may not be appropriate, the quality of the responses may shed light on otherwise missed potential. In addition, other informal assessment provides useful data to corroborate the formal assessment results. Data from multiple outside sources may be used to estimate performance in those areas or domains that cannot be tested formally. Throughout the process, examiners should guard against generalizing from too narrow a sampling of tasks. When it is not possible to accumulate sufficient evidence to support inferences, these inferences should not be proffered.

By its very nature, nonverbal assessment restricts the range of language and verbal abilities that can be sampled. Just as some native English speakers exhibit a relative strength in the verbal domain, so too might limited standard-English speaking examinees possess a relative verbal strength in their mother tongue. Reports describing results of nonverbal assessment should acknowledge the limited sampling from the verbal domains.

Nonverbal assessment can provide a useful cross-check for traditional, verbal assessment. Whenever there is a question about the role of language in the assessment process, best practice calls for examiners to test the hypothesis that the verbal aspect of traditional assessment is depressing the examinee's test performance and masking the examinee's true potential. Using nonverbal assessment measures the examiner may uncover strengths and potential capabilities that support this hypothesis. When this occurs, reports describing the results should highlight the new evidence and treat the verbal assessment as a biased indicator of potential. While the verbal assessment might be an accurate reflection of the examinee's current verbal performance, the scores are invalid for making inferences or generalizing regarding the examinee's potential.

On the other hand, when no new insights emerge from nonverbal assessment, it is important to consider the range of the tasks that were sampled. Performance on too narrow a range of tasks yields insufficient evidence to reject this hypothesis and conclude that the verbal aspect of testing is inconsequential to the examinee's performance. Therefore, unless the assessment process included a broad range of nonverbal measures as well as data from other sources (for example, parent and teacher interviews, adaptive behavior information) and less formal indicators (such as observations in a variety of settings, testing of limits in order to assess processes, and so forth), caution should be taken in eliminating the role of language as an inhibiting factor.

Nonverbal assessment does not guarantee that performing the task is "language free." While the instructions and response to a given task may not require verbal communication, there may be verbal mediation in the processes used by successful examinees in responding. For example, some sequencing tasks require the examinee to arrange a set of pictures in an order that tells a story. Examinees need not verbalize the story or the rationale for their response. Nonetheless, "telling" the story in one's mind presumes some language. The language need not be English, or any recognized language for that matter. However, success on the item presupposes facility with some language or strategy that allows the examinee to construct meaning in the task. Similarly, matrices that require the examinee to identify a relationship and memory tasks involving objects may be facilitated by verbal mediation.

Performance on the same task may be determined by quite different abilities for individuals who use different problem-solving approaches. The kinds of processes used by examinees to respond to the same task may be different for different individuals (Brody, 1988). This was illustrated by Sternberg and Weil (1980), who used error analysis on deductive reasoning problems to identify two groups: one group relied on a verbal approach to the solution; the other group relied on spatial analogs. The investigators found that when they correlated performance on the deductive reasoning task with verbal and spatial ability measures, there were differences between the two groups. For examinees who were characterized as using a spatial solution, the correlation of their score on the deductive reasoning task with a measure of spatial ability was .60 and with a measure of verbal ability was .08. For examinees characterized as using a verbal approach, the corresponding correlations between the reasoning task and measures of spatial and verbal ability were .28 and .76. From this study, it is evident that the same task can tap different intellectual abilities in different individuals. This study also demonstrates the danger of generalizing based on performance on too narrow a range of tasks—for some examinees, performance on a deductive reasoning task would be a good indicator of verbal ability, whereas for other examinees it would not.

Nonverbal assessment is not culture free. Early test developers hoped that nonverbal measures would eliminate the influence of cultural differences on performance, that is, that these measures would be culture free (Jensen, 1980). It is now generally accepted that culture goes beyond language (Armour-Thomas, 1992). For example, items that involve pictures representing objects or scenes that are common in Western or urban cultures are likely to be less familiar to examinees from less industrialized or rural cultures. Similarly, paper and pencil tasks often assume prior exposure to printed matter and the associated conventions (for example, left to right orientation). Exposure to and practice with puzzles, mazes, block designs, and so on is not universal. The impact of each of these instances of differential preparation needs to be evaluated on an individual basis.

Speed represents another aspect of performance that is influenced by culture. The tempo of daily life and the value attached to rapid performance vary from urban to rural settings as well as from one culture to another. Nonverbal assessment measures that include performance speed in the scoring formula may disadvantage examinees from cultures that do not emphasize the rapid completion of tasks.

Some nonverbal assessment measures put nonlanguage users at a disadvantage. While the option exists for most nonlanguage and nonverbal performance tests to be administered without spoken language, some of these tests were developed and standardized using oral directions. Also, there are some instruments in which partial credit is given when an examinee is able to provide an explanation for a response that would otherwise be considered an incorrect or partially correct response. For example, responses on the Goodenough-Harris drawing test are enhanced by the child's explanation of intent. The squiggle that looks like another strand of hair may turn out to be an ear!

When using instruments in which the standardized administration procedures rely on oral language, it is important to consider whether the current application violates the standardization, and, if so, what impact this violation may have on the examinee's performance. For example, for bilingual or limited standard-English speaking examinees, it may be possible for the directions to be translated or given successively in two languages without altering the nature of the task. Thus in some instances the difficulty of the task is not altered by the nonstandard administration. However, in other instances—for example, when the examiner is unsure whether the examinee understands the task—the violation or break with standardization is significant and invalidates the results.

Using norms to interpret findings may not be legitimate. Applying normative data as if they had validity in a situation where there is reason to suspect that scores may be depressed because of an examinee's background is inappropriate. Consider the situation in which a child for whom English is a second language has a performance intelligence score of 90 ± 5, a verbal intelligence score of 73 ± 4, and a full scale intelligence score of 79 ± 3. (This confidence interval is based on a decision to report a range that reflects a 68 percent certainty, that is, one standard error of measurement (SE_m). For this age child, the performance score $SE_m = 5$, the verbal score $SE_m = 4$, and the total score $SE_m = 3$.) Below are two portrayals of this information:

> In summary, this child appears to be of *borderline to low average ability* as measured by the WISC-III. Because of her bilingual background, her performance may have been underestimated due to the verbal demands of the WISC-III.

versus

> In summary, this child appears to be of *average to low average ability* as measured by the performance scale on the WISC-III. While her full scale and verbal IQ scores were somewhat lower, because of her bilingual background, these scores may have been depressed due to the verbal demand of the WISC-III.

The difference between these two interpretive descriptions is critical. Unfortunately, some readers of a test report turn to the test report summary for the bottom line, which in this case is found in the first sentence of the descriptions. Is the child of "borderline-low average" ability or "average-low average" ability? It is not appropriate or accurate to act as if the norms for this test can be applied and then a caveat added. From a best practice standpoint, it is more accurate to emphasize the more favorable interpretation. The potentially affected or biased information should be included only if administration of the test was appropriate and, even then, the potentially affected results should be deemphasized and clearly clarified with appropriate caveats.

Another example of the misuse of normative data arises when tests are given indiscriminately. Novice examiners often believe that if they administered a test, they must include it in the report. Unfortunately, they have sometimes administered a test that should not have been given in the first place because its use unfairly disadvantaged the examinee. For example, it is not unusual for school districts to have a recommended "standard assessment battery" for all referrals for special education. Intern or novice psychologists seeking to comply with the recommendation may administer ability measures that rely on verbal comprehension to a non-English-speaking child. Presenting the results and interpreting them using normative data—even with a caveat—is misleading, especially for readers of the report who are less familiar with the test and the invalidity of its use in this situation. While an examiner may use a variety of assessment tools to explore the examinee's limits, best practice dictates that normative data should be presented only when this interpretation is valid, and, in situations when a test has been administered inappropriately, results should be excluded altogether from the examinee's report and file.

Review of Selected Nonverbal Assessment Instruments

Based on their relative popularity in the assessment literature, the following ten nonverbal assessment instruments were selected for closer scrutiny regarding their purported measures and sensitivity to cultural differences: The Columbia Mental Maturity Scale (Burgemeister, Blum, and Lorge, 1972); the Goodenough-Harris Drawing Test (Harris, 1963); the Hiskey-Nebraska Test of Learning Aptitude (Hiskey, 1966); the Kaufman Assessment Battery for Children—Nonverbal Scale (Kaufman and Kaufman, 1983); the Leiter International Performance Scale (Leiter, 1948); the Matrix Analogies Test (Naglieri, 1985); Raven's Progressive Matrices—Standard and Coloured Forms (Raven, Court, and Raven, 1947b, 1947a); the Test of Nonverbal Intelligence, Second Edition (Brown, Sherbenou, and

Johnsen, 1990); and the Wechsler Intelligence Scale for Children, Third Edition—Performance Scale (Wechsler, 1991). Table 8.1 provides information on each of these instruments along the following dimensions: age range for use, type of test (nonreading, nonlanguage, or nonverbal performance, based on the definitions provided earlier), motor response required of examinee in responding, racial or ethnic makeup of the normative sample, multicultural application of the instrument, and latest year of revision.

The narrative information provided for each instrument is taken from the most recent test reviews and critiques published in the general testing literature. Readers are encouraged to consult the test manuals of the specific instruments listed for detailed information regarding instructions for administration and interpretation, reliability, validity and other psychometric properties of the tests.

Columbia Mental Maturity Scale

The Columbia Mental Maturity Scale (CMMS; Burgemeister, Blum, and Lorge, 1972) consists of ninety-two pictorial and figural classification items arranged in a series of eight overlapping levels, which correspond to specific ages. The level appropriate to the child's age is administered, and the task is to select the drawing that does not belong with the others. Drawings may differ in size, color, or shape, as well as in more subtle and abstract ways (Brown, 1985; Egeland, 1978; Kaufman, 1978; Petrosko, 1978).

The CMMS purportedly measures a child's general reasoning ability (Brown, 1985; Egeland, 1978), classificatory reasoning and pictorial classifying ability (Petrosko, 1978). However, some reviewers describe it as a test of mental maturity rather than one of general reasoning or mental ability (Petrosko, 1978). The test developers recommend that the CMMS be used as a quick screening device for possible learning disorders prior to administering a thorough diagnostic battery (Kaufman, 1978).

The CMMS does not require the child to read or speak English (Kamphaus, 1993), and only minimal gross motor movement is

Table 8.1. Comparison of Nonverbal Assessment Instruments.

Test Name	Age Range	Type of Test (1)		Motor Response Required (2)			Racial/Ethnic Makeup of Norms			Multicultural Application			Year Revised
		Nonreading	Performance	Pointing	Pencil	Manipulation	Diverse	Non-Diverse	Undetermined	Reported	Emphasized	Undetermined	
Columbia Scale	3-6 to 9-11	X		X			X					X	1972
Goodenough-Harris	3-0 to 15-11	X			X				X			X	1963
Hiskey-Nebraska	3-0 to 17-0	X	X	X					X	X			1966
K-ABC (3)	2-6 to 12-6	X		X			X			X			1983
Leiter International	2-0 to 18-0	X	X			X		X				X	1948
Matrix Analogies	5-0 to 17-0	X		X	X		X			X			1985
Raven's—Coloured	5-0 to 11-0	X	X	X	X				X (4)	X			1956
Raven's—Standard	6-0 to Adult	X	X	X	X				X (4)	X			1956
TONI-2	5-0 to Adult	X	X	X			X			X			1990
WISC-III (5)	6-0 to 16-0	X	X	X	X	X	X				X		1991

(1) Based on definitions provided in this chapter.

(2) Pointing = Subject points or gestures to chosen response; Pencil = Subject uses pencil to draw or indicate chosen response on paper answer form; Manipulation = Subject manipulates objects, like blocks, in making response.

(3) Refers to the Mental Processing subtests of the Nonverbal Scale only.

(4) North American norms were updated in 1986, but normative samples were not described (Kamphaus, 1993).

(5) Refers to the subtests of the Performance Scale only.

required for responding (Brown, 1985; Kaufman, 1978). The test's developers deem it particularly appropriate for use with children who have cerebral palsy, mental retardation, speech impairment, hearing loss, brain damage (Brown, 1985), and for those with limited proficiency in English or who speak English as a second language (Brown, 1985; Egeland, 1978). The CMMS should not be used with children who have visual-perceptual problems, as this may prevent them from perceiving the pictured objects and abstractions accurately (Brown, 1985; Kaufman, 1978).

The norms for the CMMS were derived from a sample of 2,600 children with 200 children included at each of thirteen age levels (Egeland, 1978; Kaufman, 1978). The standardization sample was stratified on the basis of parental occupation, sex, race, geographic location, and size of residence community (Brown, 1985; Egeland, 1978; Kamphaus, 1993; Kaufman, 1978). Children were selected from sixty-seven test centers across twenty-five states (Brown, 1985). Handicapped children were not included in the standardization sample (Egeland, 1978), and twice as many children from large cities were included than was true of the general population in 1960 (Brown, 1985). No information on possible sex differences is presented (Egeland, 1978).

As for its multicultural application, the test's stimuli appear to be reasonably (culture) "fair" (Kaufman, 1978, p. 299), and they are within the range of most American children, even those whose environmental backgrounds have been limited (Brown, 1985). However, since some items contain pictures of objects that should be familiar to children who have access to television, the authors caution the use of the CMMS with children from other countries and extremely isolated environments, because they may have difficulty with certain items (Brown, 1985). The CMMS may be administered in Spanish and directions for doing so are provided by the authors (Brown, 1985; Kaufman, 1978). The multicultural application of the CMMS is indicated as unknown because the test reviews consulted did not report any empirical studies validating its use with specific multicultural populations.

Goodenough-Harris Drawing Test

The Goodenough-Harris Drawing Test (GHDT; Harris, 1963) requires the child to draw a picture of a man, a woman, and the child him- or herself using a No. 2 pencil with an eraser and 8.5 × 11-inch unlined paper. These tasks are then followed by an informal interrogation by the examiner to clarify the child's intent (Kamphaus, 1993). The drawings are objectively scored for specific items on an all-or-none basis (Anastasi, 1972).

The GHDT purportedly measures a child's current intellectual maturity, accuracy of observation, and development of conceptual thinking (Anastasi, 1972; Fredrickson, 1985). In addition, it can indicate sensory-motor impairment, and has been used extensively as a personality and projective test even though there are no objective or standardized scoring procedures that support personality assessment or projective uses (Fredrickson, 1985).

The GHDT does not require the child to read or speak English, however, it does require the child to understand what is expected. Also, ambiguous aspects of the drawing may require clarification by asking the child to identify the body parts. This may be a disadvantage in nonlanguage administrations. The child also must have enough fine motor coordination to draw with a pencil. Though the test covers ages three years to fifteen years, eleven months, it appears to function best with ages three to ten (Kamphaus, 1993). Some test reviewers claim that the GHDT is especially useful with children manifesting hearing losses and neurological problems.

The test reviews consulted report inconsistent information concerning the standardization of the GHDT. Anastasi (1972) reports that "norms were established on a new standardization sample of 2,975 children between the ages of 5 and 15 years, representative of the occupational distribution of the U.S. in 1950, and distributed among four major geographical areas" (p. 670). Fredrickson (1985) states that "the normative scores in the revised edition contain 50 boys and 50 girls at each year from 6 to 15 years. These children were taken from a larger sample tested in rural and urban areas of Minnesota and Wisconsin and were representative of the population with respect to paternal occupation" (p. 320). Finally, both Sattler (1988) and Kamphaus (1993) write that a total of 2,975 boys and girls in the United States were selected as representative of the 1960 Census figures. Four geographical areas were used, and seventy-five children were included at each age level from five to fifteen years. This conflicting information regarding the location, age range (especially the lack of three- and four-year-olds in the sample), distribution of gender within the group, and the lack of information regarding the racial or ethnic makeup of the sample needs to be clarified.

Sattler (1988) cautions that while the test is useful as a screening instrument and appears less culturally loaded than other tests of cognitive ability, the child's cultural background may influence test scores in that "different cultures place varying emphases on body parts and clothing" (p. 313). He also comments that modernization of the scoring guidelines for the Draw-A-Woman component is needed in that criteria for appropriate dress and hair styling date back to the 1950s.

Only one reference was found with respect to the multicultural application of the GHDT. Dunn (1972) mentions that "the manual cites . . . only one study, on Canadian-Indian children, which reports correlations between the 1926 scale and the 1963 scale" (p. 672). This suggests that insufficient information is available regarding the validity of the GHDT with culturally diverse populations at this time.

Hiskey-Nebraska Test of Learning Aptitude

The Hiskey-Nebraska Test of Learning Aptitude (H-NTLA; Hiskey, 1966) is a nonreading, nonlanguage performance scale that consists of twelve subtests, five of which are administered only to children aged three to ten years, four to children aged eleven to seventeen years, and three to children of all ages (Mira and Larson, 1986). The

twelve subtests are: bead patterns, memory for color, picture identification, picture association, paper-folding patterns, visual attention span, block patterns, completion of drawings, memory for
digits, puzzle blocks, picture analogies, and spatial reasoning.

The H-NTLA purportedly evaluates a child's learning potential.
It may also be useful for defining areas of strength and weakness in
cognitive functioning of deaf children, and for measuring the intelligence of mentally retarded children (Mira and Larson, 1986). In
addition, it has been used to investigate the relationship of intellectual skills to English-language proficiency in deaf children and
used with children whose primary language was other than English
(Mira and Larson, 1986).

The H-NTLA does not require the child to read or speak English, and it can be administered entirely via pantomimed instructions (Bolton, 1978). Many of the items require only enough
fine-motor coordination to point accurately. The only population
of children for whom the test would not be appropriate are those
with visual impairments or moderate to severe upper-extremity
motor deficits (Mira and Larson, 1986).

The H-NTLA was originally developed for and standardized on
a population of deaf children. Subsequently, it was normed for hearing children as well. The test's items were administered to 1,074
deaf and 1,079 hearing children aged two years, six months, to
seventeen years, six months. The children came from ten states
nationwide (Mira and Larson, 1986). The deaf children came from
state schools for the deaf. However, the representativeness of the
deaf sample is unknown, since information about the national distribution of their parents' occupations was not available and information on other demographic characteristics was not provided
(Bolton, 1978; Mira and Larson, 1986). The hearing children were
representative of parental occupations nationwide. However,
beyond stratification by parental occupation, there is little evidence
that the sample is representative on other demographic variables,
like ethnic group or race (Kamphaus, 1993). Further, norms for both
groups are seriously out of date.

As for the application of the H-NTLA to multicultural populations, it has been used for making educational placement recommendations for Mexican American and Navajo children, and it is proving to be useful as an assessment device for bilingual children (Mira and Larson, 1986). Though there has been no legitimate translation of the H-NTLA into other languages, the author encourages users in other countries to translate the materials into their own language and to develop local norms (Mira and Larson, 1986).

Kaufman Assessment Battery for Children—Nonverbal Scale

The Kaufman Assessment Battery for Children—Nonverbal Scale (K-ABC; Kaufman and Kaufman, 1983) purportedly measures the intelligence of children aged two years, six months, to twelve years, six months, and is designed to separate the acquisition of factual knowledge from the ability to solve unfamiliar problems. The K-ABC is composed of four scales: Sequential Processing, Simultaneous Processing, Nonverbal, and Achievement. The first three are mental processing scales which measure fluid abilities, and the achievement scale assesses crystallized abilities (Menz, 1984).

The Sequential and Simultaneous Processing scales are intended to reflect the examinee's style of problem solving and information processing, and were designed to reduce the effects of verbal processing and gender and ethnic bias (Sattler, 1988). The scores from these two scales are combined to form the Mental Processing Composite—the test's measure of intelligence.

The Sequential Processing scale contains three subtests: Hand Movements, Number Recall, and Word Order. The Simultaneous Processing scale contains seven subtests: Magic Window, Face Recognition, Gestalt Closure, Triangles, Matrix Analogies, Spatial Memory, and Photo Series. Together, these ten subtests assess problem solving in novel situations. The Nonverbal scale is composed of those subtests from the Sequential and Simultaneous Processing scales (Face Recognition, Hand Movements, Triangles, Matrix Analogies, Spatial Memory, and Photo Series) that do not require words (Sattler, 1988). These seven subtests may be administered in pantomime and require only motor responses on the part of the examinee (Anastasi, 1985).

The Achievement scale assesses the examinee's factual knowledge and skills required in school and in the child's living environment. It is made up of six subtests: Expressive Vocabulary, Faces and Places, Arithmetic, Riddles, Reading-Decoding, and Reading-Understanding. These subtests are kept separate from those in the Sequential and Simultaneous scales in an effort to distinguish between knowledge gained by exposure to environmental stimuli and educational opportunities, and knowledge that results from an integration of sequential and simultaneous processing. However, Sattler (1988) faults the K-ABC for this separation because he believes "it artificially distinguishes the ways in which children acquire and process information" (p. 301).

The K-ABC was standardized on 2,000 children at thirty-four test sites in twenty-four states (Menz, 1984). Sampling was based on 1980 U.S. Census figures (Kamphaus, 1993), and the children were stratified within half-year groups by age, gender, geographic region, race or ethnicity (White, Black, Hispanic, other) (Anastasi, 1985), parental educational attainment (SES), community size, and educational placement (regular or special classes) (Anastasi, 1985; Kamphaus, 1993; Menz, 1984). However, according to Sattler (1988), "There are major sampling problems with the standardization sample. Hispanic-Americans [are] underrepresented by 24 percent, and low-educational-level blacks [are] underrepresented by 10 percent" (p. 303). In addition, when adjustments are made for sampling differences at the uppermost age level, Blacks and Whites differ by twelve points, in favor of Whites. Thus, in spite of the authors' efforts to eliminate bias in the test's materials and administration procedures, there is little evidence that the K-ABC significantly reduces the group difference found between Blacks and Whites on other intelligence tests (Sattler, 1988).

One of the primary goals of the authors of the K-ABC was to be sensitive to the diverse needs of minority group children (Page,

1985). Thus, much attention was paid to sex and race bias in item development (Coffman, 1985). The authors went to great lengths to include stimuli that were as fair as possible for boys and girls from diverse backgrounds (Page, 1985), and to remove items deemed biased by gender, region, or racial or ethnic group (Kamphaus, 1993). Moreover, the Mental Processing subtests were intentionally designed to reduce the need for language and verbal skills for successful performance. Thus, non-English-speaking children may be assessed more fairly than with other major intelligence tests (Menz, 1984). However, some test reviewers believe that the lack of verbal comprehension or reasoning items on the Mental Processing Composite is a "fundamental weakness of the K-ABC" (Sattler, 1988, p. 302) and they caution against using the K-ABC as the primary instrument for assessing intellectual abilities. As with the other instruments reviewed in this chapter, interpretations should reflect the domains that were sampled.

In spite of its imperfections, the K-ABC seems particularly well suited for use with children who have hearing impairments, speech or language disorders, learning disabilities, and with children who are non-English speaking, limited in their English proficiency, or who speak nonstandard English. A Spanish version of the Mental Processing subscales has been devised for use in Spanish speaking countries. This version may also be used to evaluate Spanish-speaking children in the United States who cannot be fairly assessed in English (Menz, 1984). The K-ABC is not useful with children who are severely impaired visually, or who have receptive language problems (Menz, 1984). In addition, because it has a low ceiling, the usefulness of the K-ABC for evaluating gifted children may be limited (Sattler, 1988).

Leiter International Performance Scale

The 1948 edition of the Leiter International Performance Scale (LEITER; Leiter, 1948) is a fifty-four-item nonlanguage performance instrument designed to measure a child's intelligence and mental maturity. It requires the child to match blocks with colors, shapes, designs, or pictures on them with the same on corresponding paper strips affixed to a wooden frame with stalls. The complexity of the matching tasks increases positively with the child's age. The content of the test items can be categorized as either perceptual or conceptual (Matey, 1984). The perceptual items consist of tasks involving shapes, colors, block designs, and visual closure. The conceptual items include tasks of judging relationships between events, categories, and classes; visual-spatial relationships; and numerical processes.

Since the LEITER does not require the subject to speak or understand English, it lends itself well to individuals with verbal communication difficulties, and those who are non-English speaking, or limited in their English proficiency (Jensen, 1980; Matey, 1984). Also, it can be used with subjects who have fine-motor and manipulative difficulties since they can indicate their responses simply by pointing to the appropriate stalls (Matey, 1984).

It was Leiter's intention to develop an intelligence test that would eliminate the language function and thus enable a fair comparison of children from different racial backgrounds (Matey, 1984). However, some items are culturally loaded, and little cross-cultural research has been done with the scale in the more than forty years since its publication (Jensen, 1980). Also, pictures are outdated, item difficulty levels are uneven, and there are too few items at each year level (Sattler, 1988).

The norms associated with the 1948 edition predate 1948 (Kamphaus, 1993) and are based on 289 middle-class White children (Jensen, 1980). In 1949, Arthur issued an adapted version because she felt the norms were too high for children aged three to eight. Although both forms use exactly the same test materials, the Arthur Adaptation covers only the age range between three and eight. In 1959, to correct for underestimated IQs, Leiter recommended that five points be added to the IQ obtained on the scale (Sattler, 1988). The available norms are thought to be so inadequate as to make it inadvisable (if not unethical) to use the test for determining a subject's IQ or percentile rank (Jensen, 1980), or for placement or decision-making purposes (Sattler, 1988). Kamphaus (1993) asserts that the psychometric properties of the LEITER are so lacking that it is an instrument of more historical than clinical value. Nonetheless, for children with language handicaps or for whom a total nonlanguage assessment is required, it may serve as an aid in the clinical diagnosis process (Sattler, 1988).

Matrix Analogies Test

The Matrix Analogies Test (MAT; Naglieri, 1985) is a nonlanguage paper-and-pencil multiple-choice test consisting of sixty-four visual stimulus items. The sixty-four items comprise four sixteen-item groups, including Pattern Completion, Reasoning by Analogy, Serial Reasoning, and Spatial Visualization. These four item groups were derived by logical organization, not empirical research. Each item is missing an element or elements in a sequence, and the child's task is to select the option from among those given that best completes the item. The stimulus elements include size, shape, color, and direction (McMorris and Steinberg, 1989).

Two forms of the MAT are available. The expanded form (MAT-EF) contains all sixty-four items and is administered only to individuals. The short form (MAT-SF) contains thirty-four items and is used as a screening instrument for group administration (Robinson, 1987).

The MAT is purported to be a nonverbal measure of intellectual ability (McMorris and Steinberg, 1989) or a single construct of nonverbal reasoning (Robinson, 1987). It was primarily designed to screen large numbers of five- to seventeen-year-old children with demonstrated learning difficulties, and potentially gifted bilingual or educationally disadvantaged students whose school performance may be adversely affected by their limited English proficiency (Naglieri, 1991a, 1991b). The nonverbal design of the MAT also makes it useful for testing individuals with general communication disorders, limited language development, or non-English-language backgrounds (Robinson, 1987).

The normative sample was stratified according to 1980 U.S. Census figures by age, sex, ethnicity, SES, and geography (Kamphaus, 1993; McMorris and Steinberg, 1989; Robinson, 1987). The expanded form was standardized using a group sample of 4,468 children, and an individual sample of 1,250 children (Kamphaus, 1993; Robinson, 1987). The test author reports a lack of gender or race differences (McMorris and Steinberg, 1989); girls and boys perform similarly, as do Blacks and Whites (Robinson, 1987).

As for the multicultural application of the MAT, test forms for Spanish-speaking or visually impaired subjects have not been developed. However, because the test format includes very simple oral directions that permit the child to respond by pointing to or stating the number of the choice, the test could be used appropriately with children of limited English proficiency or with language problems (Robinson, 1987). More research needs to be done in regards to the multicultural uses of the MAT.

Raven's Progressive Matrices—Standard and Coloured Forms

The Standard Progressive Matrices (SPM; Raven, Court, and Raven, 1947b) is a nonlanguage instrument that purportedly measures a person's general intelligence (Kamphaus, 1993), or more specifically, a person's capacity to form perceptual relationships or comparisons, to reason by analogy, and to develop a logical method of thinking independent of language and formal education (Jensen, 1980; Llabre, 1984). The Coloured Progressive Matrices (CPM) is thought to assess a child's perceptual ability and developmental readiness for deductive or analogical reasoning (Esquivel, 1984).

The SPM consists of sixty matrix items (that is, patterns constructed with a logical relationship between the horizontal and vertical dimensions) grouped into five sets of twelve items each. Each set varies the forms, relationships, transformations, and difficulty levels of the matrix. Each item contains a matrix with a missing piece. The task for the examinee is to determine which of several alternative choices best fits with the logical theme of the matrix and completes the pattern. The SPM is intended for use with persons six years of age and older (Jensen, 1980).

The CPM is a downward extension of the SPM for use with young children aged five to eleven, very elderly people, and adults with cognitive deficiencies (Esquivel, 1984; Llabre, 1984). It consists of thirty-six colored matrix items grouped into three sets of twelve. The CPM items are easier than those in the SPM, and their difficulty levels are less steeply graded (Jensen, 1980).

The nonverbal nature of the SPM and CPM makes them useful for testing children from different linguistic backgrounds as well as those with communication disorders or limited language proficiency, the deaf, and the physically handicapped (Llabre, 1984). The SPM and CPM can be individually or group administered using reusable test booklets and separate paper and pencil response forms. Individually tested examinees with limited motor abilities may also respond by pointing to the answer while the examiner records the choice (Llabre, 1984). Test instructions can be given either verbally or in pantomime (Jensen, 1980; Llabre, 1984).

The SPM and CPM were renormed in the United States in 1986. Unfortunately, the revised manual does not describe the demographic characteristics of the standardization sample. According to Kamphaus (1993), this suggests that the sample may have been one of convenience and not necessarily representative of the general population. However, Sattler (1988) believes that because large samples were employed in various school districts throughout the United States, the norms are probably representative of the school-age population. In addition, normative studies from countries around the world abound in the literature. However, many of these did not employ representative samples and so have limited usefulness (Llabre, 1984). Obviously, more detailed information is needed about these normative samples.

The SPM is one of the most widely used and researched culture-reduced, nonverbal, cognitive assessment instruments. The large amount of research data available from countries throughout the world enables users to decide its cross-cultural appropriateness (Llabre, 1984). The applicability of the CPM with children of different ethnic and SES backgrounds has been established in cross-cultural validation studies, and both versions are useful in testing children who do not speak English or who have limited command of English (Sattler, 1988). Also, they can serve as a screening device for identifying disadvantaged gifted children (Esquivel, 1984).

Test of Nonverbal Intelligence, Second Edition

The Test of Nonverbal Intelligence, Second Edition (TONI-2; Brown, Sherbenou, and Johnsen, 1990) is a culture-reduced, non-language, and motor-reduced measure of cognitive functioning (Watson, 1992), intellectual ability (Harrington, 1985), or general intelligence (Murphy, 1992). It is not a global intelligence measure, however, because it assesses only a single component of intelligence, namely problem-solving ability (Harrington, 1985).

Test items on the TONI-2 consist of abstract symbols and figural matrices. These items present a variety of reasoning tasks involving simple matching, analogies, classifications, intersections, and progressions arranged in an increasing order of complexity and difficulty (Brown, Sherbenou, and Johnsen, 1991; Harrington, 1985; Kamphaus, 1993). The task of the examinee is to select the response from among four choices that best completes the problem (Kamphaus, 1993). The TONI-2 is published in parallel forms, A and B, of fifty items each (Harrington, 1985).

Since the TONI-2 does not require the examinee to speak, write, or read English, it is optimally useful for assessing individuals aged five and up who have poor or impaired language skills, different linguistic or cultural backgrounds (Harrington, 1985), or impaired motor skills (Murphy, 1992). Directions are usually pantomimed by the examiner, and the examinee responds by pointing to the chosen answer (Harrington, 1985; Kamphaus, 1993; Watson, 1992).

The original TONI was standardized on a sample of 2,764 individuals (Watson, 1992). The sample reflected the age range of five to eighty-five, and it was stratified by sex, race, ethnicity, geographic region, and parental educational-occupational attainment for school-age children, and current educational-occupational attainment for the adult sample (Kamphaus, 1993). However, the number of non-English-speaking persons included in the sample is not specified (Watson, 1992).

According to Harrington (1985), the problem-solving format of the TONI reduces the cultural loading of the major standardized intelligence tests. In addition, the nonverbal item content and pointing response adaptation makes the TONI a much fairer measure of intellectual ability for ethnic minorities. As a culturally-reduced instrument, the TONI provides examiners with a method for assessing culturally different individuals in a more nonbiased manner than they have had in the past (Harrington, 1985).

Wechsler Intelligence Scale for Children, Third Edition, Performance Scale

The Performance Scale of the Wechsler Intelligence Scale for Children, Third Edition (WISC-III; Wechsler, 1991) is composed of five subtests: Picture Completion, Picture Arrangement, Block Design, Object Assembly, and Coding. Additionally, there are two supplementary subtests, Mazes and Symbol Search, which are not included in the computation of the Performance Scale IQ. However, the Mazes subtest may be substituted for any one of the five standard Performance subtests, and the Symbol Search may be used in place of the Coding subtest only.

The Performance Scale of the WISC-III is commonly regarded as a measure of general intelligence for children ages six to sixteen years. However, Kamphaus (1993) argues that the Performance IQ should be conceptualized as a measure of what a child has learned. While the subtests of the WISC-III Performance Scale do not require the examinee to read, write, or speak English, and therefore are considered nonreading and nonlanguage, some subtests require the comprehension of wordy verbal directions and most are timed stringently. Both of these factors could affect the performance of children who have verbal comprehension difficulties or fine-motor deficits (Kamphaus, 1993).

The WISC-III was normed in early 1989 using a sample of 2,200 children, 200 children in each of eleven age groups from six to sixteen years. The sample appears to be representative of the general U.S. population. The normative group was stratified based on the 1988 U.S. Census statistics along the following variables: Age, sex, race-ethnicity, geographic region, occupation of head of household, and urban-rural residence. In addition, great efforts were made to modernize item artwork, reduce biased or offensive content, ease administration and scoring, and add items to increase the test's range of item difficulty (Kamphaus, 1993). (More information regarding the specific use of the WISC-III is provided in Chapter Six of this book.)

Implications for Decision Making

Assessment does not occur in a vacuum. When we collect data about a child's intellectual functioning, we expect that what we learn will lead to improved diagnosis and intervention for the child. Nonverbal assessment offers a strategy for collecting data to improve decision making particularly with individuals for whom the validity of more verbally based measures is not established.

Recent treatises have questioned whether intelligence can be measured (Sternberg, 1992), whether cognitive processing strategies are more useful than traditional intelligence scales (Armour-Thomas, 1992; Reschly and Wilson, 1990), and whether standardized tests of intelligence have utility for educational decision making (Armour-Thomas, 1992; Reschly and Wilson, 1990). Nonverbal measures of ability are not exempted from this debate. Certainly, psychologists must repeatedly question whether the knowledge gained from the assessment process (whether it includes nonverbal or verbal measures) leads to better decisions, better-matched interventions, and improved outcomes for the examinee.

Although theories of intelligence abound, and there has been a great deal of discussion about the cognitive processes underlying intelligent behavior, theoretical specificity about them remains elusive. As Armour-Thomas asks, "Exactly what are the processes tapped by intelligence tests? How do individuals combine these processes to produce the behavior that assessors use as a criterion?" (1992, p. 554). Despite decades of debate, new and revised theories continue to be proffered and no consensus is in sight.

In the absence of consensus, examiners are left with the challenge of sampling multiple abilities in an effort to gain insight into the components of intellectual functioning. When verbal or language-based tests may disadvantage the examinee, the sampling process is restricted. The need to be clear on what is and is not being measured becomes more important, as does the need to evaluate the hypothesis that language-based tests of ability underestimate the examinee's ability. Hopefully, the caveats and recommendations of this chapter provide useful guidelines for this endeavor.

References

Anastasi, A. (1972). Goodenough-Harris Drawing Test. In O. K. Buros (Ed.), *The seventh mental measurements yearbook* (Vol. 1, pp. 666–671). Highland Park, NJ: Gryphon Press.

Anastasi, A. (1985). Review of Kaufman Assessment Battery for Children. In J. V. Mitchell, Jr. (Ed.), *The ninth mental measurements yearbook* (Vol. 1, pp. 769–771). Lincoln, NE: Buros Institute of Mental Measurements.

Anastasi, A. (1988). *Psychological testing* (6th ed.). New York: Macmillan.

Armour-Thomas, E. (1992). Intellectual assessment of children from culturally diverse backgrounds. *School Psychology Review, 21*(4), 552–565.

Arthur, G. (1949). The Arthur Adaptation of the Leiter International Performance Scale. *Journal of Clinical Psychology, 5*, 345–349.

Bolton, B. F. (1978). Hiskey-Nebraska Test of Learning Aptitude. In O. K. Buros (Ed.), *The eighth mental measurements yearbook* (pp. 307–308). Highland Park, NJ: Gryphon Press.

Brody, N. (1988). *Personality in search of individuality*. San Diego, CA: Academic Press.

Brown, L., Sherbenou, R. J., and Johnsen, S. K. (1990). *The Test of Nonverbal Intelligence* (2nd ed.) Austin, TX: Pro-Ed.

Brown, L., Sherbenou, R. J., & Johnsen, S. K. (1991). The Test of Nonverbal Intelligence-2 (TONI-2). In R. C. Sweetland & D. J. Keyser (Eds.), *Tests: A comprehensive reference for assessments in psychology, education, and business* (3rd ed., p. 63). Austin, TX: Pro-Ed.

Brown, S. W. (1985). Columbia Mental Maturity Scale. In D. J. Keyser & R. C. Sweetland (Eds.), *Test critiques* (Vol. 2, pp. 182–190). Kansas City, MO: Test Corporation of America.

Burgemeister, B. B., Blum, L. H., & Lorge, I. (1972). *Columbia Mental Maturity Scale*. Cleveland, OH: Psychological Corporation.

Coffman, W. E. (1985). Review of Kaufman assessment battery for children. In J. V. Mitchell, Jr. (Ed.), *The ninth mental measurements yearbook* (Vol. 1, pp. 771–773). Lincoln, NE: Buros Institute of Mental Measurements.

Dunn, J. A. (1972). Goodenough-Harris Drawing Test. In O. K. Buros (Ed.), *The seventh mental measurements yearbook* (Vol. 1, pp. 671–672). Highland Park, NJ: Gryphon Press.

Egeland, B. R. (1978). Columbia Mental Maturity Scale (3rd ed.). In O. K. Buros (Ed.), *The eighth mental measurements yearbook* (pp. 29–299). Highland Park, NJ: Gryphon Press.

Esquivel, G. B. (1984). Coloured progressive matrices. In D. J. Keyser & R. C. Sweetland (Eds.), *Test critiques* (Vol. 1, pp. 206–213). Kansas City, MO: Test Corporation of America.

Fredrickson, L. C. (1985). Goodenough-Harris Drawing Test. In D. J. Keyser & R. C. Sweetland (Eds.), *Test critiques* (Vol. 2, pp. 319–325). Kansas City, MO: Test Corporation of America.

Harrington, R. G. (1985). Test of nonverbal intelligence. In D. J. Keyser & R. C. Sweetland (Eds.), *Test critiques* (Vol. 2, pp. 787–798). Kansas City, MO: Test Corporation of America.

Harris, D. B. (1963). *Goodenough-Harris Drawing Test, Manual*. Cleveland, OH: Psychological Corporation.

Hiskey, M. S. (1966). *Hiskey-Nebraska Test of Learning Aptitude*. Lincoln, NE: Author.

Jensen, A. R. (1980). *Bias in mental testing*. New York: Free Press.

Kamphaus, R. W. (1993). *Clinical assessment of children's intelligence*. Needham Heights, MA: Allyn & Bacon.

Kaufman, A. S. (1978). Columbia Mental Maturity Scale (3rd ed). In O. K. Buros (Ed.), *The eighth mental measurements yearbook* (pp. 299–301). Highland Park, NJ: Gryphon Press.

Kaufman, A. S., & Kaufman, N. L. (1983). *K-ABC: Kaufman Assessment Battery for Children*. Circle Pines, MN: American Guidance Service.

Leiter, R. G. (1948). *Leiter International Performance Scale*. Chicago: Stoelting.

Llabre, M. M. (1984). Standard progressive matrices. In D. J. Keyser & R. C. Sweetland (Eds.), *Test critiques* (Vol. 1, pp. 595–602). Kansas City, MO: Test Corporation of America.

Matey, C. (1984). Leiter International Performance Scale. In D. J. Keyser & R. C. Sweetland (Eds.), *Test critiques* (Vol. 1, pp. 411–420). Kansas City, MO: Test Corporation of America.

McMorris, R. F., & Steinberg, W. J. (1989). Review of the Matrix Analogies Test: Expanded Form. In J. C. Conoley & J. J. Kramer (Eds.), *The tenth mental measurements yearbook* (pp. 479–481). Lincoln, NE: Buros Institute of Mental Measurements.

Menz, W. R., Sr. (1984). Kaufman Assessment Battery for Children. In D. J. Keyser & R. C. Sweetland (Eds.), *Test critiques* (Vol. 1, pp. 393–405). Kansas City, MO: Test Corporation of America.

Mira, M., & Larson, A. D. (1986). Hiskey-Nebraska Test of Learning Aptitude. In D. J. Keyser & R. C. Sweetland (Eds.), *Test critiques* (Vol. 3, pp. 331–339). Kansas City, MO: Test Corporation of America.

Murphy, K. R. (1992). Review of the Test of Nonverbal Intelligence, second edition (TONI-2). In J. J. Kramer & J. C. Conoley (Eds.), *The eleventh mental measurements yearbook*. Lincoln, NE: Buros Institute of Mental Measurements. 969–970.

Naglieri, J. A. (1985). *Matrix Analogies Test–Expanded Form, examiner's manual*. Columbus, OH: Merril.

Naglieri, J. A. (1991a). Matrix Analogies Test: Expanded Form (MAT-EF). In R. C. Sweetland & D. J. Keyser (Eds.), *Tests: A comprehensive reference for assessments in psychology, education, and business* (3rd ed., p. 593). Austin, TX: Pro-Ed.

Naglieri, J. A. (1991b). Matrix Analogies Test: Short Form (MAT–SF). In R. C. Sweetland & D. J. Keyser (Eds.), *Tests: A comprehensive reference for assessments in psychology, education, and business* (3rd ed., pp. 593–594). Austin, TX: Pro-Ed.

Naglieri, J. A., & Prewett, P. N. (1990). Nonverbal intelligence measures: A selected review of instruments and their use. In C. R. Reynolds & R. W. Kamphaus (Eds.), *Handbook of psychological and educational assessment of children: Intelligence and achievement* (pp. 348–370). New York: Guilford.

Page, E. B. (1985). Review of Kaufman Assessment Battery for Children. In

J. V. Mitchell, Jr. (Ed.), *The ninth mental measurements yearbook* (Vol. 1, pp. 773–777). Lincoln, NE: Buros Institute of Mental Measurements.

Petrosko, J. M. (1978). Columbia Mental Maturity Scale, third edition. In O. K. Buros (Ed.), *The eighth mental measurements yearbook* (pp. 301–302). Highland Park, NJ: Gryphon Press.

Raven, J. C., Court, J. H., & Raven, J. (1947a). *Coloured progressive matrices*. London: Lewis.

Raven, J. C., Court, J. H., & Raven, J. (1947b). *Standard progressive matrices*. London: Lewis.

Reschly, D. J., & Wilson, M. S. (1990). Cognitive processing versus traditional intelligence: Diagnostic utility, intervention implications, and treatment validity. *School Psychology Review, 19,* 443–458.

Robinson, A. (1987). Matrix Analogies Test. In D. J. Keyser & R. C. Sweetland (Eds.), *Test critiques* (Vol. 6, pp. 336–340). Kansas City, MO: Test Corporation of America.

Sattler, J. M. (1988). *Assessment of children* (3rd ed.). San Diego, CA: Author.

Sternberg, R. J. (1992). Ability tests, measurements, and markets. *Journal of Educational Psychology, 84,* 134–140.

Sternberg, R. J., & Weil, E. M. (1980). An aptitude-strategy interaction in linear syllogistic reasoning. *Journal of Educational Psychology, 72,* 226–234.

Watson, T. S. (1992). Review of the Test of Nonverbal Intelligence, second edition. In J. J. Kramer & J. C. Conoley (Eds.), *The eleventh mental measurements yearbook* (pp. 970–972). Lincoln, NE: Buros Institute of Mental Measurements.

Wechsler, D. (1991). *Wechsler Intelligence Scale for Children-Third Edition*. San Antonio, TX: Psychological Corporation.

9

Achievement Testing with Culturally and Linguistically Diverse Students

Kenneth W. Howell and Robert Rueda

Taking tests is part of going to school. Some students have taken intelligence tests, others have taken specific tests of reading skill, and others have taken tests designed to determine if they have disabilities. But almost all students in the United States, at some point in their academic lives, have taken that long walk down to the school cafeteria to pick up a No. 2 pencil and fill in the bubbles on an achievement test. This chapter is written to help the reader understand why that journey occurs, what benefits (if any) it yields, and how it may be a different sort of journey for some students than for others.

Achievement Testing: Definition and Characteristics

Standardized Norm- or Criterion-Referenced Achievement Tests (SNATs) have been a part of the educational setting for decades. Their influence on the way we make decisions about teaching and learning extends well beyond the individual student (Wang, Haertel, and Walberg, 1993). While criticisms of traditionally configured SNATs abound, their use continues. In this respect, they apparently share a common destiny with basal readers—to be universally hated—and to be universally used. Eighty percent of the tests used across whole school systems are SNATs and 71 percent are multiple-choice SNATs (General Accounting Office, 1993).

Achievement tests are devices used to summarize student performance within general domains of school curriculum (Haertel, 1990). There are individually administered achievement tests, and there are group administered SNATs. This chapter focuses primarily on group administered instruments. However, most of the observations and findings reported here are also applicable to individually administered tests. One difference between group and individual tests is that the latter are typically given to determine if a student qualifies for services under one of the special programs supported by categorical funding (such as Chapter I or Special Education). Readers interested in the utility of these measures, and the practicality of combining the construct of "achievement" with the assumptions of categorical programming (Ried, Maag, and Vasa, 1994), may wish to review the sizable body of literature dealing with procedures for determining eligibility for special education (Ysseldyke, Algozzine, and Thurlow, 1992), and for sorting students in general (Glaser and Silver, 1994).

SNATs are characterized by certain formats and technical characteristics:

- SNATs are generally group administered.

- SNATs are used for summative evaluation.

- SNATs characteristically require students to identify answers, usually in a multiple-choice format, rather than to produce answers.

- SNATs cover a wide range of curricular content beginning with very "easy" items and moving in sequence to those that are "harder" (meaning that the number of items selected to appear on the test for any particular segment of curriculum is very small).

- SNATs tend to be "construct-driven" (Messick, 1994) rather than "task-driven" in that they attempt to summarize the general notion of achievement rather than competence at any specific skill.

- SNATs tend to be "answer-driven." They focus on the answers students give, rather than the processes students follow to arrive at answers or the levels of assistance that students require. In addition, they treat all answers, regardless of complexity, using the same measurement rules (that is, one answer equals one point).

- SNATs employ structured items rather than open-ended questions.

- SNATs are supposedly employed uniformly across geographic, political, ethnic, racial, cultural, economic, and language groups.

- SNATs are given infrequently, for example, to students in Grades 5, 8, and 12. In addition, the schedule of administration has nothing to do with the needs of any particular student or the desires of any particular teacher; test schedules are set by school boards or legislatures.

- SNATs compare student performance to standards derived through sampling processes driven by traditional thinking about reliability and validity (Moss, 1994).

- SNATs yield "scores" rather than behavioral statements. An obtained score of "12" does not mean that a student does twelve of anything; performance must be translated from its obtained form (into some form of standard score) before it can be interpreted.

- SNATs use time as a mechanism for imposing an absolute limitation on score variability (therefore increasing reliability) rather than as an indicator of proficiency.

- SNATs are not sensitive to instruction—massive instructional efforts are required to make significant changes in the scores these instruments yield.

Taken together, this list presents an image of assessment that is completely nonaligned (Spady, 1988) with instruction. It is probably for this reason that SNATs are such popular targets for criticism (Haney and Madaus, 1989; Darling-Hammond, 1993). However, much of this dissatisfaction can be attributed as much to confusion about the purpose of SNATs as it can to their structural characteristics.

Achievement Testing and Minority Students

If any assessment procedure is to have legitimate impact, it must be carried out fairly. As long as factors such as prior knowledge, communication skills, content relevance, incompatible formats, and scoring bias are distributed equally across populations, concerns about the quality of the measure are merely technical. However, if there is differential influence within or upon particular groups of students, the concern becomes one of fairness.

Although the differential achievement of racial, ethnic, and linguistic minority group students on standardized achievement tests (and school in general) is well documented in the literature (Armour-Thomas, 1992; Duran, 1983, 1988; Gandara, Keogh, and Yoshioka-Maxwell, 1980; Goldman and Hewitt, 1976; Powers, Escamilla, and Haussler, 1986; Zeidner and Moss, 1992), there is increasing attention to this problem in the social science literature. In the past, explanations for this pattern often tended to be reduced to nature-versus-nurture accounts. However, more recent views are more differentiated and complex. For example, Sue and Padilla (1986) have characterized various explanations as falling into one of the following: genetic or cultural deficit, cultural difference, and context-related factors.

Another system for categorizing explanations for the differential performance of culturally or linguistically diverse (CLD) students on SNATs has been proposed by Trueba (1989). This author outlined five differentiated hypotheses:

- Cultural patterns or norms shared by members of a given group may come into conflict with those embedded in achievement tests.

- Low status and income level alone are sufficient to limit the participation of members of affected groups in educational activities. (This hypothesis recognizes differences in minority group response to low status—that is, it holds that groups may collectively respond to low social and economic status in different ways. Some groups view this status as better than what they had, while others view it as the continuation of discrimination and prejudice.)

- Differential achievement is rooted in culture-specific parental attitudes and beliefs about achievement.

- Inherited mental endowments related to achievement or abilities are tapped by standardized tests, which really do measure genetic or inborn characteristics.

- Achievement and abilities are context specific, that is, "situated" in specific social and cultural contexts. (From this sociocultural perspective, overall group differences on tests are thought to be more related to the conditions under which those abilities are measured than to the characteristics of group members based on approaches to learning and achievement.)

Factors Impacting the Use of SNATs with Minority Students

While each of the hypotheses in the previous list can explain (with varying levels of success) systematic differences among group means on academic achievement measures, none of them necessarily explain the actual mechanisms of partition. Figueroa (1990) has provided a comprehensive review of the use of both intelligence and achievement tests with minority students from both an historical and a contemporary context. Many of Figueroa's conclusions fit into one or more of the categories just listed. For example, relative to the cultural discontinuity hypothesis, the author states that the assumption of a uniform curriculum and schooling experience across ethnic, language, and socioeconomic groups (an underlying assumption of SNATs that is critical to test interpretation) is highly debatable.

A great deal of research in the past decades has been focused on the context-specific sociocultural hypothesis and the related presumption that variables such as time limits, test attitudes, examiner-examinee rapport, motivation, and anxiety account for the low performance of CLD students. While the literature offers surprising little support for this hypothesis (Figueroa, 1990; Zeidner, 1988), some authors have responded to this scarcity by calling for more differentiated and conceptually refined treatment of the variable we know of as "culture" (Helms, 1992). At any rate, the fact that culture has powerful effects on learning is well established in the literature (Heath, 1989; Tharp, 1989).

Language interference may be a major factor. As Figueroa (1990) correctly notes, the impact of language on testing has been relatively uninvestigated. This is a serious omission because, in addition to the complexities surrounding cultural influences in assessment, there are language-related factors that must also be considered (Cortes, 1986; Cummins, 1986; Garcia and Pearson, 1994). What follows is a brief summary of some of the language principles that may explain the disparate SNAT scores of CLD students:

Linguistic threshold. For students who are not native speakers of English, the degree to which both the primary and secondary language are developed is associated with positive academic outcomes. When neither language is developed to proficiency, verbally mediated cognitive functions tapped in both schooling and achievement measures are diminished. This effect is especially negative if the more poorly developed language is also the language of instruction.

Dimensions of language proficiency. Although the dichotomy has been criticized as oversimplified, Cummins (1981) and others have argued that one dimension of language proficiency is characterized as that used in everyday conversation, while a second is used for the context-reduced and cognitively demanding purpose of school learning. While the first dimension is acquired relatively easily and quickly (on the order of two to three years), the second is not. When mastery of everyday communication is mistaken for academic communication the impact on assessment can be especially disastrous.

Common underlying proficiency. When complex language-related competencies are acquired in the first language, these transfer relatively effortlessly to the second. Because it is primarily these higher-order skills that are tapped in both schooling and SNATs, the interpretation of scores cannot be left to considerations of simple communication proficiency. The student's opportunity to develop complex thinking must also be considered, even if proficiency in academic language has been developed.

Some changes in assessment practices for students with limited English proficiency have taken place. For example, bilingualism is no longer automatically viewed as an impediment to learning, cognition, and achievement. In fact it is increasingly being viewed as an advantage. Additionally, for Hispanic students at least, native language assessments are increasingly available and more and more widely used.

However, problems clearly remain. The most obvious of these is that verbally loaded items continue to produce the worst performance among minority test takers. And, although items and formats without verbal loading continue to be touted as a more appropriate approach for students who are not native speakers of English, their use remains inconsistent at best.

Current and Changing Practice Regarding Test Quality

Traditional discussions of the character of assessment have focused on a uniform set of criteria for test quality. These have been customarily articulated in the form of subsets of reliability and validity (that is, predictive validity, internal consistency, and test-retest reliability). However, more recent discussions on the topic have established *purpose* as the central aspect of quality by making the point that a tool is best judged in relation to the task it is meant to perform and the consequences of its use (Moss, 1992). Of course, such discussions unfailingly lead to other forms of partition—in this case, subdivisions of purpose and consequence.

Inside and outside. While numerous conceptualizations of purpose have been presented, the subdivision suggested by Baker and O'Neil (1994) is particularly appealing. These authors suggest that purposes of testing can be divided into those with loci outside the classroom and those with inside loci. Some examples of *outside* purpose are: accountability of state, school district, school, or teacher; screening for students who might be eligible for placement into a special program; classification of students into disability or other program categories; retention of students; and grading. These activities have little to do with the services delivered to students within classes or with the decisions teachers make about those services.

Purposes for assessment that might be considered *inside* include those that inform teacher decisions and have immediate impact on the services students receive. Some examples of these are: deciding what and how to teach an individual student; charting the prior knowledge of a student so as to select lessons at the correct level of complexity; monitoring student learning to recognize when objectives should be altered or discontinued; judging the effectiveness of an instructional procedure; setting learning aims; and collecting feedback for the teacher in terms of his or her own effectiveness.

These inside and outside purposes for assessment are somewhat analogous to the *proximal* and *distal* variables of learning. Wang, Haertel, and Walberg (1993), for example, discuss variables in terms of those that are closely related to learning (the proximal variables) and those that are not (the distal variables). Proximal variables, such as student prior knowledge, teacher classroom management skills, and the teacher's use of effective instruction are closely tied to student learning. On the other hand, distal variables (such as district and state policies on things like teacher credentialing, school-site management, and funding) are less directly related to student learning. Extension of this comparison to testing leads to the idea that, when one is testing for an inside purpose, one is collecting information for use in manipulating proximal variables.

High-stakes. It can be argued that the public policy (outside) purpose of assessment also has impact on the learning of students, but that this impact tends to be delayed and unrelated to the individual student. The group-administered variants of SNATs are characteristically given to address what has come to be known as the high-stakes agendas of teacher accountability, state or district monitoring, and image building (Porter, 1993). The topic of high-stakes testing is thoroughly covered in Chapter Eighteen. The term *high stakes* refers, once again, to the purpose for which the assessment is being conducted—not to the format of the instrument. In this case, the stakes are said to be high because the testing results are used for decisions relative to allocations of resources and the authorization of particular programmatic agendas. SNATs are used for these agendas because they seem to provide the benchmark data needed to guide the restructuring of education.

Given the information already provided regarding the performance of CLD students on SNATs, it should be clear that, if the data base used to inform restructuring are drawn from SNATs, restructuring itself may not reflect the needs of CLD students. The clearest evidence of this potential may be seen not in the data on low performance of CLD students but in the data on their exclusion from high-stakes exercises (McGill-Franzen and Allington, 1993).

All states exclude some students from standardized achievement testing programs. Two groups commonly excluded are special education and limited-English proficiency (LEP) students. The rate of this exclusion increases when high-stakes testing is implemented (Behrmann, 1993). In addition, the proportion of students excluded varies widely from state to state, and the criteria for exclusion are inconsistent (National Academy of Education [NAE], 1993). This variability is related to the proportion of CLD students in a state's population. But it is also related to variability in state and school district definitions of LEP as well as to the local exclusion policy (with some schools excluding all LEP students). New Mexico and Utah, for example, appear to classify all Native Americans as LEP regardless of their English proficiency (NAE, 1993). When interpreting this material, we encourage the reader to remember that there is a certain irony revealed by the coalition of high-stakes testing and SNATs. That is, given the outside nature of SNATs, one can only assume that the stakes are high for someone other than the learner.

Problems with SNATs

Beyond the more lofty topic of purpose, there are also certain functional issues related to test quality. These considerations typically have to do with the measurement aspects of an instrument, and the degree to which the process of measurement embodied in the device reflects both legitimate measurement practice and accurate definition of the quantities intended for measurement. Exhibit 9.1 provides a listing of measurement problems often exhibited by SNATs, along with a brief explanation of each. An examination of

Exhibit 9.1. Test Problems and Solutions.

Problem	Recommended Solution
Tests do not have clearly defined purposes.	Know the purpose and limitations of the instrument being used. Determine whether it is meant for inside or outside use.
SNATs do not measure defined content and behavioral domains.	Be able to cross-reference items and procedures to content and behavioral domains.
SNAT items are not keyed to objectives.	Develop a test plan that cross-references items to objectives.
Few SNATs permit examination of strategic behavior.	Decide whether product evaluation is sufficient. If not, devise a way to make students' thought processes observable.
Many SNATs do not permit evaluators to collect an adequate sample.	Select tests that supply a large number of items covering content the student is expected to know.
SNATs do not allow the collection of rate data.	Design or select alternative tests that collect rate data by assuring the random distribution of item difficulty, adequate sample size, and opportunity to respond.
SNATs are not designed for use as repeated measures.	Identify applied tasks that reflect the use of subskills, or design multiple versions of specific skill tests.
Many SNATs feature stimulus formats that are inappropriate.	Select or develop tests that ask students to do things like the things they do in class.
SNATs use insensitive scoring procedures.	Select tests that employ measurement rules that assign points to smallest educationally relevant unit.

these problems, particularly those dealing with issues of classroom utility, shows that many of them are related to purpose.

SNATs are designed to highlight the relative status of groups by using devices that accentuate the differences between them. The most obvious of these devices is the presentation of a large range of content that forces students to attend to material that may or may not have been taught in their class or school. This presentation of a range of content assures variability in scores, thereby supporting the contrasting function of the test. However, this efficient revelation of variability is obtained at the cost of specificity and sufficiency. Because all the students must attend to items that are below, above, or outside of the curriculum within which they are working, there is less time available to collect an adequate sample of work on the material they really have been studying (and that a teacher has been delivering to them). In simpler terms, this means that the content of six weeks of math instruction may end up being reflected on a SNAT in a single fraction-to-decimal conversion item. That is fine if one is comparing the scores of a hundred students in two different math programs, but it is not fine if one is trying to decide, with confidence, which of those students can convert a fraction to a decimal.

In summary, many of the problems listed in Exhibit 9.1 are the result of efforts to efficiently collect information about the standing of groups relative to each other, in order to make comparison-based decisions that affect groups. To meet this objective, SNATs employ formats and procedures that make them unsatisfactory sources of the information needed to inform singular teaching decisions (an inside purpose).

Alternatives and Issues

In the next section, we will consider some of the alternatives for assessment that have been developed in response to the shortcomings of the SNATs.

Curriculum-Based Measurement

In general, Curriculum-Based Measurement (CBM) approaches all share the common concern of measuring achievement of an individual student in terms of the expected curricular outcomes of a given school. The primary focus is on developing outcomes that are always connected to the local curriculum and on making them measurable.

The reliability and validity of CBM measures has been demonstrated by a variety of authors (Deno, 1989; Marston and Magnusson, 1988), as has the favorable comparison of these measures to SNATs (Jenkins and Jewell, 1993). Chapter Seven of this book covers CBM in considerable depth. However, there are certain elements of CBM that deserve some additional emphasis here. The first of these is that CBM makes use of standard overlay formats, or *scoring shells*, which are applied to classroom tasks. Because the stimulus materials utilized are native to the classroom, these scoring shells, and the guidelines for interpreting the results of their application, are what constitutes the actual CBM technology. This reliance on tasks evolved from the classroom context tends to improve the utility of the procedure for inside purposes (a characteristic CBM shares with the "portfolio" variant of performance assessment).

Another characteristic of CBM that tends to set it apart from other techniques is its use of rate, or fluency, as a matrix for indexing performance. Rate tests are not "speeded," as that term is often used, because they do not simply time students on a set of mixed items (that is, items covering various content, ordered by complexity, to be worked within a set interval). Instead, rate procedures are designed to summarize the fluency with which a student can work particular tasks. Therefore, while traditional SNATs do not allow the rate at which a student works on one particular task to be disaggregated from the total score, this is allowed on most CBM measures.

As a consequence, the measures yield information about the student's knowledge in terms of quickness, or alacrity, not simply accuracy. By recognizing and summarizing this additional proficiency dimension, the developers of CBM have produced a set of procedures that are more sensitive to learning than traditional alternatives.

CBM is also extremely efficient (Deno, 1985). The procedures have been shown to duplicate the information supplied by SNATs at a fraction of the cost in money and student time (Marston and Magnusson, 1988). For a thorough review of the issues associated with the use of CBM with diverse populations, see Chapter Seven.

Performance Assessment

Performance Assessment (PA) is being widely advanced as an alternative to SNATs (Poteet, Choate, and Stewart, 1993). In part, this advocacy is based on the belief that SNATs provide a very decontextualized and cognitively simple view of learning. The level of student understanding needed for success on SNATs is said to be low because the items are presented in isolation and without supporting context. In distinction, performance measures, which tend to make use of sizable projects rather than sequences of test items, are designed to reveal deeper understandings by allowing more time for students to work. This work is also designed to be more authentic because it involves doing things (as opposed to answering questions), working on tasks that are thought to be important, and solving problems (Coutinho and Malouf, 1993; Feuer and Fulton, 1993; Gitomer, 1993). Example performance tasks might include: planning and building a model to illustrate mathematics skill; writing an article for a local newspaper to illustrate written expression; or writing a review of a book to document reading skills.

Two other important characteristics of PA are that students may receive assistance during the examination and that the performance samples can be collected over time to illustrate trends in the formation of learning.

The issue of assistance is of particular interest relative to current views of learning that emphasize a student's awareness of the work at hand (Paris and Winograd, 1990). Often in PA, the student is expected to monitor his or her own work and to select resources as needed. These resources may include reference materials or the cooperation of teachers or peers. Therefore, both the process of task completion and the quality of the finished product are taken into account when summarizing performance. This means that two students completing equally sophisticated products could get different scores because of differences in the ways those products were produced (for example, one with considerable teacher support and one with little teacher support).

The formative application of PA is illustrated most clearly in *portfolio assessment*. In portfolio assessment, student work samples are collected across time to illustrate either the total mass of student work, improvement, or the illustration of exemplary products. By including the passage of time as well as levels of performance among the factors educators can consider when judging student work, PA can be used to inform decisions about the relative effectiveness of instructional procedures for individual students. This formative characteristic is shared with CBM (Fuchs and Fuchs, 1992).

Problems and Issues with Alternatives

Because of the controversial legal and psychological aspects of standardized tests, curriculum-based measures and performance-based assessment have often been seen as the "final solution" for an agglomerate of problems. However, these assessment approaches are not problem free by any means. Potential problem areas are noted in the following paragraphs.

Curriculum-Based Measurement

Although CBM was initially rooted in, and identified with, behaviorist approaches to learning, this focus has expanded. For example, Howell, Fox, and Morehead (1993) present curriculum-based evaluation in the context of an information processing model. Nevertheless, there are still behaviorist elements common to CBM that tend to distinguish it from other approaches and that may affront some educators. For example, the focus on observable behavior and the task-analytic decomposition of complex domains are characteristic (Tindal and Marston, 1990). This gives CBM at least the appearance of a skills-based and decontextualized approach. Such an appearance could be of particular concern for teachers of language minority students, as the most common techniques used for literacy instruction with language minority students in the United States are more "holistic" or "whole-language" approaches (Freeman and Freeman, 1992; Peitzman and Gadda, 1992). And it seems likely that advocates of these approaches would view the apparent skills focus of CBM as antithetical to the tenets of whole-language instruction and assessment.

Another potential problem is that many general education teachers may see CBM as appropriate only for special education settings. CBM has gained much support in special education as the emphasis on skills in CBM represents a shift away from the previous focus on invalidated and hypothetical psychological learning traits (Deno and Espin, 1991). However, the use of CBM in general education is still not widespread. It is possible that general education teachers may also view the CBM process as unrealistic for their own classrooms, particularly as they require a highly developed knowledge of curriculum in the various content areas. Such in-depth knowledge of curricular content is not characteristic of all teachers, and it is likely that the development of that knowledge would appear to be too time consuming and labor intensive to many.

Performance Assessment

PAs are regularly designed to reflect long-term learning (that is, across a semester as in a portfolio or across years as in some state-level performance tests), are based in large part on naturally occurring classroom tasks and content, allow for multiple processes and ways to build and display knowledge, and yield products that may include information by teachers or other relevant participants such as parents.

If these tests are to be used for outside purposes, the first obvious concern is cost. Aside from the considerable cost required to retrain school personnel in the use of performance measures (this same cost would be incurred with CBM), it appears that the cost of collecting performance data on a student is many times that of collecting data using a SNAT. For example, the Arizona Student Assessment Plan (ASAP) is a performance-based process recently developed to replace the Iowa Test of Basic Skills. According to the March 1993 ASAP summary statistics, 44,196 eighth graders took the English nonmediated version of the reading, mathematics, and writing assessments. There are three forms of these tests at each grade level (the tests are given at Grades 3, 8, and 12) and, depending on how much progress a student makes during the year, a student may take only one form, or all three (Arizona Department of Education, 1993). For the sake of this example, we only discuss the writing tests and will assume that the average eighth-grade student took two forms during the year. The test form reviewed by the authors was eight pages long, and that means that, within our example, the average eighth grader would use sixteen pages of paper for the writing section of the ASAP alone. That makes a total of 707,136 pages. Because the ASAP forms are distributed to schools and photocopied on site, local districts are required to absorb the costs of reproducing the tests, which would include paper, machine maintenance, personnel time, and distribution. Note that this list of costs does not include time to administer and score the tests or summarize the results.

However, the potential for bias in performance measures may be of more direct concern to readers of this text. Part of the appeal of performance measures is that they are seen as alternatives to identification-formatted tests on which students simply fill in a bubble to indicate the answer. However, any move to increase the sophistication of student responses must also increase the degree to which resulting scores will reflect the student's skill at displaying knowledge (for example, through written or oral expression). That is fine as long as the test is a communications test; it is not fine for a history test.

The equity issue is whether PA will have equal impact across diverse groups and contexts (for example, in poor versus rich schools). When equity is considered, one of characteristics of performance testing that is thought to be a strength, the use of complex and interactive tasks, may also be a weakness—particularly if that characteristic interacts differentially with different student populations. Complex measures are more likely to interact with unintended factors than simple measures. Factors described above (for example, cognitive classification styles, language thresholds, and common proficiency), which are sufficiently powerful to differentiate between cultures, can be expected to have an impact on test scores unless they are systematically controlled. And control, which has yet to be satisfactorily demonstrated with traditional measures, can be expected to decrease with the complexity of the new measures. Unfortunately, these concerns are primarily speculative—there is little, if any, empirical information regarding differential effects of performance measures on CLD students (Baker and O'Neil, 1994).

There is, however, some information available about the way complex measures are scored. Tests have a format (shell) and they have content. The format must be somewhat constraining and clearly understood before test results can be attributed to difference in knowledge of the content. In the case of complex measures, in which the format is unstructured, the degree to which one can attribute different levels of student performance to different levels of student knowledge is diminished. The solution to this problem is to compensate for the complex format with a structured set of standards for judging performance: the rubric. However, if the rubric contains elements that are not interpreted the same way by all teachers, or addressed in all cultural contexts, then its application may affect the resulting judgment just as surely as that judgment might be affected by a nonrepresentative norming sample or a culturally unfair test item.

Traughber (1994) found limited agreement among different

groups of teachers (that is, general education, special education, various grade levels) in their use of rubrics. This was true even after considerable training. In addition, the equitable application of a written expression rubric was examined by Howell, Bigelow, Moore, and Evoy (1994). In this study, the spelling, handwriting, syntax, and organization of two writing samples were held constant. While no personal information was provided to scorers regarding the hypothetical author, minor changes in wording were used to convey the possibility that the author of one version was a CLD student. The two versions were randomly distributed to seventy-nine teachers for scoring. It was found that, given the same rubric and equivalent writing samples, the samples of students whom teachers perceived to be of minority status were scored significantly higher than those perceived to be of majority status.

When confronted with results like those just presented, advocates of PA will often insist that bias can be controlled through scorer training or through developing rubrics with less room for interpretation. It is no doubt possible to standardize scoring by training scorers to high levels of agreement. It may also be possible to avoid bias, or low reliability, by more specifically defining the descriptive nature of rubrics. However, both of these activities have the ironic effect of focusing on observable behavior and decomposing complex domains. Those were the same complaints leveled earlier against CBM and give PA the same appearance of a skills-based and decontextualized technology. For a comprehensive review of PA, see Chapter Eleven.

Problems of Perspective

While much has been made in this chapter and others of the noncorrespondence between achievement measures and classroom curriculum, it is important to consider that while the apparent lack of relation between SNATs and classroom tasks seems bad, this may not be the case if the classroom tasks are themselves unrelated to the broader constructs of achievement, literacy, and social competence. It is certainly possible for the curriculum itself to be biased

(Messick, 1994), or for it to interfere with a student's language or cultural characteristics. Externally developed and mandated testing initiatives can be one buffer against this risk. However, this prospect puts educators interested in supporting CLD students in the uncomfortable position of deciding which of two negative outcomes they fear the most: their loss of local control over what is taught or their fear that CLD students may be receiving qualitatively inferior educations.

Any thorough program evaluation must include information derived from an independent source (Tyler, 1991). Measurement of a quantity from multiple perspectives, sometimes referred to as *triangulation* (Kansas State Board of Education, 1992), defines the quantity more clearly. In addition, arguments for external validity can only be made if one of these perspectives is outside of the system. The goal, common to both CBM and PA, of clearly describing what is happening inside a classroom is admirable. But it must be remembered that that goal can be met even if what is happening there is trivial. Therefore, the utility of either of these alternatives must ultimately be linked to efforts at clarifying what students should be taught.

Comparing the Options

Today, SNATs, PAs, and CBMs all have their advocates. In Exhibits 9.2, 9.3, and 9.4, each of these options will be briefly described across a set of common properties in order to allow the reader to contrast them. To assist in interpreting these exhibits, each property will be briefly explained (some of the properties, such as purpose, have already been covered at some length and others have not). These explanations are provided to allow the reader to understand the comments made in each table, rather than to convince the reader that they are true (the comments themselves present the author's judgments). It should also be noted that there are many variations in the specific applications that might fall under each

Exhibit 9.2. Standardized Published (Criterion- or Norm-Referenced) Achievement Tests.

Attributes: Traditional approach; based on theories of sampling and psychometrics; developed by testing industry; often group administered; given infrequently; summarize what has been taught (that is, summative); widely criticized as misleading, unfair, and of limited instructional utility.

View of Knowledge: There is a relatively stable quantity known as *achievement*; achievement is indicated by the production of specific answers; achievement can be summarized statistically.

Sensitivity to Learning: Very low.

Domains Sampled: General samples of content across a wide range of grade levels; content typically selected by test publisher; items selected according to measurement concerns and utility for discriminating among students; alignment with local curriculum and/or instructional materials may be low; content specifications are typically limited.

Behaviors Sampled: Testing carried out in groups, typically outside of the classroom; assistance not allowed; use predominantly multiple-choice, select-answer formats; responses marked on separate form; work not shown or graded.

Standards Used: National sampling in most cases although local norms are sometimes available; proportion of standardization sample falling into major subgroup categories reported; disabled students often excluded from sample; CLD students often excluded from sample; "criterion-referenced" standards based on performance of the standardization sample (typically the mean at each grade level); comparison of behavior to standards summarized in a wide choice of standard scores (for example, percentile, stanine, grade equivalence).

Cost: Much more expensive than CBM, cheaper than PA.

Compatibility with Holistic Learning Orientation: Low.

Compatibility with Direct Instruction Orientation: Low.

Usefulness for Inside Purposes: Very limited.

Usefulness for Outside Purposes: Good as long as the weaknesses (listed above) are understood by those interpreting the results; provides perspective from outside of the class, school district, or state.

Exhibit 9.2. Standardized Published (Criterion- or Norm-Referenced) Achievement Tests, Cont'd.

Strengths: Long history of use; provides outside perspective; reliability, validity, and technical adequacy known and described; likelihood of fraudulent use by teachers, schools, or districts is relatively low because tests are considered to be secure; highly correlated to grades.

Weaknesses: Summative only; little instructional utility; nonaligned with local curriculum; expensive; apparently biased.

Exhibit 9.3. Curriculum-Based Measurement.

Attributes: Tasks drawn directly from curriculum and materials found in classroom; scores derived from summaries of performance on either integrated tasks or isolated skills; uses repeated measures to determine performance and learning trends; frequently summarizes performance in terms of rate; measures take very little time, often a minute or less.

View of Knowledge: Knowledge is indicated by demonstration of outcomes specified in the curriculum; success depends on the acquisition of prior knowledge.

Sensitivity to Learning: Very high.

Domains Sampled: Samples employ common classroom tasks that rely upon, and therefore reflect, prerequisite skills (prior knowledge); performance is linked to highly specified content and behavior domains; only tasks appearing in the curriculum and taught in classes are used.

Behaviors Sampled: The student makes the same responses as during lessons; tests are frequently timed to allow for the collection of rate data.

Standards Used: When used for outside purposes, locally obtained norms are used; when used for inside purposes, performance criteria—often obtained by sampling successful students—are used; idiosyncratic standards are evoked through repeated measurement and determination of trend to allow monitoring and adjustments in instruction.

Cost: Very low.

Compatibility with Holistic Learning Orientation: Decomposition of complex skills for scoring purposes seems incompatible with holistic orientation;

Exhibit 9.3. Curriculum-Based Measurement, Cont'd.

however, use of complex behavior samples drawn from the classroom context does seem compatible.

Compatibility with Direct Instruction Orientation: Very high.

Usefulness for Inside Purposes: Very high.

Usefulness for Outside Purposes: Reported to be highly useful for screening and determination of eligibility for special programs; however, no history of use for accountability of teachers or schools.

Strengths: Directly samples and summarizes the student's knowledge of what is being taught; focus on prior knowledge (in the form of subtasks and strategies) makes the procedure useful for educational problem solving; extremely quick and economical; highly correlated with SNATs; useful for formative evaluation.

Weaknesses: If the curriculum it reflects is flawed, CBM will be flawed; CBM is generally unknown outside of special education and school psychology; although CBM has recently been extended to preschool and secondary education, in the past it has been largely limited to the sampling of basic skills; "behavioral" image; perceived as being incompatible with the holistic learning orientation.

Exhibit 9.4. Performance-Based Assessment.

Attributes: Innovative; based on theories of learning; usually applies standard "shells" to locally selected tasks (although statewide implementation may use tools developed by testing industry); group or individually administered; can be given frequently and infused into instruction; typically summative but can be used to monitor progress (formative); allows multiple ways to demonstrate knowledge.

View of Knowledge: Learning is fluid and contextual; the quality of learning is negotiated within each social context (for example, a classroom); knowledge is best indicated by planning and assembling products.

Sensitivity to Learning: Potentially high because of alignment with classroom instruction. However, if the measures are imported, the alignment could be lost. Also, sensitivity may decrease with the complexity of the

Exhibit 9.4. Performance-Based Assessment, Cont'd.

task, problems separating individual performance from the participation of peers or the assistance of teachers, quality of rubrics, and the inconsistency of judges.

Domains Sampled: Complex and interactive tasks requiring the use of both basic skills and problem solving; content typically selected locally; work is compared to "rubrics" containing categories derived from the analysis of completed products.

Behaviors Sampled: Items selected according to ideas about authenticity; testing is typically carried out in groups within the classroom; assistance is allowed; projects, or portfolio formats, are employed to allow the student to choose the way to demonstrate what is known; work is shown and graded.

Standards Used: Performance judged by raters; training of raters is usually done locally or at the state level; disabled and CLD students are often excluded from the testing and their work is not used for training of raters; and, rubrics usually contain content statements (for example, "punctuation used") but not criteria (for example "punctuation correct 95 percent of the time").

Cost: More expensive than SNATs and much more expensive than CBM.

Compatibility with Holistic Learning Orientation: High.

Compatibility with Direct Instruction Orientation: Low.

Usefulness for Inside Purposes: High.

Usefulness for Outside Purposes: Low.

Strengths: Rich behavior samples can provide useful information to teachers who wish to analyze the work samples; students who have difficulty displaying knowledge through traditional formats may do better in this arrangement; assessment tasks are meant to be "authentic" representations of real and meaningful work.

Weaknesses: Very little information on reliability and validity; extremely expensive; extreme risk of rater bias; risk that complex nature of the tasks may confound interpretation of results.

general technique, and the distinctions made here are clearer in discussion than in practice.

Attributes

This category lists characteristics of the procedures that are thought to be definitional to their nature. These attributes may be philosophical, operational, measurement-based, or political. The purpose of the attribute list is to quickly illustrate the procedure, not to explain it.

View of Knowledge and Instruction

Different instructional and evaluative techniques often seem to be more or less compatible with different ideas about knowledge and how it is acquired. In the next paragraphs, we will try to briefly summarize the differences and detail the implications of these as they impact assessment practice.

Standardized Achievement Measures

Standardized achievement tests are not usually associated with any specific model of learning. Rather, they reflect a psychometric, or statistical, model of achievement. In this sense, they are standard procedures designed to sample a specified set or domain of measurable behaviors (Crocker and Algina, 1986). Data produced by SNATs are characterized by the fact that they are explicit, quantitative, and reproducible, with a special focus on reliability and validity. The scores produced by SNATs are quantitative in nature and are used to draw inferences about how much of a theoretical construct (in this case achievement) an individual can be said to possess relative to the distribution of scores displayed by a reference (that is, norm) group.

When translated into measures of literacy, SNATs rely on a limited number of carefully sampled facsimiles of classroom tasks that are then used to derive a composite index of academic achievement. Since these are normally restricted to a paper-and-pencil format with strict time limits, the types and numbers of formats tend to be limited. In summary, SNATs illustrate learning as learning is often presented in traditional classrooms—in separate bundles and associated with the production of answers.

Curriculum-Based Measurement

Once again, a major influence in the development of CBM is the behavioral approach to learning. As Malone (1990) correctly points out, there are many variants of behaviorally based learning theories and the rigid mind-behavior dichotomy often ascribed to behavioral theories (versus more cognitive-based theories) is not as fixed as some have argued. Nevertheless, as Ormrod (1990) has explained, there are some basic assumptions about learning shared by most behaviorally oriented approaches. These might include, for example, the ideas that learning can only be assumed to have occurred when a change in behavior is observed (conversely, if no behavior change is evident, learning is assumed not to have taken place); or that the learning of all behaviors, from the most simple to the most complex, should be explained by as few learning principles as possible (parsimony and conciseness are preferred in explaining learning and behavior).

CBM approaches in general share this focus on observable and measurable behavior. With respect to the assessment of literacy, these approaches also typically share the assumption that complex curricular domains can be reduced to smaller units of skills or strategies (Howell, Fox, and Morehead, 1993) that can then be independently assessed. However, advocates of CBM do not typically recommend that these skills be measured in isolation. Passage reading, for example, is preferred over the reading of words or letters (Fuchs and Fuchs, 1992). Nor do CBM advocates suggest that material be taught as small units, or in isolation. In fact in some ways, advocates of CBM do not take any position as to what instructional methodology should be used to promote learning. Instead, they believe that because "with our current assessment technology and scientific data base, unfortunately, we cannot predict with certainty an intervention that will be effective with any given student," and therefore, "treatment outcomes for specific students must be evaluated frequently and in a timely manner. Effective interventions should be maintained. Ineffective interventions should be modified" (Shinn and Hubbard, 1992, pp. 4–5).

Because advocates of CBM take the position of valuing accountability, as opposed to advocating for a particular instructional approach, they focus on the use of measures that can be efficiently incorporated within repeated performance sampling and direct observation recording of both permanent products and transitory events within fixed time (Fuchs, Fuchs, Hamlett, Walz, and Germann, 1993). They also focus on techniques that allow the graphic display of the resultant data over time. In summary, CBM takes the view that learning is a fluid quality that cannot be separated from the conditions of instruction.

Performance Assessment

In contrast to the behavioral roots of CBM and the statistical roots of SNATs, performance measures are largely based on a constructivist model of learning. Learning, from this perspective, means the active construction of knowledge in gradually expanding networks of ideas through interactions with others and materials in the environment (Marshall, 1992). As Marshall indicates:

> According to constructivist views, learning consists of building on what the learner brings to the situation and restructuring initial knowledge in widening and intersecting spirals of increasingly complex understanding. Because learners come with different background knowledge, experience, and interests, they make different connections in building their knowledge over time. . . .

> Within a constructivist framework, learning of skills and concepts is not seen as occurring in an isolated and hierarchical manner, but rather within meaningful and integrated contexts. Learning does not occur all at once, but is built over time as initial knowledge is revised and when new questions arise and old knowledge is challenged [p. 11].

Unlike the view of learning embodied in SNATs and CBM, PA seems tightly bound to a particular view of instruction. To return to Marshall, "The teacher does not serve as the main source of knowledge transmission; both students and teachers assume multiple roles. Students, too, can generate knowledge, challenge the thinking of others, and assume responsibility for their continued learning" (p. 11).

Although all constructivists believe that learning is an active process, many make the distinction between cognitive and social constructivism (Marshall, 1992; Sternberg and Wagner, 1994). In essence, the variants differ regarding the nature and influence of the social world in the process of knowledge construction. Briefly, cognitive constructivist views suggest that the learner *individually* constructs knowledge, although sometimes the role of an expert providing guidance is included. On the other hand, social constructivist views suggest that *social interaction* is the basis through which contexts, knowledge, and meanings in everyday life are constructed. In other words, learning, thinking, and higher-order cognitive processes are situated in social contexts rather than occurring at the individual level (Wertsch, 1985; Vygotsky, 1978). Importantly, these interactional processes are seen as embedded in cultural and historical contexts.

When constructivist principles are translated to the academic arena, literacy, for example, is seen as a set of *practices* that are embedded in specific social and cultural settings rather than as a set of independent skills or strategies that can be instructed in isolation

(Cooper, 1993; Hiebert, 1991; Moll, 1990; Zebroski, 1994). Given this framework, assessment relies on tasks that are authentic (that is, are meaningful to students) rather than facsimiles; focus on the process of problem solving or meaning-taking rather than the product; require the integration of higher-order cognitive processes in a holistic fashion; and reflect skills, knowledge, or abilities with real-world connections. These expectations are highly compatible with the so-called natural approach to second-language instruction described by Krashen and others (Krashen, 1980; Krashen, 1982; Krashen and Terrell, 1983; Scarcella and Krashen, 1980).

Sensitivity to Instruction

Sensitivity to instruction refers to the usefulness of the procedure for illustrating changes in a student's skill and knowledge (as illustrated by changes in the student's performance on the measure). Because the context of this chapter is schooling, the learning we are interested in here is principally that resulting from classroom activities. Therefore, an assessment technique is considered *sensitive* if its summary of student performance will change after only a brief instructional intervention. An assessment technique will be considered *insensitive* if long-term instruction is required to produce meaningful changes in performance on the measure.

The idea of sensitivity is not easily condensed into the simple ratings presented in these tables. (It is hard, for example, to determine the qualitative difference between a fairly bland intervention that went on for months and an intense intervention that only lasted a week.) However, the concept of sensitivity is critical to formative evaluation (Shinn and Hubbard, 1992), as well as to "Assisted Assessment" and "Dynamic Assessment" (Brown and French, 1979; Campione and Brown, 1985).

Domains Sampled

This descriptor, along with the next one, attempts to explain what the measurement procedure is measuring. These descriptions will not be content specific (for example, reading comprehension) as each of the procedures may be used in numerous content categories. The emphases will be on describing what a student needs to know in order to do well on the test.

Behaviors Sampled

This descriptor attempts to explain the kinds of things students do when working on one of the measurement tasks. The emphasis is on what the procedure requires a student to do in order to display the requisite knowledge.

Standards Used

Comparison is pivotal to evaluation. In order for an educator to make decisions or render judgments about a student's performance on any measure, the educator must have expectations about the quality of performance. While discussions of standards may be quite complex, the comments in the exhibits are limited to the following:

Normative standards are those evolved by summarizing the performance of other students on the same measure. The goal of normative comparison is to place the student within the context of his or her peers and to allow the evaluator to determine if performance is typical or atypical.

Behavioral standards are those developed to represent the functional level of a skill, regardless of the number of peers who may or may not have reached that level. Behavioral criteria are set by sampling the performance of selected populations, or exemplars, in order to determine how well someone must do something. Behavioral criteria may also be set through research activities that establish the relationship of performance levels to external criteria such as success in subsequent learning.

Idiosyncratic standards reside in the previous performance of a student. The idiosyncratic standard is the student's prior performance, and the student is thought to succeed if new performance surpasses that standard. This standard must be available in order for decisions to be made about personal growth.

Cost

The expense of a procedure may be determined by the cost of developing or purchasing it, administering it, and scoring it. The cost in terms of the teacher and student resources required to produce the learning and the time lost to the evaluation activity may also be factored into this summary.

Compatibility with Holistic Instruction

This category, and the next, attempt to relate each procedure to the tenets of two instructional philosophies. In this case the dichotomy of Holistic (Freeman and Freeman, 1992) and Direct (Rosenshine and Stevens, 1986) instruction will be used. Each of these orientations has been adequately described elsewhere. However, to summarize the authors' thinking, we are viewing *Holistic* as compatible with "constructivist," "whole language," and "student centered" instruction.

Today, as in every period, there is considerable conflict about what is or is not the appropriate vision of curriculum and instruction. If that vision is holistic, then broad-based measures that attempt to capture an image of general competence would seem to be preferred. If, however, the vision includes ideas about the need to guide learning and to focus instruction, then direct procedures seem called for.

Compatibility with Direct Instruction

The authors are treating *Direct* instruction as compatible with "supplantive," "outcome-based," and "teacher regulated."

Usefulness for Inside Purposes

As explained earlier, a measure is used for an inside purpose when it is employed to decide what and how to teach individual students or classes. Inside purposes include decision making about the difficulty level of an assignment, the effectiveness of instruction for a student, the setting of aims and monitoring of student learning, and the collection of information to update one's view of a student.

Usefulness for Outside Purposes

Many of the problems educators have with SNATs are reflected in Exhibit 9.1. However, the form SNATs take, while problematic, is dictated by the function they are meant to provide. Therefore, it is not adequate to simply argue for alternatives that avoid those problems. One must also argue that the alternatives can meet the function for which SNATs are currently being used. That function seems to be to obtain the sort of global and external perspective derived by collecting the masses of data needed to engineer initiatives affecting school policy (Simmons and Resnick, 1993). For example, efforts at teacher, school, district, or state accountability require the illumination of differences among teachers, schools, districts, and states. Such outside agendas are, by definition, political. And politics does not necessarily change with the introduction of new information about teaching or assessment (Stanovich, 1994).

Both PA and CBM, because they are grounded more directly in the context of classrooms, share a problem SNATs do not have. They may be *too* descriptive of classroom practice to be of use for outside purposes. Education probably needs an outside check now and then, and if SNATs are not to be used for that purpose, it is legitimate to wonder if performance measures or CBM will be useful replacements.

Summary

This chapter has sought to explain the nature of achievement testing, and two principal alternatives, in relationship to CLD students. It has been noted that CLD students score lower on achievement tests than majority students, and several possible explanations for this occurrence have been presented. It has also been noted that the quality of any testing instrument is irrevocably tied to the purpose for which it is used. It is interesting to note that, when the purpose of assessment is one of high-stakes, CLD and disabled students are routinely excluded from testing—and as long as this is common practice, it hardly matters at all what test is being used.

References

Arizona Department of Education. (1993, March). *Arizona Student Assessment Program*. (Working paper). Phoenix, AZ: Author.

Armour-Thomas, E. (1992). Intellectual assessment of children from culturally diverse backgrounds, *School Psychology Review, 21*(4), 552–565.

Baker, E. L., & O'Neil, H. F. (1994). *Diversity, assessment, and equity in education reform*. Los Angeles: University of California, National Center for Research on Evaluation, Standards and Student Testing.

Behrmann, J. (1993). Special education counts jump with high stakes testing. *Counterpoint, 13*(3), 1–107.

Brown, A. L., & French, L. (1979). The zone of potential development: Implications for intelligence testing in the year 2000, *Intelligence, 3*, 255–273.

Campione, J. C., & Brown, A. L. (1985). *Dynamic assessment: One approach and some initial data* (Tech. Report No. 361). Urbana: University of Illinois, Center for the Study of Reading.

Cooper, J. D. (1993). *Literacy: Helping children construct meaning*. Boston: Houghton Mifflin.

Cortes, C. (1986). The education of language minority students: A contextual interactive model. In California State Department of Education, *Beyond language: Social and cultural factors in schooling language minority students* (pp. 143–186). Los Angeles: Evaluation, Dissemination, and Assessment Center, California State University.

Coutinho, M., & Malouf, D. (1993). Performance assessment and children with disabilities: Issues and possibilities. *Teaching Exceptional Children, 25*(4), 62–67.

Crocker, L., & Algina, J. (1986). *Introduction to classical and modern test theory*. Troy, MO: Holt, Rinehart, & Winston.

Cummins, J. (1981). The role of primary language development in promoting educational success for language minority students. In Office of Bilingual and Bicultural Education, California State Department of Education (Ed.), *Schooling and language minority students: A theoretical framework* (pp. 3–50). Los Angeles: California State University, Evaluation, Dissemination and Assessment Center.

Cummins, J. (1986). *Empowering minority students*. Sacramento: California Association for Bilingual Education.

Darling-Hammond, L. (1993). Reframing the school reform agenda: Developing capacity for school transformation. *Phi Delta Kappan, 74*(10), 752–761.

Deno, S. L. (1985). Curriculum-based measurement: The emerging alternative. *Exceptional Children, 52*, 219–232.

Deno, S. L. (1989). Curriculum-based measurement and alternative special education services: A fundamental and direct relationship. In M. R. Shinn (Ed.), *Curriculum-based measurement: Assessing special children* (pp. 1–17). New York: Guilford.

Deno, S. L., & Espin, C. A. (1991). Evaluation strategies for preventing and remediating basic skills deficits. In G. Stoner, M. Shinn, & H. Walker (Eds.), *Interventions for achievement and behavior problems* (pp. 79–97). Silver Springs, MD: National Association of School Psychologists.

Duran, R. P. (1983). *Hispanic education and background: Predictors of college achievement*. New York: College Entrance Examination Board.

Duran, R. P. (1988). Testing of linguistic minorities. In R. Linn (Ed.), *Educational measurement* (3rd ed., pp. 573–587). New York: Macmillan.

Feuer, M. J., & Fulton, K. (1993). The many faces of performance assessment. *Phi Delta Kappan, 74*(6), 478–479.

Figueroa, R. A. (1990). Assessment of linguistic minority group children. In C. R. Reynolds & R. W. Kamphaus (Eds.), *Handbook of psychological and educational assessment of children: Intelligence and achievement* (pp. 671–696). New York: Guilford.

Freeman, Y. S., & Freeman, D. E. (1992). *Whole language for second language learners*. Portsmouth, NH: Heinemann Educational Books.

Fuchs, L. S., & Fuchs, D. (1992). Identifying a measure for monitoring student reading progress. *School Psychology Review, 21*(1), 45–58.

Fuchs, L. S., Fuchs, D., Hamlett, C. L., Walz, L., & Germann, G. (1993). Formative evaluation of educational progress: How much can we expect? *School Psychology Review, 22*(1), 27–48.

Gandara, P., Keogh, B. K., & Yoshioka-Maxwell, B. (1980). Predicting academic performance of Anglo and Mexican-American kindergarten children. *Psychology in the Schools, 17,* 174–177.

Garcia, G. E., & Pearson, P. D. (1994). Assessment and diversity. In L. Darling-Hammond (Ed.) *Review of Research in Education* (20th ed., pp. 337–391). Washington, DC: American Educational Research Association.

General Accounting Office. (1993). *Student testing: Current extent and expenditures with cost estimates for national examination*. Washington, DC: U.S. General Accounting Office, Program Evaluations and Methodology Division.

Gitomer, D. H. (1993). Performance assessment and educational measurement. In R. E. Bennett & W. C. Ward (Eds.), *Construction versus choice in cognitive measurement* (pp. 241–263). Hillsdale, NJ: Erlbaum.

Glaser, R., & Silver, E. (1994). Assessment, testing, and instruction: Retrospect and prospect. In L. Darling-Hammond (Ed.) *Review of research in education* (20th ed., pp. 393–419) Washington, DC: American Educational Research Association.

Goldman, R. D., & Hewitt, B. N. (1976). An investigation of test bias for Mexican American college students. *Journal of Educational Measurement, 12,* 511–516.

Haertel, G. D. (1990). Achievement tests. In H. J. Walberg & G. D. Haertel (Eds.) *The international encyclopedia of educational evaluation* (pp. 485–489). New York: Pergamon Press.

Haney, W., & Madaus, G. (1989). Searching for alternatives to standardized tests: Whys, whats, and whithers. *Phi Delta Kappan, 70*(9), 683–687.

Heath, S. B. (1989). Oral and literate traditions among Black Americans living in poverty. *American Psychologist, 44,* 367–373.

Helms, J. E. (1992). Why is there no study of cultural equivalence in standardized cognitive ability testing? *American Psychologist, 47*(9), 1083–1101.

Hiebert, E. H. (Ed.). (1991). *Literacy for a diverse society: Perspectives, practices, and policies.* New York: Teachers College Press.

Howell, K. W., Bigelow, S. S., Moore, G. L., & Evoy, A. M. (1994). Bias in authentic assessment. *Diagnostique, 19*(1), 387–400.

Howell, K. W., Fox, S. L., & Morehead, M. K. (1993). *Curriculum-based evaluation: Teaching and decision making.* (2nd ed.). Pacific Grove, CA: Brooks/Cole.

Jenkins, J. R., & Jewell, M. (1993). Examining the validity of two measures for formative teaching: Reading aloud and maze. *Exceptional children, 59*(5), 421–432.

Kansas State Board of Education (1992). *Building a school profile: The QPA needs assessment process.* Topeka, KS: Author.

Krashen, S. (1980). The theoretical and practical relevance of simple codes in second language acquisition. In R. C. Scarcella & S. S. Krashen (Eds.), *Research in second language acquisition* (pp. 7–18). Rowley, MA: Newbury House.

Krashen, S. (1982). *Principles and practice in second language acquisition.* New York: Pergamon Press.

Krashen, S., & Terrell, T. (1983). *The natural approach: Language acquisition in the classroom.* Hayward, CA: Alemany Press.

Malone, J. C. (1990). *Theories of learning: A historical approach.* Belmont, CA: Wadsworth.

Marshall, H. H. (1992). Seeing, redefining, and supporting student learning. In

H. H. Marshall (Ed.), *Redefining student learning: Roots of educational change* (pp. 1–32). Norwood, NJ: Ablex.

Marston, D., & Magnusson, D. (1988). Curriculum-based measurement: District level implementation. In J. L. Graden, J. E. Zins, & M. C. Curtis (Eds.), *Alternative educational delivery systems: Enhancing instructional options for all students* (pp. 137–172). Washington, DC: National Association of School Psychologists.

McGill-Franzen, A., & Allington, R. L. (1993). Flunk 'em or get them classified: The contamination of primary grade accountability data. *Educational Researcher, 22*(9) 19–22.

Messick, S. (1994). The interplay of evidence and consequences in validation of performance assessment. *Educational Researcher, 23*(2), 13–24.

Moll, L. C. (Ed.). (1990). *Vygotsky and education: Instructional implications and applications of sociohistorical psychology.* New York: Cambridge University Press.

Moss, P. A. (1992). Shifting conceptions of validity in educational measurement: Implications for performance assessment. *Review of Educational Research, 62,* 229–258.

Moss, P. A. (1994). Can there be validity without reliability? *Educational Researcher, 23*(2), 5–12.

National Academy of Education. (1993). *The trial assessment: Prospects and reality.* Stanford, CA: Author.

Ormrod, J. E. (1990). *Human learning: Theories, principles, and educational applications.* New York: Merrill.

Paris, S. G., & Winograd, P. (1990). Promoting metacognition and motivation of exceptional children. *Remedial and Special Education, 11*(6), 7–15.

Peitzman, F., & Gadda, G. (Eds.). (1992). *With different eyes: Insights into teaching language minority students across the disciplines.* Los Angeles: University of California, Center for Academic Interinstitutional Programs.

Porter, A. C. (1993). School delivery standards. *Educational Researcher, 22*(5), 24–30.

Poteet, J. A., Choate, J. S., & Stewart, S. C. (1993). Performance assessment and special education: Practices and prospectives. *Focus on Exceptional Children, 26*(1), 1–20.

Powers, S., Escamilla, K., & Haussler, M. M. (1986). The California Achievement Test as a predictor of reading ability across race and sex. *Educational and Psychological Measurement, 46,* 1067–1070.

Ried, R., Maag, J. W., & Vasa, S. F. (1994). Attention deficit hyperactivity disorder as a disability category: A critique. *Exceptional Children, 60*(3), 198–214.

Rosenshine, B. V., & Stevens, R. (1986). Teaching functions. In M. C. Wittrock (Ed.), *Handbook on research and teaching* (3rd ed., pp. 392–431). New York: Macmillan.

Scarcella, R. C., & Krashen, S. S. (1980). *Research in second language acquisition.* Rowley, MA: Newbury House.

Shinn, M. R., & Hubbard, D. D. (1992). Curriculum-based measurement and problem-solving assessment: Basic procedures and outcomes. *Focus on Exceptional Children, 24*(5), 1–20.

Simmons, W., & Resnick, L. (1993). Assessment as the catalyst of school reform. *Educational Leadership, 50*(5), 11–15.

Spady, W. G. (1988). Organizing for results: the basis of authentic restructuring and reform. *Educational Leadership, 46,* 4–8.

Stanovich, K. E. (1994). Romance and reality. *The Reading Teacher, 47*(4), 280–291.

Sternberg, R. J., & Wagner R. K. (Eds.). (1994). *Mind in context: Interactionist perspectives on human intelligence.* New York: Cambridge University Press.

Sue, S., & Padilla, A. (1986). Ethnic minority issues in the United States: Challenges for the educational system. In California State Department of Education, *Beyond language: Social and cultural factors in schooling language minority students* (pp. 143–186). Los Angeles: Evaluation, Dissemination, and Assessment Center, California State University.

Tharp, R. G. (1989). Psychocultural variables and constants, effects on teaching and learning in schools. *American Psychologist, 44,* 349–359.

Tindal, G. A., & Marston, B. (1990). *Classroom-based assessment.* Columbus, OH: Merrill.

Traughber, B. (1994). *Aim line.* Kansas City, KS: Discretionary Special Projects IDEA Grant #9317.

Trueba, H. T. (1989). *Raising silent voices: Educating the linguistic minorities for the 21st century.* New York: Newbury House.

Tyler, R. W. (1991). General statement on program evaluation. In M. W. McLaughlin & D. C. Phillips (Eds.), *Evaluation and education: At quarter century.* Chicago: University of Chicago Press.

Vygotsky, L. S. (1978). *Mind in society: The development of higher psychological processes.* Cambridge, MA: Harvard University Press.

Wang, M. C., Haertel, G. D., & Walberg, H. J. (1993). Toward a knowledge base for school learning. *Review of Educational Research, 63*(3), 249–294.

Wertsch, J. V. (1985). *Vygotsky and the social formation of mind.* Cambridge, MA: Harvard University Press.

Ysseldyke, J. E., Algozzine, B. J., & Thurlow, M. L. (Eds.). (1992). *Critical issues in special education.* Boston: Houghton Mifflin.

Zebroski, J. T. (1994). *Thinking through theory: Vygotskian perspectives on the teaching of writing*. Portsmouth, NH: Heinemann.

Zeidner, M. (1988). Sociocultural differences in examinees' attitudes towards scholastic ability exams. *Journal of Educational Measurement, 25*, 67–76.

Zeidner, M., & Moss, R. (1992). An introduction to psychological testing. In M. Zeidner & R. Moss (Eds.), *Psychological testing: An inside view* (pp. 1–48). Palo Alto, CA: Consulting Psychologists Press.

10

Multiculturalism and Neuropsychological Assessment

Carol A. Friedman and Robert J. Clayton

Clinical neuropsychology is currently defined by the National Academy of Neuropsychology and the Division of Clinical Neuropsychology of the American Psychological Association as "the study of brain-behavior relationships based on a combination of knowledge from basic neurosciences, functional neuroanatomy, neuropathology, clinical neurology, psychology assessment, psychopathology and psychological interventions" ("Professional Issues," 1994, p. 15). The full extent of the relevance of cultural, racial, and ethnic issues to all aspects of this definition of clinical neuropsychology is far beyond the scope of this chapter. Rather, this chapter is an introductory consideration of some multicultural concerns as they impinge upon the neuropsychological assessment.

In order to identify the pertinent literature in the area of neuropsychological assessment, the authors conducted a search of two relevant computer data bases, one psychological, the other medical. Considering the scant number of citations identified, it was apparent that issues of race, culture, and ethnicity do not, for the most part, guide research in neuropsychological assessment. A similar conclusion was reached by the authors of the recently published book, *Neuropsychological Evaluation of the Spanish Speaker* (Ardila, Rosselli, and Puente, 1994). This observation stood in stark contrast to the discussion of the importance of social and cultural issues by Lezak (1983) in her standard text on neuropsychological assessment. In one concise paragraph, she expressed an understanding of the importance of potential multicultural issues with respect to not only the interpretive issues in a neuropsychological assessment, but to the possible etiological role social factors may play in the development of neuropsychological deficits. As neuropsychological services have become relevant for an ever-expanding set of conditions (Benton, 1992), and as these services are provided to a wider and more diverse population, considerations of racial, cultural, and ethnic factors have come more to impinge on the assessment process. The recent publication of the text by Ardila and others (1994) clearly attests to a more formal appreciation of Lezak's concern with multicultural issues and neuropsychological assessment.

In this notable absence of a body of established and cohesive research directly relating multicultural concerns to neuropsychological assessment, this chapter is a structured attempt to demonstrate the relevancy of such considerations. To begin, a broad perspective will be taken with the notion of assessment. While at the core of the neuropsychological assessment lies the use of tests whose measures are assumed to reflect aspects of cortical function, the assessment in totality is far more than the administration and scoring of these test materials. The assessment finds its significance in the interpretation of the test results within the context of the individual's life history (Lezak, 1983), with its function not merely to define the nature of cognitive and behavioral deficits resulting from brain dysfunction but also to guide the design of rehabilitation programs for the individual (Gass and Brown, 1992). From this perspective, apparent multicultural concerns can be seen as of importance not only with respect to the psychometric properties of test materials but also during the entire diagnostic process from the neuropsychological interview to the provision of test feedback, rehabilitation, treatment, and counseling.

While the focus of this discussion is on assessment issues, the first section of this chapter will be a consideration of the relationship between risk factors for the development of neuropsychological deficits and the possible etiological role of social factors. The following section will provide a brief introduction to the organization of the neuropsychological assessment. This will include a brief outline of the basic theoretical issues pertinent to test selection in a neuropsychological assessment in general and to issues specific to pediatric populations. Multicultural issues will then be addressed in sections concerned with test translation and sources of bias during client intake and interview, and during the administration of tests. Following the conclusion of the chapter are two case studies that illustrate the importance of multicultural considerations.

Risk Factors for Neuropsychological Deficits

While obesity, hypertension, and elevated serum cholesterol levels are well-known risk factors for cardiovascular disease, there are also risk factors associated with the secondary development of neuropsychological deficits that are often overlooked by educational and health care providers. As some of these risk factors are differentially distributed over various racial and ethnic groups, the possible development of the associated neuropsychological deficits are then also differentially distributed. For instance, Berkman (1986) has observed that both educational attainment and socioeconomic status are associated with almost every cause of morbidity and mortality. Since all the risk factors for diverse populations are too numerous to mention, a selection of risk factors and diversity issues will be used to illustrate this point.

D'Amato (1990) has reviewed the role of the neuropsychological assessment with the student experiencing academic difficulties. As D'Amato observed, the neuropsychological approach assists in the differentiation of biologically rooted difficulties from emotional-behavioral disorders. For example, as the educational implications of the neuropsychology sequelae of low-level lead toxicity in inner-city children are realized (Bellinger and Needleman, 1992), the use of neuropsychological assessments in special education to assist in the differential diagnosis of developmental disabilities, and the subsequent design of remedial programs, become more important.

While race may not be the causative risk factor in the development of a particular disorder, membership in a specific racial group may expose people to pervasive forms of societal pressures that ultimately find biological expression. With a failure to consider this possibility, race in and of itself may then appear to have biological consequences. As an example, the higher incidence of hypertension among African Americans may be viewed as a race-based risk factor for the possible development of neuropsychological problems. Essential hypertension is a significant risk factor for cerebrovascular disease (Waldstein, Manuck, Ryan, and Muldoon, 1991). Further, significant performance decrements on neuropsychology measures of attention, memory, and abstract reasoning have been found to be associated with essential hypertension (Waldstein and others, 1991). Considering the well-documented mortality rates from cerebrovascular disease and morbidity rates for essential hypertension in the African American population (Chaturvedi, McKeigue, and Marmot, 1993), there is a clear need to consider those African Americans with essential hypertension at risk for the development of cognitive deficits.

The uninsured in the United States are primarily low-income working individuals and their families, with minorities being overrepresented in this group (Bazzoli, 1986). Research has indicated that medical insurance is crucial in determining both access to health care (Aday and Andersen, 1978) and the quality of health care received (Burstin, Lipsitz, and Brennan, 1992). Several studies have noted an associative relationship between lack of medical insurance and adverse health outcomes (Braveman, Oliva, Miller, Reiter, and Egerter, 1989). Therefore, a simple lack of health insurance can legitimately be considered a risk factor for the development of neuropsychological problems.

A recent study (Stoddard, St. Peter, and Newacheck, 1994) examined the availability of medical insurance and the utilization of medical services for specific childhood conditions. The study concluded that, compared with insured children, those children lacking medical insurance were less likely to obtain appropriate medical care for their conditions. Consequently, those children failing to obtain medical care for their conditions were considered to be at an increased risk for the development of further complications.

The importance of early medical intervention is illustrated by a disease common to early childhood—otitis media and effusions of the middle ear (Giebink, 1984). Without appropriate medical care for the acute condition, the child is under an increased risk for development of the chronic condition and subsequent complications. Recent longitudinal studies of the sequelae of chronic otitis media (Chalmers, Stewart, Silva, and Mulvena, 1989; Teele and others, 1990) drew the conclusion that when this disorder is present during the first three years of life, it is associated with long-lasting developmental consequences including speech articulation and language development problems, lower school achievement scores, lower IQ scores, reading difficulties, and teacher-reported behavior problems. Since normal sensory-system development requires in part appropriate levels of environmental stimulation (Greenough, Black, and Wallace, 1987), conductive hearing loss resulting from the chronic otitis media may interfere with the normal development of the auditory cortical structures. These studies suggest a critical period during the first three years of life when the presence of chronic otitis media is associated with the development of the observed subsequent difficulties. Clearly, lack of adequate medical treatment during this period can have dire consequences for development.

Mental health providers and physicians in general practice are among the various sources of referrals for neuropsychological assessment (Sweet and Moberg, 1990). The understanding that certain behavioral and cognitive problems may have a neurological basis results in referrals to address that possibility (Sbordone and Rudd, 1986). Epidemiologic data point to the underutilization of mental health services in economically disadvantaged (Tarnowski, 1991) and culturally diverse populations (Wilson and MacCarthy, 1994). For instance, Wilson and MacCarthy found that when reporting symptoms to their family doctor, Asian patients are more somatic and White patients more psychological, differentially affecting subsequent referrals. Although preliminary evidence suggests that minority clients are more likely to utilize services and show improved functioning following treatment in ethnic-specific treatment centers (Yeh, Takeuchi, and Sue, 1994), the availability of these centers and even the availability of ethnic-specific therapists unfortunately remains quite limited (Vargas and Willis, 1994).

Introduction to Neuropsychological Assessment

Distinct from the psychological assessment, which is generally considered to focus on some determination of the intellectual potential of an individual (Matarazzo, 1972, 1990), the neuropsychological assessment has a fundamental concern with the identification and definition of cognitive and behavioral deficits associated with cerebral dysfunction (Anastasi, 1988; Kaplan, 1989; Lezak, 1983; Reitan and Wolfson, 1993a; Weintraub and Mesulam, 1985). To this end, there are available numerous standardized tests that can identify the neuropsychological deficits associated with brain dysfunction (Benton, 1994). However, there is no one standard approach to a neuropsychological assessment, nor is there a standard set of tests with which to conduct such an assessment (Hartmann, 1991; Kane, 1991; Milberg, Hebben, and Kaplan, 1986; Reitan, 1986). There is even some professional disagreement about what is the proper question concerning brain damage that is to be addressed by such an assessment (Hartmann, 1991; Loring, 1991). It has been argued that with the arrival and widespread use of the current generation of neuroimaging technology, neuropsychological assessment should not be merely concerned with the simple documentation of brain damage (Mapou, 1988). Rather, the trend in test development is "toward a refinement in both the detection and the delineation of the specific nature of the (neuropsychological) deficits (Slick and Craig, 1991, p. 79).

Approaches to Assessment

One neuropsychological test administered in isolation can neither determine the presence of brain damage nor capture the complexity of the cognitive and behavioral consequences of brain damage (Lezak, 1983; Russell, 1992). Consequently, tests are administered in groups, or batteries. There are three approaches that guide the selection of tests used in an assessment: the standardized fixed battery approach, the flexible battery approach, and the process approach. Space limitations of this chapter will allow for only the briefest description, and the inevitable oversimplification, of each method. For more information, please consult the references cited for each approach.

The *standardized fixed battery approach* (Kane, 1991) is best exemplified by the Halstead-Reitan Neuropsychological Test Battery (Reitan and Wolfson, 1993a, 1993b) and the Luria-Nebraska Neuropsychological Battery (Golden, Purisch, and Hammeke, 1985). This approach consists of a fixed set of standardized individual tests that are administered to every patient, whatever the referral question (Kane, 1991). With the *flexible battery approach*, the specific referral question, such as dementia or closed head injury, determines the particular set of tests making up the battery to be administered to the patient (Sweet and Moberg, 1990). Lastly, in the *process approach*, test selection is based both on the goal to identify and quantify the specific neuropsychological deficits of the patient and on the need to understand the qualitative nature of the patient's behavior (Milberg and others, 1986). As Sweet and Moberg (1990) have observed, while there is a general impression that the use of standardized, fixed batteries dominates the assessment approach, in reality, this approach received the least amount of endorsement. In their survey, the flexible battery approach was endorsed by 53.8 percent of practicing neuropsychologists, while only 17.6 percent endorsed a fixed, standardized battery approach.

Whatever the approach, the battery of tests administered should measure a wide spectrum of cognitive and behavioral abilities. A standard list of abilities measured by a comprehensive neuropsychological examination includes language functions, visual-motor abilities, memory, attention, affect, visual constructional abilities, motor functioning, and sensoriperceptual functioning (Weintraub and Mesulam, 1985). A neuropsychological assessment must also include measures considered to assess higher brain functions, such as abstract reasoning, judgment, insight, planning, foresight, and personality (Reitan and Wolfson, 1993a). While the specific neuropsychological instruments that are considered to measure these various functions are numerous, the tests that are used nearly universally by neuropsychologists are the Wechsler IQ batteries (Wechsler, 1974, 1981), because a global measure of intellectual functioning is usually the cornerstone of the assessment (Russell, 1986). Whether the Wechsler subtests specifically measure some of these neuropsychological constructs has been called into question (Matarazzo, 1990).

Under ideal circumstances, an individual's level of performance on a neuropsychological test should be indicative of cerebral function only. However, both normal and brain-damaged individuals' level of performance on certain test measures of basic sensory and motor processes, and cognitive functions such as language, attention, memory and abstract reasoning have all been found correlated with certain demographic variables (Finlayson, Johnson, and Reitan, 1977; Heaton, Grant, and Matthews, 1986; Reitan and Wolfson, 1992a). Age, educational attainment, IQ, and sex have been identified as demographic variables affecting performance on many neuropsychological tests (Leckliter and Matarazzo, 1989; Reitan and Wolfson, 1992a, Vannieuwkirk and Galbraith, 1985). These statistical relationships have been reported to affect the accuracy of the diagnostic classification resulting in differential misclassification rates (Heaton, Grant, and Matthews, 1991). As Leckliter and Matarazzo observe, norms developed with a psychiatric or medical control group that collapse across both age and education may not be appropriate for all individuals. If such norms, they argue, are used to assess the performance of a ninth-grade educated male, aged fifty-nine, different diagnostic conclusions may be drawn than if age and education-referenced norms were used. It seems then that at least some neuropsychological test measures may have a differential sensitivity to the detection of cerebral dysfunction across certain demographic variables, such as educational level or age. However, the full implications for the definition of the norm reference group for diverse populations are not yet fully understood. Further, it has also been argued that these demographic variables may be of etiological significance in the development of deficits or in providing some resistance to the consequences of brain damage (Berkman, 1986). Reitan and Wolfson's position (1986) on the aging process as an etiological factor in the development of brain damage is consistent with this interpretation. Age norming, for Reitan and Wolfson, would then be considered inappropriate, for it, in effect, masks the possible identification of neuropsychological deficits that are considered the result of the normal aging process on the brain. These observations highlight the need to define the appropriate reference group to which the individual's performance is compared.

A wide range of individual neuropsychological instruments is available for use in the neuropsychological assessment. In a recent survey of neuropsychological test usage at 124 public psychiatric hospitals, 136 different tests were listed as in use (Slick and Craig, 1991). Unfortunately, the large-scale normative standardization studies that mark the development of the nationally used IQ and achievement tests do not characterize the development of neuropsychological tests (Anastasi, 1988). Professional concern with the psychometric limitations of many popular neuropsychological tests has been expressed by several authors (Franzen, 1989; Russell, 1986, 1987; Spreen and Strauss, 1991). In a review of psychometric considerations in clinical neuropsychology, Russell (1987) has argued that most neuropsychological tests even fail to meet the criteria set forth in the American Psychological Association manual, *Standards for Educational and Psychological Testing*. The psychometric properties of many of these tests, including reliability, validity, standard error of measurement estimates, and the demographic characteristics of the norm reference group, are not readily available. Ardila and others (1994) have observed that most neuropsychological tests generate their normative data by comparing neurologically normal and brain-damaged, middle-class, English-speaking subjects. The applicability of these norms to multicultural populations is of serious concern (Simonian, Tarnowski, Stancin, Friman, and Atkins, 1991); so much so that some instruments give explicit warning concerning the inappropriateness of their accompanying norms in a population with ethnic differences (Spreen and Strauss, 1991). Surprisingly, the courtroom is driving some research toward population validity of normative data (Matarazzo, 1990). As the neuropsychological assessment is more widely used for litigation in cases such as compensation after injury, the psychometric properties of tests are being more closely scrutinized. This attention to the need to validate measurements with diverse populations will greatly add to this field.

Currently, there are a few comprehensive compendia of neuropsychological tests that discuss the administration, norms, and psychometric properties of some commonly used tests and batteries. This list includes Lezak's *Neuropsychological Assessment* (1983), Franzen's *Reliability and Validity in Neuropsychological Assessment* (1989), and Spreen and Strauss's *A Compendium of Neuropsychological Tests: Administration, Norms, and Commentary* (1991). Additionally, the reader is referred to the Ardila and others (1994) text on assessment with the Spanish-speaking population. There are individual papers that address the issue of neuropsychological assessment in populations with physical limitations. These references should be used with caution, as some of these journal papers do not contain the normative data and psychometric properties of the particular test battery that was used in the study being described.

Neuropsychological Assessment of Children

While the discipline of child neuropsychology is considered a recent development (Hooper and Hynd, 1993), several assessment instruments are available, varying in their validity. As with adult evaluations, pediatric assessment can be divided into three approaches: standardized fixed battery, flexible battery, and process.

Several standardized batteries are currently available for neuropsychological evaluation of children. The most frequently used fixed batteries are the two Halstead-Reitan tests: the Halstead-Reitan Neuropsychological Test Battery for Older Children, for children aged nine through fourteen (Reitan and Wolfson, 1992b), and the Reitan-Indiana Neuropsychological Test Battery for Younger Children, for children aged five through eight (Reitan and Wolfson, 1993b). Both are downward extensions of the Halstead-Reitan Neuropsychological Adult Test Battery. Both batteries also include the administration of the appropriate Wechsler Intelligence Test and recommend as well the administration of the Wide Range Battery Achievement Test-Revised (Jastak and Wilkinson, 1984).

An alternate fixed battery is the children's version of the Luria-Nebraska Neuropsychological Battery (Golden, 1987). The battery is normed for children aged eight to twelve years and consists of 497 discrete tasks. It should be noted that test items from the adult battery assumed to assess frontal lobe functions have been deleted from this test, based on Luria's early interpretation of the development of the frontal lobes after this age (Schaughency and others, 1989). Normative information and psychometric properties for this battery are available in the test manual. Children above the age of twelve years can be tested with the adult battery.

As with adult assessment, survey information from practicing child neuropsychologists indicates a clear preference for a flexible approach to assessment rather than the use of fixed batteries (Ebben,

1994). The most frequently used tests in the flexible approach include the Wechsler Intelligence Scale for Children-Revised (WISC-R;Wechsler, 1974), the Trail Making Test (Reitan and Wolfson, 1993a), the Wide Range Battery Achievement Test-Revised (Jastak and Wilkinson, 1984), Woodcock-Johnson: Tests of Achievement (Woodcock and Johnson, 1989, 1990), the Kaufman Assessment Battery for Children (K-ABC; Kaufman and Kaufman, 1983), and the Minnesota Multiphasic Personality Inventory (Hathaway and McKinley, 1943; Donders, 1992; Sellers and Nadler, 1992; Ebben, 1994). The reader should note that while newer versions of some of the above-mentioned tests are currently available, such as the Wechsler Intelligence Scale for Children-Third Edition (WISC-III; Wechsler, 1991) and the Minnesota Multiphasic Personality Inventory-Second Edition (MMPI-2, MMPI-A; Butcher, Dahlstrom, Graham, Tellegen, and Kaemmer, 1989; Butcher and others, 1992), the literature reviewed for the chapter referred almost exclusively to the older versions of the tests. It is assumed that most clinicians now use the current editions of these tests. The comparison between versions of each test needs to be established empirically. While the above psychological instruments are in general well standardized, they have yet to be thoroughly normed for patients with cerebral injury, making the legitimacy of their use as neuropsychological tests for pediatric populations still not firmly established.

Some observations are pertinent when the WISC-R is used as one component of a neuropsychological assessment. The traditional clinical uses of Verbal IQ and Performance IQ score differences and intrasubtest scatter as markers for certain conditions such as Learning Disability, or as evidence for cerebral dysfunction, has been drawn into serious question (McLean, Kaufman, and Reynolds, 1989). Since the majority of the listed instruments used to assess children with the flexible approach are more global measures of cognitive function, Matarazzo's warning (1990) on the neuropsychological interpretation of subscale scores is particularly pertinent. Considering the general factor structure of the Wechsler tests, and the complex nature of cognitive functions, individual subtests should not be construed as reflecting discrete cognitive functions. For example, there is some evidence that the factor structure of the WISC-R may change when given to patients with metabolic disorders. Research with children diagnosed with insulin-dependent diabetes mellitus shows that the Perceptual Organization factor may be reconfigured into a visual discrimination factor and a spatial conceptual factor (Holmes, Cornwell, Dunlap, Chen, and Lee, 1992). The lack of stability of the factors calls the use of them in clinical diagnosis and treatment into question.

The Kaufman Assessment Battery for Children (K-ABC; Kaufman and Kaufman, 1983) is a test of intellectual ability whose theoretical orientation was drawn from neuropsychological studies of cerebral lateralization. The cognitive portion of the test is composed of two scales. The Simultaneous Processing scale emphasizes gestalt-like or holistic processing, and is frequently considered spatial in nature. The second scale is the Sequential Processing scale, which relies on the temporal or serial order of stimuli when problem solving. In an attempt to be more sensitive to minority performance, the authors provide supplemental sociocultural norms for race and parental education level. However, in a review of the validity of the K-ABC as a specific neuropsychological instrument, Donders (1992) concludes that the battery is not superior to the WISC-R in terms of sensitivity to cerebral dysfunction and should not be considered a sophisticated neuropsychology test.

In contrast to the global measures, there are available tests that can be considered more discrete measures of brain-behavior function. For example, two such tests considered to be sensitive to spatial processing and graphomotor skills, are the Rey-Osterrieth Complex Figure test (Spreen and Strauss, 1991; Waber and Holmes, 1985) and the Clock Face Drawing (Spreen and Strauss, 1991; Edmonds, Cohen, Riccio, Bacon, and Hynd, 1994). Recent research with both tests indicates the presence of clear development trends in the children's performance. Again the reader is referred to the previously mentioned reviews for information on specific tests for children.

Translated Tests

Whatever the sophistication of the approach to translation, and the final linguistic accuracy of the translation, there are still the requirements to norm the translated test version and to validate the test as a neuropsychological instrument in the new target population (Mahurin, Espino, and Holifield, 1992). Beyond the translation, the individual test items must also be culturally sensitive. The construction of the reference norms must consider the relevant demographic characteristics of the target group. Research on properly translated neuropsychological tests has demonstrated that significant statistical differences can still occur between linguistic groups on different versions of the test (Taussig, Henderson, and Mack, 1992). Both cultural and ethnic differences, besides the often-observed age and educational effects, have been shown to affect performance on translated neuropsychological tests.

In the construction of a test battery to be used for the differential diagnosis of Alzheimer's disease in a Hispanic population, Taussig and others (1992) translated a group of standardized English-language neuropsychological instruments into Spanish. Significant statistical differences were found on four tests of the battery for the English- and Spanish-speaking controls. When the individual tests were examined for explanations of the group differences, educational attainment, cultural relevance of individual test items, differences in relative word frequency, and even Spanish dialectal differences were all found pertinent to explain the intergroup differences.

In the normative research for another Spanish-language neuropsychological battery, age and educational attainment were found related to the subject's level of performance on many tests that assessed various cognitive, sensory, and motor domains (Ardila and others, 1994). Since this battery was addressing the need to assess both an elderly Hispanic population and a segment of the Hispanic population with limited educational attainment, reference norms were constructed that reflected both demographic characteristics.

The Hispanic population in the United States is quite diverse, varying along racial, national, and ethnic lines (Robert, 1994). The construction of norms using only a Spanish-speaking reference group, classified by age and educational attainment, to define Hispanic performance may be of limited validity. There is some evidence that tests normed with a monolingual population in one country may not be appropriate with a bilingual population in another country (Figueroa, 1989). The Spanish translation of the Wechsler Adult Intelligence Scale—the Escala de Inteligencia Wechsler para Adultos—was normed in Puerto Rico (Green and Martinez, 1968). When used to assess elderly Hispanics in the United States, it was discovered that both dialect and cultural issues made generalizations to a Mexican American or Cuban American population problematic (Lopez and Taussig, 1991). Even with these caveats, the current research being conducted with Hispanic populations does represent the proper direction to be taken for the construction of culturally sensitive neuropsychological instruments.

Sources of Bias During Neuropsychological Intake and Interview

An integral part of the neuropsychological assessment is the patient interview. During the interview, pertinent information concerning the patient's medical, educational, employment, and social history, and current symptom status, must be obtained (Parker, 1990). Within the framework provided by this personal information, the tests' results will be interpreted (Lezak, 1983), including recommendations for rehabilitation or remedial programs, implications for future employment, or school placement (Gouvier, Webster, and Blanton, 1986). Background information should also be confirmed or supplemented from historical information such as school records, previous achievement or cognitive tests, and employment, medical, and military records to gain an unbiased record of the patient's medical status and previous level of functioning (Matarazzo, 1990). Clearly, the accuracy of the information obtained affects the validity of the assessment.

One potential source of bias is the failure to disclose relevant information by a competent patient. Behavioral issues, such as family dynamics, which may be relevant to the neuropsychologist, might appear irrelevant or too personal to some patients (Parker, 1990). Questions concerning current cognitive and emotional status may not be deemed appropriate, particularly in diverse populations. Questions may also be phrased in such a manner as not to be understood by the patient. Patients from culturally diverse backgrounds, particularly when different from the examiner, may differentially report symptomatology. For example, emotional status—including self-perception of emotional distress and how it is reported to clinicians—differs across ethnic groups (Wilson and MacCarthy, 1994).

Interview bias may be compounded in developmental assessments, where parental interviews are required. Parents may be uncomfortable in sharing pertinent details about the child's psychosocial history or status with the clinician (Simonian and others, 1991). The parents may even disagree on the need for an evaluation. Considering that child-rearing practices vary across cultures, questions of parental style may be seen as implicit criticism, resulting in embarrassment by parents, or anger, leading to a failure to report relevant information. Parents may also feel threatened about truthfully answering certain questions, such as those asking about a history of maternal drug use during pregnancy.

A second area of concern is the interview of the patient who is not fluent in English. Care must be taken that the patient is competent in the language of the interviewer when the patient is questioned in the nondominant language. In non-English-dominant patients, a strong effort to minimize any errors that can be introduced by using translators must be made (Vasquez and Javier, 1991). Untrained interpreters may add omissions, additions, or substitutions to the statements of both interviewer and patient (Ergueta, 1991). The seriousness of a cognitive deficit or change in emotions may be minimized or exaggerated by the translators (Sabin, 1975).

The use of structured interviews, of both standardized and individualized formats, to obtain both historical and psychological information is traditional in neuropsychological assessment (Parker, 1990). However, there is evidence that structured interviews can be biased. For example, the error rates on the Mini-Mental State Examination, used to assess cognitive status, are confounded by age, educational level, ethnicity, and language of the interview (Escobar and others, 1986). Psychosocial and cognitive functioning as well as the appropriateness of specific behaviors are undoubtedly influenced by cultural and environmental factors (Simonian and others, 1991). Clearly, the clinician needs to be sensitive to these areas of bias in administration and interpretation of the interview.

Sources of Bias During Test Performance

The neuropsychologist must elicit a level of test performance that is an accurate estimate of the patient's abilities. In all populations, motivational problems, depression, or anxiety—all resulting from the cerebral damage—can confound the patient's performance on the tests (Prigatano, 1992). Sattler (1970) has shown the operation of racial "experimenter effects" in psychological testing and interviewing situations. The racial characteristics of the experimenter were shown to alter the performance of minority students on a variety of tasks. While such effects have not been formally shown to operate during a neuropsychological assessment, related clinician variables have been shown to affect test performance. For instance, the characteristics of the interviewer can alter standardized test performance (Parsons and Stewart, 1966). Parsons and Stewart (1966) found that brain-damaged patients performed significantly better when the interviewer was perceived as interested, warm, and supportive as opposed to factual and disinterested. Thus emotional tone, technique, and social content of the interview could impinge on the patient's test taking, resulting in an inaccurate measure of abilities, leading to a possible misdiagnosis. Sensitivity to cultural traditions and ethnic mores, allowing the patient to feel at ease, may reduce these effects with a diverse population.

Summary and Conclusion

The issues of race, culture, and ethnicity have been shown to influence significant aspects of the process by which a neuropsychological assessment is constructed. Rather then provide a traditional research review, this chapter is an elaboration of Lezak's (1983) earlier observations concerning the importance of multicultural issues in neuropsychology. We hope our arguments have been sufficiently forceful so others will come to consider this work as a point of departure for their future research.

Case Study: DL

DL was an eleven-year-old Chinese American boy who was referred for neuropsychological testing by Dr. Smith, a psychologist who was the coordinator of a program for gifted children in a highly competitive public school. Dr. Smith had first been consulted about DL when he was in the second grade because of concerns about academic underachievement. DL's level of intellectual functioning fell within the Superior range, yet he was having difficulty in his regular academic placement. At the school's urging, following an unsuccessful trial period in the third grade, DL was retained in the second grade. At that point, DL did well academically. During that year, he was hit by a car while crossing the street. Subsequent to the accident, his academic performance declined. Two years later, because of academic underachievement, he was referred to a head trauma program for neuropsychological testing by Dr. Smith. Upon a review of DL's records by the staff of the head trauma program, it was suggested that DL would benefit from a comprehensive evaluation to include achievement, personality, and neuropsychological testing. There were indications from the child's history that emotional variables may have been affecting academic performance even before the accident. It was not clear if these issues had ever been identified or resolved. From a mental health perspective, extensive evaluation was war-

ranted to accurately diagnose DL's status and to tease apart emotional issues from problems arising from neuropsychological dys-
functions. The neuropsychologist let the family know of her
recommendations and was later told that the family was not interested in pursing the evaluation. In later conversations with the referring psychologist and the neuropsychologist, the parents agreed to
a limited evaluation when specific objectives were better defined and
the scope of the evaluation was limited. However, they did not follow
the more extensive recommendations made by the head trauma program, and postponed indefinitely the comprehensive evaluation of
their child.

The neuropsychologist later came to understand the issues that
were inadvertently raised by a recommendation that the family participate in the evaluation process. Part of the standard evaluation included
an interview with a social worker, who would be concerned with family matters. An unexpected issue of privacy was raised, as DL's family
considered this interview to be an unacceptable intrusion into their personal lives. A second unexpected issue was the family's attitudes to
the emotional and cognitive sequelae of the traumatic brain injury the
child had sustained. Where the family was clearly able to understand
and to emotionally deal with the child's injuries, the family did not wish
to view the psychological sequelae of the injury as consequences of
the accident. To do so would be for the family to admit to the possibility that the problems could be long term. The family chose to understand DL's current difficulties in terms of the child's personality and saw
a need for DL to perhaps apply himself more assiduously to his studies.
In the past, DL's parents had only pursued evaluation of DL under the
auspices of a gifted student program.

This case illustrates a possible cultural conflict between the
examiner and the client's family. The neuropsychologist was concerned about DL's lack of academic achievement following his closed
head injury and thought that a comprehensive evaluation, including
a neuropsychological examination, might clarify current levels of functioning and needs. In spite of the length of time since the accident,

the evaluation of the long-term sequelae, both cognitive and behavioral, of closed head injury in children is recommended (Fletcher, Ewing-Cobbs, Miner, Levin, and Eisenberg, 1990). Following a severe traumatic brain injury, there is now ample evidence of long-term cognitive deficits in children, particularly concerning memory, attention, and adaptive problem solving (Jaffe and others, 1992). It is hypothesized that the immature brain that sustains a severe injury then follows an abnormal trajectory, inhibiting the normal acquisition of cognitive skills (Reitan and Wolfson, 1993b). As a consequence of these deficits, these children are now recognized as being at risk for academic difficulties and in need of remedial services (Johnson, 1992).

Case Study: DM

DM was seven years, eleven months old when referred for a neuropsychological evaluation due to poor scholastic achievement. Her academic profile ranged from average to severely delayed. Her birth history included an ABO blood incompatibility, respiratory distress, and a report of large head size. Before the age of one, a premature fusion of the sagittal sutures was noted. With development, she had a history of ear infections, hypotonia, and poor balance.

DM was brought to the evaluation by her mother and father, and waited with her parents in the waiting room. She presented herself as a shy youngster but was still willing to accompany the evaluator to the testing room. DM was not willing to initiate conversation. The examiner made an effort to put her at ease and rapport was slowly established. DM cooperated with the examiner's requests and appeared to be involved with the test materials from the onset of the evaluation. Her demeanor changed during a measure of verbal recall, when she was presented with a story about a birthday party. As the story was read, DM's mood noticeably changed. She retracted in her seat, tensing her arm and shoulder muscles. She appeared to the examiner to be visibly agitated. DM told the examiner that she could no longer continue with the testing. The evaluator then spoke with her mother, who explained that the family's members were Jehovah's Witnesses, who do not celebrate birthdays. DM thought that she was violating her religious beliefs by listening to the story.

Mrs. M spoke to DM and assured her that she had done nothing improper. She encouraged her daughter to continue with the testing. DM agreed to continue. Before the testing could continue, the examiner had to reestablish rapport with the child. Obviously, the birthday story had to be omitted.

This case illustrates the importance of a consideration of cultural factors in the test administration. Familiarity with the patient's ethnic background and religious beliefs can be crucial in evaluating test findings. Even a thorough interview cannot prepare the evaluator for all possible contingencies, but eliciting background information from the patient and family members can be helpful in alerting the examiner to possible issues of diagnostic significance. In this case, the child's behavior was a clear indicator of problems with a particular test item. If DM had not expressed emotional displeasure, and had simply chosen not to respond to the test item concerned with the birthday story, a biased estimate of the child's verbal memory could have resulted in an underestimation of that cognitive function. Further, the child's performance on the remaining parts of the battery could have been influenced by the incident. In other cases, particularly with adults, a patient's negative response to an offending test item may not be as obvious. The clinician should be sensitive to changes in affect, demeanor, and other behavioral features.

References

Aday, L. A., & Andersen, R. (1978). Insurance coverage and access: Implications for health policy. *Health Services Research, 13,* 369–377.

Anastasi, A. (1988). *Psychological testing* (6th ed.). New York: Macmillan.

Ardila, A., Rosselli, M., & Puente, A. (1994). *Neuropsychological evaluation of the Spanish speaker*. New York: Plenum.

Bazzoli, G. J. (1986). Health care for the indigent: Overview of critical issues. *Health Services Research, 21,* 353–393.

Bellinger, D., & Needleman, H. L. (1992). Neurodevelopmental effects of low-level lead exposure in children. In H. L. Needleman (Ed.), *Human lead exposure* (pp. 191–208). Boca Raton, FL: CRC Press.

Benton, A. (1992). Clinical neuropsychology: 1960–1990. *Journal of Clinical and Experimental Neuropsychology, 14,* 407–417.

Benton, A. (1994). Neuropsychological assessment. *Annual Review of Psychology, 45,* 1–23.

Berkman, L. F. (1986). The association between educational attainment and mental status examinations: Of etiologic significance for senile dementias or not? *Journal of Chronic Diseases, 39,* 171–174.

Braveman, P., Oliva, G., Miller, M. G., Reiter, R., & Egerter, S. (1989). Adverse outcomes and lack of health insurance among newborns in an eight-county area of California, 1982 to 1986. *New England Journal of Medicine, 321,* 508–513.

Burstin, H. R., Lipsitz, S. R., & Brennan, T. A. (1992). Socioeconomic status and risk for substandard medical care. *Journal of the American Medical Association, 268,* 2383–2387.

Butcher, J. N., Dahlstrom, W. G., Graham, J. R., Tellegen, A. M., & Kaemmer, B. (1989). *Minnesota Multiphasic Personality Inventory-2 (MMPI-2): Manual for administration and scoring*. Minneapolis, MN: University of Minnesota Press.

Butcher, J. N., Williams, C. L., Graham, J. R., Archer, R., Tellegen, A., & Ben-Porath, Y. S. (1992). *MMPI-A manual for administration, scoring, and interpretation*. Minneapolis: University of Minnesota Press.

Chalmers, D., Stewart, I., Silva, P., & Mulvena, A. (1989). *Otitis media with effusion in children: The Dunedin study*. Philadelphia: Lippincott.

Chaturvedi, N., McKeigue, P. M., & Marmot, M. G. (1993). Resting and ambulatory blood pressure differences in Afro-Caribbeans and Europeans. *Hypertension, 22,* 90–96.

D'Amato, R. C. (1990). A neuropsychological approach to school psychology. *School Psychology Quarterly, 5,* 141–160.

Donders, J. (1992). Validity of the Kaufman Assessment Battery for Children when employed with children with traumatic brain injury. *Journal of Clinical Psychology, 48,* 225–230.

Ebben, P. A. (1994). The practice of clinical child neuropsychology in the United States. *Archives of Clinical Neuropsychology, 9,* 124.

Edmonds, J. E., Cohen, M. J., Riccio, C. A., Bacon, K. L., & Hynd, G. W. (1994). The development of clock face drawing in normal children. *Archives of Clinical Neuropsychology, 9,* 125.

Ergueta, E. (1991). Hospital interpreting. *The Jerome Quarterly, 7,* 12–13.

Escobar, J. I., Burnam, A., Karno, M., Forsythe, A., Landsverk, J., & Golding, J. M. (1986). Use of the Mini-Mental State Examination (MMSE) in a community population of mixed ethnicity: Cultural and linguistic artifacts. *Journal of Nervous and Mental Disease, 174,* 607–614.

Figueroa, R. A. (1989). Psychological testing of linguistic-minority students: Knowledge gaps and regulations. *Exceptional Children, 56,* 145–152.

Finlayson, M.A.J., Johnson, K. A., & Reitan, R. (1977). Relationship of level of education to neuropsychological measures in brain-damaged and non-brain-damaged adults. *Journal of Consulting and Clinical Psychology, 45,* 536–542.

Fletcher, J. M., Ewing-Cobbs, L., Miner, M. E., Levin, H. S., & Eisenberg, H. M. (1990). Behavioral changes after closed head injury in children. *Journal of Consulting and Clinical Psychology, 58,* 93–98.

Franzen, M. D. (1989). *Reliability and validity in neuropsychological assessment.* New York: Plenum.

Gass, C. S., & Brown, M. C. (1992). Neuropsychological test feedback to patients with brain dysfunction. *Psychological Assessment, 4,* 272–277.

Giebink, G. S. (1984). Epidemiology and natural history of otitis media. In D. J. Lim, C. D. Bluestone, J. O. Klein., & J. D. Nelson (Eds.), *Recent advances in otitis media with effusion* (pp. 5–9). Saint Louis, MO: Mosby.

Golden, C. J. (1987). *Luria-Nebraska Neuropsychological Battery: Children's revision.* Los Angeles: Western Psychological Services.

Golden, C. J., Purisch, A. D., & Hammeke, T. A. (1985). *Luria-Nebraska Neuropsychological Battery: Forms I and II manual.* Los Angeles: Western Psychological Services.

Gouvier, W. D., Webster, J. S., & Blanton, P. D. (1986). Cognitive retraining with brain-damaged patients. In D. Wedding, A. M. Horton, & J. Webster (Eds.), *The neuropsychology handbook: Behavioral and clinical perspectives* (pp. 278–324). New York: Springer.

Green, R. F., & Martinez, J. N. (1968). *Manual para la Escala de Inteligencia Wechsler para Adultos.* New York: The Psychological Corporation.

Greenough, W. T., Black, J. E., & Wallace, C. S. (1987). Experience and brain development. *Child Development, 58,* 539–559.

Hartmann, D. E. (1991). Reply to Reitan: Unexamined premises and the evolution of clinical neuropsychology. *Archives of Clinical Neuropsychology, 6,* 147–165.

Hathaway, S. R., & McKinley, J. C. (1943). *Manual for administering and scoring the MMPI*. Minneapolis: University of Minnesota Press.

Heaton, R. K., Grant, I. G., & Matthews, C. G. (1986). Differences in neuropsychological test performance associated with age, education, and sex. In I. G. Grant & K. M. Adams (Eds.), *Neuropsychological assessment of neuropsychiatric disorders* (pp. 100–120). New York: Oxford University Press.

Heaton, R. K., Grant, I. G., & Matthews, C. G. (1991). *Comprehensive norms for an expanded Halstead-Reitan Battery: Demographic corrections, research findings, and clinical applications*. Odessa, FL: Psychological Assessment Resources.

Holmes, C. S., Cornwell, J. M., Dunlap, W. P., Chen, R. S., & Lee, C. Y. (1992). Anomalous factor structure of the WISC-R for diabetic children. *Neuropsychology, 6*, 341–350.

Hooper, S. R., & Hynd, G. W. (1993). The neuropsychological basis of disorders affecting children and adolescents: An introduction. *Journal of Clinical Child Psychology, 22*, 138–140.

Jaffe, K. M., Fay, G. C., Polissar, N. L., Martin, K. M., Shurtleff, H., Rivara, J. B., & Winn, H. R. (1992). Severity of pediatric traumatic brain injury and early neurobehavioral outcome: A cohort study. *Archives of Physical Medicine and Rehabilitation, 73*, 540–547.

Jastak, S., & Wilkinson, G. (1984). *The Wide Range Achievement Test-Revised: Administration manual*. Wilmington, DE: Jastak Associates.

Johnson, D. A. (1992). Head injured children and education: A need for greater delineation and understanding. *British Journal of Education Psychology, 62*, 404–409.

Kane, R. L. (1991). Standardized and flexible batteries in neuropsychology: An assessment update. *Neuropsychology Review, 2*, 281–339.

Kaplan, E. (1989). A process approach to neuropsychological assessment. In T. Boll & B. K. Bryant (Eds.), *Clinical neuropsychology: Research, measurement, and practice* (pp. 125–166). Washington, DC: American Psychological Association.

Kaufman, A. S., & Kaufman, N. L. (1983). *Kaufman Assessment Battery for Children: Administration and scoring manual*. Circle Pines, MN: American Guidance Service.

Leckliter, I. N., & Matarazzo, J. D. (1989). The influence of age, education, IQ, gender, and alcohol abuse on Halstead-Reitan Neuropsychological Test Battery performance. *Journal of Clinical Psychology, 45*, 484–512.

Lezak, M. (1983). *Neuropsychological assessment* (2nd ed.). New York: Oxford University Press.

Lopez, S. R., & Taussig, I. M. (1991). Cognitive-intellectual functioning of
    Spanish-speaking impaired and nonimpaired elderly: Implications for cul-
    turally sensitive assessment. *Psychological Assessment, 13*, 448–454.

Loring, D. W. (1991). A counterpoint to Reitan's note on the history of clinical
    neuropsychology. *Archives of Clinical Neuropsychology, 6*, 167–171.

Mahurin, R. K., Espino, D. V., & Holifield, E. (1992). Mental status testing in
    elderly Hispanic populations: Special concerns. *Psychopharmacology Bul-
    letin, 28*, 391–399.

Mapou, R. L. (1988). Testing to detect brain damage: An alternative to what
    may no longer be useful. *Journal of Clinical and Experimental Psychology,
    10*, 271–278.

Matarazzo, J. D. (1972). *Wechsler's measurement and appraisal of adult intelligence*
    (5th ed.). New York: Oxford University Press.

Matarazzo, J. D. (1990). Psychology assessment versus psychology testing. *Ameri-
    can Psychologist, 45*, 999–1017.

McLean, J., Kaufman, A. S., & Reynolds, C. R. (1989). Base rates of WAIS-R
    subtest scatter as a guide for clinical and neuropsychology assessment.
    Journal of Clinical Psychology, 45, 919–926.

Milberg, W., Hebben, N., & Kaplan, E. (1986). The Boston process approach to
    neuropsychological assessment. In I. Grant & K. M. Adams (Eds.), *Neuro-
    psychological assessment of neuropsychiatric disorders* (pp. 65–86). New York:
    Oxford University Press.

Parker, R. S. (1990). *Traumatic brain injury and neuropsychological impairment.*
    New York: Springer-Verlag.

Parsons, O. A., & Stewart, K. D. (1966). Effects of supportive versus dis-
    interested interviews on perceptual-motor performance in brain-
    damaged and neurotic patients. *Journal of Consulting Psychology, 30*,
    260–266.

Prigatano, G. (1992). Personality disturbances associated with traumatic brain
    injury. *Journal of Consulting and Clinical Psychology, 60*, 360–368.

Professional Issues. (1994). *Bulletin of the National Academy of Neuropsychology,
    11*, 15.

Reitan, R. (1986). Theoretical and methodological bases of the Halstead-Reitan
    Neuropsychological Test Battery. In I. G. Grant & K. M. Adams (Eds.),
    Neuropsychological assessment of neuropsychiatric disorders (pp. 3–30). New
    York: Oxford University Press.

Reitan, R., & Wolfson, D. (1986). The Halstead-Reitan Neuropsychological
    Test Battery and aging. *Clinical Gerontologist, 5*, 39–61.

Reitan, R., & Wolfson, D. (1992a). Conventional intelligence measurements and neuropsychological concepts of adaptive abilities. *Journal of Clinical Psychology, 48*, 521–529.

Reitan, R., & Wolfson, D. (1992b). *Neuropsychological evaluation of older children*. Tucson, AZ: Neuropsychology Press.

Reitan, R., & Wolfson, D. (1993a). *The Halstead-Reitan Neuropsychological Test Battery: Theory and clinical interpretation* (2nd ed.). Tucson, AZ: Neuropsychology Press.

Reitan, R., & Wolfson, D. (1993b). *Neuropsychological evaluation of young children*. Tucson, AZ: Neuropsychology Press.

Robert, S. (1994). *A portrait of America based on the latest U.S. census*. New York: Times Books.

Russell, E. W. (1986). The psychometric foundation of clinical neuropsychology. In I. Weiner (Series Ed.) & S. B. Filskov & T. Boll (Vol. Eds.), *Handbook of clinical neuropsychology: Vol. 2.* (pp. 45–80). New York: Wiley.

Russell, E. (1987). A reference scale method for constructing neuropsychological test batteries. *Journal of Clinical and Experimental Neuropsychology, 9*, 376–392.

Russell, E. W. (1992). Reliability of the Halstead Impairment Index: A simulation and reanalysis of Matarazzo and others (1974). *Neuropsychology, 6*, 251–259.

Sabin, J. E. (1975). Translating despair. *American Journal of Psychiatry, 132*, 197–199.

Sattler, J. M. (1970). Racial "experimenter effects" in experimentation, testing, interviewing, and psychotherapy. *Psychological Bulletin, 73*, 137–160.

Sbordone, R. J., & Rudd, M. (1986). Can psychologists recognize neurological disorders in their patients? *Journal of Clinical and Experimental Neuropsychology, 8*, 285–291.

Schaughency, E. A., Lahey, B. B., Hynd, G. W., Stone, P. A., Piacentini, J. C., & Frick, P. J. (1989). Neuropsychological test performance and the attention deficit disorders: clinical utility of the Luria-Nebraska Neuropsychological Battery-Children's Revision. *Journal of Consulting and Clinical Psychology, 57*, 112–116.

Sellers, A. H., & Nadler, J. D. (1992). A survey of current neuropsychological assessment procedures used for different age groups. *Psychotherapy in Private Practice, 11*, 47–57.

Simonian, S. J., Tarnowski, K. J., Stancin, T., Friman, P. C., & Atkins, M. S. (1991). Disadvantaged children and families in pediatric primary care settings: II. Screening for behavior disturbance. *Journal of Clinical Child Psychology, 20*, 360–371.

Slick, D. J., & Craig, P. L. (1991). Neuropsychological assessment in public psychiatric hospitals: The changing state of the practice—1979 to 1989. *Archives of Clinical Neuropsychology, 6*, 73–80.

Spreen, O., & Strauss, E. (1991). *A compendium of neuropsychological tests.* New York: Oxford University Press.

Stoddard, J. J., St. Peter, R. F., & Newacheck, P. W. (1994). Health insurance status and ambulatory care for children. *New England Journal of Medicine, 330*, 1421–1425.

Sweet, J. J., & Moberg, P. J. (1990). A survey of practices and beliefs among ABPP and non-ABPP clinical neuropsychologists. *The Clinical Neuropsychologist, 4*, 101–120.

Tarnowski, K. J. (1991). Disadvantaged children and families in pediatric primary care settings: I. Broadening the scope of integrated mental health service. *Journal of Clinical Child Psychology, 20*, 351–359.

Taussig, I. M., Henderson, V. W., & Mack, W. (1992). Spanish translation and validation of a neuropsychology battery: Performance of Spanish- and English-speaking Alzheimer's disease patients and normal comparison subjects. *Clinical Gerontologist, 11*, 95–107.

Teele, D. W., Klein, J. O., Chase, C., Menyuk, P., Rosner, B., & the Greater Boston Otitis Media Study Group. (1990). Otitis media in infancy and intellectual ability, school achievement, speech, and language at age 7 years. *Journal of Infectious Diseases, 162*, 685–694.

Vannieuwkirk, R. R., & Galbraith, G. G. (1985). The relationship of age to performance on the Luria-Nebraska Neuropsychology Battery. *Journal of Clinical Psychology, 41*, 527–532.

Vargas, L. A., & Willis, D. J. (1994). Introduction to the special section: New directions in the treatment and assessment of ethnic minority children and adolescents. *Journal of Clinical Child Psychology, 23*, 2–4.

Vasquez, C., & Javier, R. A. (1991). The problem with interpreters: Communicating with Spanish-speaking patients. *Hospital and Community Psychiatry, 42*, 163–165.

Waber, D. P., & Holmes, J. M. (1985). Assessing children's copy productions of the Rey-Osterrieth Complex Figure. *Journal of Clinical and Experimental Neuropsychology, 7*, 264–280.

Waldstein, S. R., Manuck, S. B., Ryan, C. M., & Muldoon, M. F. (1991). Neuropsychological correlates of hypertension: Review and methodologic considerations. *Psychological Bulletin, 110*, 451–468.

Wechsler, D. (1974). *Manual for the Wechsler Intelligence Scale for Children-Revised.* San Antonio, TX: Psychological Corporation.

Wechsler, D. (1981). *Manual for the Wechsler Adult Intelligence Scale-Revised*. San Antonio, TX: Psychological Corporation.

Wechsler, D. (1991). *Manual for the Wechsler Intelligence Scale for Children-Third Edition*. San Antonio, TX: Psychological Corporation.

Weintraub, S., & Mesulam, M.-M. (1985). Mental state assessment of young and elderly adults in behavioral neurology. In M.-M. Mesulam (Ed.), *Principles of behavioral neurology* (pp. 71–123). Philadelphia: Davis.

Wilson, M., & MacCarthy, B. (1994). GP consultation as a factor in the low rate of mental health service use by Asians. *Psychological Medicine, 24,* 113–119.

Woodcock, R. W., & Johnson, M. B. (1989, 1990). *Woodcock-Johnson Psycho-Educational Battery-Revised*. Allen, TX: DLM Teaching Resources.

Yeh, M., Takeuchi, D. T., & Sue, S. (1994). Asian-American children treated in the mental health system: A comparison of parallel and mainstream outpatient service centers. *Journal of Clinical Child Psychology, 23,* 5–12.

. . . .

11

Multicultural Implications of Performance-Based Assessment

Anthony A. Cancelli and Sabrina Teresa Arena

Performance-based assessment (PBA), one of education's hot top-ics, has taken center stage in the continuing discussion regarding the measurement of educational achievement in our schools. Policy makers at all levels of government are talking about PBA as the core of a national examination system (Baker, O'Neil, and Linn, 1993). Indeed, PBA is the centerpiece of the Goals 2000 proposal of the Clinton administration (Goals 2000: Educate America Act, 1993). It is purported to be not only a method for assessing national standards but also a means to help ensure that these standards are met (Wiggins, 1989). Increased interest in PBA is also found among teachers for use in their assessment of learning in the classroom. Although teachers have been using PBA to assess classroom learn-ing for years (Airasian, 1994), more and more teachers are being encouraged to adopt PBA as the major component in their assess-ment practice (see, for example, Wiggins, 1989). Yet, in the midst of our rush to develop and use these new assessment techniques, it is important that we stop to consider how much we know about PBA and what we need to learn before we implement it on a large scale. As stated by Linn, Baker, and Dunbar (1991) in discussing the use of PBA as an alternative to standardized multiple-choice

Note: The authors wish to thank Vincent Alfonso for his comments on an earlier version of this chapter.

. . . . .

tests (SMCTs), "It is not premature to pose questions about the standards of quality that alternative assessments ought to satisfy, given that they may become increasingly prominent in assessment programs of the 1990s" (p. 16).

Much has been written on the limitations of SMCTs (for example, Archibald and Newman, 1988; Resnick and Resnick, 1992; Shepard, 1991) and the idea of shifting from SMCTs to alternative forms of assessment is enticing. Reflecting the beliefs of many, Wiggins (1989) writes that SMCTs tell us "too much about a student's short-term recall and too little about what is most important: a student's habits of mind" (p. 706). However, many discussions of PBA focus on what it is not (Baker and others, 1993) rather than what it is and how it can be used effectively in our schools. Therefore, the important question to answer becomes, What exactly are we moving to?

The need to proceed cautiously becomes even more imperative when discussing implementation with children who are culturally and linguistically diverse. Our history of using individual and group tests in schools is replete with evidence of unfairness and bias. Judgments about deficient cognitive functioning have been influenced by educational tests indifferent to the language backgrounds of children. Children of color have been classified, sorted, and disproportionately placed in special and remedial education classes of dubious educational value. We have spent decades trying to sort through issues of bias and fairness in the use of tests in schools, and before we move toward adopting alternative forms of assessment, we should use the knowledge gained from this dialogue to assess the potential bias in PBA and reflect on the fairness of its use.

In this chapter, we examine what we know and do not know about PBA. We discuss some of the issues that should be explored to ensure equitable treatment for all children, regardless of their cultural and language backgrounds. We begin with an overview that provides a definition of PBA. Next, we discuss the importance of the concept of validity in examining bias and fairness in testing. We offer a unified and expanded definition based on the work of Messick (1989a, 1989b) that provides a framework for examining the impact of PBA on culturally and linguistically diverse groups of children. Each aspect of the definition is examined, and what we know and still need to know about PBA in each area is presented.

Overview of Performance-Based Assessment

Performance-based assessment, as its name implies, is an assessment that entails "observing and judging a pupil's skill in actually carrying out a physical activity (e.g., giving a speech) or producing a product (e.g., building a birdhouse)" (Airasian, 1994, p. 426). Many times, PBA tasks themselves are actual simulations of a valued criterion (Linn, 1993). PBA is considered different from multiple-choice, true-false, and norm-referenced tests (Baker and others, 1993) in that "It calls for the *demonstration* of understanding and skill in *applied, procedural,* or *open-ended* settings" (italics added) (p. 1210). In other words, it calls for *demonstration,* in that the assessment requires actual performance in the task to be measured; it is *applied,* in that the selected tasks are intended to tap real-life use of knowledge; it is *procedural,* in that it assesses the procedures used in applying knowledge; and finally, it is *open-ended,* in allowing the examination of different perspectives and approaches that may be employed in answering a question or solving a problem.

There are many classroom situations in which teachers have always used PBA to assess the ability of students to show what they can do in real-life situations (Wiggins, 1992). For example, teachers regularly assess communication skills by having students demonstrate that they can follow directions, write essays, or give speeches (Airasian, 1994). PBA is also used regularly by teachers to measure psychomotor skills such as using scissors or conducting a science experiment. However, only recently has the use of PBA been seriously considered as a way to measure the acquisition of concepts and affective skills (Airasian, 1994). Proponents of PBA argue that assessing only knowledge of concepts does not tell us anything about whether or not students can use that knowledge in real-life situations. For example, we do not measure students' knowledge of writing essays by having them tell us how to write essays. Rather, we ask them to demonstrate that knowledge by actually producing an essay. Similarly, it is argued, when we teach students how to think inductively, we should require that they demonstrate their ability to draw conclusions given bits of evidence in real-life situations rather than asking them on SMCTs how one reasons inductively.

Posing the Questions

Is PBA a procedure that can be used in a nonbiased and fair way with culturally and linguistically diverse groups of children? To address issues of bias, researchers have used the concept of validity to frame their questions. The major question posed asks if a test is valid to the same degree for respondents who differ in such factors as gender, culture, or language background. Bias is not demonstrated when the mean performance of children across groups differs on a test. Although such evidence may make a test suspect, bias is only evidenced if this mean difference is the result of the test not measuring the same thing or measuring the same thing to a different degree. This is reasonable. Differences between groups may exist for a variety of reasons that are external to the test. The purpose of the test is to tell us what is, and if group mean differences exist, the test should reflect that difference.

Discussions of fairness, on the other hand, focus on the implications the use of tests holds for different groups of children and for society. For example, even if a test is nonbiased in a technical sense, is it fair to use it if it results in the disproportional selection and placement of children of color in special education classes? If mean score differences across groups exist on a test and the test is used to make decisions, there may be consequences that are not in the best interest of anyone. By the nature of fairness questions, such discussions require conclusions based on one's beliefs about what is fair and what is not. Regardless, Messick (1989a) argues that such discussions are intrinsic to the use of tests and must be considered when evaluating the overall validity of a test.

The study of the validity of PBA, let alone of differences in its validity across groups, has not been a high priority of its proponents. Linn and others (1991) write, "Simply because the measures are derived from actual performance or relatively high-fidelity simulations, it is too often assumed that they are more valid than multiple choice tests" (p. 16). Indeed, just because one may reasonably argue that inferences drawn from PBA are reduced because of their close approximation to relevant criteria, it does not mean that PBA's developers are absolved from having to demonstrate its validity and reliability and to provide evidence that it could be used in a nonbiased and fair way. Regardless of how small the inferences are, they are inferences nonetheless, subject to the threats and biases that challenge the measurement of any construct, regardless of the method used to assess it.

The Concept of Validity

For the past quarter of a century, our understanding of the concept of validity has been rapidly evolving. As reflected in the *Standards for Educational and Psychological Testing* (American Educational Research Association, American Psychological Association, and National Council on Measurement in Education, 1985), validity has grown to be understood as a unitary concept with content, criterion-related, and construct validity describing three types of validity evidence rather than three separate types of validity (Cole and Moss, 1989). Since publication of the 1985 revision of the *Standards*, the concept of validity has continued to evolve (Moss, 1992). Led by the writings of Cronbach (1988) and Messick (1989a, 1989b) the concept of validity continues to be unified as well as broadened to address issues related to the social consequences and value implications of test interpretation and use. Only through this expanded and unified definition can we effectively assess the validity of any test and thoroughly examine the unique features of PBA (Linn and others, 1991).

In contrast to the traditional tripartite conceptualization (construct, content, and criterion-related validity), Messick (1989a) writes that we should move to a view of validity as "an integrated evaluative judgment of the degree to which empirical evidence and theoretical rationales support the *adequacy* and *appropriateness* of *inferences* and *actions* based on test scores or other modes of assessment" (p. 5). Thus, Messick's definition reveals four aspects of one validity that should be investigated: namely, *adequacy of inferences, adequacy of actions, appropriateness of inferences,* and *appropriateness of actions.* Evaluations based on each of these aspects contributes to an overall judgment of the construct validity of a test.

Searches for validity have traditionally focused on the *adequacy of inferences.* The question posed is: How well does a test measure the construct it purports to measure? All educational tests, including PBA, are administered with the idea that the samples of behavior collected have meaning beyond the specific items asked on the test. For example, from five or six items on an achievement test, judgments are made about a child's mastery of an entire domain of knowledge. How adequate is the construction of that domain? How consistently can it be measured? Is performance on the domain related to items measuring other domains as one would expect? The answer to these and other similar questions all impact the confidence one has in the test's adequacy in measuring the construct. When examining bias, each of these questions is asked simultaneously for different groups, and the results are examined to determine differences.

The second aspect of validity, *adequacy of actions,* poses the question: How useful is a measure of the construct in making decisions? Messick (1989a) writes, "In practical testing applications, there needs to be some means of assuring that *general* evidence supportive of construct validity includes *specific* evidence of the relevance of the test to the applied purpose and of the utility of the scores in the applied setting" (p. 9). This aspect of validity recognizes that tests are not administered in a vacuum. Rather, decisions are made with their use, and there are consequences as a result of that use. Because a test measures a construct well does not mean that decisions made with an understanding of that construct will be useful. For example, SMCTs are used regularly in schools to make decisions about how to group students, for whom special instruction should be provided, how successful one school is in educating children in comparison to another, and how to distribute resources in a school district. With respect to these decisions, this aspect of validity asks, Is the probability of making a "good" decision increased with the use of data from SMCTs? In other words, does the use of the test enhance the probability of predicting a desired outcome? When investigating bias, the question posed asks if decisions made with a test are equally effective in predicting the desired outcome for different groups of children.

Appropriateness of inferences is the aspect of validity that examines the values implicit in inferences drawn from tests. How we decide to measure educational attainment is determined by our theories about how children learn and express their knowledge. Implicit in the decisions we make in the construction of tests is our understanding of the structure of knowledge and how questions can be posed to assess the degree to which this knowledge is possessed by test takers. It is imperative to recognize that the very questions we pose and the way we pose them rest on assumptions about the learner that are bound by our culture.

Most test practices in this country are grounded in a positivist or postpositivist tradition (for an excellent review, see Denzin and Lincoln, 1994). These traditions suggest that there is a world of knowledge independent of the learner that, within the limits of individual capabilities, may be acquired through effective instruction. For testing, the issue becomes how to construct a test whose results most closely approximate the true level of the acquisition of this knowledge. The intellect responsible for acquiring the knowledge is viewed as a unitary and immutable trait possessed by students in varying degrees. It accumulates knowledge in a linear sequence of acquisitions culminating in complex understandings when capable. Given this perspective, testing has come to rely on the measurement of the molecular components that make up the various strands of knowledge and rests comfortably on the assumption that children who have attained the most in schools are those most capable of responding correctly to the bits and pieces of the various strands of knowledge (see Wolf, Bixby, Glenn, and Gardner, 1991).

In typical SMCTs, there is an additional assumption that this knowledge may be gathered through tests that emphasize speed and efficiency. The amount of time given to respond to questions is limited and children who do poorly because they do not use their time efficiently are assumed to have attained less. Also assumed is that the expression of knowledge is a private affair. The ability to harness resources to display knowledge is explicitly disallowed. Test instruction to SMCTs forbid collaboration and usually caution the test administrator to offer little more than a paraphrasing of the instructions when a student asks for clarification (Wolf and others, 1991). When we consider the content of these exams, these precautions seem justified. The real question then becomes, Why are we asking questions that require such restrictions on the expression of knowledge? Is this the way we expect children to use the knowledge and skill we teach them outside of school? Are the outcomes represented by these tests too narrow to judge adequately educational attainment? When examining the *adequacy of the inferences* we make with tests, we ask if what we ask in tests and how we ask it is valid and nonbiased. Typical test validation practice used in gathering evidence about the adequacy of inferences asks these questions after tests have been constructed from a certain point of view. When examining the *appropriateness of inferences*, we ask if the *what* and *how* of testing captures the essence of what we really want to know and if it does so in sufficient ways to assure that the achievements of all children are measured equally well. These questions should be posed *before* as well as after we construct the test.

The relevance of what we ask in testing and its ability to predict meaningful outcomes is not a new concern. In 1915, William James wrote:

> No elementary measurement, capable of being performed in a laboratory, can throw light on the actual efficiency of the subject; for the vital thing about him, his emotional and moral energy and doggedness, can be measured by no single experiment, and becomes known only to the total results in the long run. . . . Be patient, then, and sympathetic with the type of mind that cuts a poor figure in examination. It may, in the long examination which life sets us, come out in the end in better shape than the glib and ready producer, its passions being deeper, its purposes more worthy, its combining power less commonplace, and its total mental output consequently more important [as quoted in Wolf and others, 1991, pp. 135–143].

Questions posed to assess the *appropriateness of inferences* of tests become all the more important when children from diverse cultural and language backgrounds are treated differently than children raised in mainstream because of the tests that are used in schools. How children express their knowledge is dependent on what they already know and the way their culture has encouraged them to express it. When assessing children whose cultural and language experiences are different, bias becomes a potential problem if the testing practices reflect one type of acquisition and expression over others. When we concern ourselves with the appropriateness of the inferences we make with tests, we acknowledge the contributions the learner makes to the acquisition and expression of knowledge. The question posed here is: What is the appropriateness of inferences made about children with the use of a test in light of the potential narrow focus on what one has chosen to assess and how it is being assessed? With respect to bias, the question in which we become most interested is, If test results provide evidence of differences across groups, is it because of our parochial perspectives on what we are measuring and how we are measuring it?

Also concerned with the values implicit in tests is the *appropriateness of action*, which has to do with the fair use of tests. Regardless of their psychometric integrity, all tests have an impact in the real world. What are the educational, social, economic, and political effects of the use of the test? This aspect of validity acknowledges that there are implications to the use of a test that have little to do with its technical adequacy. Thus, the difference between *adequacy of action* and *appropriateness of action* is that the former focuses on the validity of a test to predict outcomes, while the latter focuses on the fairness of the use of the test to make decisions, regardless of its technically adequate validity. Tests affect all of our institutions and that effect needs to be evaluated so that we understand the potential harm or good that may result from their use. For example, SMCTs affect the way teachers deliver the curriculum, the way children feel about themselves, and the way others view them. Also, the use of tests may perpetuate disproportional representation of minorities in certain career choices. The question here is whether a test is appropriate to use given the long-range values held by the institution employing the test and by society in general.

In the remaining sections of this chapter, we will examine each of these aspects of validity as they relate to PBA. We will review what we know, what we need to learn, and the special issues raised in the use of PBA with multilingual and multicultural populations.

Adequacy of Inferences

The growing consensus among measurement scholars is that evidence traditionally gathered in support of the validity of a measure all bears on the measure's construct validity (Messick, 1989a). Thus, information about stability and consistency (typically referred to as reliability), the generalizability of an item to a content domain (typically referred to as content validity), and the relationship of test scores to other tests and practical outcomes (typically referred to as criterion-related validity), all serve our overall understanding of *construct* validity. If the construct validity of a test cannot be established, the test is not measuring what it is supposed to measure and should not be used to assess the construct or to make decisions that imply an understanding of the construct.

We extend this definition of construct validity when examining bias in tests. Specifically, if a test is construct valid for some groups but not for others, it is biased. This understanding provides the framework for examining bias in most of our current measures of ability and achievement. Research in this area typically examines indices of validity to see if there are differences between groups based on gender, race, ethnicity, and language ability. Any complete study of the adequacy of inferences made with PBA should include a full investigation of construct bias. Frechtling (1991) writes, "Simply shifting from a product-oriented assessment to a process-oriented assessment does not guarantee an unbiased test" (p. 24).

Task generalizability. Proponents of PBA view the placement of assessment into a real-life context or simulation of it to be one of its greatest advantages (Baker and others, 1993). Ironically, it is the very aspect of PBA that makes it so appealing that is a problem for the generalizability of test results. One of the major findings concerning PBA is that not much consistency in performance has been found in student responses that are supposed to measure content in the same domain (Baker and others, 1993; Linn, 1993; Mehrens, 1992). For example, Shavelson, Baxter, and Pine (1992) found little relationship in the performance of students on the same science tasks using different methods of assessment (that is, hands-on manipulation with notebook recordings, computer simulation, and paper-and-pencil tests). Thus, when PBA is used, we are unsure what children know when they complete a complex task successfully other than how to complete the exact task represented on the test.

The lack of generalizability across tasks in PBA is understandable. Research in cognitive psychology has yielded a two-part interactive model of knowledge structures. The two types of knowledge that are believed to coexist are declarative knowledge and procedural knowledge. *Declarative knowledge* refers to specific content knowledge (such as historical dates, mathematical facts, and vocabulary words). *Procedural knowledge* refers to knowledge about how to do things (such as, brushing your teeth, driving a car, or using a computer to solve a math problem) and is highly context specific. "Context often determines how a problem will be perceived as well as the strategies a child will deploy to solve it" (Ceci and Ruiz, 1993, p. 179). Indeed, some research has shown that variations in context have significant effects on mathematical performance dependent on whether it was presented in street- or school-like settings (Saxe, 1991). Since PBA tasks are usually complex, often requiring significant use of context-specific procedural knowledge as well as declarative knowledge (Mehrens, 1992), two tasks are not likely to be similar even when they appear to be measuring the same thing. This has been less of a problem with multiple-choice tests, since items included in these tests are often less complicated and require limited use of procedural knowledge (Mehrens, 1992).

In order to make inferences to a content domain, several tasks must be included; however, given the time requirements to complete complex PBA tasks, a dilemma is created. Linn (1993), for example, shows that in order to achieve a generalizability coefficient of .90 or greater for the PBA type questions on the College Board's Advance Placement examinations, testing time would range from a lower boundary of one hour and fifteen minutes for the physics exams on electricity and magnetism to thirteen hours for European history. This would be in addition to the time required to complete the multiple-choice part of the exams. Thus, in order to make PBA practical, breadth in sampling a domain is sacrificed for depth (Mehrens, 1992). This impacts on the validity of PBA. As Mehrens concludes, "the major problems for valid performance assessment relate to the limited sampling and lack of generalizability from the limited sample to any identifiable domain" (p. 7).

This inherent problem with PBA enhances the likelihood of bias. We know from the limited information we have about PBA that the differences we find in mean performance between minority and nonminority groups in SMCTs are also found in PBA (Linn and others, 1991). If PBA tasks inadequately sample a domain, faulty inferences about what performance means results in an increase in measurement error. This increases the potential for bias, because measurement error erroneously accentuates differences between groups (Jensen, 1980). For example, if the mean performances of African American and nonminority children differ on a math test, the more unreliable the test, the more likely the difference will be larger than the true difference.

Interrater reliability. Since PBA is designed to be a holistic approach to assessment, the scoring criteria established for successful performance typically require subjective judgments. The scoring criteria, called rubrics, should be clearly delineated during test development, and those who will be rating the tests should be trained to apply them. It is best that more than one scorer analyze each response—and follow-up analyses are necessary to determine the degree to which judges agree. Most of the empirical research on PBA to date has focused on interrater reliability (Baker and others, 1993). Findings suggest that when clear criteria are established and raters trained in their use, reliable ratings can be obtained (Baker and others, 1993; Linn, 1993; Shavelson and others, 1992).

Rubrics aid examiners to evaluate student performance by providing guidelines for different levels of performance on a given task (for example, see Exhibit 11.1). Each criterion describes different levels of performance within the domain and delineates a score for each; the higher the score the higher the level of performance. Note that a score of four is offered (for all three components) when

Exhibit 11.1. Rubric: Reasoning Strategy of Comparison.

Components	Rating
a. Selects appropriate items to compare.	*Four Points:* Selects items that are extremely suitable for addressing the basic objective of the comparison and that show *original or creative thinking.* *Three Points:* Selects items that provide a means for successfully addressing the basic objective of the comparison. *Two Points:* Selects items that satisfy the basic requirements of the comparison but create some difficulties for completing the task. *One Point:* Selects items that are inappropriate to the basic objective of the comparison.
b. Selects appropriate characteristics on which to base the comparison.	*Four Points:* Selects characteristics that encompass the most essential aspects of the items and *present a unique challenge or provide an unusual insight.* *Three Points:* Selects characteristics that provide a vehicle for meaningful comparison of the items and address the basic objective of the comparison. *Two Points:* Selects characteristics that provide for a partial comparison of the items and may include some extraneous characteristics. *One Point:* Selects characteristics that are *trivial* or do not address the basic objective of the comparison. Selects characteristics on which the items cannot be compared.
c. Accurately identifies the similarities and differences among the items, using the identified characteristics.	*Four Points:* Accurately assesses all identified similarities and differences for each item on the selected characteristic. *Additionally, the student provides inferences from the comparison that were not explicitly requested in the task description.* *Three Points:* Accurately assesses the major similarities and differences among the identified characteristics.

Exhibit 11.1.   Rubric: Reasoning Strategy of Comparison, Cont'd.

Components	Rating
	Two Points: Makes some important errors in identifying the major similarities and differences among the identified characteristics.
	One Point: Makes many significant errors identifying the major similarities and differences among the identified characteristics.

Note: Comparison involves describing the similarities and differences between two or more items. The process includes three components that can be assessed, labeled a, b, and c.

Source: Marzano, Pickering, and McTighe (1990), p. 68. Reproduced in adapted and modified form with permission from McREL Institute, the copyright holder.

students offer something more to the given circumstances: a creative thought or insight, a unique challenge, or inference. This particular example heeds the warning in Wolf and others (1991) against creating scoring rubrics that delineate a single approach to success that stunt serious thought and progression in support of "multiple paths to excellence" (p. 63).

Although seemingly most appropriate for mathematical reasoning exercises, rubrics can facilitate the objective scoring of essays tapping higher-order thinking. Rubrics, for example, can be used for comparative essays in subjects ranging from social studies to biology where students are given the opportunity to express the depth of their knowledge in the given area of study. Exhibit 11.2 provides two examples of comparison questions, one for social studies and one for biology, and several levels of responses scored using the rubric described in Exhibit 11.1.

Note that a score of four is given when students offer something more in their response: a creative thought or insight, or a unique challenge or inference. Since the first response to the social studies question brought about another comparison or insight as to how yet

Exhibit 11.2. Examples of Scored Responses to PBA Comparison Questions.

Comparison Question	Scored Response
Social Studies The two main types of government studied in this unit were democracy and communism. Identify some of the ways these two types of government are similar and some of the ways these two types of government are different.	*Four Point Response* Democracy and communism are both types of government that have particular philosophies of rule behind them. Although they are both "for" the people, they are for them in different ways. Democracy is for the rights of all the individual people that make up the society and entrust in their right to govern themselves. However, in American society this right is transferred to the elected public officials who are more directly involved in governing. Theoretically, individuals are compensated according to their worth or job input and they are allowed to own property. Communism is for the people in that the government provides the jobs and related services that are needed. People are compensated according to the needs of society so that there is a type of sharing and equality among the people in that most of the people are equally compensated regardless of their level of contribution to society. All property is owned and controlled by the government. Thus, it is a community of people whose individual rights are sacrificed for the good of the community, or at times, for the good of the government. *Socialism is a type of government that seems to be a near half-way point between democracy and communism. Socialism and communism both believe in public ownership of a nation's property. However, socialism values the rights of the individual in so far as the property that is needed or*

Exhibit 11.2. Examples of Scored Responses to PBA Comparison
Questions, Cont'd.

Comparison Question	Scored Response
Social Studies	*Four Point Response* *taken by the government is thus compensated in* *addition to the amount of property that is owned* *by the government is decided via constitutional* *and legal means.* Three Point Response (same response as above without italics) One Point Response Democracy and communism are different types of people. All democratic peoples are good and all communist peoples are bad. Democratic people are rich and communist people are poor.
Biology ·During this unit, we've learned about the unity and diversity among living things. Identify some of the similarities and differences among the different living things.	*Four Point Response* All living things share certain basic functions of life. The eight identified in this unit are: nutrition, transport, respiration, excretion, synthesis, regulation, growth, and reproduction. . . . (with a brief description of each life function). However, all living things differ in the manner in which they go about these life functions. For example, . . . All living things are made of cells that are similar in structure and function. However, they are again different because they are made up of different numbers of cells. In the multi-cellular organisms there is also specialization of cells where each cell is different in that it is made to carry out a particular function; whereas, in the single cellular organisms, that cell carries out all of the life functions. *Finally, all living things are similar in that they all have souls but differ in their closeness to God.*

Exhibit 11.2. Examples of Scored Responses to PBA Comparison
Questions, Cont'd.

Comparison Question	Scored Response
	or
	This type of specialization and working together is similar to how different types of people perform various jobs which contribute to the functioning of society as a whole.
	Three Point Response (same response as above without italics)
	One Point Response All living things eat and drink. Rocks aren't alive because they don't eat or drink. Humans eat plants and animals; and animals can eat plants, and sometimes humans; but plants don't eat; plants only take in water. . . .

another form of government relates to the ones discussed, it was
scored as a four-point response. Although both four-point responses
offer something more than the three-point answers, the governmental response may be less debatable as to its appropriateness as
a four-point response than the responses to the biology question.
The four-point biology response brings into it something more than
may have been intended. This response of the soul being a similarity of all living beings brings forth a different dimension related
to cultural and religious beliefs. Thus, the question remains: Should
such a response be considered worthy of four points? This question
cannot be answered without considering values. This issue will be
elaborated on later in this chapter in the section headed "Appropriateness of Inferences."

Rubrics help ensure the reliability of judgments when using PBA
and are more easily adopted for large-scale testing programs than
for teachers in the classroom. Shavelson and others (1992) provide
some evidence that, with properly constructed PBA, teachers may

be capable of making fairly reliable judgments on their own. However, are the performance-based tests typically administered by teachers well constructed? Can we be confident that those guides that help ensure consistency in judgment are being used by teachers in the classroom? Stiggins and Bridgeford (1985) provide evidence that most teachers do not feel confident in developing or conducting performance assessments. Teachers generally feel that they do not possess sufficient knowledge about PBA—and their lack of confidence seems justified. One-third of the teachers in the Stiggins and Bridgeford (1985) study indicated that they did not provide students with information about what constituted good performance beforehand, their scoring or rating procedures were not planned prior to conducting their assessment, and the criteria for adequate performance were not established beforehand.

Linn (1993) writes that "proponents of the 'new objective tests' in the early 1900s argued against performance-based tests by arguing that subjective judgments of student essays were inherently unfair" (p. 9). This concern is just as relevant today as it was ninety years ago. If teacher-made performance tests are designed, administered, and scored inadequately, it is reasonable to hypothesize that the resulting measurement error may be systematic. In other words, such poorly constructed tests may invite bias. Nisbett and Ross (1980) write that teachers' judgments can be influenced by a variety of factors, including their prior knowledge of students, their first impressions, or their personal prejudices or beliefs. The more subjective the scoring procedures are and the more informally the assessment is conducted, the more potential exists for a teacher's prejudgments, whether conscious or unconscious, to bias the results of a test (Stiggins, 1987).

Adequacy of Actions

It is one thing to provide evidence that a test is measuring what it is supposed to measure but another to demonstrate that the measured construct is useful in making decisions. Traditionally, the type of evidence about a test's utility has been conceptualized separately from the study of validity. However, since test use is so interwoven with the fabric of test development, construction, and interpretation, trying to separate issues of use from the study of test validity is artificial at best.

The best way to enhance the validity of any decision made with a test is to draw few inferences about what test behaviors represent. If one wants to be able to make a judgment about whether or not a child can solve a particular type of science problem, replicate in the assessment the problem you want solved and the context in which you want it solved. Then, when interpreting a child's performance, draw few inferences about what the scores represent. That is, do not draw too many conclusions about what other types of solutions a child can perform and in what other contexts a child would be able to perform them.

It is argued that the low levels of inferences drawn from PBA is the strength. PBA is closely aligned with school curricula and PBA tasks require the types of performance we expect from children as a consequence of instruction. It is for this reason that PBA is referred to by some as *authentic* assessment (Baker and others, 1993). Wiggins (1989) writes, "Authentic assessments replicate the challenges and standards of performance that typically face writers, business people, scientists, community leaders, designers, or historians. These include writing essays and reports, conducting individual and group research, designing proposals and mock-ups, assembling portfolios, and so on" (pp. 703–704).

Clearly, the closeness in relationship between the score derived from PBA and the desired criterion performance is an undeniable strength. The discussion above notwithstanding, when PBA is used by teachers in classrooms to make judgments about the mastery of specific curricular goals, PBA has a face validity that makes it very appealing. Even those who caution that we go slowly in our adoption of PBA, favor the use of PBA by teachers who integrate it with their instruction (see, for example, Mehrens, 1992).

However, when we attempt to use PBA to make decisions based

on inferences about performance on other tasks and in other settings, such as we do in high-stakes testing (for example, in school-wide testing programs, discussed in more detail in Chapter Eighteen), we find PBA fraught with validity concerns that have yet to be addressed. Indeed, many of the concerns are the same that exist with the use of SMCTs (Mehrens, 1992).

When tests are used to make important selection or placement decisions in schools, we must ask ourselves if we achieve our intended outcomes as a consequence of the use of the test. For example, when we use a test to help determine if a child should be placed in a remedial class in reading, the validity question that should be posed is, Does the use of the test enhance the probability of improving the child's chances for success in that subject area? It is not enough to be satisfied that the test used to place the child is actually measuring reading achievement. Evidence that the child would achieve more in that special class than he or she would if not placed in that class is the type of validity evidence required here.

When examining the consequences of test use, bias would be evident if the remedial reading placement mentioned above was useful for some groups of students but not for others. For example, if the remedial reading placement enhanced the performance of nonminority children above what their performance would have been had they not been placed but was found to be of no benefit (or a detriment) to the performance of children of color, the test would be biased for that use. Such a finding would stimulate the need to find alternative ways of providing remedial instruction to children of color. Needless to say, validity and bias evidence of this sort is scant in educational decision making for any type of test. Nonetheless, it should become part of our validation process regardless of whether we are validating standardized achievement tests or PBA.

Appropriateness of Inferences

The formation and use of rubrics arose from two concerns. The first is directly related to overcoming the limited reliability of PBA as discussed in the section on the adequacy of inferences. The second, which will be the focus of this section, has to do with the concern that multiple-choice tests "often enforce a view of single correct answers at the expense of recognizing culturally varied forms of excellence or contrasting approaches to displaying understanding" (Cummins, 1986, as quoted in Wolf and others, 1991, p. 32). Values guide judgments on what is correct and incorrect and thus what will be rewarded. For example, most standardized exams are timed, artificial learning experiences leaving students with the impression that "speed and correctness outweigh overall quality and risk" (Wolf and others, 1991, p. 45). Armed with the knowledge that these tests are timed, well-intentioned teachers hope that their practice on these types of exams will pay off. However, they are reinforcing the underlying values of speed and correctness that are counterproductive to the now-realized importance of teaching to develop critical thinking (as opposed to factual knowledge).

Values, as just mentioned, not only play an important role in what is taught in the classroom but also in the evaluation of what is correct and appropriate in a given situation or task. Values have been defined by Rokeach as "being an enduring organization of beliefs concerning preferable modes of conduct or end-states of existence along a continuum of relative importance" (as quoted in Fernald, 1987, p. 318). Values not only play a role in determining what possible alternatives exist but also influence the order in which these alternatives will be placed. Moreover, Fernald states that these cultural and social values are what determine personal values.

Wolf and others remind us that "our conceptions of learning and what is worth being learned evolve at the high speed of culture rather than the gradual speed of biology. That only a century ago, to be literate was to be able to sign your name or read a highly familiar test, but neither of these definitions is sufficient today" (1991, p. 64)

In fact, even our conception of what intelligence is has undergone considerable change. Intelligence was once considered a unitary hereditary trait that was fixed and unalterable. Later, others argued that the environment determined every aspect of behavior, including intelligent behavior. Today, intelligence is generally believed to be determined by a combination of both, whereby heredity provides a potential range and the environment in which one is raised helps to determine where one falls within that range. Perhaps more importantly, our understanding of intelligence has evolved to believe that there is no single form of intelligence, rather that "the human ability to process and understand is the result of the interaction of *multiple intelligences* such as an acute understanding of verbal, spatial, or kinesthetic information" (Sternberg and Wagner, 1985, quoted in Wolf and others, 1991, p. 49).

Such a belief has implications for how intelligence is measured and for who is deemed intelligent, as well as what type of instruction these and other students receive. First, a single score of intelligence, or even achievement for that matter, no longer provides us with accurate and appropriate information for educational planning. Second, students who display intelligence in other fashions than through extraordinary verbal capacity may continue to be overlooked. Thus, education may need to focus on the development of students' strengths to overcome their weaknesses rather than utilizing their weaknesses as excuses for low achievement and expectations. Wolf and others (1991) note that the utilization of the normal curve as an indicator of intelligence allows us to accept that there are those students who are naturally underachievers. Shifting the yardstick of measurement away from other students and toward a profile of achievement places us in a more data-based, action-oriented position to educate according to students' needs.

In this regard, PBA holds promise in the area of multicultural assessment. PBA is a complex process that typically requires immediate judgments on the part of the examiner. This allows the examiner to "see" if the examinee comprehends the directions and the questions or tasks being posed. The opportunity then arises to assess whether it is a language barrier that impedes correct performance or a lack of "know how." In the case of multiple-choice questions, one does not readily have this opportunity. In fact, the opportunity to guess may mask the child's linguistic or cultural incomprehension. Thus, with PBA, the examiner can clarify any misunderstandings or miscommunications and interpret the results accordingly.

Culture and its values remain a factor in any type of assessment. Examiners must recognize that what they deem creative or trivial may be a matter of cultural preference and not a matter of fact. PBA scoring rubrics open the doors to "multiple paths of excellence." However, it is up to the examiners to keep the doors open by being open-minded themselves. In addition, because some cultures appreciate the individual attention that is offered by performance-based means, while other cultural groups may find it difficult to perform in ways they may view as showing off or being disrespectful, examiners need to be well versed in the role that culture plays and its expression in diverse groups of people. Examiners may need to assess how well this type of assessment fits the mold of their examinee's life and evaluate its use in that light. PBA affords the examiner the time and flexibility to do so.

Appropriateness of Actions

Regardless of the technical validity of an instrument in measuring a particular construct or despite its established usefulness, using a procedure for making important decisions has a variety of implications that must be considered in judging any assessment procedure. Just as we must examine the appropriateness of inferences we draw when we use tests, we must evaluate the appropriateness of actions taken with them.

Cole and Moss (1989) draw a distinction between intended and unintended outcomes of testing that focuses our attention on several critical issues that should be discussed when examining the appropriateness of actions. Intended outcomes, whether implicit or explicit, are those that guide the selection of a test. For example, let us consider a decision to use a SMCT to select children for a remedial reading class. Evidence about whether selected children benefit from the class (more than they would if not in the class) would be necessary to establish the adequacy of actions. However, in addition to this intended outcome may be unintended outcomes or side effects, some of which may be negative. For example, children who are identified for this class may suffer lower self-esteem, teachers may fail to challenge identified students with sufficiently difficult material, or a disproportional number of minority children may be selected. The identification of negative unintended outcomes inevitably leads to discussions about whether or not the benefits of making the decisions outweigh the costs. In other words, is the purpose worthy in light of the negative side effects? Such decisions require judgments based on values. As Cole and Moss state, "The importance or worthiness of the purpose is basically a matter of value judgments about which not all persons will necessarily agree" (p. 215).

Considering the appropriateness of actions is just as imperative when using PBA as it is when employing other forms of assessment. There is no reason to believe that some of the same decisions we now make with traditional SMCTs will not be made with PBA. Nor is there any reason to believe that some of the negative side effects will disappear. Specifically, as mentioned previously, there is reason to believe that the same mean group differences found in test results using SMCTs are also found in PBA results (Linn and others, 1991). Thus, whether we use SMCTs or PBA to make norm-referenced decisions in schools, disproportional representation remains an issue about which the risks and benefits must be discussed.

However, PBA holds a potential advantage for many of the purposes SMCTs are currently used in schools. Many of the potential negative side effects that accompany testing that compares children to each other may be avoided with PBA. In this sense, PBA holds the same advantage as criterion-referenced testing in that the child is compared to a standard rather than to other children in the class. Such a referencing system avoids having to assign single grades that rank children in a class and force competition where none is required. Instead, multifaceted profiles of the strengths and weaknesses of each child can be developed.

Teachers often use SMCTs in their classes because they are either provided the instruments by those who publish the texts they use or because they are not adequately skilled in alternatives (Airasian, 1994). As we continue to establish the psychometric integrity of PBA and develop the skills among our teachers for using PBA, an alternative becomes available that may better fit a school's purpose as it examines the appropriateness of actions it takes with the tests that currently serve its purposes.

Conclusions

While the application of a unified and expanded conceptualization of validity is important to validation research with all types of assessment systems, its use in validating PBA is essential. As discussed in the section on potential uses, PBA is being touted as a means of bringing about meaningful change in schools. Yet we still know little about whether or not their use would be more or less equitable for children from different cultural and language backgrounds. The potential uses of these measures in high-stakes testing to determine, for example, who is eligible to receive a high school diploma, or who should be admitted to college, should be carefully examined to determine if its validity differs for different groups. As Wolf and others (1991) point out, "Whereas there is considerable criticism of the approaches taken by standardized tests, as yet we have no such critical tradition for new modes of assessment. And we cannot be without one" (p. 60).

Yet in the face of the voluminous work that has to be completed, the potential of PBA has an allure that motivates, especially among those who hold serious questions about the equity of our current practices. Above all, PBA is a system that holds real-world knowledge as the criterion for judging educational attainment. Implicit is a respect for all of the elements of learning that are prerequisite to masterful performance. PBA offers hope that we will no longer need to infer mastery of complex performances by assessing incomplete parts whose sum we are unsure equal the whole. No longer will we need to disrespect aspects of learning by excluding them from our assessments—aspects such as working cooperatively with others, gathering and using resources critical to the successful completion of a task, thinking creatively and accepting inefficiency if it is part of a process that ultimately yields better results, or having the capacity to improve our performance through feedback. Also respected is the learner's capacity to demonstrate performance, when appropriate, other than that prescribed by a test designer. But most of all, PBA offers the promise that teachers will be able to become more intimate with the thoughts of their students. The more teachers understand the ways their children think, the more able they will be to recognize and acknowledge diversity as a strength in our children rather than a weakness.

References

Airasian, P. W. (1994). *Classroom assessment.* New York: McGraw-Hill.

American Educational Research Association, American Psychological Association, and National Council on Measurement in Education. (1985). *Standards for educational and psychological testing.* Washington, DC: Authors.

Archibald, D. A., & Newman, F. M. (1988). *Beyond standardized testing: Assessing authentic academic achievement in secondary schools.* Washington, DC: National Association of Secondary School Principals.

Baker, E. L., O'Neil, H. F., & Linn, R. L. (1993). Policy and validity prospects for performance-based assessment. *American Psychologist, 48,* 1210–1218.

Ceci, S. J., & Ruiz, A. I. (1993). Inserting context into our thinking about thinking: Implications for a theory of everyday intelligent behavior. In M. Rabinowitz (Ed.). *Cognitive science foundations of instruction* (pp. 173–188). Hillsdale, NJ: Erlbaum.

Cole, N. S., & Moss, P. A. (1989). Bias in test use. In R. L. Linn (Ed.), *Educational measurement* (3rd ed., pp. 201–219). New York: Macmillan.

Cronbach, L. J. (1988). Five perspectives on validity argument. In H. Wainer (Ed.), *Test validity* (pp. 3–17). Hillsdale, NJ: Erlbaum.

Denzin, N. K., & Lincoln, Y. S. (1994). Introduction: Entering the field of qualitative research. In N. K. Denzin & Y. S. Lincoln (Eds.), *Handbook of qualitative research* (pp. 1–18). Newbury Park, CA: Sage.

Fernald, L. W. (1987). Values and creativity. *Journal of Creative Behavior, 21,* 312–324.

Frechtling, J. A. (1991). Performance assessment: Moonstruck or the real thing? *Educational Measurement: Issues and Practice, 10,* 23–25.

Goals 2000: Educate America Act, H.R. 1804, 103d Cong., 1st Sess. (1993).

Jensen, A. R. (1980). *Bias in mental testing.* New York: Free Press.

Linn, R. L. (1993). Educational assessment: Expanded expectations and challenges. *Educational Evaluation and Policy Analysis, 15,* 1–16.

Linn, R. L., Baker, E. L., & Dunbar, S. B. (1991). Complex, performance-based assessment: Expectations and validation criteria. *Educational Researcher, 20,* 15–21.

Marzano, R., Pickering, D., & McTighe, J. (1990). *Assessing student outcomes: Performance assessment using the dimensions of learning.* Aurora, CO: McREL Institute.

Mehrens, W. A. (1992). Using performance assessment for accountability purposes. *Educational Measurement: Issues and Practice, 11,* 3–9, 20.

Messick, S. (1989a). Meaning and values in test validation: The science and ethics of assessment. *Educational Researcher, 18,* 5–11.

Messick, S. (1989b). Validity. In R. L. Linn (Ed.), *Educational measurement* (3rd ed., pp. 13–103). New York: Macmillan.

Moss, P. A. (1992). Shifting conceptions of validity in educational measurement: Implications for performance assessment. *Review of Educational Research, 62,* 229–258.

Nisbett, R. E., & Ross, L. (1980). *Human inference: Strategies and shortcomings of social judgment.* Englewood Cliffs, NJ: Prentice Hall.

Resnick, L. B., & Resnick, D. P. (1992). Assessing the thinking curriculum: New tools for educational reform. In B. R. Gifford & M. C. O'Connor (Eds.), *Changing assessment: Alternative views of aptitude, achievement, and instruction* (pp. 37–75). Boston: Kluwer.

Saxe, G. B. (1991). *Culture and cognitive development: Studies in mathematical understanding.* Hillsdale, NJ: Erlbaum.

Shavelson, R. J., Baxter, G. P., & Pine, J. (1992). Performance assessments: Political rhetoric and measurement reality. *Educational Researcher, 21,* 22–27.

Shepard, L. A. (1991). Psychometricians' beliefs about learning. *Educational Researcher, 20,* 2–16.

Stiggins, R. J. (1987). Design and development of performance assessments. *Educational Measurement: Issues and Practice, 6,* 33–42.

Stiggins, R. J., & Bridgeford, N. J. (1985). The ecology of assessment. *Journal of Educational Measurement, 22,* 271–286.

Wiggins, G. (1989). A true test: Towards more authentic and equitable assessment. *Phi Delta Kappan, 70,* 703–713.

Wiggins, G. (1992). Creating tests worth taking. *Educational Leadership, 49,* 26–33.

Wolf, D., Bixby, J., Glenn, J., III, & Gardner, H. (1991). To use their minds well: Investigating new forms of student assessment. *Review of Research in Education, 17,* 31–74.

Part IV

· ·

Emerging Issues in Assessment

Part IV of the *Handbook of Multicultural Assessment* is composed of chapters pertaining to relatively new areas in measurement, which have specific relevance to multicultural populations. The wide range of topics makes it clear that multicultural assessment is moving in many directions. It is imperative that researchers, clinicians, and educators remain updated regarding these complex and contemporary issues.

In Chapter Twelve, Edward Yansen and Ellen Shulman critically examine the process of evaluating students from culturally, ethnically, and linguistically different backgrounds. Assessment of language dominance and proficiency, second language acquisition, use of interpreters or translators, and specific language measures are addressed. The authors also provide language assessment procedure guidelines. The chapter concludes with two case studies to illustrate the importance of integrating language issues in the assessment process.

Assessment of diverse family systems is the focus of Chapter Thirteen, by Jane Close Conoley and Lorrie Bryant. The authors stress the importance of valid measures in this area to plan for effective family interventions. Family roles, therapeutic issues, personality factors, belief systems, interpersonal and interactional styles, and acculturation are just some of the topics covered. These issues are examined with respect to racial and ethnic group differences. Various assessment instruments and approaches to family assessment are reviewed.

In Chapter Fourteen, Leo Goldman highlights the benefits of qualitative assessment in the multicultural area. Specific methods such as card sorts, in-boxes, work-samples, games, and exercises are provided. This applied chapter will provide readers with suggested ways to integrate qualitative methods into the assessment process.

Multicultural issues in the assessment of alcohol and drug use are the focus of Chapter Fifteen, by Mitchell Schare and Norweeta Milburn. The authors note that many cultures use various substances for medicinal, spiritual, and ritual purposes. Various assessment instruments and interview methods are reviewed. Epidemiological research is summarized with respect to racial or ethnic group membership.

S. Alvin Leung critically examines the usage of vocational assessment procedures across diverse populations in Chapter Sixteen. Research on the use of particular instruments with racial or ethnic minority groups is examined, and guidelines for vocational assessment are provided. Case studies are used to illustrate multicultural themes. Directions for future research are highlighted in the conclusion of this chapter.

Cultural issues in the assessment of infants and preschool children are the focus of Chapter Seventeen, by Paul Meller and Phyllis Ohr. Recent legislative landmarks and the controversies surrounding the assessment of young children are discussed. General psychometric issues and reviews of the most popular preschool measures are provided. Factors influencing the administration and interpretation of preschool assessments are examined. The authors also provide two case examples to illustrate multicultural issues that can impact the evaluation of young children.

The impact of high-stakes testing on racial or ethnic minority students is addressed in Chapter Eighteen. Richard Valencia and Irma Guadarrama note the exclusive use of test scores to make educational decisions about students, teachers, and schools. A brief history of this movement is provided, along with highlights of the controversies stimulated by these practices. The authors provide specific examples of the use of high-stakes testing in Texas. A more adaptive model is suggested in terms of performance-based assessment procedures.

Eric Kohatsu and Tina Richardson provide an in-depth examination of racial and ethnic identity assessment procedures in Chapter Nineteen. They provide a review of both racial identity and ego-ethnic identity models and explanations regarding the differences between stage-process and typology models. Attention is also given to selected instruments, which are reviewed with respect to their validity and reliability.

Chapter Twenty, by Joseph Ponterotto and Charlene Alexander, highlights the importance of assessing the multicultural competence of counselors and clinicians who are conducting the evaluations. The authors examine the current status of multicultural training in psychology programs, and provide reviews of objective measures of counseling competence. Recommendations are made regarding future research needed in this area.

In Chapter Twenty-One, Lisa Suzuki, Paul Meller, and Joseph Ponterotto discuss present trends and future directions in the field of multicultural assessment. Recommendations regarding best practices in the area of multicultural assessment are highlighted.

. . . .

Language Assessment

Multicultural Considerations

Edward A. Yansen and Ellen L. Shulman

The public school system in the United States is faced with the increasingly difficult task of successfully educating large groups of culturally, ethnically, and linguistically diverse students. The majority of these students attend public schools in densely populated urban centers such as New York, Los Angeles, and Chicago. In addition to the diversity of the student population, factors such as high mobility, poverty, and social deprivation make the task of educating these students even more challenging.

The purpose of this chapter is to examine some of the issues clinicians and educators should address in evaluating students from culturally, ethnically, and linguistically different backgrounds. The authors will analyze some current assessment practices and discuss instruments that are used in the assessment process. The authors will propose ways of effectively evaluating these students and provide case histories to illustrate the process.

Clinicians and educators constantly face the daunting challenge of evaluating and educating students from different cultural and linguistic backgrounds. These tasks have become even more challenging with the immigration of students from Latin America, Eastern Europe, the West Indies, Asia, and East and West Africa. These students form a mosaic of ethnic, racial, cultural, and linguistic diversity in the community and in the schools. These ethnically diverse groups have expanded the quilt of the other ethnic or minority groups such as Native Americans, African Americans, and Hispanics. The non-White population in the United States has grown significantly. It is estimated that by year 2000, the non-White and Spanish-speaking youth under the age of eighteen years will constitute 30 percent of the nation's youth population (U.S. Bureau of the Census, 1986). In addition to this national demographic shift of population, some regions have experienced a rapid influx of large groups of ethnic and linguistic minorities into their communities due to political and social conflicts in other countries.

The presence of these diverse ethnic and linguistic groups in the schools creates opportunities and dilemmas. These students bring with them a rich cultural and linguistic heritage that should be used to enrich the rest of the student body. In addition, they are good examples of our efforts to understand and embrace people who are different from mainstream American culture. The dilemma is that the heterogeneity of these students presents teachers and clinicians with the task of better planning and organizing to provide these students with equal access and opportunities to succeed. Clinicians and educators need to acquire the skills and competencies to work with these groups.

Unfortunately, many professionals inappropriately view these students' difficulties as disabilities and place the students in classes for the mentally retarded, learning disabled, or emotionally disturbed. Advocates are challenging this practice. The famous case, *Larry P. v. Riles* (1979/1984), forced the state of California to outlaw the use of intelligence tests to place minority students in classes for the educable mentally retarded. A fundamental problem in the assessment process is the fact that clinicians and educators do not use a formal or informal test of acculturation. Olmedo (1979, 1981) stresses that "acculturation is also related to testing issues because it involves the acquisition of language, values, customs, and cognitive styles of the majority culture, all factors that may substantially affect performance on tests" (Olmedo, 1981, p. 1082). In essence, in order to reduce the inappropriate diagnosing and misdiagnosing of minority students, the authors are suggesting that clinicians and educators assess the degree of acculturation that the students have reached before administering formal tests. As Berry, Trimble, and Olmedo note (1986), acculturation is a fluid and never-ending process. Therefore, it has major psychological impact on students' performance. The acculturation process reaches an optimum level when the student is able to "pass" as a member of the new culture, nation, or group (Berry, 1980).

One of the major criticisms that clinicians and educators face in assessing students from different cultural backgrounds is that the tests that are used with these students are biased. This point of view was essentially supported by the courts (*Larry P. v. Riles*, 1979/1984; *Jose P. v. Ambach*, 1979/1982). However, the placement of minority students in special education classes in excess of their representation in the normal population continues to be a major problem. Researchers such as Oakland (1977), Reschly (1981), and Hilliard (1976) have indicated the overrepresentation of minority students in special education classes continues to be a major problem.

The federal regulations (Office of the Federal Register) address the issue of bias by requesting that students be tested in their native language or other mode of communication. They also require that the tests must have been validated for the specific purpose for which they are used. Finally, the tests must be administered by trained personnel in conformance with the instructions provided by the producer.

The issue of language in the assessment process is very important for all students. Minority students bring cultural, linguistic, and dialectal differences as part of their communication styles. This phenomenon is true for African American students who speak English. Research by Baratz and Baratz (1969) suggests that African American children grow up in a distinct culture that gives rise to a distinct language system in addition to distinct behavioral characteristics that are often ignored in the educational process.

The incidence of speech impairment as a disability among non-White students seems again to follow the pattern of overrepresentation similar to that seen in the special education classes. The clinician needs to determine if these students are in fact experiencing delays in the dominant language in areas such as syntax, morphology, fluency, phonology, grammar comprehension, and receptive and expressive language. It is important to note that it takes sometimes seven to ten years (Holland, 1960) to become proficient in the second language. Examiners often classify these students as speech impaired when in fact the students' language reflects regional or dialectal differences. This problem further underscores the need for clinicians and educators to be very knowledgeable about the students' culture and language in order to conduct a nonbiased assessment.

In many school districts, students who have been classified as having disabilities receive speech as a related service when the primary disability is a condition other than speech impairment. This service is frequently provided to students who are emotionally disturbed, learning disabled, and mentally retarded. Speech services are provided to these students as a secondary disability. Clinicians and educators often place these students in self-contained special education classes after the students fail to make significant gains in the classes for speech-impaired students. The classification of speech impairment as a disability is viewed by clinicians and educators as the least harmful disability for students. In some instances, it is considered benign. However, this practice does not address the problem of providing effective educational programs for students. It also fails to deal with the issues of culture and language of these students. Cole (1971) strongly suggests that we must understand the culture of African American children if we are to gain insights into their learning styles.

In order to assess linguistically and culturally diverse students, clinicians must begin a sequential process. This process begins with assessing the students' language dominance and proficiency skills and ends with recommendations for placement in an appropriate educational setting.

Language Dominance and Proficiency

According to the Education of All Handicapped Children Act (1975), all students should be evaluated in their dominant language.

Therefore, all students who speak a language other than English should be tested to determine language dominance and proficiency. Language proficiency refers to the level of skill or the degree to which the student exhibits control over language use (Payan, 1984). The dominant language is generally the one that is more developed; it is preferred, when, from the point of view of both the speaker and the listener, the two languages are equally appropriate; or it intrudes on the phonological, syntactic, lexical, or semantic system of the other (for example, when Spanish syntax is used in English utterances, as in the case of saying "the car blue" for the blue car). While dominance data suggest the language of instruction, proficiency data indicate the type of intervention program most likely to meet the student's needs (Ortiz, 1992).

Language proficiency is measured on a continuum from a nonspeaker of a language to a fluent speaker. Here are the proficiency levels:

Levels	Description of Proficiency (L1 and L2)
1	Nonspeaker
2	Very Limited Speaker
3	Limited Speaker
4	Functional Speaker
5	Fluent and Proficient Speaker

Once proficiency levels have been ascertained, language dominance may be determined. For example, a student may be a very limited speaker of English and a functional speaker of Vietnamese. Therefore, Vietnamese is the dominant language. One method of determining dominance and proficiency is to use standardized tests. One of the more popular tests available is the Language Assessment Scale I and II (LAS; DeAvila and Duncan, 1977). The LAS I is used for younger students in Grades K–5 (ages five to twelve), while the LAS II is used for students in Grades 6 and higher (ages twelve and up). The LAS I and II assess sound discrimination, phoneme production, lexicon (vocabulary), sentence comprehension (grammatical understanding), and production (storytelling).

There are several dominance and proficiency tests available, however, that can tap into different aspects of language (syntax or vocabulary or overall oral skills). These tests are only screening instruments and give just a brief description of the student's oral language proficiency. The results can vary. For example, a student may be dominant in syntax of the first language but could be dominant in vocabulary of the second language (Mattes and Omark, 1991). Proficiency and dominance tests do not assess academic language. This raises the question of validity for predicting academic success. Cummins (1984) argued that tests must have predictive validity for academic achievement if they are to be of value in the educational placement of bilingual children.

A home language survey (HLS) is used to determine whether a language other than English is spoken in the home. The HLS can reveal valuable information about language use patterns in the home, the language the child learned first, and the one he or she prefers to use with adults and siblings (Ortiz, 1992). The questions asked on the HLS are outlined in the following list, reproduced from Ortiz (1992).

Home Language Survey

1. Which was the first language learned by your child?

2. Which is the language most frequently used by your child at home?

3. Which language do you use most frequently with your child?

4. Which language do adults in the home use most frequently with each other?

5. Which language do your other children use most frequently when speaking to (family member's name)?

6. Does your child understand (family member's name)?

7. Does your child understand English?

Another way of assessing language dominance and proficiency is to have the student narrate a story from a set of pictures or a book without words. This should be tape recorded and analyzed later to give the clinician an idea of the student's capacity for self-expression in the first and second languages. A native speaker of the student's first language may listen to the tape and analyze the vocabulary, grammatical structure, and so forth. Use of a language sample will not provide the examiner with a score but will provide an impression of which is the student's stronger language.

Once dominance has been obtained, the clinician must determine which language to use for subsequent testing: cognitive, academic, speech-language areas, and so on. There are several factors to consider when choosing the language of testing, including dominance, language of instruction, and language of preference. If a student is bilingual (has the same proficiency levels in both the first and second language, referred to as L1 and L2), the clinician may choose to switch between languages throughout the testing session. That is, the clinician should present test items in both languages simultaneously. This affords the student all possibilities for success. Students often may know some facts or vocabulary items in one language and not in the other. By presenting the items in L1 and L2, the student has the opportunity to respond in either language. The same premise is applied to students who are equally limited in both languages. These students have weak, underdeveloped linguistic systems in L1 and L2. Equally proficient or limited students should be given the opportunity to choose the language of testing.

Many students may come from homes where languages other than English are spoken but are enrolled in English monolingual classrooms. Therefore, their academic skills could possibly be stronger in English (depending on the length of time in these classes). If in a bilingual program, the students could have equal abilities or weaknesses. It is very important to remember that a student must have a well-developed linguistic base in his or her first language before being able to successfully acquire a second language (Cummins, 1984).

Sometimes, students believe they are expected to speak English in school and will request that they be tested in that language. It is imperative that the clinician permit the student to request testing in his or her dominant language.

In the classroom, a bilingual student may appear very fluent within a social context. Oral language proficiency may be rather deceiving. For example, a student may appear very orally proficient in his or her L2 in conversations and social situations but may not have developed adequate skills in academic areas. It is essential to remember that it takes an individual two to three years to acquire oral language proficiency or social language. These are called Basic Interpersonal Communication Skills (BICS; Cummins, 1984). However, it takes between five and seven years to acquire language skills needed for academic tasks. These are referred to as Cognitive Academic Language Proficiency (CALP; Cummins, 1984). Students need to be given time to acclimate to a new culture and linguistic system before they are expected to succeed academically. Social language does not require reading or writing and therefore places fewer demands on the speaker. As a result, it is much quicker to be developed.

It is important for the clinician to be familiar with code switching. Code switching is a systematic and rule-governed process whereby a speaker switches from one language to the other at will and in accordance with appropriate situations or contexts (Ortiz, 1984). A student may begin a sentence in one language and switch to the other within the same sentence. The grammatical structures remain intact, however. This is very typical of second language learners and regarded as normal behavior. As bilinguals learn the usage norms of two languages within the community, they use them to facilitate the total act of communication (Dulay, Burt, and

Krashen, 1982). When bilingual students code switch, they have the advantage of drawing from both languages to communicate their message to others. Code switching gives the clinician another perspective on a child's dominant language.

Preassessment Considerations

Educational personnel often are concerned when students who are limited English proficient are not making quick academic gains in the classroom (Cummins, 1984). Many concerns are very legitimate, while others may be premature in nature. There are many factors to consider before evaluating a child for a potential placement in special education services. There are also several alternatives to attempt before a full evaluation is completed. Clinicians and educators who work in urban or rural school districts frequently face the task of evaluating a unique group of students. In the rural communities, some students' families are migrant farm workers who move from place to place to harvest the crops. The students move from school to school within the same state and also from school to school between states. Unfortunately, some of these students never remain in one school for more than a year.

This phenomenon is also seen in urban school districts with some ethnic minority students (Cummins, 1984). Typically, the students are Hispanic from Puerto Rico or Latin America. They come to the United States and attend school for a year or less and return to Puerto Rico or to their native country. They then return to the United States after a few months or a year and reenter the same school or a different school.

The third group of students are those who move frequently from one city to another or from one neighborhood to another within a year. It appears that the families of these students move from place to place depending on their abilities to cope with crises in their lives. In this group also are families who have been dislocated because of poverty and its attendant ills. These children—the urban nomads—move from temporary shelters several times before finding permanent homes. Therefore, they never attend the same schools for any prolonged period of time.

There are numerous implications associated with the high mobility rate of these students. They are deprived of the opportunity to have a continuous instructional program. Their skill levels in many academic areas show gaps and fragmentations. They sometimes have difficulties mastering basic academic skills. They are deprived of the opportunities of forming and maintaining healthy peer group and adult relationships. Educators and clinicians often find educational experiences of these children so fragmented that they are often in a quandary as to determining the most effective instructional program for them. Because the needs of these students are so complex, the authors are recommending that the students be placed in transitional classes for at least one year. This gives the students some time to adapt to the school environment, and it also gives educators and clinicians the opportunities to do a more comprehensive assessment. The authors strongly recommend that educators and clinicians use great caution before recommending special educational programs for these students.

It is very important to consider the amount of time the student has been in the United States. If the student has recently entered the country (less than one year), then there has not been adequate time to learn the new language and culture. This may be the student's very first exposure to English, and therefore it is important to allow the student enough time to begin to learn the new language. If the student has no history of learning difficulties, a referral for testing at this time would be highly inappropriate. Many LEP students have been misdiagnosed as having handicapping conditions because they were expected to acquire English at an unreasonably rapid rate (Shulman, 1988).

When the student comes from a home where a language other than English is spoken, he or she may take longer to acquire the second language. For educational purposes, however, a referral for additional services may be warranted if the student has not acquired some English after a year. It is interesting to note that Hispanic students are often recognized earlier than other minority groups, usually within the first six months, because Spanish is a language that is more familiar to some educators. Therefore, errors and delays are easier to detect (Dew, 1984).

A student's academic history should be considered. If the child has done well in school, with instruction in his or her native language, then a referral for special education is not warranted. If he or she had difficulty academically in the first language, then a true learning problem may exist. A referral (after at least one year) would be valid. If a student has true cognitive delays that were substantiated in the student's country of origin, testing may be administered in this country, as long as it is done by a qualified, bilingual professional.

On the other hand, a student may come from a country where more emphasis is placed on helping in the fields, baby-sitting, and similar activities than on attending school. Attendance is weak and will set the student behind. These students, when evaluated, present as learning disabled or mentally retarded, when in actuality, they have been deprived of an education. They are not truly handicapped due to the circumstances of the family, but may appear so "on paper" to the examiner. The examiner should interpret these results with caution and consider the factors involved.

If a student has had instruction only in English but is clearly dominant in another language, then he or she needs to be considered for bilingual education. Emphasis should be given to native language development to help assure that the student is proficient in his or her native language and has the language skills necessary to handle academic tasks (Ortiz, 1984).

In other cases, a student may be dominant verbally in the first language but academically dominant in English. This could be attributed to the fact that he or she has never received native language instruction. The home language may be maintained orally, but the parents prefer that their children learn only English in school. School personnel should honor the wishes of parents who refuse to allow their child to participate in a program in which instruction is offered in the native language (Ortiz, 1984).

Some students believe that they have to speak English in school because it is expected of them. They may not truly be as proficient in English as they would like us to believe. In fact, expressive skills may sometimes exceed comprehension. Ordinarily, it is safe to assume that a child who says something also understands the content and has mastered requisite structures (Metz, 1989). Bilingual students can appear more proficient than they truly are in their second language. Educational personnel should not make assumptions about a student's language proficiency without confirming it through testing. Academic and speech-language testing should always be done in the student's dominant language. Although a student may state a preference for the second language, no evaluation should be done without properly assessing language dominance.

Before considering evaluating a student for special education services, several other factors should be considered. Socioeconomic status should be considered. Some students come in with far fewer experiences and advantages than others. These students are at risk for lower language abilities. Regional backgrounds may differ. Some students come from very rural areas where education was not emphasized, while others may come from urban areas. Dialects may differ between regions and socioeconomic status levels within the same language. For example, a student from Mexico and a student from Puerto Rico both speak Spanish but have different vocabulary for some words. (For example, the Mexican word for swimming pool is *alberca*, while speakers from Puerto Rico will say *piscina*.) There are numerous dialects in Chinese that vary so much that speakers from different regions may not be able to communicate at all with each other. A speaker of Mandarin, for example, may not be able to communicate with a speaker of Cantonese. We must remember these dialectal differences when considering evaluations for speakers of languages other than English. If we are unable to speak the child's language ourselves, we must secure an interpreter who speaks the student's dialect. We must be sensitive to speakers of English who speak different dialects based on ethnic background, regional differences (northern versus southern United States, and so on). Table 12.1 will help identify dialectal differences (Shulman, 1988).

Data should be collected to document that the problem occurs in a variety of settings and is considered deviant by more than one educator who works with the student. It is also important to get parents' perceptions of the problems. If parents also consider the behavior to be deviant, the presence of a handicapping condition is more likely (Ortiz, 1992).

Finally, we must consider any prior referrals for special education services that may have been submitted on the student. If this is the first time he or she is being referred, we must consider all of the variables mentioned earlier: country of origin, rural versus urban background, amount of schooling in native country, mobility rate (locations, schools, and so on), length of time in the United States, exposure to English, academic history, language of instruction, socioeconomic status, regional dialects, and cultural influences. If this is not the first referral, it indicates that this is a problem that was identified earlier but has not been remediated. The classroom teacher must evaluate his or her own teaching style—if it has been successful with other limited-English-proficient speakers in the classroom, then this student may be in need of additional help. A referral at this time would be warranted.

To understand what is considered normal language development, the clinician must have an understanding of acquisition in the first and second languages. This will help in determining if a language disorder or difference exists.

Second Language Acquisition

Many educators believe that young children are the quickest, most efficient acquirers of a second language. The optimal age for beginning second language acquisition, however, is debatable. Increasing

Table 12.1. Articulation and Language: Dialectical* Differences as Compared to Standard American English (SAE).

Black Dialect	Spanish	Southeast Asian Languages:** Lao, Vietnamese, Khmer
b/v substitutions	Spanish phonemes that do *not* exist in English.	w/v substitutions
f/θ (th) substitutions	ñ (mañana)	v/w substitutions
d/ð (th) substitutions	rr (perro)	r/l substitutions
i/e substitutions		l/r substitutions
omission of many final consonants	Phonemes that exist in Spanish and English, but the articulation is slightly different:	*Vietnamese*
	t, d, c	-no /f/, but there is /ph/ in written language
	English phonemes that do not exist in Spanish:	-/u/ vowel is very gutteral, made in back of throat
	/ɛ/ th<u>e</u>m /l/ b<u>i</u>	The most difficult sounds to produce: /s, ʃ, th, t, e, i/ and consonant clusters.
	/θ/ <u>th</u>in /ʌ/ b<u>u</u>t	
	/ʒ/ plea<u>s</u>ure /oɛ/ b<u>a</u>t	
	/ʃ/ <u>sh</u>all /u/ b<u>oo</u>k	
	/z/ <u>z</u>oo /ju/ b<u>eau</u>ty	-no /s/ in the final position of words. The final /s/ is only used in written language but is not pronounced.
	/v/ <u>v</u>oice /at/ b<u>i</u>ke	-no /z/
	These phonemes do not exist in the *final* position of words in Spanish:	-q/w substitutions
	/p,t,k,b,g,f,z/	-tend to drop final consonants because they are not in the language.
	These phonemes do not exist in the *initial* position of words in Spanish:	
	sl, sm, sp, st, sk, sf, sn, spl, spr, spy, str ski, skr, sk, sty	

Intonation patterns: Differences exist in level of pitch, intensity, and rhythm of speech chain.

Rules:

If a word ends in a vowel or in a consonant n/s, the stress falls on the *next to last syllable.*

If a word ends in a consonant other than n/s, or a vowel, the stress falls on the last syllable.

There are some exceptions to these rules.

Vowels:

-Spanish vowels are short and pure.

-English vowels tend to be longer.

Common phonological differences:

s/z -all /z/'s are pronounced as /s/

b/v -in initial position: a strong b/v medial position: lighter contact

/d/ -when between 2 vowels, it becomes more dentalized and sounds like a /θ/

/d^F/ -sounds like a /θ/

/j/ or ll -in some dialects, sounds like /d$_3$/ or /ʒ/

ʃ/tʃ -fairly consistent substitution of ʃ/tʃ

/s^F/ -in many dialects, the final /s/ is often omitted. The /s/ in the medicla position is sometimes omitted as well.

*The term used in text is *dialectal.*

**The Southeast Asian languages have different alphabets from English.

Table 12.1. Articulation and Language: Dialectical Differences as Compared to Standard American English (SAE), Cont'd.

Black Dialect	Spanish	Southeast Asian Languages: Lao, Vietnamese, Khmer
Morphology *Noun plurals:* -Absence of /-s/ or /-es/ endings often occurs (e.g., She got five dollar.)	**Morphology** *Noun plurals:* -In regular plurals, /-s/ and/-es/ endings are used (e.g., gatos, arboles)	**Morphology** *Noun plurals:* -Do not exist in these languages. -When plurals are used, speaker will overcompensate (e.g., I drink many *waters*.)
Noun possessives: -Often omitted (e.g., the boy car) -Double possessives sometimes used, (e.g., It Jim's Brown's car.)	*Noun possessives:* -No apostrophe /s/ (e.g. Esta es la casa de mama.) Translation: This is mother's house. Literal translation: This is the house of mother.	*Noun possessives:* -No apostrophe /s/
Third person singular: -Omission of /-s/ or /-es/ marker	*Third person singular:* -Omission of /-s/ or /-es/ marker of third person singular	*Third person singular:* -No /-s/ used for third person singular form
Forms of to be: -Usually omitted	*Forms of to be:* -In Spanish, two forms are used: permanent (ser) and temporary (estar), e.g., (ser) Soy mujer. (I *am* a woman.) estar (Estoy enferma. (I am sick.)	*Forms of to be:* -The forms of to be are included and used the same as in S.A.E. -Sometimes omitted in Vietnamese
Past tense: -The /-ed/ ending is usually omitted	*Past tense:* Two forms are used: the preterite and the imperfect. 1. *Preterite:* indicates an action that was finalized 2. *Imperfect:* indicates an action that was continuous over a period of time	*Past tense:* No past tense. The verbs do not change (e.g., Yesterday, I walk to the store) -Verb tense can change by adding word *before* noun in Vietnamese (tense markers are optional)

Future tense:
-"Is" and "are" may be deleted when indicating the future, (e.g., I gonna do it. He gonna drive.)

Comparatives/Superlatives:
-The /-er/ and /-est/ endings often put at end of multi-syllabic words, instead of using adverbs "more" or "most," (e.g., She is beautifuller than her sister.)

Adverbs:
/-ly/ endings may be omitted

Future tense:
Used by adding endings on to the infinitive. (There are some exceptions.)

Comparatives/Superlatives:
-no /-er/ or /-est/ endings exist
-Most comparatives and superlatives are regular, e.g., más bonita (prettier), la ma bonita (prettiest), peor (worse), lo peor (worst)

Adverbs:
Uses the adverbial suffix /-mente/, e.g., rapido (quick), rapidamente (quickly)

Contractions:
-Few contractions exist, e.g., del: of the (de + el), al: at the or to the (a + el)

Agreement:
-Gender
-Quantity

Ordinals:
-In many dialects, ordinals are used in numbers 1 to 10.
-After 10, ordinals are generally not used, e.g., the third book: el tercer libro; the twelfth floor: el doce piso (the twelve floor).

Future tense:
No future tense. The verbs do not change (e.g., Tomorrow, I walk to the store.)

Comparatives/Superlatives:
-Use "more" and "most" (e.g., John, Bill more tall is. More tall John is than Bill.)

Adverbs:
-There are no adverbial suffixes

Agreement:
-Nouns don't vary according to quantity

Table 12.1. Articulation and Language: Dialectical Differences as Compared to Standard American English (SAE), Cont'd.

Black Dialect	Spanish	Southeast Asian Languages: Lao, Vietnamese, Khmer
Syntax *Negation:* -May substitute "ain't" for don't -Often use double negatives (e.g., He didn't do nothing.) *Interrogatives:* -Often ask questions through indirect question forms (e.g., I asked where she was going.)	**Syntax** *Negation:* 1. Use double negatives, e.g., *No hay nada aquí.* (There is nothing here.); *No quiero nadie.* (I don't want anyone.) 2. Negatives precede verb, e.g., *El hombre no es alto.* (The man isn't tall.) *Interrogatives:* -Most questions formed by inversion, changing the order of nouns and verbs -Some questions use words similar to S.A.E. "Wh" question forms, e.g., *Dónde están los libros?* (*Where are the books?*) *Adjectives:* -Adjectives succeed the noun, e.g., el árbol verde (the green tree) (the tree green) *Direct & indirect objects:* -Direct and indirect objects precede the noun, e.g., *El me dijo que quiso dinero.* (He told me that he wanted money.); *La maestra me lo dio.* (The teacher gave it to me.)	**Syntax** *Negation:* -Negatives precede the verb. *Interrogatives:* -Interrogatives are formed the same as in S.A.E. -Question words appear in middle or at end of question (e.g., Mr. Nam is *where?*) *Direct and indirect objects:* -Direct and indirect objects precede the verbs.

Semantics

Colloquial terms:

-Generally not to be interpreted literally

Idioms:

-Generally not to be interpreted literally

Nonverbal communication:

-An exaggerated use of arm movements, facial expressions, hands, etc., may be misinterpreted as signs of aggression. These movements are an acceptable way of expressing oneself within the black community.

Semantics

Colloquial terms:

-Cannot be translated literally

Idioms:

-Cannot be translated literally, e.g., Me cuesta un ojo de la cara. *Translation:* It cost me an arm and a leg. *Literal translation:* It cost me an eye from my face.

Nonverbal communication:

1. In conversation, in a group setting, interruptions are allowed without excusing oneself.
2. Low-voiced comments (jokes), while someone is speaking are permissible.
3. If a teacher allows "chattering" to go on in the classroom, the students see this as a loss of control and lose respect for the teacher.

Miscellaneous:

-Articles are not in Southeast Asian languages and are often omitted in English

-"Do" as an auxillary verb does not exist

-No genders in pronouns

Semantics

Colloquial terms:

-Cannot be translated literally

Idioms:

-Cannot be translated literally, e.g., Shui lo shih ch'u. (Chinese) *Translation:* The truth came out. *Literal translation:* The tide went out and the rock was revealed.

Nonverbal communication:

1. Children are accustomed to learning by rote and usually do not participate in discussions.
2. Cambodian children do not want their heads to be touched.
3. Frustration, anger, and disagreement are usually expressed in an indifference, silence, or a reluctant smile.

Table 12.1. Articulation and Language: Dialectical Differences as Compared to Standard American English (SAE), Cont'd.

Black Dialect	Spanish	Southeast Asian Languages: Lao, Vietnamese, Khmer
	4. When being reprimanded, children from Hispanic cultures look down as a sign of respect. 5. When a student's eyes are wide open, the face very serious staring at the teacher who has just said something, this indicates they need it repeated, because it was not understood.	4. Students are fearful of giving a wrong answer or do not want to show off, therefore, are hesitant to volunteer answers. 5. Many of these children are visually-oriented learners.

Note: Nonverbal communication could be misinterpreted and often results in miscommunication.

Sources: 1. Nguyen, K. H.: Tips to American educators in dealing with Vietnamese students. Language and Cultural Consultant. Vietnamese Program Regional Cross-cultural Training and Resource Center, Board of Education of the City of New York.

2. Curt, C.J.N. Non-verbal communication in Puerto Rico. TESOL Convention, Denver, CO, March 5, 1974.

3. Le Xuan Khoa, Dung Thiet Phan, Hong Hoeung Doeung, Kue Chaw, Phuc Gin Pham, Thai Bounthinh, J. V. Deusen, and B. Miller. Southeast Asian social and cultural customs: Similarities and differences, Part 2.

4. Semel, E. M., and Wiig, E. H. (1980). Dialectical variations. In *Clinical evaluation of language functions manual.* Charles E. Merrill Publishing Co., 1980.

5. Shulman, E. L.: Interview with Somphith Phichith on the Lao Language. Unpublished paper, November 1984.

6. Bridging the Asian language and cultural gap: Handbook for teachers. Division of Career and Continuing Education, Los Angeles Unified School District, 1971–74.

7. Linguistic and syntactic differences and likenesses between English and Vietnamese. Institute for Cultural Pluralism. San Diego State University, San Diego, CA.

8. Tri Buu, Logan, L., Gordon, F. N.: Han hanh duoc gap (Happy to meet you). Division of Curriculum, Pennsylvania Department of Education, 1976.

research evidence indicates that the age questions cannot be separated from another key variable in second language acquisition: cognitive development and language proficiency in the first language (Collier, 1989).

Research has shown that first language acquisition is not a quick and easy process; it takes a minimum of twelve years (Collier, 1989). From birth through age five, children acquire enormous amounts of first language phonology, vocabulary, grammar, semantics, and pragmatics. However, the process is not at all complete by the time children reach school age. From age six to twelve, children still have to develop in the first language the complex skills of reading and writing, in addition to continuing acquisition of more complex rules of morphology and syntax, elaboration of speech acts, expansion of vocabulary, semantic development, and even some aspects of phonological development (Collier, 1989).

Second language acquisition research has found that this process of the first language has a significant influence on the development of second language proficiency. One important finding is that the lack of continuing first language cognitive development during second language acquisition may lead to lowered proficiency levels in the second language and in reduced cognitive growth (Cummins, 1984).

Normal development indicates that children first learn to talk and then use language for learning. Requiring that a child use language to learn before learning to talk in a particular language can place significantly greater cognitive and psychological demands on that child. It is only reasonable, therefore, that learning content cannot be expected of young children (handicapped or not) until they have learned the language in which that content is couched (Metz, 1989).

At times, children learning a second language may tend to borrow parts of their intact first language and use them in their second language sentences. Sometimes this borrowing helps a child, while at other times it results in grammatical errors in the second language.

This is similar to code switching. One difference, however, is that when students borrow from the other language (L1), they will do so within a single word. For example, a student may say, *"Yo quiero ir a la norsa."* (I want to go to the nurse). The word for *nurse* in Spanish is *enfermera*, but in this case, an "English-like" word was substituted. Whether errors in the new language are made because students are simplifying the language, making incorrect assumptions about how it works, or transferring portions of their first language inappropriately, these error-producing processes and strategies are part of the normal second language acquisition process (Collier, 1989).

Second language learners should be encouraged to be risk takers and to experiment with the use of their second language. Educators should focus on what is being said, as opposed to how it is said. They should look at content as opposed to form (grammatical structures). This is an example of comprehensible input. According to Krashen (1982), language acquisition takes place best when the input provided is comprehensible, interesting, relevant, not grammatically sequenced, and is provided in sufficient quantity.

The most efficient and effective way to acquire a second language is to learn it as you did your first language: developmentally. Young children acquire their native language subconsciously and without knowledge of rules. This is how a second language should be taught—informally and naturally (Krashen, 1982).

There are several different theories as to how one actually acquires a second language. Many researchers support the theory that the processes involved in the acquisition of grammar in the second language are similar, in many respects, to those involved in first language acquisition (Dulay and others, 1982). In fact, the majority of grammatical errors produced by second language learners appear to be developmental errors similar to those observed among children learning a first language (see Hakuta, 1986). Others, however, have found that second language learners progress through stages in the acquisition of English language structures but that these stages are not identical to those observed among native English speakers (Cancino, Rosansky, and Schumann, 1978; Ravem, 1968).

Each language has its own developmental milestones. These milestones indicate at what age speech and language skills are developed. They apply to phonological as well as semantic, syntactical, and morphological development. There are also listening skills and pragmatic skills to consider. For the purposes of this chapter, we will focus on the purely linguistic areas.

In most languages, children generally begin to speak anywhere from approximately ten months of age to eighteen months. This includes single word utterances such as "Daddy, Mommy, milk," and so on. At approximately eighteen months to thirty months of age, children begin to speak in two to three word utterances. By age two, children generally have a speaking vocabulary of around 300 words. By age three, they are speaking in at least three- to four-word utterances and have vocabularies of up to 1,000 words. By age four, they speak in at least four- to five-word utterances and have a vocabulary of nearly 1,500 words (Brooks and Engmann, 1976).

Languages are learned developmentally with certain grammatical structures and concepts acquired at certain stages. The following lists demonstrate how English and Spanish are developed.

In English, grammar is acquired in the following order (Brown, 1973):

1. Present progressive (-ing)
2. Prepositions ("on" and "in")
3. Regular plurals (s, -es)
4. Irregular past tense (went, saw, read, etc.)
5. Possessives (Mommy's, boy's, etc.)
6. Uncontractible copula verb (go, see, etc.)
7. Articles (the, a, an, etc.)
8. Regular past tense (looked, baked, fixed, etc.)

9. Regular third person singular (sits, reads, etc.)

10. Irregular third person singular (went, goes, etc.)

11. Uncontractible auxiliary (was, can, etc.)

12. Contractible copula (am, are, etc.)

13. Contractible auxiliary (have, would, will, etc.)

In Spanish, for example, the order of grammatical acquisition is as follows (Werner and Kresheck, 1989):

1. Plural noun

2. Prepositions (in, on, of, with)

3. Possessive noun (Mother's, boy's)

4. Personal pronouns (he, she, they, etc.)

5. Locative adverb clause (Here you have to see, etc.)

6. Conditional clause (If it were sunny, we could play outside.)

7. Comparison of quantity (I want more candy.)

8. Negation (I don't want to.)

9. Copula ("to be" verbs)

10. Comparison of equalities (He was big like an elephant.)

11. Temporal adverbial clause (before, until, when)

These lists should give the educator some examples of how the acquisition of first and second languages may be very similar but still have some differences in chronology. It is very common for students to skip some stages of development and master more complicated steps before they have mastered the earlier stages. Although language acquisition follows some basic doctrines, the chronology of linguistic events is not the same for each child. Much of the development is additionally influenced by external factors, including environment and the amount of language stimulation.

Once the clinician has an understanding of factors that may

influence academic performance and the processes of language acquisition, the physical act of evaluating students may begin. The clinician must begin to carefully select assessment tools with minimal or no cultural and linguistic biases.

Assessment Tools

Evaluating students from culturally and linguistically diverse backgrounds is a difficult task for educators and clinicians. The two main problems facing professionals are their own limitations in working with these students, and the lack of adequate evaluation instruments. Educators and clinicians generally use some of the following scales to measure cognitive functioning: the Wechsler Intelligence Scale for Children-Third Edition, the Wechsler Preschool and Primary School Scales of Intelligence-Revised, the Differential Ability Scales, the Kaufman ABC, the Stanford-Binet (4th Edition), the Wechsler Adult and Adolescent Intelligence Scales-Third Edition, the Kaufman Adult and Adolescent Intelligence Test, the Test of Nonverbal Intelligence-Second Edition, the Peabody Picture Vocabulary Test-Revised, the Ravens Standard and Progressive Matrices, and the Leiter International Performance Scale. There are Spanish translations for some of the Wechsler scales. There are no translations in other languages such as Chinese, French, Ukranian, and none for Native Americans.

These instruments do provide the clinician with information about the students' cognitive abilities. They also help educators in grouping these students for instructional purposes. However, using these instruments with ethnic minority children poses numerous problems. Sattler (1982, 1988) suggests that these instruments are adequate as they are; if the clinician uses caution, it is possible to overcome present bias problems. However, other researchers such as Davis (1971), Mercer (1979), Reschly (1981), and Williams (1970, 1971) suggest the assessment instruments that clinicians use do not give ethnic minorities the same advantages as White students.

Educators and clinicians find that some ethnic minorities score lower on the verbal scale and higher on the performance scale. These students often score lower on general cognitive abilities than their White peers. It is also not unusual to see Hispanic and African American students score lower on the verbal scale than on the performance scale in spite of several years of special educational services. Among some of the limitations of the instruments are that they have been normed on the U.S.-born population. Others are Spanish translations of the instruments. This distinction is important. They are not instruments for Hispanic students. Some of the tests are old; for example, the Leiter International Performance scale has not been renormed since 1960. The Spanish translation of the Wechsler Adult Intelligence scale has not been renormed since 1974.

Clinicians face the difficulty of using these instruments with immigrant students from the West Indies, Latin America, Southeast Asia, and East and West Africa. Many students from these different cultures have no experiential basis to respond to some of the items on the tests. In addition, there are no equivalent translations of the questions in the students' languages.

The authors are suggesting that educators and clinicians who have no access to native speakers or native professionals as resources to evaluate ethnic minority students use *cultural mediators*. For the purpose of this chapter, a cultural mediator is defined as someone who has successfully assimilated into his or her culture and the mainstream American culture. These individuals are able to act as cultural and linguistic bridges between the student, school, community, and home environment. The authors also want to stress the importance that all assessments include the family and the community in which the student lives. The data obtained from this type of evaluation help to develop a holistic profile of the student since school is often viewed by some ethnic minorities as a hostile environment.

The authors recognize the constraints that educators and clinicians face when they try to evaluate students in their native language. There is a paucity of professional staff who are bilingual and bicultural to evaluate non-English-speaking students or students who speak English with a nonstandard dialect. Educators and clinicians are reluctantly forced to use interpreters and translators to conduct the evaluations. The primary role of the interpreter and translator in the school setting is to act as a conduit in all forms of communication between the school and the family. *Interpreters* are operationally defined as people who translate oral communication from one language to another. *Translators* are operationally defined as people who translate written communication from one language to another. The authors recommend that educators and clinicians secure the services of people who are competent in both areas.

Assessing culturally and linguistically diverse students is a challenge. The assessment process should include the student and his or her family. Language affects all areas needing to be assessed: cognitive, academic, perceptual, social-emotional, and so on. A full evaluation of any student must involve a complete assessment of linguistic abilities.

Language Assessment

Language and cognition cannot be separated, and language permeates all areas of academic growth. According to Heath (1986), from a sociolinguistic perspective, student's academic success depends less on the specific language they know than on the ways of using language they know.

In order to assess students whose first language is other than English, we must evaluate them with instruments with little or no cultural and linguistic biases. Ideally, the diagnostic instruments should be normed on the population we are testing. This should account for cultural and linguistic differences, including dialects, as well as socioeconomic status and other factors. These instruments should be administered by trained professional bilingual, bicultural clinicians. In the best of all possible worlds, all of these factors would be considered and implemented. However, the fact is that there is a shortage of personnel as well as a shortage of available diagnostic instruments.

There are several diagnostic instruments available for language assessment. The language proficiency and dominance tests are screening instruments that give an indication of basic language skills. However, the tests administered by the speech-language pathologist are more specific and analyze the deep structures of language.

General Issues

Clinicians should choose instruments based on the specific areas they would like to assess (phonology, syntax, semantics, morphology, processing, pragmatics, and so on). They should look for tests that are normed on the population to be tested. If none are available, they may look for translated versions of the commercially available tests for monolingual English speaking students. These tests should be interpreted with caution, however, as the norms were not derived from students of the same background as the student being tested. Most of these instruments were not normed on LEP students and thus should not be used to make special education eligibility decisions. Scores for these instruments should not be reported because doing so may communicate that the speech-language pathologist or diagnostician is presenting these scores as accurate representations of student abilities (Ortiz, 1992).

Screening Process

In order to quickly and effectively assess a student's language abilities, the speech-language pathologist utilizes screening instruments. The easiest way to screen a student would be to update the language proficiency and dominance scores. Then one major diagnostic instrument could be used to assess language functioning. If the student performs adequately, no further testing is necessary. However, if the student exhibits difficulty, further testing is warranted. At this time, a full diagnostic assessment must be completed.

Diagnostic Assessment

Once the screening process has been completed, the evaluator must make diagnostic decisions. If the student failed the language screening, a full diagnostic battery should be administered. Instruments should be chosen based on the student's age and the areas of language to be assessed: morphology, syntax, semantics, auditory processing, and pragmatics. The evaluation tools should be norm referenced. Informal measures may also be utilized, such as a language sample. A combination of norm-referenced and criterion-referenced diagnostic instruments in the dominant language can provide the examiner with an accurate assessment of the student's true linguistic abilities.

The use of local test norms in many cases should be considered. Local test norms may be developed for existing tests by administering these tests to a representative sample of students from the local student population. However, it must be noted that students within the local community differ from one another in the extent to which they have been exposed to the language being tested (Mattes and Omark, 1991).

Once an appropriate test has been selected, procedures are needed to ensure that the instrument is administered in a manner that will yield valid assessment data. The examiner should be thoroughly familiar with the procedures for administering and scoring the test prior to assessing the child (Mattes and Omark, 1991).

During the evaluation, the student may exhibit code switching behaviors. As stated earlier, code switching is a common practice of second language learners. Responses given in the other language should be scored as correct if semantically appropriate. However, if the response is invalid in both English and the native language, it should be scored as incorrect. It is especially important at this time to have a bilingual, bicultural clinician assessing the child to determine if the responses are indeed appropriate.

As difficult as it may be to assess a LEP child with minimal cultural and linguistic biases, it is often more of a challenge to correctly interpret the obtained data. Mattes and Omark (1991) outlined four major guidelines to use when determining if students are communicatively handicapped. First, test scores should not be used as the sole basis for identifying children with communication disorders. When children achieve low scores on tests, it is important to examine the reason for their poor performance: lack of motivation, test anxiety, inability to understand the directions, or whatever it may be.

Second, the contexts in which the child has had opportunities to use each language need to be considered in the analysis of responses produced on tests. The student may know the answer in his or her first language but has had no exposure to its label in the second language. Therefore, he or she knows the concept but can only express it in the first language.

Third, the extent to which test performance is influenced by cultural and environmental factors unique to the individual being assessed needs to be explored. Often, students from similar cultural backgrounds may have different value systems, beliefs, and so on that may yield different test results.

Finally, test results should always be used in conjunction with information obtained from natural communication samples. Some children tend to do poorly on structured tests but perform much better in more naturalistic contexts. It is also important to assess the student's functional use of language through observations, and so on.

As a general rule of thumb, if a student's language skills are strong in the first language but delayed in the second (English), then the student does not have a language disorder. He or she is merely in the process of acquiring a second language. However, if skills are delayed in both languages, it is most likely that a handicapping condition exists in the area of communication. At this time, speech-language therapy services should be considered. In both cases, these students would also benefit from English as a Second Language (ESL) services.

Once all of this information has been obtained, results must be shared with the interdisciplinary team members. Language and auditory processing skills are essential to consider when looking at the whole student. The school psychologist's findings often reflect what the speech-language pathologist has found. The team members and the student's teachers may then analyze the student's learning styles (multisensory, visual-tactile, and so on) and may then develop an appropriate educational plan.

Making Recommendations

The main purpose of conducting a comprehensive assessment is to provide the student, parents, and school staff with information that would help increase the student's access to services and opportunities for academic success. The interdisciplinary team approach process that the authors highly recommend is the best way for gathering and sharing information about the student and his or her family. In this forum, the teachers, social worker, speech pathologist, school psychologist, school nurse, building administrator, cultural mediator, and other personnel should develop a profile of the student, taking into account the student's cultural and linguistic backgrounds. This process allows clinicians and educators the opportunity to develop recommendations for services or instructional strategies that would benefit the student. It is important to stress that clinicians and educators need to guard against the tendency to make the student fit into existing programs rather than creating an instructional program to meet the needs of the student.

Clinicians and educators are often confronted with the challenge of trying to determine what is the student's primary disability. The problem is often exacerbated by the fact that some students have had very little previous school experience prior to entering the United States. In addition, school personnel are not able to obtain reliable medical or school records from countries where the student previously lived. These factors—in addition to the paucity of adequate assessment instruments—make the evaluation process a very difficult one. There is often great difficulty in making a differential diagnosis. One of the more problematic areas for clinicians and educators is to differentiate between speech impairment, learning disability, and mental retardation with this population. The lack of valid and reliable cognitive instruments to be used with these students makes it difficult to get a fair estimate of their cognitive ability.

There is also the difficulty of differentiating between language disorders and language differences. Because school personnel do not often have access to reliable medical or school records on some ethnic minority students, it is very problematic to resolve the question whether the student is language impaired or language deficient. The authors are suggesting that professionals exercise great caution when faced with these situations and err on the side of language difference when in doubt. Schools are required by law to provide ethnic minorities who speak languages other than English with services for the students to become proficient in English. This service—English as a Second Language (ESL)—is frequently provided to students in addition to speech-language services. The authors are suggesting that clinicians and educators consider whether these services are duplicative or if they can be provided in different ways.

The service delivery models are also important to consider. Generally, services are provided to individual students or groups of students who are removed from the classroom (pulled out) by their service provider for a specified period of time each day. The services may also be provided in a format whereby the service provider goes directly into the classroom and provides the services to the students who are mandated to receive them. Clinicians and educators should carefully consider the student's cultural and linguistic background and level of acculturation when deciding which model would best meet the student's needs.

Accessing Testing Materials

Locating diagnostic instruments for limited-English-proficient students has always been a challenge. The clinician generally has very few avenues to pursue. There are many criterion-referenced tests available to assess English language skills but very few norm-referenced materials available in languages other than English.

It is strongly suggested that the clinicians contact their State Education Department (SED). The SED will most likely be able to provide a list of diagnostic instruments in the areas of cognition, achievement, processing, language, and so on. References may be limited for language groups other than English. Spanish instruments will be easier to access than other language groups, although tests are still limited.

Mattes and Omark (1991) provide an extensive list of references for limited-English-proficient students. Their appendix provides information on several language tests for speakers of Spanish, Chinese, Japanese, Vietnamese, Tagalog, Arabic, Greek, Italian, Korean, and a few other Asian languages. It should be noted, however, that some of these tests are literal translations of English tests that have not been validated for use in other languages (Mattes and Omark, 1991).

The tests available are mostly translated or often normed on specific populations. For example, the clinician should explain that it was necessary to use a test with norms from Mexico while testing a Puerto Rican student. Therefore, the test results should be interpreted with caution. Regional and dialectal differences should be taken into account when testing, scoring, and interpreting the results.

When the norms on certain tests are not appropriate for the population to be tested, the clinicians should consider developing local norms. Although a lengthy and cumbersome process, local norms can provide more accurate results.

The following case studies help illustrate several of the issues discussed in this chapter. They give examples of preassessment considerations, the diagnostic process (nonbiased evaluations, test interpretation, synthesis of data from interdisciplinary team members), and recommendations for educational placement.

Case Study 1

Felix was born in Santo Domingo in the Dominican Republic. He came to Brooklyn, New York, at age eight. Two years later, Felix entered school in Rochester, New York, in the fourth grade, at age ten. Felix was struggling academically after only a few months in school. He was referred to the Committee on Special Education (CSE) by his classroom teacher because of difficulty in all academic areas, reading and oral comprehension, and some behavior problems. Felix received daily English for Speakers of Other Language (ESOL) services. When he first entered, Felix was a nonspeaker of English and a proficient speaker of Spanish. While in the Dominican Republic, Felix missed a great deal of school.

The bilingual psychologist evaluated Felix and found him to be functioning in the educable mentally retarded (EMR) range of cognitive ability. His auditory and visual perceptual skills also fell within the mentally retarded range. Academically, Felix was functioning, in Spanish, at the first-grade level in reading and written language and at the end of second-grade level in math. The scores on the adaptive behavior scale and social-emotional profiles fell within the EMR range as well.

The bilingual speech-language pathologist evaluated Felix's communication abilities. Felix exhibited normal hearing, articulation, voice, and fluency skills. When compared to his mental age, Felix exhibited moderate receptive/expressive language delays and severe auditory processing skills.

The medical history revealed that at eight days old, Felix had seizures and meningitis. Forceps were used at birth. Overall, Felix is a healthy child. Felix wears glasses but usually leaves them at home.

A social history revealed that Felix had no preschool experience. He attended school in Santo Domingo (although sporadically) and in Brooklyn.

The CSE reviewed all of the information and made a recommendation. They recommended that Felix was to remain nonhandicapped due to sporadic school attendance, recent entry into the United States, and reluctance of school personnel and his father to classify Felix as handicapped. However, after the CSE meeting, Felix was put back in the third grade, where his academic skills were better addressed.

Two years later, Felix was still struggling in school. He was still at least two years behind academically. His cognitive abilities increased by approximately nine points. It was recommended that Felix be classified as Learning Disabled (LD) in a bilingual classroom, with speech and language services ninety minutes a week. Felix received these services in a middle school.

Three years after being in a bilingual LD classroom, Felix was tested for his state-mandated triennial reevaluation. He was then in secondary school. Felix scored in the low average to borderline range of cognitive abilities. He was functioning at the fifth-grade level in reading and math and at the mid second-grade level in written language. Felix's language skills were within normal limits, with mild-to-moderate auditory processing delays. Felix also reached a higher level of English proficiency than a few years before. It was recommended that Felix continue his classification as LD but that he enter an English monolingual classroom. He was dismissed from speech-language services and was to continue with ESOL services.

Case Study 2

Rhonda is an eleven-year, eight-month-old African American student who is currently in a regular fifth-grade classroom at Public School

#60 in Rochester, New York. She was referred by her classroom teacher because of poor academic progress and behavioral problems. Specifically, it was noted that she has difficulties decoding and exhibits aggressive behaviors toward peers. The teacher estimated her academic skills to be at the middle of the third-grade level.

School history: Rhonda entered a preschool program at age four years and was classified as speech impaired and received speech therapy for three years. She has a history of difficulties in reading, spelling, and written language problems beginning in first grade. She attended preschool at P.S. #5 and transferred to P.S. #43 kindergarten. She repeated kindergarten at P.S. #34 and then transferred to P.S. #56 in the first grade. She transferred to P.S. #43 in the second grade. She finished the second grade at P.S. #43 but then transferred to P.S. #9 in the third grade. She transferred in the middle of the school year to P.S. #44, where she completed the third grade. She reentered P.S. #9 and completed the fourth grade but transferred back to P.S. #43 in the fifth grade. Rhonda's family moved about eight times between her preschool and fifth-grade years. It is also significant to note that Rhonda has attended school from preschool to fourth grade for only 80 percent of the school year.

Previous Assessment: Rhonda's cognitive ability as measured by the Wechsler Preschool and Primary Scale of Intelligence-Revised (WPPSI-R) indicated that she has borderline ability. She demonstrated mild-to-moderate delays in expressive and receptive language.

Current Assessment: A psychosocial evaluation was done by the social worker who visited the home. Rhonda's father, who is a member of the household, was hospitalized for mental illness and has ceased to take his medication. Rhonda's mother is employed and supports the family. There is evidence that one of Rhonda's older siblings is abusing drugs. Rhonda's mother moves frequently to allow the children to be in a better neighborhood. The family is close-knit and relies on its own resources. There are two other school-age children in the family. Rhonda is the youngest and only female. The family moved to Rochester from the Deep South and still speaks with a heavy, accented southern dialect. The health assessment indicated that Rhonda was a healthy student who does not like to wear her corrective lenses.

The psychological evaluation, using the Wechsler Intelligence Scale-Third Edition (WISC-III) indicated that Rhonda had low average cognitive ability. Her visual and auditory perceptual skills showed a two-year delay as compared to her chronological age of eleven years, eight months. Academically, her achievement ranges from 3.7 in written language (standard score 88) to 5.8 in math problem solving (standard score 104).

The speech and language assessment indicated mild-to-moderate delays in short-term memory, vocabulary, and expressive language.

The multidisciplinary team met. The classroom teacher felt strongly that Rhonda was an emotionally disturbed student. The Pupil Personnel Services Team reviewed Rhonda's mobility and attendance problems, lack of reasonable opportunities to form healthy peer group relationships, lack of consistent school curriculum, and cultural and ethnic background and recommended that Rhonda remain in a regular program.

Summary

Clinicians and educators have been charged with the responsibility of evaluating and educating students from culturally and linguistically diverse backgrounds. Each student is afforded the right to fair and unbiased testing by qualified bilingual-bicultural evaluators. This will eliminate the problem of inappropriate classification of students as handicapped.

Language dominance and proficiency must be determined in order to test students in their strongest language. There are numerous preassessment factors (including educational, medical, and family history) to consider before determining if a student is at risk for a handicapping condition. Clinicians must have an understanding of first and second language acquisition processes and reasonable timelines for making academic growth. Assessment tools need to be selected carefully for different students. Tools with relevant normative data and with minimal cultural and linguistic biases are the best instruments to use. Unfortunately, there is a significant lack of appropriate diagnostic instruments available for students who speak languages other than English or who speak dialects other than mainstream English. Students should be evaluated in all areas: cognitive, academic, processing, social-emotional, and language, with little or no cultural biases involved. Caution must be taken when utilizing translators or interpreters.

Once all areas have been appropriately assessed, the multidisciplinary team can make recommendations for placement. Recommendations need to be based on language proficiency and cognitive and academic needs. Learning styles and educational and social history should also be heavily weighed into the decision-making process. Finally, it is very difficult to access test materials for students who come from culturally and linguistically diverse backgrounds. The development of local norms is encouraged in order to best meet a specific population's needs. Although the demands have increased for working with a wide variety of students, educators and clinicians are now more prepared to face the challenges ahead.

References

Baratz, S. S., & Baratz, J. C. (1969). Negro ghetto children and urban education: A cultural solution. *Social Education 33*, 400–404.

Berry, J. W. (1980). Acculturation as varieties of adaptation. In A. M. Padilla (Ed.), *Acculturation: Theory, models and some new findings* (pp. 9–25). Boulder, CO: Westview.

Berry, J. W., Trimble, J., & Olmedo, E. L. (1986). Assessment of acculturation. In W. J. Lonner & J. W. Berry (Eds.), *Field methods in cross-cultural research* (pp. 291–324). Newbury Park, CA: Sage.

Brooks, M., & Engmann, D. (1976). *Speech and language milestones*. Lawrence, KS: H & H Enterprises.

Brown, L., Sherbenou, R. J., & Johnsen, S. K. (1990). *The Test of Nonverbal Intelligence* (2nd ed.) Austin, TX: Pro-Ed.

Brown, R. (1973). *A first language: The early stages*. Cambridge, MA: Harvard University Press.

Cancino, H., Rosansky, E. J., & Schumann, J. (1978). The acquisition of English negatives and interrogatives by native Spanish speakers. In E. M. Hatch (Ed.), *Second language acquisition*. Rowley, MS: Newbury House.

Cole, M. (1971). *The cultural context of thinking and learning*. New York: Basic Books.

Collier, V. P. (1989). How long? A synthesis of research on academic achievement in a second language. *TESOL Quarterly, 3*(3), 509–511.

Cummins, J. (1984). *Bilingualism and special education: issues in assessment and pedagogy*. San Diego, CA: College-Hill.

Davis, W. M., Jr. (1971, September). Are there solutions to the problems of testing black Americans? In M. M. Meier (Chair), *Some answers to ethnic concerns about psychological testing in the schools*. Symposium conducted at the meeting of the American Psychological Association, Washington, D.C.

DeAvila, E. A., & Duncan, S. E. (1977). *Language assessment scales*. Corte Madera, CA: Linguametrics Group.

Dew, N. (1984). *Instructional Strategies for Special Needs ESL Students*. Paper presented at ESL teachers workshop, National Origin Desegregation Assistance Center, Teachers College, Columbia University, New York.

Dulay, H., Burt, M., & Krashen, S. (1982). *Language two*. New York: Oxford University Press.

Dunn, L. M., & Dunn, L. M. (1981). *Peabody Picture Vocabulary Test (Revised)*. Circle Oaks, MN: American Guidance Service.

Education of All Handicapped Children Act, 20 U.S.C. § 1401–1485 (1975).

Hakuta, J. (1986). *Mirror of language*. New York: Basic Books.

Heath, S. B. (1986). Sociocultural contexts of language development. In California State Department of Education, *Beyond language: Social and cultural factors in schooling language minority students* (pp. 143–186). Los Angeles: Evaluation, Dissemination, and Assessment Center, California State University.

Hilliard, A. (1976). *Alternatives to IQ testing. An approach to the identification of gifted minority children*. Final report to the California State Department of Education.

Hilliard, A. (1987). *Testing African-American students*. San Francisco: Richardson.

Holland, W. R. (1960). Language barrier as educational problem of Spanish-speaking children. *Exceptional Children, 27*, 42–50.

Jose P. v. Ambach, 669 F.2d 865 (2nd Cir. 1982).

Kaufman, A. S., & Kaufman, N. L. (1992). *Kaufman Adolescent and Adult Intelligence Test*. Circle Pines, MN: American Guidance Service.

Krashen, S. (1982). *Innovative approaches to language teaching*. Rowley, MA: Newbury House.

Larry P. v. Riles, 495 F supp. 926 (N. D. California 1979), *aff'd.*, 793 F.2d 969 (9th Cir. 1984).

Leiter, R. G. (1960). *Leiter International Performance Scale*. Los Angeles: Western Psychological Services.

Mattes, L., & Omark, D. (1991). *Speech and language assessment for the bilingual handicapped*. Oceanside, CA: Academic Communication Associates.

Mercer, J. R. (1977). *Identifying the gifted Chicano child: Chicano psychology* (pp. 153–173). New York: Academic Press.

Mercer, J. R. (1979). *Technical manual: System of multicultural pluralistic assessment (SOMPA)*. New York: Psychological Corporation.

Mercer, J. R., & Lewis, J. F. (1977). *System of multicultural pluralistic assessment (SOMPA)*. New York: The Psychological Corporation.

Metz, I. B. (1989). *English language development of linguistically diverse preschoolers*. Buffalo, NY: Crossroads.

Oakland, T. (Ed.). (1977). *Psychological and educational assessment of minority children*. New York: Brunner/Mazel.

Office of the Federal Register, National Archives and Records Administration. *34 code of federal regulations* (CFR 300.532). Washington, DC: U.S. Government Printing Office.

Olmedo, E. L. (1979). Acculturation: A psychometric perspective. *American Psychologist, 34*, pp. 1061–1070.

Olmedo, E. L. (1981). Testing linguistic minorities. *American Psychologist, 36*(10), 1078–1085.

Olmedo, E. L., Martinez, J. L., & Martinez, S. R. (1978). Measure of acculturation in Chicano adolescents. *Psychological Reports 42*, 159–170.

Ortiz, A. A. (1984). Choosing the language of instruction for exceptional bilingual children. *Teaching Exceptional Children, 16*(3) 208–212.

Ortiz, A. A. (1992). Considerations in the assessment of language minority students with communication disorders. *Best practices in school speech-language pathology*, 107–113.

Payan, R. (1984). Language assessment for bilingual exceptional children. In

L. M. Baca & H. T. Cervantes (Eds.), *The bilingual special education interfaces* (pp. 125–137). St. Louis, MO: Mosby.

Ravem, R. (1968). Language acquisition in a second language environment. *International Review of Applied Linguistics, 6,* 175–185.

Reschly, D. J. (1981). Psychological testing in educational classification and placement. *American Psychologist, 36,* 1094–1102.

Sattler, J. M. (1982). *Assessment of children's intelligence and special abilities* (2nd ed.). Needham Heights, MA: Allyn & Bacon.

Sattler, J. M. (1988). *Assessment of children* (3rd ed.). San Diego, CA: Author.

Shulman, E. L. (1988). Speech and language of the limited English proficient (LEP) child. *Seminars in Speech and Language, 9*(4), 383–397.

Thomas, A., & Grimes, J. (1990). *Best practice in school psychology—II.* Washington, DC: National Association of School Psychologists.

U.S. Bureau of the Census. (1986). *Projections of the Hispanic population: 1983–2080.* (Current Population Reports, Series P-25, No. 995). Washington, DC: U.S. Government Printing Office.

Werner, E., & Kresheck, D. (1989). *Structured Photographic Expressive Language Test-Preschool.* Sandwich, IL: Janelle.

Williams, R. L. (1970). Danger: Testing and dehumanizing black children. *Clinical Child Psychology Newsletter, 9*(1), 5–6(a).

Williams, R. L. (1971). Abuses and misuses in testing black children. *Counseling Psychologist, 2*(3), 62–73.

13

. . . .

Assessing Diverse Family Systems

Jane Close Conoley and Lorrie E. Bryant

In contrast to individual assessment, family assessment approaches are not as well developed. As other chapters in this book attest, assessing individuals who are members of minority or recent immigrant groups creates special and critical challenges for psychologists committed to equitable practice (Dana, 1993). The goal of accomplishing valid family assessments is daunting in its own right, and culturally sensitive procedures of family evaluation are, perhaps, even more difficult to conceptualize and administer.

The objectives associated with this chapter include presenting our view of cultural sensitivity; suggesting constructs related to family function and dysfunction and how these constructs vary across U.S. minority and recent immigrant groups; reviewing the most frequently used paper-and-pencil assessment devices relative to ethnic diversity concerns; and providing some suggestions to promote valid assessment procedures.

Family practitioners rely on valid measurement and interpretations to plan for effective treatments. Families are not diagnosed in the ways in which individuals are (for example, personality traits or intelligence), but they are frequent consumers of mental health services. Clients from ethnic minority families present interesting assessment concerns for the practitioner.

Cultural Sensitivity

Culture is an intricate web of meanings through which people, individually and as a group, shape their lives. Culture does not have, however, absolute predictive power concerning the behavior of members of a group. Further, every culture continues to evolve. It is a set of tendencies of possibilities from which to choose.

Although best practice demands that cultural paradigms be recognized and understood, these paradigms must be viewed as broadly composed of cultural tendencies that individual families may accept, deny, modify, or exhibit situationally. Forcing a family or an individual to fit within any preconceived cultural model is not cultural sensitivity—it is stereotyping (Anderson and Fenichel, 1989; Steele, 1990).

It seems clear that culturally sensitive assessments of families would be characterized by an acceptance that certain differences and similarities exist in families across cultural groups. These differences are neither good or bad; better or worse; less or more intelligent. The awareness of this possibility and a flexible repertoire of responses are the important components of multicultural assessments of families.

What Is Known About Healthy Families?

A growing list of competencies or attributes of families that predict or correlate with positive adjustment for the family has appeared. Some of the important constructs include: good communication skills, excellent problem solving, provision of emotional support, authoritative child socialization strategies, provision of child supervision, satisfaction with work, positive orientation toward education, good mental health (or at least the absence of serious psychopathology), no substance abuse, physical affection toward children, successful infant attachment, and good marital or relationship quality (Seifer, Sameroff, Baldwin, and Baldwin, 1992). Successful families are good at managing the stresses within their nuclear or extended group and dealing with the press of other environmental demands (Barocas and others, 1991).

In contrast, poverty, unemployment, residence in violent neighborhoods, a history of antisocial behavior in the family, and parental failures in school are all risk factors for family and child adjustment (Reid, 1993).

Some of the family dynamics or situations just mentioned may present fairly straightforward assessment targets (for example, where people live, whether there are two responsible adults or an adaptive network of adults to care for children, whether the adults are employed). Others, however, may be difficult to measure in any family and hard to interpret across cultural groups (for example, marital quality, socialization strategies, or problem solving) (Beavers and Hampson, 1990; Oster and Caro, 1990).

Later in this chapter, constructs and methods useful with families from the majority culture are reviewed. The application of identical procedures and interpretative norms with minority families may, however, result in unreliable and invalid measurement. Results of analyses of minority members' scores on individual personality measures (Campos, 1989; Dahlstrom, 1986; Greene, 1987; Padilla and Ruiz, 1975; Velasquez, 1992) point out the dangers of using majority culture expectations to interpret minority performance on tests. Such threats to validity are likely to exist at the family level of assessment as well, due to differences among family cultural patterns.

Minority Groups in the United States

Because our analysis of families has included only a few of the so-called minority groups, this chapter outlines information about several ethnocultural groups. By the middle of the twenty-first century, today's minorities will make up nearly one-half of all Americans (O'Hare, 1992). These demographic changes have important implications for family therapists, who are likely to encounter increases in their minority client populations.

It is common in both everyday language and in professional literature to describe groups of people using "ethnic glosses" (Trimble, 1990–91). That is, most writers (ourselves included) use the terms

Native Americans, African Americans, Hispanic Americans, and Asian Americans as if each of these groups contained very similar people (few within-group differences) and were quite different from each other (many between-group differences). Neither of these assumptions is made safely. Within each racial category there are several ethnic groups. Ethnicity refers to cultural attributes of a group while race refers to the physical or biological characteristics of a group.

Native Americans

The federal government recognizes 517 separate entities of Native American peoples. The states recognize 36 tribes whose members still speak a total of about 149 different languages with many, many related dialects (LaFromboise, 1988; LaFromboise and Low, 1989; Manson and Trimble, 1982). There are about two million Native Americans in the United States. There are many differences among these peoples, whose homes range from the arctic regions of Alaska to the deserts of Southwest and the shores of New England.

African Americans

African Americans are the slowest-growing minority group, yet the group is growing three times faster than the European American population. They represent the largest, and in some ways, the most homogenous minority group (O'Hare, 1992). African Americans account for about 12 percent of the U.S. population. African Americans tend to share a group identity based on a common historical experience of racism and oppression.

Concepts of cultural orientation and Nigrescence have been used to differentiate individuals within this group (Cross, 1971, 1978; Thomas, 1971; Parham, 1989; Whatley and Dana, 1989). Four cultural orientations have been described: Afrocentrist, Anglocentrist, bicultural, and marginal. The distinctions refer to an individual's commitment to and pride in traditional African values, or identification with Anglo-American priorities, or attempt to be part of both cultures, or finally, to lack a clear commitment to either culture and attempt to survive through cooperation, toughness, suppression of feelings, and a belief in luck and magic (Pinderhughes, 1982).

Nigrescence is a continuum of racial identity that describes an individual's movement from dependence with suppressed rage on White society (that is, Negromarchy) through steps leading to transcendence that identifies the individual with all of humankind.

Hispanic Americans

By the year 2020, it is estimated that the Hispanic population will grow from 9 percent of the U.S. total to 15 percent. There are four major groups of Hispanics (Mexican Americans, Puerto Ricans, Cubans, and Other). The Other group includes sixteen groups of Hispanic Americans that have been identified as ethnic minorities in the United States, including groups from Central and South America.

The other three groups have different histories of migration to the United States and some significant demographic variations among them. Many Mexican Americans came to the United States from rural, poverty-stricken backgrounds. They arrived with little formal education. In contrast, some groups of Cubans who came were highly educated and relatively affluent. Many of that group thought their stay in the United States would be brief. They awaited the overthrow of Fidel Castro in fairly segregated enclaves in southern Florida. This generalization does not apply to recent waves of poor, mentally ill, and jail inmate Cubans who were probably sent by the Castro government to the United States. In contrast, Puerto Ricans (already American citizens) tended to come to New York to find better-paying jobs but returned often to their island homes. In fact, the expression *Nuyoricans* has grown up to describe this group.

Asian Americans

Asian Americans are the fastest growing and most culturally diverse minority group (O'Hare, 1992). Asian Americans comprise about thirty-two groups. They represent 4 percent of the U.S. population and are concentrated in California, New Jersey, Texas, Rhode Island, and Oregon. The primary groups are Chinese, Filipinos, Koreans, Japanese, Asian Indians, and other Southeast Asian groups such as the Vietnamese, Laotians, Cambodians, Hmong, and ethnic Chinese. This Southeast Asian group contains at least an additional eleven cultural groups. Southeast Asians have a birth rate comparable to Hispanic Americans and are, therefore, a fast-growing group in comparison to other Asian groups, whose birth rate is lower than the European American birth rate (Leung and Sakata, 1988).

The different groups have distinct immigration and acculturation experiences. Kitano and Daniels (1988) have done a comprehensive review of these processes. Each group has faced violent racism upon entry to the United States, which continues today for many of the recent immigrants (Carlson and Rosser-Hogan, 1993; Starr and Roberts, 1982).

Most of the research on Asian Americans is based on Japanese and Chinese samples (Marsella, 1993; Morishima, Sue, Teng, Zane, and Cram, 1979; Nakanishi, 1988). The more recently immigrated Chinese and other groups have often arrived in the United States with major health problems, and many of them have been victims of terroristic political persecution or overwhelming economic deprivation.

Summary

It should be clear from the previous brief paragraphs that generalizations about our usual ethnic glosses are dangerous. However, in order to provide some guidance to those wishing to improve their cultural competencies with families, it is still useful to examine cultural patterns associated with each of these groups. And, further, to comment on how such patterns may change as families interact with the American host culture. These patterns and changes may be described in numerous ways. For the purposes of this chapter, issues related to family interactions and definition and preferred service providers and systems will be highlighted.

Who Is in the Family

The definition of family membership may differ across ethnic groups. Individuals from all the groups mentioned above may describe complicated relationships of obedience, cooperation, respect, and obligation to people beyond a nuclear family. This extended family may include individuals who are not blood relatives, especially for Native and African Americans. Assumptions, therefore, about roles in family life and the intensity of various relationships beyond the nuclear family require careful attention (McAdoo, 1979; Myers, 1982; Wilson, 1993).

Roles in the Family

Asian and Hispanic Americans may hold very rigid views about appropriate age and gender roles within families. In particular, Asian American families may be strictly organized with male leadership and unquestioning obedience to parents and grandparents. Hispanic American families may exhibit traditional values of *machismo* (role of the father to lead, protect, and provide for the family) and *marianismo* or *hembrismo* (role of the wife and mother to be virtuous, nurture the children, and be submissive to her husband's wishes).

In Hispanic American families in which the woman works outside the home, some greater equality in decision making and family income expenditures may be evident. As least in some Hispanic subgroups, however, women remain completely responsible for domestic duties (Zavella, 1987).

Native American families are more difficult to characterize. Individuals may feel responsibility to many people in their community and a traditional respect for elders. In some tribes, women hold visible and influential roles in both tribal governance and family decision making.

African American families, although overtly headed by males, may be best understood by the mother's and other female relatives' leadership. Female children are socialized to be strong and responsible for family welfare (Boyd-Franklin, 1989; Staples, 1988).

Motherhood among African American women is not necessarily biological. The notion of motherhood is embedded in the community and in addition to kin may include "pseudokin" (Collins, 1991). The model of the African mother is not that she, herself, is powerful, but that she empowers others to accomplish their goals.

Franklin (1993) presents a case study and analysis of the struggles endured by a middle-class African American family man that illustrates the pervasive effects of racism on families. Hersch (1993) examines the experience of two gifted African American children, suggesting the same finding that the experience of unremitting racism affects families and individuals in profound ways—often misunderstood by European American psychologists.

Service Provision

Service providers who are unaware of the cultural expectations of each group are likely to have high drop-out rates from therapy and low utilization from minority groups (LaFromboise, 1988). Some illustrations regarding these expectations may be helpful to the reader.

Asian American families may expect deference and careful courtesy from every person involved in a mental health clinic or office. Providers are often expected to meet and greet the family in the waiting room and direct conversation to the oldest member of the family. These families may evaluate providers upon their obvious expertise in terms of credentials, publications, and other accomplishments. Older, male providers will have more immediate credibility than younger females.

Native American, Hispanic, and African American families tend to value egalitarianism from the service provider. Families may expect the provider to chat with them and be very friendly and cordial. In fact, they may build rapport more readily if the provider has several connections with them (for example, is a friend of a friend, a relative, or known in another capacity). The usual trappings and distance of professionalism may impede the development of a therapeutic relationship (Bailey, 1987; Farris, 1978; Locust, 1986; Samora, 1979). Native American families expect providers to be respectful, tolerant, accepting of life and other people, family-oriented, generous, cooperative, flexible, and have a sense of humor (Kemnitzer, 1973). They may respect advisers for the kind of people they are rather than for their specific skills, task orientation, or material possessions (Lewis and Gingerich, 1980).

The Spanish word *simpatia* captures the interactional script expected by some Hispanic Americans and likely useful with Native Americans and African Americans as well. This refers to the providers' tendency to be positive and to avoid negative, competitive, and assertive interactions. Other informative Spanish descriptors of interactional style are *respeto, personalismo, platicando,* and *ambiente* (Triandis, Marin, Lisansky, and Betancourt, 1984).

"*Respeto,* or respect, is accorded by younger to older persons, by women to men, and to persons in authority or higher socioeconomic positions. *Personalismo* refers to a preference for personal, informal, individualized attention in relationships, including those at work and in politics. *Platicando,* or chatting, is used to create a warm and accepting atmosphere that is called '*ambiente*' and is characteristic of personalismo" (Dana, 1993, p. 70).

Therapeutic Issues

Members of each minority group may behave in ways that do not match the expectations of European American providers. Further, these clients' basic understandings of health and illness may be unfamiliar to European American providers.

Behavior

African American men and women and Hispanic American men may speak easily on certain topics to service providers from any cultural background but may be quite reluctant to discuss personal issues at any meaningful depth. Native Americans, Hispanic American women, and most Asian Americans tend to be very quiet. Their silence might be mistaken for resistance. In fact, they have learned that silence in the face of an authority figure is courteous behavior. Among many Native American groups, lots of talking is generally considered impolite behavior. Asian Americans may expect the provider to learn what is wrong in rather indirect ways and provide directives for change. Rehashing family attempts to solve problems may be seen as disrespectful and useless.

Although African American women are likely to speak for the family no matter who is present, women from the other families tend to defer to the adult men. Even if the women disagree with the men or have other therapeutic agendas, it is possible these will not be mentioned unless the women are seen alone.

Service providers might expect very long rapport-building periods with African and Native Americans. A relationship called *confianza en confianza* (trusting mutual support) must be established for genuine therapeutic alliances to be forged. African and Native Americans have every reason not to trust European American providers. The provider may have to prove him or herself worthy over time. This worthiness will be judged not by the usual trappings of expertise (that is, how many diplomas on a wall) but by the attitudes, trustworthiness, and availability of the provider (Gibbs, 1988).

Even well-intentioned providers can fail this test because they have been taught to interpret certain behaviors in ways that are probably not universally correct. For example, some therapists interpret a client's tardiness or unwillingness to engage in future planning as resistance to therapy. Minority families, however, may not view appointment times as very important. In fact, they may find the lock-step office procedures of many mental health service centers to be offensive, or at least unhelpful. They may be late for appointments and seem unmoved by the fact they have fifty minutes to discuss their difficulties. Such discussion may take significantly longer or be quite brief. The notion that personal relationships are ordered by time periods may seem very foreign to some clients. They may also not connect to future orientations and long-term planning as being relevant to their current difficulties.

African American families may contain some very angry members. The assertive expression of this anger is frightening to some European American therapists. Its suppression, however, is likely to make genuine communication unlikely (Franklin, 1993). A therapist may have to show the street-smart skill of meeting the unwavering, angry gaze of an African American with calmness, compassion, and perseverance.

Understanding of Difficulties

Most dominant culture members understand physical illness as due to biological difficulties. Their understanding of mental illness is likely to be less clear, but often they believe that with personal effort their psychological problems can be alleviated.

Hispanic and Native Americans may have a more spiritually based understanding of illness. They may believe illness represents a life that is out of balance because of bad behavior or that evil forces are acting upon the sick or disturbed patient. They may feel most comfortable turning to traditional healers within their own communities to assist them in dealing with illness (Delgado, 1988). Traditional healers often have other jobs (in addition to healing) but still occupy influential positions in many ethnic minority cultures.

Asian American families rarely come to psychologists for emotional or personality problems. Their most frequent use of mental health services concerns vocational and educational counseling (Tracey, Leong, and Glidden, 1986). It is likely they would care for emotionally disturbed family members without professional intervention until such home care became completely impossible (K. M. Lin, Inui, Kleinman, and Womack, 1982). Mental illness may still carry a significant stigma in Asian American families, representing a failure of the parents to raise children with the appropriate behaviors.

Some Asian Americans may somatize their psychological difficulties. Physical symptoms due to emotional distress appear commonly in Asian American communities (T. Y. Lin, 1982, 1983). Neurasthenic reactions may be observed in reaction to a variety of social and personal stresses (T. Y. Lin, 1990).

All of the U.S. minorities may have difficulty believing that discussion of difficulties has any value. If their orientations are somewhat external (that is, the problem is out there and must be fixed by an expert) then European American talk therapies appear irrelevant at best. The therapeutic demands for self-disclosure may seem very dangerous, given the way most minority groups have been victimized by the dominant culture (Boyd-Franklin, 1993). Readers may find work by Sue and Sue helpful in conceptualizing the challenges associated with delivering services to various ethnic groups (D. W. Sue, Arredondo, and McDavis, 1992; S. Sue, 1988, 1992).

Key Questions

A review of existing literature and analysis of our clinical experiences suggest that dominant culture service providers should ask questions and pay special attention to family roles, interpretations concerning personality factors, belief systems, interactional or interpersonal styles, and level of acculturation characteristic of client families. Each of these constructs may vary in ways that make diagnostic impressions based on European American norms invalid and typical intervention suggestions inappropriate.

Questions About Family Roles

What are the differential expectations toward sons and daughters? Are the son's accomplishments or his obedience seen as vitally important to the family's honor and long-term viability? Is the daughter viewed as only a visitor who will someday contribute to her husband's family?

Does the daughter-in-law owe special allegiance and obedience to her mother-in-law? Does the son have his most intense relationship with his mother rather than his wife?

How influential is the extended family? Is their approval required before decisions can be made?

Are both husband and wife expected to be monogamous? What are the accepted responses toward infidelity?

Are the couple and family comfortable with rigid gender roles? Are the roles complementary in terms of providing senses of purpose and worth to each member?

How are children to be raised? What are the expectations concerning their behavior in terms of reaching developmental milestones (such as toilet training) and in their interaction with adults (for example, silent and docile, or argumentative and assertive)? What is used to manage their behavior? Considerations of shame and honor may be more powerful than appeals to personal accomplishments or mastery.

How is the family defined? Are there members who are not related by blood or marriage but are nonetheless important sources of support or disturbance?

Personality Factors

Are family members best characterized as optimistic about their abilities to change their situation or pessimistic and fatalistic about their position? Fatalistic world views are common among some minority groups and do not suggest depression or lack of problem-solving skills.

Does the family value independence and individuation or emphasize interdependence (Guisinger and Blatt, 1994)? Families may not recognize the value of adult children going off on their own or be impressed by or supportive of individual achievements.

How open is the family? Self-disclosure is valued by mainstream therapists but may be quite offensive to some family members. Because their individual assessments of a situation are not considered important and are likely to cause confrontation, talking about personal feelings and opinions may be considered bad manners and irrelevant.

What are the family members' construction of "self?" The Lakota Sioux word *tiospaye* refers to an extended self-concept that includes all family and other relationships necessary for survival. Personal self and needs and rights to become self-actualized may be confusing concepts outside of European American groups.

Belief Systems

How is formal education viewed? Is it seen as equally relevant to men and women? How do family members prefer to learn? Native American clients report finding informal settings in which they can listen and observe without evaluation or demands for contributions to be the most beneficial.

How powerful is religion or spiritual systems among family members? Sensitivity to religious beliefs is always an important therapeutic issue. This mandate is made more complex by the relative lack of information European American practitioners may have about Native and Hispanic American spirituality and Eastern religions.

What is the time orientation of the family? Does a future orientation to problem solving make sense with all families? What are the norms of the family regarding punctuality or scheduling?

How is illness understood? Is there shame? Does a particular symptom represent a punishment? Some Native American groups believed that epilepsy was a punishment for sibling incest. Some Hispanic Americans may believe their difficulties are due to *mal ojo*, that is, an evil curse from another.

Does dominant culture intervention seem relevant to etiological and other cultural beliefs? Should traditional healers from certain groups be involved in treatment programs?

Interpersonal and Interactional Styles

Is rapport and understanding possible if English is used as the second language? Some writers feel that bilingualism is an absolute necessity to really understand what the family is reporting.

What are the parameters associated with personal space? How much touching is considered appropriate? Who can touch whom?

What are nuances of body language? Some Native American groups consider pointing at another to be extremely rude. Some African Americans use what seems to be a signal to move away (arm and hand waving away from the body) that may actually be an invitation to come closer.

What are the norms of courtesy? Eye contact is sometimes considered to be impolite. In some families, only the oldest member should be addressed. How much small talk should be used before (what the service provider considers to be) the session begins? Can first names be used? The safest strategy is to address any older male by a title until given permission to use a first name.

How is dress interpreted? Asian Americans may find a casually dressed provider to be unacceptable, while Native Americans may find those clothed in suits and ties to be too distant to be helpful.

What does yes mean? Among some Southeast Asian immigrant groups a yes means, "I heard you." It does not mean, "I will follow your suggestions." Among traditional Japanese Americans, "That would be difficult" means "I can't or won't do this."

Does the family value a personal connection to the service provider? In contrast to typical professional norms, some families may want to consult relatives and friends regarding problems. They may come because of knowing the provider in another capacity. The meaning of multiple relationships (problematic to mainstream therapists) may be difficult to translate to some groups.

Acculturation

All the dynamics suggested in the preceding sections are influenced by the degree to which client families are acculturated to the dominant U.S. culture. Acculturation refers to the learning that occurs among members of minority cultures as a result of their interface with the dominant culture (Padilla, 1980).

Berry (1980) suggests that acculturation occurs in individuals across six dimensions of psychological functioning: language, cognitive styles, personality, identity, attitudes, and acculturative stress. The most obvious measure of acculturation is language. Other signs of increasing acculturation are food preferences, choices of media and entertainment events, knowledge of national history (that is, which history is known—the new host culture or the original culture), choices of friends for recreational events, and adoption of the norms and values of the host culture.

The level to which minority group members have acculturated to the dominant culture has been shown to have an effect on their mental health status. In general, high levels of acculturation are related to substance abuse, increased risk-taking behaviors, reductions in social support, and general decreases in mental health adjustment ratings (Graves, 1967; Padilla, 1980; Newton, Olmedo, and Padilla, 1982; Szapocznik and Kurtines, 1989).

This finding may appear paradoxical. It seems that current measurement may capture a dimension of acculturation—that is, loss of the culture of origin—without ascertaining if another adaptive framework has been developed. Mental health difficulties may arise because individuals have left one system but have little comfort with or acceptance in the other system. African Americans who are described as marginal fit this definition.

Some families may seek professional help because of conflict caused by the discrepancy between the acculturation levels of different generations. Japanese Americans have names for each generation away from birth in Japan (*issei, nisei, sansei,* and *yousei*). A common conflict within this group is the younger generation's rejection of traditional religious, family, and social norms.

Assessment Approaches

There are multiple strategies for evaluating family functioning and multiple targets to consider. Paper-and-pencil normative tests are not as widely used for families as they are for individual assessment. Interviews, observation, and enactments are more frequently utilized.

Critique of Existing Paper-and-Pencil Family Assessments

Paper-and-pencil measures may not be the most culturally sensitive methodology a practitioner can employ to assess a family from an ethnic minority culture. Most models of family relationships are based on European American, middle-class families. As a result, most paper-and-pencil measures used to assess family relationships have not been validated with families from diverse ethnic backgrounds.

Family Adaptability and Cohesion Evaluation Scales

The Family Adaptability and Cohesion Evaluation Scales (FACES; Olson, Portner, and Lavee, 1985) is the benchmark for family assessment. Unfortunately, the norms for the *FACES III* do not consider cultural and ethnic diversity. The authors of the *FACES* suggest a practitioner account for cultural ethnic diversity by having family members complete the scale twice. Once in reference to how they perceive the family and again for how they ideally would like their family to operate. Olson and others (1985) also suggest that completion of the Family Satisfaction Scale (Olson and Wilson, 1982) by ethnic minority culture family members will provide helpful information to a practitioner.

If a practitioner wishes to compare a family to the normative group, however, it must be remembered that the *FACES* norm group may not have included members of the particular ethnic culture. Further, a review of certain items that make up the constructs of cohesion and adaptability may give rise to some concern regarding cultural sensitivity.

Family cohesion is defined as emotional bonding that family members have toward one another. It is measured by items such as:

- Family members have feelings of closeness to each other

- Family members have feelings of special closeness to people outside the family rather than to other family members

- In our family everyone goes his or her own way

- Our family does things together

- Family members avoid each other at home

- Family members know each other's close friends

- Family members consult other family members on their decisions

- We have difficulty thinking of things to do as a family

Family adaptability is defined as the ability of the marital or family system to change its power structure, role relationships, and relationship rules in response to situational and developmental stress. It is measured by such items as:

- Family members say what they want

- Each family member has input in major family decisions

- Children have a say in their discipline

- When problems arise, we compromise

- In our family, everyone shares responsibilities

- It is difficult to get a rule changed in our family

- In our family it is easy for everyone to express his or her feelings

- Discipline is fair in our family

It seems clear that at least several of these items across the two dimensions of cohesion and adaptability may mean something in the European American culture and something very different among certain minority families.

Family Environment Scale

Another frequently cited assessment tool, the Family Environment Scale (FES) developed by Moos and Moos (1986), may be used by practitioners to measure the social-environmental characteristics of families from a variety of backgrounds. This scale has been translated into eleven languages, including Chinese, French, Korean, and Spanish, which may aid the practitioner who administers it to families with primary languages other than English. In addition, the normative sample includes a small group of Hispanic and African American families. Due to the norming sample not being matched on community size or socioeconomic status, however, the results must be interpreted with caution when used with families from minority cultures.

The FES describes a family's characteristics on the dimension of relationships, personal growth, and system maintenance. The constructs included within these dimensions are cohesion, expressiveness, conflict, independence, achievement orientation, intellectual-cultural orientation, active-recreational orientation, moral-religious emphasis, organization, and control. In name, some of these constructs consider cultural diversity. Because well-constructed norms are not available for minority groups, however, a client's responses may be misinterpreted by a practitioner using the FES for family assessment. Items on the FES that may be problematic include:

- Family members are private about their feelings

- There is a lot of conflict in our family

- Political and social problems are frequent topics of conversation

- Family members are regular attendees at religious services

- Independence is highly valued by our family

- Most of the decisions are made by one family member
- Family members strongly encourage each other to stand up for their rights

Like statements on the FACES, the above FES items may have multiple meanings across various minority families.

Other Approaches

Many familiar and innovative methods may be useful with families if a careful analysis is done to ensure the methods are congruent with the cultural norms of the family (Patterson, Reid, Jones, and Conger, 1975; Reid, 1978). Parent interview formats have been described by several authors (Aponte, 1976; Fine and Holt, 1983; Friedman, 1969; Golden, 1983).

If family interviewing is impractical, information from the child-administered assessments can also be instructive (Anderson, 1981). For example, the California Test of Personality (Thorpe, Clark, and Tiegs, 1953), Mooney Problem Checklist (Mooney and Gordon, 1950); Offer Self-Image Questionnaire for Adolescents (Offer, 1979); and the Self-Concept and Motivation Inventory (Farrah, Milehus, and Reitz, 1977) are all general personality tests that have scale scores reflecting family processes.

More specific devices to administer to children include the Behavior Rating Profile (Brown and Hammill, 1983); Child Report of Parent Behavior Inventory (Schaefer, 1965); Child's Attitude Toward Mother and Father Scales (Guili and Hudson, 1977); and the Family Relations Test (Bene and Anthony, 1978).

A number of instruments can also be completed by parents to derive information about their child and about their child in the home. Some of these include the Becker Adjective Checklist (Patterson and others, 1975); Revised Behavior Problem Checklist (Quay, 1987); Child Behavior Profile (Achenbach and Edelbrock, 1991); Eyberg Child Behavior Inventory (Eyberg, Hiers, Cole, Ross, and Eyberg, 1980); and the Parent Daily Report (Patterson and others, 1975).

Another very simple but useful assessment, goal setting, and monitoring device is an *ecomap* (Newbrough, Walker, and Abril, 1978). The ecomap graphically represents each system involved with the identified child (for example, family, church, YWCA, peers, probation) and notes the quality of the relationships among all of the systems. Goals to make the system supportive of change are set and monitored by updates of the ecomap. Essentially, the ecomap turns attention to the qualities of the boundaries surrounding clients as well as to their individual experiences.

Conclusions

Although this brief critique suggests the most frequently cited family assessment tools are not useful for normative comparisons, a therapist may be able to obtain important information under certain conditions. If a measure can be administered in the primary language of the family and the family's priorities match the constructs measured by the instruments, the therapist may use change on the measure following therapy as a means for tracking family members' views on aspects of family life.

Interviews, Observations, and Enactments

Family assessment may be done with the greatest cultural sensitivity and competence using interviews, observations, and enactments. An important axiom to consider is that the solution to any family problem lies within the family's own definition of reality. If practitioners believe this, then a deep understanding of the family ecosystem must be attained before therapists can have confidence in their interpretations and suggestions.

Interviews

An interview format that may be helpful follows. The key ingredients are excellent listening and suspension of personal cultural assumptions. Own up to ignorance when appropriate and ask questions that illustrate an interest in knowing about the family's background.

1.   Determine what language should be used. If an interpreter must be used, the person should be one trusted by the family and knowledgeable about nuances in both languages. Even with an interpreter, the validity of the assessment may be compromised.

2.   A focus on family strengths will be most respectful. Seeking out family successes and resources is far more useful than trying to determine a psychiatric diagnosis for family members. Many families will not have understandings of difficulties that come close to DSM-IV categories, and language difficulties tend to make minority members appear more pathological than they are. In addition, most interventions that will be suggested rely on existing behavioral repertoires. Identification of these is likely to be most critical. For at least these three reasons, an emphasis on strengths is desirable.

3.   What are this family's priorities? Service providers make frequent mistakes by assuming what changes are desired by families. Although family therapy may result in clients learning and using strategies modelled or taught by a therapist, therapists should not teach clients to act like European Americans. Therapists aim to make existing systems work within the framework of general understandings of mental health.

4.   What aspects of family life does the family see as important and affecting their priorities? Cause and effect relationships are sensitive to cultural interpretations. It is best to find out what family members believe about how they are involved in problem definition and maintenance before offering an interpretation.

5.   What are the family's perceptions of situations and events that affect them? It is common to misconstrue the importance of certain phenomena across cultures. The trust in a therapist will be shattered if no common understanding of what really matters can be reached.

6.   Check frequently if goals are being met and if services are matching expectations. For example, S. Sue and Zane (1987) suggest that Asian American clients need some immediate results from therapeutic intervention (for example, reduction of anxiety, nor-

malization of symptoms, relief of depression) for them to continue with services. On the other hand, some Native Americans may take some time to build trust and not anticipate much change on the basis of their work with therapists.

7.   If certain paper-and-pencil instruments must be used, they require scrutiny by culturally aware professionals, community leaders, and family members prior to administration.

8.   In contrast to other paper-and-pencil devices (for example, Moos and Moos, 1986; Olson, Fournier, and Druckman, 1982; Olson, McCubbin, and others, 1982; Olson, Portner, and Lavee, 1985), practitioners might consider careful use of family *genograms* (McGoldrick and Gerson, 1985). Genograms focus attention on the complexity of family interrelationships allowing family members to describe the intensity and quality of each of the interactions via graphic representations.

Genograms allow the practitioner and family members to develop hypotheses regarding how a clinical difficulty may be connected to the family system and the evolution of the difficulty over time. McGoldrick and Gerson (1985) provide an interview format that practitioners may find useful. It is a tool for gaining important information from family members about the present living situation, the extended family context, social context, family relationships and roles, and individual issues. Because nuclear and extended family members are included in a genogram, its use may be especially useful when serving families from minority cultures.

Common Pitfalls

Some of the interpretive pitfalls associated with interviewing minority families may be illustrated by the following. Waterman (1982) suggests a very useful set of questions to use with families who have children with disabilities. Consider each of these from the perspectives of the minority groups described throughout this chapter. (Waterman's questions are paraphrased in italics. Our commentary follows each.)

Do both parents participate with the children? It is a modern European American ideal that both parents have an equitable interaction with their children (especially children with difficulties). Would families from other cultures expect this? Probably not. Who are the caretakers of sick children or children with disabilities in minority families? Can we assume the mother and father of the nuclear family are the most likely ones to shoulder this responsibility?

Are parents overprotective or rejecting or disengaged? What do these terms mean in different cultures? Some Hispanic American girls are never permitted to play out of doors except under the direct supervision of an adult. Is that overprotective? Asian Americans may care for their children with disabilities at home and seek help only in the most serious cases. Is that overprotection, rejection, or disengagement? If a child's disability is seen as punishment for family wrongdoing, is that evidence of rejection? Lin and others (1982) describe a pattern of love, denial, and rejection to characterize Asian American families' reaction to mental illness within the family.

Some Native American families have been seen as rejecting and disengaged toward their children because of the flexible kinship structure in which adults may informally share responsibility for children and the apparently permissive style of parenting that predominates (Attneave, 1982; Locust, 1988; Medicine, 1981).

Do the parents project their anger on each other or on a child? What are cultural expressions of anger? Will it always be recognized by a therapist? How much anger is normative given experiences of racism and oppression? Is anger the most likely emotion to be evoked by a child with a disability? Perhaps guilt, shame, and dishonor are more typical reactions.

Can the children access the parents appropriately? What levels of interaction are normal for different groups? How do children usually get the attention of adults in their culture? Are they supposed to ask for attention?

Is information kept within subsystems? What are the operative subsystems? Some groups may expect women relatives to speak together about family matters or that male elders will be consulted on all decision making. It may be hard to identify triangulation in communication when a therapist is not sure who is supposed to know information in certain systems. European American therapists emphasize the husband-wife dyad as appropriately the most intense in a family. This may not be true for many Asian American families (Tamura and Lau, 1992) in which the mother-child dyad (especially between mother and son) is the strongest.

Is nurturing and support available within and across subsystems? What are the cultural norms for support? What does nurturing behavior look like? There may be very high expectations for help from extended families that seem unreasonable to a European American therapist but normative to certain groups. Expressions of love may be verbal, or physical, or through tangible gifts or goods. Some groups may find expressions of affection to be irrelevant to the quality of their relationships with each other.

Does each system have time alone with its members? To understand "alone," a therapist must understand the conception of self. Dominant-culture Americans view self in terms of separateness. Many Asians may see self more holistically, feeling identity as belonging to a group of family members, classmates, or company colleagues. In addition, cultural expectations regarding private times may vary as a function of cultural preferences or as a result of economic pressures. There is no word for privacy in Japanese, indicating that at least among traditional Japanese the notion of privacy was not valued (Tamura and Lau, 1992). Families who live in one or two rooms, work sixteen hours each day, and are responsible to an extended family network are not likely candidates for private times between spouses.

Observations and Enactments

Important family functions can be assessed using behavioral observations. Reliability will vary, of course, depending on the particular techniques and time allotted for the observation. Validity will depend on the practitioner's abilities to choose important observation targets and to interpret the meaning the family members ascribe to the behaviors.

Naturalistic observations are often difficult to arrange. Asking the family to enact various scenarios creates some threats to validity but does allow the practitioner to see family members in action with each other. Family members can be asked to accomplish a task (for example, to plan an outing or decide on a way to manage a child's school problems) during a therapy session. Choice of the task would be dictated by the presenting priorities and culturally relevant information. Practitioners could gain information about communication patterns, problem solving, family roles, and socialization strategies with just these two tasks.

Another facet of using observational data as the basis for assessment is the possibility of obtaining multirespondent information. In addition to getting individual family members' descriptions of family issues, practitioners can often access teacher descriptions of child behavior. Multimethod and multisource assessments may be very useful as long as family norms for privacy and communication are carefully followed. In some families, individual sessions may be necessary to gather impressions because family members may not confront each other directly.

Common Mental Health Objectives

Although mental health probably has many different definitions across U.S. ethnic minority groups (for example, are you in touch with your feelings or do you successfully repress them for a common good?), there are some goals common to all forms of therapeutic intervention (Madanes, 1990). Each of the goals may be reached in diverse ways, depending on cultural expressions and preferences. Whatever the cultural group under consideration, therapists who accept these goals are likely to do less harm than those who do not use them as standards.

Therapists should be seeking information and developing interventions that help them to assist their clients to: control their actions so as to be successful in their chosen tasks; control their thoughts so as to focus their cognitive and emotional energy in productive ways; control violence and anger so that innocent victims are not created and negative cognitive and emotional cycles are avoided; promote empathy so that clients understand the position of others and can choose to use that information if they wish; promote hopefulness in either individual action or collective success— all clients must be able to imagine they will be successful; promote tolerance so that energy can be focused on adjustment and not wasted on hatred of other individuals or groups; encourage forgiveness so that a present or future orientation may be used, thus allowing for action in the present; and promote harmony and balance that permits a range of human behavior to emerge.

Conclusions

Careful study of multicultural family measurement issues suggests that culturally sensitive assessment requires broad and deep understandings and a commitment to *emic* (ideographic, case study knowledge) assessment approaches (Triandis and others, 1993). There are many potential sources of confusion when attempting a multicultural practice (S. Sue, 1991). The most pervasive danger is applying some normative (or *etic*) constructs to a group without careful validity studies. At this point in time, only emic approaches can be attempted with any safety.

Another problem may be a practitioner's beliefs about assimilation versus pluralism (S. Sue, 1991). Some psychologists may still believe in the melting pot metaphor and expect (in fact, demand) that ethnic differences will disappear over time. They may assume such homogeneity is preferable to enduring ethnic differences. These practitioners may fear the conflict caused by the clash of cultural norms.

Others believe the differences among the peoples who make up our nation (that is, a commitment of memory to ethnic group strengths) is what provides the unique and remarkable success of the United States. From this perspective, differences are embraced as complementary patterns that provide for cultural resilience. Practitioners from this orientation may be interested in acculturation measures as moderators to performance on various psychological tests, but would consider variations among people to be strengths.

Another common cause of confusion, introduced early in this chapter, is a tendency to develop descriptions of group personalities that limit our abilities to recognize individual differences among members of a group. The process of trying to understand minority and recent immigrant groups can inadvertently lead to stereotyping if general statements are confused with personal realities.

Finally, throughout the experience of minority families, are the unremitting, humiliating, enraging realities of racism. Those who practice professional psychology must confront racism in their own assumptions and behaviors and learn to identify the effects of racism on their clients. For many of the families who might seek mental health assistance, their everyday life is spent in a toxic environment of hatred, fear, and aggression. We must all be wary of blaming our clients for the environmental stress they endure by using assessment procedures that are insensitive to their contexts.

A challenge of family assessment is to characterize a group of people in meaningful ways. The further challenges of assessing multicultural families are to identify valid targets for measurement and assessment strategies that take into account the costs of being different in the United States of America.

References

Achenbach, T. M., & Edelbrock, C. (1991). *Revised Child Behavior Profile.* Burlington, VT: University Associates in Psychiatry.

Anderson, C. (1981, April). *Family-oriented assessment techniques for school psychologists.* Paper presented at the annual meeting of the National Association of School Psychologists, Detroit, MI.

Anderson, P. P., & Fenichel, E. S. (1989). *Serving culturally diverse families of infants and toddlers with disabilities*. Washington, DC: National Center for Clinical Infant Programs.

Aponte, H. J. (1976). The family-school interview: An eco-structural approach. *Family Process, 15*, 303–311.

Attneave, C. (1982). American Indians and Alaska Native families: Emigrants in their own homeland. In M. McGoldrick, J. K. Pearce, & J. Giordano (Eds.), *Ethnicity and family therapy* (pp. 55–83). New York: Guilford.

Bailey, E. (1987). Sociocultural factors and health care-seeking behavior among Black Americans. *Journal of the National Medical Association, 79*, 389–392.

Barocas, R., Seifer, R., Sameroff, A. J., Andrews, T. A., Croft, R. T., & Ostrow, E. (1991). Social and interpersonal determinants of developmental risk. *Developmental Psychology, 27*, 479–489.

Beavers, W. R., & Hampson, R. B. (1990). *Successful families: Assessment and intervention*. New York: Norton.

Bene, E., & Anthony, J. (1978). *Family Relations Test*. London: NFER Publishing.

Berry, J. W. (1980). Acculturation as varieties of adaptation. In A. M. Padilla (Ed.), *Acculturation: Theory, models, and some new findings* (pp. 9–25). Boulder, CO: Westview Press.

Boyd-Franklin, N. (1989). *Black families in therapy: A multisystems approach*. New York: Guilford.

Boyd-Franklin, N. (1993). Pulling out the arrows. *Networker, 17*(4), 54–56.

Brown, L. L., & Hammill, D. D. (1983). *Behavior Rating Profile*. Austin, TX: Pro-Ed.

Campos, L. P. (1989). Adverse impact, unfairness, and bias in the psychological screening of Hispanic peace officers. *Hispanic Journal of Behavioral Sciences, 11*, 127–135.

Carlson, E. B., & Rosser-Hogan, R. (1993). Mental health status of Cambodian refugees ten years after leaving homes. *Journal of Orthopsychiatry, 63*, 223–231.

Collins, P. H. (1991). *Black feminist thought*. New York: Routledge & Kegan Paul.

Cross, W. E., Jr. (1971, July). The Negro-to-Black conversion experience. *Black World*, 13–27.

Cross, W. E., Jr. (1978). The Thomas and Cross models of psychological Nigrescence: A literature review. *Journal of Black Psychology, 5*, 13–31.

Dahlstrom, L. E. (1986). MMPI findings on other American minority groups. In W. G. Dahlstrom, D. Lachar, & L. E. Dahlstrom (Eds.), *MMPI patterns of American minorities* (pp. 50–86). Minneapolis: University of Minnesota Press.

Dana, R. H. (1993). *Multicultural assessment perspectives for professional psychology*. Needham Heights, MA: Allyn & Bacon.

Delgado, M. (1988). Group in Puerto Rican spiritism: Implications for clinicians. In C. Jacobs & D. D. Bowles (Eds.), *Ethnicity and race: Critical concepts in social work* (pp. 34–47). Silver Spring, MD: National Association of Social Workers.

Eyberg, S., Hiers, T., Cole, K., Ross, A. W., & Eyberg, S. (1980). *Parent-child interaction training*. Charleston, SC: CAMHC.

Farrah, G. A., Milehus, N. J., & Reitz, W. (1977). *The Self-Concept and Motivation Inventory: What face would you wear?* Dearham Heights, Mich.: Person-O-Metrics.

Farris, L. (1978). The American Indian. In A. L. Clark (Ed.), *Culture/childbearing/health professionals* (pp. 20–33). Philadelphia: Davis.

Fine, M. J., & Holt, P. (1983). Intervening with school problems: A family systems perspective. *Psychology in the Schools, 20*, 59–66.

Franklin, A. J. (1993). The invisibility syndrome. *Networker, 17*(4), 32–39.

Friedman, R. (1969). A structured family interview in the assessment of school learning disorders. *Psychology in the Schools, 6*, 162–171.

Gibbs, J. T. (1988). Young, Black, and male in America: An endangered species. Dover, MA: Auburn House.

Golden, L. (1983). Brief family interventions in a school setting. *Elementary School Guidance & Counseling, 17*, 288–293.

Graves, T. D. (1967). Acculturation, access, and alcohol in a tri-ethnic community. *American Anthropologist, 69*(3–4), 306–321.

Greene, R. L. (1987). Ethnicity and MMPI performance: A review. *Journal of Consulting and Clinical Psychology, 55*, 497–512.

Guili, C. A., & Hudson, W. W. (1977). Child's attitude toward mother and father. *Journal of Social Service Research, 1*, 77–92.

Guisinger, S., & Blatt, S. J. (1994). Individuality and relatedness: Evolution of a fundamental dialectic. *American Psychologist, 49*, 104–111.

Hersch, P. (1993). Young, gifted and trapped. *Networker, 17*(4), 40–49.

Kemnitzer, L. S. (1973). Adjustment and value conflict in urbanizing Dakota Indians measured by Q-Sort technique. *American Anthropologist, 75*, 687–707.

Kitano, H.H.L., & Daniels, R. (1988). *Asian Americans: Emerging minorities*. Englewood Cliffs, NJ: Prentice Hall.

LaFromboise, T. D. (1988). American Indian mental health policy. *American Psychologist, 43*, 388–397.

LaFromboise, T. D., & Low, K. G. (1989). American Indian children and adolescents. In J. T. Gibbs & L. N. Huang (Eds.), *Children of color: Psychological interventions with minority youth* (pp. 114–147). San Francisco: Jossey-Bass.

Leung, P., & Sakata, R. (1988). Asian Americans and rehabilitation: Some important variables. *Journal of Applied Rehabilitation Counseling, 9*(4), 16–20.

Lewis, R. G., & Gingerich, W. (1980). Leadership characteristics: Views of Indian and non-Indian students. *Social Casework: The Journal of Contemporary Social Work, 61*(8), 494–497.

Lin, K. M., Inui, T. S., Kleinman, A. M., & Womack, W. M. (1982). Sociocultural determinants of the help-seeking behavior of patients with mental illness. *Journal of Nervous and Mental Disease, 170,* 78–85.

Lin, T. Y. (1982). Culture and psychiatry: A Chinese perspective. *Australian and New Zealand Journal of Psychiatry, 16,* 235–245.

Lin, T. Y. (1983). Psychiatry and Chinese culture. *Western Journal of Medicine, 139,* 862–867.

Lin, T. Y. (1990). Neurasthenia revisited: Its place in modern psychiatry. *Culture, Medicine and Psychiatry, 14,* 105–129.

Locust, C. (1986). *Hopi beliefs about unwellness and handicaps.* Tucson: University of Arizona Press.

Locust, C. (1988). Wounding the spirit: Discrimination and traditional American Indian belief systems. *Harvard Educational Review, 58,* 315–330.

Madanes, C. (1990). *Sex, love, and violence: Strategies for transformation.* New York: Norton.

Manson, S. M., & Trimble, J. E. (1982). American Indian and Alaska Native communities. In L. R. Snowden (Ed.), *Reaching the underserved: Mental health needs of neglected populations* (pp. 143–163). Newbury Park, CA: Sage.

Marsella, A. J. (1993). Counseling and psychotherapy with Japanese Americans: Cross-cultural considerations. *Journal of Orthopsychiatry, 63,* 200–208.

McAdoo, H. (1979). Black kinship. *Psychology Today,* May, 67–110.

McGoldrick, M., & Gerson, R. (1985). *Genograms in family assessment.* New York: Norton.

Medicine, B. (1981). American Indian family: Cultural change and adaptive strategies. *Journal of Ethnic Studies, 8*(4), 13–23.

Mooney, R. L., & Gordon, L. V. (1950). *Mooney Problem Checklist.* Cleveland, OH: Psychological Corporation.

Moos, R., & Moos, B. (1986). *Family environment scale manual.* Palo Alto: Consulting Psychologists Press.

Morishima, J., Sue, S., Teng, L. N., Zane, N., & Cram, J. (1979). *Handbook of*

Asian American/Pacific Islander mental health research. Rockville, MD: National Institute of Mental Health.

Myers, H. F. (1982). Research on the Afro-American family: A critical review. In B. A. Bass, G. E. Wyatt, & G. J. Powell (Eds.), *The Afro-American family: Assessment, treatment, and research issues* (pp. 35–68). Philadelphia: Grune & Stratton.

Nakanishi, D. T. (1988). Seeking convergence in race relations research: Japanese-Americans and the resurrection of the internment. In P. A. Katz & D. A. Taylor (Eds), *Eliminating racism: Profiles in controversy* (pp. 159–180). New York: Plenum.

Newbrough, J. R., Walker, L., & Abril, S. (1978, April). *Workshop on ecological assessment*. New York: National Association of School Psychologists.

Newton, F., Olmedo, E. L., & Padilla, A. M. (1982). *Hispanic mental health research: A reference guide*. Berkeley: University of California Press.

Offer, P. (1979). *The psychological world of the teenager: A study of normal adolescent boys*. New York: Basic Books.

O'Hare, W. P. (1992). American minorities—The demographics of diversity. *Population Bulletin, 47*, 1–42.

Olson, D. H., Fournier, D. G., & Druckman, J. M. (1982). *ENRICH*. Minneapolis: PREPARE-ENRICH.

Olson, D. H., McCubbin, H. I., Barnes, H., Larsen, A., Muxen, M., & Wilson, M. (1982). *Family inventories*. St. Paul, MN: Family Social Science, University of Minnesota.

Olson, D. H., Portner, J., & Lavee, Y. (1985). *FACES III*. St. Paul, MN: Family Social Science, University of Minnesota.

Oster, G. D., & Caro, J. E. (1990). *Understanding and treating depressed adolescents and their families*. New York: Wiley.

Padilla, A. M. (1980). *Acculturation, theory, models, and some new findings*. Boulder, CO: Westview Press.

Padilla, A. M., & Ruiz, R. A. (1975). Personality assessment and test interpretation of Mexican Americans: A critique. *Journal of Personality Assessment, 39*, 103–109.

Parham, T. A. (1989). Nigrescence: The transformation of Black consciousness across the life cycle. In R. L. Jones (Ed.), *Black adult development and aging* (pp. 151–166). Berkeley, CA: Cobb & Henry.

Patterson, G. R., Reid, J. B., Jones, R. R., & Conger, R. E. (1975). *A social learning approach to family intervention: Vol. 1. Families with aggressive children*. Eugene, OR: Castalia.

Pinderhughes, E. (1982). Afro-American families and the victim system. In

M. McGoldrick, J. K. Pearce, & J. Giordano (Eds.), *Ethnicity and family therapy* (pp. 108–122). New York: Guilford.

Quay, H. C. (1987). *Revised behavior problem checklist.* Odessa, FL: Psychological Assessment Services.

Reid, J. B. (Ed.) (1978). *A social learning approach to family intervention: Vol. 2. Observation in home settings.* Eugene, OR: Castalia.

Reid, J. B. (1993). Prevention of conduct disorder before and after school entry: Relating interventions to developmental findings. *Development and Psychopathology, 5,* 243–262.

Samora, J. (1979). Conceptions of health and disease among Spanish-Americans. *American Catholic Sociological Review, 22,* 314–323.

Schaefer, E. S. (1965). Child report of parent behavior. *Child Development, 36,* 413–423.

Seifer, R., Sameroff, A. J., Baldwin, C. P., & Baldwin, A. (1992). Child and family factors that ameliorate risk between 4 and 13 years of age. *Journal of the American Academy of Child and Adolescent Psychiatry, 31,* 893–904.

Staples, R. (1988). The Black American family. In C. H. Mindel, R. W. Habenstein, & R. Wright, Jr. (Eds.), *Ethnic families in America: Patterns and variations* (pp. 303–324). New York: Elsevier.

Starr, P. D., & Roberts, A. E. (1982). Attitudes toward new Americans: Perceptions of Indo-Chinese in nine cities. In C. B. Marrett & C. Leggon (Eds.), *Research in race and ethnic relations: A research annual* (Vol. 3, Part 2, pp. 165–186). Greenwich, CT: JAI Press.

Steele, S. (1990). *The content of our character: A new vision of race in America.* New York: St. Martin's Press.

Sue, D. W., Arredondo, P., & McDavis, R. J. (1992). Multicultural counseling competencies and standards: A call to the profession. *Journal of Counseling and Development, 70,* 477–487.

Sue, S. (1988). Psychotherapeutic services for ethnic minorities: Two decades of research findings. *American Psychologist, 43,* 301–309.

Sue, S. (1991). Ethnicity and culture in psychological research and practice. In J. D. Goodchilds (Ed.), *Psychological perspectives on human diversity in America* (pp. 51–85). Washington, DC: American Psychological Association.

Sue, S. (1992). Ethnicity and mental health: Research and policy issues. *Journal of Social Issues, 48,* 187–208.

Sue, S., & Zane, N. (1987). The role of culture and cultural techniques in psychotherapy: A critique and reformulation. *American Psychologist, 42,* 37–45.

Szapocznik, J., & Kurtines, W. M. (1989). *Breakthroughs in family therapy in drug abusing and problem youth*. New York: Springer.

Tamura, T., & Lau, A. (1992). Connectedness versus separateness: Applicability of family therapy to Japanese families. *Family Process, 31*, 319–340.

Thomas, C. S. (1971). *Boys no more*. Beverly Hills, CA: Glencoe Press.

Thorpe, P., Clark, W. W., & Tiegs, E. W. (1953). *California Test of Personality*. New York: CTB/McGraw-Hill

Tracey, T. J., Leong, F.T.L., & Glidden, C. (1986). Help seeking and problem perception among Asian Americans. *Journal of Counseling Psychology, 33*, 331–336.

Triandis, H. C., Betancourt, H., Iway, S., Leung, K., Salazar, J. M., Setiadi, B., Sinha, J.B.P., Touzard, H., & Zaleski, Z. (1993). An etic-emic analysis of individualism and collectivism. *Journal of Cross-Cultural Psychology, 24*, 366–383.

Triandis, H. C., Marin, G., Lisansky, J., & Betancourt, H. (1984). *Simpatia* as a cultural script of Hispanics. *Journal of Personality and Social Psychology, 47*, 1363–1375.

Trimble, J. (1990–1991). Ethnic specification, validation prospects, and the future of drug use research. *International Journal of the Addictions, 25*(2A), 149–170.

Velasquez, R. J. (1992). Hispanic-American MMPI research (1949–1992): A comprehensive bibliography. *Psychological Reports, 70*, 743–754.

Waterman, J. (1982). Assessment of the family system. In G. Ulrey & S. J. Rogers (Eds.), *Psychological assessment of handicapped infants and young children* (pp. 172–178). New York: Thieme-Stratton.

Whatley, P. R., & Dana, R. H. (1989). *Racial identity and MMPI group differences*. Unpublished paper, Department of Psychology, University of Arkansas, Fayetteville.

Wilson, M. N. (1993). A view of African American family life: Thoughts and implications for social research and intervention. *Focus: Notes from the Society for the Psychological Study of Minority Issues, 7*(2), 14–15.

Zavella, P. (1987). *Women's work and Chicano families: Cannery workers of the Santa Clara Valley*. Ithaca, NY: Cornell University Press.

14

Qualitative Assessment and
Multicultural Issues

Leo Goldman

Q *ualitative assessment* as used here is a concept that encompasses a variety of methods and techniques, some of which have been used for years. The term was first applied by the writer in an article that described the limitations of standardized tests in general for counseling use and proposed that most counselors would contribute more to their clients by using nonquantitative methods such as card sorts, in-boxes, work-samples, and a number of games and exercises (Goldman, 1982). The concept, as a model for counselors, is very similar to one that has been used in theme groups and workshops; Drum (1992) uses the term "facilitative assessment" for those applications, and later in his article combines the two terms into "qualitative/facilitative assessment."

These conclusions were outgrowths of earlier articles (Goldman, 1972, 1973) that spelled out the limitations inherent in standardized tests themselves when used in counseling: the error of *measurement* resulting from reliability coefficients typically in the .70s for interest and personality measures and in the .80s (sometimes into the .90s) for ability tests; and the error of *estimate* resulting from

---

Note: I want to express my gratitude to Silvia Greenberg and Gayle Fried, both graduate students in counseling at Hunter College of the City University of New York, for their contributions in trying out two of the qualitative assessment activities with their own classes.

validity coefficients typically in the .60s at best. When used for selection and placement, which is what most standardized tests were developed for originally, this level of inaccuracy can be justified in terms of the financial and other savings that can result from even small reductions in the number of students or workers who fail. Used in counseling, however, where one is assisting individuals and groups in estimating their probability of success or satisfaction in school or work, the predictions should properly be presented in such wide bands of percentile or standard scores (to take account of the errors of measurement and estimate) as to be of very limited value. Those bands, even when adding and subtracting one standard error of measurement to and from the obtained score, often span 20 to 30 percentile points; that does not take into account the even wider band that would result from application of the error of estimate.

A second major reason for questioning the usefulness of standardized tests in counseling in general (not just limited to multicultural factors, which aggravate the situation, as is explained below) is the limited competence of most master's-level counselors in the statistical and other technical areas of knowledge required to use the quantitative tests adequately—to be able to read a test manual and related journal articles and test reviews with critical comprehension. The qualitative methods by contrast require almost none of those competencies.

In later articles expounding on qualitative assessment, one of the major advantages claimed for those methods is their flexibility and adaptability to diverse clientele: diverse in terms of age, physical and mental condition, and ethnic and color identity (Goldman, 1990, 1992). Among the factors contributing to that flexibility and adaptability are the following:

1. In most qualitative assessment methods, time is not a factor, so that, for example, people for whom English is a second language, or anyone else with language limitations due to life history, are not at a disadvantage.

2. Because of the informal approach used with many qualitative assessment methods, an adequate translation to other languages

is less of a problem than it is with standardized tests. With the latter, translation could change the nature of the task or situation presented by an item, enough so that established norms would no longer be usable, nor would validity data be applicable.

3.   Comparison with established norm groups is in fact rarely part of qualitative assessment methods; the emphasis instead is on understanding and describing what is being assessed—whether that be abilities, interests, personality, values or other areas—in as holistic a manner as possible. The goal is to describe that individual's functioning in specified life situations rather than to add items to get numbers that compare the person with others—the others, by the way, usually being insufficiently known to allow for a truly meaningful comparison.

4.   Qualitative assessment methods frequently focus on the individual's response to, and interaction with, real-life stimulus situations and people, or at least to simulations thereof. Toward this end, the methods often present a lifelike situation rather than the narrow tasks and abstractions typical of standardized tests, such as spatial visualization or items making up a dominance scale on a temperament inventory. As Drum (1992) has commented, this newer approach "reveals client personality characteristics and capabilities in action and provides insight into interpersonal interaction. Because they are usually oriented to exercise or activity and are carried out in the presence of others, these techniques evoke affect and cognition simultaneously, yielding a far more complete client image than do traditional assessment procedures" (p. 622).

Perhaps the essential point is that quantitative assessments present their findings in terms of numbers—whether percentile or standard scores, or, even worse, the grade or age equivalent scores that measurement textbooks have criticized for decades. When one's client is from any culture different from the usual majority sample making up most norm groups, or even from a sample that includes some people from other cultures, one is usually at a loss to know how to adjust the numbers to take account of language, attitudinal differences, or other differences between one's client and the published norm groups. By contrast, the focus in qualitative assessment is usually on the entire *process* rather than just a bottom line number. As a result, the assessor is able to observe and interpret all the behaviors in the activity and to see more clearly, for example, what culture-related perceptions, cognitions, attitudes, and assumptions were involved.

When used in a multicultural group, these techniques add a dimension to the assessment of an individual, a dimension in which people from different backgrounds can increase their awareness of how their own and others' attitudes, perceptions, values, and styles of behavior actually interact. The structure of the particular qualitative technique allows for a controlled study of these phenomena as a microcosm of the real world. Perhaps the best way to convey to the reader the flavor of qualitative assessment is to give an example using one of these methods.

Friendship Inventory

One informal method I learned about at a summer institute is called the Friendship Inventory. The inventory may be used with an individual or group; each has its advantages, but a heterogeneous group is especially valuable, because each person can then see his or her own patterns more sharply through comparison with those of the other members of the group.

On an 8½ × 11-inch sheet are ruled columns where the individual writes the name of each friend and for each, the person's age, ethnic identity, color, marital status, religion, occupation, how long known, who initiated the friendship, who maintains it, what they do together, how they stay in touch. (These categories can be modified, deleted, or added to as the assessor prefers; there is no standardization protocol to be concerned about.) Used thus in a group, one first allows enough time for all to fill in the columns for as many friends as they choose to include—usually about thirty minutes. Then they are asked to comment on any trends they see in their inventories. A variety of such comments emerge; for our present purposes, the most pertinent usually are found with reference to the columns for ethnic, color, and religious identity, areas in which most people report a lack of diversity in their friendships; this of course lends itself ideally to use with multicultural groups. It might be of interest to note that often one or two people in a group will ask for a definition of friendship; I do not provide one, because individual differences on that point offer excellent material for discussion. Some people include only a small number of people with whom they are very close and see often. Others include people with whom they are in touch only once in months, and then perhaps by mail or phone; one such group member said that, for her, friends are people with whom she discusses intimate topics. Some include siblings, boyfriends, or girlfriends; others do not. Another interesting discussion point is the finding that some people have friends going back to childhood, others go back only a few years. All of these provide a basis for insight-producing discussions of individual lifestyles, needs, and things they would like to change.

A graduate student at Hunter College, Silvia Greenberg, herself a fairly recent immigrant to the United States from Argentina, tried the technique with a group of her undergraduate students in a Spanish course, with the results reported in the following section.

. . . .

College Group

The group was a small class of ten undergraduates in a suburban college. Included were five African American (Black), one Asian American, and four European Americans. Eight were female, two Black. After completing the inventory, they first discussed the results in a group, and then five were interviewed individually; the entire process was audiotaped. The following is drawn from the tapes and the individual inventories. The number of friends ranged from four to thirteen. There was a wide range as to the religion of each person's friends:

four listed people almost all of the same religion, while four had friends from different religions, and two said they did not know the religions of most of their friends.

As to ethnic identity, the friends of seven were limited to one ethnic group, while three had friends from several ethnic groups. Color was the most limited: nine of the ten had friends all, or almost all, of their own color. These facts alone provided interesting discussion material about the reasons for this kind of self-segregation.

In addition, there was some discussion by several of the females to the effect that most of their friends are males: females, they said, are more competitive, get into more arguments, talk about people's clothes and boyfriends, while males, they said, are more "laid-back" and think, "I can be myself more with guys." These latter comments are particularly interesting because so often one has heard in recent years that men are more competitive with each other and that more androgenous men prefer to talk with women about feelings. Perhaps in both instances we are hearing from nontraditional, more androgenous men and women.

One Black female said that until she entered college she had had almost no White fellow students or faculty (she lived in a predominately Black suburb). She listed only four friends—one of them her brother—and all were Black.

Another student of mixed European ancestry listed eight names of diverse ethnic backgrounds, but all were Catholic or Orthodox in religion. What she stressed in her interview is her preference for friends who had similar family values, which she characterized as "strict," meaning valuing education and strongly discouraging getting married or even "serious" before completing one's college education.

One unusually mature young woman described her "independence"—having many friends (thirteen were listed) of diverse ages but most older, going into the thirties, and diverse ethnic backgrounds, but all White and all Catholic. She was very critical of people her age who have no interest in foreign films, for example, and whose idea of a fun evening is getting drunk, and who do not learn from each other and in fact are not much interested in learning at all. Though she has many male and female friends and a boyfriend, she often goes out for an evening by herself to meet new people at clubs and other places. Yet, despite her independence and seeming sophistication, she listed no friends of color or of any religion other than her own.

As an informal method, the inventory can be modified for one's specific assessment purposes without concern about deviating from standardized methods. The columns as used here provided much interesting assessment information regarding, for example, the extent to which people take the initiative in beginning or maintaining a friendship; their narrowness or variety of activities engaged in with different friends; whether or not they have long-term friendships, going back to childhood in some instances, and what this implies about their relationships; whether a person's occupation is an important factor in their choosing or keeping friends (some people keep friendships from childhood even if the friend goes a very different route regarding length of schooling or the level of occupation they enter, while others let those friendships end); and many other such issues. An assessor, however, may freely change any of the column headings, deleting or adding to adapt to the particular group or to topics of special interest.

For the multicultural focus of this book, however, probably the most pertinent kinds of data have to do with ethnicity, color, and religious factors. In many administrations to graduate classes in counseling and to workshops, I have found that analysis and discussion of those three columns have made a major impact and have led to productive examination of attitudes, perceptions, and feelings regarding the reasons that people do or do not have friends from other groups than their own.

As with most other qualitative assessment methods, this one is usable with almost any individual or group, is readily translated into other languages, and can be interpreted, and serve as a stimulus for self-examination, without reference to norm tables or validity data.

Certificate of Accomplishment

A simple assessment technique, the Certificate of Accomplishment, requires only a blank sheet of paper or, at most, a page made to look like a formal certificate for presentation. Participants—individually or in groups—are asked to place themselves at some point in the future and to assume that they have been selected to receive an award for outstanding achievement. Each is to write the statement that will appear on the certificate. The purpose here is to stimulate people to fantasize and project their important values and goals; because I have found that so many people describe just ordinary career activities, I now stress that the achievement should be very special and important. Even with this stress, there is usually a wide range from very modest to very outstanding achievements. This is itself valuable information and helps people to see how achievement-oriented and ambitious they are compared to others.

In addition to the fact that this technique can readily be used with a multicultural population, regardless of language, age, or other demographics, it offers a special opportunity to bring into the open any cultural differences as to ambition, level of expectations, types of achievements valued, modesty, and perceived barriers. For example, some cultures (for example, some Asian and Native American) consider it inappropriate to draw attention to one's personal accomplishments. Counselors need to be sensitive to such factors when processing the results.

I usually ask groups to break into dyads or triads and try to interpret each other's statements; then I ask for volunteers to share some of their interpretations with the group. People are often fascinated to hear the different kinds of response; some are truly moved by the candid expressions of goals and ambitions.

Elementary School Experience

A graduate student at Hunter College, Gayle Fried, tried to use the Certificate of Accomplishment with a small group of fifth graders in the school where she is a teacher. This group met regularly with a guidance counselor and included Black, White, and Latino children. One boy drew a basketball scene and verbally told about his wish that he could be a successful athlete. Another, a special education student, wrote only a few words but orally said that he wants to be in politics, explaining that he wants to help people through leading them in a persuasive manner. A third drew a basketball player and someone he labeled as a "skating player," and also wrote "basketball player," tennis player," and "game artist." When asked to explain, he indicated that he likes both to compete in sports and to draw. Whether any of these expressed goals are realistic and will continue, the children appeared to be very interested in the activity itself and in talking about their values and goals in general. Fried expressed great enthusiasm for the usefulness of this simple technique, even for a group so young and so much in need of counseling help. She did express the opinion that the counselor's work with this group had probably contributed toward their ability to talk about themselves. In any case, it is impressive that a group of that age, some of them with academic and other problems, were able to make productive use of this assessment procedure.

Vocational Card Sort

Even more impressive is the administration of the Vocational Card Sort (VCS) to that same group of elementary school pupils. Before reporting the results of this administration, the VCS must be described in some detail; it is one of the most well-developed qualitative assessment methods (Dewey, 1974; Dolliver, 1967; Goldman, 1983; Jones, 1980; Tyler, 1961).

The VCS is a method for exploring work values and goals. It differs from standardized interest inventories in having no preset interest scales or categories that the items fall into or contribute to. Instead, the method permits, indeed requires, that each individual project onto a set of cards his or her own idiosyncratic classification system for, in effect, what the individual would like to get out of or avoid in a job. The method is essentially projective in nature and is deceptively simple, considering how powerful it can be in evoking personal values and needs.

In the version developed by Dewey (1974), which built on earlier work by Tyler (1961) and Dolliver (1967), there are seventy-six occupational titles, all presented in nonsexist language, each typed or printed on a small card or slip of paper. The VCS may be used with an individual or a group; as with most qualitative assessments, group administration is especially valuable, in this case because it permits each individual to see his or her work-related values or needs more clearly by hearing contrasting values and needs of other people. For this reason, the value is enhanced by having in the group people with very different work goals (for example, money, security, intrinsic satisfaction, fame) and different interests and needs (for example, data, people, things, competitiveness, autonomy).

First, each person separates his or her cards into two groups: those the individual finds attractive and would consider, and those that the person finds unappealing for whatever reasons. After that sort, one works with either of the two piles separately; I usually use the negative group first because it seems to evoke more feeling and more involvement. (Some, by the way, use a third group—occupations the individual is uncertain about—but I prefer to force choices in order to obtain as much data as possible to work with.) The instruction then is to divide the negative group into subpiles, as few or as many as the individual wishes, such that the occupations in each subpile have in common the *reason* for rejection. It is important to avoid discussing individual occupations because what makes the VCS process distinctive is the focus on the projection of the individual's reasons (values, needs, and so forth), which become in effect the interest scales for that individual. In fact, one should not answer questions about any of the occupational titles; for purposes of this process, it does not even matter whether the individual has a correct understanding of the occupations, any more than it matters whether someone taking the Rorschach or Thematic Apperception Test sees the "real" picture in the inkblots or the "real" story in the scenes depicted. The counselor can at a later time correct any misconceptions about specific occupations; for now, the purpose is to facilitate the individual's digging personal and idiosyncratic values and needs out of his or her insides.

The results are fascinating and of endless variety. People develop such categories as "in all these occupations someone is always looking over your shoulder, and I can't stand that" or "these all require more years of study than I am willing or able to invest" or "I hate doing the same thing all day" or "I'm uncomfortable with anything involving math" and on and on. Most of the categories produced do not resemble categories or scales to be found on standardized interest inventories or values inventories. In fact, I have heard hundreds of different "categories" or "scales" from individuals taking the VCS, as contrasted with the preconceived ten or fifteen or whatever number is found on any one standardized inventory. Even more important is that individuals are not *forced* into a preset, limited framework. Some produce as few as three or four categories, others ten or more. That alone is a valuable bit of information; it reveals something about the individual's cognitive structure regarding work-related values and needs—from simple to very complex—a variable that may be related to cultural factors. One also has the opportunity to observe the individual's style of sorting: speed of decisions, whether changes are made after the first sort, impulsiveness versus thoughtfulness, and others.

The flexibility, open-endedness, and lack of norms contribute to the multicultural applicability of the VCS. The occupational titles can be translated into other languages or even presented in pictorial form. The specific occupations included can be changed to those that would be meaningful to the specific individual or group; the only requirement is that they include among them a diversity of settings, functions, and relationships with others.

The second subsort—of the positive group of occupational cards—also produces a wide variety of categories: "I like to be able to move around during the course of a day, and these occupations all permit that" or "I love being outdoors and working with nature" or "these would all give me a chance to use my creativity" or "I'm good at solving problems, which is what all these involve," and another endless list of responses that have been given.

In this entire process, whether dealing with positive or negative valences, the individual is fully participating in the process rather than answering questions without awareness of where they will eventually lead in terms of scores or profiles. The results are instantly obvious in the very process itself. Further, from a counseling point of view, assessment and counseling flow together; to a client's statement of a commonality among a subsort of cards, the counselor can immediately respond with a reflection, an interpretation, or a probe that encourages the individual to say more, to dig deeper, rather than having to wait until a test is scored and then go over the numbers and react to them a week or more later.

VCS Administration to Elementary School Children

Fried administered the VCS to the group of five fifth-grade children described earlier in connection with the Certificate of Accomplishment. Because of the limited time available and the limited attention span of the children, she did only the first sort—Yes or No, in effect—and then asked the children to explain their choices. The following are excerpts from her written report of the experience:

Just as you had suggested in class, I noticed significant differences in the ways in which each child did his or her sorting. One child (the one I would not have expected to be so, based upon his behavior on this day) was so cautious in the way he separated his cards into the groups. Despite the fact that he was being somewhat disruptive, can I assume that he was really taking the activity very seriously? He is somewhat of a perfectionist. Maybe his sorting technique could have been related to that? But this boy refused to share how he "came to" either his Yes or No piles. After looking at them myself, it seemed obvious that his Yes pile consisted of very high reaching goals; there was a large variety—several helping occupations, some in which he would be able to exert his influence over other persons and run things, as well as some involving creativity. Since he refused to talk about them, I can only speculate about his reasons.

Another child, who was very cooperative, went through all of his cards in about five to ten minutes and, even with my help, was able to find only one occupation that really interested him. Was he so sure of what it was that interested him or was he a little tired? And is there a correlation between his proclaimed desire to be a politician/president of the U.S. (in the Certificate of Accomplishment assessment) and his desire to be a police officer in the VCS? When I asked him about this, he said in essence that both as the president and as a police officer he would be able to exert his influence to obtain order and help people. Yet this boy had no expressed desire to become a president of a company or do any job that had to do with schooling. Very interesting!

Then there was one boy who seemed to want to follow in his parents' footsteps, who wished to make a lot of money and who was interested in using his creativity and thought processes. Another child selected a wide range of occupations and gave very different reasons for each. The last boy, who had first stated that he had no interest in anything suddenly came up with some vocations that he was interested in. Though he didn't want to share his reasons, I think that this activity had the greatest effects on him because he found out that he did have some interests after all, which I hope made him feel a little less sad (as he seemed to be very uninterested in everything and very sad on this day). Yet, when doing the qualitative accomplishment assessment, he seemed more excited. And he finally decided to deliberately look through the cards to find the same vocation he chose last time: chemist. This boy seems to like the excitement of creating new things.

Another interesting point I noticed is that the children seemed to choose many fewer Yes cards than the students in the college class. Could it be that maybe they didn't understand some of the vocations (though we did discuss them and did modify the cards for the children)? Or maybe young children are a little more sure of themselves or see fewer options open to them? Or maybe this was, for the most part, just a very self-aware and decisive group.

Though I must admit that this "lesson" certainly did not go as smoothly as I had hoped for, I do think that the children did get a lot out of the activity and that this activity really does have great implications to help students in their efforts to clarify their values.

. . . .

As a footnote to this report, one should note that the VCS is essentially a process of making abstractions and generalizations. This implies that the process has limitations when used with populations who are more concrete in their cognition and who have difficulty with abstractions and generalizations; included are children, some people with learning disabilities, and those ethnic and socioeconomic groups that traditionally function at a more concrete level. With such populations, one may need to do as Fried did: simplify the process but still stay with the essence of the VCS, which is to emphasize *reasons* why, even if the people cannot really think in terms of commonalities among a group of occupations.

There are literally hundreds of games, exercises, and structured activities similar to the three that have been described thus far.

They come out of programs and processes called psychological education, theme groups, workshops, gestalt therapy, group guidance, sociodrama, and others. Unfortunately, these are not found in any one source book; many in fact are unpublished and therefore unavailable in libraries. A list is appended to this chapter of some of the major publishers of this kind of material. In addition, attendance at selected workshops and institutes will provide assessors with additional techniques.

We now turn to somewhat different kinds of qualitative assessment methods, methods that have in common a hands-on approach and that are used with a major emphasis on abilities, though still include temperament and other factors.

Hands-On Assessment of Abilities

A number of qualitative assessment activities might be characterized as hands-on, in that they present the individual with a concrete task, using some sort of materials, that simulates a real-life task, usually work-oriented in some way. Some of these grew out of methods developed by the U.S. Office of Strategic Services (OSS) during World War II (OSS Assessment Staff, 1948). Faced with the charge to select people who would be effective in difficult assignments, often behind enemy lines and involving contacts with guerrilla resistance forces in occupied European countries, the OSS decided that paper-and-pencil tests of abilities and personality were not adequate for the purpose. Instead, they designed field situations in which the candidates were presented with challenging and dangerous tactical problems that had to be solved under time pressure using their wits and whatever materials they could use imaginatively, such as tree branches or rocks.

Two examples of current assessment procedures of this nature follow. These do not involve the OSS kind of stress, but exemplify the principle of presenting the individual with a microtask that taps some of the abilities and temperamental qualities needed to do the real-life task that is being simulated. Both also exemplify a basic belief that higher predictive validities will result from a gestalt approach—that is, from presentation of a total task, rather than separate tests of the specific abilities, aptitudes, knowledge, and temperament that job analysis or task analysis indicate are required to perform that task. The rationale here is that predictive validity is diminished when, for example, separate tests of spatial visualization, mechanical comprehension, and arithmetic abilities (even hands-on tests such as wooden form-boards) are used to estimate how well an individual will function in a mechanical task that calls for all those abilities. The rationale also states that the individual's functioning in the total simulated task with a piece of wood or metal or part of a motor involves the *integration* of all the component competencies with three-dimensional materials and tools, and that therefore the highest order of validity will result from the use of the total task simulation.

With reference to multicultural issues, this kind of approach avoids some of the problems found when using standardized tests (especially paper-and-pencil tests) with people from groups other than the majority population for whom the tests were developed and on whom they were standardized—their norms, reliability, validity, and time limits. The qualitative approach usually avoids the handicaps that standardized tests present to someone for whom English is a second language. The approach also presents less of an obstacle to people whose life history makes them uncomfortable and awkward when taking paper-and-pencil tests; among the groups thus affected are the less-educated and those ethnic groups that emphasize concrete rather than abstract, and manual rather than verbal activities.

Two examples now follow.

Work-Samples

Actually, this category title could be used for many other kinds of qualitative assessment, but it has traditionally been used with materials developed for use in programs of rehabilitation of people with disabilities. These tasks tend to be relatively simple, such as assembly of parts, filing papers, blueprint reading, mail sorting, and message taking. The person being assessed is usually instructed by a film or videotape or by the assessor as to what the task involves and is then observed over a period of time—hours or days—with an eye to the ease and skill with which the task is learned, understood, and accomplished. This can be viewed as a mini-training session, with immediate evaluation, so that it is a sample of the individual's aptitude for learning and performing full-scale jobs of this kind. Evaluation of some of the major systems of work-sample assessment as used in rehabilitation counseling may be found in Batterbusch (1976).

In-Basket

A work-sample type of qualitative assessment is the in-basket procedure. This could be developed for many kinds of tasks where decisions must be made and stimuli of various kinds responded to. This could include, for example, the work of receptionists and supervisors of various kinds. It seems to be used mostly for assessing candidates for managerial positions in industry, schools, and other settings.

An actual desktop in-basket might be used, though increasingly one would expect that the many types of presentation offered by computer terminals will make that the method of choice in the future. Whatever the method, the person being assessed is presented with a sample of the types of messages, letters, phone calls, and other communications that a corporate manager or school administrator might receive during the course of a day. For each, the candidate writes or dictates to a recording machine the immediate action he or she would take: phone the person, ask the secretary to arrange an appointment with the person, arrange a meeting with several people, dictate a letter right then, or indicate that this is a matter not to be acted upon at this time. In a hiring situation, the assessor might evaluate the responses based on criteria previously established as good practices, taking into account everything else known about the candidate from interviews, application forms, and other sources. In a counseling setting, the assessor might review each decision with the client, trying together to understand the person's reasoning, on the basis of which the assessor could offer feedback that could help the client decide whether that is a promising type of work to try to enter.

Both methods—work-sample and in-basket—share with most other types of qualitative assessment ready adaptability to multicultural populations. The work-sample directions and the in-basket contents can be presented in any language and to people of any age, gender, color, disability, or ethnic identity. This contrasts markedly with traditional standardized tests of ability, where any modification in the contents threatens the applicability of published norms and predictive correlations. Furthermore, there is a very basic principle here of multicultural fairness: people are evaluated on the basis of their demonstrated ability to perform the job tasks rather than on the basis of predictions deriving from paper-and-pencil tests on which those people might not perform as well as they would on the real-life tasks.

Games and Exercises

As mentioned earlier, there are undoubtedly hundreds of activities, games, and exercises that have been developed (and unfortunately never compiled) that could be included within the scope of games and exercises. Two may be worth brief mention.

Lifeline

The Lifeline asks each individual to display graphically on a sheet of paper the major events of his or her own life, with an indication of its effects—positive, negative, or neither—on the person's current condition, feelings, or status. The method is very powerful and may arouse strong feelings of pleasure, sadness, anger, or nostalgia. It is an excellent way to begin a series of sessions intended to enhance self-awareness and growth. Its adaptability to almost all cultural groups results from the fact that each individual provides his or her own structure and selections rather than being confined to specific questions and categories.

Kidney Machine Game

A second example is the Kidney Machine Game. It shares with other comparable methods a set of stimuli that require the participants to make uncomfortable choices and decisions about a group of people, some of whom face certain death as a result of the decisions. In the case of the Kidney Machine (or Kidney Transplant, as I have used it recently), the participants are given brief descriptions of several people, each of whom will die without immediate access to a kidney machine (or a transplant). There is only one machine (or transplant) available, and therefore only one of the people listed will survive. The candidates differ as to age, gender, ethnic identity, past contributions to society in the areas of art, science, or medicine, political orientation, parenthood, and whatever else the assessor might want to add to the list. The participants are usually placed in groups of four to six and instructed to serve as the hospital's committee to decide who will survive. Working under time limits, the groups usually get very involved in considerations of values and attitudes. Some groups refuse to choose and propose instead to use a random method; I insist that they must choose. The purpose here, which is in congruence with the purpose of the entire activity, is to evoke different values and attitudes and afterward to debrief the experience by asking participants to consider what factors contributed to those values and attitudes (for example, family of origin, religion, ethnic group, neighborhood, and so on). A second focal point for debriefing is the role played by each participant in his or her group; this presents an additional opportunity for increased self-awareness.

With a multicultural emphasis, one would make certain that the brief biographical sketches of the candidates included the variables that one wants to examine with the group. Used with a multicultural group, the technique offers rich opportunities to explore each others' perceptions and opinions regarding different cultures. A skilled group leader can use this as a base for developing increased understanding and reduced distance.

Criticisms of Qualitative Assessment

The methods clustered here as qualitative assessments have been criticized on several points.

First is the amount of time required to use most of these methods. No doubt, standardized tests could be administered to large groups, scored, and even reported briefly in the time needed to use one of the qualitative techniques with a group of, say, ten people. One response to this criticism is that qualitative methods are so intimately interwoven with counseling that they should be acknowledged as performing many functions during the time period, and performing them more meaningfully because they are so integrated. A second response is that the qualitative methods have far more impact than most quantitative tests and that in the long run more service is provided to the participants.

A second criticism is that using qualitative techniques requires much skill on the part of the assessor or counselor. It is certainly true that the value of the experiences is likely to be highly correlated with the competencies of the professional person using them. The response is that standardized tests also require a high order of competence, even more perhaps because they demand understanding of statistics and technical data about reliability and validity if they are to be used properly. It is, then, a matter of what *kind* of competencies each approach requires, rather than how much.

A third criticism is that reliability and validity data are lacking for the qualitative methods. This is indeed a matter requiring consideration, although the traditional statistical methods usually do not apply. However, reliability and validity do not seem to be as much of a concern with these methods because they are so much closer to real life than standardized tests, and also because most of these methods are so open to and understandable by the participants. Both reliability and validity can therefore be discussed with the client (for example, Are these behaviors typical of you? Do they occur in other parts of your life?). This is far from a perfect answer, but one must compare it with the reality of predictive validity and concurrent validity, where the criterion problem remains a major obstacle, and where the correlations at best are in the .60s, and typically much lower.

Conclusions

Qualitative assessment methods are an ideal approach for the work of psychologists, counselors, and others who deal with people of different ethnic backgrounds, language, religion, color, gender, sexual orientation, or ability. Perhaps the one most common characteristic is that they simulate real-life processes or qualities and thus help clients to project and then examine their ways of functioning in various life situations, including interpersonal relations with people who differ from them in those regards.

Second, qualitative assessment methods are readily adaptable to people who differ from the middle-class majority on which quantitative tests are usually standardized. Even if some tests or inventories do include other than the predominant population in their norms or reliability and validity studies, all are usually included in a single set of norms or in the statistical studies. This leaves the assessor still unable to conclude what each person's abilities, interests, or personality traits are, if that person is in some way different culturally from the standardization population.

Third, standardized tests, certainly paper-and-pencil tests, usually provide only the bottom line; that is, the number scores that result from adding up all of a person's responses to the individual questions that comprise each scale. The qualitative methods, by contrast, reveal directly, or in later debriefing and discussions of the experience, the *process* that each person went through cognitively, the feelings the person experienced, and the problem-solving behaviors the person utilized.

All in all, qualitative assessment includes a body of methods and techniques worth serious consideration by professionals who seek to assist people of diverse backgrounds and current identities to know themselves better, to solve problems, to make decisions, to grow more fully in many areas of their lives, and to plan how they want to live the rest of their lives.

Appendix

•••••••••••••••••••••••••••••••••
Sources of Qualitative Assessment Materials

American Guidance Service
Publishers' Building
Circle Pines MN 55014

Cambridge Career Products
One Players Club Drive
Charleston WV 25311

Chronicle Guidance Publications
Aurora Street
Moravia NY 13118

The College Board
45 Columbus Avenue
New York NY 10023

Educational Media Corporation
Box 21311
Minneapolis MN 55421

Pro-Ed
8700 Shoal Creek Boulevard
Austin TX 78758

Research Press
Box 3177
Champaign IL 61821

Whole Person Press
1702 East Jefferson Street
Duluth MN 55812

References

Batterbusch, K. (1976). *Descriptions and comparisons of seven commercial evaluation systems*. Menomenie: Stout Vocational Rehabilitation Institute, University of Wisconsin.

Dewey, C. R. (1974). Exploring interests: A non-sexist method. *Personnel and
Guidance Journal, 52*, 311–315.

Dolliver, R. H. (1967). An adaptation of the Tyler Vocational Card Sort. *Personnel and Guidance Journal, 45*, 916–920.

Drum, D. J. (1992). A review of Leo Goldman's article "Qualitative assessment:
An approach for counselors." *Journal of Counseling and Development, 70*,
622–623.

Goldman, L. (1972). Tests and counseling: The marriage that failed. *Measurement and Evaluation in Guidance, 4*, 213–220.

Goldman, L. (1973). Test information in counseling: A critical view. In *Proceedings of the 1973 Invitational Conference on Testing Problems* (pp. 28–34).
Princeton, NJ: Educational Testing Service.

Goldman, L. (1982). Assessment in counseling: A better way. *Measurement and
Evaluation in Guidance, 15*, 70–73.

Goldman, L. (1983). The Vocational Card Sort: A different view. *Measurement and Evaluation in Guidance, 16*, 107–109.

Goldman, L. (1990). Qualitative assessment. *The Counseling Psychologist, 18*, 205–213.

Goldman, L. (1992). Qualitative assessment: An approach for counselors. *Journal of Counseling and Development, 70*, 616–621.

Jones, L. K. (1980). Issues in developing an occupational card sort. *Measurement and Evaluation in Guidance, 12*, 206–215.

OSS Assessment Staff. (1948). *Assessment of men.* New York: Rinehart.

Tyler, L. E. (1961). Research explorations in the realm of choice. *Journal of Counseling Psychology, 8*, 195–202.

15

Multicultural Assessment of
Alcohol and Other Drug Use

Mitchell L. Schare and Norweeta G. Milburn

The use of mind-altering substances such as alcohol and other drugs is a universal phenomenon found throughout the history of the human species. As early as the Paleolithic period (approximately 750,000 B.C.E.), our forebears ingested a variety of caffeine-bearing plants for their psychoactive properties (Gilbert, 1986). The discovery of Stone Age beer jugs from the neolithic period (approximately 15,000 B.C.E.) provides factual evidence for the drinking of fermented beverages (Poznanski, 1959).

Within written records of humankind, numerous references are noted concerning the consumption of psychoactive substances. Ancient references to the usage of marijuana can be found in the Hebrew Bible, as well as early writings from China, Greece, and India (Brecher, 1972). Likewise, discussions about the production and use of both beer and wine are found in numerous works of the ancient Egyptians, Jews, Greeks, and Romans (Poznanski, 1959). Even the use of inhalants is talked about in the writings of the Egyptians, Jews, and Greeks (Preble and Laury, 1967).

Global exploration, particularly during the sixteenth century, increased knowledge and usage of various psychoactive substances throughout the world. For example, the smoking of tobacco was originally a practice of Native American groups. Following the initial exposure of Columbus and other early explorers to tobacco, trade began to flourish in this commodity. "Magellan's crew smoked tobacco, and left seeds in the Philippines and other ports of call. The Dutch brought tobacco to the Hottentots: the Portuguese brought it to the Polynesians. Soon, wherever sailors went—in Asia, Africa, even Australia—they found tobacco awaiting them. The natives tended the plants, and learned to smoke the leaves themselves" (Brecher, 1972, p. 209). Likewise, other local products and practices became part of international trade. The production and importation of tea and coffee became important, particularly for Dutch and British traders (Gilbert, 1986). As demonstrated by the preceding examples, the use of substances, while typically found to be indigenous to certain geographic regions and people, has been shared universally among all cultural groups.

The use of substances among many cultures is deeply ingrained because of their medicinal, spiritual, or ritual properties. For example, the chewing of the coca leaf (containing cocaine) is practiced among the indigenous cultures of the Andes mountains (Brecher, 1972). Ritual use of substances may even mitigate against abuse in some cultural groups. Classic studies of alcoholism have attributed the observed low rates of problem drinking among Jews to the primary use of wine for ritual purposes (Snyder, 1958; Waylan and Mintz, 1976).

Modern cross-cultural study finds the use of alcohol and other drugs to be problematic and of international concern. For example, the abusive consumption of alcohol is a problem of considerable proportions. Of those European countries reporting to the World Health Organization, an average death rate of 14.7 per 100,000 persons in the population was attributed to cirrhosis and chronic liver disease, a likely result of alcohol consumption (World Health Organization, 1989). Comparable statistics can be found for the American, African, and Western Pacific regions.

The cross-cultural study of alcohol and other drug use is complicated by a number of issues. One such problem involves the determination of when the usage of a drug becomes abusive. While such a division may be evident for drugs readily seen as dangerous (such as inhalants or heroin), for socially acceptable substances (nicotine, caffeine, alcohol) the distinction may not be as clear.

Where substance abuse is recognized, operational definitions of the problem may still be quite diverse, particularly when complicated by multicultural considerations. Some cultural groups do not define the use of substances as atypical or problematic. For example, little universal agreement has been obtained in the complex issue of defining the term alcoholism (Armor, Polich, and Stambul, 1978; Heath, 1982; Pittman, 1982; Westermeyer, 1981).

When addressing issues of assessment in the context of alcohol and other drug use and abuse, a question arises as to the nature of the assessment to be undertaken. Assessment aimed at the level of the individual typically addresses problems of a clinical nature. Within this domain, persons may be identified as needing treatment services due to, or in conjunction with, alcohol and other drug abuse that typically impairs some aspect of daily functioning. The group level of assessment seeks to gather data to enhance our understanding of cultural and community norms while also being able to address issues of prevention of abuse; thereby reducing the rate of alcohol and other drug abuse within various cultural and community groups (Caplan, 1964; Rappaport, 1977; Leukefeld and Bukoski, 1991). This chapter will be devoted to giving the reader an overview of the two levels of assessment as typically conceptualized in the alcohol and substance abuse field.

Individual Assessment Level

As stated above, the primary purpose of alcohol and other drug use assessment at the level of the individual is directed toward treatment. However, the true nature and extent of drug-related problems may be unknown when patients come into contact with treatment professionals. In some cases, the background of a patient is unknown because the referral was for other types of treatment issues (for example, depression or domestic violence) rather than for chemical dependency. In this case, an assessment for alcohol and other drugs should be conducted as part of a general assessment in an exploratory fashion. Likewise, in working with a patient, a clinician who suspects the presence of such a problem needs to seek further data. For the purposes just described, general screening procedures tend to work well.

General screening procedures may identify persons warranting a deeper level of alcohol and substance abuse assessment. In situations when chemical dependencies present themselves as an explicit part of the referral, the assessment should begin at a more thorough level of analysis in order to understand the extent of the substance abuse problem. General screening procedures may be bypassed for more detailed procedures. Both general screening procedures and specific detailed instruments are discussed in this chapter.

Before moving ahead to review procedures of assessment, it is necessary to review a few of the issues related to these instruments and to concepts of multiculturalism. Most of the well-established psychometric development has occurred around alcohol and not other drugs. This is likely due to the acknowledgment of the pandemic nature of problem drinking associated with this legal drug. However, it suggests that there are severe limitations in our ability to find valid and reliable measures of polysubstance use or abuse. Therefore, limited extrapolations may be made from alcohol instruments provided that they can be confirmed by other sources such as a thorough clinical interview, which is always central in this process.

Despite a growing sensitivity to working with individuals from differing cultural backgrounds, little can be found regarding formal assessment issues of diversity in the professional literature. The trend in research is to formulate studies with cross-cultural comparisons on the basis of alcohol or substance use patterns. For example, Williams, Newby, and Kanitz (1993) compared the drinking patterns of African American college students to White students and concluded that alcohol consumption was more of a problem for the White students. Similarly, a five-year, longitudinal study of adolescents belonging to four ethnic groups (White, Asian, Black, Hispanic) resulted in eight identifiable single and multiple substance use patterns (Maddahian, Newcomb, and Bentler, 1985). While interesting, these studies contribute little to developing standardized assessment instruments or procedures, either because ethnic differences and similarities in psychometric properties were not addressed or because nonstandardized measures were used.

Thomas and Schare (in press) studied outpatient alcoholics and medical patient controls in Panama and the United States. Subjects completed standardized drinking measures, the Alcohol Use Inventory (AUI), and the MacAndrew Alcoholism Scale (MAC), as well as other instruments. Panamanian alcoholics were found to drink more for socialization purposes and to experience more alcohol-induced delirium, unusual thinking, feelings of guilt, anxious thoughts, and hangover episodes than the other groups. While this research has limited generalization, it demonstrates that cross-cultural investigations can be undertaken with standardized measures and appropriate controls. It is through this type of work that cultural differences can be studied and understood.

Individualized instruments aimed at assessing specific cultural groups do not exist. Over the years, the inclusion of diverse populations into normative reference groups has served as a control for cultural variance. This approach has been debated for years in the MMPI literature, where individuals have long called for the establishment of culturally sensitive T score corrections or entirely separate norms for diverse groups of people. Despite the apparent strength of the arguments, a major research project on the MMPI has found little variance due to race or culture that substantially biases or distorts the test while using the established norms (Dahlstrom, Lachar, and Dahlstrom, 1986). Furthermore, it was argued that the use of subgroup norms could result in the underidentification of persons truly in need of services. Nonetheless, Dahlstrom, Lachar, and Dahlstrom argue that when a deviant pattern of responding is observed, one should "take special pains to explore in detail the life circumstances of that individual in order to understand as fully as possible the nature and degree of his or her problems and demands" (p. 204). It is this suggestion with which the assessment section will begin.

Interviewing with Multicultural Sensitivity

Ultimately, it is up to the clinician to make a judgment while assessing a patient as to the presence of problems necessitating therapy. Such clinical judgment cannot be made in isolation from the person's cultural background, or from current behavior and medical conditions affected by drug ingestion. In order to understand a person's background, direct, simple questions should be asked regarding the person's cultural, racial, and religious identification. However, simple demographic information alone is insufficient; questions should be wide ranging. For example, one should assess the degree to which "old world" or neighborhood patterns *were* part of the patient's socialization or *are* part of current behavior. The degree of current religious practice and orthodoxy are as important as merely seeking religious identification. All of these issues come to bear on the questions of alcohol and substance abuse.

Cultural contributions in understanding typical alcohol and other drug use behavior patterns must be studied by the clinician conducting the assessment. Information for such study can be obtained from a variety of sources. Obviously, written sources may be obtained as beginning references. One outstanding book (McGoldrick, Pearce, and Giordano, 1982) is titled *Ethnicity and Family Therapy*. It contains chapters written by therapists representative of differing ethnic and racial groups. Many have explicit information on substance use. For example, in her chapter on Irish families, McGoldrick (1982) presents a combination of historical and sociological analysis of the high alcoholism rates of Irish American families that is quite enlightening to the naive reader.

Community-based resources can be used to further understand

cultural contributions to patient's behaviors. Typically, members of the clergy are most helpful when approached for such information. Furthermore, local schools and community centers often have personnel who may be of service in answering questions and suggesting other sources of information. Community mental health centers and social service agencies may also be helpful resources for information.

Specific Instruments

As mentioned earlier, screening instruments serve the purpose of helping identify individuals who may have a substance abuse problem. The advantage of this type of instrument is that it is fairly short and therefore may be rapidly administered. Despite the brevity of such instruments, they have been found to be extremely useful in formulating clinical hypotheses and serving as jumping-off points for more in-depth assessment instruments.

The three instruments presented are screening instruments that are specifically oriented toward alcohol-related issues. They share the characteristic of being quite obvious in the nature of their questions. While specific cultural norms are not readily available for these instruments, their direct behavioral nature renders them less likely to be biased. Of course, the assessor must always be aware of the behavioral norms that are acceptable for any given group.

CAGE

The CAGE questionnaire is an extremely brief screening questionnaire consisting of only four items (Mayfield, McLeod, and Hall, 1974). The name of this instrument is an acronym based on key words from these questions: Have you ever felt you should Cut down on your drinking? Have people Annoyed you by criticizing your drinking? Have you ever felt bad or Guilty about your drinking? Have you ever had a drink first thing in the morning (an Eye-opener) to steady your nerves or get rid of a hangover? In a year-long validation study of hospitalized psychiatric patients, 90 percent of an alcoholic subgroup were correctly identified. The obvious nature of the CAGE clearly leaves the respondent ample opportunity to give socially desirable responses. Yet the developers claim that two or three yes responses were generally obtained from persons who would have had reason to keep their drinking problem hidden.

MODCRIT

The MODCRIT is a thirty-six-item checklist elicited through interview and observation by the rater. The assessor is instructed to give a weighted score on a five-point scale for each test item. This instrument is designed to give the evaluator an explicit indication of the degree to which a patient is manifesting symptoms of an alcohol problem. The name of this test comes from its derivation: it is a modified version of a more extensive form of the criteria for the diagnosis of alcoholism (CRIT) developed in association with the National Council on Alcoholism (Jacobson, 1979). As a briefer form of the original instrument, Jacobson and colleagues have found ample validity and reliability in its use with a variety of populations, including drunk drivers and welfare recipients (Jacobson, Niles, Moberg, Mandehr, and Dusso, 1979; Jacobson and Lindsay, 1980). As with the CAGE, the MODCRIT is quite susceptible to biased responding.

Michigan Alcoholism Screening Test

The Michigan Alcoholism Screening Test (MAST) is one of the best-known alcohol-related behavior screening instruments (Selzer, 1971). The test is a twenty-five-item list of the most common symptoms of alcohol dependence. It is quickly administered, with a score of five or more items usually sufficient to suggest a possible drinking problem. However, as suggested by Jacobson (1979), such a low cutoff might be not most suited to the population that you are targeting and other corroborating information should be sought out. A score of twelve or higher is a likely indicator of an alcohol problem of a substantial magnitude. Many studies of the MAST have found it to be a valid instrument—although as with the other screening instruments mentioned above, the MAST is susceptible to fake responding by patients (Jacobson, 1976, 1979).

Subtle Screening Instruments

The following sections contain scales designed to measure aspects of alcohol and substance use and abuse. Except for the Alcohol Use Inventory, these are quite subtle as to the nature of what is being assessed, unlike the previously reviewed measures. Furthermore, they are based upon the Minnesota Multiphasic Personality Inventory (MMPI) and thus, when given within the context of a full test administration, are not very likely to be individually biased by the test respondent. Unlike the first two measures discussed, these scales are not very behavior-specific but rather reflect personality tendencies. The scales were chosen for this chapter due to the nature of the norms available within the recently published versions of the MMPI.

MacAndrew Scale—Revised

The MacAndrew Scale—Revised (MAC-R) is an empirically criterion-keyed scale originally developed by Craig MacAndrew (1965) for the correct identification of alcoholics within a psychiatric population. The forty-nine-item revision, published with the MMPI-2 (1989), is designed to be a subtle indicator of characteristics associated with alcohol and substance abuse. Unlike the previously discussed screening instruments, the MAC-R cannot be obviously faked by the respondent. However, the validity of the MAC-R score must be considered within the context of the full MMPI validity determination. The MMPI manual suggests that the MAC-R may actually measure people with tendencies of "general-addiction proneness rather than with alcoholic tendencies alone" (p. 38). Research has supported this assertion, finding MAC-R relationships with drug abuse and pathological gambling (Butcher and Williams, 1992). The MAC-R is based upon the

MMPI-2's normative sample, which was specifically designed to reflect the ethnic and racial makeup of the American census based upon proportionality (MMPI-2, 1989). However, although separate ethnic norms are found in the MMPI-2 manual for the main clinical scales, such breakdowns are not provided for the MAC-R.

Addiction Potential Scale

The Addiction Potential Scale (APS) is a newly developed measure based on the MMPI-2 and thus reflects the same multicultural normative base as discussed for the MAC-R. The APS is a thirty-nine-item scale designed to measure personality factors underlying the development of addictive disorders in adults (Weed, Butcher, Ben-Porath, and McKenna, 1992). The content of this new scale overlaps somewhat with that of the MAC-R, and interpretive guidelines can be found in Butcher and Williams (1992). A thirty-six-item version of this scale, called the Alcohol/Drug Problem Proneness scale (PRO) was published with the introduction of the adolescent version of the MMPI, the MMPI-A, in 1992. The actual item content of the PRO is somewhat different from the adult version of the scale, though its expressed purpose is for similar early identification of substance abuse problems (MMPI-A, 1992). As with the MMPI-2, the MMPI-A was developed to include a fair representation of children from diverse cultural backgrounds. However, separate ethnic norms are not provided in the test manual.

Addiction Acknowledgment Scale

The Addiction Acknowledgment Scale (AAS) is another recently developed scale based on the MMPI-2 (Weed and others, 1992). It is a thirteen-item measure designed as an assessment of a person's willingness to acknowledge problems with alcohol or drugs. The interpretative guidelines, found in Butcher and Williams (1992), suggest this scale may also measure a person's self-awareness of problems. An adolescent counterpart of the AAS, published within the MMPI-A, is called the Alcohol/Drug Problem Acknowledgment scale (ACK). The ACK was developed "to assess the willingness of a young person to acknowledge the problematic use of alcohol and other drugs and the symptoms associated with such use" (MMPI-A, 1992, p. 72). As discussed previously, neither the MMPI-2 nor MMPI-A manuals contain racial breakdowns of the norms for these measures, although the normative sample is clearly ethnically diverse.

Alcohol Use Inventory-Revised

A number of extensive instruments for the assessment of alcohol abuse have been developed over the years. Yet, as we have found throughout the process of writing this review, none are specifically aimed at different cultural groups, nor do they appear to contain normative samples with specific racial or ethnic breakdowns. The Alcohol Use Inventory (AUI-R) will be reviewed as an example of the types of measures available.

In its current revised form (Horn, Wanberg, and Foster, 1987; Wanberg, Horn, and Foster, 1977), the AUI-R is made up of 228 forced-choice items. The instrument is multidimensional in nature, with the scoring procedure resulting in seventeen scales representing differing aspects of drinking problems. Furthermore, there are six additional scorable dimensions of alcohol use, based upon composites of the other scales, which are thought to represent more global aspects of alcohol consumption. Within the normative sample of approximately 1,200 people admitted for their first alcohol treatment, African Americans make up 21 percent and Hispanics 8 percent of the group. As discussed in the previous sections regarding the MMPI, separate racial breakdowns are not contained in the test manual.

Summary

The foregoing brief review is not intended to be a comprehensive overview of clinical assessment procedures for people with alcohol or other drug use problems. The reader can easily find this information elsewhere. Its intent is to give some direction to the reader for finding resources that may be more culturally sensitive. However, it should also be apparent that measures have not been and need to be developed with more culturally sensitive components in place, such as normative breakdowns by race.

Group Assessment Level

This section will focus on the assessment of alcohol and other drug problems at the group level for cross-cultural work. Assessment at this level is paramount when one is interested in moving beyond the treatment of alcohol and other drug problems to the prevention of alcohol and other drug problems by identifying those at risk for such problems. The purpose of group-level assessment will be addressed by reviewing several specific measurement instruments that are used in group level assessment; issues related to the reliability and validity of these measurement instruments; issues related to the use of these measurement instruments for diagnostic purposes; and the appropriateness of within- and between-group comparisons using these measurement instruments.

Purpose of Epidemiologic Research

The assessment of alcohol and other drug problems at the group level, such as the assessment of alcohol problems among African, Latino (Hispanic), Asian or European American adults, is often done through epidemiologic research. The purpose of epidemiologic research in the mental health field—more specifically, the alcohol and other drug subfields within mental health—is to identify the incidence and prevalence of alcohol and other drug use and abuse, and the risk factors, such as demographic characteristics, personality characteristics, or lifestyle behaviors, for this use and abuse (for example, see Huba, Wingard, and Bentler, 1980; Leukefeld and Bukoski, 1991; Schaps, Churgin, Palley, Takata, and Cohen, 1980; Tobler, 1986).

Prevalence estimates that are typically used are the respondent's lifetime use, use within the past year (annual use), and use within the past month (current use). Incidence usually refers to the number of new cases of users that arise over a period of time. For example, the number of adults within a given population (such as African American adults age eighteen and older who live in Newark, New Jersey, who are currently experiencing alcohol abuse), the number of new cases of adults who became alcohol abusers during a set time period (e.g., 1989 to 1994), and their risk factors for alcohol abuse can be determined.

Epidemiologic studies are usually community-based surveys with large samples of respondents. One such study, the 1990 National Household Survey on Drug Abuse (NHSDA), which assessed alcohol and other drug use in the general American population of people twelve years and older in the contiguous forty-eight states, used a probability-based, cluster sampling technique to draw a nation-wide sample of 9,259 individuals. Within this sample, 5,241 (56.6 percent) respondents were European American, 1,842 (19.9 percent) were African American, 1,915 (20.7 percent) were Latino (Hispanic) American and 261 (2.8 percent) were "other" American (National Institute on Drug Abuse [NIDA], 1991). Epidemiologic research can encompass single or multiple sites depending upon the nature of the research. For example, an epidemiologic study can be an investigation of drug use among African American homeless adults in a specific city such as Washington, D.C. (Milburn and Booth, 1992), or the NHSDA—which draws samples from a hundred sites across the contiguous United States (NIDA).

Epidemiologic research offers several advantages for investigations of alcohol and other drug use. One advantage is both the prevalence of licit and illicit drug use can be examined simultaneously without respondents being unduly stigmatized or labeled as abusers or addicts. Licit drug use includes the use of substances such as alcohol, nicotine, and prescribed medications, whereas illicit drug use includes the use of substances such as cocaine (crack) or marijuana and the nonmedical use of prescribed drugs. The 1990 NHSDA, for example, queries respondents about their lifetime, annual, and current use of specific illicit drugs, such as marijuana, as well as alcohol, cigarettes, and smokeless tobacco (NIDA, 1991). Moreover, the data from epidemiologic studies are aggregated and comparisons are at the group level. Findings from a survey such as the 1990 NHSDA can be used to compare the current percentage of heavy drinkers (those who had five or more drinks at one time on five or more days during the past month) among European (12.2 percent), African (7.2 percent) and Latino (Hispanic) (9.7 percent) Americans aged eighteen to twenty-five years (NIDA, 1991).

Another advantage of epidemiologic research is that it is a cost-effective way to assess alcohol and other drug use in large samples, since most of the measurement instruments can be administered by trained interviewers who are not clinicians. Furthermore, certain instruments may be self-administered. The sample size for the 1990 NHSDA is 9,259 individuals. A sample of this size is more than sufficient to make intergroup and intragroup comparisons among racial or ethnic groups. Annual cigarette use can be compared between African (28.2 percent) and European (38.3 percent) American women aged eighteen to twenty-five years—an intergroup comparison—or between African American men (30.2 percent) and women (28.2 percent) aged eighteen to twenty-five years—an intragroup comparison (NIDA, 1991). Epidemiologic research, consequently, can be used for the prevention of alcohol and other drug use and abuse as well as treatment, since individuals who are at risk for alcohol and other drug problems can be identified within various populations.

Specific Instruments

Several measurement instruments have been more widely used in epidemiologic studies of alcohol and other drug use. They are the National Household Survey (NHS), the Monitoring the Future survey, and the Diagnostic Interview Schedule (DIS). The former two are used more to assess alcohol and other drug use and the latter is used to assess alcohol and other drug abuse or dependence. All three, however, can be used to examine abuse in terms of quantity, frequency, age of onset, and recency of use. The 1990 version of the NHS also asked specifically about dependence (for example, trying to cut down on use, needing to use larger amounts of the drug, and so on) for several licit and illicit drugs (NIDA, 1991). All three can be used to provide lifetime, annual, and current prevalence rates for use and abuse. Two of these instruments will be described in some detail in the sections that follow.

National Household Survey

The National Household Survey (NHS) is a questionnaire that ascertains the duration, frequency, and quantity of use of illicit drugs (marijuana, cocaine, inhalants, hallucinogens, heroin, and the non-medical use of prescription drugs) and licit drugs (alcohol and nicotine). In addition, information on how drugs are ingested, treatment for drug use, perceptions of risk associated with drug use, perceptions of the availability of drugs, drug dependence, and use of drugs in the workplace is assessed. Demographic information, such as age, gender, race and ethnicity, income, source of income, health insurance, and so forth, is also assessed. Psychological and emotional problems are also ascertained.

The NHS is administered through a face-to-face interview. The interviewer reads the questions and responses to the respondent. Answers to the questions on demographics and psychological or emotional problems are recorded by the respondent, who marks answer sheets that are not seen by the interviewer. The answer sheets are sealed in an envelope by the respondent at the end of the interview. This is done to ensure privacy, maintain confidentiality, and encourage truthfulness. The NHS is designed for respondents aged twelve and older.

Diagnostic Interview Schedule

The Diagnostic Interview Schedule (DIS) was designed for use in epidemiologic research for nonclinicians to make clinical diagnoses that are commonly used by psychiatrists and psychologists (Robins,

Helzer, Croughan, and Ratcliff, 1981). The DIS has two subscales that assess alcohol and other drug use or abuse and dependence. Specific items ascertain heavy drinking behavior, behavioral and physiological problems associated with drinking, help-seeking for problem drinking, use of other drugs, age of onset of other drug use, frequency of drug use, perceptions about drug dependence, and physical, emotional, and behavioral problems associated with drug use.

The DIS is administered through a face-to-face interview. The interviewer records the respondent's answers to the questions. The questions are asked within the context of other questions about behaviors and symptoms related to mental health disorders.

Epidemiologic research is widely used in group-level assessments of alcohol and other drug use, but there are problems associated with this type of research. These include: reliability and validity issues, specificity versus severity issues, and within- versus between-group comparison issues.

Reliability-Validity Issues

Epidemiologic research relies heavily on self-report measures. Self-report measures of alcohol and other drug use and abuse have been criticized about the underreporting of use and abuse (Mensch and Kandel, 1988). Procedures have been implemented to minimize underreporting, including assessing use with multiple items, having multiple informants, having respondents self-record, adding physiological measures, and using the "bogus pipeline procedure" wherein respondents are led to believe they will be assessed through physiological measures (Johnston and O'Malley, 1986; Forman and Linney, 1991). The NHS, for example, tries to minimize underreporting by relying on multiple items and having respondents record their responses so the interviewer is not aware of their answers.

Specificity-Severity

Concerns have also been raised about the appropriateness of the measurement instruments that have been used in epidemiologic research as "gold standards" for diagnostic purposes. Some researchers question whether these measurement instruments provide sufficient information to accurately diagnose a disorder. Does the DIS, for example, provide an adequate assessment for diagnosing alcohol abuse? Research suggests that it does (Robins and others, 1981). Moreover, such instruments are needed to do large-scale, community-based research on alcohol and other drug use where it would not be feasible to rely solely on clinicians for data collection.

Intergroup-Intragroup Comparisons

Epidemiologic research has been used primarily to make intergroup comparisons to identify ethnic or racial differences in alcohol and other drug use and abuse, so as to determine groups whose members are most at risk for alcohol and other drug problems. For example, alcohol abuse rates for African Americans are compared to those for Hispanic, Asian, or European American youth (for example, Bachman, and others, 1991). This type of research has been important for determining groups to target for interventions (Trimble, Padilla, and Bell, 1987). Intragroup comparisons that look at within-group differences in specific ethnic or racial groups are more appropriate to develop the best interventions. Comparisons to determine risk factors would involve, for example, comparing native-born African Americans to immigrant African Americans from the Caribbean or comparing African Americans across social class, educational attainment, and ethnic identity characteristics. Such comparisons can be done in the context of epidemiologic studies.

In summary, assessment at the group level is an important component of the investigation of alcohol and other drug use; especially when multicultural issues are taken into account. The measurement instruments that were reviewed were by no means an exhaustive list of measures, but they are some of the more well-known epidemiologic tools. Other measures, such as the MAST (discussed in the individual assessment section) have been used in community-based studies. What distinguishes individual and group level assessment measures is the use of the results; whether they are used to identify individuals for immediate treatment and therapy or used to identify groups for future intervention and treatment.

Concluding Comments

Despite a growing sensitivity to multicultural issues, the general area of assessment concerning alcohol and other drug use has been slow to develop. For the clinician to be effective, assessment procedures for a given individual must include information about the specific cultural beliefs and norms of behavior regarding alcohol and other drug ingestion. A cultural understanding, along with the necessary specific quantity and frequency information of drug and alcohol consumption, will allow a clinician to effectively identify, diagnose, and work with problematic individuals. The clinical assessment literature needs to develop more culturally sensitive norms and instruments to reflect the diversity of patient backgrounds.

Epidemiologic research may ultimately provide clinicians with a better understanding of cultural norms regarding the ingestion of alcohol and other drugs. Yet the goal of such research is more oriented toward the prevention of alcohol and other drug problems by identifying those at risk for such problems through inter- and intragroup comparisons. As the individual (clinical) and group (epidemiological) levels of assessment interact, a greater multicultural sensitivity will develop, promoting improved assessment procedures for all.

References

Armor, D., Polich, M., & Stambul, H. (1978). *Alcohol and treatment*. New York: Wiley.

Bachman, J. G., Wallace, J. M., O'Malley, P. M., Johnson, L. D., Kurth, C. L., & Neighbors, W. (1991). Racial/ethnic differences in smoking, drinking and illicit drug use among American high school seniors, 1976–89. *American Journal of Public Health, 79*, 634–636.

Brecher, E. M. (1972). *Licit and illicit drugs*. Boston: Little, Brown.

Butcher, J. N., & Williams, C. L. (1992). *Essentials of MMPI-2 and MMPI-A interpretation*. Minneapolis: University of Minnesota Press.

Caplan, G. (1964). *Principles of preventive psychiatry*. New York: Basic Books.

Dahlstrom, W. G., Lachar, D., & Dahlstrom, L. E. (1986). *MMPI patterns of American minorities*. Minneapolis: University of Minnesota Press.

Forman, S. G., & Linney, J. A. (1991). Increasing the validity of self-report data in effectiveness trials. In *Drug abuse prevention intervention research: Methodological issues-NIDA Research Monograph #107* (ADM 91–1761) (pp. 235–247). Rockville, MD: National Institute of Drug Abuse.

Gilbert, R. J. (1986). *Caffeine: The most popular stimulant*. New York: Chelsea.

Heath, D. (1982). Sociocultural variants in alcoholism. In E. Pattison & E. Kaufman (Eds.), *Encyclopedic handbook of alcoholism* (pp. 426–440). New York: Gardner Press.

Horn, J. L., Wanberg, K. W., & Foster, F. M. (1987). *Guide to the Alcohol Use Inventory*, Minneapolis, MN: National Computer Systems.

Huba, G. J., Wingard, J. A., & Bentler, P. M. (1980). Applications of a theory of drug use to prevention programs. *Journal of Drug Education, 10*(1), 25–38.

Jacobson, G. R. (1976). *The alcoholisms: detection, assessment, and diagnosis*. New York: Human Sciences Press.

Jacobson, G. R. (1979). Identification and assessment of problem drinkers. In *Proceedings of the 2nd National DWI Conference* (pp 35–43). Falls Church, VA: AAA Foundation for Traffic Safety.

Jacobson, G. R., & Lindsay, D. (1980). Screening for alcohol problems among the unemployed. In M. Galanter (Ed.), *Currents in alcoholism: Vol. 7. Recent advances in research and treatment* (pp. 357–371). Philadelphia: Grune & Stratton.

Jacobson, G. R., Niles, D. H., Moberg, D. P., Mandehr, E., & Dusso, L. (1979). Identifying alcoholic problem-drinking drivers: Wisconsin's field test of a modified NCA Criteria for the diagnosis of alcoholism. In M. Galanter (Ed.), *Currents in alcoholism: Vol. 6. Recent advances in research and treatment* (pp. 273–293). Philadelphia: Grune & Stratton.

Johnston, L. D., & O'Malley, P. M. (1986). Why do the nation's students use drugs and alcohol: Self-reported reasons from nine national surveys. *Journal of Drug Issues, 16*, 29–66.

Leukefeld, C. G., & Bukoski, W. J. (1991). *Drug abuse prevention intervention research: Methodological issues*. (NIDA Research Monograph 107). Washington, DC: U.S. Government Printing Office.

MacAndrew, C. (1965). The differentiation of male alcoholic outpatients from nonalcoholic psychiatric outpatients by means of the MMPI. *Quarterly Journal of Studies on Alcohol, 26*, 238–246.

Maddahian, E., Newcomb, M. D., & Bentler, P. M. (1985). Single and multiple patterns of adolescent substance use: longitudinal comparisons of four ethnic groups. *Journal of Drug Education, 15*, 311–326.

Mayfield, D., McLeod, G., & Hall, P. (1974). The CAGE questionnaire: validation of a new alcoholism screening instrument. *American Journal of Psychiatry, 131*, 1121–1123.

McGoldrick, M. (1982). Irish families. In M. McGoldrick, J. K. Pearce, & J. Giordano (Eds.), *Ethnicity and family therapy* (pp. 310–339). New York: Guilford.

McGoldrick, M., Pearce, J. K., & Giordano, J. (1982). *Ethnicity and family therapy*. New York: Guilford.

Mensch, B. S., & Kandel, D. B. (1988). Under reporting of substance use in a national longitudinal cohort. *Public Opinion Quarterly, 47*, 557–566.

Milburn, N. G., & Booth, J. A. (1992). Illicit drug and alcohol use among homeless Black adults in shelters. *Drugs and Society, 6*(1), 115–155.

MMPI-A (1992). *Minnesota Multiphasic Personality Inventory-A, manual for administration, scoring, and interpretation*. Minneapolis: University of Minnesota Press.

MMPI-2 (1989). *Minnesota Multiphasic Personality Inventory-2, manual for administration and scoring*. Minneapolis: University of Minnesota Press.

National Institute on Drug Abuse. (1991). *National Household Survey on Drug Abuse: Main findings*. (DHHS Publication No. ADM 91–1788). Washington, DC: U.S. Government Printing Office.

Pittman, D. (1982). The police court system and the public intoxication offender. In E. Pattison & E. Kaufman (Eds.), *Encyclopedic handbook of alcoholism* (pp. 938–945). New York: Gardner Press.

Poznanski, A. (1959). Our drinking heritage. In R. G. McCarthy, (Ed.), *Drinking and intoxication* (pp. 42–43). New Haven, CT: College and University Press.

Preble, E., & Laury, G. V. (1967). Plastic cement: The ten cent hallucinogen. *International Journal of the Addictions, 3*, 271–272.

Rappaport, J. (1977). *Community psychology: Values, research, and action*. New York: Holt, Rinehart & Winston.

Robins, L. N., Helzer, J. E., Croughan, J., & Ratcliff, K. S. (1981). National Institute of Mental Health Diagnostic Interview Schedule. *Archives of General Psychiatry, 38*, 381–389.

Schaps, E., Churgin, S., Palley, C. S., Takata, B., & Cohen, A. Y. (1980). Primary prevention research: A preliminary review of program outcome studies. *International Journal of the Addictions, 15 (5)*, 657–676.

Selzer, M. L. (1971). The Michigan Alcoholism Screening Test: The quest for a new diagnostic instrument. *American Journal of Psychiatry, 127*, 89–94.

Snyder, C. R. (1958). *Alcohol and the Jews.* New York: Free Press.

Thomas, T., & Schare, M. L. (in press). An analysis of alcoholism and social alienation in Panama and the United States. *International Journal of Psychology Research.*

Tobler, N. S. (1986). Meta-analysis of 143 adolescent drug prevention programs: Quantitative outcome results of program participants compared to a control or comparison group. *Journal of Drug Issues, 16*, 537–568.

Trimble, J. E., Padilla, A. M., & Bell, C. S. (1987). *Drug Abuse Among Ethnic Minorities* (DHHS Publication No. ADM 87–1474). Rockville, MD: U.S. Government Printing Office.

Wanberg, K. W., Horn, J. L., & Foster, M. F. (1977). A differential assessment model for alcoholism: The scales of the Alcohol Use Inventory. *Journal of Studies on Alcohol, 38*, 512–543.

Waylan, L., & Mintz, N. L. (1976). Ethnic differences in family attitudes towards psychotic manifestations. *International Journal of Social Psychiatry, 22*, 86–95.

Weed, N. C., Butcher, J. N., Ben-Porath, Y. S., & McKenna, T. (1992). New measures for assessing alcohol and drug abuse with the MMPI-2: The APS and AAS. *Journal of Personality Assessment, 58*, 389–410.

Westermeyer, J. (1981). Research on treatment of drinking problems: Importance of cultural factors in alcoholism. In D. Heath, J. Waddell, and M. Topper (Eds.), Cultural factors in alcohol research and treatment of drinking problems. *Journal of Studies on Alcohol* (Suppl. 9), *42*, 44.

Williams, J. E., Newby, R. G., & Kanitz, H. E. (1993). Assessing the need for alcohol abuse programs for African-American college students. *Journal of Multicultural Counseling and Development, 21*, 155–167.

World Health Organization. (1989). *World health statistics annual.* Geneva: Author.

16

Vocational Assessment Across Cultures

S. Alvin Leung

Vocational assessment is viewed as an indispensable step in the process of career counseling (Walsh, 1990). An accurate vocational assessment is a prerequisite for effective career intervention. A survey of the literature on career assessment and counseling (for example, Herr, 1988; Herr and Cramer, 1992; Zunker, 1994) suggests at least three major purposes for vocational assessment. First, in the context of career intervention, vocational assessment provides the counselor with useful information (for example, aptitudes, interests, vocational maturity) about an individual or a group of individuals that are useful in formulating intervention goals and objectives. Second, assessment information (such as aptitudes and interests) can be used to predict the probabilities that an individual may attain future success and satisfaction in different educational and occupational areas. Third, vocational assessment devices can be used to evaluate the effectiveness and outcomes of career intervention programs, including individual and group-oriented programs. Vocational assessment often involves the use of standardized instruments. Several categories of tests are commonly used for vocational assessment, including measures of interests, aptitudes, values, personalities, vocational development, and decision making.

The quality of vocational assessment is affected by a number of factors, including the appropriateness of the selected tests in meeting the needs of the client, the reliability and validity of these test instruments, and the ability of a counselor to accurately interpret the test scores and use them to benefit a client. An important factor to consider in the selection, administration, and interpretation of vocational tests is the cultural background of a test taker. Many assessment instruments commonly used in vocational assessment are developed from a Euro-American cultural perspective, and may not be appropriate for racial or cultural minorities whose perspectives about work are different. Also, many counselors are not adequately trained in multicultural counseling, and consequently are not able to accurately interpret the test scores in light of the cultural background of a client.

The purpose of this chapter is to examine vocational assessment with culturally different individuals. Due to the limitation in length, the focus of this chapter is primarily on assessing members of minority groups in the United States in the context of career counseling intervention. In the first section, the research on the use of vocational assessment instruments with ethnic minorities is examined. In the second section, some guidelines on multicultural vocational assessment, including the use and interpretation of test information, are discussed. In the third section, a case example is used to illustrate vocational assessment with an ethnic minority person. In the fourth section, some directions for future research are suggested.

Vocational Assessment Instruments

There are at least three major issues concerning the use of vocational tests across cultures. The first issue is related to the concurrent and predictive validity of vocational assessment instruments. For example, one of the major functions of vocational interest inventories is to predict occupational choice and satisfaction, yet there is some evidence suggesting that the predictive validity of interest inventories might be lower for minority persons than for White individuals (see Carter and Swanson, 1990). A second issue is related to differences in test scores between Whites and ethnic minorities. For example, some studies have found differences between Whites and ethnic minority individuals in career interest scores (see Hansen, 1987), and in career maturity scores (for example, Leong, 1991a; Westbrook, Cutts, Madison, and Arcia, 1980). Differences in scores between Whites and ethnic minorities could be due to biases in testing instruments, and could lead to inaccurate conclusions about the test taker. The third issue is related to the theoretical structure of testing instruments. Most vocational assessment instruments are based on theoretical structures that reflect a Eurocentric world view. The use of theoretical models inappropriate for minority members could result in inaccurate data and conclusions about individuals.

It is only in the past ten to fifteen years that researchers and practitioners have become aware of the potential biases of vocational assessment instruments against culturally different individuals. Only a limited number of research studies are available in the literature about cross-cultural vocational assessment, and most studies in this body of literature have examined the use of interest inventories across cultures. These studies and their implications are examined in this section. Also, selected research studies related to the use of career development and choice process instruments are examined. Due to the limitation in the length of this chapter, several categories of instruments that are used in vocational assessment, including personality, aptitude, and values tests, are not reviewed in this chapter.

Vocational Interest Inventories

The most commonly used category of vocational assessment instruments is interest inventories. The assessment of vocational interest is based on a trait-factor assumption that career satisfaction could best be attained by matching the interests of an individual with the characteristics of occupations. In recent years, this trait-factor assumption has been further expanded to become a person-environment-fit perspective, in which the goal of interest assessment is to maximize the match between a person and the characteristics of the work environment (Holland, 1985a; Rounds and Tracey, 1990). Existing research studies on the cross-cultural assessment of interests have focused mainly on the Strong Interest Inventory (Hansen and Campbell, 1985) and the Self-Directed Search (Holland, 1985c).

Strong Interest Inventory

The Strong Interest Inventory (SII) is the most popular interest inventory (Zytowski and Warman, 1982). Hansen (1986) indicated that about one million Strong profiles are scored annually. The most current version of the SII is the fourth edition (Hansen and Campbell, 1985). The SII is designed for a wide spectrum of individuals who are making educational, career, and lifestyle decisions, including high school and college students, adults, career changers, and individuals who are returning to work. The SII is one of the most researched assessment instruments (Walsh and Betz, 1990), and its reliability and validity have been well documented in the research literature (Hansen, 1986; Hansen and Campbell, 1985).

The SII provides the user with a variety of information. There are 6 General Occupational Themes (GOT), 23 Basic Interest Scales (BIS), and 207 Occupational Scales representing 106 different occupations. The GOT, BIS, and the Occupational scales are organized according to the Holland (1973; 1985a) theory of vocational interest in which vocational interests are organized into six different types: Realistic, Investigative, Artistic, Social, Enterprising, and Conventional. These six vocational interest types are often represented by the acronym RIASEC. The RIASEC ordering of interests is presented in a hexagonal model in which the degrees of similarities and dissimilarities between any two interest types are indicated by the distance between the types in the hexagon.

An Introversion-Extraversion scale provides information about preferences in terms of working with ideas, things, and people. An Academic Comfort scale provides information about a person's degree of interest in an academic environment. Several Administrative Indexes provide information about the validity of the profile. Information about the SII scales, and the reliability and validity of the instrument, is presented in the SII Manual (Hansen and Campbell, 1985) and User's Guide (Hansen, 1992a).

A number of studies have investigated the validity of the SII among Black Americans (for a review, see Carter and Swanson, 1990). In a study by Borgen and Harper (1973), the Strong Vocational Interest Blank (SVIB), an early edition of the SII, was administered to a sample of Black and White male National Merit Scholars, and a follow-up on the participants was performed after three years. Borgen and Harper (1973) found that the Occupational scales were equally valid for both racial groups. The use of a multiple discriminant function method revealed that the percentage of accurate prediction using the Basic Interest scales was higher than chance prediction, and the hit rates were higher for Whites than for Blacks. One limitation of this study was the use of a highly gifted college student sample, and the results might not be generalized to a general college student sample. Whetstone and Hayles (1975) examined the concurrent validity of the SVIB profile for White and Black male college students. They asked raters to judge if the declared majors of students were consistent, questionable, or inconsistent with their SVIB profiles. The SVIB was found to be predictive of the college majors of both racial groups. Both of these two studies support the predictive validity of the SVIB for Black American students.

In a study by Swanson (1992), the SII scores of a sample of African American college students were compared with the men-in-general and women-in-general normative sample of the SII. Swanson (1992) found that African American women scored higher than the women-in-general sample on the GOT Social scale, and higher than the combined-gender normative sample on the Realistic, Investigative, and Artistic scales. African American men scored higher than the men-in-general sample on the Social,

Enterprising, and Conventional scales, and scored lower than the combined-gender normative sample on the Realistic scale. Swanson (1992) also performed a multidimensional scaling (MDS) procedure using the GOT scores to examine the structure of interests of the African American students. For females, a good fit was found between the data and the RIASEC hexagonal framework by Holland (1973; 1985a). The degree of fit between the data and Holland's model was less for male students, and the resultant configuration supported the RIASEC ordering, but not the hexagonal shape. Swanson's (1992) study supports the construct validity of the SII among African American college students.

The use of the SII among Hispanic Americans has also been examined in a number of research studies. The first was a study by Hansen and Fouad (1984) to establish a valid translation of a Spanish version of the SII. A three-step procedure was used consisting of translation, back-translation, and field-testing. Hansen and Fouad found high correlations between the correspondent scales of the two language versions of the SII in a group of Hispanic and Anglo bilingual students and adults. No differences were found between the correspondent scale scores (a total of 220 scales) of the two language versions. Also, there was no difference between the two language versions at the level of individual profile. These findings support the equivalence of the two language versions of the SII.

In a study by Fouad, Cudeck, and Hansen (1984), a confirmatory factor analysis was performed on the Spanish and English SII, utilizing responses from a group of Hispanic, bilingual high school students. The resultant factor structure supported the validity of Holland's (1973, 1985a) hexagonal model of interests among Hispanic students.

In a series of studies, Fouad and colleagues (Fouad and Dancer, 1992; Fouad and Hansen, 1987; Fouad, Hansen, and Arias, 1986, 1989) examined the structure of interest among Mexican engineering students and professionals. The findings from these studies support the cross-cultural validity of the SII for Hispanic persons.

First, the predictive accuracy of the Spanish SII was equal for both the Mexican and U.S. engineer samples, suggesting that the norms and scales of the SII are valid for Mexicans (Fouad and Hansen, 1987). Second, the structures of interests of Mexican engineering students and professionals were similar to their counterparts in the U.S. (for example, Fouad and Dancer, 1992), except that for Mexican engineering students, the ordering of the GOT themes deviated slightly from the Holland framework. Third, there were more similarities between Mexican and U.S. engineers than between Mexicans in different occupations (Fouad and others, 1986). Fourth, there were differences between Mexican and U.S. engineers in some SII themes (for example, medical services, social services) that might be related to differences in avocational interests (Fouad and others, 1989). A limitation of these research studies is that only male engineering students and professionals were included. Further research is needed to validate the SII on males and females from other selected occupational groups (for example, selected Social Occupations).

Several studies examined the cross-cultural validity of the SII for Asian Americans. D. W. Sue and Kirk (1972) compared the SVIB interest profiles of Chinese American students with the rest of the 1966 incoming freshmen at the University of California, Berkeley. Chinese American male students were more interested in physical sciences, skill technical trades, and business occupations than other male students, but were less interested in social service and welfare, sales, and verbal-linguistic occupations than the latter. Chinese female students were more interested in technical-applied fields, biological and physical sciences, business and office activities than other female students, and they were less interested than the latter in aesthetic-cultural fields, social sciences, and verbal-linguistic occupations. In another study using the same Berkeley freshmen data base, D. W. Sue and Kirk (1973) compared the interest patterns of Chinese and Japanese American students as measured by the SVIB. While there were many areas of similarity between the two groups, Japanese Americans as a group were more similar to the White students than Chinese American students. D. W. Sue and Kirk (1973) explained the observed differences in interests between the two Asian student groups in terms of differences in levels of acculturation.

While the studies by D. W. Sue and Kirk (1972, 1973) were descriptive in nature and the validity of the Strong was not tested directly, a recent study by Haverkamp, Collins, and Hansen (1994) used a multidimensional scaling (MDS) procedure to analyze the GOT scores of the SII to examine the interest structure of Asian American college students. The MDS configurations for both males and females did not support the Holland hexagonal ordering of the six interest types. Haverkamp and others (1994) suggested that the MDS configurations revealed three occupational clusters, which were Artistic, Realistic-Investigative, and Social-Enterprising-Convention. These findings questioned the validity of the SII for Asian Americans.

The validity of the SII among American Indians was examined in a study by Haviland and Hansen (1987). The authors examined how well the GOT score of the SII predicted the declared college major of a sample of American Indian college students. The hit rates for women and men were 64 percent and 44 percent, respectively. Haviland and Hansen (1987) suggest that these findings supported the concurrent validity of the Strong for American Indians. The lower hit rate for male students was explained in terms of a tendency for male American Indian students to lack persistence in completing college.

The Self-Directed Search

The Self-Directed Search (SDS) is one of the most widely used interest inventories (for example, see Zytowski and Warman, 1982). The SDS is based on Holland's theory (1973; 1985a) of vocational interests. The SDS is divided into five sections: Occupational Daydreams, Activities, Competencies, Occupations, and Self-Estimates.

The Occupational daydream section asks the test takers to report occupations they have considered. In each of the other sections, items are arranged according to the six Holland interest types, and a respondent indicates either like or dislike for each item. Afterward, the test taker computes a total score for each of the six Holland interest types in the summary score section. The summary scores are then transformed into a three-letter interest code.

The SDS has several unique features. First, the SDS is an example of what Spokane (1990) called a "self-guided interest inventory." It can be self-administered, self-scored, and self-interpreted. The test taker receives immediate feedback on the test. Second, Holland (1985c) suggested that taking the SDS is a process of vocational counseling for those who do not want (or do not have access to) a counselor. Third, the SDS summary scores and profile can be interpreted without referring to a normative comparison group. The test taker is instructed to explore occupations suggested by the three-letter code, and other combinations of the three letters if necessary (Holland, 1985c). The test user is encouraged to use the Occupations Finder (Holland, 1985d) and the College Majors Finders (Holland, 1985e) to identify occupational and educational alternatives suggested by the interest code. A large volume of research has been accumulated about the validity of Holland's theory and that of the SDS (see Holland, 1985a, 1985c; Holland and Rayman, 1986).

The SDS has been adapted and translated into twenty languages (Holland and Gottfredson, 1992). A number of studies were mentioned in the SDS Manual (Holland, 1985c) supporting the international use of the SDS. However, the amount of published research about its application for ethnic minorities in the United State is still quite limited.

Kimball, Sedlacek, and Brooks (1973) investigated the use of the SDS among Black and White college students and found that both groups were equally satisfied with the experience. The authors also found that Black students were more likely than White students to obtain higher Social scores, whereas White students were more likely to score higher in the Realistic and Investigative areas.

The SDS was found to have predictive validity for Black Americans. In a study by O'Brien and Walsh (1976), the SDS and another inventory developed by Holland, called the Vocational Preference Inventory (VPI; Holland, 1985f), were administered to a sample of Black males in a variety of occupations, including maintenance persons, X-ray technicians, musician-entertainers, youth leaders, salespersons, and inventory clerks. The SDS interest codes were found to correspond to the Holland occupational codes assigned to the actual occupations of the participants. In another study, Ward and Walsh (1981) found that the SDS high-point codes of a sample of nondegreed Black women (teacher aides, sales clerks, and clerk-typists) were accurate in predicting the occupational code of their actual occupations. It was also found that the Social scores of the participants were generally higher than the other SDS scale scores, regardless of their chosen occupational areas.

Two studies compared the SDS scores of Black and White participants and reported no racial effects. Walsh, Bingham, Horton, and Spokane (1979) compared the SDS scores (only Realistic, Investigative, and Enterprising scales) of a sample of college-degreed Black women engineers, physicians, and lawyers, with a comparison sample of White women. The Investigative scale of the SDS was found to differentiate between the three occupational groups, but no difference between Black and White participants was found in the SDS scores. In another study, Hecht (1980) examined the SDS profiles of Black and White nursing students and found no differences between the two racial groups in the SDS scales.

The use of the SDS for a group of American Indian high school students was examined by Gade, Fuqua, and Hurlburt (1984). The high school students consisted of two groups. The first group attended schools in an all-White district using a compensatory educational model. The second group consisted of students who attended schools that use an integrative model in which the Indian cultural heritage was promoted. Significant differences in the Realistic, Social, and Conventional scales of the SDS were found between the Native American sample and the normative sample. There were also differences between the two American Indian samples in the Social, Conventional, and Investigative scales. Students educated under a compensatory model were more likely than students educated under an integrative model and the SDS normative group to have inconsistent SDS interest codes and a restricted range of occupational interests. The authors attributed the observed differences in SDS scores between the two American Indian samples to differences in cultural and socialization experiences. Based on the above findings, Gade and others (1984) suggest that local norms should be developed for American Indian students.

Summary

The research studies conducted so far have supported the use of the SII and SDS in cross-cultural assessment. On the SII, there is a body of research to support the predictive and construct validity of the instrument for ethnic minority groups. An interesting development is the publication of three recent studies that examined the structure of vocational interests of Black Americans (Swanson, 1992), Hispanic Americans (Fouad and Dancer, 1992), and Asian Americans (Haverkamp and others, 1994). All three studies have identified some aspects of the interest structures of ethnic minority groups that deviated from the Holland hexagonal model, which is the conceptual framework of the SII. Hansen (1992b) examined some of the above research studies and suggested that these deviations may represent important aspects of the vocational interests among ethnic minorities. It is important for researchers to further explore the implications of these findings on the development and use of interest inventories among diverse cultural groups (Hansen, 1992b).

The research on the use of the SDS with ethnic minorities has identified some evidence indicating both predictive and concurrent validity. However, most of the existing research has been confined to Black Americans, and research studies with other ethnic groups are needed. Overall, additional research is needed to investigate the construct validity of the instrument for minority populations.

Career Development Instruments

A category of career assessment instruments commonly used in career counseling is career development and choice process scales. A number of career development and choice process instruments are available (see Betz, 1988 and Savickas, 1990 for reviews), such as the Career Maturity Inventory (Crites, 1978), the Career Decision Scale (Osipow, 1987), and the My Vocational Situation (Holland, Daiger, and Power, 1980). Career development and choice process instruments are useful in two ways. First, these instruments provide information about one's readiness (for example, career maturity) in making career-related decisions. If a client is not ready to make a career decision (for example, due to insufficient motivation or limited exposure to the world of work), an assessment of vocational interest may not produce meaningful information (Super, 1983; Savickas, 1990). Second, career development and choice process instruments provide information about barriers one encounters in the career decision-making process. The elimination of these barriers is essential before one can make appropriate career choices.

Only a small number of studies have examined the use of career development and choice process instruments with ethnic minority groups. Most of these studies have focused on the Career Maturity Inventory (Crites, 1978). Several studies have also examined the cross-cultural use of the My Vocational Situation (Holland and others, 1980). These research studies are summarized in the following section.

The Career Maturity Inventory

The construct of career maturity was first proposed by Super (1957) in his theory of career development. Based on Super's theoretical work, Crites (1978) developed a hierarchical and multidimensional model of career maturity. The Career Maturity Inventory (CMI) was developed to measure two major components in this model, career choice competencies and career choice attitudes. The Competence scale of the CMI consists of five subscales: Self Appraisal, Occupational Information, Goal Selection, Planning, and Problem Solving. The Attitude scale of the CMI consists of five subscales: Decisiveness, Involvement, Independence, Orientation, and Compromise. Reviews about the reliability and validity of the CMI have been mixed (for example, see Betz, 1988; Katz, 1978; Westbrook and others, 1980). There are concerns about the validity of the subscales, the high correlations between the subscales, and the high correlations with measures of cognitive ability and career decision.

The majority of studies on the cross-cultural use of the CMI used a descriptive approach and compared the CMI scores of Black and White students. The findings of these studies suggested quite consistently that there were differences in the CMI scores between the two racial groups. Westbrook and others (1980) report two studies that involved samples of ninth graders and technical college students. For both samples, significant differences in the CMI scores (Attitudes and Competence scales) between Black and White students were found. Westbrook and others suggests the need for separate CMI norms for ethnic minority groups. Similar differences in the Attitude and Competence scales between Black and White high school students were found in a study by Westbrook and Sanford (1991). A study by Westbrook, Sanford, Merwin, Fleenor, and Gilleland (1988) found that Black ninth graders scored lower than the White students on the Goal Selection subscale of the Competence scale. In a related study by Westbrook, Sanford, Gilleland, Fleenor, and Merwin (1988), Black students were found to score lower than White students in the Appraisal subscale of the competency scale.

Leong (1991a) used a descriptive approach and found that the CMI-Attitude scale scores of a group of Asian American college students were lower than the scores from a comparison group of White students. Leong (1991b) cautioned that the lower CMI scores could be due to the cultural values of Asian students, rather than developmental deficits.

The differences in scores in career maturity between Whites and racial minority groups should be interpreted cautiously. Smith (1975, 1983) argued that the construct of career maturity was based on a set of White middle-class assumptions that might not be applicable to ethnic minorities. For example, a study by Smith (1976) demonstrated that the CMI scores of a group of Black high school students from a lower socioeconomic background were related to the reference group orientations of the students. Students who adopted a middle-class reference group orientation scored higher than those who adopted a lower-class reference group orientation. Smith (1976) suggested that the CMI measured career maturity based on middle-class work values, and might not be appropriate for Black students who came from a lower socioeconomic level. Accordingly, because of possible racial and social class biases related to the construct of career maturity, lower CMI scores among minority clients when compared to the normative sample might reflect cultural differences in career planning and decision making, rather than deficits in career development.

My Vocational Situation

The My Vocational Situation (MVS; Holland and others, 1980) consists of three scales. The Vocational Identity scale (VI, eighteen true-false items) measures the degree to which an individual possesses a clear and stable picture of career goals, interests, personality, and talents. The Occupational Information scale (four true-false items) measures a person's need for vocational information, and the

Barriers scale (four true-false items) measures perception of external obstacles to chosen occupational goals. A recent article by Holland, Johnson, and Asama (1993) summarized the existing research about the reliability and validity of the MVS.

The career development of racial minorities is affected by variables such as racial identity development and societal barriers (Leung, 1995). The constructs of vocational identity, information needs, and barriers measured by the MVS have the potential to be relevant for ethnic minorities. However, only a small number of studies have examined the use of the MVS among ethnic minorities. In a study by Leong (1991a), the VI scale of the MVS was administered to a group of Asian American college students along with two other career development and values measures. The scores of the Asian American students were compared to the scores of a group of White students. No difference was found on the VI scores between the two racial groups, which supports the cross-cultural use of the MVS. In another study by Mosley-Howard and Anderson (1993), the MVS was administered to a group of auto workers who were laid off by the auto plant, including a small subgroup of African Americans. The workers in this sample scored significantly lower than the MVS normative sample in all the three MVS scales. Also, the MVS scores of African American workers were lower than the other workers. It is unclear whether the racial differences in the MVS scores were due to race-related or other variables. Lastly, a study by Miller and Wells (1988) examined the VI scale scores of a group of lower SES African American teenagers. Neither gender nor age differences in vocational identity were found. Age differences in vocational identity were expected because of the developmental nature of the constructs.

Summary

As a whole, the amount of research examining the reliability and validity of the CMI and MVS among ethnic minorities is insufficient. Counselors should be cautious in drawing conclusions regarding possible deficits based on the scores of clients. There is a need for more research to examine the cross-cultural applications of not just the two instruments mentioned in this section, but other instruments that are used in measuring career development and decision making.

Guidelines for Career Assessment with Ethnic Minorities

Betz (1990) suggests that the goal of assessment for individuals from all segments of our society is to enhance self-development and occupational success. The following are some guidelines that can maximize the benefits of ethnic minority clients in career assessment.

Training in Multicultural Counseling and Career Development

Counselors need to understand the cultural backgrounds and characteristics of minority clients, including world views, values, beliefs, immigration history, acculturation, and racial identity. Formal training in multicultural counseling, including training in racial attitudes awareness, cultural knowledge, and cross-cultural counseling theories and techniques, is a necessary prerequisite for counselors who engage in cross-cultural career assessment (for example, Pederson, 1988; D. W. Sue, Arredondo, and McDavis, 1992). In addition to course work in measurement, assessment, and career development, the counselor should be familiar with the current literature on the career development of ethnic minorities (for example, Leong, 1991b; Leung, 1995; Savickas, 1993; Smith, 1983). All of the above constitute a necessary theoretical and technical foundation for effective career assessment and counseling.

Instrument Selection

Career assessment should be preceded by a thorough interview to determine the needs of a client. It is important for counselors to select the instrument that can provide useful information related to the vocational needs of the client. The counselor should be familiar with the intended purposes and structure of an instrument, as well as its technical strengths and limitations, such as norms, reliability, and validity (Womer, 1988), especially in relation to the use of this instrument with ethnic minorities. For minority clients whose native language is not English, the language ability of the test taker should be assessed to see if the language level of the selected instrument is appropriate. Most interest inventories consist of items with occupational titles. Individuals who are socialized in a cultural background different from the United States may not be familiar with these titles, or may attach different meanings to them based on their cultural backgrounds and experience. In administering career instruments to a non-native-English speaker, the effects of language and cultural experience on the comprehension of test items should be assessed before test administration and during the test interpretation process.

A number of career interest inventories have different language versions. The counselor should consult the test authors or publishers to identify these non-English versions if the situation calls for their use.

Assessing the Cultural Background of Minority Clients

Knowledge about the general cultural characteristics of a minority group cannot be used to replace an assessment of the cultural background and characteristics of culturally different clients. In each cultural group, there exists an array of within-group differences. Each individual is unique and may or may not possess the characteristics and experience common to his or her cultural group. Lonner and Ibrahim (1989) suggested that if a formal assessment of a minority client is called for, a preassessment procedure can be done to examine the cultural beliefs, values, racial identity, and levels of acculturation of the client. The information can then be integrated with formal career assessment data. Reviews of instruments related to racial and cultural identity can be found in Ponterotto and Casas (1991), and Sabnani and Ponterotto (1992).

Communicating Test Data

While perception of counselor expertness and credibility are important dimensions in the counseling process (Strong, 1968), these dimensions seem to be particularly salient for ethnic minority clients (D. W. Sue and D. Sue, 1990; S. Sue and Zane, 1987). Some ethnic minorities, such as Asian Americans, tend to perceive counselors as experts, and test data as opinions from an authority source (Leong and Leung, 1994). This perception may reduce the potential benefit of assessment data because it prevents clients from recognizing and sharing their reactions to the test scores, especially to interpretive ideas that are not consistent with their own. The counselor may deal with this perception in at least three ways. First, before formal assessment, the counselor should make sure a client understands the limitations of assessment. Second, the tentative nature of test information should be clearly communicated before and during career assessment. Third, the counselor should closely observe the verbal and nonverbal reactions of a client during interpretation so that both positive and negative reactions can be explored in the counseling process. The counselor should solicit feedback from a client so that personal reactions to test data can be thoroughly explored.

Assessment Data as Agenda Items in Career Counseling

Career assessment data can be used as stimuli for counseling discussion (Campbell, 1990; Duckworth, 1990). First, test content (for example, test items) or scores can help a client identify and select themes to focus on during career counseling. This process allows the client and counselor to individualize career counseling according to the needs and cultural views of the client. Second, test content and scores may serve as stimuli to identify topics or issues that are difficult for the client to express. For example, a minority client may hesitate to discuss an experience related to employment discrimination. In the context of test interpretation, when issues related to perceived vocational barriers and cultural experience are introduced, the client may feel more at ease to bring up this issue. Third, test content and scores can serve as a medium for a client to identify aspects of career development that are unique to his or her culture. For example, a discussion of test items from an instrument about career decision can lead to an exploration about how individuals in the client's culture make important decisions, and how this process is different from the White majority culture.

Assessment to Increase Perception of Choices

Career assessment can be viewed as a process of empowerment in which clients develop an increased sense of control over their career problems through participating actively in the career assessment process, including the selection of instruments, the integration of test information, and identification of relevant goals to resolve career concerns (Healey, 1990). An empowering assessment process is especially important for ethnic minorities because of the adverse social (for example, racial discrimination) and economic (for example, disadvantaged socioeconomic status) conditions that minorities have experienced in their lives. These adverse conditions may reduce the actual and perceived vocational alternatives available to the person (Leung, 1995). A desirable outcome of career assessment with ethnic minorities is an expansion of their awareness of occupational alternatives. The effort to expand choice perception, however, does not imply a disregard for social and environmental constraints. The process of expanding one's awareness of alternatives should be accompanied by an analysis of the reality of work, and for minority persons, an analysis of social discrimination and prejudice that may limit available choices.

Case Example

Nancy is a twenty-four-year-old Chinese American female who sought counseling to help her make decisions about the choice of an academic major. Nancy immigrated to the United States from Hong Kong when she was about sixteen years old and completed the last two years of high school here. Since Nancy graduated from high school, she has been enrolled as a part-time student in an urban university, while at the same time working in a part-time position to meet economic needs. Nancy indicates that her progress in college has been slow, mainly because of a lack of a clear vocational direction. Since Nancy has accumulated enough credit hours at the university to be a junior, she has to declare a college major in order to continue her enrollment. Nancy admits that she is not familiar with the occupational structure of the United States, even though she has been living in the country for a number of years. To some extent, Nancy feels restricted in her occupational choices because of her language and cultural background. Nancy wanted to be a high school teacher before she immigrated to the United States, but she has given up this aspiration because she feels that the teaching profession does not receive adequate respect and reward here. Recently, Nancy has thought about becoming a commercial artist.

During the initial interview, some background information related to Nancy's career concerns was collected. It was decided that vocational assessment instruments would provide useful information to assist Nancy in making decisions about her education and career. I asked Nancy to complete a measure of Asian acculturation called the Suinn-Lew Asian Self-Identity Acculturation Scale (SL-ASIA; Suinn, Rickard-Figueroa, Lew, and Vigil, 1987), as well as the MVS (Holland and others, 1980) and the SDS (Holland, 1985b).

Rationales for the Choice of Instruments

The SL-ASIA is used to provide an assessment of Nancy's level of acculturation to the U.S. culture. The information can be used to assist in the interpretation of the vocational assessment instruments (Lonner and Ibrahim, 1989).

The MVS provides data about Nancy's career decision-making needs and barriers. Even though normative information may not be appropriate in the interpretation of the MVS, an exploration of the test items may help identify issues to explore during career counseling.

While research evidence tends to support the validity of both the SDS and the SII for ethnic minorities, the SDS was chosen over the SII for three reasons. First, the SDS allows the test taker to generate an interest code by comparing ratings in the six Holland interest areas instead of comparing them to a normative population. Since Nancy's socialization and cultural upbringing is primarily Chinese, the use of norms established in the United States may not be appropriate. Second, the SDS is developed to maximize career exploration and perceptions of choices. The process of completing the SDS is designed to be a self-exploration exercise to enhance one's sense of control (Holland, 1985c). Nancy should benefit from such a process. Third, Nancy can take home the College Majors Finders (Holland, 1985d) and the Occupations Finders (Holland, 1985e) upon completing the SDS. The availability of these resources can help Nancy to expand her perception of choices.

Test Scores and Interpretation

SL-ASIA. The SL-ASIA consists of twenty-one multiple-choice items (ranging from 1 to 5) related to language, identity, behaviors, generation and geography, and attitudes. The final score is an average of the twenty-one items. According to Suinn and others (1987), a score of 5 represents a high level of acculturation, which is termed Western-identified. A score of 1 denotes a strong preference for Asian culture and values, which is termed traditional Asian. A score at the midpoint reveals a bicultural orientation. Nancy's average score is 2.09, suggesting that she has a slight preference toward the traditional Asian culture in comparison to the Western culture. The SL-ASIA is not designed to be a diagnostic tool. However, an inspection of Nancy's responses may reveal some useful information about her adjustment and acculturation in the United States, and it is possible to draw some hypotheses about the relationship between acculturation and perceptions of career choices. For example, Nancy rated herself as more proficient in her native language (Chinese) than in English. This perception may limit her consideration of occupations to those that do not require significant language skills.

MVS. Nancy scored 6 points in the VI scale (range between 0 and 18 points) of the MVS, compared to a mean score of 11.25 for college students, according to normative information provided in the MVS Manual (Holland and others, 1980). The relatively low score on the VI scale indicates that Nancy does not have a clear and stable view of herself in terms of goals, interests, and abilities (Holland, 1985a). Nancy may be lacking in self-confidence and may not have developed a focused vocational direction. Nancy responded in the "true" direction to many items in the VI scale. A review of these items indicates that Nancy is unsure of herself (for example, strengths and weaknesses), and does not know how to approach a career decision (for example, how to make a decision). Nancy scored 0 points in the Information scale (ranged between 0 and 4) of the MVS, in comparison to a mean of 2.39 for college students based on the normative sample. This score indicates that Nancy perceives a strong need for career information. Nancy scored 2 points on the Barrier scale (ranged between 0 and 4), in comparison to a mean of 3.35 among college students based on the normative sample. This score indicates that Nancy perceives many barriers in her career decision making and implementation. An examination of the items on this scale indicates that Nancy is uncertain about whether she has the ability and talent to complete training and attain her chosen career.

The SDS. In the Occupational Daydream section of the SDS, the occupations that Nancy has considered so far are: teacher (SEC), interior designer (AES), social worker (SEA), graphic designer (AES), and commercial designer (AEI). All the occupations that Nancy has considered are in the Artistic and Social areas. Artistic is the first code in three of the five occupations. Holland (1985c) details how the Occupational Daydream section can be used to verify the interest code derived from the SDS. One way is to determine the degree of agreement between the Holland codes assigned to the occupations reported in the Daydream section and the summary occupational code. A disagreement may indicate career choice instability and a need for further crystallization of occupational interests (Holland, 1985c). The occupations reported in the Daydream section can also be viewed as a history of vocational aspirations. An exploration of the developmental changes in career aspirations can help clients to understand career choice crystallization as a developmental process.

Nancy's SDS summary scores section is presented in Figure 16.1. The highest two scores are Social and Artistic (35 and 32, respectively). The two scores are not separated by eight or more points, and applying the "rule of eight" by Holland (1985c), there may not be a meaningful difference in the degree of preference in the two interest areas. Since Enterprising and Conventional are separated by only three points, the third code can be either one of the two. Using Holland's (1985c) "rule of full exploration," I would suggest that Nancy browse through all the college majors and occupational titles listed under the Social/Artistic and Artistic/Social sections of the *College Major Finder* (Holland, 1985d) and the *Occupations Finder* (Holland, 1985e), especially those with Enterprising or Conventional as a third code. I would ask Nancy to write down all the majors and occupational titles that appeal to her for a more in-depth exploration in the future.

Further examination of the scores in the subsections of the SDS reveals that Nancy scored the same number of points in the Artistic and Social areas in the Occupations scales, but her ratings of abilities (that is, the Competencies and Self-Estimates scales) are higher in the Social than in the Artistic area. These scores are consistent with Nancy's VI and Barrier scales scores on the MVS, which indicate that Nancy has doubts about whether she has the talents and abilities to implement her career choice.

Figure 16.1. The Summary Score section of Nancy's SDS.

How to Organize Your Answers

Start on page 4. Count how many times you said L for "Like." Record the number of Ls or Ys for each group of Activities, Competencies, or Occupations on the lines below.

Activities
(pp. 4–5)   R   I   A   S   E   C

Competencies
(pp. 6–7)   R   I   A   S   E   C

Occupations
(p. 8)   R   I   A   S   E   C

Self-Estimates
(p. 9)   R   I   A   S   E   C
What number
did you circle?

                       R   I   A   S   E   C

Total Scores
Add the five R
scores, the five   R   I   A   S   E   C
I scores, the 5
A scores, etc.

The letters with the three highest numbers indicate your summary code.
Write your summary code below.
(If two scores are the same or tied, put both letters in the same box.)

Summary Score

Highest   2nd   3rd

Using the normative table for college students provided in the SDS Manual (Holland, 1985c), the raw scores of the SDS can be transformed into percentile scores. The percentile scores for Nancy are: Realistic 55, Investigative 3, Artistic 74, Social 53, Enterprising 53, and Conventional 51. The use of percentile scores based on the normative sample resulted in Artistic being the primary interest area. The percentile score can be used to help further distinguish Nancy's Artistic interest from other interest areas. Holland (1985c), however, suggested the use of raw scores over standardized scores in the interpretation of the SDS.

The three-letter interest code derived from the SDS can be examined in terms of the degree of consistency and differentiation, based on Holland's theory (1985a). Consistency refers to whether a person's vocational interests are compatible, and is indicated by the distance of the first two interest codes in the Holland hexagon. Nancy's highest codes, A and S, are adjacent in the hexagon, and thus her career interests have a high degree of consistency. Differentiation refers to whether a clear pattern of interests is exhibited in the interest profile, and is indicated by the arithmetic difference between the scale with the highest score and the one with the lowest score. Nancy's differentiation score is 28, which can be converted into a percentile score of 19 based on the normative information from the SDS Manual (Holland, 1985c). Therefore, Nancy's interest scores indicate a low level of differentiation. Both consistency and differentiation are hypothesized to be related to the stability and satisfaction of career choice. However, both concepts have only received mixed support in terms of their predictive validity (for example, Holland, 1985a; Leung, Conoley, Scheel, and Sonnenberg, 1992), and their validity for ethnic minorities has not been adequately examined.

Translating Assessment Data into Treatment Intervention

Several themes emerged from the assessment data that have implications for career counseling with Nancy:

• Nancy appears to be unsure of herself both in terms of what she wants in her life and what her strengths and limitations are. The test interpretation process can help Nancy gain a better understanding of herself (for example, interests, values, and aptitudes). Career counseling can also help Nancy examine her aspirations to be a teacher (a Social occupation) and a designer (an Artistic occupation). Nancy may benefit from an exploration of her work values (for example, need for status), and an appraisal of her language and artistic abilities. I would also explore with Nancy some variables that have been identified as important for Asian Americans, such as family structure and prestige (for example, Leong and Gim, in press; Leung, Ivey, and Suzuki, 1994).

• Nancy would benefit from learning how to make a career decision. Her responses on the MVS indicate an apprehension and a lack of knowledge about the decision-making process (for example, stages of career decision making). I would try to help Nancy identify a decision-making strategy that is consistent with her cultural values.

• The low score in the MVS Information scale indicates that Nancy has a strong need for occupational information. Nancy would benefit from a systematic process of collecting information about careers, including printed literature and information interviewing.

• It is useful to explore with Nancy the issues of her cultural identity, the ways she has coped with the immigration changes, and her adjustment in the United States. A related issue is whether Nancy perceives her minority cultural background as a barrier to her career development. The perception of barriers and a lack of familiarity with the U.S. occupational structure might have created feelings of fear and helplessness, preventing Nancy from participating actively in a career choice process. Career counseling can empower Nancy so that she recognizes the strengths and resources in herself that she is not aware of because of her immigration transition. Through this process, Nancy should experience an increased awareness of choices and alternatives.

- The SDS scores can be used to examine Nancy's avocational interests (for example, leisure). If Nancy cannot fulfill her Social interest in a career choice, she can be involved in leisure activities that allow her to express this interest.

Conclusions

There are two major challenges confronting the area of cross-cultural career assessment. The first is the development of assessment instruments that are valid, reliable, and useful for ethnic minorities. Unfortunately, with few exceptions, many career assessment instruments have not been adequately researched in terms of their cross-cultural application. The second challenge is the development of cross-cultural competencies among psychologists and counselors who work with ethnic minority clients. The appropriate usage of test instruments can only be realized if a counselor is knowledgeable about the cultural background of minority clients, and if the counselor can accurately assess how cultural factors influence the meaning of test scores. A valid and reliable career assessment instrument can be misused by a test user who is prejudiced against racial minorities, or who is not sensitive to issues of racial and cultural diversity.

Cross-cultural career assessment is still in its infancy. Further research is clearly needed to develop assessment instruments that are valid and reliable for ethnic minorities. First, current research on cross-cultural assessment has focused mostly on career interest inventories. Research should expand its scope to include other types of inventories, such as career development and decision-making inventories. Second, most current research has relied on a racial comparison approach, in which the test scores of White participants are compared with the scores from one or more racial minority groups. Another useful approach that has received increasing attention is to examine whether the theoretical structure of an instrument is appropriate for ethnic minorities (Hansen, 1987). A number of recent studies (for example, Fouad and others, 1984; Haverkamp and others, 1994; Swanson, 1992) have utilized techniques such as multidimensional scaling and structural equation models to examine the structure of interests among ethnic minorities. Construct validation is crucial in determining the cross-cultural application of career assessment instruments. Lastly, research should examine the relationship between career assessment with ethnic minorities and treatment outcomes. It is important for researchers to determine how a process of formal assessment, in the context of multicultural career counseling, can lead to resolution of career concerns, and the growth and development of individuals.

References

Betz, N. E. (1988). The assessment of career development. In W. B. Walsh & S. H. Osipow (Eds.), *Career decision making* (pp. 77–136). Hillsdale, NJ: Erlbaum.

Betz, N. E. (1990). Contemporary issues in testing use. In C. E. Watkins & V. L. Campbell (Eds.), *Testing in counseling practice* (pp. 419–450). Hillsdale, NJ: Erlbaum.

Borgen, F. H., & Harper, G. T. (1973). Predicting validity of measured vocational interests with Black and White college men. *Measurement and Evaluation in Guidance, 6,* 19–27.

Campbell, V. L. (1990). A model for using tests in counseling. In C. E. Watkins & V. L. Campbell (Eds.), *Testing in counseling practice* (pp. 1–7). Hillsdale, NJ: Erlbaum.

Carter, R. T., & Swanson, J. L. (1990). The validity of the Strong Interest Inventory with Black Americans: A review of literature. *Journal of Vocational Behavior, 36,* 195–209.

Crites, J. O. (1978). *Administration and use manual for the Career Maturity Inventory* (2nd ed.). Monterey, CA: MTB/McGraw Hill.

Duckworth, J. D. (1990). The counseling approach to the use of testing. *The Counseling Psychologist, 18,* 198–204.

Fouad, N. A., Cudeck, R. A., & Hansen, J. C. (1984). Convergent validity of the Spanish and English Forms of the Strong-Campbell Interest Inventory for bilingual Hispanic high school students. *Journal of Counseling Psychology, 31*, 339–348.

Fouad, N. A., & Dancer, L. S. (1992). Cross-cultural structure of interests. *Journal of Vocational Behavior, 40*, 129–143.

Fouad, N. A., & Hansen, J. C. (1987). Cross-cultural predictive accuracy of the Strong-Campbell Interest Inventory. *Measurement and Evaluation in Counseling and Development, 20*, 3–10.

Fouad, N. A., Hansen, J. C., & Arias, F. G. (1986). Multiple discriminant analyses of cross-cultural similarity of vocational interests of lawyers and engineers. *Journal of Vocational Behavior, 28*, 85–96.

Fouad, N. A., Hansen, J. C., & Arias, F. G. (1989). Cross-cultural similarity of vocational interests of professional engineers. *Journal of Vocational Behavior, 34*, 88–99.

Gade, E. M., Fuqua, D., & Hurlburt, G. (1984). Use of the Self-Directed Search with Native Americans. *Journal of Counseling Psychology, 31*, 584–587.

Hansen, J. C. (1986). Strong Vocational Interest Blank/Strong-Campbell Interest Inventory. In W. B. Walsh & S. H. Osipow (Eds.), *Advances in vocational psychology (Vol. 1): The assessment of interests* (pp. 1–29). Hillsdale, NJ: Erlbaum.

Hansen, J. C. (1987). Cross-cultural research in vocational research. *Measurement and Evaluation in Counseling and Development, 19*, 163–176.

Hansen, J. C. (1992a). *User's Guide: Strong Interest Inventory (Rev. ed.)*. Palo Alto, CA: Consulting Psychologists Press.

Hansen, J. C. (1992b). Does enough evidence exist to modify Holland's theory to accommodate the individual differences of diverse populations? *Journal of Vocational Behavior, 40*, 188–193.

Hansen, J. C., & Campbell, D. P. (1985). *Manual for the SVIB-SCII* (4th ed.). Palo Alto, CA: Consulting Psychologists Press.

Hansen, J. C., & Fouad, N. A. (1984). Translation and validation of the Spanish Form of the Strong-Campbell Interest Inventory. *Measurement and Evaluation in Guidance, 16*, 192–197.

Haverkamp, B. E., Collins, R. C., & Hansen, J. C. (1994). Structure of interests of Asian-American college students. *Journal of Counseling Psychology, 41*, 256–264.

Haviland, M. G., & Hansen, J. C. (1987). Criterion validity of the Strong-Campbell Interest Inventory for American Indian college students. *Measurement and Evaluation in Counseling and Development, 19*, 196–201.

Healey, C. C. (1990). Reforming career appraisals to meet the needs of clients in the 1990s. *The Counseling Psychologist, 18,* 214–226.

Hecht, A. B. (1980). Nursing career choice and Holland's theory: Are men and Blacks different? *Journal of Vocational Behavior, 16,* 208–211.

Herr, E. L. (1988). The counselor's role in career assessment. In J. T. Kapes & M. M. Mastie (Eds.), *A counselor's guide to career assessment instruments* (2nd ed., pp. 39–46). Alexandria, VA: National Career Development Association.

Herr, E. L., & Cramer, S. H. (1992). *Career guidance through the life-span* (4th ed.). Boston: Little, Brown.

Holland, J. H., & Gottfredson, G. D. (1992). Studies of the hexagonal model: An evaluation (or, the perils of stalking the perfect hexagon). *Journal of Vocational Behavior, 40,* 158–170.

Holland, J. H., & Rayman, J. R. (1986). The Self-Directed Search. In W. B. Walsh & S. H. Osipow (Eds.), *Advances in vocational psychology (Vol. 1): The assessment of interests* (pp. 55–82). Hillsdale, NJ: Erlbaum.

Holland, J. L. (1973). *Making vocational choices: A theory of careers.* Englewood Cliffs, NJ: Prentice-Hall.

Holland, J. L. (1985a). *Making vocational choices: A theory of vocational personalities and work environments* (2nd ed.). Englewood Cliffs, NJ: Prentice-Hall.

Holland, J. L. (1985b). *The Self-Directed Search: Professional manual.* Odessa, FL: Psychological Assessment Resources.

Holland, J. L. (1985c). *The Self-Directed Search.* Odessa, FL: Psychological Assessment Resources.

Holland, J. L. (1985d). *The Occupations Finders.* Odessa, FL: Psychological Assessment Resources.

Holland, J. L. (1985e). *The College Majors Finders.* Odessa, FL: Psychological Assessment Resources.

Holland, J. L. (1985f). *Manual for the Vocational Preference Inventory.* Odessa, FL: Psychological Assessment Resources.

Holland, J. L. (1994). *Self-Directed Search Assessment Booklet.* Odessa, FL: Psychological Assessment Resources.

Holland, J. L., Daiger, D. C., & Power, P. G. (1980). *My Vocational Situation: Description of an experimental diagnostic form for the selection of vocational assistance.* Palo Alto, CA: Consulting Psychologists Press.

Holland, J. L., Johnson, J. A., & Asama, N. F. (1993). The Vocational Identity Scale: A diagnostic and treatment tool. *Journal of Career Assessment, 1,* 1–12.

Katz, M. R. (1978). [Review of *The Career Maturity Inventory*.] In O. K. Buros (Ed.), *The eighth mental measurement yearbook* (Vol. 2, pp. 1562–1565). Highland Park, NJ: Gryphon Press.

Kimball, R. L., Sedlacek, W. E., & Brooks, G. C., Jr. (1973). Black and White vocational interests in Holland's Self-Directed Search (SDS). *Journal of Negro Education, 42*, 1–4.

Leong, F.T.L. (1991a). Career development attributes and occupational values of Asian American and white American college students. *Career Development Quarterly, 39*, 221–230.

Leong, F.T.L. (1991b). Guest editor's introduction to special issue: Career development of racial and ethnic minorities. *Career Development Quarterly, 29*, 196–198.

Leong, F.T.L., & Gim, R.H.C. (in press). Career assessment and intervention with Asian Americans. In F.T.L. Leong (Ed.), *Career development and vocational behavior of racial and ethnic minorities*. Hillsdale, NJ: Erlbaum.

Leong, F.T.L., & Leung, S. A. (1994). Career assessment with Asian Americans. *Journal of Career Assessment, 2*, 240–257.

Leung, S. A. (1995). Career development and counseling: A multicultural perspective. In J. G. Ponterotto, J. M. Casas, L. A. Suzuki, & C. M. Alexander (Eds.), *Handbook of multicultural counseling*, (pp. 549–566). Newbury Park, CA: Sage.

Leung, S. A., Conoley, C. W., Scheel, M., & Sonnenberg, R. T. (1992). An examination of the relationship between vocational identity, consistency, and differentiation. *Journal of Vocational Behavior, 40*, 95–107.

Leung, S. A., Ivey, D., & Suzuki, L. (1994). Factors affecting the career aspirations of Asian-Americans. *Journal of Counseling and Development, 72*, 404–410.

Lonner, W. J., & Ibrahim, F. A. (1989). Assessment in cross-cultural counseling. In P. B. Pedersen, J. G. Draguns, W. J. Lonner, & J. E. Trimble (Eds.), *Counseling across cultures* (3rd ed., pp. 299–333). Honolulu: University of Hawaii Press.

Miller, M. J., & Wells, D. (1988). Learning more about the vocational "barriers" of Black youths. *Psychological Reports, 62*, 405–406.

Mosley-Howard, G. S., & Anderson, P. (1993). Using My Vocational Situation with workers facing plant closing. *Journal of Career Development, 19*, 289–300.

O'Brien, W. F., & Walsh, W. B. (1976). Concurrent validity of Holland's theory for non-college-degreed Black working men. *Journal of Vocational Behavior, 8*, 239–246.

Osipow, S. H. (1987). *The Career Decision Scale manual*. Odessa, FL: Psychological Assessment Resources.

Pedersen, P. (1988). *A handbook for developing multicultural awareness*. Alexandria, VA: American Counseling Association.

Ponterotto, J. G., & Casas, J. M. (1991). *Handbook of racial/ethnic minority counseling research*. Springfield, IL: Thomas.

Rounds, J. B., & Tracey, T. J. (1990). From trait and factor to person-environmental fit counseling: Theory and process. In W. B. Walsh & S. H. Osipow (Eds.), *Career counseling: Contemporary topics in vocational psychology* (pp. 1–44). Hillsdale, NJ: Erlbaum.

Sabnani, H. B., & Ponterotto, J. G. (1992). Racial/ethnic minority-specific instrumentation in counseling research: A review, critique, and recommendations. *Measurement and Evaluation in Counseling and Development, 24*, 161–187.

Savickas, M. L. (1990). The use of career choice process scales in counseling practice. In C. E. Watkins & V. L. Campbell (Eds.), *Testing in counseling practice* (pp. 373–417). Hillsdale, NJ: Erlbaum.

Savickas, M. L. (1993). A symposium on multicultural career counseling. *The Career Development Quarterly, 42*, 3.

Smith, E. J. (1975). Profile of the Black individual in vocational literature. *Journal of Vocational Behavior, 6*, 41–59.

Smith, E. J. (1976). Reference group perspectives and the vocational maturity of lower socioeconomic Black youth. *Journal of Vocational Behavior, 8*, 321–336.

Smith, E. J. (1983). Issues in ethnic minorities' career behavior. In W. B. Walsh & S. H. Osipow (Eds.), *Handbook of vocational psychology* (Vol. 1, pp. 161–222). Hillsdale, NJ: Erlbaum.

Spokane, A. R. (1990). Self-guided interest inventories as career inventories: The Self-Directed Search. In C. E. Watkins & V. L. Campbell (Eds.), *Testing in counseling practice* (pp. 285–316). Hillsdale, NJ: Erlbaum.

Strong, S. R. (1968). Counseling: An interpersonal influence process. *Journal of Counseling Psychology, 15*, 215–224.

Sue, D. W., Arredondo, P., & McDavis, R. J. (1992). Multicultural counseling competencies and standards: A call to the profession. *Journal of Counseling and Development, 70*, 477–486.

Sue, D. W., & Kirk, B. A. (1972). Psychological characteristics of Chinese-American students. *Journal of Counseling Psychology, 19*, 471–478.

Sue, D. W., & Kirk, B. A. (1973). Differential characteristics of Japanese-American and Chinese-American college students. *Journal of Counseling Psychology, 20*, 142–148.

Sue, D. W., & Sue, D. (1990). *Counseling the culturally different: Theory and practice*. (2nd ed.) New York: Wiley.

Sue, S., & Zane, N. (1987). The role of culture and cultural techniques in psychotherapy: A critique and reformulation. *American Psychologist, 42*, 37–45.

Suinn, R. M., Rickard-Figueroa, K., Lew, S., & Vigil, P. (1987). The Suinn-Lew Asian Self-Identity Acculturation Scale: An initial report. *Educational and Psychological Measurement, 47*, 401–407.

Super, D. E. (1957). *The psychology of careers*. New York: HarperCollins.

Super, D. E. (1983). Assessment in career guidance: Toward truly developmental counseling. *Personnel and Guidance Journal, 61*, 555–562.

Swanson, J. L. (1992). The structure of vocational interests for African-American college students. *Journal of Vocational Behavior, 40*, 144–157.

Walsh, W. B. (1990). A summary and integration of career counseling approaches. In W. B. Walsh & S. H. Osipow (Eds.), *Career counseling: Contemporary topics in vocational psychology* (pp. 263–282). Hillsdale, NJ: Erlbaum.

Walsh, W. B., & Betz, N. (1990). *Tests and assessment* (2nd ed.). Englewood Cliffs, NJ: Prentice Hall.

Walsh, W. B., Bingham, R., Horton, J. A., & Spokane, A. (1979). Holland's theory and college-degreed working Black and White women. *Journal of Vocational Behavior, 15*, 217–223.

Ward, C. M., & Walsh, W. B. (1981). Concurrent validity of Holland's theory for non-college degreed Black women. *Journal of Vocational Behavior, 18*, 356–361.

Westbrook, B. W., Cutts, D. D., Madison, S. S., & Arcia, M. A. (1980). The validity of Crites' model of career maturity. *Journal of Vocational Behavior, 16*, 249–281.

Westbrook, B. W., & Sanford, E. E. (1991). The validity of career maturity attitude measures among Black and White high school students. *The Career Development Quarterly, 39*, 199–208.

Westbrook, B. W., Sanford, E., Gilleland, K., Fleenor, J., & Merwin, G. (1988). Career maturity in grade 9: The relationship between accuracy of self-appraisal and ability to appraise the career-relevant capabilities of others. *Journal of Vocational Behavior, 32*, 269–283.

Westbrook, B. W., Sanford, E., Merwin, G., Fleenor, J., & Gilleland, K. (1988). Career maturity in grade 9: Can students who make appropriate career choices for others also make appropriate choice for themselves? *Measurement and Evaluation in Counseling and Development, 21*, 64–71.

Whetstone, R. D., & Hayles, V. R. (1975). The SVIB and Black college men. *Journal of College Student Personnel, 12*, 253–258.

Womer, F. B. (1988). Selecting an instrument: Chore or challenge. In J. T. Kapes & M. M. Mastie (Eds.), *A counselor's guide to career assessment instruments* (2nd ed., pp. 27–35). Alexandria, VA: National Career Development Association.

Zunker, V. G. (1994). *Using assessment results for career development* (3rd ed.). Pacific Grove, CA: Brooks/Cole.

Zytowski, D. G., & Warman, R. E. (1982). The changing use of tests in counseling. *Measurement and Evaluation in Guidance, 15*, 147–152.

17

. . . .

The Assessment of Culturally Diverse
Infants and Preschool Children

Paul J. Meller and Phyllis S. Ohr

Although the history of the assessment of human abilities dates back over four millennia (Meller, 1994), the assessment of infants, toddlers, and preschool children is a relatively recent undertaking. Driven initially by the attempt to scientifically document the nature and sequence of developmental processes, assessment has begun to play more of a role in early intervention programs. Starting with the passage of PL 94–142 (U.S. Congress, 1975), which mandated the provision of a free and appropriate education to all children between the ages of five and twenty-one, the need for reliable and accurate assessment instruments for young children grew.

The recent emphasis on cultural diversity in the assessment of young children has emerged because of the consideration of several factors. Principal among these is the federal mandate to incorporate the family into the planning of early intervention strategies. This change in legislation forces psychologists to take a broader view of assessment. In addition, the changing demographics of the United States is a critical factor in that the number of children from racial and ethnic groups other than White (Anglo) is increasing rapidly and may exceed the number of Anglo children by the twenty-first century (Henry, 1990). With the acknowledgment of the need to assess children within the context of their development, there is an increase in attention being paid to the cultural fit between the evaluation instruments and the child (Gopaul-McNicol, 1993).

Psychologists and other professionals who work with young children and their families are frequently confronted with issues such as the stigma of labeling at an early age, the limitations regarding the predictability of standardized tests, and the validity of test results. Perhaps the most overlooked issue is the impact of cultural diversity as it applies to the cognitive and behavioral functioning of young children who are being assessed for possible developmental delay.

There are three primary goals of this chapter. First, a broad historical and conceptual foundation of the issues of cultural diversity in early childhood assessment will be reviewed. In addition, a conceptual framework will be developed to help guide practitioners through the quagmire of early childhood assessment. Finally, a brief review of the literature regarding the efficacy of major assessment instruments with culturally diverse populations will be presented.

History

The specific issues and challenges associated with the assessment of culturally diverse young children with developmental disabilities or delays has only recently become an area of focus. Many school psychologists have acknowledged that cultural influence has its strongest impact on the functioning of the child who has yet to enter kindergarten. Although there has been an increase in the number of young children going to preschool, the cognitive and social experiences of most children below the age of five are still primarily dependent on the type of interactions and stimulation available in their home environment. To adequately assess young children, psychologists are now attending to the different attitudes and behaviors of culturally diverse families.

The development and expansion of early intervention services has accelerated the drive for culturally appropriate, reliable, and valid methods for assessing young children. The evolution of early intervention services is highlighted by federal legislation extending back to the 1960s. Below is a brief review of the most important pieces of legislation with regard to early childhood assessment.

Economic Opportunity Act (U.S. Congress 1964). The Economic Opportunity Act, passed by Congress in 1964, established Head Start. This law was especially significant because it represented the first national commitment to educating young children. The Head Start legislation specifically targeted economically disadvantaged young children and was based on the finding that children from impoverished environments did poorly in the lower grades, and that differences increased as students progressed through school. The original Head Start was designed to decrease the likelihood of school failure by giving low-income students the skills to succeed in elementary schools. However, the legislation did not provide for services for young children with disabilities.

Economic Opportunity Act Amendment (U.S. Congress, 1972). This legislation opened the doors of Head Start centers to children with disabilities, by mandating that at least 10 percent of the children enrolled in Head Start must have some handicapping condition. This is particularly significant because it reflects the first national commitment to providing comprehensive services for a group of children with disabilities.

Public Law 99–457 (U.S. Congress, 1986). This law is an amendment of Public Law 94–142, the Education for All Handicapped Children Act, passed in 1975 and now called the Individuals with Disabilities Education Act (IDEA), which established free and appropriate education for children with special needs. Public Law 99–457 extended all the rights and protections of IDEA to children ages three to five years by providing initiatives to encourage states to provide more comprehensive early intervention services for preschool children with disabilities. This law also established a program to encourage and assist states to design a comprehensive statewide early intervention system for infants and toddlers with disabilities (or at risk for disabilities) and for their families.

Public Law 99–457 is noteworthy in that it mandates an Individualized Family Service Plan (IFSP) for infants and toddlers with disabilities, an acknowledgment of the significant influence of parents and the home environment at this particular developmental level.

Controversies

The theoretical basis of the legislation that established early intervention programs aimed at economically disadvantaged preschool children has been an area of controversy. In particular, debate has ensued regarding whether the legislation reflects the cultural disadvantage approach, a dominant, theoretical framework regarded by some as accounting for the educational failure of children from diverse cultural backgrounds.

Cultural Disadvantage Theory

Cultural disadvantage theory maintains that children from adverse or diverse cultural backgrounds fail academically because they are not provided with the types of social and cultural interactions necessary for the development of the cognitive, preacademic, and social skills required for school success.

One issue that has created a great deal of confusion and controversy is the stereotyping of economic disadvantage as equivalent to cultural disadvantage or diversity. Children from culturally diverse backgrounds differ along a number of dimensions including, for example, race, ethnicity, socioeconomic status, and level of acculturation. They are most similar in that their cultural backgrounds differ from mainstream American culture.

Critics of the cultural disadvantage approach argue that this theory posits individual change, rather than systemic change, which makes it limited in its effectiveness (see Allen and Boykin, 1992; Howard and Scott, 1981). Cultural disadvantage theory also ignores the general finding in psychology that there is more variability in functioning within a given racial or ethnic group than across groups.

Serious questions have been raised about the assumptions or premises of legislation that established early programs aimed at decreasing the likelihood of school failure for children from economically deprived environments. Much research has been generated and differing viewpoints have emerged regarding whether such legislation stems from the cultural disadvantage view as well as the effectiveness of the programs.

Those who adhere to the view that legislation that established Head Start reflects cultural disadvantage theory maintain that these programs are designed to alleviate the negative effects of "inferior" social and cultural experiences by providing "rich" social, cultural and cognitive experiences (Allen and Boykin, 1992; Barclay and Allen, 1982; Boykin, 1986; Springle and Schaefer, 1985). Others assert that Head Start was designed to be different from other early intervention programs by deliberately not using a cultural disadvantage or "deficit" model (see, for example, Zigler and Berman, 1983). In contrast to the deficit model, which assumed that learning experiences are lacking in impoverished environments, some maintained that Head Start focused on a "cultural relativistic approach" that respected the children's diverse cultural backgrounds.

Research evaluating the effects of Head Start are mixed and far from conclusive. Some of the earliest outcome studies suggest that Head Start does not sufficiently improve the academic performance of economically disadvantaged children (Allen and Boykin, 1992; Lee, Brooks-Gunn, Schnur, and Liaw, 1990; Springle and Schaefer, 1985). The first large-scale study examining the impact of Head Start on later school achievement, the 1969 Westinghouse study, concluded that the IQ improvements of those children participating in Head Start tended to fade out (Datta, 1974, 1979). Other studies have also found that although students may perform better academically in the lower grades, the gains disappear as students move to the upper grades (Lee and others, 1990). The conclusions suggested by the Westinghouse study were so strongly negative with regard to early intervention programs that any positive outcomes were not widely acknowledged.

Since the Westinghouse report, numerous studies have emerged discussing its shortcomings. Among these were observations that the evaluation criteria did not reflect the fundamental goals of Head Start, and that the outcome measures, particularly the IQ score, may have been inappropriate for use (for discussion, see Zigler and Seitz, 1982; Zigler and Trickett, 1978).

Several researchers have also presented findings that have refuted some of the conclusions of the Westinghouse study. A follow-up comparison of participants in the Perry Preschool Program, a specially funded Head Start project (Weber, Foster, and Weikart, 1978), declared that other academic as well as nonacademic gains could be found and were more enduring. Specifically, children participating in the project were less likely to repeat a grade or be placed in special education programs, or to be on public assistance. They were more likely to have higher projected lifetime earnings, attend college or job training, and support themselves. Similar findings on other intervention programs were obtained by the Consortium for Longitudinal Studies (Lazar and Darlington, 1982), which pooled information from several of the older studies.

Those arguing for the need for early intervention programs for certain populations have used the positive findings of outcome studies as justification for the usefulness of such programs. Still others have used the negative findings to strengthen the view that governmental funding of such programs be discontinued. Some proponents of the cultural disadvantage view who assert that Head Start reflects disadvantage ideology suggest that the finding that Head Start does not sufficiently improve the academic performance of African American children is evidence that supports cultural disadvantage theory.

Social and Cultural Context of Development

Many of the issues that are associated with assessing culturally diverse children, such as bias and validity, reflect the argument over how to assess the culturally disadvantaged. However, it is important not to lose sight of the fact that assessment of young children is merely a tool designed to measure the developmental process and outcome in young children. As such, the social and cultural context of development must be explored prior to determining the efficacy and appropriateness of evaluation instruments, techniques, and processes.

Critics of the cultural disadvantage explanation posit alternative views to explain the relationship between cultural and child development. Among these are Vygotsky's cultural perspective (1978), Ceci's bio-ecological perspective (1990), Gardner's multiple intelligences (1983), Sternberg's triarchic theory of intelligence (1985), and the work of Piaget (1983). All of these theories suggest a dynamically interactive relationship between cultural experiences and child development. However, Vygotsky's theory is particularly relevant to early childhood assessment in that the child's early sociocultural milieu is viewed as, perhaps, the most significant influence on social, emotional, and cognitive functioning. This refers to the child's experiences as an infant, toddler, and preschooler.

Vygotsky stressed the role of social interaction in individual development. Children developed, according to this theory, as a result of their interaction with a more competent partner, usually an adult or older child. The importance given to adult-child social interactions is illustrated in children's development of self-regulating language (for a discussion, see Pelligrini, Perlmutter, Galda, and Brody, 1990) and problem-solving behavior (for a discussion, see Vygotsky, 1978).

Culture is hypothesized as shaping cognitive development within the constructs of Vygotskian theory (Armour-Thomas, 1992). First, as indicated, social interaction with competent individuals in a child's culture is responsible for the transmission of knowledge. The particular cognitive skills that are modeled and reinforced by competent individuals in that child's environment are determined by the needs and demands of the particular culture of that individual. The culture determines the criteria that establish whether the child has learned the task successfully. Finally, cultural expectations help the competent individual determine what cognitive tasks are viewed as challenging and the appropriate degree of support and guidance necessary in order to foster independence in thinking.

The influence of cultural diversity on the development of cognitive abilities in children has been an area of recent investigation (Cole, 1988; Laboratory of Comparative Human Cognition, 1982; Simmons, 1985) and is supportive of the Vygotskian perspective. According to the model presented by the Laboratory of Comparative Human Cognition (1983), cognitive competence is content specific in that it is representative of competence in specific tasks rather than a "central cognitive processor" as suggested by Piaget. Furthermore, it is suggested that in order to make valid comparisons about the cognitive performance of individuals from two culturally different groups, the stimulus attributes of tasks being assessed must be equivalent. The model describes this as "functional stimulus equivalence." If the skill in question has been equally modeled and reinforced by competent individuals in both cultures, it is likely that one is measuring a cognitive competence that is not culturally biased (Armour-Thomas, 1992).

One of the most consistent characteristics found across developmental theories is the centrality of the social context of learning and development. Theorists as diverse as Piaget (1983), Feuerstein (1980), and Vygotsky (1978) all viewed development as a phenomenon that occurred within a social (that is, cultural) context, and that this social context played a direct and seminal role in creating developmental outcomes.

Piaget (1983) suggested that three primary factors underlie the development of young children; maturation, experience, and social transmission. Much of Piaget's research had focused on the first two variables, however, toward the end of his career, he discussed in detail the impact of social transmission on development. Piaget suggested that social transmission takes two forms. First, children develop and grow utilizing culturally bound tools such as language, math symbol systems, and alphabets, which serve as both media and catalysts for development. Social transmission also incorporates the process by which significant people in a child's world act as social mediators of development.

The construct of social mediation has been expanded by Sigel and his colleagues in their development of the distancing hypothesis (Sigel, 1970; Sigel and Cocking, 1977; Copple, Sigel, and Saunders (1984). The *distancing hypothesis* states that children develop representational competence through interactions with their physical and social environments. Social environments that maximize children's development are those in which parents, teachers, or other adults create learning conditions in which children deal with objects or events in ways that are separate from concrete time and space. That is, social facilitation requires the creation of a cognitive distance between the solution and the concrete event. Parents and teachers are not purveyors of information but rather catalysts that create learning environments for children to discover and actively learn through cognitive and physical manipulation.

Another constructivist view of social context of learning was developed by Feuerstein (1980) and included the notion of mediated learning experiences. Feuerstein suggested that information available in the environment is transformed by the mediating agent such as parent or teacher. The mediator, who is strongly influenced by cultural values and expectations, organizes the learning world for the child. Organization occurs by selecting, framing, and scheduling stimuli, as well as structuring the environment in ways similar to those proposed by Sigel (1970).

Stigma of Labeling

A second area that has provoked much discussion—and disagreement—regards the stigma of labeling the young, culturally different child. Professionals and legislation (Public Law 99–457) acknowledge that effective early intervention requires a multispecialist approach. Several team members (for example, a psychologist, a communication specialist, and a developmental pediatrician) must coordinate their assessments and collaborate when formulating recommendations in order to meet the needs of young children and their families (Neisworth and Bagnato, 1987). To be effective as a team, team members need to develop trust and respect for each other's expertise and be open to sharing judgments as a way to solve problems. While many teams function quite effectively, disagreements naturally exist among professionals who determine if a young child is developmentally delayed and if early intervention is warranted. Inherent in this is the attitude held by different professionals regarding the impact that labeling might have on the young child and his or her family.

Those who object to labeling children early in life argue that labels are stigmatizing in that they create negative bias that may be perpetuated throughout the child's life (Neisworth and Bagnato, 1987). Cultural differences, specifically race and ethnicity, influence the expectations professionals hold for different children and may influence the decision about a diagnosis of developmental delay for a specific child. For example, delayed language development in a preschool child from a bilingual household is not unusual, and some professionals will label such a child as developmentally disabled, while others will see the same child as "at risk" for future language difficulties but not give the child a label.

The labeling of prenatally drug-exposed young children as developmentally delayed is an area of recent interest and controversy. Research has indicated that many children born to substance-abusing mothers are likely to demonstrate language and cognitive delays when very young (Chasnoff, Griffith, Freier, and Murray, 1992; van Baar, 1990). However, although not all children exposed to drugs in utero demonstrate developmental delay, they may be labeled as developmentally delayed or at risk because problems are expected to appear. Many professionals have objected to this "expectancy" labeling because it creates a negative bias toward a group of racially and ethnically diverse children. Although cognitive and language development are identified as possible areas affected by in utero drug exposure, longitudinal research has not yet provided definitive results regarding long-term outcome (Hawley and Disney, 1992). In fact, a longitudinal study recently conducted in the Netherlands (van Baar, 1990) found that prenatally drug-exposed children performed as well as comparison children by age thirty months on a task assessing nonverbal cognitive abilities.

Labeling of very young children, particularly those from culturally diverse backgrounds, may also be inappropriate because of limitations regarding the validity of the test results from major standardized infant and toddler tests. A major criticism of standardized testing of young children is that tasks used to assess infant and toddler intelligence do not tap the same cognitive domain tapped by later tests. Only when assessment involves more focus on language is reliability improved. In spite of this, many children are diagnosed as developmentally delayed during early childhood. Historically, children from ethnic minority backgrounds perform more poorly than Anglo children on standardized measures. Therefore, they are more likely to be given diagnoses of disability based on assessment techniques that do not reliably predict later performance.

Psychometric Issues

Young children demonstrate unique assessment needs that make the task of diagnosing risk and developmental disability exceptionally complex. Preschoolers with developmental problems do not fall neatly into general etiological categories. It is particularly difficult to determine the long-term impact of organic and environmental factors, which makes it hard to project developmental courses and outcomes. Additionally, categories used for reporting handicapping conditions in school-age children are often inappropriate for use with younger children. Young children frequently go in and out of risk depending on the basis for the risk itself, external circumstances and intervention.

There are substantial concerns regarding the reliability and validity of standardized measures used to assess the cognitive functioning of children below the age of five (Reynolds and Clark, 1983). The appropriateness of standardized assessment measures for use with young children from culturally diverse backgrounds produces additional concerns. Problems most often cited in the use of tests with culturally diverse preschoolers typically include inappropriate standardization samples in that specific ethnicities are underrepresented, the inclusion of material not adequately sampled by many children of diverse background, lack of familiarity with the demands of the testing situation, examiner and language bias, and the failure of the test to predict for culturally diverse group members although the test may predict for members of the cultural majority (Reynolds and Kaiser, 1990). Issues to be discussed include inadequate test floors, sampling bias, predictive validity, item bias, and standardization.

Inadequate Test Floors

A significant concern regarding many evaluation instruments designed for use with young children is inadequate test floor, that is, too few items assessing the lowest ability levels (Bracken, 1987). In general, lack of an adequate floor makes it hard to distinguish between children of average and low average intelligence and of differing degrees of developmental delay. Culturally diverse preschoolers may be particularly negatively affected by inadequate floors, as such children frequently miss early items because they need time to become familiar with the items and the appropriate way of responding, but then pass more difficult items once they understand the demands of the task.

Subject Sampling

A primary issue in the assessment of young children is the psychometric adequacy of the instruments available. One concern is the *myth of universality of psychometric properties*. Specifically, the myth involves the assumption, whether implicit or explicit, that an assessment device's psychometric properties are consistent across settings, circumstances, and populations. When assessing young infants and preschool children from diverse cultural backgrounds, the myth of universality of psychometric properties affects validity by employing devices that were not standardized using an appropriately representative sample, or by employing an instrument that may be age appropriate but not valid to address the referral concern. Any evaluation instrument is only valid to answer specific questions with specific populations (Meller, 1994). Inadequate subject sampling is a principal problem in developing one-size-fits-all tests.

Perhaps the most blatant example of a sampling bias was found in the original Bayley Scales of Infant Development (Bayley, 1969). The Bayley manual stated that children with developmental disabilities were specifically excluded from the standardization sample. That is, the population for which the test was intended to be used was not represented in the norms. Although this type of blatant and systematic sampling bias is unusual, more subtle forms of sampling bias exist. For example, Bracken (1985) indicated that the reduced differences in scores on the Kaufman Assessment Battery for Children between Anglos and African American and Latino children (that is, seven and three points respectively) is an artifact of sampling a disproportionate number of ethnic minority students from high socioeconomic backgrounds and undersampling ethnic minority children from low SES. Other research in which subjects were blocked along both ethnic minority status and SES suggested differences between Anglo and ethnic minority children of approximately twelve points (Bracken, 1983; Das, 1984).

Predictive Validity

One of the crowning achievements of the testing movement has been the ability to predict future academic performance based on current test performance. However, this ability has been elusive for those interested in measuring development of infants. The majority of standardized infant intelligence tests sample skills readily observable in very young children and important for later functioning (such as sensory-motor ability and rudimentary symbolic function), but not identical to the abilities measured on later tests of cognitive functioning (such as visual-motor problem solving or verbal reasoning). This limits the predictive value of infant intelligence tests, and as contrasted with the variety of assessment techniques that can be used for diagnosis with school-age children, many fewer valid and reliable instruments are available for use with young children.

There are very few studies linking the impact of cultural diversity on the predictive validity of assessment instruments. However, when data are available there appears to be as good predictive capability for ethnic minority children as Anglo children (for example, Blachman, 1981; Valencia, 1982).

Test-Retest Reliability

There are several developmental issues that may reduce an instrument's reliability, or the ability to accurately measure the reliability of the instrument. First, test-retest reliability, or the relationship between performance on an evaluation instrument administered on two separate occasions (Anastasi, 1982) is dependent on the assumption that development follows a predictable trajectory in which skills and abilities are developing in a fixed sequential pattern. McCall, Eichorn, and Hogarty (1977) describe this pattern as *homotypic development*. Alternatively, these authors have also described a pattern of development that does not follow a temporally juxtaposed pattern, which they refer to as *heterotypic development*. One example of heterotypic patterns of development occurs in infants learning to walk. Thelan (1984) asserts that the development of walking entails a series of developmental milestones that are moderated by infants being placed in a vertical position. Precursors of walking such as the stepping reflex have long been documented (Vasta, Haith, and Miller, 1992). However, Thelan (1984) demonstrated that the stepping motion, which is viewed as a precursor to walking, often disappears from an infant's behavioral repertoire for a while, only to return later in a more refined and adaptive form. This temporary disappearance of abilities is called reciprocal interweaving. The large variability of reciprocal interweaving across infants and skills make reliable assessment of infants' abilities more difficult.

Issues with Standardization

Norm-referenced standardized assessment procedures have been the form of assessment that has been most criticized for use with culturally diverse young children. Before these controversies can be explored, standardized testing must be defined. Standardization in testing refers to a uniformity of procedures in administering, scoring, and interpreting the test (Anastasi 1982; Robertson, 1990). Standardization makes no assumptions concerning the purpose, form, or content of evaluation. It merely refers to the rules governing how a test should be given, how it should be corrected or tabulated, how to make sense of the results, and the limitations of those results (Meller, 1994).

Likewise, no assumptions are made regarding the method of evaluating a student's performance. That is, standardized tests may be norm-referenced, whereby a student's performance can be compared to others who have already taken the test, or criterion-referenced, in which a student's performance is evaluated against some set criteria. Therefore, both norm-referenced and criterion-referenced tests may be used to assess learning processes and acquired knowledge.

The purpose and intent of standardized tests are almost as diverse as the number of procedures available. The only common link among these procedures is a prescription for uniform administration, scoring, and interpretation. Therefore, the more descriptive term, standardized procedures, is preferred.

The primary goals of standardizing evaluation procedures is to enhance the reliability and interpretability of the results. Through standardization, incorrect slanting or bias introduced into the assessment through evaluator subjectivity is greatly reduced. Modifications of teachers' behaviors based upon their expectations of students' abilities are well documented (Dusek, 1985). Evaluator subjectivity may include unrealistic expectations, halo effects with known children, gender biases, and other prejudices. Standardized procedures, therefore, seek to provide a fair evaluation environment for each child across multiple settings. Additionally, they attempt to substantially reduce evaluator bias by providing specific, set instructions.

One of the principal benefits of standardized evaluation procedures is that they help to reduce evaluator bias that may infringe upon a child's fair and accurate assessment. It would be a great disservice to children if subjective and biased evaluation procedures permeated the educational system. Standardized evaluation procedures prevent the adjustment of evaluation results based on irrelevant criteria such as behavioral patterns, biased expectations, stereotypes, or prejudices.

Standardized evaluation procedures also allow for accurate comparisons of children's performance across time and setting. That is, if a child is evaluated on a specific skill (for example, reading comprehension, reading speed, or arithmetic reasoning) at two different times using identical testing procedures but different evaluation procedures, it would be impossible to compare the results of these evaluations. One could never be certain if the difference in the child's performance were due to true differences in ability, or merely a reflection of the differences between the methods by which the child's abilities were evaluated. Imagine the difficulty you would have determining your gas mileage if every gas station gave you a different size "gallon."

Research on children's learning also suggests that the method of evaluation will have a predictable effect on a child's performance. For example, both Feuerstein (1980) and Vygotsky (1978) demonstrated the impact of a human mediator in the learning process. Vygotsky described the area between where a child can function independently and where a child can function without assistance as the zone of proximal development. The zone is merely that point in which the child can perform with varying levels of aid. Vygotsky believed the zone of proximal development is the place where all instruction should take place. People have described the support that is available in the zone of proximal development as scaffolding. Varying test procedures would offer children varying levels of support within the zone of proximal development, and hence lead to a fluctuation in assessment results. The only way a true estimate of abilities can be obtained is if the procedures are consistent (that is, standardized) or we determine a mechanism for measuring and factoring the degree of scaffolding that was available during the assessment process.

Culturally Sensitive Assessment of Infants and Toddlers

Although professionals rarely agree upon a single theory to account for the complexity of child development, there are some well-accepted general constructs. One specific construct that can be applied to early childhood assessment posits that, from the beginning of life, a child's development is influenced by numerous, inter-dependent factors (Neisworth and Bagnato, 1987). Of particular relevance to multicultural assessment is the influence of environmental factors that may impact upon the young child's ability to develop optimally, specifically the child's family.

The contributions of family members to child development is perhaps greatest for infants and toddlers. These youngsters often have limited exposure to stimulation outside the home given that they may not yet attend school. The cognitive experiences of infants and toddlers are then dependent primarily on the stimulation provided primarily by parental figures. The type of context provided by parents depends to a large degree upon the cultural identification of the family. Cultural experiences thus represent a critical component of the very young child's home environment.

In order to diagnose delayed development in very young children it is, thereby, essential to understand multicultural factors that influence development in the earliest years of life. To meet the requirements in PL 99–457 that assessment be comprehensive, recent early childhood intervention has put much emphasis on the assessment of the child's home environment (see, for example, Guralnick, 1991). Infants and toddlers cannot be adequately assessed unless they are viewed within their broader cultural context.

As suggested, early developmental delay may result from differences in children's learning opportunities and their experiences with structured tasks similar to the test items (see, for example, Allen and Boykin, 1992). Children from diverse cultural backgrounds enter the testing situation with differing life experiences and therefore may perform poorly on tests assessing abilities they have not been geared to master. This, in turn, may result in a disproportionate number of very young children from ethnic minority backgrounds being given diagnoses of developmental delay.

Guidelines for Infant and Toddler Assessment and Diagnosis

Several aspects of working with infants and toddlers in general make the traditional styles of evaluating children less tenable (Neisworth and Bagnato, 1987). Infants and toddlers are limited in their response repertoire because they are not yet verbal. This has implications for the type of standardized assessment procedures appropriate for this population.

In addition, while it is appropriate to expect a school-age child to understand that he or she has to sit at a table and answer questions, few infants and toddlers would understand what is expected of them in the testing situation. They will normally be less attentive, less cooperative, more active and distractible, and need many more breaks and tangible reinforcers to continue (Bracken, 1983). Parents often remain in the room during the assessing of young children. It is often very difficult to recognize and address parental needs and concerns while, at the same time, set strict limits regarding the role of parents during the assessment. Yet any professional working with children recognizes that gaining rapport with both child and parent is essential to obtaining an accurate assessment of the needs of the child and family (Neisworth and Bagnato, 1987).

The task of diagnosing developmental disability, stable over time, in infants and toddlers is complex regardless of cultural background. The number of young children with a handicapping condition can change at any point in time, since young children go in and out of risk depending on the basis for the risk itself, current environmental factors, and intervention. In addition, categories used for reporting handicapping conditions in school-age children are often inappropriate for use with younger children and, therefore, do not fall neatly into general etiological categories.

A thorough developmental assessment of infants and toddlers within a multicultural framework incorporates both test-based information as well as the experiential and cultural background of each child assessed. Formal evaluation of the young child may include assessment of current cognitive development, symbolic function and play skills, rudimentary language, gross and fine motor skills, and other areas of concern (Walsh and Bagnato, 1991). As previously discussed, children's cultural experiences play a role in determining the contextual conditions for learning that, in turn, can facilitate or hinder cognitive performance (see, for example, Allen and Boykin, 1992). Therefore, it is important to consider the situational specificity of young children's learning. To do this, one might, for example, supplement standardized assessment with nonstandardized presentation of tasks using material with which the child is already familiar.

Multiple sources of information should be included in a thorough multicultural assessment of infants and toddlers. Parental interview is critical to ascertain current medical information, health history of child, and records of milestones, psychosocial history, and assessment of home environment—including stimulation and models of learning available in the home. Informal assessment may include the reciprocal interaction between parent and child behavior. Observation of parent-child interactions may yield information including, for example, verbal and nonverbal interactions and parental discipline (McIntyre, 1992).

Understanding cultural contributions to parental reaction during the assessment procedure is another aspect of assessment and is critical in developing rapport with culturally diverse families. The assessment process is often a family's first introduction to the educational system. While establishing rapport with parents, in general, is essential, it is frequently difficult when cultural expectations for authority figures differ from background to background. Once rapport has been gained, an assessment of the young child's home environment, including the impact of culturally-related experiences on cognitive and social development, can be made. Public Law 94–457 mandates that the needs of families be addressed in the young child's individualized family service plan. Therefore, the assessment of the young child needs to be more than the reporting of scores and levels of functioning. Family members should be an integral part of the assessment process and, later, the intervention process.

Cultural factors make accurate diagnosis of infants and toddlers particularly difficult due to the extreme degree very young children depend on their home environment for stimulation that, in turn, is influenced by cultural factors. Since it is hard to determine in young children the impact of organic and environmental factors, it is very difficult to make projections. An assessment that results in a diagnosis of developmental delay may be the result of inexperience stemming from multicultural diversity rather than resulting from test scores and would be interpreted more appropriately as a functional rather than a specific delay.

Infant Assessment Instruments

This section discusses the instruments often used to measure development of infants from culturally diverse populations.

Bayley Scales

The Bayley Scales of Infant Development-Second Edition (BSID-II; Bayley, 1993) is a measure of current developmental status of infants and children, one month to forty-two months of age. It consists of three scales: the Mental Scale, Motor Scale, and Behavior Rating Scale (BRS). Levels of cognitive, language, personal-social, and fine and gross motor development are assessed by the Mental and Motor Scales that yield developmental indexes with a mean of 100 and a standard deviation of 15. The BRS assesses the child's behavior during the testing situation. The BSID-II is a revision of the Bayley Scales of Infant Development (BSID; Bayley, 1969) and includes updated norms, extended age range, improved and updated content coverage and stimulus materials. The psychometric quality of the scale was improved, as was its clinical utility, in that data were collected on children with high-incidence clinical diagnoses, including young children with Down's syndrome and children born HIV positive. The most cited limitation has been the equivocal ability of the BSID and BSID-II to predict later intelligence (Bayley, 1993). Increased predictability has been noted for severely delayed young children and for measurement taken later in the preschool period (that is, beyond two years).

The original Bayley Scale of Infant Development had a long and well-documented history of use across many cultures world-wide. Unfortunately, the BSID-II has not been available long enough to have a sufficient data base supporting its use with infants from diverse ethnic backgrounds.

Brazelton Neonatal Behavioral Assessment Scale

While the Bayley Scale has set the standard for structured assessment for infants and toddlers, it is not designed to assess children younger than three months of age. The Brazelton Neonatal Behavioral Assessment Scale (NBAS; Brazelton, 1973) is an infant assessment device that is designed to assess developmental functioning of infants in the first month of life. The NBAS is composed of twenty-eight items and nine supplemental items (NBAS with Kansas Supplements; Horowitz, Sullivan, and Linn, 1978), which are scored on a nine-point scale. The authors suggest that evaluations occur within the first two or three days after birth, at seven to ten days, and finally at two to four weeks. Items on the NBAS reflect an infant's early motor development, level of alertness, sensory processes, and emotional functioning. Although the authors report adequate reliability and concurrent and predictive validity of the scales, some research has questioned the factor structure (Azuma, Malee, Kavanaugh, and Deddish, 1991) and the interrater reliability (DiPietro and Larsen, 1989).

There have been numerous studies conducted throughout the world using the NBAS. Although these studies have demonstrated the adaptability of the NBAS to a variety of cultures, including Japanese (Eishima, 1992), Hmong (Muret-Wagstaff and Moore, 1991), Italian (Valenza, Simion, dalla-Barba, and Calabro, 1992), Norwegian (Mathiessen, 1988), Navajo (Chisolm, 1991) and German (Grossman and Grossman, 1986), each of these studies has accepted the myth of universality of psychometric properties. That is, each study accepted the NBAS as a reliable and valid measure of early infant development and used this assumption to document specific developmental processes, or to demonstrate developmental differences between groups. The problem with these studies is that if the assumption is not true, reported development differences may be error variance due to differential psychometric properties of the test. Future research needs to be conducted on the factor structure, concurrent and predictive validities, and reliability of the NBAS across these diverse populations.

Denver Developmental Screening Test

One of the most commonly used instruments for screening infants at risk for developmental delays is the Denver Developmental

Screening Test (DDST; Frankenburg, Dodds, Fandal, Kazuk, and Cohrs, 1975). The DDST is a 105-item instrument that may be used to assess functioning in four developmental domains: personal, fine motor, language, and gross motor. Because of the ease of administration and the short administration time (approximately twenty minutes) the Denver is frequently used by pediatricians (Ensher and Clark, 1986) and paraprofessional examiners (Gerken, 1991).

Despite its widespread acceptance and use, several psychometric weaknesses have been noted with the DDST. First, the standardization sample systematically excluded children who were at risk or demonstrated a handicapping condition. This served to underrepresent the targeted population and artificially inflate the norms. In addition, Salvia and Ysseldyke (1988) suggested that there was a disproportionate representation of Anglo children from middle-class homes in the standardization sample.

Although some research has suggested adequate concurrent and face validity of the DDST (Salvia and Ysseldyke, 1988), these findings have not been consistent throughout the literature. Frankenburg, Camp, and van Natta (1971) note that scores on the DDST were somewhat discrepant with scores on the Bayley scales. In fact, the authors suggested that as many as 13 percent of the children who should be identified as developmentally delayed will not be identified as such by the DDST. Werner (1972) also found the DDST to underidentify children less than thirty months old, and overidentify children older than four years old. In one study (Harper and Wacker, 1983), the DDST did not identify two-thirds of the children who earned scores in the mentally retarded range on the Stanford-Binet, Form L-M. A review of five studies using the DDST found sensitivity (the ability to identify children who need special services) to be a consistent problem with the DDST (Greer, Bauchner, and Zuckerman, 1989). In this review, over 80 percent of children who have had poor developmental outcomes were not identified by the Denver. Greer et. al suggest that the lack of sensitivity was so severe that the DDST should not be used to make diagnostic or therapeutic decisions.

Similar difficulties plague the Denver Developmental Screening Test-Revised (RDDST; Frankenberg, Fandal, Sciarillo, and Burgess, 1981). In a five-year follow-up of kindergarten children who were given the RDDST as part of their kindergarten screening, Diamond (1987) found the RDDST to misclassify the majority of children who were in need of special education services as typical.

The goal of a screening program is to identify those children who are at risk for developmental delays as early as possible, so that early intervention programs can be implemented. Systematic false negatives, which are common on the DDST, remove children from the early intervention cycle at the detriment of their development. Therefore, despite its widespread use and acceptance, the DDST should be used with extreme caution when making diagnostic or therapeutic decisions, and then only in conjunction with other, more validated indicators of developmental functioning.

There have been many cross-cultural studies employing the DDST using populations as diverse as children from Turkey (Kemhali and Sarp, 1989), China (Xin, Chen, Tang, and Lin, 1992), Australia (Najman, Bor, Morrison, and Anderson, 1992), Finland (Martikainen, 1992), India (Rastogi, Srivastava, Dutt, and Singh, 1987), and Japan, the Philippines, and the Netherlands (Williams and Williams, 1987). These studies may be classified into three groups: cross-cultural comparisons, validation of other instruments of unknown validity, and basic research on developmental processes. Unfortunately, a review of the literature did not reveal a single validation study in which the concurrent and predictive validity of the DDST was assessed for these diverse populations. Given the difficulties associated with the original DDST employed with children in the United States, it is premature to accept the DDST as a standard by which to compare other tests or to make cross-cultural comparisons.

Ordinal Scales of Infant Development/Infant Psychological Development Scales

One of the most unique and interesting measures of infant abilities is the Ordinal Scales of Psychological Development (Uzgiris and

Hunt, 1975). Based upon the research and theory of Piaget, the Ordinal Scales are designed to assess the development of cognitive schemes throughout the sensory-motor period. The six scales include: the Development of Visual Pursuit and the Permanence of Objects, the Development of Means for Obtaining Desired Environmental Events, the Development of Vocal and Gestural Imitation, the Development of Operational Causality, the Construction of Object Relations in Space, and the Development of Schemes Relating to Objects.

Developed from a Piagetian framework, the Ordinal Scales were designed to yield qualitative information regarding development and no specific scores are generated. However, based upon the needs of professionals working in early intervention programs, Dunst (1980) developed a scoring system that includes age norms and an Estimated Developmental Age.

Consistent with Piagetian research, the Ordinal Scales were not developed with the intention of assessing developmentally delayed or handicapped children (Uzgiris and Hunt, 1975). Piaget did not attend to issues of atypical developmental trajectories. Despite this focus on typical development, the Ordinal Scales have been demonstrated to be a reliable and valid instrument for assessing infants and toddlers with a wide range of abilities (Dunst, 1980; Dunst and Gallagher, 1983; Dunst and Rheingrover, 1983; Hefferman and Black, 1984; Uzgiris and Hunt, 1987). An interesting caveat to this high level of validity is that the Ordinal Scales may not be assessing constructs that are different from more standardized measures. For example, Hefferman and Black (1984) report a correlation of .92 between the Ordinal Scales and the Bayley Scales of Infant Development. This correlation suggests that there is over 85 percent common variance between the two scales, and that performance on either measure is highly predictive of performance on the other. Further research is needed to determine whether or not measures such as the Bayley Scale are truly measuring the same developmental processes, or if this relationship is an artifact of providing additional structure to the Ordinal Scales.

Although there has not been any systematic research on the Ordinal Scales with culturally diverse populations, they appear to have much potential for this use. Assessment in a play-based forum is a more natural context in which to observe and assess infants, and may yield more valid results. In addition, the Ordinal Scales are linked to a curriculum (Dunst, 1980) so that assessment and intervention become part of a single process. Questions still remain as to whether a wide array of infants from a variety of racial and ethnic backgrounds will find Piagetian tasks equally familiar. Miller (1986) indicates that parents of preschool children are far less accurate in assessing their children's abilities on Piagetian tasks than on the Stanford-Binet. Miller attributes this difference to the parents' reported lack of familiarity with the demands of the Piagetian tasks. If parents of infants appear to be unfamiliar with Piagetian tasks, than it is important to determine whether or not there is a differential familiarity of these materials among infants from diverse ethnic groups.

Curriculum-Based Measures

Perhaps the most promising technologies for the assessment of culturally diverse infants involve curriculum-based assessment (CBA). Curriculum-based assessment was developed as a means of using the content of interventions as a basis of assessment and decision making. Two of the most common curricula that incorporate a built-in assessment process are the Carolina Curriculum for Handicapped Infants (Johnson-Martin, Jens, and Attermeier, 1979) and the Hawaii Early Learning Profile (Furuno and others, 1979). When implementing either of these curricula, assessment is not an event in which a team of professionals huddle around the infant and demand performance of a variety of skills, but rather, assessment becomes a process in which professionals observe and interact with infants and their families in a natural learning context over a long period of time. It is this dynamic interaction with significant adults and learning within a cultural context that was highlighted earlier in this chapter. The use of curriculum-based instruments is highly conducive to meeting both of these conditions necessary for understanding the infant in cultural context, but further research is necessary to validate this process. For a comprehensive review of the use of CBA with culturally diverse children, see Chapter Seven.

Case Example

Crista was brought in for a developmental assessment at an early intervention program at eighteen months of age, and was followed up one year later. She was born in Guatemala and lived there for the first one-and-a-half years in hospitals and with various foster families. She reportedly had a history of sensory deprivation and physical abuse, but no medical difficulties were noted. Crista was adopted by a bilingual, bicultural Anglo-Latino American couple who had no other children; she came to live with them approximately six weeks prior to the assessment. During the evaluation, the following formal standardized instruments were administered: Bayley Scales of Infant Development (Bayley, 1969), Vineland (Sparrow, Balla, and Cicchetti, 1984), Lowe-Costello Symbolic Play Test (Lowe and Costello, 1988), and the Home Observation for Measurement of the Environment (Caldwell and Bradley, 1978). Standardized assessment revealed Crista to be nonverbal (the only sounds noted were snorts and shrieks) and nonwalking, with limited social interaction (no eye contact or seeking of physical contact), significant cognitive delays, limited symbolic play skills, and self-stimulatory behaviors. However, an informal at-home assessment of Crista's environment as well as informal observation of parent-child interactions revealed an appropriate home environment in which it was believed that skills might have the opportunity to develop. Importantly, when informally observing Crista playing with familiar toys at home, it was revealed that her symbolic play ability was appropriate for an eighteen-month-old and she was heard to use some Spanish terms of endearment, including the putting together of two words (beautiful doll). Follow-up at one year determined that Crista's language, motor, and cognitive ability as assessed by standardized tests was near age-appropriate levels. Interpretations of the evaluation results outside of a sociocultural context could have led to a premature and inaccurate diagnosis of mental retardation. Cultural differences and extreme isolation during her first year of life masked Crista's potential on the formal assessment instruments. The inclusion of informal assessment techniques as well as interpreting the results in an appropriate cultural context resulted in a more optimistic and accurate prognosis.

Assessment Goals for Preschool Children

The goal of the assessment of preschool children is to uncover information that may be useful in facilitating the development of their cognitive, linguistic, perceptual, social, or emotional processes. As such, evaluation must be viewed as only one part of a larger problem-solving process involving the educational professionals and family members who will have an impact on the child's development (Meller, 1994). Assessment must be viewed as an intermediary information-gathering stage between the initial identification of risk factors and the provision of services. A report or series of scores must not be the end point of the process, but rather the point of departure for intervention.

Paget (1990) and Rubin (1990) outlined four principal goals of preschool assessment. These included screening, diagnosis of developmental difficulties, gathering of formative or summative information, and program evaluation. The goal of screening is to quickly, accurately, and in a cost-efficient manner identify children whose behaviors or development sequelae fall outside of the typical range. The purpose of screening is to help direct children into the next appropriate level of service. Through a systematic screening procedure children may be identified who are at risk for later behavioral, academic, or developmental difficulties. These children may be referred for early intervention or preventive programming. Screening may also serve as the mechanism for the initial identification of those children who are already exhibiting more severe developmental difficulties. For these children, the next step would be a more comprehensive diagnostic evaluation.

One of the biggest difficulties in providing screening services with young children is that there are few institutions with ongoing access to the majority of preschool children. Although PL 94–142 and PL 99–457 both mandate school districts to seek out and identify all children from birth to age twenty-one who may be in need of special services, there are no effective conduits for screening the mass of infant and preschool children. Even programs like Head Start can not bear the burden of screening children, as there are only enough slots in Head Start Programs to serve one-third of the eligible children. In addition, Head Start may not provide these services to infants or to children whose families did not meet the eligibility requirement. Pediatricians can also provide the first level of screening. Unfortunately, without universal health care coverage for all children, gaps still exist in the screening net. Because of this lack of formal structure for the provision of services to young children, systematic and comprehensive screening generally does not take place until children are entering kindergarten.

It would appear that, by their very nature, screening procedures would need to trade off some accuracy and precision for expediency. Paget and Nagle (1986) suggest that screening procedures are vulnerable to a large number of both false positives and false negatives. However, careful validation of screening instruments will greatly reduce these imprecisions. For example, Hightower, DeMeis, and Meller (in preparation) accurately classified the placement (for example, first grade versus kindergarten/first grade bridge or retention in kindergarten) of 91.5 percent of kindergarten children with a battery that included the AML-R Behavior Rating Scale and the Gesell School Readiness Screening Test.

While screening is designed to identify the broadest array of children who may be in need of services, diagnostic evaluations provide detailed information regarding the nature and extent of the child's developmental difficulties as well as specific strengths that may be employed to help remediate or compensate for the difficulty. As part of the consultative process, assessment results should be easily incorporated into the development of Individual Educational Programs or Individual Family Service Plans. Although differential diagnosis or classification may be necessary to secure the appropriate services, in order to best meet the needs of the child the principal goal of the diagnostic evaluation must be generating information that can be directly incorporated into the development of a treatment plan. As such, in the course of providing a diagnostic evaluation, one should assess levels of current functioning as well as levels of learning and social processes.

Once a child is receiving services, it is necessary to maintain an ongoing record of progress, in order to determine the efficacy of the intervention, as well as modifying the intervention as the data suggest. This ongoing process of evaluation is a formative evaluation. Formative evaluation requires ongoing assessment of the child's growth and development relative to the specific curriculum. Therefore, criterion-referenced instruments are most frequently utilized in this role. In fact, a number of programs such as the Carolina Curriculum and the Hawaii Early Learning Profile integrate both curriculum and assessment materials into a single package.

The final level of evaluation is program evaluation. The focus here is not on the child but rather on the efficacy of a program. The goal is to build on or modify programs, not directly change an individual child's functioning.

Guidelines for Evaluating Culturally Diverse Preschool Children

The nature of evaluations of preschool children will vary as a function of the goal of the assessment. The following guideline pertains primarily to diagnostic, formative, and summative evaluations. Conceptually, the evaluation of preschool children must entail the collection and integration of information that may be used to describe a child's current functioning as well as facilitating the development of the child. Toward this end, information must be gathered regarding the child's developmental history, the cultural influences on this development, family background and support, as well as an assessment of strengths and weaknesses across multiple domains. A framework integrating these data was outlined by Barona (1990) and Santos de Barona and Barona (1991). These authors suggest a four-step process, including an initial interview, language assessment, assessment of developmental processes, and placing the assessment data into a natural learning context.

In addition to providing a comprehensive set of data collected from multiple sources in multiple ways, Santos de Barona and Barona's model serves to increase the treatment validity and the social validity of the assessment process. Bagnato and Neisworth (1981) suggest that assessment of preschool children should yield information that may be used by significant adults in the child's life such as parents and teachers to facilitate the child's growth and development. That is, assessment must be more than diagnostic, it must also demonstrate a high level of treatment validity.

Parents and teachers must also be empowered to act as the facilitators of the child's development. Therefore, the evaluation process must be socially acceptable to the parent and viewed as a reasonable and accurate measure of the child's abilities. Wolff (1978) refers to this general acceptability of psychological services as *social validity*. The strength of the Santos de Barona and Barona model (1991) is that it provides formal linkages to interventions, as well as a broad and varied assessment approach that will also increase the social validity of the process.

Initial Interview

The current functioning of any child must be understood in the context of the developmental path taken to reach this point. It is therefore essential that accurate developmental information be collected as the first stage of any diagnostic evaluation of a preschool child. The initial interview can be conceptualized as consisting of two components, a developmental phase and a sociocultural phase.

Assessment of preschool children must include accurate information regarding the developmental trajectory of the child. In order to understand the context of development, information must be gathered regarding prenatal care and development, the course of perinatal development, and any pregnancy or birth complications. In addition, accurate information must be gathered with regard to developmental milestones, including fine and gross motor development, language development, cognitive development and problem solving, social and emotional development, and medical history. It is important to note that there are great individual differences found for these developmental milestones, and interpretation of a developmental history must be made in light of these great variations. Many factors are associated with this individual variability, including genetics, medical history, and life experiences. Therefore it is important to interpret the developmental history in light of familial and sociocultural histories.

The sociocultural portion of the preassessment phase should include gathering information regarding the parents' expectations of the child's development, as well as their degree of acculturation, language use and proficiency, and available social support networks.

Language Assessment

For a comprehensive review of issues associated with the assessment of language, refer to Chapter Twelve. It is also important to note that the most common form of developmental delay in early childhood is in speech and language processes. Therefore, examiners who are assessing the abilities of a young child who may not have English as the dominant language, may have limited proficiency in both languages and language processes. Therefore, examiners who assess young children must exhibit some caution, as many young children who do not have English as their dominant language may also demonstrate limited proficiency in their native language. A final issue to consider when assessing language development in preschool children is the language history of the child. To facilitate the assessment of the child, it is important to note to what extent is English being spoken in the home, and to which other sources of English is the child exposed. Development of language in general is not the issue.

Developmental Processes

The third phase of the assessment process is the direct evaluation of the child. Similar to any case, the selection of assessment techniques for evaluating culturally diverse children should be based upon the referral question. With young children, the referral question should contain two components. The first addresses the question of the child's current level of functioning across developmental domains. This portion of the assessment should include a detailed analysis of the strengths and weakness demonstrated by the child. Analysis of the strengths and weaknesses drives the second portion of the referral question, that is, how to help increase the adaptiveness of this child. Hence, information about the child must be collected in a way that will allow the application of these results to the consultation process with the parents or guardian, as well as the generation of the individualized educational plan. To address both components of the referral question, it is often necessary to employ formal norm-referenced procedures, curriculum-based criterion-referenced procedures, and other, less formal processes.

Norm-referenced assessment devices are assessment instruments that are administered in a standardized fashion where the child's performance is judged relative to the performance of other children of similar age. Norm-referenced instruments provide a standard and a general level of functioning, information necessary to address the first part of the referral question. Validity is always an issue with norm-referenced standardized tests. Before any instrument is

employed, a thorough review of the manual and subsequent literature must be undertaken to ensure that there are no biases or sampling problems.

Unlike the infant assessment instruments there is fairly good predictive validity among the many of the norm-referenced preschool
instruments. Good psychometric properties still should not give
license to develop prognoses based upon these test results. If prog-
nostication is undertaken, the validity of the instrument may become
a self-fulfilling prophecy. That is, if a child is thought to be moderately mentally retarded, and a program and parental expectations are
developed based on this information, the child's development may
be hindered by inappropriate distancing and presentation of new
material to be learned. Rather than engage in prognosis, it is far more
beneficial to the child to use the predictive nature of the instruments
to determine the level of risk the child is at and develop an appropriate intervention to address the risk factors.

Another danger is the use of these assessment devices as high-
stakes instruments. Please refer to Chapter Eighteen for a comprehensive review of this topic.

Criterion-referenced instruments address the prescriptive portion
of the referral question (Neisworth and Bagnato, 1986). Often times,
criterion-referenced assessment devices are directly linked to the curriculum, as with informal curriculum-based assessment or formal systems such as the Carolina Curriculum and the Hawaii Early Learning
Profile. Other forms of criterion-based assessment include theoretically based devices such as the Ordinal Scales of Infant Development, the Developmental Activities Screening Inventory-II (Fewell
and Langley, 1984), and the Development Indicators for the Assessment of Learning-Revised (DIAL-R; Mardell-Czudnaiski and Goldenberg, 1983), the Battelle Developmental Inventory (BDI; Newborg,
Stock, Wnek, Guidubaldi, and Svinicki, 1988), and the Brigance
Diagnostic Inventory of Early Development (Brigance, 1978). The
advantages of these more formal norm-referenced procedures are the

direct linkage of assessment to curriculum. In addition, the assessment is conducted in a more naturalistic environment, which can be used for both formative and summative purposes.

Informal Procedures

There are a number of informal procedures that may provide a great deal of information regarding the development of culturally diverse preschool children. These procedures may be conceptualized as passive or active techniques.

Passive techniques are those assessment approaches where the examiner does not actively engage the child during the assessment process. Rather, the examiner observes the children in a variety of situations (for example, structured versus unstructured) with a variety of people. Passive techniques may be structured to some degree. For example, an examiner may ask a parent to teach a child to put together a puzzle in order to assess the dynamics of the parent-child interaction. Observations that help us to understand preschool children within their multiple systems include those performed in the classroom during free play and structured activities, as well as observations of parent-child interactions.

The quality and type of play often mirrors a child's developmental capabilities (Paget, 1990; Rubin, 1990). Observation of children's play provides a window of opportunity to determine how cognitive, linguistic, fine and gross motor, social, and emotional development are integrated in the day-to-day reality of the child.

Active informal assessment involves engaging a child in a task that will shed light on the child's current level of development and the processes the child uses to learn. One of the most common forms of active informal assessment is Dynamic Assessment. Dynamic Assessment refers to a set of assessment procedures that are characterized by: a test-teach-test sequence, an emphasis on assessment of processes rather than outcomes, and assessment of generalizable skills. The procedure identifies strengths and weaknesses, and differentiates performance and potential (Haywood, Brown, and Wingenfeld, 1986). Dynamic Assessment is the natural outgrowth of the theoretical work of developmentalists such as Vygotsky and Piaget.

Diagnostic Placement or Intervention

There is an adage in developmental psychology that states if you want to learn about the development of some phenomenon you must try to change it. Applying this adage to early intervention programs translates into giving a child a diagnostic placement in order to assess the child's capabilities and find the most effective means of teaching the child. Barona (1990) suggests that development placements should extend over a period of three to six months. This allows the child to acclimate to the classroom, the other children, and the educational professionals. A significant period of assessment also allows educational professionals to engage in an ongoing series of classroom observations, curriculum-based assessments, and dynamic assessments. During the course of the diagnostic placement, educational professionals may be able to gather information regarding cultural background and degree of acculturation, parental expectations, language history, and parental involvement. All of these issues are essential in developing an effective individual educational plan. In conjunction with formal assessment procedures, diagnostic placement provides educational professionals and parents the information essential for the development of an individual educational program that will help to maximally facilitate the child's development.

Preschool Assessment Instruments

This section discusses the instruments often used to measure development of young children from culturally diverse populations.

Kaufman Assessment Battery for Children

The Kaufman Assessment Battery for Children (K-ABC; Kaufman and Kaufman, 1983) measures cognitive and achievement ability in children ages two through twelve, and is made up of the following four scales: sequential processing, simultaneous processing, achievement, and nonverbal. The sequential and simultaneous processing scales were designed to reflect problem-solving and information-processing style although the meaning of each is somewhat unclear and ambiguous. The sequential and simultaneous processing scales combine to form an index of mental ability, called the Mental Processing Composite (MPC), that has a mean of 100 and a standard deviation of 15. The achievement and nonverbal scales likewise yield means of 100 and standard deviations of 15. A noted limitation is that a number of the subtests of the K-ABC recommended for children below the age of three have inadequate floors, with subtests added at ages four and five having inadequate floors as well (Sattler, 1992). In addition to the English version of the K-ABC, a Spanish version of the test (K-ABCM), which was normed in Mexico City, is available. Questions about the standardization sample and the psychometric properties of the test warrant caution when interpreting the results (Figueroa, 1990). Due to these circumstances, the rest of this review of the K-ABC will focus on the English version.

The K-ABC has been one of the most researched evaluation instruments with reference to cross-cultural applicability. A review of the literature suggests the K-ABC is quite applicable to addressing a number of referral questions across a number of diverse populations.

Since reliability is a necessary condition for validity, it is necessary to demonstrate both consistency and stability of scores for target populations. Hernandez and Wilson (1992) examined the internal consistency of the K-ABC Composite and subtests for Mexican American and Anglo children. Analyses were performed on the standardization sample, which included children at eleven age groups ranging from two years, six months, to twelve years, six months. Results indicated similar reliability coefficients across groups for each age group. Similar results were found by Matazow, Kamphaus, Stanton, and Reynolds (1991) with Anglo and African American samples.

The K-ABC also appears to produce scores that are similarly stable over time for low-SES, African American and Anglo children. Lamp and Krohn (1990) administered the K-ABC to thirty-nine Anglo and thirty-two African American children at the ages of four and six. Children in both groups showed expected increases in performance on the K-ABC, and correlations indicating test-retest reliability were identical for both groups.

Earlier in this chapter, it was stated that the average difference between African American, Latino, and Anglo students' scores reported by Kaufman and Kaufman (1983) (seven and three points respectively) is approximately one-half of the difference reported on other measures of cognitive functioning. Further, it was suggested that this diminished group difference is probably due to a sampling bias rather than a true reflection of group differences or similarities. Several researchers have further investigated this question, and their results suggest group differences similar to other cognitive measures (that is, twelve to fifteen points). Specifically, Naglieri (1986) evaluated eighty-six African American and eighty-six Anglo children with the K-ABC and WISC-R. Although only a six-point difference was found between African American and Anglo students' scores, this difference was of similar magnitude to differences in scores on the WISC-R. These results do not support the contention that group differences on performance on the K-ABC are approximately 50 percent of the differences found in the WISC-R.

In a similar study of Mexican American and Anglo students, Whitworth and Chrisman (1987) found no significant differences on K-ABC composite scores between these groups. In addition, both groups showed similarly high and positive correlations with the WPPSI, suggesting consistent concurrent validity across groups also.

The one psychometric property of the K-ABC that has not been demonstrated to be consistent across ethnic and racial groups is predictive validity. It is interesting to note that this bias has been found for both the Mental Processing Composite (MPC) as well as the Nonverbal Composite Score. For example, Glutting (1986) predicted teacher-given academic grades using K-ABC Composite Scores and the MPC for African American, English-dominant Latino students, Spanish-dominant Latino students, and Anglo students. Results indicated bias on the Nonverbal Scale Score such that lower-scoring African American students' academic grades were significantly underestimated compared to the other samples. In addition, the MPC as a predictor tended to overestimate achievement for the ethnic minority students. Other studies have not been supportive of the predictive validity of the K-ABC. For example, Naglieri and Hill (1986) were not able to support the prediction of K-ABC Achievement scores based upon MPC scores.

In general, the K-ABC has been demonstrated to be a reliable and valid instrument with Anglo, African American, and Latino students. Research has been inconsistent with regard to the predictive validity of these scales. In addition, further research needs to be conducted with students who are members of other ethnic and racial groups.

McCarthy Scales

The McCarthy Scales of Children's Abilities (MSCA; McCarthy, 1972) is used with children ages two years through eight years. The MSCA assesses strengths and weaknesses across the following domains: verbal, nonverbal reasoning ability, number aptitude, short-term memory, and coordination. The General Cognitive Index, a measure of intellectual functioning, yields a mean score of 100 and a standard deviation of 16. The remaining five scales (verbal, perceptual-performance, quantitative, memory, and motor) have mean scores of 50 and standard deviations of 10. The MSCA has a number of positive attributes, including an excellent normative sample, good reliability, and colorful, child-oriented stimulus materials. Testing begins with nonverbal tasks and gradually moves toward verbal interaction. A significant limitation, however, is the GCI floor of 50, which limits the scale's usefulness in determining the abilities of severely mentally retarded children and children below the age of three who have below-average cognitive abilities (Sattler, 1992).

A comprehensive review of the literature of the McCarthy Scales was conducted by Valencia (1990). His integration of the research on the use of the McCarthy with culturally diverse populations yielded encouragement and concern. Of greatest concern is the almost complete lack of research on the psychometric properties of the McCarthy Scales with most ethnic minority groups except for Mexican American children. In fact, after reviewing over 175 published articles and dissertations, Valencia was unable to find one study that establishes the concurrent validity or stability of scores with typical African American children. In addition, there were no studies that addressed issues of content validity or reliability for typical African American children or those with special needs. An updated review of the literature performed for this chapter did not reveal any new studies in these areas since Valencia's review.

The encouraging news is that research has suggested good predictive validity of the McCarthy Scales with African American children (Blachman, 1981), Mexican American children (Valencia, 1982), and Puerto Rican children (Shellenberger, 1982). It is important to note that although the McCarthy Scale does demonstrate predictive validity with these groups, the Verbal scale, which is the single best predictor of academic success in Anglo children, is not nearly as strong a predictor with ethnic minority children. It appears that when research has been conducted regarding the use of the McCarthy Scales with diverse student populations, results suggest them to be reliable and valid measures of children's cognitive functioning. Unfortunately, such information is available only for Mexican American and Puerto Rican students. Future research needs to be conducted in order to build confidence in the use of the McCarthy Scales with other populations.

Wechsler Preschool and Primary Scale of Intelligence-Revised

The Wechsler Preschool and Primary Scale of Intelligence-Revised (WPPSI-R; Wechsler, 1989) assesses the intelligence of children ages three years, zero months, through seven years, three months. The WPPSI-R, first published in 1967 and revised in 1989, is a downward extension of the Wechsler Intelligence Scale for Children-Revised (WISC-R; Wechsler, 1974) and the Wechsler Adult Intelligence Scale-Revised (WAIS-R; Wechsler, 1981). Each of the Wechsler tests was designed to assess an individual's overall capacity to process information presented verbally (Verbal scale) and visually (Performance scale). Verbal and Performance scale scores combine to form a Full-Scale Score with all three scales having a mean of 100 and a standard deviation of 15. Standardization procedures for the WPPSI-R are quite good and, in fact, the WPPSI was one of the first major intelligence tests to adequately sample racial minorities (Sattler, 1992). Other psychometric properties of the test are strong as well, including internal consistency (Full-Scale IQ = .96; Verbal IQ = .95; Performance IQ = .92) and test-retest reliability (Full-Scale IQ = .91; Verbal IQ = .90; Performance IQ = .88). Unfortunately, the WPPSI-R is still a relatively new test and as yet there have been no published studies attesting to its efficacy with children from diverse ethnic and cultural backgrounds.

Battelle Developmental Inventory

A relatively recent entry into the field of preschool assessment, the Battelle Developmental Inventory (BDI; Newborg and others, 1988) is an individually administered instrument appropriate for children from birth through eight years old. The BDI assesses functioning in six developmental domains, including Personal-Social, Adaptive Functioning, Motor Development, Communications, and Cognition. A unique and highly desirable feature for working with ethnically diverse children is the ability to employ the BDI as both a norm-referenced and a criterion-referenced instrument. Although additional research needs to be conducted on the BDI, its structure, ease of linkage to intervention, and flexible administration procedures demonstrate good promise for use with ethnically diverse populations.

Case Example

James is an outgoing four-year, eight-month-old African American boy who was born following prenatal exposure to crack cocaine, alcohol, and other controlled substances. He lives in a highly economically depressed urban center. James is enrolled in a preschool program for crack-exposed children and is currently in familial foster care with his elderly grandmother.

An evaluation was conducted to determine the extent of his progress through the preschool program, as well as to help determine the most effective kindergarten placement for him. The evaluation included standardized norm-referenced tests (K-ABC), criterion-referenced test (Battelle Developmental Inventory), informal play-based assessment (using a dynamic process, that is, test-teach-test), classroom observations, and observations of guardian-child interactions. In addition, objective behavior rating scales were completed by the teacher and grandmother. Results of the evaluation revealed substantial delays in cognitive, language, social, and emotional development. Convergent data suggested self-regulation, planning, and inability to meaningfully integrate natural cues and feedback as primary sources of interference with his development across each of these domains. To determine the most effective school placement for James, he was enrolled in a local Head Start program on a trial basis. During this time, the Head Start teachers kept logs of James's daily activities and evaluated his ongoing progress. After six months, a team meeting was held to share and integrate all of the assessment data, and to update and formalize an educational plan.

Summary and Conclusions

The assessment of young children from diverse ethnic and cultural backgrounds poses unique and complex difficulties for psychologists.

Psychologists must consider a myriad of variables, including culture and degree of acculturation, language development and history, the social context of development, as well as individual differences among children, in order to develop effective assessment and intervention plans. In addition, caution must be taken when choosing assessment instruments. It is apparent from this review of the literature that even the most sophisticated instruments still have gaps and weaknesses when applied to diverse populations. It is important to consider that validity is a property of a test that is specific to a situation, assessment question, and population. If there are any variations in these factors, validity must be reestablished. Perhaps the single most important point to consider when assessing young children is that flexibility in assessment and information gathering using multiple techniques are necessary to develop an accurate portrait.

References

Allen, B. A., & Boykin, A. W. (1992). African-American children and the educational process: Alleviating cultural discontinuity through prescriptive pedagogy. *School Psychology Review, 21*, 586–596.

Anastasi, A. (1982). *Psychological testing* (5th ed.) New York: Macmillan.

Armour-Thomas, E. (1992). Intellectual assessment of children from culturally diverse backgrounds. *School Psychology Review, 21* (4), 552–565.

Azuma, S. D., Malee, K. M., Kavanaugh, J. A., & Deddish, R. B. (1991). Confirmatory factor analysis with preterm NBAS data: A comparison of four data reduction models. *Infant Behavior and Development, 14*(2), 209–225.

Bagnato, J. T., & Neisworth, S. J. (1981). *Linking developmental assessment and curricula: Prescriptions for early intervention.* Rockville MD: Aspen Systems.

Barclay, A., & Allen, J. (1982). Effects of Head Start programs on factor structure of mental ability. *Psychological Reports, 51*, 512–514.

Barona, A. (1990). Assessment of multicultural preschool children. In B. Bracken (Ed.), *The psychoeducational assessment of preschool children* (2nd ed., pp. 374–397). Needham Heights, MA: Allyn & Bacon.

Bayley, N. (1969). *Bayley Scales of Infant Development: Birth to Two Years.* San Antonio, TX: Psychological Corporation.

Bayley, N. (1993). *Bayley Scales of Infant Development* (2nd ed.). San Antonio, TX: Psychological Corporation.

Blachman, B. A., (1981). *The relationship of selected language measures and the McCarthy Scales to kindergarten and first-grade reading achievement.* Unpublished doctoral dissertation, University of Connecticut.

Boykin, A. W. (1986). The triple quandary and the schooling of Afro-American children. In U. Neisser (Ed.), *The school achievement of minority children* (pp. 57–92). Hillsdale, NJ: Erlbaum.

Bracken, B. A. (1983). Observing the assessment behavior of preschool children. In K. D. Paget & B. A. Bracken (Eds.), *The psychoeducational assessment of preschool children* (pp. 63–79). Philadelphia: Grune & Stratton.

Bracken, B. A. (1985). A critical review of the Kaufman Assessment Battery for Children (K-ABC). *School Psychology Review, 14,* 21–36.

Bracken, B. A. (1987). Limitations of preschool instruments and standards for minimal levels of technical adequacy. *Journal of Psychoeducational Assessment, 5,* 313–326.

Brazelton, T. B. (1973). *Neonatal Behavioral Assessment Scale.* Philadelphia: Lippincott.

Brigance, A. H. (1978). *Brigance Diagnostic Inventory of Early Development.* Woburn, MA: Curriculum Associates.

Caldwell, B. M., & Bradley, R. H. (1978). *Home observation measurement of the environment.* University of Arkansas: Authors.

Ceci, S. J. (1990). *On intelligence . . . more or less: A bio-ecological treatise on intellectual development.* Englewood Cliffs, NJ: Prentice Hall.

Chasnoff, I., Griffith, D. R., Freier, C., & Murray, J. (1992). Cocaine/polydrug use in pregnancy: Two-year follow-up. *Pediatrics, 89,* 284–289.

Chisolm, J. (1991). Biology, culture, and the development of temperament: A Navajo example. In J. K. Nugent, B. M. Lester, & T. B. Brazelton (Eds.), *The cultural context of infancy: Vol. 2.* New York: Ablex.

Cole, M. (1988). Cross-cultural research in the sociohistorical tradition. *Human Development, 31,* 137–157.

Copple, C., Sigel, I. E., & Saunders, R. (1984). *Educating the young thinker: Classroom strategies for cognitive growth.* Hillsdale, NJ: Erlbaum.

Das, J. P. (1984). Simultaneous and successive processes and the K-ABC. *Journal of Special Education, 18*(3), 229–238.

Datta, L. (1974). The impact of the Westinghouse/Ohio evaluation of Project Head Start: An examination of the immediate and longer term effects and how they came about. In C. C. Abt (Ed.), *The evaluation of social programs.* Newbury Park, CA: Sage.

Datta, L. (1979). Another spring and other hopes: Some findings from national evaluations of Project Head Start. In E. Zigler & J. Valentine (Eds.), *Project Head Start: A legacy of the war on poverty.* New York: Free Press.

Diamond, K. E., (1987). Predicting school problems from preschool developmental screening: A four year follow-up of the Revised Denver Developmental Screening Test. *Journal of the Division of Early Childhood, 11*, 247–253.

DiPietro, J. A., & Larsen, S. K. (1989). Examiner effects in the administration of the NBAS: The illusion of reliability. *Infant Behavior and Development, 12*(1), 119–123.

Dunst, C. J. (1980). *A clinical and educational manual for use with the Uzgiris Hunt Scales of Infant Psychological Development.* Baltimore: University Park Press.

Dunst, C. J., & Gallagher, J. L. (1983). Piagetian approaches to infant development. *Topics in Early Childhood Special Education, 3*(1), 44–62.

Dunst, C. J., & Rheingrover, R. M. (1983). Structural characteristics of sensorimotor development among Down's Syndrome infants. *Journal of Mental Deficiency Research, 27*(1), 11–22.

Dusek, J. B. (1985). *Teacher expectancies.* Hillsdale, NJ: Erlbaum.

Eishima, K. (1992). The effects of obstetrics conditions on neonatal behavior in Japanese infants. *Early Human Development, 28*(3), 253–263.

Ensher, G. L., & Clark, D. (1986). *Newborns at risk: Medical care and psychoeducational interventions.* Rockville, MD: Aspen.

Feuerstein, R. (1980). *Instrumental enrichment: An intervention for cognitive modifiability.* Baltimore: University Park Press.

Fewell, R. R., & Langley, M. B. (1984). *Developmental Screening Inventory-II.* Austin, TX: Pro-Ed.

Figueroa, R. A. (1990). Assessment of linguistic minority group children. In C. R. Reynolds and R. W. Kamphaus (Eds.), *Handbook of psychological and educational assessment: Intelligence and achievement.* New York: Guilford.

Frankenberg, W. K., Camp, B. W., & van Natta, D. R. (1971). Validity of the Denver Developmental Screening Test, *Child Development, 42*, 475–485.

Frankenberg, W. K., Dodds, J. B., Fandal, A. W., Kazuk, E., & Cohrs, M. (1975). *Denver Developmental Screening Test.* Denver: LADOCA Project and Publishing Foundation.

Frankenburg, W. K., Fandal, A. W., Sciarillo, W. D., & Burgess, D. (1981). The newly abbreviated and revised Denver Developmental Screening Test. *Journal of Pediatrics, 99*, 995–999.

Furuno, S., O'Reilly, K. A., Hosaka, C. M., Inatsuka, T. T., Allman, T. L., & Zeisloft, B. (1979). *Hawaii Early Learning Profile (HELP): Activity guide.* Palo Alto, CA: VORT Corporation.

Gardner, H. (1983). *Frames of mind: The theory of multiple intelligences.* New York: Basic Books.

Gerken, K. C. (1991). Assessment of preschool children with handicaps. In

B. A. Bracken (Ed.), *The psychoeducational assessment of preschool children* (2nd ed., pp. 392–429). Boston: Allyn & Bacon.

Glutting, J. J. (1986). Pothoff bias analysis of the K-ABC MPC and Non-Verbal Scale IQ among Anglo, Black, and Puerto Rican kindergarten children. *Professional School Psychology, 1*(4), 225–234.

Gopaul-McNicol, S. (1993). Understanding and meeting the psychological and educational needs of African-American and Spanish-speaking students. *School Psychology Review, 21,* 529–531.

Greer, S., Bauchner, H., & Zuckerman, B. (1989). The Denver Developmental Screening Test: How good is its predictive validity? *Developmental Medicine and Child Neurology, 31*(6), 774–781.

Grossman, K. E., & Grossman, K. (1986). Phylogenetic and ontogenetic aspects of the development of the parent-child bond and of children's problem solving competence. *Zeitschrift fur Entwick Lungspsychologie und Pedogogische Psychologie, 18,* 287–315.

Guralnick, M. J. (1991). The next decade of research on the effectiveness of early intervention. *Exceptional Children, 58*(2), 174–183.

Harper, D. C., & Wacker, D. P. (1983). The efficiency of the Denver Developmental Screening Test with rural disadvantaged preschool children. *Journal of Pediatric Psychology, 8,* 273–283.

Hawley, T. L., & Disney, E. R. (Winter, 1992). Crack's children: The consequences of maternal cocaine abuse. *Social Policy Report, 6*(4). Ann Arbor, Mich.: Society for Research in Child Development.

Haywood, H. C., Brown, A. L., & Wingenfeld, S. (1986). Dynamic approaches to psychoeducational assessment. *School Psychology Review, 19*(4), 411–422.

Hefferman, L., & Black, F. W. (1984). Use of the Uzgiris and Hunt Scales with handicapped infants: Concurrent validity of the Dunst age norms. *Journal of Psychoeducational Assessment, 2,* 159–168.

Henry, W. A. (1990, April 9). Beyond the melting pot. *Time,* p. 28.

Hernandez, A. E., & Wilson, V. (1992). A comparison of Kaufman Assessment Battery for Children reliability for Mexican American and non-Hispanic Whites. *Hispanic Journal of Behavioral Science, 14*(3), 394–397.

Hightower, A. D., DeMeis, J. A., & Meller, P. J. (in preparation). An examination of the Gesell School Readiness Screening Test.

Hightower, A. D., Lotyczewski, B. S., & Spinell, A. P. (1990). *The AML-R behavior rating scale.* Rochester, New York: Primary Mental Health Project.

Horowitz, F. D., Sullivan, J. W., & Linn, P. (1978). Stability and instability in newborn infants: The quest for elusive threads. In A. J. Sameroff (Ed.), *Organization and stability of newborn behaviors: A commentary on the Brazel-*

ton Neonatal Behavioral Assessment Scale. Monographs of the Society for Research in Child Development, 43 (5–6, Serial No. 177).

Howard, A., & Scott, R. (1981). The study of minority groups in complex societies. In R. H. Munroe, R. L. Munroe, & B. B. Whitings (Eds.), *The handbook of cross-cultural human development* (pp. 113–152). New York: Garland.

Ilg, F. G., Ames, L. B., Haines, J., & Gillespie, C. (1980). *The Gesell school readiness screening test*. New Haven, CT: Programs for Education.

Johnson-Martin, W., Jens, K. G., & Attermeier, S. M. (1979). *The Carolina curriculum for handicapped infants and infants at risk*. Baltimore: Rookes.

Kaufman, A. S., & Kaufman, N. L. (1983). *K-ABC: Kaufman Assessment Battery for Children*. Circle Pines, MN: American Guidance Service.

Kemhali, A. S., & Sarp, N. (1989). The growth and development of children living in residential units in Turkey. *Maladjustment and Therapeutic Education, 7*(3), 163–168.

Laboratory of Comparative Human Cognition. (1983). Culture and cognitive development. In W. Kessen (Ed.), *Handbook on child development: Vol. 1. History, theory, and methods* (pp. 295–356). New York: Wiley.

Lamp, R. E., & Krohn, E. J. (1990). Stability of the Stanford-Binet Fourth Edition and K-ABC for young Black and White children from low income families. *Journal of Psychoeducational Assessment, 8*(2), 139–149.

Lazar, I., & Darlington, R (1982). The lasting effects of early education: A report from the Consortium for Longitudinal Studies. *Monographs of the Society for Research in Child Development, 195*(47), 2–3.

Lee, V. F., Brooks-Gunn, J., Schnur, E., & Liaw, F. R. (1990). Are Head Start effects sustained? A longitudinal follow-up comparison of children attending Head Start, no preschool, and other preschool programs. *Annual Progress in Child Psychiatry and Child Development*, 600–618.

Lowe, M., & Costello, A. J. (1988). *Symbolic play test* (2nd ed.). London: NFER-Nelson.

Mardell-Czudnaiski, C., & Goldenberg, D. (1983). *Developmental indicators for the assessment of learning—revised*. Edison, NJ: Childcraft Education.

Martikainen, M. A. (1992). Effects of intrauterine growth retardation and its subtypes on the development of preterm infants. *Early Human Development, 28*, 7–17.

Matazow, G. S., Kamphaus, R. W., Stanton, H. C., & Reynolds, C. R. (1991). The reliability of the K-ABC for Black and White students. *Journal of School Psychology, 29*(1), 37–41.

Mathiessen, B. (1988). The preverbal dialogue: A study of some aspects of mother-infant interaction during the first year of life. *Tidsskrift for Norsk Psykologforening, 25*, 109–117.

McCall, R. W., Eichorn, D., & Hogarty, P. (1977). Transitions in early mental development. *Monographs of the Society for Research in Child Development, 43* (Serial No. 171).

McCarthy, D. A. (1972). *Manual for the McCarthy Scales of Children's Abilities.* San Antonio, TX: Psychological Corporation.

McIntyre, T. (1992). A primer for cultural diversity for educators. *Multicultural Forum, 1,* 6–7, 12.

Meller, P. J. (1994). Authenticity in assessment: A psychometric perspective. In A. M. Saturnelli (Ed.), *In pursuit of excellence and equity: Transforming testing in New York State* (pp. 73–84). Albany, NY: New York State Council of Education Associations.

Miller, S. A. (1986). Parents' belief about their children's cognitive abilities. *Developmental Psychology, 22,* 276–284.

Muret-Wagstaff, S., & Moore, S. G., (1991). The Hmong in America: Infant behavior and rearing practices. In J. K. Nugent, B. M. Lester, & T. B. Brazelton (Eds.), *The cultural context of infancy* (Vol. 2. pp. 168–199). New York: Ablex.

Naglieri, J. A. (1986). WISC-R and K-ABC comparison for matched Black and White children. *Journal of School Psychology, 24*(1), 81–88.

Naglieri, J. A., & Hill, D. S. (1986). Comparison of WISC-R and K-ABC regression lines for academic prediction with Black and White children. *Journal of Consulting and Clinical Psychology, 15*(4), 353–355.

Najman, J. M., Bor, W., Morrison, J., & Anderson, M. (1992). Child developmental delay and socio-economic disadvantage in Australia: A longitudinal view. *Social Science and Medicine, 34*(8), 829–835.

Neisworth, J. T., & Bagnato, S. J. (1986). Curriculum-based developmental assessment: Congruence of testing and teaching. *School Psychology Review, 15,* 180–199.

Neisworth, J. T., & Bagnato, S. J. (1987). *The young exceptional child: Early development and education.* New York: Macmillan.

Newborg, J., Stock, J. R., Wnek, L., Guidubaldi, J., & Svinicki, J. (1988). *The Battelle Developmental Inventory.* Allen, TX: DLM Teaching Resources.

Paget, K. D. (1990). Assessment of intellectual competence in preschool age children: Conceptual issues and challenges. In C. R. Reynolds & R. W. Kamphaus (Eds.), *Handbook of psychological and educational assessment of children: Intelligence and achievement* (pp. 751–760). New York: Guilford.

Paget, K. D., & Nagle, R. J. (1986). A conceptual model of preschool assessment. *School Psychology Review, 15*(2), 154–165.

Pelligrini, A. D., Perlmutter, J., Galda, L., & Brody, E. H. (1990). Joint reading between Black Head Start children and their mothers. *Child Development*, *61*, 443–453.

Piaget, J. (1983). Piaget's theory. In P. H. Mussen (Ed.), *Handbook of child psychology* (Vol. 1, 4th ed.) New York: Wiley.

Rastogi, A. K, Srivastava, V. K., Dutt, K., & Singh, J. V. (1987). Pattern of development in preschool children of a rural community. *Indian Journal of Clinical Psychology*, *14*(1), 29–31.

Reynolds, C. R., & Clark, J. (1983). Assessment of cognitive abilities. In K. D. Paget & B. A. Bracken (Eds.), *The psychoeducational assessment of preschool children* (pp. 163–189). Philadelphia: Grune & Stratton.

Reynolds, C. R., & Kaiser, S. M. (1990). Test bias in psychological assessment. In C. R. Reynolds & T. B. Gutkin (Eds.), *The handbook of school psychology* (pp. 487–525). New York: Wiley.

Robertson, C. G. (1990). A practical model for test development. In C. R. Reynolds & R. W. Kamphaus (Eds.), *Handbook of psychological and educational assessment of children: Intelligence and achievement* (pp. 62–85). New York: Guilford.

Rubin, K. H. (1990). *New directions for child development: Children's play.* San Francisco: Jossey-Bass.

Salvia, J., & Ysseldyke, J. E. (1988). *Assessment in special and remedial education* (4th ed.). Boston: Houghton Mifflin.

Santos de Barona, M., & Barona, A. (1991). The assessment of culturally and linguistically different preschoolers. *Early Childhood Research Quarterly*, *6*, 363–376.

Sattler, J. M. (1992). *Assessment of children* (3rd ed.). San Diego, CA: Author.

Shellenberger, S. (1982). Assessment of Puerto Rican children: A cross-cultural study with the Spanish McCarthy Scales of Children's Abilities. *Bilingual Review*, *9*, 109–119.

Sigel, I. E. (1970). The distancing hypothesis: A causal hypothesis for the acquisition of representational thought. In M. R. Jones (Ed.), *The effects of early experience* (pp. 37–61). Miami, FL: University of Miami Press.

Sigel, I. E., & Cocking, R. R. (1977). *Cognitive development from childhood to adolescence: A constructivist perspective.* New York: Holt, Rinehart & Winston.

Simmons, W. (1985). Social class and ethnic differences in cognition: A cultural practice perspective. In S. F. Chipman, J. W. Segal, & R. Glaser (Eds.), *Thinking and learning skills: Vol. 2. Research and open questions* (pp. 519–536). Hillsdale, NJ: Erlbaum.

Sparrow, S. S., Balla, D. A., & Cicchetti, D. V. (1984). *Vineland adaptive behavior scales.* Circle Pines, MN: AGS.

Springle, J. E., & Schaefer, L. (1985). Longitudinal evaluation of effects of two compensatory preschool programs on fourth through sixth grade students. *Developmental Psychology, 21*, 702–708.

Sternberg, R. J. (1985). *Beyond IQ: A triarchic theory of human intelligence.* New York: Cambridge University Press.

Thelan, E. (1984). Learning to walk: Ecological demands and phylogenetic constraints. In L. P. Lipsett & C. Rovee-Collier (Eds.), *Advances in infancy research: Vol. 3.* Norwood, NJ: Ablex. 213–250.

U.S. Congress (1964). *Economic Opportunity Act of 1964,* PL-89–16, Stat. 108, as amended in scattered sections of 42 USC.

U.S. Congress (1972). *Economic Opportunity Act Amendments of 1972,* PL-92–424, Stat 2425, as amended in scattered sections of 42 USC.

U.S. Congress (1975). *Education for All Handicapped Children Act of 1975,* PL-94–142, Stat 773, as amended in scattered sections of 42 USC.

U.S. Congress (1986). *Education of the Handicapped Act of 1986,* PL-99–457, Stat 1145–1177, as amended in scattered sections of 20 USC.

Uzgiris, I., & Hunt, J. M. (1975). *Assessment in infancy: Ordinal Scales of psychological development.* Urbana: University of Illinois Press.

Uzgiris, I., & Hunt, J. M. (1987). *Infant and experience: New findings with the Ordinal Scales.* Urbana: University of Illinois Press.

Valencia, R. A. (1982). Predicting academic achievement of Mexican American children: Preliminary analysis of the McCarthy Scales. *Educational and Psychological Measurement, 42,* 1269–1278.

Valencia, R. A. (1990). Clinical assessment of young children with the McCarthy Scales of Children's Abilities. In C. R. Reynolds & R. W. Kamphaus (Eds.), *Handbook of psychological and educational assessment of children: Intelligence and achievement* (pp. 209–258). New York: Guilford.

Valenza, E., Simion, F., dalla-Barba, B., & Calabro, L. (1992). Neurobehavioral organization of the newborn in sleep state. *Eta Evolutivas, 43,* 22–35.

van Baar, A. (1990). Development of infants of drug-dependent mothers. *Journal of Child Psychology and Psychiatry, 31,* 911–920.

Vasta, R., Haith, M. M., & Miller, S. A. (1992). *Child psychology: The modern science.* New York: Wiley.

Vygotsky, L. S. (1978). *Mind in society: The development of higher psychological processes.* Cambridge, MA: Harvard University Press.

Walsh, A. D., & Bagnato, S. J. (1991). What is unique about working with infants? In S. N. Elliot & J. C. Witt (Eds.), *Assessment for early intervention: Best practices for professionals* (pp. 110–129). New York: Guilford.

Weber, C. U., Foster, P. W., & Weikart, D. P. (1978). An economic analysis of the Ypsilanti Perry Preschool Project. *Monographs of the High Scope Educational Research Foundation, 5*. Ypsilanti, MI: High Scope Press.

Wechsler, D. (1974). *Wechsler Intelligence Scale for Children-Revised*. San Antonio, TX: Psychological Corporation.

Wechsler, D. (1981). *Wechsler Adult Intelligence Scale-Revised*. San Antonio, TX: Psychological Corporation.

Wechsler, D. (1989). *Wechsler Preschool and Primary Scale of Intelligence-Revised*. San Antonio, TX: Psychological Corporation.

Werner, E. E. (1972). The Denver Developmental Screening Test. In O. K. Buros (Ed.), *The seventh mental measurements yearbook*. Highland Park, NJ: Gryphon Press. 734–736.

Whitworth, R. H., & Chrisman, S. M. (1987). Validation of the Kaufman Assessment Battery for Children comparing Anglo and Mexican-American preschoolers. *Educational and Psychological Measurement, 47*(3), 695–702.

Williams, P. D., & Williams A. R. (1987). Test norms: A cross-cultural comparison. *Journal of Pediatric Psychology, 12*(1), 39–59.

Wolff, M. (1978). Social validity: The case for subjective measurement or how behavior analysis found its heart. *Journal of Applied Behavior Analysis, 11*, 203–214.

Xin, R., Chen, S. K., Tang, H. Q., and Linn, X. F. (1992). Behavioral problems among preschool age children in Shanghai. *Canadian Journal of Psychiatry, 37*(4), 250–258.

Zigler, E., & Berman, W. (1983). Discerning the future of early childhood intervention. *American Psychologist, 38*, 894–906.

Zigler, E., & Seitz, V. (1982). Future research on socialization and personality development. In E. Zigler, M. Lamb, & I. Childs (Eds.), *Socialization and personality development* (2nd ed., pp. 185–199). New York: Oxford University Press.

Zigler, E., & Trickett, P. E. (1978). IQ, social competence, and evaluation of early childhood intervention programs. *American Psychologist, 33*, 789–798.

18

High-Stakes Testing and Its Impact on Racial and Ethnic Minority Students

Richard R. Valencia and Irma Guadarrama

The contemporary United States is experiencing an unprecedented activity and preoccupation with testing in education. "Tests have moved from recorders of the effects of educational reform to initiators of reform, from passive instruments to intrusive devices that threaten test takers and seek to dictate the ends of the instructional system. Tests have moved from descriptive indices to certification devices" (Airasian, 1988, pp. 304–305). Never before in American educational history has testing taken on such a powerful role in decision making. As of 1990, forty-seven states had requirements that students be assessed—at some point in time—on competency tests. Of the forty-seven states, 83 percent ($n = 39$) mandated the use of state-developed, state-selected, or state-approved tests (Allington and McGill-Franzen, 1992a).

The purposes of the present chapter are to describe this testing campaign and to examine its impact on racial and ethnic minority students (hereafter referred to as minority students). Our target populations are minority students who have experienced persistent, pervasive, and disproportionately low academic achievement in public schools (that is, Mexican Americans, Puerto Ricans, African

---

Note: Portions of the discussions of high school competency tests and teacher certification tests have been excerpted with minor revisions from Valencia and Aburto (1991b, pp. 224–225 and pp. 222–223, 230).

Americans, and American Indians). The focal grade levels are elementary and secondary; impact on minority college students is also discussed, but in the context of teacher competency tests.

The type of testing discussed here falls in the rubric of state-mandated, *high-stakes testing*. We define high-stakes testing as *the exclusive or near-exclusive use of a test score to make significant educational decisions about students, teachers (prospective and incumbent), and schools*. Such decisions can have desirable or undesirable consequences for students, teachers, and schools. That is, a great deal rides on the results of certain tests. A significant gain or loss can result from test score outcomes (hence the notion of high-stakes). For example, twenty states mandate the use of a minimum competency test at the secondary school level to determine who receives a high school diploma (Suarez and Gottovi, 1992). Students who pass such tests are awarded a high school diploma, and students who fail are denied a diploma. Diploma denials can occur even in instances where a student has an acceptable grade point average and has passed all course requirements (for example, see Lott, 1993a). In sum, high-stakes testing emphasizes the decision-making aspects of tests. Such tests have "significant contingencies associated with the test results" (Popham, 1991, p. 12).

The negative contingencies connected to high-stakes testing are potentially severe in practice. Suarez and Gottovi (1992) provide examples of stakes for students, teachers, and schools that exhibit poor test performance. Contingencies for students involve participation in cocurricular activities, placement in remedial classes, grade-to-grade promotion, and graduation from high school. For teachers, the contingencies deal with pay and teacher certification (both initial and continued). For schools, they involve financial resources, certification, and takeover.

Our coverage of the subject at hand is as follows: First, we provide a brief history of high-stakes testing. Second, we discuss a number of controversies associated with high-stakes testing, with particular focus on the impact of high-stakes testing on minority students. We emphasize minority students because of the widespread finding that, compared to their White peers, minorities tend to perform lower on most educational tests (for example, see Valencia, 1991a). Third, we discuss alternative assessments to high-stakes testing, with special attention on implications for assessment of minority students.

Brief History of High-Stakes Testing

It appears that the term high-stakes testing was adopted by Madaus (1988a). The actual appearance of high-stakes testing, however, can be traced to the late 1970s, apparently appearing out of the blue (Airasian, 1988). "In the late 1970s, after two decades of focus on policies designed to enhance educational equity, concern began to be expressed about the quality of American schools and pupils" (p. 304). There was a great deal of discussion by educators and policymakers about falling test scores and a growing mediocrity of schooling quality, as evidenced by student test performance. The best-known of this rash of "excellence" studies documenting lowered standards and mediocre test performance was *A Nation At Risk*, a report by the National Commission on Excellence in Education (1983).

Beginning in the late 1970s, a wide range of reform tactics were advanced as responses to the perceived need to improve educational quality in the country. The strategies that surfaced as the winners can be characterized best as "new forms of standardized testing and accountability programs" (Airasian, 1988, p. 305). During the ten years that spanned the initial activity of the high-stakes testing movement (late 1970s to late 1980s), Airasian notes that *all* state legislatures encountered the issue of the new state-mandated, high-stakes testing programs. Most state legislatures have adopted such programs, conveying this message to students, teachers, and schools: You are all to be held accountable for academic performance.

The new tests and programs are quite different from the conventional standardized achievement testing practiced in America's schools for decades. Airasian (1988) observes that the new-sprung tests are different in three significant ways. First, they are *mandated* by the state. With few exceptions, all schools and pupils within a state are required to take the tests. Exceptions tend to be limited; for example, seventeen states have test exemption policies for limited-English proficiency (LEP) students (Lam and Gordon, 1992). Second, local school districts have lost a great deal of discretion in the development, administration, scoring, and interpretation of the tests. These facets of testing are now controlled by the state, which governs all aspects of single, state-approved tests administered across all school districts. Third, as discussed previously, these are high-stakes tests with sanctions built in based on statewide standards.

In sum, high-stakes testing—as currently conceptualized—has been in existence since the late 1970s. It is important to note, however, that such testing is part of a larger movement—public accountability in education. The accountability movement has a long history, beginning around the turn of the century. Milliken (1970) describes the accountability notion as a collective sense "that people are increasingly demanding to know how their children are learning, what they are learning, and why they are being taught whatever they are being taught" (p. 17). Tests are typically used to meet the public's demand for accountability (Resnick, 1979). Current high-stakes testing has assumed powerful roles in holding students, teachers, and schools accountable for improving educational quality via test scores. These new centralized programs and tests with their potent gatekeeping roles, however, are not without controversies, a subject we turn to next.

Controversies Surrounding High-Stakes Testing

Suffice it to say, high-stakes testing is not a value-free and apolitical reform strategy. Given the sudden appearance of this nonempirically validated educational innovation, the loss of control of local schools over their own testing programs, and the gains or losses to students, teachers, and schools resulting from such mandated testing, it is not surprising that a number of controversial issues surround high-stakes testing. In our review of the high-stakes testing literature, we have identified seven issues. They are:

- Symbolic validation (that is, the manner in which high-stakes testing seeks its legitimacy, as opposed to scientific validation)

- Lack of psychometric integrity

- Measurement-driven instruction

- Failure to demonstrate school effectiveness

- Untrained standard setters

- Test abuse in early childhood educational promotional practices

- Impact on minority students

Symbolic Validation

In a riveting treatise, Airasian (1988) contends that high-stakes testing has sought its legitimacy in nonempirical sources—that is, through "symbolic validation." (He notes that despite scholarly advice urging systematic, empirical substantiation of educational innovations before implementation, *most* educational innovations are adopted by policymakers in the absence of scientific, technical evidence of effectiveness.) Airasian sees high-stakes testing as but another one of these unproven innovations. High-stakes testing mandated by state governments possesses three basically distinct forms of symbolic appeal: "First, they [high-stakes tests] symbolize order and control in a system where autonomous local control is perceived to be weak. Second, they symbolize, in the constructs they are perceived to measure, important educational outcomes. Third, they symbolize a distinct value or moral outlook that the public wishes to see reflected in its schools" (p. 306).

As such, high-stakes testing—through the legitimizing process of symbolic validation—becomes a powerful symbol of accountability and gatekeeping. Airasian's analysis (1988) helps to explain, in part, the massive public embrace and policymaker adoption of high-stakes testing. One major implication stemming from such an analysis is that high-stakes testing has taken on a life of its own, with proponents ignoring the point that the items on these tests measure very small samples of behavior. As well, such testing programs forget that other assessment and reform strategies could be tried. High-stakes testing serves as a public barometer of our society's educational progress. Having such a gauge is not inherently troublesome. What is of concern, however, is that high-stakes testing legitimacy is derived from symbolic validation, not scientific bases.

Lack of Psychometric Integrity

Although Airasian (1988) does not concern himself with the technical properties of state-mandated, high-stakes testing, other scholars do. For example, Madaus (1986) in reference to teacher competency tests, contends that "present methods of determining content validity are simply insufficient" (p. 13). He points out that content validity is determined by a "tightly closed circle" (p. 13) of test contractors and a small number of educators, and thus external and independent review does not typically occur. In addition, he notes that contractors fail to relate test knowledge and skills to actual classroom performance by teachers, thus criterion-related validity is clearly lacking.

Valencia and Aburto (1991a), also focusing on teacher competency tests, "conclude that existing psychometric research is, in general, weak and irrelevant, and that although there have been attempts to debias existing tests, differential criterion validity research across ethnic groups is sorely needed" (p. 195). Regarding criterion validity research, in general, Valencia and Aburto's summary conclusion of existing research is that a prospective teacher's score on teacher tests (for example, National Teachers Examination Common Examinations) has no predictive validity to how effective or competent a teacher is in day-to-day classroom instruction. Finally, Valencia and Aburto's coverage of technical issues of teacher testing concludes that problems abound in standard setting procedures (for example, operationally defining the notion of "competence").

Measurement-Driven Instruction

One of the most frequently voiced criticisms of high-stakes testing is that teachers—more and more—are "teaching to the tests." In current educational parlance, this practice is referred to as "measurement-driven instruction" (for coverage of this issue, see for example, Madaus, 1986, 1988b; Meisels, 1989; Suarez and Gottovi, 1992). The main point critics argue is that the contingencies tied to high-stakes testing "drive" curricular instruction. As Madaus notes, "A high-stakes outcome such as graduation or teacher accountability grafted to test performance is the fuel of measurement-driven instruction" (1988b, p. 34). There are some scholars, however, who argue that measurement-driven instruction is beneficial (for example, Popham, Cruise, Rankin, Sandifer, and Williams, 1985). Their contention is that if a test measures specific skills and knowledge, then preparing students for such a test can improve learning.

Of the concerns raised about the consequences of measurement-driven instruction via high-stakes testing, four primary issues are most frequently discussed (Suarez and Gottovi, 1992). First, an inordinate amount of class time is spent on test preparation. Given the pressure teachers are under to make sure their students succeed on high-stakes tests, excessive (and valuable) class time is devoted to test-taking skills, exposing students to the type of test content they are to face, and introducing students to the types of thinking required by the impending tests. Second, there is a gradual narrowing of the curriculum. Greater attention is paid to the basics, for example, in the language arts and mathematics. Because of this curricular shift, less time is available for other areas such as foreign language instruction and the arts. Third, similar to concern number two, there is a gradual curricular shift, but this concern deals with the quality of instruction. High-stakes testing overwhelmingly covers basic competencies (for example, recall of knowledge; fundamentals of reading), and the common test item format is select-type (that is, multiple-choice testing). As a result of the preparation required for this type of test content and format, students are often deprived of opportunities to engage in instructional strategies that involve higher-level thinking (for example, synthesis) via test situations using supply-type items (for example, essays). Fourth, measurement-driven instruction in high-stakes testing programs sends messages to educators, as well as to students and parents, "that the purpose of education is solely for academic achievement rather than for the social, intellectual, emotional, and physical development of young people" (Suarez and Gottovi, 1992, p. 84). This exclusionary nature of measurement-driven instruction is certainly troublesome. Education becomes very narrowly defined as a cognitive mission, ignoring the affective and physical components of human development. Also, as Suarez and Gottovi observe, this cognitive preoccupation of instruction is particularly disturbing in that it comes at a time when our schools are becoming increasingly culturally diverse, and therefore students have greater needs to meet the challenges of living in a diverse society.

Failure to Demonstrate School Effectiveness

A major assumption of high-stakes testing is that such assessment will make schools more accountable. That is, there is a widespread belief among high-stakes testing proponents that there will be increased accountability in schools and such pressure will exert its intended outcome—the improvement of school effectiveness (Allington and McGill-Franzen, 1992a, 1992b). To what degree is this significant assumption true? Existing research does not support this major supposition of high-stakes testing policy (see Allington and McGill-Franzen; also see Gottfredson, 1986, and Walker and Levine, 1988, cited in Allington and McGill-Franzen, 1992a).

For example, Allington and McGill-Franzen (1992a) examined third-grade reading achievement test data from New York's accountability program. Their major finding was that the state-reported accountability profiles (as measured by high-stakes testing) were spurious. That is, the percentages of students achieving state minimum competency standards were inflated. New York State has a discretionary policy of exempting handicapped (special education) students and pupils who are retained from taking the state-mandated assessments. And if such students take the examinations, their scores are *not* included in the aggregate reported by the state. The research query posited by Allington and McGill-Franzen (1992a) was, "How does a school's policy on retaining students or identifying them as handicapped influence the reading achievement levels reported by that school for high-stakes testing?" (p. 4). The authors compared the test scores of third-grade students attending seven elementary schools. They looked at the percentage of students who passed the third-grade competency test (excludes scores of handicapped and retained students) with the percentage of students who would have passed the test if the *entire* age cohort had been tested. Each of the seven comparisons showed substantial percentage gaps between the exclusive cohort (higher pass rates) and the inclusive cohort (lower pass rates). This led Allington and McGill-Franzen to conclude: "The increasing use of retention and special education placement in the primary grades can produce an increase in the proportion of children reported as achieving state minimum competency standards with no actual increase in school effectiveness or improvement in the reading achievement levels of students" (p. 10).

Suffice it to say, the research references cited above constitute a very small number of empirical studies investigating whether high-stakes testing improves school effectiveness. Given the pervasive use of high-stakes testing and the many concerns raised in this chapter, it seems to us that school effectiveness research of high-stakes testing should be a high priority for policymakers and researchers. In a related vein, some researchers have advocated that—given the educational entrenchment of high-stakes testing programs—there needs to be a redesign of state-mandated, high-stakes testing reports to provide sounder evidence of school effectiveness (Allington and McGill-Franzen, 1992b). Much too much is at stake to allow such testing to continue in the absence of empirical support.

Untrained Standard Setters

An essential feature of a high-stakes test is the pass score, sometimes referred to as the cut-off score. The determination of the standard that identifies those individuals who pass or fail the test is clearly arbitrary. This in itself constitutes a problem. As Valencia and Aburto comment, "A number of . . . specialists in the measurement community . . . have indicated that the process of standard setting is open to repeated criticism, particularly along lines of the difficulty in executing the process and defending it psychometrically" (1991a, p. 207).

An exacerbating aspect of current standard setting in high-stakes testing is the growing number of state and local school boards that are required to determine the pass score (Popham, 1987). For example, as discussed by Popham, all local school boards in California are mandated to set pass scores for high school graduation tests. Popham also notes that there are increasing cases where local school boards (for example, Charleston County, South Carolina) are setting standards for teacher and administrator competency tests. The main problem associated with these new standard setters is that they "establish passing standards for important tests [and] typically do so with little or no standard-setting experience" (Popham, 1987, p. 77). In light of the inherent technical problems associated with standard setting (see Valencia and Aburto, 1991a), adding the questionable reliability of human judgment makes a sensitive measurement issue even more vulnerable to criticism.

Given that amateurs abound in standard setting on high-stakes tests, Popham (1987) advocates that formal training be given to policymakers who engage in standard-setting tasks. Popham discusses ten factors that might be covered in formal preparation (that is, one- to two-hour training sessions). Some of these factors involve "decision implications" (such as, What are the potential consequences for one who fails?), "quality of the examination" (that is, How reliable is the test? Are parallel forms equidifficult?), and "adequacy of preparation" (that is, Have all examinees had the same opportunity to learn the instructional material on which they will be tested?). The training session ideas presented by Popham make sense. If such preparation is widely implemented, then the arbitrariness of current standard-setting practices could be reduced.

Test Abuse in Early Childhood Education

One of the most tragic high-stakes testing practices is seen in the use of such tests in early childhood education to identify young children who will be promoted or retained. Meisels (1989), in a highly critical paper, discusses the 1986 Georgia Quality Basic Education (QBE) Act. Georgia mandated that all pupils seeking to matriculate to Grades 1 and 4 must first pass an academic test (as well as satisfy a teacher, who also assesses the child's readiness). The test chosen by the Georgia Department of Education was the California Achievement Test (CAT), level 10 (CTB/McGraw-Hill, 1988).

Meisels (1989) criticizes the Georgia high-stakes, early childhood education testing plan on several counts. For example: only 44 percent of the total CAT items are administered, and this modification was done without psychometric validation. Thus, the short-form version may not share the psychometric properties of the parent version. In any case, the CAT manual contains no data on predictive validity. The Georgia CAT contains only the three subtests of mathematical concepts, sound recognition, and visual recognition; no assessment of other important samples of behavior (such as attention, rate of learning, or expressive language) are done. In addition, the Georgia plan ignores the substantial body of empirical evidence that kindergarten retention does not improve academic achievement. Based on these and other criticisms, Meisels voices: "The Georgia plan for kindergarten testing and retention is the *reductio ad absurdum* of high-stakes testing, where an entire state (and so far the only state) has transferred control over its early childhood education program to a single group-administered paper-and-pencil test" (p. 20). (It should be noted that the Georgia Board of Education rescinded the kindergarten provisions of the QBE Act as a reaction to public criticism (Wodtke, Harper, Schommer, and Brunelli, 1989).)

In addition to concluding that such high-stakes testing is a flawed policy, Meisels (1989) offers a reformulation of early childhood education and curricular organization (for example, limitation of class size, and increased home-school communication) and alternative testing (that is, "low-stakes testing" in which test scores are used for diagnostic and remediation purposes). His suggestions are well taken.

Impact on Minority Students

In that the focus of this chapter is the impact of high-stakes testing on minority students, for organizational purposes we present the discussion of this controversy in a separate section of its own. Minority students as a whole typically score lower than their White peers on various conventional group-based and individually administered achievement tests. It must be emphasized that these between-group comparisons are based on aggregated test scores for each group, and such comparisons are sometimes confounded by socioeconomic status. For example, Oakland (1978) compared lower-class and middle-class Anglo, African American and Mexican American students on reading and mathematics achievement (test scores). It was found that Mexican American and African American middle-class students performed higher than their Anglo lower-class peers on academic achievement.

However, the disproportionately lower performance of low socioeconomic status (SES) Mexican American, Puerto Rican, American Indian, and African American students is one of the most persistent and pervasive findings seen in the schooling literature. It is not surprising, therefore, that minority students—compared to White students—also perform lower on the new high-stakes tests. Given the frequently low performance of low-SES minority students on such tests—coupled with the contingencies associated with high-stakes testing—then it is also not surprising that high-stakes testing generally has disparate, negative impact on minorities. We explore this impact in this section.

Our contention is that the utilization of high-stakes, singular data sources is an improper use of educational testing. As Gronlund (1985) admonishes, "In all . . . educational decisions, test scores provide just one type of information and should always be supplemented by past records of achievement and other types of assessment data. *No major educational decision should ever be based on test scores alone*" (p. 480). Furthermore, the practice of high-stakes testing poses a particularly troublesome situation for minority students (for example, Mexican Americans) who, as a group, typically experience massive school failure (Valencia, 1991a).

For many Mexican American students, high-stakes testing has become another hurdle heaped on existing obstacles (such as school segregation and inequities in school financing), thus intensifying the difficulties of these students as they seek to attain school success.

In the following discussion, we cover the impact of three types of high-stakes testing on minority students. First, we examine the disproportionate failure rate of minority students on state-mandated competency tests that high school students take to determine whether they will be awarded or denied a high school diploma. Second, we discuss the disparate, negative impact of teacher competency tests on minority students who seek teaching certification. Such tests are powerful determinants of who becomes state certified to teach. Third, we explore the impact of what we call "school-based competency tests" on students who attend predominately minority schools. This type of high-stakes testing uses the local school as the unit of analysis. Based on test results, inter- and intradistrict comparisons can be made. For schools that perform at unacceptable levels, the extreme negative impact is one of "takeover" (loss of accreditation, school closure, and subsequent receivership by the state).

As a data source for these three types of high-stakes testing, we will use the state of Texas to illustrate how state-mandated, high-stakes testing programs have disparate impact on minority students. Texas is a useful example first because it is a multiethnic state. According to a Texas Education Agency report, in fall 1990 there were 3.4 million students attending grades kindergarten through twelve (K-12) in Texas public schools (Garcia, 1991). Of this total, 49.5 percent were White, 33.9 percent were Hispanic (overwhelmingly Mexican American), 14.4 percent were Black, 2 percent were Asian, and .2 percent were American Indian. Thus, Texas can provide some insights to comparative high-stakes testing across racial and ethnic groups. In addition, such data, for the most part, are readily available.

High School Competency Tests for Diploma Award or Denial

The type of high-stakes testing used to determine a high school student's eligibility for a diploma is frequently called minimum competency testing (MCT). Our coverage begins with a brief, general overview of MCT impact on minorities. Second, we discuss the impact of MCT on minority students in Texas.

Of the many criticisms leveled against MCT, several relate to questions concerning its impact on minorities. From the start, opponents argued that MCT programs posed substantial risks for students from minority backgrounds, who, through no fault of their own, experience school failure. Rather than forcing those students who fail competency tests to take their education more seriously, some critics believed the diploma sanction would instead lower student motivation for attending school, thus causing increased academic and disciplinary problems and higher drop-out rates (Serow, 1984). Unless tied to an effective remediation program monitored by sensitive administrators, MCT could also be used to justify a new sort of segregation by placing failing students with the worst teachers or in less effective curriculum tracks (Paulson and Bell, 1984). Above all, competency testing further reinforces a stigma of failure for low-achieving students, and in the long run perpetuates racial and economic inequality (Serow). Though few studies have examined the consequences of MCT, it appears many negative premonitions have come to pass.

Failure rates on minimum competency tests for minorities, particularly African Americans, Mexican Americans, and other Latinos, are much higher than they are for White students. For example, early MCT trial run information from Florida showed that of 115,901 students taking the state's MCT in 1977, 36 percent failed. Of those who failed, 78 percent were African American, even though African Americans constituted only about 20 percent of those taking the exam (Paulson and Bell, 1984). In 1978, it was reported that some 77 percent of Blacks, 39 percent of Latinos, and 24 percent of Whites failed the reading test and writing portions (Jensen, 1980). Those students failing received a certificate of completion rather than a standard diploma. This is a significant impact when one considers that a certificate of completion is not considered a diploma for purposes of employment in the state of Florida or for purposes of admission to one of Florida's nine state universities. Paulson and Bell estimated that the denial of a diploma to African American students who failed the competency test resulted in a 20 percent decline in African American enrollment in the state's universities and colleges. Competency test performance data from the states of California, North Carolina, and Virginia also confirm the expectation that minority students experience greater difficulty in passing such tests than Whites (Serow, 1984). The high failure rate of African American high school students on Florida's

MCT program led to the nation's first lawsuit challenging MCT (*Debra P. v. Turlington*, 1979/1981/1983; cited in Bersoff, 1984). See Bersoff for a brief discussion of the plaintiff's claims (Debra P. was an African American student; the suit was a class action), and the court's decision. Supplementary data from the state of North Carolina revealed that students from lower-SES backgrounds were about one-third less likely to pass the exam on their first attempt than students from higher-SES backgrounds (Serow, 1984). As is well known, minorities are usually concentrated in the lower-SES categories.

Texas is one of twenty states that use MCT as a gatekeeper to the high school diploma: Pass the test, you will be awarded a diploma; fail the test, you will be denied a diploma. Of course, students also have to take the required courses to graduate. The current state-mandated, high-stakes test used in Texas that high school students must pass to receive their diploma is the Texas Assessment of Academic Skills (TAAS), a test that measures the academic skills of writing, reading, and mathematics. TAAS was first administered in 1991, replacing the less-difficult Texas Educational Assessment of Minimum Skills (TEAMS).

Racial and ethnic pass/fail comparisons on the TEAMS and TAAS are scattered, but informative. Data from about a decade ago reveal the expected disproportionate failure rate of minorities on the MCT then used in Texas. Based on a 1985 administration of TEAMS to high school juniors, 12 percent ($n = 22,485$) of the examinees failed the mathematics section and 9 percent ($n = 16,921$) failed the English language arts sections (Archer and Dresden, 1987). Regarding racial and ethnic comparisons, the failure rates for mathematics were: African American, 19 percent; Mexican American, 18 percent; Whites, 6 percent. The failure rates for the language arts section of TEAMS were: African American, 19 percent; Mexican American, 16 percent; White, 4 percent. Data were not available for pass/fail rates for students who retook TEAMS. Archer and Dresden also report that almost 12,000 other students were at risk of not receiving a diploma. These were students who did not sit for the 1985 TEAMS administration nor any subsequent make-up dates. Although racial and ethnic breakdowns were not available for these thousands of "no shows," one can assume minority students were disproportionately represented. In sum, although data are not available for *final* diploma denials, TEAMS data from a decade ago in Texas are very suggestive that diploma denials were disproportionately imposed on African Americans and Mexican American students (Archer and Dresden, 1987).

How do present-day high school students in Texas fare on the relatively new TAAS? Data are available for the 1992–93 school year for first-time test results for eleventh-grade students (Brooks and South, 1994). (Beginning in the 1993–94 school year, students take their first administration of TAAS in the tenth grade. They have eight chances to pass TAAS in time for senior graduation.) The data presented in Table 18.1 show statewide TAAS pass rates for the aggregate (all eleventh graders) and the subgroups disaggregated by race or ethnicity (that is, White, Hispanic, and African American). Aggregated and disaggregated TAAS scores are also presented for the high schools in the Austin Independent School District (AISD). Comparative TAAS scores for Austin's high schools are shown because of the district's multiethnic makeup. AISD resembles the overall K-12 state enrollment in having no single racial or ethnic group constitute a majority population.

The TAAS statewide pass rates observed in Table 18.1 show that for the aggregated cohort (all eleventh graders), only a slight majority (54.4 percent) of students passed (first-time administration for these students). This fairly low pass rate on TAAS provides some support to the contention that TAAS is more difficult than its predecessor, the TEAMS. With respect to pass rates by race and ethnicity, slightly more than two-thirds (68.8 percent) of White juniors *passed* TAAS. In sharp contrast, and conversely, approximately two-thirds of Mexican Americans (and other Hispanics) and African Americans *failed* TAAS. The current disproportionately high failure

Table 18.1. Statewide and Austin Independent School District (AISD) TAAS Pass Rates for Eleventh Graders, 1992–93 School Year.

Unit of Analysis	Percentage Minority	Comparisons (percent passing)			
		All 11th Graders	White	Hispanic	African American
Statewide		54.4	68.8	38.5	32.1
AISD (high school)					
Anderson	24	75.9	84.9	42.9	52.6
Austin	47	56.7	76.6	29.8	27.6
Bowie	28	71.7	76.3	60.4	58.3
Crockett	49	49.0	58.2	40.2	28.0
Johnston	77	40.7	68.3	31.7	25.0
Lanier	52	37.9	64.4	28.3	9.4
LBJ	61	59.8	92.5	62.5	35.4
McCallum	39	57.1	76.8	39.2	19.3
Reagan	70	42.2	67.0	35.6	19.8
Travis	67	40.0	62.4	29.6	16.7
W. R. Robbins	na	23.2	57.1	14.3	21.4

Note: na = Not Available.

Source: Adapted from Brooks and South (1994). Numbers in "Percent Minority" column are from Lott (1992).

of Mexican Americans and African Americans on TAAS indicate that little has changed in racial and ethnic MCT comparisons since 1985. Table 18.1 also presents comparison TAAS data for Other, Hispanic, and African American eleventh graders attending high schools in Austin, Texas. On a school-by-school basis, the AISD TAAS pass rates for Whites are substantially higher than for minority students.

It can be concluded that state-mandated, high-stakes testing in Texas is taking its toll on minority students by eventually denying a disproportionate percentage of them diplomas. The disparate, negative impact of Texas' high school MCT program on minority students is very likely to escalate because of increased passing standards on TAAS. Members of the high school class of '92 were required to answer correctly 60 percent of TAAS items in order to pass the test. For the class of '93, the pass score was raised to 70 percent. These tougher standards were likely the cause of a doubling of the failure rate on TAAS. In 1992, 3.4 percent of twelfth graders failed TAAS; in 1993, the failure rate was 7.4 percent (Brooks, 1993). There are emerging data that minority students are experiencing increased disparate impact. For example, at Brownsville High School—a predominantly Mexican American high school in South Texas—20 percent of the seniors failed TAAS. This is nearly three times the rate of the statewide average of 7.4 percent (Associated Press, 1993).

Compounding the disparate, negative impact of Texas' high-stakes graduation examination on minority students is the general state of educational affairs in the state. For example, there is widespread school segregation in Texas. Mexican American (and other Latino) students who attend public schools in Texas and California experience a greater degree of segregation than African American students in Mississippi and Alabama (Orfield and Monfort, 1992). It is well documented that there are strong linkages between school segregation and adverse learning and achievement outcomes (Donato, Menchaca, and Valencia, 1991). Another major issue in Texas is the ongoing, contentious battle over school financial inequities (Valencia, 1991b). In 1989, the Texas Supreme Court in a 9–0 decision declared the state's public school system of financing to be unconstitutional (Graves, 1989). Currently, the state legislature is under court order to prepare a new, equitable financing plan that will equalize the large funding discrepancies between poor and more economically advantaged school districts.

In sum, low-SES minority students in Texas and elsewhere in the nation are often forced to traverse an obstacle-filled path in their realization of some semblance of school success. Hurdles, inequities, and adverse conditions abound. High-stakes testing in the form of MCT programs used to determine graduation from high school is one such obstacle. In our opinion, such testing constitutes test abuse. In a later section, we will present some alternative assessment strategies that could help promote nondiscriminatory assessment.

Competency Tests Used for Teacher Certification

As another child of the parental accountability movement, the teacher competency testing movement began in 1978 and has now swept the country. The term *teacher tests* is an umbrella for three forms of paper-and-pencil teacher competency tests. An *admissions* test is a basic skills test required as an entry criterion to a teacher education program. A *certification* test is also a basic skills test, a professional knowledge test, or a subject matter test required as a condition for earning an initial teaching credential granted by the state. A *recertification* test is a basic skills test required of incumbent teachers. Based on recent data, there are twenty-four states that require some type of teacher competency test for admission to a teacher education program; thirty-six states require such testing only upon graduation, as part of state certification, and eighteen states mandate both entrance (admissions) and exit testing (certification) (Eissenburg and Rudner, 1988). There are several states that require teacher competency testing for teachers currently practicing (recertification) (Shepard and Kreitzer, 1987).

Approximately a decade ago, concern was raised at public, political, and school levels about the preparedness and effectiveness of beginning teachers. Because of the continuing criticism of America's teachers and schools (such as the 1983 report, *A Nation at Risk*, by the National Commission on Excellence in Education), the public is demanding some assurance from its state agencies that teachers who become licensed are actually competent—hence the introduction of competency tests. The central idea behind such testing is that before people be allowed to teach, they must demonstrate basic skills (for example, mathematical ability, reading, and writing) that are believed to be necessary to carry on day-to-day instructional activities. Although the motive underlying teacher competency testing is clear (that is, the need to upgrade teacher quality), the nature of teacher testing is fraught with conceptual, measurement, and social problems (Valencia and Aburto, 1991a, 1991c). In the case of prospective teachers, they have been forced to carry a very disproportionate burden of teacher reform efforts. That is, minority examinees, compared to their White peers, have failed teacher tests at very high rates—one factor adding to the enormous minority teacher shortage, which is at a crisis situation. The sharp decline of minority teachers comes at a time in which the minority school-age population is growing at dramatic rates. In 1980, the total minority elementary and secondary public school enrollment nationally was 27 percent (Orfield, 1988). By the year 2000, the combined minority enrollment is predicted to be 33 percent of the total, national public school population (Smith, 1987)—a growth of 22 percent in two decades. During the same time period, the total minority teaching force in grades K-12 is projected to *decline* by 60 percent—from 12.5 percent in 1980 to less than 5 percent in the year 2000 (Smith).

The negative, disparate impact of high-stakes teacher competency tests on prospective minority teachers is a national issue. Based on some older data, typical first-time pass rates on admissions and certification tests ranged (nationally) from 71 to 96 percent for White candidates. Minority pass rates were substantially lower. They were: African American, 15 to 50 percent; Latinos, 39 to 65 percent; Asian American, 37 to 77 percent; American Indian, 20 to 70 percent (Smith, 1987). Reflecting this national trend, there are also sharp differences between White and minority examinees on teacher competency tests used in Texas. For example, based on a 1985 administration of the Pre-Professional Skills Test (PPST; the teacher competency test used then in Texas), the pass rates by race and ethnicity were: White (73 percent), Asian and American Indian (49 percent; data reported in combined fashion), Hispanic (34 percent), and African American (23 percent) (see Table 6 in Valencia and Aburto, 1991b).

How do students currently pursuing teaching certification in Texas fare on the present teacher competency tests? Individuals who seek certification as educators in Texas need to pass the appropriate Examination for the Certification of Educators in Texas (EXCET; Texas Education Code 13.032). The EXCET program is an ambitious undertaking, as indicated by this description from the *EXCET 1991–92 Report* (Texas Education Agency [TEA], 1991–92): "The EXCET program consists of 53 content specialization tests, three professional development (i.e., pedagogy) tests, and seven examinations for a professional certificate (e.g., Superintendent, Mid-management Administrator, Counselor). In general, EXCET examinees take a combination of tests—the appropriate professional development test and one or more content specialization tests in the fields in which they are seeking certification. . . . All EXCET test items are multiple-choice. Individuals may retake EXCET tests as many times as needed to pass" (p. 1).

The *EXCET 1991–92 Report* provides rich data for 28,156 examinees who attempted a particular EXCET test for the first time in 1991–92. Included in the various comparisons (for example, by gender, age) are pass rate performances by race and ethnicity. Table 18.2 presents pass rates by race and ethnicity. The EXCET tests

Table 18.2. Racial and Ethnic Pass Rates on EXCET for Total, Professional Development, and Elementary Comprehensive Test Administrations.

| | Total[a] | | | Other[b] | | | Comparisons by race/ethnicity | | | | | |
| | | | | | | | Hispanic | | | African American | | |
Name of test	no. taken[c]	no. passed	% passed	no. taken[c]	no. passed	% passed	no. taken[c]	no. passed	% passed	no. taken[c]	no. passed	% passed
Total	49,256	42,088	85.4	40,705	36,124	88.7	6,369	4,671	73.3	2,182	1,293	59.3
All-Level Prof. Develp.	1,740	1,597	91.8	1,426	1,372	96.2	208	154	74.0	106	71	67.0
Elementary Prof. Develp.	7,084	6,388	90.2	5,963	5,606	94.0	859	608	70.8	262	174	66.4
Secondary Prof. Develp.	5,024	4,610	91.8	4,331	4,093	94.5	505	386	76.4	188	131	69.7
Elementary Comprehensive	8,533	8,028	94.1	7,083	6,917	97.7	1,055	844	80.0	395	267	67.6

Note: [a] "Total" (for "name of test") refers to all content specialization, professional development, and professional certificate tests taken. [b] "Other" includes Whites, Native Americans, Asians, Pacific Islanders, and other examinees who did not report their race or ethnicity. Overwhelmingly, the Other category includes White examinees. [c] "no. taken" refers to number of tests taken in each category.

Source: Adapted from TEA (1991–92, Table 4).

compared are: the total, which refers to *all* first-time administrations ($n = 49,256$) of the specialization, professional development, and professional certificate tests taken; the three professional development tests (all-level, elementary, and secondary); and the elementary comprehensive test, which is also required for teacher certification at the elementary level. The EXCET professional development tests "measure pedagogical knowledge in areas such as instructional planning and methodology, curriculum development, classroom management, assessment and evaluation and principles of education" (TEA, 1991–92, p. 6).

The data shown in Table 18.2 echo the long-standing finding in racial and ethnic comparative pass rates on teacher competency tests: White examinees, compared to minority examinees, pass teacher tests at considerably higher rates. For example, on *all* first-time EXCET administrations (nearly 50,000) in 1991–92, Whites (overwhelmingly represented in the "Other" category) had a pass rate of 88.7 percent—about 15 percentage points higher than Hispanics and 29 percentage points higher than African Americans. Similar pass rate gaps are also seen in the three EXCET Professional Development tests and the Elementary Comprehensive test. For White examinees, the pass rates on these four frequently taken tests average in the mid to high 90 percents. Intermediately are Hispanics, whose pass rates range from the low 70 percents to about 80 percent. African American examinees have the lowest pass rates on these four tests, averaging in the mid to high 60 percents—considerably lower than their White peers.

Suffice it to say, the disproportionately low percentage of minority students in teacher education programs in Texas institutions of higher education—coupled with minority students' disproportionately high failure rate on EXCET—point to a recruitment and teacher supply problem. As the *EXCET 1991–92 Report* underscores in its "key issues" section (TEA, 1991–92): "Texas must intensify efforts to recruit minorities into careers in education. Only 17 percent of the beginning teachers (persons completing a traditional teacher education program or alternative certification program) are Hispanic and only 5 percent are African American. Teachers entering Texas from other states are 4 percent Hispanic and 5 percent African American. Students in public education [in Texas] are 34 percent Hispanic and 14 percent African American. . . . The supply of minority teachers in most certification areas, including those designated as critical need areas will probably continue to show significant gaps compared to the student population (p. i)."

In the 1991–92 school year, the percentages of Hispanics and African Americans teaching in the Texas public school population (early childhood education through grade 12) were 13.7 percent and 8.5 percent, respectively. The percentages of Hispanics and African American students enrolled in early childhood through grade 12 were 34.4 percent and 14.3 percent, respectively. In terms of a student/teacher disparity analysis, Hispanic teachers were *underrepresented* by 60 percent. African American teachers were also *underrepresented*, by 41 percent. We estimate that white teachers were *overrepresented* by about 50 percent.

The small supply of minority teachers in critical shortage presents a very pressing problem. The Texas Education Agency (TEA) has identified four critical need areas in which the current supply of teachers is not adequate. These areas are: special education, mathematics, science education, and bilingual education (TEA, 1991–92). Let us examine the latter, the bilingual education teacher shortage in Texas. As the grade level frame of reference, we focus on prekindergarten through grade six (PK-6)—the grades in which bilingual education is typically taught. As well, these levels encompass the teaching areas for those who obtain the Elementary Bilingual Education certification. As of March 1994, in Texas there were 7,084 bilingual certified teachers assigned to PK-6 bilingual education classrooms (computer printout provided by TEA Bilingual Education Office). As of January 1994, there were 315,584 PK-6 students identified by the TEA as limited-English proficient (LEP) (computer printout provided by TEA Bilingual Education Office). To calculate the estimated demand of PK-6 bilingual teachers, we use a demand calculation of 22:1 (that is, student to teacher ratio of twenty-two to one, a TEA average minimum for elementary grades). Dividing the 315,584 LEP count by 22 provides an estimated demand of 14,345 bilingual teachers. Next, we subtract the current supply (n = 7,084 PK-6 bilingual teachers) from the estimated demand (14,345 teachers). The difference (that is, the estimated shortage) is 7,261 PK-6 bilingual teachers. In short, in order for Texas to solve the severe supply shortage of bilingual teachers in PK-6 the number of teachers would need to double immediately—an unlikelihood given the obstacles we have discussed. Texas is not alone in this shortage of bilingual teachers. For example, California had 1.1 million K-12 LEP students in 1993, and an estimated shortage of 19,903 K-12 bilingual teachers (Gold, 1994).

Another issue compounding the serious shortage of bilingual teachers in Texas is that Mexican Americans—who have disproportionately high failure rates on EXCET—are also the ethnic group that disproportionately pursues teaching careers in bilingual education. In 1991–92, 1,182 examinees took (for the first time) the content specialization EXCET test in Bilingual Education. Of this total, 956 (81 percent) were Mexican American (and other Hispanic) examinees (TEA, 1991–92). Although the pass rate on this test was relatively high for Hispanics as a whole (87.3 percent), the bottleneck for eventual certification appears to be on the Elementary Professional Development test, where Table 18.2 shows a Hispanic pass rate of 70.8 percent.

In the final analysis, a strong case can be made that state-mandated, high-stakes teacher competency testing is having disparate, negative impact on prospective minority teachers (and minority students). Without an adequate supply of minority teachers, much is lost. First, minority students get shortchanged by not having an adequate number of racial and ethnic role models, and everything that entails in terms of shared identity. Second, the delivery of bilingual and multicultural education significantly suffers because of the critical teacher shortage in this area. Third, minority access to educational leadership roles (for example, the principalship) is often thwarted because of the small number of minority teachers—classroom teaching is frequently required for certification as an administrator, posing another pipeline problem for minorities. In sum, these three issues are disturbing and threatening to our ever increasingly culturally and linguistically diverse society. The main obstacles appear to be the very low percentage of minorities in college pursuing teaching careers, plus the disproportionately high failure rate of minority examinees on teacher competency tests. These alone are solvable problems, where, given the political will, researchers, policymakers, and educators could begin to rectify matters. In the final section on alternative assessments we will return to this challenge.

School-Based Competency Tests Used for Rating Campuses

A third form of high-stakes testing is what Valencia and Aburto (1991b) refer to as "school-based competency testing." Like the other two types of high-stakes testing we have discussed (high school diploma issuance and teacher certification), school-based competency testing is also state mandated. It is typical for school-based competency testing to be a component of an omnibus "school reform" package passed by a state legislature (Valencia and Aburto). Such testing programs are considered to assess minimum skills in broad-based achievement domains (for example, mathematics, reading, and writing) administered at select grade levels to elementary and secondary students.

Valencia and Aburto (1991b) coined the term *school-based competency testing* because the individual school is the unit of analysis. Test scores are reported for the aggregate (for example, the mean pass percentage for all third graders at a particular school). In turn, aggregate scores can be compared along intra- and interdistrict lines. Often, the statewide average is juxtaposed as a global frame of reference. To be sure, school-based competency testing is serving a public accountability function. The results of such testing are often presented for public scrutiny in local newspapers. Valencia and Aburto refer to these detailed newspaper reports of comparative test results as "public report cards." Interestingly, the public disclosure of local schools' test scores is, in some cases, required by law. For example, in Texas the Texas Education Agency (TEA) requires, by law, that "each board of trustees . . . to publish a report describing the educational performance of the district and of each campus, and make it available to the public" (TEA, 1993, p. 16). Underscoring the public nature of school-based competency testing, the TEA refers to the reports as "campus report cards" (p. 17).

How does school-based competency testing constitute high-stakes testing, and what are the consequences for minority students? First, some states have built-in financial incentives for schools to do well on the state-mandated, high-stakes testing. That is, local schools can reap monetary rewards for improving their test scores. For example, the Texas legislature recently created the highly competitive Texas Successful School Award system to recognize schools that show superior achievement or academic growth on the TAAS test. As a case in point, five schools in the Austin Independent School District (AISD) won cash awards in mid 1992 for outstanding academic achievement. They were among 125 schools receiving awards, out of 6,000 public schools in Texas (Todd, 1992). The monetary awards ranged from $50,079 to $136,306.

The Texas Successful School Award system uses both TAAS scores and comparative demographic indicators (such as percentage of minority students and SES), so predominantly minority schools are eligible to be award recipients. Of the five schools selected in the AISD, two were predominantly minority, two predominantly White, and one was ethnically mixed. If TAAS test performance alone was used as the criterion for identifying superior schools, then predominantly minority schools would generally be locked out of the competition. In sum, although the monetary award given to the outstanding school is quite small compared to the school's overall budget, each dollar counts in an era of fiscal austerity. Thus, state-testing programs, such as the one in Texas, that have built-in financial incentives do indeed contain elements of high-stakes testing.

A second way that school-based competency testing constitutes high-stakes testing has to do with how an individual school's reputation is shaped by the public report cards that emerge from test results. As discussed earlier, the results of school-based competency tests frequently serve as a powerful mechanism in forcing schools to be accountable to the public. Local superintendents, principals, and teachers often receive unambiguous messages about their performance. Public rebuke is not that uncommon. For example, a headline in the *Austin American-Statesman* read: "San Marcos school superintendent takes heat over test scores" (Hiott, 1993). The issue here involved school board and parental disappointment over low TAAS scores. Caught in the fray was the San Marcos School District superintendent whose three-year contract was up for consideration (San Marcos is a small city about fifteen miles south of Austin). Of course, there is the flip side of public accountability. That is, high-performing schools often flaunt their scores (for example, Lott, 1993b). This is particularly common in suburban schools where test scores are considerably higher than scores in nearby urban schools and statewide averages (see, for example, Taylor, 1992). The main concern we observe, however, about school-based competency tests and their role as public report cards is the potential impact on shaping the public's views of minority schools. A case in point is a late 1992 newspaper article, "Who's learning? Who isn't," that appeared in the *Austin American-Statesman* (Lott, 1992). The focus of the article was on the achievement gap (as measured by TAAS) between minority and White students in the AISD. Achievement gaps were reported by grade level (third, fifth, seventh, ninth, and eleventh) and school level (sixty-three elementary, thirteen middle, and ten high schools). As expected, of the numerous Black-White gaps and Hispanic-White gaps analyzed, there were (with a few exceptions) higher performances by White students. Although there is mention in the news article that the minority-White achievement gap is a "gap that is attributed by almost everyone to economics rather than ability" (Lott, 1992, p. A4), the reader tends to get a sense of futility about solving the achievement chasm. The burden of change appears to be placed on the homes of minority children rather than the learning environment in the schools. Note the following account from the news article:

> If current [growth] trends continue, Hispanic students will make up the majority of the district in about 10 to 12 years. And those students will likely remain the most economically disadvantaged in the district.
>
> That means the students AISD now struggles most to serve are becoming the majority.
>
> Superintendent Jim Hensley said the school district must try to overcome the obstacles to teaching poor children and must overcome the attitude that because of problems at home, poor children can't learn.
>
> A teacher at Travis Heights Elementary school, Roberta Wright, agrees with Hensley, but she stresses that the problems some children must overcome in order to learn are tremendous.
>
> "These are real problems," said Wright, who has written for *Texas Monthly* about her teaching experiences at Winn Elementary School. "We have (in AISD) many children born into poverty. These are mothers malnourished when their kids are in the womb, pregnant

mothers drinking too much or smoking too much. These
children are born with a high rate of learning problems"
[p. A4].

The third way that school-based competency testing represents
high-stakes testing has to do with the accreditation ratings of
schools and the consequences of such ratings, some being grave.
Once again, as our case in point, we refer to Texas. In May of 1993,
the Texas legislature enacted Senate Bill 7 (SB 7), which included
a chapter that revised and consolidated existing sections in a statute
pertinent to educational accountability (TEA, 1991–1992). SB 7
determined accreditation status ratings for districts using TAAS
scores, attendance, and drop-out rates. These academic indicators
served as standards and criteria for rating school districts and their
campuses. The four status ratings are:

- *Exemplary*—the district's performance meets the state
  exemplary standards

- *Recognized*—the district's performance meets or exceeds
  required improvement and is within 10 percent of state
  exemplary standards

- *Accredited*—the district does not attain required performance levels for exemplary or recognized; nor does its
  performance fall into the "clearly unacceptable" level
  as defined by the commissioner of education.

- *Accredited Warned*—the district's performance is
  "clearly unacceptable" as defined by criteria set by the
  commissioner. (TEA, 1993, p. 8)

In August 1993, the Texas Education Agency (TEA) made public its SB 7 ratings of Texas' public schools. Suffice it to say, newspapers throughout the state assertively covered the TEA ratings.

What received most news was the identification—by name—of schools that were rated "low-performing" or "clearly unacceptable." The major standard used to rate these poor-performing schools was the TAAS test. If only 20 percent or fewer of a school's students passed TAAS, it was cited (rated) as "clearly unacceptable." The 20 percent pass rate was for all grade levels in which TAAS was administered and for all subjects. The consequences for these schools was, potentially, grim. Under state law, low-performing campuses will undergo sanctions (TEA, 1993). After public notification of being rated clearly unacceptable, low-performing, a campus could go through a series of sanctions, beginning with a "public hearing," followed by the submission of a "student achievement improvement plan," and the possibility of the commissioner appointing a "special campus intervention team." If the low-performing school continues to perform poorly after a year or more, the commissioner has the power to suspend the powers of the local board of trustees and to appoint a "board of managers" to govern the school. The final resort, and sanction, is "campus closure." The TEA report admonishes: "Finally, if after two years of school intervention, the campus fails to improve outcomes for its students, the commissioner is authorized to order closure of the school program on the campus. In this case, the commissioner will direct the district to abolish the school and provide for transfer of students to a campus that demonstrates the ability to adequately meet the educational needs of its students" (TEA, 1993, p. 27).

When the TEA ratings were made public in August 1993, there was little surprise that the schools identified as clearly unacceptable, low-performing were predominantly minority schools. In the AISD, for example, eight schools (seven elementary and one middle) were labeled as such (Lott, 1994). The combined minority enrollments (African American and Hispanic) in the seven elementary schools ranged from 94 percent to 98 percent; the middle school had a combined minority enrollment of 82 percent (Lott, 1992). It is not difficult to imagine the state of mind of principals, teachers, students, and parents in these low-performing minority schools who are forced to get on with the business of schooling as the specter of school closure hangs over their heads. Aside from this haunting worry is the issue of public perception of their schools. As a principal of one of the TEA-rated low-performing AISD elementary schools lamented, "The whole school has been labeled because of one measurement [TAAS]" (Lott, 1993b).

In conclusion, we see no educational sense for the use of TEA ratings, particularly the rating of "clearly unacceptable, low-performing schools." To use threats (that is, possible school closure) as a means to improve academic achievement in low-performing minority schools is not sound educational policy. At worst, it constitutes institutionalized bullyism. Furthermore, the TEA campus rating policy of poor-performing schools is grounded in "deficit thinking," a construct that contends school failure lay in cognitive and motivational shortcomings of students, as well as in their economic and familial backgrounds. Deficit thinking, a person-centered explanation of school failure, "pays little, if any, attention to how schools are institutionally implicated in ways that exclude students from learning" (Ronda and Valencia, 1994, p. 6). The TEA campus rating policy ignores the systemic educational problems that abound in Texas (for example, massive school segregation, inequities in school financing, and underserving of the limited-English proficiency student population). For the TEA to sidestep these issues and to place the burden of school reform solely on the local campus is an indefensible policy.

Alternative Assessments to High-Stakes Testing

There is growing evidence that high-stakes testing is fraught with problems, particularly the negative impact on minorities. To be sure, assessment reform is needed. Improving the assessment systems to make them more responsive in quality and equity to minority students requires addressing several issues at all levels. This section addresses some of the major issues involved in assessment reform, starting with accountability issues, then issues in attaining equity, and finally, alternative means to assessing and testing at the classroom and school levels.

Creating Responsive Accountability Models

The kinds of assessment and testing appropriate for evaluating the effectiveness of schools can be successfully used only if they are congruent with a school's accountability system. An appropriate and responsive accountability system is one that creates and nurtures effective practices and continual self-evaluation as reflected in its stated goals and policies (Darling-Hammond and Ascher, 1991). Ideally, accountability systems are created for the sole purpose of improving the schools that ultimately lead to effective instruction. However, in the process of creating a manageable system of standardized quality, schools may lose sight of this important purpose, and in effect create problems that are particularly unfair to minority student populations. In this chapter we have discussed, in some detail, how state-mandated (criterion-referenced), high-stakes testing has led to serious consequences for minorities.

Another example of an accountability system that is specifically inappropriate is one that relies heavily on norm-referenced testing and the practice of judging schools' effectiveness by comparing norm-referenced test scores across schools. When schools with large numbers of minority students are compared (using norm-referenced test data) with schools that are predominantly White, the results are usually in favor of the latter schools. Such practices are clearly ineffectual and unfair toward minority students, and are socially irresponsible since they often lead to negative consequences (see, for example, Neill, 1993).

Issues of effective accountability systems can be examined by analyzing the various types of accountability. Systems of accountability are essential to maintaining quality of life in a society. Among the various accountability mechanisms that exist as described by Darling-Hammond (1989; cited in Darling-Hammond and Ascher, 1991), are political accountability, legal accountability, bureaucratic accountability, professional accountability, and market accountability. Two of these, bureaucratic and professional accountability systems, are especially relevant in determining the role and purpose of accountability that is responsive to a high-quality and equitable education. Bureaucratic accountability deals with ensuring a quality and standardized education, adhering closely to established guidelines and policies. Professional accountability encompasses the complex and specialized knowledge and decision-making abilities necessary to meet the individual, varied needs of students. Each is important in promoting quality schooling for all students, but the goals and roles of each are markedly different.

Bureaucratic accountability is the best known and is usually synonymous with overall accountability. It deals with maintaining order and uniformity in the operation of the institutions, as well as in the delivery of instruction. It assumes that students are homogeneous enough that standardized processes will produce the desired effect; that knowledge of how to provide a quality education can be both defined and translated into practice; and that practitioners can responsibly implement the prescribed programs. In this model of accountability, tests are used regularly and faithfully, and their results relied upon for indications of general effectiveness or ineffectiveness.

In the professional accountability model, the focus is on the practitioner, who makes responsible decisions concerning the individual needs of the students. This involves a specialized knowledge base, and requires the institution to ensure that the practitioners are well versed in their field and kept abreast of the current changes. Most importantly, the practitioner focuses on the students: their individual differences, their special needs, their backgrounds, and their histories.

A New Paradigm?

The tools for evaluation in each of the bureaucratic and the professional accountability models are purposely different. The bureaucratic model requires assessment tools and strategies that provide a view of the total educational environment, specifically to ensure that procedures and rules are followed. The professional model necessitates strategies and tools that focus on developing ways to accurately assess the knowledge and skills of the students, and attaining appropriate and sufficient feedback that is used to inform classroom instruction.

The question of which tools and strategies to use for effectively assessing schools is hardly moot when considering the fact that each testing instrument has a designated purpose, and deciding which instruments to use is the purview of the practitioner who must evaluate students for a specific purpose. Thus, by examining the goals that promote quality and equity in an evaluation system, one can determine appropriate means of evaluating for specific purposes.

The pros and cons of performance-based and norm-referenced tests have been adequately discussed in the literature (see, for example, Frechtling, 1991; Mehrens, 1992). Performance-based assessment has been touted by many experts as a viable alternative to norm-referenced testing because of its promise to safeguard and improve quality and equity in education (see, for example, Baker, O'Neil, and Linn, 1993; Darling-Hammond, 1994; LaCelle-Peterson and Rivera, 1994; Linn, Baker and Dunbar, 1991; Messick, 1994; Wiggins, 1989). Others have criticized norm-referenced testing (see Frederiksen, 1984; Shepard, 1991) because of its lack of alignment to both the instructional goals and practices and to current thought in cognitive development.

The key to an effective evaluation system is in the selection of the instrumentation, and in using the data to strengthen the schooling process. An important source of data for bureaucratic accountability may be norm-referenced testing, but because of its negative consequences for minority students, it should be used sparingly and judiciously. The most important sources of data for professional accountability are the progress and completion profiles of students within a well-planned and cohesive curriculum. Norm-referenced testing data may not be as valuable to a teacher who works with students in a variety of tasks and activities as the feedback from student performance on specific instructional tasks.

Data generated from student performance are valuable to a teacher who uses them to make decisions that affect the instruction and curriculum of the student. Performance-based testing may yield such data, facilitating the decision-making process for practitioners. Yet, these data may have little value for central administration officials who need information for assessing schools as part of entire school district effort. Presently, very little data are available to substantiate the use of performance-based assessment at a global scale. Nevertheless, efforts are underway in several states in the nation to use performance-based assessment instead of norm-referenced testing or the large-scale, criterion-referenced testing programs (for example, high school MCT) (see Darling-Hammond, 1994; Mehrens, 1992). Successful efforts will require, however, the collaboration of proponents from performance-based, norm-referenced testing, and large-scale, criterion-referenced testing—the latter two whom must adopt a broader data base to systematically accommodate the performance-based data into their global schema.

The features of a new paradigm, then, include a combination of assessment strategies and instrumentation that focus on a system that is well-planned, clearly stated, and part of a continual process, and whose goals and policies reflect an affirmation and commitment to ensuring equity for all students. The paradigm also requires valuable and timely feedback, so the teachers and other practitioners may use it to make decisions that benefit the learner, and substantial face validity to aid in conveying a message of support and nurturance, especially to teachers, students, and their parents. Most importantly, the proposed assessment paradigm must deal in a proactive, responsible manner to eliminate test abuses associated with testing minority students.

Is Test Equity Attainable?

A general consensus prevails among assessment experts who believe that the science of constructing tests is typically void of cultural bias as reflected in the following statement: "Well-constructed multiple-choice tests generally fare well under psychometrically accepted definitions of test bias" (Mehrens, 1992, p. 4). The question that remains is what is the psychometrically acceptable definition of bias and does it reflect the changing view held by practitioners who seek equity in education? See Valencia and Lopez (1992) for a discussion of the notions of *test bias* and *test unfairness*. The former is concerned with an inherent feature of a test while the latter deals with how we use test results in decision-making. Even if tests are debiased, the fact that tests are *used* as high-stakes assessments further magnifies the arguments against the use of these tests. In addition, the context validity of such tests is questioned by Linn and others (1991): "It does not follow, for example, that because a multiple-choice, paper-and-pencil test has relatively good predictive validity in low-stakes assessment contexts, the test will lead to valid inferences about the achievement of important educational goals when that test is used in a high-stakes assessment context or to make wise decisions about the educational system" (p. 20).

Performance-based testing as an alternative to norm-referenced testing and large-scale, criterion-referenced testing does not guarantee instant equity for all students. As stated in Linn and others (1991), "it is clear that questions of fairness will loom as large for performance-based measures as they do for traditional tests" (p. 18). Indeed, to simply replace the norm-referenced testing and large-scale, criterion-referenced testing with performance-based testing is merely scratching the surface without impacting the heart of the problem. That performance-based assessment is a tool and not a panacea is exemplified well in the following statement: "If performance assessment is used for high-stakes accountability purposes, many of the same kinds of problems that have occurred with multiple-choice tests will exist for performance-based assessment" (Mehrens, 1992, p. 3).

What constitutes test equity? This question can be explored in a number of ways. From the standpoint of instruction and curriculum, an achievement test should properly and adequately reflect the content, and delivery of the content should be appropriate and successful. If minority students are shortchanged and schools do not effectively provide for adequate and meaningful education, then students will obviously fare poorly in this test, but not because they are cognitively incapable of doing well. Rather, the issue is that students are denied the opportunity to perform well. Whether the test was properly constructed and validated is irrelevant; the administration of the test to the students under these circumstances constitutes an impropriety and injustice. Further, if the results of the test are used to make decisions of a high-stakes nature, the students are doubly denied an equitable educational opportunity.

Another way to analyze test equity is by determining a test's impact on the quality of instruction. As we have previously discussed, the abuses associated with tests that drive instruction have been noted for their role in reducing the quality of instruction (for example, Shepard, 1991). This type of test abuse, however, is especially serious among minority students who, because they experience failure at a greater rate than White students, are generally exposed to test preparation in megadoses, reducing the quality of instruction to a greater extent, and in some cases, worsening the problem instead of resolving it.

Test equity, then, encompasses not just the testing event but a wide array of educational practices. If test equity is to be attained at the classroom level, practitioners must focus on the alignment of instruction with authentic assessment practices. At a global scale or school district level, test equity can be attained when minority students are provided an opportunity to demonstrate their knowledge, and testing results at all levels are used for the sole purpose of facilitating students in their academic endeavors, ensuring their adequate academic and life-long preparation, and eventual graduation.

Questions That Lead to Test Equity

1. Are minority students as adequately prepared as White students to meet the challenge of the test's *content* and *format*? This question distinguishes between "teaching to the test"

and providing a quality education. Teaching to the test is the practice of using the content and format of the test as the curriculum, which does not constitute a high-quality and equitable education.

2. Does the test meet the requirements of being free of bias in terms of ethnicity and gender in the strictest sense (that is, psychometric bias; see Valencia and Lopez, 1992)?

3. Will test results be used for the primary purpose of facilitating minority students' academic growth, and not for labeling individual students or hindering their progress in any way, or for sanctioning or rewarding schools?

4. Does the test play the role of "test" or is it the driving force behind instruction, and as a consequence, dilute the quality of education?

In sum, fragmented reform in assessment holds promise to address only part of the solution to the problem. Attempts at reform that focus on partial change are far too common, and too frequently fail in their efforts to impact change substantially. A comprehensive response in the schools' efforts to resolve the problem is an essential first step. Some of these ideas are explored next.

The Adaptive Assessment Model

The move toward an *adaptive* model for schooling students, as suggested by Glaser (1990), presents a viable response to the educational needs of all students. The adaptive model expands the opportunities for student learning, while practitioners adapt the curriculum and teaching styles to meet the diverse needs, backgrounds, and experiences of their students. This contrasts with the *selective* model, which follows a narrowly defined channel offering limited possibilities and opportunities for students. In an adaptive model, assessment is integrated into the teaching and learning process. This kind of assessment, which is often called *authentic assessment*, has high instructional value that benefits both teacher and student. The assessment tasks relate to the instructional content to such an extent that they are often indistinguishable from the instructional tasks. This type of performance-based assessment can be used in both a classroom and schoolwide setting.

Performance-based assessment for the adaptive classroom has the potential of meeting the important criteria in assessing minority students in a responsible and appropriate manner. The teacher focuses on the learner, learning as much as possible about the student—what the student knows, his or her interests, experiences, family history, and so on. The instructional activities provide opportunities for students to express themselves in various ways, thus allowing teachers to make insightful observations. The students are involved in a multitude of activities—reading and writing projects such as journals, essays, stories, and books; cooperative group activities that produce, for example, projects in science, social studies, and math; community-based projects that link up with environmental organizations or develop relationships with businesses. Students are also involved in the development of portfolios to help them maintain a focus on the quality and quantity of their work, and to assess their work in collaboration with the teacher and, when appropriate, with other students. Activities that combine instruction and assessment are apt to reveal what Kornhaber and Gardner (1993) describe as the multiple intelligences and potentials of minority students that are not acknowledged, and in fact, are hidden in the traditional testing methods.

Performance-based assessment also facilitates teaching and learning processes as described in the constructivist approach to education. Shepard (1989) provides a description of the students' role in a constructivist learning model whereby they "construct their own knowledge and develop their own cognitive maps of the interconnections among facts and concepts" (cited in Marzano, Pickering, and McTighe, 1993, p. 11). In contrast to traditional modes that focus on students' acquisition of fragmented, isolated bits of information, the constructivist model allows for students to learn meaningfully, applying their knowledge to real-world situations by solving problems, making decisions, and simulating activities that will prepare them to reach their potential after graduation. In this model, performance-based assessment activities allow students to demonstrate their competencies through a variety of venues, self-evaluate their products, and chart their own progress. Thus, performance-based assessment activities promote educational equity in providing students the opportunity to demonstrate their knowledge in various ways, focusing on the unique personal qualities of each student.

Performance-Based Assessment as a Staff Development Strategy

An equity issue discussed earlier in this chapter is the training and certification of minority teachers, and how high-stakes testing constitutes test abuse for these prospective teachers. See Valencia and Aburto (1991c) for a discussion of a number of proactive strategies institutions can utilize to increase the proportion of minority teachers. An issue of a different sort is the training, or lack of training, for teachers who work with minority students. This is especially important because of the pervasive problem of a predominantly White teaching force in public schools where the student population is becoming increasingly diverse. School districts with large numbers of minority students and few minority teachers tend to follow a specific profile: the minority students fail in disproportionately high rates; minority teachers, who are underrepresented politically, view themselves as disenfranchised from the school organization; and White teachers, whose large numbers of students are perceived as failures, waver in their commitment to their teaching profession. In many instances, teachers see overpreparing their students for the next round of high-stakes testing as their only option.

Performance-based testing, however, can serve not only to strengthen the relationship between assessment and teaching, thereby improving the instructional component, but it can also serve to facilitate teachers' understanding of their students' strengths, abilities, and conceptual understandings, and of how they can better structure their lessons for increased effectiveness. Darling-Hammond (1994) reflects on this process in the following statement: "As teachers learn about how students approach tasks, what helps them learn most effectively, and what assessment tasks challenge and support the kinds of learning desired, they find themselves transforming both their teaching and their assessment strategies" (p. 22). The key to using performance-based assessment is in making informed decisions about what students need to know, integrating these notions in a well-planned set of standards and performance tasks, and recording and reporting the results in an organized, effective manner (Marzano and others, 1993). Teachers are in the best position to design a performance-based assessment program, but their understanding of this process as an *educational* tool is crucial. Implementing performance-based assessment requires the organizational commitment whereby it becomes a district-wide effort supported in policy and spirit by personnel at every level. Teacher change is more likely to result when such implementation efforts are widespread and comprehensive, and the focus is on change as a process rather than an event (Guskey, 1986).

Schoolwide Assessment

We have argued elsewhere for the importance of assessment reform as an integral part of a comprehensive plan toward educational reform. When viewed as an essential link to an overall process, assessment reform is likely to improve not only assessment strategies, but also play an important role in contributing to the educational reform as a whole. Assessment systems for determining program or school effectiveness are best developed by teachers and principals collaborating and using existing resources. There are several reasons why this approach is more effective than the top-down model, in which teachers are given a prescribed program without their input. First of all, teachers and principals who plan collaboratively and collectively acquire a sense of ownership unlike their noncollaborating counterparts. Ownership is extremely important and essential to any innovation's survival. Change is a very complex and difficult process in which participants must engage in developing and expanding ideas, as well as dealing creatively with problems on a daily basis. The progress of an innovation is most evident when participants are connected to each other and to the innovation from its inception.

Second, in that implementing performance-based assessment models requires the development of standards, tasks, and scoring procedures, teachers and principals must develop these in a cohesive, well-organized manner. Students depend on this cohesive plan to progress from grade to grade with smooth, effective transitions.

Third, to ensure quality and equity, the assessment plan must involve continuous self-evaluation and renewal. This again requires teachers and principals to work in collaboration in identifying areas of needed improvement and creating ways to make them.

Many schools have explored the idea of restructuring at the school level with considerable success. Snyder and Darling-Hammond (1993) report on one school's efforts to define and implement change in collaboration between teachers, parents, and administrators. Part of their plan included a year-long self-study, in which they posed the following questions:

- How do we know how well we are achieving what we want to accomplish?

- What happens at our school? With what effects on whom?

- What approaches to assessment do—and can—we use to help us answer these questions?

- Are these approaches appropriately matched to our values and goals?

- Do these approaches give us information that helps us understand, explain, and improve on what we do? (p. 23)

These questions are not out of the ordinary. What is extraordinary is the efforts of the school's teachers, administrators, and parents to work toward a common goal that is unique to their school's goals and culture. Other efforts describe school and university collaborations in determining ways of using local knowledge to initiate, plan, and implement change (see, for example, Falk and Darling-Hammond, 1993; Guadarrama, 1992). These examples demonstrate how schools are willing to take the first steps toward a difficult process of change.

There is a growing discontent with high-stakes testing. We have identified a number of controversies surrounding such testing, particularly the negative, disparate impact on minority students. As well, we have identified a number of proactive ideas that might be considered for reforming current high-stakes testing. In the final analysis, we are optimistic about workable assessment reform. To facilitate this process, policymakers and practitioners must carefully examine the issues at hand and strive for an assessment system that is truly student-centered and sensitive to the needs of minority students.

References

Airasian, P. W. (1988). Symbolic validation: The case of state-mandated, high-stakes testing. *Educational Evaluation and Policy Analysis, 10*, 301–315.

Allington, R. L., & McGill-Franzen, A. (1992a). Does high-stakes testing improve school effectiveness? *ERS Spectrum, 10*, 3–12.

Allington, R. L., & McGill-Franzen, A. (1992b). Unintended effects of educational reform in New York. *Educational Policy, 6*, 397–414.

Archer, E. L., & Dresden, J. H. (1987). A new kind of dropout: The effect of minimum competency testing on high school graduation in Texas. *Education and Urban Society, 19*, 269–279.

Associated Press. (1993, May 27). 20 percent of Brownsville seniors fail TAAS, won't graduate. *Austin American-Statesman*, p. A15.

Baker, E., O'Neil, H., Jr., & Linn, R. (1993). Policy and validity prospects for performance-based assessment. *American Psychologist, 48*, 1210–1218.

Bersoff, D. N. (1984). Legal constraints on test use in the schools. In C. W. Daves (Ed.), *The uses and misuses of tests: Examining current issues in educational and psychological testing* (pp. 107–125). San Francisco: Jossey-Bass.

Brooks, A. P. (1993, May 25). TAAS failures double '92 rate. *Austin American-Statesman*, pp. A1, A6.

Brooks, A. P., & South, J. (1994, April 24). Exam slights minorities, critics say. *Austin American-Statesman*, pp. A1, A13.

CTB/McGraw-Hill. (1988). *California Achievement Test, Grade K*. Georgia Edition. Monterey, CA: CTB/McGraw-Hill.

Darling-Hammond, L. (1989). Accountability for professional practice. *Teacher's College Record, 91*, 59–80.

Darling-Hammond, L. (1994). Performance-based assessment and educational equity. *Harvard Educational Review, 64*, 5–30.

Darling-Hammond, L., & Ascher, C. (1991). *Creating accountability in big city school systems*. New York: Columbia University, Teacher's College, National Center for Restructuring Education, Schools, and Teaching.

Debra P. v. Turlington, 474 F. Supp. 244 (M. D. Fla. 1974), *affirmed in part and remanded in part*, 644 F. 2d 397 (5th Cir. 1981), *on remand*, 564 F. Supp. 177 (M. D. Fla. 1983).

Donato, R., Menchaca, M., & Valencia, R. R. (1991). Segregation, desegregation, and integration of Chicano students: Problems and prospects. In R. R. Valencia (Ed.), *Chicano school failure and success: Research and policy agendas for the 1990s* (pp. 27–63). The Stanford Series on Education and Public Policy. Basingstoke, England: Falmer Press.

Eissenburg, T. E., & Rudner, L. M. (1988). State testing of teachers: A summary. *Journal of Teacher Education, 39*, 21–22.

Falk, B., & Darling-Hammond, L. (1993). *The primary language record at P. S. 261: How assessment transforms teaching and learning*. New York: Columbia University, Teacher's College, National Center for Restructuring Education, Schools, and Teaching.

Frechtling, J. (1991). Performance assessment: Moonstruck or the real thing? *Educational Measurement: Issues and Practices, 10*, 23–25.

Frederiksen, N. (1984). The real test bias: Influences of testing on teaching and learning. *American Psychologist, 39*, 193–202.

Garcia, J. E. (1991, September 7). Minorities in Texas' schools are the majority. *Austin American-Statesman*, pp. A1, A6.

Glaser, R. (1990). *Testing and assessment: O tempora! O mores!* Pittsburgh, PA: University of Pittsburgh, Learning Research and Development Center.

Gold, N. C. (1994, April). *State educational agency strategies in meeting the need for bilingual education teachers: A progress report.* Paper presented at the meeting of the American Educational Research Association, New Orleans.

Gottfredson, G. D. (1986). *You get what you measure, you get what you don't: Higher standards, higher test scores, more retention in grade* (Report No. 2a). Baltimore: Center for Research on Elementary and Middle Schools, Johns Hopkins University.

Graves, D. (1989, October 7). School finance woes echo across nation. *Austin-American Statesman*, pp. A1, A5.

Gronlund, N. E. (1985). *Measurement and evaluation in teaching* (5th ed.). New York: Macmillan.

Guadarrama, I. (1992). *Self-assessment profiles facilitate decision-making in bilingual education.* Denton: Texas Woman's University, Mentor Teacher Network.

Guskey, T. (1986). Staff development and the process of teacher change. *Educational Researcher, 24,* 5–12.

Hiott, D. (1993, January 19). San Marcos school superintendent takes heat over test scores. *Austin American-Statesman*, p. B1.

Jensen, A. R. (1980). *Bias in mental testing.* New York: Free Press.

Kornhaber, M., & Gardner, H. (1993). *Varieties of excellence: Identifying and assessing children's talents.* New York: Columbia University, Teachers College, National Center for Restructuring Education, Schools, and Teaching.

LaCelle-Peterson, M., & Rivera, C. (1994). Is it real for all kids?: A framework for assessment policies for English language learners. *Harvard Educational Review, 64,* 55–75.

Lam, T.C.M., & Gordon, W. I. (1992). State policies for standardized achievement testing of limited English proficient students. *Educational Measurement: Issues and Practice, 11,* 18–20.

Linn, R. L., Baker, E. L., & Dunbar, S. B. (1991). Complex, performance-based assessment: Expectations and validation criteria. *Educational Researcher, 20,* 15–21.

Lott, T. (1992, November 22). Who's learning? Who isn't? *Austin American-Statesman*, pp. A1, A4, A6-A7.

Lott, T. (1993a, May 25). School board rejects failed students' pleas. *Austin American-Statesman*, pp. B1, B2.

Lott, T. (1993b, October 17). 4 Austin schools may look the same, but a performance gap divides them. *Austin American-Statesman*, pp. A1, A14-A15.

Lott, T. (1994, February 26). 8 schools in AISD get reprieve from state. *Austin American-Statesman*, pp. A1, A5.

Madaus, G. F. (1986). Measurement specialists: Testing the faith—a reply to Mehrens. *Educational Measurement: Issues and Practice*, 5, 11–14.

Madaus, G. F. (1988a). The influence of testing on the curriculum. In L. N. Tanner (Ed.), *Critical issues in curriculum* (pp. 83–121). Eighty-seventh Yearbook of the National Society for the Study of Education. Chicago: University of Chicago Press.

Madaus, G. F. (1988b). The distortion of teaching and testing: High-stakes testing and instruction. *Peabody Journal of Education*, 65, 29–46.

Marzano, R., Pickering, D., & McTighe, J. (1993). *Assessing student outcomes: Performance assessment using the dimensions of learning model*. Alexandria, VA: Association for Supervision and Curriculum Development.

Mehrens, W. A. (1992). Using performance assessment for accountability purposes. *Educational Measurement: Issues and Practices*, 11, 3–9, 20.

Meisels, S. J. (1989). High-stakes testing in kindergarten. *Educational Leadership*, 46, 16–22.

Messick, S. (1994). The interplay of evidence and consequences in the validation of performance assessments. *Educational Researcher*, 23, 13–23.

Milliken, W. G. (1970). Making the school system accountable. *Compact*, 4, 17–18.

National Commission on Excellence in Education. (1983). *A nation at risk*. Washington, DC: U.S. Government Printing Office.

Neill, M. (1993). A better way to test. *The Executive Educator*, September, 24–27.

Oakland, T. (1978). Predictive validity of readiness tests for middle and lower socioeconomic status Anglo, Black, and Mexican American children. *Journal of Educational Psychology*, 70, 574–582.

Orfield, G. (1988, July). *The growth and concentration of Hispanic enrollment and the future of American education*. Paper presented at the National Council of La Raza Conference, Albuquerque, NM.

Orfield, G., & Monfort, F. (1992). Status of school segregation: The next generation. *Report to the National School Boards Association*. Alexandria, VA: Council of Urban Boards of Education.

Paulson, D., & Bell, D. (1984). Back to basics: Minimum competency testing and its impact on minorities. *Urban Education*, 19, 5–15.

Popham, W. J. (1987). Preparing policymakers for standard setting on high-stakes tests. *Educational Evaluation and Policy Analysis*, 9, 77–82.

Popham, W. J. (1991). Appropriateness of teachers' test-preparation practices. *Educational Measurement: Issues and Practice*, 10, 12–15.

Popham, W. J., Cruise, K. L., Rankin, S. C., Sandifer, P. D., & Williams, P. L.

(1985). Measurement-driven instruction: It's on the road. *Phi Delta Kappan, 66,* 628–635.

Resnick, L. B. (1979). The future of IQ testing in education. *Intelligence, 3,* 241–253.

Ronda, M. A., & Valencia, R. R. (1994). "At-risk" Chicano students: The institutional and communicative life of a category. *Hispanic Journal of Behavioral Sciences, 16,* 363–395.

Serow, R. C. (1984). Effects of minimum competency testing for minority students: A review of expectations and outcomes. *The Urban Review, 16,* 67–75.

Shepard, L. (1989). Why we need better assessments. *Educational Researcher, 46,* 4–9.

Shepard, L. A. (1991). Psychometricians' beliefs about learning. *Educational Researcher. 20,* 2–16.

Shepard, L. A., & Kreitzer, A. E. (1987). The Texas teacher test. *Educational Researcher, 16,* 22–31.

Smith, G. P. (1987). *The effects of competency testing on the supply of minority teachers.* A report prepared for the National Education Association and the Council of Chief State School Officers.

Snyder, J., & Darling-Hammond, L. (1993). Learner-centered accountability in action: The Brooklyn new school. In L. Darling-Hammond, J. Snyder, J. Ancess, L. Einbender, A. Goodwin, & M. Macdonald (Eds.), *Creating learner-centered accountability* (pp. 21–27). New York: Columbia University, Teacher's College, National Center for Restructuring Education, Schools, and Teaching.

Suarez, T. M., & Gottovi, N. C. (1992). The impact of high-stakes assessments on our schools. *NASSP Bulletin, 76,* 82–88.

Taylor, C. (1992, January 17). Suburban schools see fewer passing state test. *Austin American-Statesman,* p. B2.

Texas Education Agency. (1991–92). *EXCET 1991–92 Report.* Austin: Division of Professional Educator Assessment, Texas Education Agency.

Texas Education Agency. (1993). *Statewide accountability system: An overview of the accreditation procedures as revised by Senate Bill 7.* Austin: Office of Accountability, Texas Education Agency.

Todd, M. (1992, July 19). Austin-area schools reap awards for improved test scores. *Austin American-Statesman,* pp. B1, B8.

Valencia, R. R. (Ed.). (1991a). *Chicano school failure and success: Research and policy agendas for the 1990s.* The Stanford Series on Education and Public Policy. Basingstoke, England: Falmer Press.

Valencia, R. R. (Ed.). (1991b). The plight of Chicano students: An overview of schooling conditions and outcomes. In R. R. Valencia (Ed.), *Chicano school failure and success: Research and policy agendas for the 1990s* (pp. 3–26). The Stanford Series on Education and Public Policy. Basingstoke, England: Falmer Press.

Valencia, R. R., & Aburto, S. (1991a). Research directions and practical strategies in teacher testing and assessment: Implications for improving Latino access to teaching. In G. D. Keller, J. Deneen, & R. Magallán (Eds.), *Assessment and access: Hispanics in higher education* (pp. 195–232). Albany, NY: State University of New York Press.

Valencia, R. R., & Aburto, S. (1991b). The uses and abuses of educational testing: Chicanos as a case in point. In R. R. Valencia (Ed.), *Chicano school failure and success: Research and policy agendas for the 1990s* (pp. 203–251). The Stanford Series on Education and Public Policy. Basingstoke, England: Falmer Press.

Valencia, R. R., & Aburto, S. (1991c). Competency testing and Latino student access to the teaching profession. In G. D. Keller, J. Deneen, & R. Magallán (Eds.), *Assessment and access: Hispanics in higher education* (pp. 167–194). Albany: State University of New York Press.

Valencia, R. R., & Lopez, R. (1992). Assessment of racial and ethnic minority students: Problems and prospects. In M. Zeidner & R. Most (Eds.), *Psychological testing: An inside view* (pp. 399–439). Palo Alto, CA: Consulting Psychologists Press.

Walker, J., & Levine, D. U. (1988, April). *The inherent impact of non-promoted students on reading scores in a big city elementary school.* Paper presented at the meeting of the American Educational Research Association, New Orleans, LA.

Wiggins, G. (1989). Teaching to the authentic task. *Educational Leadership, 46,* 41–47.

Wodtke, K. H., Harper, F., Schommer, M., & Brunelli, P. (1989). How standardized is school testing? An exploratory observational study of standardized group testing in kindergarten. *Educational Evaluation and Policy Analysis, 11,* 223–235.

Racial and Ethnic Identity Assessment

Eric L. Kohatsu and Tina Q. Richardson

A ddressing cultural issues in the science and practice of psychology has gained increasing importance in recent years. In particular, one within-group variable that has stimulated a significant amount of research has been racial identity development. A number of models have been proposed, both for people of color (for example, Cross, 1971; Helms, 1990a; Jackson, 1976; Milliones, 1980; D. W. Sue and Sue, 1990) and for White Americans (for example, Hardiman, 1982; Helms, 1984, 1990a; Ponterotto, 1988; Rowe, Bennett, and Atkinson, 1994; Sabnani, Ponterotto, and Borodovsky, 1991). In addition, measures assessing racial identity according to these models have also emerged. This chapter will provide an overview of racial identity theory and models and a selective review of the psychometric properties of these scales.

The first half of the chapter will cover racial and ethnic identity theory and important methodological issues associated with these constructs. More specifically, we begin by reviewing both racial identity and ego/ethnic identity models. Nigrescence and Afrocentric-based models of racial identity for people of color and White Americans will be discussed separately, and then *ethnic* identity models will be presented. Then we will provide an explanation of the conceptual differences between the two primary kinds of racial

Note: The first author would like to thank members of his research team, especially Sharon W. Lo, Trinh Luong, and Carol Soudah, for their administrative assistance in preparing this chapter.

identity models; that is, stage/process and typology. Most of the research and instrument development has focused on stage models. We will conclude by discussing the utility of racial identity as a within-group variable and its conceptual differences with ethnic identity, and presenting a number of recent theoretical advances made in racial identity research.

The second half of the chapter focuses on a review of psychometric issues regarding the selected instruments. The first section will review widely used measures that are based primarily (or partly) on Nigrescence theory, namely the Racial Identity Attitude Scale (RIAS), Developmental Inventory of Black Consciousness (DIB-C), and the White Racial Identity Attitude Scale (WRIAS). Recently developed scales, such as the Cultural Identity Attitude Scale/Visible Racial/Ethnic Group Member Identity Attitude Scale (CIAS/VIAS), the African Self-Consciousness Scale (ASC), the Oklahoma Racial Identity Attitude Scale-Preliminary (ORAS-P), and the White Racial Consciousness Development Scale (WRCDS), that hold promise for future research, will be discussed in the second section. In the third section, a number of new, not widely used, or unpublished instruments will be briefly discussed (for example, White Racial Identity Reactions System-WRIRS). Last, in the fourth section, the Multigroup Ethnic Identity Measure (MEIM), an ethnic identity measure, will be reviewed. In addition, brief summary evaluations of each of the instruments will be presented.

Racial Identity Models

The various racial identity models are based on different conceptual frameworks. In this chapter, the racial identity models are classified as either Nigrescence, Afrocentric, Minority (Visible Racial/Ethnic Group Member, or VREG), or White identity-based. Please note that the VREG models were influenced to a large degree by Nigrescence theory. Before reviewing these models, it is important to define what we mean by racial identity. The clearest definition of racial identity was offered by Helms (1990a). According to Helms, racial identity refers to a person's sense of a collective or group identity based on one's perception that he or she shares a common racial heritage with a particular racial group. In addition, racial identity has to do with the quality or manner of a person's racial group identification. An integral component of racial identity theory is that identification with the "larger" group (meaning race) is tempered by how the individual internalizes racism and oppression.

Nigrescence Models

In an attempt to highlight one aspect of the process of identity development for Black people, African American psychologists proposed models of Nigrescence (process of becoming Black) or Racial Identity Development (N/RID; for example, Cross, 1971, 1978, 1991; Cross, Parham, and Helms, 1991; Helms, 1984, 1990a; Jackson, 1976; Milliones, 1973, 1980; Thomas, 1971). These models attempted to define the direction of healthy Black identity development and proposed that overidentification with Whites and/or White culture was a psychologically unhealthy way of resolving identity issues in the midst of a racist society. The N/RID models are stage models, where individuals could potentially move from least healthy, White-defined stages of identity, to most healthy, self-defined racial transcendence (Helms, 1990a).

Although there is variability in the labeling of the stages, the underlying structure of the models is relatively consistent (see Helms, 1990a). For example, Thomas (1971) proposed a five-stage process by which Blacks shed a devalued sense of self and dependence on White society for self-definition: *Withdrawal* occurs when one takes the first step away from White definition toward a new Black identity; *Testifying* is characterized by confronting the anxiety about becoming a self-defined Black person; *Information processing* refers to the process of acquiring knowledge about one's Black heritage and the Black experience; *Activity* is characterized by involvement in activities to find communion within the Black experience; and *Transcendental* entails the individual being relatively free of conflict regarding issues of race, age, sex, and social class.

Somewhat similar to Thomas' model was the Nigrescence model developed by Cross (1971) at roughly the same time. Undoubtedly, the most widely used model in research has been Cross's Nigrescence model. Cross originally proposed a five-stage model wherein each stage was characterized by self-concept issues which had implications for a person's feelings, thoughts, and behaviors. The first stage, *Preencounter,* is characterized by an idealization of Whites and White culture and a denigration of Blacks and Black culture. *Encounter* entails some type of external racial event(s) that challenges the Eurocentric perspective held by the Preencounter Black. *Immersion/Emersion,* the third stage, occurs when the Black person immerses himself or herself in the Black experience (for example, reading Black literature, joining Black cultural organizations) with a corresponding denigration of Whites and White culture. The next stage, *Internalization,* characterizes individuals who have internalized a positive and personally relevant Black identity. The last stage in Cross's (1971) model was *Internalization/Commitment* and entailed social activism; that is, one sought to challenge and eliminate systems of oppression.

Approximately twenty years later, Cross (1991) revamped his theory of Nigrescence, particularly the Preencounter stage. Thus, Nigrescence is a resocializing experience in that one transforms a preexisting, non-Afrocentric identity into one that is Afrocentric. Briefly, Cross proposed that to account for the diversity of Preencounter Blacks the notion of *salience of race* became central to his theory. No longer was the Preencounter Black person simply anti-Black, but one could simply have a low salience for race. That is, a person who has low salience for race does not deny being Black, but being "Black" in the physical sense was thought to play an insignificant role in his or her life (Cross, 1991).

Afrocentric Models

A second group of racial identity models is based primarily on those personality characteristics developed out of an Afrocentric-embedded context. That is, an underlying assumption in Afrocentric approaches is that adherence to a set of beliefs consistent with an African world view is a more optimal and healthier state for Blacks to be in (Burlew and Smith, 1991). For example, Baldwin's (1984) Afrocentric theory of personality formed the basis for the African Self-Consciousness Scale.

Briefly, Baldwin proposed that the Black personality is composed of a complex biopsychical structure consisting of two core components: the African self-extension orientation and African self-consciousness (Baldwin, 1980, 1981, 1984, 1986, 1987; Baldwin and Bell, 1982, 1985; Baldwin, Duncan, and Bell, 1987). The African self-extension orientation represents the fundamental organizing principle of the Black personality system and is an unconscious process that is defined by spirituality or Africanity. Spirituality provides the interconnecting energy that allows the self to extend into the total communal experience of Black people. Thus, the African self-extension orientation gives coherence, continuity, and "Africanity" to the basic behaviors and psychological functioning of Black people (Baldwin and others, 1987).

The second major component of the African personality system is African self-consciousness, which refers to the conscious level expression of the African self-extension orientation, and it represents the conscious collective survival thrust of African people (Baldwin, Brown, and Rackley, 1990). Baldwin (1984) proposed that African self-consciousness plays a vital role in defining the normal-natural psychological function of the Black personality. In addition, there are four basic characteristics or indices of African self-consciousness (Baldwin and others, 1987; Baldwin and others, 1990), which will be discussed later. When these four indices of

African self-consciousness are fully operational in the Black personality, they generate self-affirmative behaviors (Baldwin and others, 1990). Baldwin (1984) suggested that under normal-natural conditions, these two components of the Black personality operate as one unified or undifferentiated process.

VREG Models

Stimulated by the theoretical advances made by Black psychologists during the 1970s and early 1980s, a number of alternative *process/stage* models articulating the identity development of VREG (Cook and Helms, 1988) groups other than African Americans were proposed (for example, Atkinson, Morten, and Sue, 1983, 1989; Kim, 1981; Lee, 1988; D. W. Sue and Sue, 1990). Many of these alternative models are similar to the Cross model in terms of the essential dynamics and conflicts contained in each of the stages of development (Kohatsu, 1992). For example, the Minority Identity Development Model (MID) originally was composed of five racial identity stages: Conformity, Dissonance, Resistance/Immersion, Introspection, and Integrative Awareness (Atkinson and others, 1983, 1989; see also the racial/cultural identity model of D. W. Sue and Sue, 1990). Briefly, *Conformity* entails a strong preference for Whites and White culture and deprecation of one's own culture. *Dissonance* involves a series of experiences that challenge one's former White cultural frame of reference. *Resistance/Immersion* takes place when the VREG individual becomes immersed in his or her own respective culture while rejecting Whites and White culture. *Introspection* entails a more realistic appraisal of the shortcomings of his or her ethnic minority cultural perspective and a deeper sense of other minority groups' experiences of racism. Finally, *Integrative Awareness* involves a positive internalization of both White and ethnic minority culture(s) into one's self-concept.

The MID/RCID (Racial Cultural Identity Development) model theoretically captures the core conflicts that all oppressed people in the United States experience and ultimately resolve in developing a crystallized racial identity. Further, each "stage" is comprised of attitudes toward oneself, one's racial group, Whites, and other racial and ethnic groups. Recently, research utilizing the MID/RCID model with VREG groups has emerged (for example, Kohatsu, 1992; Pannu and Helms, 1993); it will be reviewed in a later section.

White Identity Models

An interesting corollary to the work done on VREG racial identity has been the growing body of literature on models of White racial identity (for example, Hardiman, 1982; Helms, 1984, 1990a; Ponterotto, 1988; Rowe and others, 1994; Sabnani and others, 1991; D. W. Sue and Sue, 1990). One of the most influential and widely researched models has been Helms's (1984, 1990a) White racial identity model.

According to Helms (1990a, 1992), developing a healthy White racial identity is a two-phase process: (a) abandoning racism; and (b) developing a nonracist identity. Each phase in her model encompasses three distinct racial identity statuses. The first status in Phase One is *Contact*, where a person is oblivious to his or her Whiteness and naive about the implications of race in American society. *Disintegration* is characterized by confusion and guilt from realizing the implications of being White and the moral dilemmas associated with such a privileged racial membership. The *Reintegration* racial identity status reflects an underlying belief in the superiority of Whites, and the inferiority of Blacks and other minorities. Any previous awareness of societal restrictions and limitations for people of color is thwarted by the belief that "people get what they deserve."

The remaining three racial identity statuses (that is, Pseudo-Independent, Immersion/Emersion, and Autonomy) are associated with the conflicts inherent in developing a positive nonracist White identity. The *Pseudo-Independent* individual approaches racial issues from an intellectualized stance and also helps other Whites to understand VREGs. The *Immersion/Emersion* status involves an active search for personal meaningfulness to being White in the United States and a commitment toward encouraging other Whites to explore their own Whiteness and to abandon racism. Lastly, in *Autonomy*, the individual continues to internalize a positive White identity and appropriately integrates knowledge and experiences dealing with racial issues.

In contrast to the Helms model (1984, 1990a), another camp of White racial identity theory has recently developed (Rowe and others, 1994). Rowe and others used Helms's (1984) definition of White racial consciousness as the basis for their model and conceptualized racial consciousness in terms of two forms of identity statuses which, in turn, encompass seven attitude types. There are two types of statuses, achieved and unachieved. Achieved statuses require some kind of exploration of racial issues and a concomitant commitment to these beliefs. Unachieved statuses entail a lack of either exploration or commitment, or both of these components.

Achieved statuses are characterized by four relatively stable internalized attitude types; namely *Dominative, Conflictive, Reactive,* and *Integrative* attitudes. Within the unachieved status, the three attitude types share a noninternalized set of expressed racial attitudes. The three attitude types are *Dependent, Avoidant,* and *Dissonant*. Please refer to Rowe and others (1994) for an extensive discussion of these attitude types.

Ego and Social Identity Models

The models reviewed earlier (for example, Nigrescence-based) share a degree of similarity in their conceptual underpinnings. Researchers working in these areas of VREG identity have been fairly consistent about the usage of race as it pertains to the formation of *racial identity*. The case is not as clear with the ego identity models and theorists.

In direct contrast to these aforementioned groups of racial identity models are the ego and social identity theorists who are primarily based in developmental and adolescent psychology. In addition, the research generated from the ego identity models has emphasized *ethnic identity* as opposed to *racial identity*, although the differentiations between these two constructs are not always clear. Nonetheless, most of the research has been generated from the ego identity theorists; hence, the focus of this section will be on ego identity models and not on social identity theory.

As an extension of Erikson's work (1968), Marcia (1966, 1980) suggested four ego identity statuses based on whether an individual has explored his or her identity options and made a decision about these options. *Diffusion* occurs when the individual has not made a commitment or engaged in exploration. *Foreclosed* status describes the person who makes an identity commitment without exploration, usually on the basis of external influences (such as parents). *Moratorium* involves the exploration of an identity without having made a commitment; and lastly, *Achieved* status is characterized by the person making a firm commitment after having explored the options. One of the primary problems with Marcia's ego identity theory is that issues of racial and ethnic identity for the most part have not been addressed (Phinney, 1990; Ponterotto and Pedersen, 1993).

The application of Marcia's ego identity theory (1980) to "ethnic" (racial) issues among adolescents was done by Phinney and her colleagues (Phinney, 1989, 1990; Phinney and Alipuria, 1990; Phinney and Chavira, 1992; Phinney, DuPont, Espinosa, Revill, and Sanders, 1994; Phinney, Lochner, and Murphy, 1990; Phinney and Tarver, 1988). Phinney (1989, 1990) proposed a three-stage progression ranging from an unexamined ethnic identity, through a period of examination, to an achieved or committed ethnic identity. Stage one (*unexamined ethnic identity*) is characterized by the lack of exploration of one's ethnicity. Essentially, the adolescent is ignorant and/or may not be interested in racial or ethnic issues. This stage is comparable to Marcia's diffusion and foreclosure ego identity statuses.

Stage two (*ethnic identity search/moratorium*) is triggered by a traumatic encounter that forces the VREG individual to think about the meanings surrounding race and ethnicity. Thereafter, the individual actively undergoes the process of learning more about his or her respective ethnic culture. This stage is similar to Marcia's *moratorium* ego identity status.

Last, stage three (*ethnic identity achievement*) entails the individual attaining a deeper understanding and appreciation of his or her ethnicity. That is, the VREG adolescent has internalized a clear sense of what his or her ethnicity is or means. Stage three corresponds to Marcia's *achieved* ego identity status.

It is important to note that the ego identity research (for example, Adams, Ryan, Hoffman, Dobson, and Nielsen, 1985; Adams and Shea, 1978; Jones and Hartman, 1988; Marcia, 1966; Phinney, 1989, 1990; Phinney and Alipuria, 1990; Phinney and Chavira, 1992; Phinney and others, 1990; Phinney and Tarver, 1988) examined ethnic identity issues primarily among adolescents and not adults. However, the Nigrescence and Afrocentric theories were applied primarily to adult populations in order to examine *racial identity* development. In addition, it is clear that the sociopolitical underpinnings of these models differ greatly as well—for example, the Nigrescence models were based on mapping out how racism and oppression imposed by White Americans impacts the VREG person's sense of self. Yet the dynamics of racism and oppression are not, implicitly or explicitly, addressed in the ego identity models. Indeed, the dynamics of race and of one's relationship with the dominant culture are not dealt with in Phinney's work, either (for example, 1989, 1990).

Stage Versus Typology Models

Although many racial identity models have been proposed, the underlying conceptual premises of these models may not be clearly understood or differentiated. One useful strategy is that racial identity models can be classified into two different groups—a typology versus a stage/process model. *Typology models* articulate specific modal personality and psychological characteristics, and each type is presumed to adapt differently to environmental racial oppression (Helms, 1990b). Each type provides a specific category that individuals can be grouped into depending on how racial issues have been resolved. Emotions, attitudes, values, and behaviors are thought to be characteristically different for each type, and one could presumably predict behaviors of an individual from each of these discrete types (Helms, 1990a, 1990b). However, typology models have a number of shortcomings. For example, they do not provide any theoretical rationale for how a person develops a particular type, nor do they explain how one moves from one type to another. A number of typology models have been developed for the various VREG groups in the United States; for example, Asian Americans (see Kitano, 1982; S. Sue and Sue, 1971), Hispanics (see Ruiz and Padilla, 1977; Szapocznik, Scopetta, Kurtines, and Aranalde, 1978), and American Indians (see Carroll, 1978; Chance, 1965; Lowrey, 1983).

In contrast, *stage/process models* propose a process of racial identity development that consists of certain identifiable stages rather than discrete types or categories. Each stage entails a specific constellation of attitudes and emotions, and moreover, a healthier resolution of racial issues is assumed to occur at the later rather than the earlier stages (Helms, 1990a). In addition, stage models propose that each person can move through the different stages of identity development, although not necessarily in the same stage or time sequence. A number of stage/process models have been developed for the various VREG groups in the United States; for example, Asian Americans (see Lee, 1988; D. W. Sue and Sue, 1990), and Hispanics (see Ruiz, 1990). Recent innovative developments of these stage/process models will be discussed in a later section.

Racial Identity as a Within-Group Variable

As mentioned previously, racial identity has gained a great deal of attention as a powerful within-group variable. Nonetheless, researchers have often confused or confounded racial identity with other within-group variables, such as acculturation (Kohatsu, 1992; Kohatsu, Suzuki, and Bennett, 1992).

As reviewed by Kohatsu (1992), many cross-cultural studies purporting to analyze racial or ethnic identity were actually examining acculturation issues (for example, Connor, 1974; Masuda, Matsumoto, and Meredith, 1970; Meredith and Meredith, 1966). A critical conceptual difference between racial identity and acculturation is that acculturation does not deal with the psychological process by which a VREG person internalizes meanings of racism and oppression. Although there has been little conceptual conciseness regarding this construct historically (Celano, 1986), acculturation primarily involves the extent to which a person adopts White cultural values, beliefs, and attitudes, while either maintaining or losing their own respective cultural beliefs and attitudes (Kohatsu, 1992).

Similarly, racial identity has often been treated as being synonymous with ethnic identity. Much of the confusion has to do with the systemic problem in the field of psychology of not clearly defining race and ethnicity (Betancourt and Lopez, 1993; Helms, 1994b; Zuckerman, 1990). Hence, this confusion of terms has spilled over into conceptualizations of racial and ethnic identity. Ethnic identity refers to a sense of a group identity based on the extent to which the individual perceives him- or herself to share a common membership or affiliation with a particular ethnic or cultural group rather than with the larger group (or category) of racial membership (Garcia, 1982; Kohatsu, 1992). In contrast to racial identity, ethnic identity models do not account for racism and oppression. One theoretical approach for understanding these two different collective identities is that ethnic identity is a subset of or can be subsumed under racial identity. Nonetheless, a VREG person could presumably develop both a racial and an ethnic identity, particularly those individuals who are of Asian or Hispanic descent. For example, an Asian could theoretically develop both a racial identity as an Asian and an ethnic identity as a Japanese American.

Another problematic area in the field of racial identity research is the aligning of racial labeling or identification as an accurate barometer of one's racial identity development. The fundamental error that seems to have occurred is that researchers inferred the levels of racial identity from such simple (and often singular) labels that VREGs selected for themselves. As Parham and Helms (1981) suggested, racial labels might be more of a transitory indicator of the current social environment rather than an accurate depiction of a person's racial identity structure. Therefore, although information gained from racial labeling may be important (Phinney, 1990), it should not be equated as being representative of a person's overall racial identity.

Recent Innovative Developments

A number of innovative theoretical advances have been offered since the early models of Black identity were first published in the 1970s. For instance, Helms (1984) refined Cross's Nigrescence model by suggesting that each "stage" be considered a world view. That is, each stage is akin to a cognitive template that people use to organize information about themselves, other people, the environment, and institutions (Helms, 1984). In addition, these world views are the result of an individual's cognitive maturation interacting with social and environmental forces.

Helms (1989, 1990a) also suggested that it might be useful to think of each of the racial identity stages as bimodal. That is, each stage has two potentially distinguishable forms of expression. Further, in order to get away from the static, linear notions of developmental stage models, Helms (1992) proposed, as a heuristic device, that each of the racial identity attitudes could coexist at different levels (that is, levels in a cylinder), with one set of attitudes predominating at any given point in time. Helms (1990a, 1990c) has also applied racial identity theory to interpreting dyadic and small-group interactions.

In addition, Parham (1989) extended Cross's Nigrescence model into the context of lifespan development with his constructs of recycling, stagnation, and stagewise linear progression. Essentially, Parham theorized about how an individual's racial identity attitudes are expressed at different stages of the adult life cycle. For example, recycling entails the Black person reinitiating the process of racial identity struggle and resolution after having gone through the process at an earlier point in life. Parham and Williams' (1993) study provides some preliminary support for identity resolution through the lifespan of African Americans.

More recently, Helms (1994a, 1994b) essentially reconceptualized her racial identity model, originally based on Cross's Nigrescence theory, with elements from other racial identity and ego or social identity theories. Instead of four sets of racial identity attitudes or "stages" (Preencounter, Encounter, Immersion/Emersion, Internalization), Helms proposed six racial identity ego statuses that theoretically evolve from the simplest to the most complex; that is, increasingly more sophisticated differentiations of the ego take place (Helms, 1994a, b, c). Her six racial identity ego statuses for people of color are *Conformity*, *Dissonance*, *Immersion*, *Emersion*, *Internalization*, and *Integrative Awareness*. Briefly, Conformity, Dissonance, and Immersion are externally defined ego statuses; that is, these statuses are dependent on external factors. In contrast, Emersion, Internalization, and Integrative Awareness ego statuses are internally defined statuses. For each of these six racial identity ego statuses, Helms (1994c) proposed corresponding information processing strategies characteristic of that particular status.

Psychometric Issues

Although there has been a proliferation of racial identity models as discussed earlier, there has been little corresponding activity in developing psychometrically sound instruments. The remainder of this review will focus on a number of widely used scales, followed by recently developed and promising measures, then several new, unpublished instruments will be highlighted, and lastly, an ethnic identity measure will be discussed.

First-Tier Measures

The first group of measures that will be discussed are all based on some form of the Nigrescence model of Black identity, are well known, and widely used in current research. The RIAS, DIB-C, and the WRIAS will be reviewed in this section.

Racial Identity Attitude Scale

The Black Racial Identity Attitude Scale (RIAS-B; Parham and Helms, 1985; Helms and Parham, 1990; cited in Helms, 1990a) was developed to assess the stages of Black racial identity proposed by Cross (1971). The scale consists of thirty and fifty items (short and long form, respectively), to which participants are asked to respond using a five-point Likert scale (1 = strongly disagree; 5 = strongly agree). The subscales are scored by averaging the appropriately keyed items such that each respondent receives a scale score for each of the four types of racial identity attitudes. Higher mean subscale scores indicate a greater degree of that racial identity attitude. Cronbach's alpha coefficients for the four subscales ranged from .51 to .80 for the long form and .66 to .71 for the short form (Burlew and Smith, 1991; Carter, 1987; Helms, 1990a; Sabnani and Ponterotto, 1992).

In the only extant published psychometric study of the RIAS-B (short form), Ponterotto and Wise (1987) analyzed the construct validity of the scale using oblique factor analysis. First, as summarized by Ponterotto and Wise, alpha coefficients for the four racial identity attitude scales in past studies were: Preencounter = .67–.69; Encounter = .45–.72; Immersion/Emersion = .66–.67; and Internalization = .35–.79. In their study, the following Cronbach's alphas were reported: Preencounter = .63; Encounter = .37; Immersion/ Emersion = .72; and Internalization = .37. The empirical evidence just cited seems to suggest that the RIAS has adequate internal consistency, although the Encounter subscale in particular appears to be problematic.

Ponterotto and Wise (1987) performed oblique factor analyses with three-, five-, six-, and seven-factor models and concluded that the three-factor solution was the best model. The three factors were Immersion-Emersion, Preencounter, and Internalization, and accounted for 30.5 percent of the common variance prior to rotation; these three factors appeared to match the theoretical constructs of Cross's model. Interestingly enough, they conducted a reliability test on the newly derived subscales (Preencounter; Immersion-Emersion; Internalization) which were .74, .62, and .70, respectively. It is important to note that little empirical support was found for the Encounter attitudes subscale. This finding is consistent with the relatively low coefficient alphas indicated earlier.

Evidence that supported the measure's convergent validity was presented by Grace (1984), who reported that the scores on the Racial Identity Attitudes Scale and Milliones's (1980) DIB-C were appropriately correlated with respect to direction. Also, Helms (1990a) summarized the research literature providing validity evidence for the RIAS-B—for example, racial identity attitudes were significantly related to self-esteem, affective states, demographic similarity, and preference for therapists' race in a manner fairly consistent with racial identity theory (see also Helms and Carter, 1991; Ponterotto and Wise, 1987).

In summary, the RIAS has been the most widely used measure of racial identity in the research literature. The alpha coefficients for the four subscales have been variable, particularly for the Encounter scale. However, adequate evidence exists to support the reliability of the Preencounter, Immersion-Emersion, and Internalization scales (for example, Helms, 1990a; Sabnani and Ponterotto, 1992). Regarding validity, there is a growing body of recent work employing the RIAS (especially using the long form) that supports the construct validity of the RIAS (for example, Carter, 1991;

Mitchell and Dell, 1992; Mumford, 1994; Parham and Williams, 1993; Pyant and Yanico, 1991; Taub and McEwen, 1992). An important cautionary note is that researchers have used both the long and short form of the RIAS and the results from these different scale versions may not be interchangeable (Pyant and Yanico, 1991). In fact, the consistent use of the long-form version of the RIAS scale (fifty items) may present entirely different psychometric data in the future. Subsequent psychometric work, such as factor analysis, will provide additional information about the RIAS long form. We recommend that in using the RIAS, researchers keep in mind what Helms (1989) suggested; namely, that the reliability estimates may vary depending upon the particular environment in which the scale is being used and the racial identity levels of the respondents in the study. Likewise, some caution should be used in interpreting the results with the Encounter scale due to the difficulties in measuring such a changeable and dynamic phenomenon.

Developmental Inventory of Black Consciousness

The Developmental Inventory of Black Consciousness (DIB-C; Milliones, 1980) was designed to assess levels of Black consciousness related to Cross's (1971) Negro-to-Black Conversion Model and Thomas's (1971) model of Black consciousness. The DIB-C's four subscales are as follows: Preconscious—person not engaged in the conversion experience; Confrontation—person is engaged in the conversion process and expresses extreme anti-White and pro-Black sentiments; Internalization—person begins to incorporate positive values associated with the Black experience, along with a decrease in anti-White sentiments; and Integration—person is committed to a plan of action to eradicate oppression and dehumanization of people.

Only limited reliability and validity data are available on this measure (for example, Denton, 1985; Milliones, 1980, 1983). The results of Item Discrimination, Test of Homogeneity, Reliability Index, and Differential Validity Index supported a sixty-five-item measure (note: an eighty-four-item scale also exists; see Burlew and

Smith, 1991; Sabnani and Ponterotto, 1992). Each item selected for the final scale from all of these tests was significant at the .05 level. The items are responded to on a seven-point Likert scale (1 = strongly disagree, 7 = strongly agree). Construct validity of the DIB-C subscales was indicated by significant correlations between Preconscious and Integration subscales and Taylor's Nadanolitization scale (degree of internalization among African Americans of racist anti-Black attitudes propagated by Whites) scores as expected (Milliones, 1980). For example, Preconscious individuals are more prone to internalize stereotypical attitudes held by Whites about African Americans than are those individuals in the Integration stage. In addition, Milliones (1983; cited in Burlew and Smith, 1991) reported split-half reliabilities ranging from .66 to .88. Denton (1985) reported psychometric support for three of the existing factors according to Milliones's model, but found two additional groupings which he termed Encounter and Double Consciousness stages. As summarized by Burlew and Smith (1991), Denton's findings suggested that scores on the DIB-C were correlated with measures of Black Nationalism and internationalized racism.

Published research utilizing the DIB-C has not been extensive and seems to be restricted to dissertations. Likewise, there is a limited amount of information on reliability and validity of this scale. Although some support for the factor structure of the DIB-C was found (Denton, 1985), further factor analysis of the scale needs to be done. Given the lack of psychometric data, a complete evaluation of the usefulness of the DIB-C can not be made at this time.

White Racial Identity Attitudes Scale

There are several measures of Whites' attitudes toward other racial and ethnic groups or prejudice (Hamersma, Paige, and Jordan, 1973; Sedlacek and Brooks, 1970; Woodmansee and Cook, 1967), but only a few measures of White racial consciousness (Helms, 1992). In an attempt to measure one aspect of White racial consciousness, Helms developed the White Racial Identity Attitudes Scale

(WRIAS; 1990a). The scale was designed to measure the five types of racial attitudes described in her model (1984). The model was developed as a result of a series of informal interviews with White people, as well as adapting theories of culture shock (Adler, 1975; Casse, 1981). According to Helms's model, the five types of attitudes are Contact, Disintegration, Reintegration, Pseudo-Independence, and Autonomy.

The WRIAS consists of fifty rationally derived items, responded to on a five-point Likert scale (1 = strongly disagree; 5 = strongly agree) and the five subscale scores are obtained by summing each of the respective 10-items. The reliability coefficients reported for Contact, Disintegration, Reintegration, Pseudo-Independence, and Autonomy attitudes are .53, .77, .80, .71, and .67, respectively (Carter, 1987). Helms and Carter (cited in Helms, 1990a) also reported Cronbach's alphas ranging from .55 to .74. More recently, Pope-Davis and Ottavi (1994) administered the WRIAS to 243 college students and reported the following alpha coefficients: Contact = .50; Disintegration = .73; Reintegration = .76; Pseudo-Independence = .68; and Autonomy = .64. Construct validity studies indicated that White racial identity attitudes were differentially related to value orientations (Carter and Helms, 1987), counselor intentions (Carter, 1987), symbolic racism (Westbrook, cited in Helms, 1990a), strength of preferences for White counselors (Helms and Carter, 1991), racism (Carter, 1990; Pope-Davis and Ottavi, 1994), and interpersonal relationships (Taub and McEwen, 1992).

However, one of the limitations of the WRIAS is the absence of a scale to assess the Immersion-Emersion level of White racial identity. Corbett, Helms, and Regan (1992) addressed this issue by developing a measure of the Immersion-Emersion (IE) Status. The measure, which can be used as a subscale of the WRIAS measure, consists of ten rationally derived items. The items use the word "race" but not "White" (for example, "I am making an effort to decide the type of person I want to be in terms of my race"). The response format is based on a 5-point Likert scale (1 = strongly disagree, 5 = strongly agree). Point values for each of the items are averaged and the higher the score, the more descriptive the scale is for the respondent.

Some preliminary validity and reliability data are available on this scale. When the IE scale was correlated with the Social Desirability Scale (Crowne and Marlowe, 1964), the relationship proved nonsignificant ($r = .12$; Corbett and others, 1992). However, there was a moderate correlation between the IE scale and Wilhoit's Racial Self Esteem Scale ($r = .20, p < .05$). Regan (1992), using interview data, found significant relationships between the IE Scale and ratings of search about racism ($r = .34, p < .05$), ratings of search about the meaning of being White ($r = .42, p < .01$), and search for answers to questions about ethnicity ($r = .37, p < .01$) and religious beliefs ($r = .25, p < .01$).

Meijer (1992) explored relationships between White racial identity attitudes and reactions to race-related topics in a classroom lecture. The IE scale and the WRIAS were administered at two times during the semester. The IE scale scores were positively related with Autonomy subscale scores at Time 2 ($r = .23$ and $.22$, respectively, $p < .05$). In addition, the Time 2 IE Scale was positively correlated with Pseudo-Independence at Time 2 ($r = .18, p < .05$). Also, Immersion/Emersion attitudes contributed uniquely to the prediction of Whites' strategies for coping with race-related lecture material. Thus, some evidence of internal consistency was obtained for the IE scale, test-retest reliability was relatively high for a twelve-week interval, and preliminary evidence of construct validity of the measure was also indicated.

Clearly, the WRIAS has become an important research measure for examining White racial identity issues. Existing psychometric information, albeit not extensive, suggests that the five subscales are somewhat variable regarding internal consistency. However, there is a growing body of evidence for the validity of the scale. Additional factor analyses of the scale would provide more information about the domains in the WRIAS.

Second-Tier Measures

The second group of instruments that will be reviewed are recently developed scales that are potentially promising psychometric additions to the repertoire of available measures of racial identity. The CIAS/VIAS, ASC, ORAS-P, and the WRCDS will be discussed.

VREG Identity Attitudes Scale
(Formerly the Cultural Identity Attitudes Scale, CIAS)

The VIAS preliminary and VIAS final form (VREG Identity Attitudes Scale; Helms and Carter, 1990) is a thirty-five- and fifty-item inventory, respectively, which assesses attitudes representing four of Atkinson and others' Minority Identity Development stages (1989). Participants are asked to respond to each item in the CIAS/VIAS using a five-point Likert scale (1 = strongly disagree to 5 = strongly agree). Higher scores on each of the four subscales indicate stronger levels of the relevant racial identity attitudes. Conformity, Dissonance, Resistance, and Integrative Awareness attitudes are assessed with this scale. Items from the Introspection scale were merged with the Dissonance scale to create the Dissonance/Introspection scale. The VIAS was developed to measure the racial identity attitudes of Asian, Black, Hispanic, and American Indian participants.

Helms and Carter (1990) conducted initial reliability studies of the CIAS-final form. Reliabilities ranged from .62 to .87 for Blacks, and from .74 to .82 for the "other racial/ethnic" sample. For the combined sample (n = 131), Helms and Carter reported the following alpha coefficients for the four scales: Conformity = .79; Dissonance = .72; Resistance = .79; and Integrative Awareness = .82.

Interscale correlations were also computed by Helms and Carter (1990) with their sample of Blacks, other racial/ethnic minorities, and with the combined sample. Conformity and Integrative Awareness attitudes were significantly negatively related. Moreover, Dissonance/Introspection and Integrative Awareness attitudes were also significantly negatively correlated.

Recently, a number of studies have been conducted using both forms of the CIAS/VIAS with different racial groups (Kohatsu, 1992, 1994; Pannu and Helms, 1993). For example, Kohatsu examined the extent to which racial identity attitudes and acculturation (to Asian and White culture) significantly predicted levels of anxiety, assertiveness, and awareness of interpersonal and institutional racism among Asian Americans. Reliabilities for the CIAS/VIAS-preliminary were as follows (n = 267): Conformity = .71; Dissonance = .76; Resistance = .74; and Integrative Awareness = .67. In addition, support for the validity of the CIAS/VIAS was also found (Kohatsu, 1992) as predictions regarding the relationships between racial identity attitudes and acculturation with anxiety, assertiveness, and awareness of racism were supported. For example, Kohatsu found that the more strongly one adhered to Resistance attitudes, the more aware one tended to be of interpersonal racism.

Pannu and Helms (1993) examined the extent to which racial and ethnic identity and acculturation contributes to perceptions of family functioning among Asian Indians (n = 101). In their study, Cronbach's alphas for the fifty-item CIAS/VIAS-final form were initially as follows: Conformity = .58; Dissonance = .64; Resistance = .68; and Integrative Awareness = .36. Subsequently, in order to reduce the length of the questionnaire, a split-half approach was employed. The reported alpha coefficients for the odd-numbered version were: Conformity = .64; Dissonance = .77; Resistance = .89; Integrative Awareness = .73. For the even-numbered version, they were: Conformity = .83; Dissonance = .49; Resistance = .75; and Integrative Awareness = .70.

The CIAS/VIAS-final form holds promise as a reliable and valid instrument to assess racial identity attitudes among many diverse racial and ethnic groups. Moreover, the MID/RCID model also seems to be a useful theoretical framework to use in studying racial identity issues among VREGs.

Although a limited number of studies have used the CIAS/VIAS-final form, the existing evidence does suggest that the scale has good reliability and validity, particularly for use with African

Americans and Asian Americans. In light of the inclusive nature of the MID model, the research possibilities with the CIAS/VIAS-final form are numerous. That is, the CIAS/VIAS-final form was intended to be used with all the major racial groups in the United States and so it is not restricted to measurement of racial identity attitudes for just one racial group. Nonetheless, how the scale functions with other racial groups, such as Latinos, is not clearly known and consequently, should be studied more closely. Moreover, factor analysis of the measure needs to be done, as well as examining its convergent validity.

African Self-Consciousness Scale

The African Self-Consciousness Scale (ASC) was developed by Baldwin and Bell (1982, 1985). The scale assesses four competency and six expressive dimensions. The competency dimensions are, awareness/recognition of African identity and heritage; ideological and behavioral priorities placed on Black survival, liberation, and proactive-affirmative development; specific activity priorities placed on self-knowledge and self-affirmation (that is, Africentric values, customs, institutions, and so forth); resistance toward anti-Black forces and threats to Black survival in general. The six expressive dimensions encompass the areas of education, family, religion, cultural activities, interpersonal relations, and political orientation.

The forty-two-item ASC is scored on an eight-point Likert scale (1–2 = strongly disagree, 3–4 = disagree, 5–6 = agree, 7–8 = strongly agree). Odd-numbered items are negatively skewed for the African self-consciousness construct and are scored as the reverse of their scaled values (that is, an odd-scaled value of 8 = 1, 7 = 2, 6 = 3, and so on), and even-numbered items are positively skewed for the construct and are scored by computing their scaled scores directly. The scale can be scored by computing either the total score or the mean total score. Baldwin and Bell (1985) reported a test-retest reliability of .90 over a six-week period with a sample of 109 Black college students. Convergent validity was demonstrated by a significant correlation (r = .68, p < .001) between scores on the ASC and the Black personality questionnaire (Baldwin and Bell, 1985; Burlew and Smith, 1991; Sabnani and Ponterotto, 1992). Lastly, content validity was indicated by a significant correlation (.70) between teachers' ratings of fifty students (twenty-five with the lowest and twenty-five with the highest ASC scores) using a ten-item ASC checklist and scores on the ASC (Burlew and Smith, 1991). However, there is a lack of information on internal consistency estimates and no published factor analyses have been done on the ASC.

As an approach to studying racial identity attitudes, the ASC presents an interesting alternative to the Nigrescence-based measures. Given the paucity of research done using the ASC, it is not clear how sound the instrument is and whether the African self-consciousness construct functions as proposed. Further psychometric studies should explore the factor structures in the ASC (Sabnani and Ponterotto, 1992). It would also be interesting to examine the relationships between the RIAS and the ASC in order to ascertain the amount of shared variance these two measures may or may not have among African Americans.

Oklahoma Racial Identity Attitudes Scale-Preliminary Form

The Oklahoma Racial Identity Attitudes Scale-Preliminary Form (ORAS-P) was developed by Bennett and Behrens (1994) and consists of forty-two rationally derived items. There are thirty-one items for measuring Achieved statuses, ten items for the Unachieved statuses, and one filler item. Respondents use a five-point Likert scale format to endorse each item (1 = strongly disagree, 5 = strongly agree). Raw values are used to score the items; thus, the higher the raw score value for a particular subscale, the more descriptive that racial identity status is of the person.

Limited reliability and construct validity is available for this measure (Bennett and Behrens, 1994). Cronbach alphas for each subscale were as follows: .68 (Avoidant); .82 (Dependent); .75 (Dissonant); .77 (Dominative); .80 (Reactive); .72 (Conflictive); and

.79 (Integrative). Test-retest reliabilities, calculated for forty-nine subjects with a four-week interval between administration, were as follows: .51 (Dependent), .68 (Avoidant), .46 (Dissonant), .67 (Dominant), .67 (Conflictive), .76 (Reactive), and .60 (Integrative).

An exploratory factor analysis with promax rotation was conducted on the ORAS-P and revealed a five factor solution. Items loading positively on Factor 1 were designed to measure dominative type attitudes while negatively weighted items measure integrative types. Positively loaded items on Factor 2 represented conflictive types and negatively loading items reflected reactive types. Factors 3, 4, and 5 matched with dependent, dissonant, and avoidant types of attitudes, respectively. Bennett and Behrens (1994) reported intercorrelations between the various attitude types which provide additional support for the validity of the ORAS-P. For example, Dominative type attitudes were positively related to both dissonance and avoidance.

As a new instrument, the ORAS-P offers a different approach to measuring White racial identity. Preliminary data do seem to suggest that this measure has adequate reliability and validity. However, given the very limited amount of psychometric information, no other evaluations of the instrument can be made at this time. Consequently, more research is needed in order to validate this instrument.

White Racial Consciousness Development Scale

The White Racial Consciousness Development Scale (WRCDS; Claney and Parker, 1989) is conceptually based on Helms's model of White racial identity. This fifteen-item scale contains three items pertaining to each of the five stages of development described by Helms (1984). (Note: The Immersion-Emersion stage was not present in this version of the model.) Respondents rate each of the items using a five-point Likert scale (1 = strongly agree, 5 = strongly disagree). The measure is scored by obtaining a mean value for each of the subscales. The items are inversely scored, thus a low score indicates a greater degree of strength of that stage of racial identity.

Very limited data are available regarding the validity and reliability of the measure. Claney and Parker (1989) reported factor analytic results using a varimax rotation indicating six factors accounting for 67 percent of the total variance. An "eigenvalue > 1" criterion confirmed the six-factor solution, which justified reconfiguring the measure according to six subscales (Contact, Disintegration, Reintegration, Pseudo-Independence, Autonomy, and a sixth scale that assesses a behavioral aspect of the Autonomy stage). In addition, Parker, Moore, and Neimeyer (1994) used the WRCDS to examine the impact of multicultural training on the development of White racial identity and interracial comfort. However, the reliability and validity of the instrument was not indicated or made available in the report of that research.

Given the shortness of the WRCDS (total fifteen items), it is not surprising that estimates of internal consistency and validity information are not known at this time. Initial factor analysis of the measure indicates that at least five of Helms's White identity stages were operating. Obviously, extensive work needs to be done on this scale and researchers need to be careful about reporting reliability and validity information in greater detail.

Third-Tier Measures

The third group of instruments that will be reviewed are unpublished research scales and recently developed instruments that have promising psychometric properties. These measures represent the next generation of scales that will enhance the quality of racial identity assessment.

White Racial Identity Reactions System

In response to the potential limitations of attitudinal measures of racial identity, Richardson and Helms (1991) developed a projective measure of White racial consciousness. The White Racial

Identity Reactions System (WRIRS) was developed to take into consideration the interplay between attitudes and behavior, to reveal more complex thinking about White racial identity issues, and to generalize to a wider range of social contexts than is possible with attitudinal measures.

The measure uses an open-ended response format allowing participants to respond to stimulus items on a variety of levels (such as affective, behavioral, and cognitive). The WRIRS consists of twenty-four sentence-completion items intended to elicit reactions concerning respondents' awareness of their Whiteness, manner of viewing themselves racially, race-related cultural values, and awareness of sociopolitical implications of being White. Helms's (1990a) six racial identity statuses were used as the scoring categories for the WRIRS responses. Each of the responses to the stimulus items were assigned to one of six racial identity reaction categories (Contact, Disintegration, Reintegration, Pseudo-Independence, Immersion-Emersion, Autonomy). A miscellaneous reactions category was used in the event a response did not clearly fit into any of the six other categories. Each response is assigned to only one category as indicated by a score of 1. Thus, the score for each category can potentially range from 0 to 24 for each participant. High scores or frequencies on a category indicate a higher level of that racial identity attitude.

Kappa Coefficients computed on sixteen raters for six of the seven reaction categories ranged from .67–.88 (the Miscellaneous was not included in the analyses). Support for the instrument's validity was evidenced in analyses that compared WRIRS's reaction categories to the WRIAS (Helms, 1990a). For example, four of the WRIRS categories significantly correlated with Helms's WRIAS subscales. Convergent validity was demonstrated by positive relationships between similarly named scales, Reintegration ($r = .47$ $p < .001$), and the Autonomy ($r = .25$, $p < .01$) attitudes.

Further, WRIRS reaction categories predicted scores from Stephan and Stephan's Intergroup Relations Inventory (1985) in a manner consistent with racial identity theory. The combination of racial identity reactions categories predicted perceptions of racial dissimilarity, Intergroup Contact, and Intergroup Anxiety. Thus, there is limited construct validity for the measure and further research is needed.

The WRIRS presents an interesting alternative method to measuring White racial identity. Due to the projective nature of the measure, the scoring of the WRIRS is fairly complex. Hence, it is important to keep in mind that the attitudinal measures provide a faster means of assessing White racial identity than projectives. Although primarily an unpublished research instrument, the WRIRS does hold promise for the future as an assessment device for understanding the complexities of White racial identity.

New Instruments

A number of very promising measures have been developed fairly recently, yet have not been as widely used by other researchers in the field or are relegated to an unpublished status. Some of the more promising instruments are as follows: the Belief Systems Analysis Scale (BSAS; Brookins, 1994; Montgomery, Fine, and James-Myers, 1990), the Multi-Construct African Identity Questionnaire (MCAIQ; Smith and Brookins, 1993; Smith, Walker, Fields, and Seay, 1994), the Multidimensional Racial Identification Questionnaire (Sanders Thompson, 1991, 1994), the Scale for the Effects of Ethnicity and Discrimination (SEED; Cardo, 1994) and the Asian Cultural Identity Attitudes Scale (Lee, 1988).

Multigroup Ethnic Identity Measure

In contrast to the racial identity models discussed earlier, the last section of this review will present an ethnic identity measure. Although the Multigroup Ethnic Identity Measure (MEIM) purports to measure ethnic rather than racial identity, and has been used primarily with adolescents, it will be reviewed in this section due to its increasing usage in the research literature. The MEIM consists of fourteen items assessing three aspects of ethnic identity: positive ethnic attitudes and sense of belonging (five items); ethnic identity achievement (seven items); and ethnic behaviors or practices (two items). A four-point Likert scale (1 = strongly disagree, 4 = strongly agree) is used and scores are obtained by summing across items and obtaining the mean; hence, scores can range from 1 (low) to 4 (high ethnic identity). There are also six items assessing other-group orientation.

Initial reliability estimates were calculated with a high school sample ($n = 417$) and a college sample ($n = 136$) and were as follows: Overall reliability was .81 for high school sample and .90 for the college sample. The five-item affirmation/belonging subscale reliabilities were .75 and .86, respectively. For the seven-item ethnic identity achievement subscale, reliabilities were .69 and .80, respectively, for the two samples. No Cronbach's alphas could be calculated for the two-item ethnic behaviors subscale (Phinney, 1992).

Principle axis factor analyses were done with both samples—a two-factor solution was obtained with the high school sample and a five-factor solution with the college sample. For the high school sample, the first factor included all the items measuring ethnic identity and the second factor consisted of those items measuring other-group orientation. Regarding the college sample, a five-factor solution was obtained; however, three of the factors were highly intercorrelated and the other two factors appeared to be subfactors of the Other-group orientation domain (Phinney, 1992). Hence, a two-factor solution was chosen, reflecting the same two dimensions derived for the high school sample.

Some preliminary validity support was demonstrated by correlations of scores on the MEIM with demographic variables and self-esteem in the expected directions, developmental trends (that is, higher ethnic identity scores in college than high school students), and positive correlations with school achievement and engagement (for example, Phinney, 1992; Taylor, Casten, Flickinger, Roberts, and Fulmore, 1994). At this date, it appears that the MEIM has good potential as a research instrument.

However, Birnbaum (1991) conducted an extensive psychometric investigation of the MEIM and the PII (Personal Identity Inventory; London, Birnbaum, Dalit, and Rothery, 1990; London and Hirschfeld, 1989) and found that the MEIM items comprising the ethnic identity dimension did not load on the three interrelated components as suggested by Phinney (1992). In contrast, the revised PII (a twenty-six-item ethnic identity measure) was found to have five clearly distinguishable factors (in-group preference, in-group pride, perceived prejudice, rootedness and affiliation, and individual as group-member in society) and high reliability (Cronbach's alpha = .90). Birnbaum suggested that the MEIM tapped too few of the potentially relevant dimensions of ethnic identity, that Phinney's college sample was too small and thus constrained her factor analysis, that the subscale correlations were too high (.59–.73), and that the MEIM scores were not standardized before factor analyzing the entire sample.

As an ethnic identity measure, the MEIM appears to have fairly good reliability in spite of the small number of items. Although there is some preliminary evidence on the validity of the scale, further research needs to done in this area. Given the contradictory results of Birnbaum's (1991) psychometric work, additional factor analysis of the MEIM with different groups would shed further light on the factor structures of the measure. Unlike the racial identity scales, the MEIM is applicable primarily to adolescents and hence the brief nature of the measure can be an advantage. Nonetheless, there are some precautions to be taken when using this measure. First, race and ethnicity do not seem to be clearly differentiated in the scale and may impact the scores and the interpretation of the results. Second, the use of a single score representing different phases of ethnic identity development may be a disadvantage in that such a unidimensional approach collapses discrete identity phases into one undifferentiated continuous phase.

Summary and Conclusion

Racial issues have been and will continue to be among the most important psychosocial and emotional problems in our country. Such a serious and pervasive social issue requires, in turn, serious and methodologically sound research. Therefore, social scientists need to be more specific about the ways in which they conceptualize and operationalize constructs such as race, ethnicity, and culture (Helms, 1994b, c). One of the ways in which psychologists have grappled with racial issues is by developing theories and models of how individuals develop a racial identity and, to a lesser extent, ethnic identity.

As discussed in this chapter, many of the prominent theories of racial identity were based on Nigrescence and Afrocentric theory. Although the early models addressed the racial identity development of African Americans, subsequent research has extended into theorizing and assessing racial identity issues among other VREG groups and White Americans. Indeed, a growing movement of sorts is the burgeoning of research on White racial identity development. A corollary to this phenomenon is the reality that White Americans now have some tools by which to understand what it means to be White for them in this country. On the other hand, there does not appear to be a similar spurt of growth in the research on other VREG groups, such as Asian Americans. Therefore, it is imperative that more research be conducted on racial identity issues among Asian Americans, Hispanics, and American Indians.

Racial identity theory and assessment has enjoyed a relatively short history, yet its importance has become increasingly clear. As a within-group variable, this variable has been used to better understand the links between identity development and various aspects of psychological functioning among VREGs and White Americans. Important innovative developments continue to emerge, such as Helms's (1994a, b, c) reconceptualization of the racial identity stage model into that of racial identity ego statuses. As these innovative developments become integrated into the research enterprise, the outcome will undoubtedly be the continual refinement of racial identity theory.

Future Directions

Assessment research in racial identity is at an exciting juncture in its development. More sophisticated instruments are being created and tested on a number of racial and ethnic groups. In order to accurately and comprehensively assess the complexity of racial identity development, measures of other domains besides attitudes could be developed. Indeed, the use of projective-type instruments as well as qualitative methods could be fruitfully employed to broaden our understanding of racial identity development as a multifaceted phenomenon. Such qualitative approaches as participant observation, life and oral histories, and interviews could complement quantitative approaches (Sabnani and Ponterotto, 1992).

In addition, the intersections between racial and ethnic identity (as well as other aspects of identity) should be systematically studied. By so doing, researchers can attain a deeper understanding of how the various components of a person's identity come together. Although developed with different theoretical models and generating rather disparate data sets, collaborative work in the assessment of racial and ethnic identity can only enhance our knowledge base of this incredibly rich process. Likewise, tracking the developmental pathways of racial identity over the lifespan is another area of inquiry that promises to yield important information. Too often, instruments are used as static pictures of an individual at a given point in time and we need to follow the intricate changes that take place through the lifespan.

In conclusion, new models of racial identity are appearing and we can hope that more sophisticated instruments to assess racial identity will continue to appear as well. The development and maintenance of racial identity is a complex process. Researchers therefore need to develop more sensitive (that is, psychometrically sound) instruments to capture the inherent complexity of this process. Continuing the efforts to probe the complexity of issues embedded in the development of one's racial identity can only lead researchers into a better realm of understanding of how individuals function as racial beings.

References

Adams, G. R., Ryan, J. H., Hoffman, J. J., Dobson, W. R., & Nielsen, E. C. (1985). Ego identity status, conformity behavior, and personality in late adolescence. *Journal of Personality and Social Psychology, 47,* 1091–1104.

Adams, G. R., & Shea, J. H. (1978). The relationship between identity status, locus of control, and ego development. *Journal of Youth and Adolescence, 8,* 81–89.

Adler, P. (1975). The transnational experience: An alternative view of culture shock. *Journal of Humanistic Psychology, 15,* 13–23.

Atkinson, D. R., Morten, G., & Sue, D. W. (1983). Proposed minority identity development model. In D. R. Atkinson, G. Morten, & D. W. Sue (Eds.), *Counseling American minorities* (2nd ed., pp. 32–42). Dubuque, IA: Brown.

Atkinson, D. R., Morten, G., & Sue, D. W. (1989). A minority identity development model. In D. R. Atkinson, G. Morten, & D. W. Sue (Eds.), *Counseling American minorities* (3rd ed., pp. 35–52). Dubuque, IA: Brown.

Baldwin, J. A. (1980). An Africentric model of Black personality. In *Proceedings of the 14th Annual Convention of the Association of Black Psychologists,* (pp. 23–25). Washington, DC: Association of Black Psychologists.

Baldwin, J. A. (1981). Notes on an Africentric theory of Black personality. *The Western Journal of Black Studies, 5,* 172–179.

Baldwin, J. A. (1984). African self-consciousness and the mental health of African-Americans. *Journal of Black Studies, 15,* 177–194.

Baldwin, J. A. (1986). Black psychology and Black personality. *Black Books Bulletin, 4,* 6–11, 65.

Baldwin, J. A. (1987). African psychology and Black personality testing. *The Negro Educational Review, 38,* 56–66.

Baldwin, J. A., & Bell, Y. (1982). *The African self-consciousness scale manual.* Florida A & M University, Psychology Department.

Baldwin, J. A., & Bell, Y. (1985). The African self-consciousness scale: An Africentric personality questionnaire. *The Western Journal of Black Studies, 9,* 61–68.

Baldwin, J. A., Brown, R., & Rackley, R. (1990). Some sociobehavioral correlates of African self-consciousness in African-American college students. *The Journal of Black Psychology, 17,* 1–17.

Baldwin, J. A., Duncan, J. A., & Bell, Y. R. (1987). Assessment of African self-consciousness among Black students from two college environments. *Journal of Black Psychology, 13,* 27–41.

Bennett, S., & Behrens, J. T. (1994). *Development of the Oklahoma Racial Attitudes Scale-Preliminary form (ORAS-P).* Unpublished manuscript, University of Oklahoma, Oklahoma City.

Betancourt, H., & Lopez, S. R. (1993). The study of culture, ethnicity, and race in American psychology. *American Psychologist, 48,* 629–637.

Birnbaum, A. (1991). *Measuring level of ethnic identity: A comparison of two new scales.* Unpublished doctoral dissertation, Rutgers University, NJ.

Brookins, C. C. (1994). The relationship between Afrocentric values and racial identity attitudes: Validation of the belief systems analysis scale on African-American college students. *Journal of Black Psychology, 20,* 128–142.

Burlew, A. K., & Smith, L. R. (1991). Measures of racial identity: An overview and a proposed framework. *The Journal of Black Psychology, 17,* 53–71.

Cardo, L. M. (1994). Development of an instrument measuring valence of ethnicity and perception of discrimination. *Journal of Multicultural Counseling and Development, 22,* 49–59.

Carroll, R. E. (1978, October). Academic performance and cultural marginality. *Journal of American Indian Education,* 11–16.

Carter, R. T. (1987). *An empirical test of a theory on the influence of racial identity attitudes on the process within a workshop.* Unpublished doctoral dissertation, University of Maryland, College Park.

Carter, R. T. (1990). The relationship between racism and racial identity among White Americans: An exploratory investigation. *Journal of Counseling and Development, 69,* 46–50.

Carter, R. T. (1991). Racial identity attitudes and psychological functioning. *Journal of Multicultural Counseling and Development, 19,* 105–114.

Carter, R. T., & Helms, J. E. (1987). The relationship between Black value orientations and racial identity attitudes. *Measurement and Evaluation in Counseling and Development, 19,* 185–195.

Casse, P. (1981). *Training for the cross-cultural mind.* Washington, DC: Society for Intercultural Education and Research.

Celano, M. (1986). *Acculturation, adjustment, and length of residence of Vietnamese refugees.* Unpublished doctoral dissertation, University of Maryland, College Park, MD.

Chance, N. (1965). Acculturation, self-identification, and adjustment. *American Anthropologist, 67,* 372–393.

Claney, D., & Parker, W. M. (1989). Assessing White racial consciousness and perceived comfort with Black individuals: A preliminary study. *Journal of Counseling and Development, 67,* 449–451.

Connor, J. W. (1974). Acculturation and changing need patterns in Japanese American and Caucasian American college students. *Journal of Social Psychology, 93,* 293–294.

Cook, D. A., & Helms, J. E. (1988). Visible racial/ethnic group supervisees' satisfaction with cross-cultural supervision as predicted by relationship characteristics. *Journal of Counseling Psychology, 35,* 268–274.

Corbett, M. M., Helms, J. E., & Regan, A. M. (1992, August). *A measure of Helms' Immersion/Emersion stage of White racial identity development.* Paper presented at the 100th Convention of the American Psychological Association, Washington, D.C.

Cross, W. E., Jr. (1971, July). The Negro-to-Black conversion experience. *Black World,* 13–27.

Cross, W. E., Jr. (1978). The Thomas and Cross models on psychological nigrescence: A literature review. *Journal of Black Psychology, 4,* 13–31.

Cross, W. E., Jr. (1991). *Shades of Black: Diversity in African-American identity.* Philadelphia: Temple University Press.

Cross, W. E., Jr., Parham, T. A., & Helms, J. E. (1991). The stages of Black identity development: Nigrescence models. In R. L. Jones (Ed.), *Advances in Black psychology* (3rd ed., pp. 319–338). Berkeley, CA: Cobb & Henry.

Crowne, D. P., & Marlowe, D. (1964). *The approval motive: Studies in evaluative dependence.* New York: Wiley.

Denton, S. E. (1985). A methodological refinement and validational analysis of the DIB-C. Unpublished doctoral dissertation, University of Pittsburgh.

Erikson, E. H. (1968). *Identity: Youth and crisis.* New York: Norton.

Garcia, J. A. (1982). Ethnicity and Chicanos: Measurement of ethnic identification, identity, and consciousness. *Hispanic Journal of Behavioral Sciences, 4,* 295–314.

Grace, C. A. (1984). *The relationship between racial identity attitudes and choice of typical and atypical occupations among Black college students.* Unpublished doctoral dissertation, Columbia University Teachers College, New York. (University Microfilms No. 8411267).

Hamersma, R. J., Paige, J., & Jordan, J. E. (1973). Construction of a Guttman facet design cross-cultural attitude-behavior scale toward racial-ethnic interaction. *Educational and Psychological Measurement, 33,* 565–576.

Hardiman, R. (1982). *White identity development: A process oriented model for describing the racial consciousness of White Americans.* Unpublished doctoral dissertation, University of Massachusetts, Amherst.

Helms, J. E. (1984). Toward a theoretical explanation of the effects of race on counseling: A Black and White model. *The Counseling Psychologist, 12*, 153–165.

Helms, J. E. (1989). Considering some methodological issues in racial identity counseling research. *The Counseling Psychologist, 17*, 227–252.

Helms, J. E. (Ed.) (1990a). *Black and White racial identity: Theory, research, and practice*. New York: Greenwood Press.

Helms, J. E. (1990b). Three perspectives on counseling and psychotherapy with visible racial/ethnic group clients. In F. C. Serafica, A. I. Schwebel, R. K. Russell, P. D. Issac, & L. B. Myers (Eds.), *Mental health of ethnic minorities*, (pp. 171–201). New York: Praeger.

Helms, J. E. (1990c). *Training manual for diagnosing racial identity in social interactions*. Kansas: Content Communications.

Helms, J. E. (1992). *A race is a nice thing to have*. Topeka, KS: Content Communications.

Helms, J. E. (1994a, February). *Helms's version of racial identity theory*. Workshop presented at the 11th Annual Teachers College Winter Roundtable Conference, Columbia University, New York.

Helms, J. E. (1994b). How multiculturalism obscures racial factors in the therapy process: Comment on Ridley and others (1994), Sodowsky and others (1994), Ottavi and others (1994), and Thompson, et al. (1994). *Journal of Counseling Psychology, 41*, 162–165.

Helms, J. E. (1994c). Racial identity and career assessment. *Journal of Career Assessment, 2*, 199–209.

Helms, J. E., & Carter, R. (1990). *A preliminary overview of the Cultural Identity Attitude Scale*. Unpublished manuscript.

Helms, J. E., & Carter, R. T. (1991). Relationships of White and Black racial identity attitudes and demographic similarity to counselor preferences. *Journal of Counseling Psychology, 38*, 446–457.

Helms, J. E., & Parham, T. A. (1990). Black Racial Identity Attitude Scale. In J. E. Helms (Ed.), *Black and White racial identity: Theory, research, and practice* (pp. 245–247). New York: Greenwood Press.

Helms, J. E., & Piper, R. E. (1994). Implications of racial identity theory for vocational psychology. *Journal of Vocational Behavior, 44*, 124–138.

Jackson, B. W. (1976). Black identity development. In L. Golubschick and B. Persky (Eds.), *Urban social and educational issues* (pp. 158–164). Dubuque, IA: Kendall/Hunt.

Jones, R. M., & Hartman, B. R. (1988). Ego identity: Developmental differences and experimental substance use among adolescence. *Journal of Adolescence, 11*, 347–360.

Kim, J. (1981). The process of Asian American identity development: A study of Japanese-American women's perceptions of their struggle to achieve personal identities as Americans of Asian ancestry. *Dissertation Abstracts International, 42,* 1551A. (University Microfilm No. 81–18010).

Kitano, H. H. (1982). Mental health in the Japanese American community. In E. E. Jones and S. J. Korchin (Eds.), *Minority mental health* (pp. 149–164). New York: Praeger.

Kohatsu, E. L. (1992). The effects of racial identity and acculturation on anxiety, assertiveness, and ascribed identity among Asian American college students. (Doctoral dissertation, University of Maryland, College Park, 1992). *Dissertation Abstracts International, 54(2-B),* 1102.

Kohatsu, E. L. (1994, August). *Racial identity attitudes: Implications and applications for African Americans.* Paper presented at the annual convention of the American Psychological Association, Los Angeles.

Kohatsu, E. L., Suzuki, L. A., & Bennett, S. K. (1992). Racial identity research on Asian Americans and American Indians: Is racial identity misplaced or forgotten in the literature? In R. T. Carter & S. D. Johnson (Eds.), *The 1991 Teachers College Winter Roundtable Edited Conference Proceedings,* (pp. 19–26). New York: Columbia University.

Lee, S. R. (1988). Self-concept correlates of Asian American cultural identity attitudes. *Dissertation Abstracts International, 49,* 12B.

London, P., Birnbaum, A., Dalit, B., & Rothery, C. (1990). *The personal identity inventory.* Unpublished manuscript, Rutgers University, NJ.

London, P., & Hirschfeld, A. (1989). *The psychology of identity formation.* Unpublished manuscript, Rutgers University, NJ.

Lowrey, L. (1983). Bridging a culture in counseling. *Journal of Applied Rehabilitation Counseling, 14,* 69–73.

Marcia, J. (1966). Development and validation of ego-identity status. *Journal of Personality and Social Psychology, 3,* 551–558.

Marcia, J. (1980). Identity in adolescence. In J. Adelson (Ed.), *Handbook of adolescent psychology* (pp. 159–187). New York: Wiley.

Masuda, M., Matsumoto, G. H., & Meredith, G. M. (1970). Ethnic identity in three generations of Japanese Americans. *Journal of Social Psychology, 81,* 199–207.

Meijer, C. E. (1992). *White racial identity development and responses to diversity in an introduction to psychology course and curriculum.* Unpublished doctoral dissertation, University of Maryland, College Park.

Meredith, G. M., & Meredith, C. W. (1966). Acculturation and personality among Japanese American college students in Hawaii. *Journal of Social Psychology, 68,* 175–182.

Milliones, J. (1973). *Construction of the developmental inventory of Black conscious-ness.* Unpublished doctoral dissertation, University of Pittsburgh.

Milliones, J. (1980). Construction of a Black consciousness measure: Psycho-therapeutic implications. *Psychotherapy: Theory, Research and Practice, 17,* 175–182.

Milliones, J. (1983). *Descriptive statistics on the DIB–C in Black and White college settings.* Unpublished manuscript. University of Pittsburgh.

Mitchell, S. L., & Dell, D. M. (1992). The relationship between Black students' racial identity attitude and participation in campus organizations. *Journal of College Student Development, 33,* 39–43.

Montgomery, D. E., Fine, M. A., & James-Myers, L. (1990). The development and validation of an instrument to assess an optimal Afrocentric world view. *Journal of Black Psychology, 17,* 37–54.

Mumford, M. B. (1994). Relationship of gender, self-esteem, social class, and racial identity to depression in Blacks. *Journal of Black Psychology, 20,* 157–174.

Pannu, R. K., & Helms, J. E. (1993). *Asian Indian cultural identity and perception of family functioning.* Paper presented at the 101st annual convention, American Psychological Association, Toronto, Canada.

Parham, T. A. (1989). Cycles of psychological nigrescence. *The Counseling Psy-chologist, 17,* 187–226.

Parham, T. A., & Helms, J. E. (1981). The influence of Black students' racial identity attitudes on preferences for counselor's race. *Journal of Counseling Psychology, 28,* 250–257.

Parham, T. A., & Helms, J. E. (1985). The relationship of racial identity atti-tudes to self-actualization of Black students and affective states. *Journal of Counseling Psychology, 32,* 431–440.

Parham, T. A., & Williams, P. T. (1993). The relationship of demographic and back-ground factors to racial identity attitudes. *Journal of Black Psychology, 19,* 7–24.

Parker, W. M., Moore, M. A., & Neimeyer, G. J. (1994). *Altering White racial consciousness attitudes and interracial comfort through multicultural training.* Paper submitted for publication.

Phinney, J. S. (1989). Stages of ethnic identity development in minority group adolescents. *Journal of Early Adolescence, 9,* 34–49.

Phinney, J. S. (1990). Ethnic identity in adolescents and adults: Review of research. *Psychological Bulletin, 108,* 499–514.

Phinney, J. S. (1992). The Multigroup Ethnic Identity Measure: A new scale for use with diverse groups. *Journal of Adolescent Research, 7,* 156–176.

Phinney, J. S., & Alipuria, L. (1990). Ethnic identity in older adolescents from four ethnic groups. *Journal of Adolescence, 13,* 171–183.

Phinney, J. S., & Chavira, V. (1992). Ethnic identity and self-esteem: An exploratory longitudinal study. *Journal of Adolescence, 15*, 271–281.

Phinney, J. S., DuPont, S., Espinosa, C., Revill, J., & Sanders, K. (1994). Ethnic identity and American identification among ethnic minority youths. In A. Bouvy, F. van de Vijer, P. Boski, & P. Schmitz (Eds.), *Journeys into cross-cultural psychology*, pp. 167–183. Berwyn, PA: Swets & Zeitlinger.

Phinney, J. S., Lochner, B. T., & Murphy, R. (1990). Ethnic identity development and psychological adjustment in adolescence. In A. R. Stirman & L. E. Davis (Eds.), *Ethnic issues in adolescent mental health* (pp. 53–72). Newbury Park, CA: Sage.

Phinney, J. S., & Tarver, S. (1988). Ethnic identity search and commitment in Black and White eighth graders. *Journal of Early Adolescence, 8*, 265–277.

Ponterotto, J. G. (1988). Racial consciousness development among White counselor trainees: A stage model. *Journal of Multicultural Counseling and Development, 16*, 146–156.

Ponterotto, J. G., & Pedersen, P. B. (1993). *Preventing prejudice: A guide for counselors and educators.* Newbury Park, CA: Sage.

Ponterotto, J. G., & Wise, S. L. (1987). Construct validity study of the Racial Identity Attitude Scale. *Journal of Counseling Psychology, 34*, 218–223.

Pope-Davis, D. B., & Ottavi, T. M. (1994). The relationship between racism and racial identity among White Americans: A replication and extension. *Journal of Counseling and Development, 72*, 293–297.

Pyant, C. T., & Yanico, B. J. (1991). Relationship of racial identity and gender-role attitudes to Black women's psychological well-being. *Journal of Counseling Psychology,, 38*, 315–322.

Regan, A. (1992). *Search and commitment processes in White racial identity formation.* Unpublished doctoral dissertation, University of Maryland, College Park.

Richardson, T. Q., & Helms, J. E. (1991). *Using racial identity reaction categories to predict intergroup relations.* Unpublished manuscript.

Rowe, W., Bennett, S. K., & Atkinson, D. R. (1994). White racial identity models: A critique and alternative proposal. *The Counseling Psychologist, 22*, 129–146.

Ruiz, A. S. (1990). Ethnic identity: Crisis and resolution. *Journal of Multicultural Counseling and Development, 18*, 29–40.

Ruiz, R. H., & Padilla, A. M. (1977). Counseling Latinos. *Personnel and Guidance Journal, 55*, 401–408.

Sabnani, H. B., & Ponterotto, J. G. (1992). Racial/ethnic minority-specific instrumentation in counseling research: A review, critique, and recommendations. *Measurement and Evaluation in Counseling and Development, 24*, 161–187.

Sabnani, H. B., Ponterotto, J. G., & Borodovsky, L. G. (1991). White racial identity development and cross-cultural counselor training: A stage model. *The Counseling Psychologist, 19,* 76–102.

Sanders Thompson, V. L. (1991). A multidimensional approach to the assessment of African American racial identification. *The Western Journal of Black Studies, 15,* 154–158.

Sanders Thompson, V. L. (1994). Socialization to race and its relationship to racial identification among African Americans. *Journal of Black Psychology, 20,* 175–188.

Sedlacek, W. W., & Brooks, G. C. (1970). Measuring racial attitudes in situational contexts. *Psychological Reports, 27,* 971–980.

Smith, E. P., & Brookins, C. C. (1993). *Reviewing the relationship between racial preference, ethnic identity, and personal identity: Findings from an identity measure in African American youth.* Paper presented at the 1993 annual meeting of the Society for Research on Child Development, New Orleans, LA.

Smith, E. P., Walker, K., Fields, L., & Seay, R. (February, 1994). *The salience of ethnic identity and its relationship to personal identity and efficacy among African American youth.* Paper presented at the 10th anniversary biennial meeting of the Society for Research in Adolescence, San Diego, CA.

Stephan, W. G., & Stephan, W. C. (1985). Intergroup anxiety. *Journal of Social Issues, 41,* 157–175.

Sue, D. W., & Sue, D. (1990). *Counseling the culturally different: Theory and practice* (2nd ed.). New York: Wiley.

Sue, S., & Sue, D. W. (1971). Chinese-American personality and mental health. *Amerasia Journal, 1,* 36–49.

Szapocznik, J., Scopetta, M. A., Kurtines, W., & Aranalde, M. D. (1978). Theory and measurement in acculturation. *Inter-American Journal of Psychology, 12,* 113–130.

Taub, D. J., & McEwen, M. K. (1992). The relationship of racial identity attitudes to autonomy and mature interpersonal relationships in Black and White undergraduate women. *Journal of College Student Development, 33,* 439–446.

Taylor, R. D., Casten, R., Flickinger, S. M., Roberts, D., & Fulmore, C. D. (1994). Explaining the school performance of African-American adolescents. *Journal of Research on Adolescence, 4,* 21–44.

Thomas, C. S. (1971). *Boys no more.* Beverly Hills, CA: Glencoe Press.

Woodmansee, J. J., & Cook, S. W. (1967). Dimensions of verbal racial attitudes: Their identification and measurement. *Journal of Personality and Social Psychology, 7,* 240–250.

Zuckerman, M. (1990). Some dubious premises in research and theory on racial differences. *American Psychologist, 45,* 1297–1303.

· ·

20

Assessing the Multicultural Competence of Counselors and Clinicians

Joseph G. Ponterotto and Charlene M. Alexander

During the past decade, the psychology profession has devoted increasing attention to multicultural issues in research, training, and practice. Both ethical (for example, Bernal and Castro, 1994; Dana, 1994; LaFromboise and Foster, 1989; Pedersen, 1995; Ponterotto and Casas, 1991) and training accreditation (for example, Altmaier, 1993; Payton, 1993; Rickard and Clements, 1993) guidelines have been put forth and have emphasized the need for psychologists and educators to become more clinically competent cross-culturally. Concise yet comprehensive reviews of these and related issues have recently been put forth by Highlen (1994) and Reynolds (1995). In citing the well-known multicultural counseling competency report of Sue, Arredondo, and McDavis (1992), Reynolds notes, "A growing number of psychologists believe that professionals without training or competence working with clients with diverse cultural backgrounds are [increasingly seen as] unethical and potentially harmful" (p. 2).

Unlike the majority of chapters in this text, the present chapter focuses not on the cultural relevance of an assessment device or procedure but on the cultural competence of the clinician providing the assessment. A main thesis of this chapter is that despite the "cultural validity" of an assessment device with a particular ethnic group, what is of paramount importance is the clinician's multicultural awareness, knowledge, and interpretive skill. Our position is that a culture-bound (or biased) assessment device in the hands of a well-trained multicultural practitioner is preferred over a culture-fair instrument in the hands of a poorly trained multicultural practitioner.

The purpose of this chapter is three-fold. First, we review the current status of multicultural training in professional psychology programs. Second, leading paper-and-pencil measures of multicultural counseling competence are examined from a psychometric standpoint. Finally, the chapter closes with recommendations for needed research in the area of competency assessment.

Multicultural Training in Professional Psychology

In the early 1980s, the psychology profession was harshly criticized for its lack of curricular attention to multicultural issues (for example, Atkinson, 1983; Bernal and Padilla, 1982; Casas, 1984; Sue, 1981). More recently, however, the profession has begun to attend to multicultural issues in training programs. A number of writers have documented the profession's increasing strength of commitment to diversity issues in training (for example, Ponterotto and Casas, 1991; Reynolds, 1995). In this section, we will review recent survey research that has examined the status and format of multicultural training in clinical, school, community, and counseling psychology programs.

Clinical Psychology

Recently, Bernal and Castro (1994) replicated and extended the classic Bernal and Padilla (1982) survey so often referenced in clinical psychology training literature. The new survey was sent to all APA-accredited doctoral programs in clinical psychology; 104 of the programs returned completed questionnaires. The overall conclusion presented by Bernal and Castro is that progress in multicultural training over the past decade has been mixed. On the positive side, compared to the 1982 survey results, the 1994 survey found that programs providing minority-related courses had increased by 20 percent, and programs requiring such courses increased by 17 percent. Furthermore, 10 percent more programs in 1994 reported that faculty are engaged in multicultural research. The authors found numerous other signs of progress over the last decade, and the interested reader is referred to Bernal and Castro for a detailed presentation of results.

Notwithstanding the signs of progress noted above, Bernal and Castro (1994) highlight that a substantial percentage of programs continue to lack the "structural basics of minority training . . . 39 percent of accredited clinical programs still have no minority-related courses, 74 percent of programs do not require even one minority course . . . 47 percent have no clinical faculty conducting minority mental health research, and . . . 40 percent of programs do not make use of off-campus clinical settings serving ethnic minorities as standard practicum placements for their students" (p. 803).

Overall, Bernal and Castro (1994) conclude that despite some curricular progress over the last decade, clinical psychology training programs are more effective in providing some minimal exposure to cultural issues than in preparing culturally competent and proficient psychologists.

School Psychology

In the field of school psychology, Rogers, Ponterotto, Conoley, and Wiese (1992) examined curriculum surveys completed by training directors at 121 doctoral and nondoctoral school psychology programs. The results indicated that 60 percent of the programs offer at least one course in multicultural issues, and 63 percent of the programs offered two to five courses. Interestingly, this study revealed the percentage of the minority issues information that was presented in core school psychology courses (namely, Assessment, Intervention, Consultation, Roles and Function, Practicum, and Internship). Of particular interest to the present discussion was the Assessment focus. The results indicated that during the core assessment classes,

13 percent of the programs devoted 0–5 percent of class time to multicultural issues, 49 percent devoted from 6–15 percent, 29 percent devoted 16–25 percent, and 9 percent devoted 26 percent or more of class time to minority issues. Interestingly, of the four content core areas (excluding Practicum and Internship), assessment courses had the highest percentage of multicultural emphasis.

Community Psychology

Suarez-Balcazar, Durlak, and Smith (in press) surveyed fifty-six community psychology graduate programs. Among the findings of this study were the following: 48 percent of programs required at least one multicultural course; 87 percent indicated that relevant fieldwork experiences were available to interested students; and in 70 percent of programs, multicultural research was being conducted. Suarez-Balcazar and others also asked training directors to evaluate their program's success in training students to deal with multicultural issues. Thirty-eight percent of directors indicated that they were fairly successful, and 23 percent indicated success with most students. Overall, the survey found that although training directors were cognizant of the importance of multicultural issues, and were committed to increasing training in this area, only modest progress has occurred.

Counseling Psychology

In their national survey of counseling programs (masters and doctoral level), Hollis and Wantz (1990) found that new multicultural courses were added to curricula in 76 counseling programs nationwide (projected from 1989–1991). This increase represented the greatest growth (ranked first) among the thirty-four content areas identified in the survey of courses added to preexisting curriculums. In their most recent update, Hollis and Wantz (1994) surveyed counseling programs nationwide for projected 1993–1995 curriculum changes. The projection for multicultural counseling courses during this time revealed that not one program planned on drop-ping such a course, and that twenty-seven new multicultural courses were being added to training curriculums.

In an independent survey of APA-accredited counseling psy-chology doctoral programs, Hills and Strozier (1992) found that 87 percent of programs offered a multicultural course, with 59 percent of the programs requiring the course of all its students. Most recently, Quintana and Bernal (1995) mailed surveys to all sixty-one APA-accredited counseling psychology programs; forty-one pro-grams returned completed surveys. Some of the key findings of this study were as follows: 73 percent of programs had one or more spe-cific courses in minority issues, and 22 percent offered three or more such courses; 42 percent of programs require that a multicultural course be completed by all students; 59 percent of programs have at least one racial or ethnic minority faculty member, and 22 percent have 20 percent or more minority faculty representation; 34 per-cent of programs include faculty engaged in multicultural research, and 95 percent of programs have faculty willing to chair theses or dissertations on multicultural issues. In gauging the significance of their survey results with regard to training culturally competent counseling psychologists, Quintana and Bernal note that "norma-tive data from counseling psychology programs indicate that most programs are providing training that leads to, at best, multicultural sensitivity, but very few appear to be providing training that pre-pares practitioners to be multiculturally proficient" (p. 1).

D'Andrea and Daniels (1991) present an interesting qualitative analysis of the status of multicultural counseling training. Using var-ious qualitative methods (for example, interviews with a variety of educators, national leaders, practitioners, and students; journal con-tent analyses; information gathered at conferences and training workshops), the authors developed a conceptual stage model of training thought to reflect different types and levels of multicultural counseling training. Four training levels, each distinguished by the progressive "complexity and intentionality of the educational strategies selected to promote multiculturalism" (D'Andrea and Daniels, 1991, p. 80) were theorized: the Culturally Entrenched stage, where multicultural training is rarely incorporated into courses and other training experiences; the Cross-Cultural Awakening stage, characterized by a developing awareness of multicultural issues and some mention or discussion of such issues in classes; the Cultural Integrity stage, characterized by increased attention to multicultural issues and the existence of a separate multicultural counseling course; and the Infusion stage, where programs more fully integrate multicultural issues into the entire training curriculum. A detailed description of each stage is beyond the scope of this chapter, and the interested reader is referred to the cited article for a thorough presentation. Suffice it to say, the authors found that a majority of counseling programs are operating at the second stage (Cross-Cultural Awakening) of the model, with few programs operating at the more desirable third and fourth stages.

Combined Program Survey

Recently, Allison, Crawford, Echemendia, Robinson, and Knepp (1994) surveyed 1985–1987 doctoral graduates in counseling, school, and clinical psychology. Ninety percent of the respondents were White and 10 percent were of racial or ethnic minority status. Given the small number of school psychology respondents ($n = 22$), only the responses of counseling ($n = 68$) and clinical ($n = 191$) psychology graduates were tabulated. The survey focused on multicultural training and professional work with diverse racial or ethnic and cultural groups. Among the more striking findings were the following: Only a small percentage of respondents felt "extremely" or "very" competent to work with African American (38 percent), Asian American (16 percent), Hispanic American (26 percent), and Native American (8 percent) clients. There was a marked discrepancy between the percentage of respondents serving culturally diverse clients and their sense of competence for the task. Allison and others express concern that psychologists who perceive their multicultural competence to be limited continue to provide such services.

Additional findings from the Allison and others (1994) survey indicate that the sampled graduates report "minimal to moderate exposure to diverse faculty, limited access to courses that focus on cultural diversity, and restricted [training] opportunities for working with clients from specific cultural groups."

A Comparative Survey

In an interesting twist on survey research, Quintana and Bernal (1995), besides providing recent survey data on counseling psychology programs, also directly compared counseling with clinical psychology programs. The direct comparison of the status of multicultural training in APA-accredited counseling and clinical psychology programs indicated that counseling programs included a greater proportion of minority-related coursework and training, provided more systematic and formalized multicultural training, and were more likely to require students to complete at least one multicultural course. In reviewing the results of their survey, Quintana and Bernal caution the reader that although counseling programs appeared more advanced with regard to multicultural training than clinical programs, the differences were at times small and therefore not clinically meaningful.

In interpreting the surveys briefly reviewed in this section, two conclusions can be drawn. First, in comparison to surveys conducted in the 1970s and 1980s, the more recent crop of surveys indicate that, overall, programs in professional psychology are making some gains in their efforts to diversify the curriculum. However, the extent of—and mechanism for—this cultural infusion varies greatly between programs (see Bernal and Castro, 1994; D'Andrea and Daniels, 1991; Ponterotto, Alexander, and Grieger, 1995). Second, when one considers projected demographic trends, coupled with the present poor status of minority mental health services, it can be assumed that intensified multicultural training in professional psychology is needed (Mio and Morris, 1990; Ponterotto and Casas, 1991).

As programs in psychology continue to expand their cultural pluralization efforts, there will be an increasing need for mechanisms to evaluate the multicultural competence of both programs (for example, see Ponterotto, Alexander, and Grieger, (1995) and individual students or practitioners. Clearly, one component of a culturally proficient training program, regardless of specialty area, is the program's ability to objectively evaluate student (and faculty) multicultural competence. Not surprisingly, given the Quintana and Bernal (1995) findings, it is the counseling psychology subfield that has taken the lead in developing objective assessments of multicultural competencies. In the next section, we provide concise psychometric reviews of such instrumentation.

Objective Measures of Multicultural Counseling Competence

Presently, there are four multicultural competency assessment instruments with at least a moderate level of psychometric support. The four instruments are the Cross-Cultural Counseling Inventory-Revised (CCCI-R; LaFromboise, Coleman, and Hernandez, 1991), the Multicultural Awareness-Knowledge-and-Skills Survey (MAKSS; D'Andrea, Daniels, and Heck, 1991), the Multicultural Counseling Inventory (MCI; Sodowsky, Taffe, Gutkin, and Wise, 1994), and the Multicultural Counseling Awareness Scale (MCAS; Ponterotto and others, 1993). Each of the instruments is conceptually rooted, at least to some degree, in the multicultural counseling competency construct proffered by Sue and colleagues (Sue and others, 1992; Sue and others, 1982). Given the centrality of the Sue conceptualization for multicultural counseling competence assessment, we now turn to a brief discussion of the model.

Multicultural Counseling Competence Model

Building on earlier work (Sue and others, 1982; Sue and Sue, 1990), Sue, Arredondo, and McDavis (1992) developed a comprehensive model delineating competencies for effective multicultural counseling. Thirty-one specific competencies are organized within a 3 (Characteristics) by 3 (Dimensions) matrix. The counselor characteristics are: awareness of own cultural values and biases, awareness of client's world view, and appropriate intervention strategies. Within each of the characteristics there are three dimensions: beliefs and attitudes, knowledge, and skills.

For example, a "belief and attitude" competency under the first characteristic of "counselor awareness of own assumptions, values, and biases" reads, "Culturally skilled counselors are able to recognize the limits of their competence and expertise" (Sue and others, 1992, p. 482). A sample "knowledge" competency under the characteristic of "Understanding the worldview of the culturally different client" reads, "Culturally skilled counselors understand how race, culture, ethnicity, and so forth may affect personality formation, vocational choices, manifestation of psychological disorders, help-seeking behavior, and the appropriateness or inappropriateness of counseling approaches" (p. 482). Finally, a sample "skills" dimension under the characteristic of "Developing Appropriate Intervention Strategies and Techniques" reads, "Culturally skilled counselors are not averse to seeking consultation with traditional healers or religious and spiritual leaders and practitioners in the treatment of culturally different clients when appropriate" (p. 483). The competency report in its entirety can be found in Sue and others (1992); Atkinson, Morten, and Sue (1993); or Ponterotto, Casas, Suzuki, and Alexander (1995).

As noted earlier, all four multicultural competency instruments utilize the Sue and others (1992) model, or its predecessor (Sue and others, 1982), to some degree for item generation. At this point in our discussion, we turn to brief descriptions and psychometric reviews of each instrument.

The Cross-Cultural Counseling Inventory-Revised

The Cross-Cultural Counseling Inventory-Revised (CCCI-R; LaFromboise and others, 1991) is a revision of the original Cross-Cultural Counseling Inventory (CCCI; Hernandez and LaFromboise, 1985). The CCCI-R consists of twenty items that are placed on a Likert-type scale ranging from *strongly disagree* (1) to *strongly agree* (6). This instrument is completed by an evaluator or supervisor.

Items were developed based on the competencies specified in the Sue and others (1982) report. A sample skill item is "Counselor is willing to suggest referral when cultural differences are extensive."

Reliability and Validity

LaFromboise and others (1991) report a coefficient alpha (measure of internal consistency) of .95 for the CCCI-R total score. Using video analogs of a brief cross-cultural counseling vignette, three expert raters achieved an interrater reliability coefficient of .84.

Content validity for the CCCI-R was demonstrated by having graduate students classify items into one of the three competency categories after reading the Sue and others (1982) report. There was an 80 percent hit rate across items (LaFromboise and others, 1991). Criterion-related validity was established when counseling students rated as above average a videotaped counselor judged by faculty to have high levels of cross-cultural counseling competence. Additional criterion-related validity evidence for the CCCI-R was demonstrated in three analogue studies, which found videotaped counselors enacting a "culturally responsive" role to be rated higher than matched counselors in a "culturally unresponsive role" (for details, see Atkinson, Casas, and Abreu, 1992; Gim, Atkinson, and Kim, 1991; Pomales, Claiborn, and LaFromboise, 1986).

Using the principal components technique with orthogonal

rotations, LaFromboise and others (1991) examined the factor structure of the CCCI-R. The exploratory analysis yielded a single interpretable factor accounting for 51 percent of the total variance. The authors then forced a three-factor solution consistent with the Sue and others (1982) theoretical model. The resulting factors were named "Cross-Cultural Counseling Skills," "Socio-political Aware-ness," and "Cultural Sensitivity," and accounted for 63 percent of the total variance. The results of the forced three-factor extraction are not fully consistent with the Sue and others (1982) conceptu-alization, and the instrument's senior author, Teresa LaFromboise, has recommended interpreting only the total score at this point in the CCCI-R's development (see Ponterotto, Rieger, Barrett, and Sparks, 1994).

Evaluation

In summary, the CCCI-R was the first multicultural counseling competency instrument developed, and it remains the only evalu-ator-completed measure. The instrument, however, needs more val-idation work before an accurate assessment of its potential for training can be made. Immediate research is needed to examine the instrument's test-retest stability and factor structure across large samples. More detailed evaluations of the CCCI and CCCI-R can be found in Ponterotto and others (1994) and Sabnani and Pon-terotto (1992). Table 20.1 summarizes key descriptive and psycho-metric information on the CCCI-R and the self-report instruments to be reviewed next.

The Multicultural Awareness-Knowledge-and-Skills Survey

The Multicultural Awareness-Knowledge-and-Skills Survey (MAKSS; D'Andrea and others, 1991) is a sixty-item self-report measure. Items were generated from the literature and fall into three categories: awareness of personal attitudes toward minority clients, knowledge about minority populations, and cross-cultural communication skills. Twenty items measure each category, and responses are measured on

Table 20.1. Description and Psychometric Properties of the CCCI-R, MAKSS, MCI, and MCAS.

Description and Psychometrics	Instrument			
	CCCI-R	MAKSS	MCI	MCAS
Scale Length & Response Format	20 item, 6 pt. Likert-type	60 items, 2 different 4 pt. Likert-type	40 items, 4 pt. Likert-type	45 items, 7 pt. Likert-type
Previous Psychometric Critiques	Ponterotto & Casas, 1991; Ponterotto et al., 1994; Sabnani & Ponterotto, 1992	Ponterotto et al., 1994; Pope-Davis & Dings, 1995	Ponterotto et al., 1994; Pope-Davis & Dings, 1994, 1995	Ponterotto et al., 1994; Pope-Davis & Dings, 1994, 1995
Coefficient Alpha	Total = .95	Aw = .75 Kn = .90 Sk = .96	Aw = .83, .76 Kn = .79, .76 Sk = .83, .76 Re = .71, .63	Tot = .91, .90, .92, .75, .93 Kn/Sk = .92, .91, .93, .78, .90 Aw = .75, .67, .78, .78, .72
Interrater Reliability	.84	Not applicable	Not applicable	Not applicable
Test-retest Reliability	Not examined	Not examined	Not examined	Not examined

Content Validity	Trained raters	Item similarity to preexisting MCAS	Expert raters; name consensus by student judges	Expert raters; card sorts
Criterion Validity	Sensitive to training; discriminant validity established with Counselor Rating Form	Sensitive to training	Sensitive to training and experience; videotaped analogues rated in expected direction	Sensitive to training and experience; no social desirability contamination; convergent validity established with theoretically related instruments
Construct Validity via Factor Analysis	Exploratory factor analysis	Scale-specific exploratory factor analysis	Exploratory and confirmatory factor analysis (Goodness-of-fit index = .84)	Exploratory and confirmatory factor analysis (Goodness-of-fit index = .67)

Note: CCCI-R = Cross-Cultural Counseling Inventory-Revised; MAKSS = Multicultural Awareness-Knowledge-and-Skills Survey; MCI = Multicultural Counseling Inventory; MCAS = Multicultural Counseling Inventory; MCAS = Multicultural Counseling Awareness Scale.

Source: All data in table are extracted from Ponterotto and others (1994) and Pope-Davis and Dings (1994, 1995).

two different four-point Likert-type scales. An example of each format is as follows: "Psychological problems vary with the culture of the client" (1 = *strongly disagree* to 4 = *strongly agree*); and "In general, how would you rate your level of awareness regarding different cultural institutions and systems" (1 = *very limited* to 4 = *very aware*).

Reliability and Validity

D'Andrea and others (1991) report a coefficient alpha of .75 for the Awareness subscale, .90 for the Knowledge subscale, and .96 for the Skill subscale. Through the use of a fifteen-week pretest-posttest assessment, D'Andrea and others established some measure of criterion-related validity, as MAKSS scores increased significantly after multicultural training.

Interestingly, instead of factor analyzing the entire instrument, D'Andrea and others (1991) factor analyzed each subscale separately. The results of these analyses indicated that the Knowledge and Skills subscales were best interpreted as unidimensional, but the Awareness subscale seemed to be tridimensional. These results provide partial support (in terms of the Knowledge and Skills subscales) for the construct validity of the MAKSS as conceptualized by the Sue and others (1982) model.

Evaluation

The MAKSS appears to have promise as a self-report assessment. However, all the extant research is based on the single D'Andrea and others (1991) development study. More extensive validity testing is needed, particularly with regard to the factor structure of the MAKSS. Concurrent validity studies correlating the MAKSS with other self-report measures are also sorely needed. More thorough critiques of the MAKSS can be found in Pope-Davis and Dings (1995) and Ponterotto and others (1994).

The Multicultural Counseling Inventory

The Multicultural Counseling Inventory (MCI; Sodowsky and others, 1994) consists of forty items organized into four factor-analytically derived subscales: multicultural counseling skill, multicultural awareness, multicultural counseling knowledge, and the multicultural counseling relationship. Items were generated from an extensive review of the multicultural counseling literature. Scale items appear on a four-point Likert-type scale ranging from *very inaccurate* (1) to *very accurate* (4). All items are prefaced with the statement "When working with minority clients . . ." A sample multicultural counseling relationship item is "I perceive that my race causes the clients to mistrust me."

Reliability and Validity

Internal consistency (coefficient alpha) data across two samples were as follows: multicultural counseling skill, .83 and .81; multicultural awareness, .83 and .81; multicultural counseling knowledge, .79 and .78; and multicultural counseling relationship, .71 and .72.

Content validity was established through expert evaluation of item clarity and through raters classifying items into the correct subscale category. Criterion-related validity was demonstrated through the findings that students with multicultural training or more professional experience working with culturally diverse clients score higher on the MCI subscales. Finally, with regard to construct validity, both exploratory and confirmatory factor analyses provide moderate support for the four-factor model.

Evaluation

The internal consistency of the MCI is satisfactory. Of the three self-report instruments reviewed in this chapter, the MCI may be the strongest with regard to validity. Although a relatively new instrument, the MCI has accumulated impressive initial indices of validity with large, geographically dispersed samples. In their recent comprehensive review of the MCI, Pope-Davis and Dings (1995) state that the "MCI may provide the most behaviorally-based assessment of self-reported multicultural counseling Competencies" (p. 24). The reader is referred to Pope-Davis and Dings (1994, 1995) and Ponterotto and others (1994) for much more detailed reviews of the MCI.

The Multicultural Counseling Awareness Scale

The Multicultural Counseling Awareness Scale (MCAS) was first presented in 1991 (Ponterotto, Sanchez, and Magids, 1991) and then refined and further evaluated in 1993 (Ponterotto and others, 1993). The MCAS is a forty-five-item instrument consisting of two subscales, Knowledge/Skills, and Awareness. Each item is placed on a seven-point Likert-type scale ranging from *not at all true* (1) to *totally true* (7). Items were generated from an exhaustive review of the multicultural counseling literature. An example of an awareness item (one that is reverse-scored) is "I feel all the recent attention directed toward multicultural issues in counseling is overdone and not really warranted."

Reliability and Validity

Coefficient alphas across five separate samples ranged from .78 to .93 for the Knowledge/Skills factor, and from .67 to .78 for the Awareness factor (see Table 20,1 for all coefficients) (Ponterotto and others, 1993; Pope-Davis and Dings, 1994, 1995). Content validity for the MCAS was established through both quantitative (expert ratings on clarity and domain appropriateness) and qualitative (intensive focus group discussion and analysis) procedures. Additional content validity was recently demonstrated by Ponterotto (1994), who adapted the MCAS as a classroom study and assignment guide.

Moderate to high levels of criterion-related validity were established in a series of within-group comparisons (for example, scores of national experts were higher than practicing professionals and students), and through training-group comparisons (for example, those with more multicultural training scored higher). Convergent validity was established through predicted correlational relationships with related instruments. Furthermore, careful tests of social desirability contamination revealed no bias in this regard.

Finally, with regard to construct validity, both exploratory and confirmatory factor analyses support the two-factor extraction over competing theoretical extractions (for example, one global factor of general perceived multicultural competence; a three-factor model as conceptualized in Sue and others, 1982). However, confirmatory factor analytic procedures indicated that the two-factor model, despite being the best-fit of the models tested, only accounted for 67 percent of the total scale variance (this is less than desired in confirmatory analyses).

Evaluation

Notwithstanding some strong initial reliability and validity support, the MCAS is in need of more extensive validity work before the instrument could be used with confidence in training. Needed at this time are more large-scale factor analytic investigations. For more detailed critiques of the MCAS, the reader is referred to Ponterotto and others (1994), Pope-Davis and Dings (1994, 1995).

Research Agenda for Multicultural Counseling Competency Assessment

Research on multicultural competency assessment is in its infancy. Systematic, well-planned research on competency assessment should be one priority for the psychology profession. We close this chapter with the following specific recommendations for needed research in the area:

1. *Research needs to more closely examine the construct of multicultural competence.* Although conceptualized as a tridimensional (for example, Sue and others, 1982) construct, only limited factor-analytic support has been found for the three-factor model. Large-scale factor-analytic research on all four instruments is needed.

2. *Concurrent validity studies are needed to correlate the instruments reviewed here with one another and with related instruments.* Pope-Davis and Dings (1994) did in fact utilize a multitrait-multi-method procedure to examine the construct validity of the MCAS and MCI. This well-designed study revealed that the MCAS and MCI appear to be measuring different constructs. Additional

research on a larger scale is needed to test the replicability of the Pope-Davis and Dings findings. Furthermore, to help establish convergent and discriminant validity, more research is needed correlating the multicultural competency scales to hypothesized related (for example, racism and prejudice scales) and nonrelated measures.

3. *Research is needed to examine the instruments' stability over time.* The following questions need to be addressed. What would be an appropriate test-retest interval for the competency construct? Can it be expected that scale scores would increase after a one-day multicultural workshop? Or is a full semester of learning necessary to evidence change scores in competency? Ponterotto and others (1993) found that knowledge scores rose significantly after training, but awareness scores did not. One possible explanation for these findings was that awareness (also a measure of bias in the MCAS) was more immutable to change. Research needs to examine these questions more thoroughly.

4. *A crucial area of validation research for the instruments reviewed in this chapter concerns outcome study.* Little research has examined whether counselors who score higher on these scales are better counselors across cultures. Research needs to examine whether client satisfaction with counseling and perceived goal attainment is correlated with counselors' scores on the competency scales.

5. *Another research recommendation concerns broadening our methodological base to study the competency construct.* Specifically, given the early stage of research in the area, qualitative methods would serve as an effective research tool (Ponterotto and Casas, 1991). Qualitative research might focus on the following: interviewing identified experts in multicultural counseling to identify core themes of competence, interviewing clients after therapy to examine what counselor behaviors and characteristics were most impactful from a cross-cultural perspective, and conducting a participant observation study of a mental health center known to be highly respected by a minority community.

Conclusion

It is hoped that the present chapter has brought attention to the importance of accountability and assessment in multicultural counseling practice. Recent surveys indicate that training programs in professional psychology are addressing multicultural issues, but that the level of training may not yet be sufficient to meet the mental health needs of a demographically shifting U.S. population. Four paper-and-pencil assessment instruments were described and reviewed. Although they have some initial levels of reliability and validity, much more systematic research on the collective instruments is needed before they can be used with confidence. The chapter ended with specific recommendations for research on the instruments themselves and on the overriding competency construct.

References

Allison, R. W., Crawford, I., Echemendia, R., Robinson, L., & Knepp, D. (1994). Human diversity and professional competence: Training in clinical and counseling psychology revisited. *American Psychologist, 49*, 792–796.

Altmaier, E. M. (1993). Role of criterion II in accreditation. *Professional Psychology: Research and Practice, 24*, 127–129.

Atkinson, D. R. (1983). Ethnic minority representation in counselor education. *Counselor Education and Supervision, 23*, 7–19.

Atkinson, D. R., Casas, A., & Abreu, J. (1992). Mexican-American acculturation, counselor ethnicity and cultural sensitivity, and perceived counselor competence. *Journal of Counseling Psychology, 39*, 515–520.

Atkinson, D. R., Morten, G., & Sue, D. W. (Eds.). (1993). *Counseling American minorities: A cross-cultural perspective* (4th ed.). Dubuque, IA: Brown.

Bernal, M. E., & Castro, F. G. (1994). Are clinical psychologists prepared for service and research with ethnic minorities? Report of a decade of progress. *American Psychologist, 49*, 797–805.

Bernal, M. E., & Padilla, A. M. (1982). Status of minority curricula and training in clinical psychology. *American Psychologist, 37*, 180–187.

Casas, J. M. (1984). Policy, training, and research in counseling psychology: The racial/ethnic minority perspective. In S. D. Brown & R. W. Lent (Eds.), *Handbook of counseling psychology* (pp. 785–831). New York: Wiley.

Dana, R. H. (1994). Testing and assessment ethics for all persons: Beginning and agenda. *Professional Psychology: Research and* Practice, *25*, 349–354.

D'Andrea, M., & Daniels, J. (1991). Exploring the different levels of multicultural counseling training in counselor education. *Journal of Counseling and Development, 70*, 78–85.

D'Andrea, M., Daniels, J., & Heck, R. (1991). Evaluating the impact of multicultural counseling training. *Journal of Counseling and Development, 70*, 143–150.

Gim, R. H., Atkinson, D. R., & Kim, S. J. (1991). Asian American acculturation, counselor ethnicity and cultural sensitivity, and ratings of counselors. *Journal of Counseling Psychology, 38*, 57–62.

Hernandez, A. G., & LaFromboise, T. D. (1985). *The development of the cross-cultural counseling inventory.* Paper presented at the annual meeting of the American Psychological Association, Los Angeles, CA.

Highlen, P. S. (1994). Racial/ethnic diversity in doctoral programs of psychology: Challenges for the twenty-first century. *Applied & Preventive Psychology, 2*, 91–108.

Hills, H. I., & Strozier, A. L. (1992). Multicultural training in APA-approved counseling psychology programs: A survey. *Professional Psychology Research and Practice, 23*, 43–51.

Hollis, J. W., & Wantz, R. A. (1990). *Counselor preparation, 1990–92: Programs, personnel, trends* (7th ed.). Muncie, IN: Accelerated Development.

Hollis, J. W., & Wantz, R. A. (1994). *Counselor preparation, 1993–1995: Volume II: Status, trends, and implications* (8th ed.). Muncie, IN: Accelerated Development.

LaFromboise, T. D., Coleman, H.L.K., & Hernandez, A. (1991). Development and factor structure of the Cross-Cultural Counseling Inventory—Revised. *Professional Psychology: Research and Practice, 22*, 380–388.

LaFromboise, T. D., & Foster, S. L. (1989). Ethics in multicultural counseling. In P. B. Pedersen, J. G. Draguns, W. J. Lonner, & J. E. Trimble (Eds.), *Counseling across cultures* (3rd ed., pp. 115–136). Honolulu: University of Hawaii.

Mio, J. S., & Morris, D. R. (1990). Cross-cultural issues in psychology training programs: An invitation for discussion. *Professional Psychology: Research and Practice, 21*, 434–441.

Payton, C. R. (1993). Review of APA accreditation criterion II. *Professional Psychology: Research and Practice, 24*, 130–132.

Pedersen, P. B. (1995). Culture-centered ethical guidelines for counselors. In J. G. Ponterotto, J. M. Casas, L. A. Suzuki, & C. M. Alexander (Eds.),

Handbook of multicultural counseling (pp. 35–49). Thousand Oaks, CA: Sage.

Pomales, J., Claiborn, C. D., & LaFromboise, T. D. (1986). Effects of Black students' racial identity on perceptions of white counselors varying in cultural sensitivity. *Journal of Counseling Psychology, 33*, 57–61.

Ponterotto, J. G. (1994, August). Competency assessment: Moving beyond the Multicultural Counseling Awareness [and related] Scale. Paper presented in D. Pope-Davis's (Chair) Symposium: *Multicultural counseling competencies: Assessment, education and training issues.* Annual meeting of the American Psychological Association, Los Angeles.

Ponterotto, J. G., Alexander, C. M., & Grieger, I. (1995). A multicultural competency checklist for counselor education programs. *Journal of Multicultural Counseling and Development, 23*, 11–20.

Ponterotto, J. G., & Casas, J. M. (1991). *Handbook of racial/ethnic minority counseling research.* Springfield, IL: Thomas.

Ponterotto, J. G., Casas, J. M., Suzuki, L. A., & Alexander, C. M. (Eds.). (1995). *Handbook of multicultural counseling.* Thousand Oaks, CA: Sage.

Ponterotto, J. G., Rieger, B. P., Barrett, A., Harris, G., Sparks, R., Sanchez, C. M., & Magids, D. (1993, September). *Development and initial validation of the Multicultural Counseling Awareness Scale.* Paper presented at the Ninth Buros-Nebraska Symposium on Measurement and Testing: Multicultural Assessment, Lincoln.

Ponterotto, J. G., Rieger, B. P., Barrett, A., & Sparks, R. (1994). Assessing multi-cultural counseling competence: A review of instrumentation. *Journal of Counseling and Development, 72*, 316–322.

Ponterotto, J. G., Sanchez, C. M., & Magids, D. (1991, August). *Initial development of the Multicultural Counseling Awareness Scale.* Paper presented at the annual meeting of the American Psychological Association, San Francisco.

Pope-Davis, D. B., & Dings, J. G. (1994). An empirical comparison of two self-report multicultural counseling competency inventories. *Measurement and Evaluation in Counseling and Development, 27*, 93–101.

Pope-Davis, D. B., & Dings, J. G. (1995). The assessment of multicultural counseling competencies. In J. G. Ponterotto, J. M. Casas, L. A. Suzuki, & C. M. Alexander (Eds.), *Handbook of multicultural counseling* (pp. 287–311). Thousand Oaks, CA: Sage.

Quintana, S. M., & Bernal, M. E. (1995). Ethnic minority training in counseling psychology: Comparisons with clinical psychology and proposed standards. *The Counseling Psychologist, 23*, 102–121.

Reynolds, A. L. (1995). Challenges and strategies for teaching multicultural counseling courses. In J. G. Ponterotto, J. M. Casas, L. A. Suzuki, & C. M. Alexander (Eds.), *Handbook of multicultural counseling* (pp. 312–330). Thousand Oaks, CA: Sage.

Rickard, H. C., & Clements, C. B. (1993). Critique of APA Accreditation criterion II: Cultural and individual differences. *Professional Psychology: Research and Practice, 24*, 123–126.

Rogers, M. R., Ponterotto, J. G., Conoley, J. C., & Wiese, M. J. (1992). Multicultural training in school psychology: A national survey. *School Psychology Review, 21*, 603–616.

Sabnani, H. B., & Ponterotto, J. G. (1992). Racial/ethnic minority-specific instrumentation in counseling research: A review, critique, and recommendations. *Measurement and Evaluation in Counseling and Development, 24*, 161–187.

Sodowsky, G. R., Taffe, R. C., Gutkin, T., & Wise, S. L. (1994). Development of the Multicultural Counseling Inventory: A self-report measure of multicultural competencies. *Journal of Counseling Psychology, 41*, 137–148.

Suarez-Balcazar, Y., Durlak, J. A., & Smith, C. (in press). Multicultural training practices in community psychology programs. *American Journal of Community Psychology*.

Sue, D. W. (1981). *Counseling the culturally different: Theory and practice*. New York: Wiley.

Sue, D. W., Arredondo, P., & McDavis, R. J. (1992). Multicultural counseling competencies and standards: A call to the profession. *Journal of Multicultural Counseling and Development, 20*, 64–88.

Sue, D. W., Bernier, J. E., Durran, A., Feinberg, L., Pedersen, P., Smith, E. J., & Vasquez-Nuttall, E. (1982). Position paper: Cross-cultural counseling competencies. *The Counseling Psychologists, 10*, 45–52.

Sue, D. W., & Sue, D. (1990). *Counseling the culturally different: Theory and practice* (2nd ed.). New York: Wiley.

21

Multicultural Assessment

Present Trends and Future Directions

Lisa A. Suzuki, Paul J. Meller, and

Joseph G. Ponterotto

The chapters in this text have highlighted multicultural issues as they impact usage of various standardized and nonstandardized procedures that may be included in the assessment process. The multicultural issues impacting this process are complex and often must be examined in relation to the individual's family, community, environment, and educational context. The following discussion highlights present and future directions with respect to multicultural assessment. The areas to be covered include the political and economic climate associated with assessment, recommendations for appropriate assessment procedures, and future directions.

Political and Economic Climate

Assessment practices are complicated due to the different agencies and people with agendas and opinions in this area (McShane, 1989). The agencies include test development companies, educational and institutional systems, and racial and ethnic communities. Clinicians and educators must keep a balanced perspective regarding these agendas and integrate updated and empirically based information regarding the assessment of racial and ethnic minority group members. Professionals may also serve as advocates, providing information to examinees and their families regarding appropriate usage and interpretation of various measures used in assessment. This will enable people to become more knowledgeable and informed consumers of assessment results.

People who develop assessment procedures clearly have an investment in selling their wares. Both standardized and nonstandardized procedures have become big business. Consumers include educational institutions, mental health agencies, community and governmental institutions, employment agencies, and many others. Many test companies are aware of and sensitive to the issues confronting various racial and ethnic groups. The Educational Testing Service (1988, 1994) includes information regarding racial and ethnic differences on their published tests when they release test scores for minority group members (for example, GRE scores). Test developers incorporate minority expert panels to review items, stimuli, and tasks to ensure face validity. Measures are also administered to representative samples of people of color to check whether the test is reliable and valid for different racial and ethnic groups.

When these data are not available, clinicians must question test developers with respect to usage of various instruments and assessment procedures with racial and ethnic minority group members. In the absence of such material, or when discrepancies exist between sources of data, professionals must interpret the results with caution, include supplementary measures, and gather additional qualitative information.

In many settings such as schools and clinics, tests have become efficient means to obtain scores that can be used to make placement decisions and determine appropriate intervention strategies. Some assessment procedures, however, have become examples of quick-and-dirty methods with little clinical utility. Professionals are sometimes rewarded for completing assessments quickly without much thought to quality. These writers have heard clinicians state, "I don't know why I am spending so much time writing this report when no one is really going to read it."

The chapters in this text have not only examined standardized tests but also assessment procedures and methods more qualitative in nature, which may make up the assessment process. These qualitative procedures provide valid and reliable information, which may be more accurate than standardized test results in assessing particular aspects of an individual's personality or ability. Professionals must take an active stance in promoting best practices in assessment, selecting the most appropriate and culturally sensitive methods of assessment based upon the unique needs of the individual examinee.

Recommendations for Appropriate Assessment Procedures

Many researchers and clinicians have made recommendations regarding how culturally sensitive assessments can occur within various cultural contexts (for example, Armour-Thomas, 1992; McShane, 1989; Suzuki and Kugler, 1995). These recommendations are reflected throughout the chapters of this book. The following discussion addresses issues pertaining to the following: assessment purposes, test content, alternative methods and procedures, and the role of the examiner.

Assessment Purposes

Professionals engaged in the assessment process must be clear regarding the purposes of the particular evaluation or the reason for referral. While some agencies advocate a standard battery of measures to be used with all individuals entering their doors, this does not comply with ethical practice. Administering standard batteries to everyone does not take into consideration the unique needs of the individual or the specific goals of treatment or intervention. Only those evaluation techniques that show clear benefit to the person should be utilized. Evaluation procedures should be employed only when they have been shown to have clinical utility. Assessment should be one step in a process that leads to increased competency (Meller, 1994).

The individual being tested—and in some cases (that is, those involving a minor child)—the family must be aware of the purposes and procedures to be used in the assessment process, and the possible ramifications of the results. What is the testing for? What will the process entail? How will the results be used? Each of these questions refer to ethical issues regarding informed consent.

On another level, racial and ethnic groups must become proactively involved in determining the purposes of testing in their community (McShane, 1989). Assessment practices need to be related to the goals and values of the larger society *and* the objectives of the local community (McShane, 1989). Collaboration between professionals and communities is imperative, especially given the way cultural issues can impact the assessment process.

Test Content

With respect to test content, awareness and sensitivity to issues of cultural loading in assessment practices and measures need to be considered in the interpretation of results. All tests, verbal or nonverbal, involve some degree of cultural specificity. Some researchers have highlighted the need for culture-specific instruments (such as the Black Intelligence Test of Cultural Homogeneity; Williams, 1975), the development of ethnic norms (Gynther, 1972; Tanner-Halverson, Burden, and Sabers, 1993), and the need for translating tests into other dialects and languages.

Culture-specific instruments can provide professionals with information regarding an individual's behavior within a particular cultural context. However, the testing community has generally gravitated toward instruments that allow for comparison across groups. As Williams (1975) notes in relation to the BITCH Test, this can only happen if "whites are willing to engage themselves in the black experience" (p. 114).

Ethnic norming also provides assistance to professionals in comparing individuals with members of their own racial or ethnic group. However, this does not provide information with respect to why individuals perform the way they do; it does not change the actual performance of the individual within the assessment process (McShane, 1989).

Translations of measures need to follow strict guidelines. With respect to translation, a back-translation procedure is preferred. However, despite careful attention to state-of-the-art translation procedures, it is important to note that the meaning attributed to the test content may differ between racial and ethnic groups. The back-translation method ensures only equivalence in language, it does not ensure equivalence in meaning.

It is important to note that there is currently no such thing as a "culture free" or "culture fair" instrument or assessment method. Removing language factors may result in a "culturally reduced" measure, but cultural issues are still embedded in test content and procedures (Sattler, 1992).

Alternative Methods and Procedures

As noted earlier, this text has highlighted a variety of assessment procedures and areas that may be included in the evaluation. In addition, the chapters have provided recommendations regarding usage and appropriate practice. Professionals must be responsible for understanding, recommending, and providing "culturally sensitive" information throughout the assessment process. For example, curriculum-based measures, performance-based assessment, and qualitative assessment procedures are just a few of the alternative sources of information that can be used in conjunction with standardized tests or by themselves.

Guidelines regarding general assessment procedures need to be established cojointly between the individual, community, and agency professionals to ensure greater sensitivity to multicultural issues. Parents, family members, significant others, and cultural consultants may be included in the information gathering process.

Recognition of the professional's role in this interaction is imperative. Some racial and ethnic groups may tend to defer immediately to the wishes of the examiner, given that they view this person as the expert. Parents and guardians may not be aware of their rights in this process, nor of the rights of the individual being tested. They need to be provided with information so that they can make informed decisions. Professionals, family members, and the individuals being tested should be included in deciding how their children or they themselves will be assessed. At times, professionals look to having parental and family input in the assessment process as a hindrance, that is, as something that interferes with efficiency. It is important to recognize that significant others can provide vital information regarding the individual being tested.

During the assessment process, professionals must work toward establishing rapport with the examinee. An understanding of cultural differences will facilitate this process. When the evaluation commences, the professional should be alert to observations regarding behavior—motivation, problem-solving strategies, level of frustration tolerance, and so on—that may impact the results of the procedures selected.

Interpretation of findings should incorporate all of the data collected. Discrepancies or contradictions in findings must be addressed. Clinical observations should be integrated into the test report.

Test results should be shared openly with the family and individual being tested in a language and manner they can understand. This will enhance the possibility of an honest dialogue regarding the relative strengths and weaknesses of the individual and open channels regarding possible interventions involving not only the agency but the significant others in this person's life.

Role of the Examiner

McShane (1989) notes the importance of clarifying the qualifications of the examiner in testing members of diverse populations. In particular, he poses the following questions (p. 46):

- What is the extent of the professional's cultural and community specific knowledge?

- What is the level of technical competence?

- To what extent has this specific professional been able to translate and integrate cultural knowledge?

- Is this professional's "shared" knowledge base primarily based in research, or is it clinical in nature? Is her/his personal knowledge a result of systematic collection of data, or simply a result of personal interpretation of experiences? Has this professional adapted the knowledge she/he shares with other professionals in light of his own idiosyncratic knowledge in systematic ways?

- Is the professional's focus domain specific (i.e., only concerns himself with the school), or can it be characterized by systematic comprehensiveness (i.e., across biological, psychological, sociological and cultural levels)?

- Does her/his expertise lie in diagnosis, prescription, or intervention, or some combination thereof?

- Does her/his strength lie in individual or team functioning?

As professionals, we must self-monitor our personal level of assessment expertise with respect to members of racial and ethnic minorities.

Future Directions

The need for more culturally sensitive ways of assessing individuals from diverse racial and ethnic backgrounds is clear. Many professionals have continued the work being done in this area and promote actively the importance of understanding possible racial or ethnic group differences and how these may impact the usage of particular assessment methods, procedures, and measures. As noted earlier, over time the profession has become increasingly aware of these issues, and currently most tests and methods include reference to usage with diverse populations. It is important that research and training continue in this area to ensure the greater understanding of assessing the true potential of individuals within diverse settings and from different backgrounds. Future directions to be addressed in the following section include: development of alternative methods of assessment, understanding of ethnic norms, increasing collaboration with bilingual and/or bicultural professionals, development of a broader conceptual framework in assessment, increasing relevant literature and research, and increasing community involvement.

• *Developing alternative measures and procedures to be used in assessment process with diverse populations.* There was a time when assessment was equated with testing. Test scores were used unequivocally to represent the multifaceted nature of individuals and determine their potential to succeed in particular settings (for example, school, job, or relationships). We currently recognize the realistic limitations of all assessment procedures with respect to racial and ethnic minority groups. The continued development of alternative measures and procedures will facilitate movement of the profession toward more culturally sensitive assessment practices.

No educational or clinical decisions should be made based on a single source of information. This is particularly true if there is any concern about a mismatch between the culture of the individual and the instrument(s) used.

• *Understanding ethnic norms.* When we refer to ethnic norms, we mean not only those used with comparative groups on standardized instruments but also an understanding of normative behavior within a specific racial or ethnic group. For example, individuals from different cultural groups may respond differently to tasks presented based upon what is acceptable in their cultural context. Thus, the responses must be interpreted within an appropriate cultural framework. "Cultural reframing" must occur to understand how the behavior makes sense within that racial or ethnic context. Continuing to increase our knowledge with respect to the diverse populations we serve is imperative.

- *Increasing collaboration with bilingual and bicultural professionals.* It is important to note that there is a growing recognition of the need for bilingual and bicultural professionals. These individuals are more likely to be aware of the subtle nuances of their particular cultural group. They can serve not only as direct service providers but also as consultants, assisting other professionals with multicultural cases. Bilingual and bicultural professionals can also serve as bridges into various communities to establish connections for the flow of vital information between the particular agency and community with respect to the individual being assessed.

- *Developing a broader conceptual framework for the practice of psychological assessment.* Training programs must be infused with information regarding usage of particular procedures with racial and ethnic minority group members. Students need to become sensitive to within- and between-group variability in their conceptualization of assessment. Focusing only on standardized administration and scoring of instruments and procedures is only the beginning. Rote memorization of test manuals does not ensure that the professional will be able to use the tests as clinical instruments. Special practica focusing on the assessment of culturally different individuals could prove invaluable in training students and preparing them for the diverse clientele that they will eventually serve.

- *Increasing literature and research available regarding multicultural assessment procedures.* As noted throughout the text, additional research is needed to examine the actual differences between groups. While some of the psychometric literature has identified specific discrepancies between groups, more information is needed to examine the clinical implications of these differences. The moderator variables that impact this process also need further investigation and better understanding.

- *Increasing racial and ethnic community involvement in the assessment process.* As noted earlier, increased community involvement would prove beneficial in identifying specific cultural factors that impact the assessment process. This involvement may include involvement of cultural consultants familiar with the particular racial or ethnic community and aware of the psychological factors impacting the assessment process. Not only can they serve as effective translators, interpreters, or observers, but these individuals can provide invaluable information regarding subtle cultural cues for more effective practice, and consultation regarding the individual's environment.

Conclusions

Professionals engaged in multicultural assessment practices have continually raised questions regarding usage of particular instruments with different racial or ethnic minority groups. Our attempts to create "culture fair" instruments or procedures have repeatedly failed. As Williams (1975) writes: "Since the American society is pluralistic on the one hand and racist on the other, it would be virtually impossible to conceptualize an instrument which would be fair to all people: Asians, Blacks, Caucasians, Chicanos, Indians and Puerto Ricans" (p. 103). In addition, within-group differences clearly exceed between-group differences. Thus, we clearly cannot make definitive statements or predictions about how an individual will perform on particular measures.

This text has brought the reader up to date with respect to the usage of particular measures and procedures with diverse populations. At our disposal are a variety of instruments and procedures with available information regarding their usage with diverse populations. There is greater information available regarding usage of traditional measures in a variety of testing areas including personality, achievement, intelligence, nonverbal reasoning, neuropsychology, vocational interests, and infant and preschooler development. Curriculum-based measurement and performance-based assessment procedures are also readily available. Instruments are at hand to enhance our understanding of language proficiency, family systems, and ethnic identity. Clinicians can also use emerging tests in the area of multicultural competence. This listing is by no means comprehensive.

Despite increases in our understanding of the multicultural assessment process, important questions remain unanswered. Effective and appropriate assessment procedures involve an understanding of a myriad of complex factors that must be integrated with test and measurement data to form a comprehensive picture of the individual.

References

Armour-Thomas, E. (1992). Intellectual assessment of children from culturally diverse backgrounds. *School Psychology Review, 21*(4), 552–565.

Educational Testing Service. (1988). A summary of data collected from Graduate Student Record Examinations test takers during, 1986–87, *Data Summary Report #12*. Princeton, NJ: Author.

Educational Testing Service. (1994). *GRE: 1994–1995 guide to the use of the Graduate Record Examinations program*. Princeton, NJ: Author.

Gynther, M. D. (1972). White norms and Black MMPIs: A prescription for discrimination? *Psychological Bulletin, 78*(5), 386–402.

McShane, D. (1989, April). *Testing and American Indians, Alaska Natives*. Sponsored by the National Commission on Testing and Public Policy. Symposium concerning the effects of testing on American Indian and Alaska Natives, Albuquerque, NM.

Meller, P. J. (1994). Authenticity in assessment: A psychometric perspective. In A. M. Saturnelli (Ed.), *In pursuit of excellence and equity: Transforming testing in New York State* (pp. 73–84). Albany, NY: NYSCEA.

Sattler, J. M. (1992). *Assessment of children* (Revised and updated 3rd ed.). San Diego: Author.

Suzuki, L. A., & Kugler, J. F. (1995). Intelligence and personality assessment: Multicultural perspectives. In J. G. Ponterotto, J. M. Casas, L. A. Suzuki, & C. M. Alexander (Eds.), *Handbook of multicultural counseling* (pp. 493–515). Thousand Oaks, CA: Sage.

Tanner-Halverson, P., Burden, T., & Sabers, D. (1993). WISC-III normative data for Tohono O'odham Native-American children. *Journal of Psychoeducational Assessment: WISC-III Monograph*, 125–133.

Williams, R. L. (1975). The BITCH-100: A culture-specific test. *Journal of Afro-American Issues, 3* (1), 103–116.

Name Index

Subject Index

A

Abuse: and intellectual functioning, 172; and interpretation issues, 43–44

Accountability: bureaucratic and professional types of, 595–596; and high-stakes testing, 563–564, 568–570, 580, 589; responsive models for, 594–595

Accreditation of schools, 591–593

Acculturation: and assimilation or pluralism issues, 55–56, 69; and cultural sensitivity, 4–5, 14–15, 17–18; and ethical issues, 34–35, 37–38, 43, 46; and family assessment, 409–410; instruments for, 83–84; and intelligence tests, 151; levels of, 354–355; as moderator variable, 65–66; and MMPI-2, 96, 101; and projective techniques, 120–121, 125, 128–130; and racial identity, 622; and vocational assessment, 491–492

Achievement tests: alternatives to, 264–271; aspects of, 253–290; assumptions for, 13–15; characteristics of, 253–256; and classroom curriculum, 271–272; compared, 272–284; exclusion from taking, 262; high-stakes purposes of, 8–9, 261–262; knowledge and instruction in, 277–278; and language, 258–260; and minority students, 256–260; problems with, 262–272; purposes of, 260–262, 264, 283–284; and quality criteria, 260–262; standards for, 282; summary on, 284

Actions: adequacy of, 324–325, 337–339; appropriateness of, 328, 342–344. *See also* Behavior

Addiction Acknowledgment Scale (AAS), 462–463

Addiction Potential Scale (APS), 462

Adequacy: of actions, 324–325, 337–339; of inferences, 324, 328–337

Admissions, college, and high-stakes testing, 9

Adults, and intelligence tests, 155–156

African Americans: acculturation stages among, 66; and alcohol and substance abuse, 456–457, 465, 466; characteristics of, 398–399, 403, 404, 409; and diagnosis of mental illness, 34; and dialect, 366–372; and early childhood assessment, 546, 547, 548, 550; families of, 401–402, 405; friendships of, 434; and high-stakes testing, 572, 573, 574, 575–577, 578, 579, 582, 583, 584–585, 590; and hypertension, 294; identifying, 83; and intelligence tests, 144, 145, 146, 147, 148, 149–150, 154, 156, 158, 159; and interview styles, 31; and language assessment, 378, 387–389; language system of, 355, 356; and literacy, 181, 203–209, 210–217; and MMPI-2, 85–92, 103–106; nonverbal behavior of, 39–40; and nonverbal tests, 240; in normative group, 80, 413, 463; and personality assessment, 52, 54, 62; and projective methods, 117, 119, 123, 127; and racial identity